GOD, MAN, AND THE UNIVERSE

MENTAL METAMORPHISM

An Essential Encyclopedia in search of the Truth

DR. FERIDOUN SHAWN
SHAHMORADIAN

authorHOUSE®

AuthorHouse™
1663 Liberty Drive
Bloomington, IN 47403
www.authorhouse.com
Phone: 1 (800) 839-8640

Published by AuthorHouse 03/27/2020

ISBN: 978-1-7283-5760-7 (sc)
ISBN: 978-1-7283-5771-3 (e)

Print information available on the last page.

CONTENTS

MINDS OF REASON

ABOUT THE AUTHOR

Dr. Feridoun Shawn Shahmoradian showed an avid interest in learning about other cultures from a very young age. Shawn's love for people, as well as his need to quench a thirst for learning about others' way of life, inspired him to travel extensively to many parts of the world, including the Middle East, Persia, Turkey, (Istanbul, Ankara), Europe, West Africa, and North America. His travels have rewarded him with an invaluable wealth of knowledge and experience, allowing him to acquire realistic views in the context of diversified culture, philosophical, social, political, economic, and psychological endeavors.

Dr. Shawn attended many spiritual and callisthenic seminars in different parts of the world, including Morocco (Rabat, Marrakesh city, Fes, and Casablanca), Oslo, Paris, Amsterdam, Dublin (Ireland), Toronto (Canada), and Monroe (California), Santiago (California), New jersey, Orlando (Florida), Dallas, Houston, and Galveston (Texas) In the United States of America. He then visited New York, Washington, Las Vegas, San Antonio, Austin, El Paso, Corpus Christi, Texas, New Orleans, Miami Beach, Mexico (Mexico City, Cancun, Cozumel), and Bahamas.

At the age of Seventeen, Shawn attended Crawley College in Crawley England, for three consecutive years, and also attended boarding school at Birchington-On-Sea a village in northeast Kent, England. He visited London several times, resided at Brighton England for a while, and visited Hasting, Canterbury, and Sheffield England. Dr. Shawn then traveled to Fresno and San Francisco, California, and went to Lake Tahoe, Nevada, to teach. Dr. Shawn then left to study at Stockton College in Stockton, California, for two full years, taking philosophy and other social science courses. He then transferred to Galveston Texas College for one more year. A couple of years later he received his electronic engineering degree from

Texas Southern University in Houston Texas. He furthered his studies at Texas A & M and received his master's degree in economics, a minor in finance. His love for social science motivated him to attend the University of Texas at Dallas in Dallas Texas, and there he obtained a master degree in public affairs, with a minor in psychology. Dr. Shawn obsession with sports and a relentless pursuit for excellence in the art of self-defense that he pursued while facing insurmountable challenges over many years makes him a true embodiment of wisdom and strength. After extensive and thorough research in a variety of arts, Dr. Shawn finally created the Pang- Fang system a very unique and extremely practical system approved by well-known authorities in the field of self-defense. Dr. Shawn's system is highly recommended since it conveys decisive tactics with utterly significant strategy in a life and death situation. Dr. Shawn holds a nine-degree black belt in Hapkido, a Korean martial art, and holds a tenth-degree black belt in the Pang-Fang system of self-defense, second-degree black belt in Judo, first-degree black belt in Tae Kwan do, and third-degree black belt in Wu Shu Kung-Fu. He is acknowledged a prominent figure and as a holder of a non-conventional doctorate in the sport and the art of self-defense. Dr. Shawn is the author of the book Mind fighter, the book of The Anatomy of wake-up calls volume one & volume two, The book of God and the system, Minds of Reason, The Incorporeal God: An Insight into the higher realms and Mental Metamorphism.

THE INCORPOREAL GOD: AN INSIGHT INTO THE HIGHER REALMS

And Jesus said "Foxes have holes, and birds of the air have nests, but the Son of Man has nowhere to lay his head."
Mathew 8: 20

The Incorporeal God: An insight into the higher realms

In the name of the Omnipotent, omnipresent, Omni-temporal, omnibenevolent, and the Omniscient God. The most merciful, the most gracious, and the most compassionate. The proprietor of patience, time, space, and beyond. The Fiduciary, Custodian, the Adjudicator (Arbitrator, Judge) to all there is and the nonexistence. In the name of the almighty God.

> Watch your thoughts; they become words.
> Watch your words; they become actions.
> Watch your actions; they become habits.
> Watch your habits; they become character.
> Watch your character; it become your destiny
>
> Lao Tzu

"The only thing I know is that I know nothing" – Socrates

"That man is wisest who, like Socrates, realizes that his wisdom is worthless" – Plato

1

Why? Because as Anaxagoras puts it:

"In everything, there is a share of everything" – Anaxagoras

If so, it will be of no possibility to exponentially know the infinitely driven share of everything, in everything else.

Bar Elaha (oh God) I have a countenance (appearance, facial expression), a façade, bas- (enough) shrouded (mentally dispersed, with anxiety, not intelligently gathered), an inside in deep sleep, an un-awakened spirit lost in dreams. Occasionally I burn in fire and often drown into my tears. Bar Elaha (oh God), when I know the almighty, my troubles narrow, and when I don't, I am lost with self into dark alleys and plunged into the abyss. Bar Elaha (oh God), when I look upon you, I am the crown holder, and then look upon the self, I am not but just a speck of dust with massive ego tied to insatiable greed. Conveying unfathomable potential to advance, infinitely honored, which, I am. And exhilarated (intoxicated, elated) to know you, but so deprived (needy) in demeanor that I desperately seek your mercy.

SCIENCE AND PHILOSOPHY

A little philosophy inclineth man's mind to atheism; but depth in philosophy bringeth men's minds about to religion.

– Sir Francis Bacon

It is of utmost important to analyze some of the preliminary subjects that most atheists cling to when discussing God and existence. For instance, non-believers mostly purvey arguments utilizing Newtonian science, quantum physics, how's of the visible world, Darwinian evolution, the big bang, existence, matter, nothingness, infinity, entropy, and so on. In contrast, the believers resort to the philosophy of existence, whys of the world, metaphysics, the unseen world, consciousness, the quantum realm, the Omnipotent Designer, God and creation, believing in a destiny with purpose, entropy, and so on. When philosophical subjects are done without being angered or frustrated, the mind can act resolutely in finding valuable outcomes.

"Leisure is the mother of philosophy"

– Thomas Hobbes

"Philosophy is a battle against the bewitchment of our intelligence by means of language"

– Ludwig Wittgenstein

3

Both atheism, and theism views are typically based on their emotional approach of the world, neither one is nimrod (stupid, foolish). What we know and grasp is that: God is unknown, and cannot be seen, proven or unproven. What we are left with is making sense of an amazingly marvelous universe, in which is either the effect of an absolutely competent creator, creators or none. They all require some type of faith, correct, or not? Is to be left with one's own insight, and choosing to decide, where no coercions should ever make any one to believe in God, or not. I said emotional, because so many non-believers are sad and angry with an unjustified world that we live in, mistakenly holding God responsible for our pain and agony implemented by the mighty and the "pharaohs" of our time. And bear in mind that: the absence of belief is not atheism. Atheism is saying something on God. The absence of belief is agnosticism.

Obviously, enough subjects as such are byzantine (intricate), and culminating enough in which they must be coagulated with grave reasoning power. And unless they are answered correctly and insightfully, the repercussion for an undermining discussion can manifest abstruse (convoluted) outcomes.

This can leave dire socio-cultural and socioeconomic issues, with ill morals and a spiritual impact, where humanity can lose ground for hope and justice; where everyone's moral imperative can become questionable, since man's relativity in judgement cannot be taken as an absolute, since no man is free from making mistakes as we must take refuge to the all-knowing, infinitely resourceful, with infinite wisdom, and omnipotent God to render precise sagacity (judiciousness).

One should meditate on and examine one's own character conduct before delving into metaphysical realms in search of God. As Socrates said, "The unexamined life is not worth living."

We need to distinguish and understand the differences between the two concepts of science and philosophy, since both terms relate to whys and how's of the world, especially when dealing with metaphysical views, God, and existence.

It is important to clarify the differences between philosophical analogy and scientific undertakings, and to discern which is which. Philosophical inquiries need to be precise, not sporadic; they need to betoken (presage, denote) perspicacious (insightful, penetrating) answers for proving the existence of God. Philosophy and science are essential, as they are needed to be logic-oriented, where philosophy is also very decisive in metaphysical discussions beyond the physical domain.

Science can often help with comprehending natural phenomena. It conveys empirical data, meaningful information that can be investigated; it quantifies; it does examine and repeat if necessary. Science is what we know, it is the objective truth. It is normally in terms of mass, energy, velocity, and position. Science is based on perceptual realty.

Science is methodical (orderly) by nature; it follows scientific methods, which makes its founding based on the outcome of experiments and facts. It commonly starts with experimenting with a certain hypothesis (educated guess) in which it can be corroborated (verified) as truth, or it can prove maquillage (artificial, not genuine), and even wrong.

"Science is what you know. Philosophy is what you don't know"

– Bertrand Russell

For philosophy, measurements and observations, statistics and numbers, are not as crucial, since not even a laboratory is required to dissect findings and examine results, as they are as crucial for scientific endeavors that demand empirical validity with an equipped laboratory for hands-on participation.

Science is good at answering the 'how' questions. 'How did the universe evolve to the form that we see?' But it is woefully inadequate in addressing the 'why' questions. 'Why is there a universe at all?' These are the meaning questions, which many people think religion is particularly good at dealing with. (Brian Greene)

Philosophy makes subjective and objective questions. It also generates answers, while science is involved in finding answers. Science also takes answers and proves them as objectively right or wrong. Philosophy meditates on a variety of issues to produce knowledge through savvy thoughts, where science accomplishes the same thing often by observing. Science can be applicable to many areas of discipline.

Science investigates the physical world and learns to exhibit results in a correct way that shifts the responsibility to science in how things are actuated, since science delivers its findings due to probing into physical phenomena.

"An experiment is a question which science poses to Nature, and a measurement is the recording of Nature's answer"

–Max Planck

George Wilhelm Friedrich Hegel said, "Philosophy must indeed recognize the possibility that the people rise to it, but must not lower itself to people." Many philosophers believe the issue of existence is the origin of all philosophical principals; they believe the subject of existence is the core value in which all metaphysical teachings (i.e., information, knowledge, religions, and God) are centered.

Frank outlaw Referencing to the philosophy of God and the existence, validity embraces testing our reviews, where Conclusion should avoid challenging the infinite regression, and not to continually ask why?

One must warrant that reasoning and the power of inference can guarantee a rational and true conclusion.

Existence, or quiddity (nature, disposition, character), is the focal point and the essence of Existentialism. We often approach the concept of existence, since existence or existent is well-regarded as the subject of philosophy (i.e., the mind has to consider existent as belonging to all things and where the mind simultaneously does not behold it in the same way in two things). This is because man's mind cannot contrive (devise) even a single assertion (statement) unless it can narrate (relate) it to existence.

It seems that beautiful minds are influenced with premonition (foreboding, a sense of something happening in the future, anticipation of an event without conscious reason), as if they are mandated with a mission to perform gynecology into the womb of Mother Nature and give birth to yet another treasure, leaping into unveiling the mysteries of nature's obscurities to emancipate man from the clutches of ignorance.

For instance, it is heresy to believe the end justifies the mean; that you should make money every which way you can, which I am afraid a market exhausted from fair and just competition certainly ends up with a disparaging (demeaning, insulting, derogatory) outcome. Extreme income inequality materializes a huge gap between the haves and have nots, creating so much violence, crime, pain, and suffering beyond repair. Thousands and thousands of innocent lives are annually lost, solely because of financial depravity, as billons are globally being forced into poverty with no way out of their misery. One asks why that is the philosophy, and how to fix it; it takes scientific notion and expertise in economic and financial management to fix it—that is science.

Be aware of "predatory philosophy," where the culprits use psychology on masses of believers, prejudicially saying that if you are rich and influential, you are good and blessed, and if you are poor and disadvantaged, you are bad, and perhaps ungodly. But then again, Jesus was not rich.

Why a just and loving God should be so discriminatory in victimizing billions beyond repair; that is philosophy. How to fix it—in unleashing peaceful revolt without murdering innocent lives—is the science. When they use bogus anthropology and utilize false sociology to conceptualize sadistic (cruel) justification to keep different races, different nationalities apart, and crucify millions as misfits, implying they are of an inferior God, and you ask why; that is philosophy. Doing something about it—that is the science behind good socio-cultural conduct.

When neurologists tell us that billions of neurons and trillions of synapse at neurons' junctures spark in one's brain to produce thoughts; that is science. But why should they fire to create thoughts, insights, release hormones, create feelings, emotions, and thousands of other things? That is philosophy. (Which no one has been able to know why so far.)

The bottom line is, we must change the abusive narratives in which the consequences don't direct humanity into the cul-de-sac of socio-cultural and socio-economic impediments; where an intelligence-oriented society should question the root causes of our misfortunes manufactured by the few; where the epistemology (the theory of knowledge, especially with regard to its methods, validity, and scope) and the nature of every word and deed is questioned to avoid further exploitation of the children of God, as we all are, since humanity originated from the same undeniable source. And stop taking God hostage for our misdeeds and sins, as Fredrick Nietzsche said, "God is dead and we killed him."

THE MAGIC OF THE QUANTUM WORLD

The world of subatomic particles, the quantum world, has changed the physicist's mind and prominent scientists' thought process on subatomic particles and the quantum world, since the quantum realm is much different from the world we live in. What we should expect in Newtonian's laws of physics and the material world is quite different and ought not to be expected in the subatomic world.

What makes sense in our world, the world of Newton's laws of physics, does not make any sense in the realms of quantum mechanics because what is practical in our world cannot be experienced in a subatomic situation. Human beings are accustoming and in tune with the visible world. The human brain has gone through evolutionary processes for millions of years, but it is solely practical in the world we live in, as we also are relatively the product of our environment. This makes the quantum world quite strange, and not so comprehendible. That is why scientists say that those who claim knowing the quantum world should realize, they know not much.

For instance, as defined, "The term classical vacuum is used in classical electromagnetism where it refers to as an ideal reference medium, devoid of all particles, with ideal properties." Electromagnetism is referred to by scientists as free space, or the vacuum of free space, and sometime as the ideal vacuum. Also as defined by the physicists and the scientists: "In a quantum field theory, the quantum vacuum state (also called quantum vacuum state) is the quantum state with the lowest possible energy generally" it contains no physical particle. Zero-point field is sometimes used as a synonym for the vacuum state of an individual quantized field.

Here is the catch, as "perfect vacuum" is defined and believed by physicists and scientists as the empty space with no atoms or any particles in it. But they also believe there is no such thing as a perfect vacuum, or better said, nothingness, because virtual particles are always popping in and out of existence. Even empty space is seething (come to a boil) with virtual particles. And weirdly enough, in a quantum vacuum, or supposedly in the nothingness state, there is no matter or space, but it's filled with the fundamental subatomic particles that are nowhere until they are observed, and when seen, they cannot be located. Their position is never identified; they can be in more than one place at the same time.

How odd! These particles are nowhere until they are observed, then, when they notice the observer's attention, they disappear, as if they know they are being spied on, therefore making the whole power of intention futile. Scientists believe the space within the world, like a balloon getting bigger and bigger, where there is space within the balloon, but there is no space, or any place outside of it, and without dimensions.

The strange thing is that there must exist some place, some sort of coordinates, for the balloon to have room as it expands, but to no avail; there is no place to accommodate the balloon as it grows bigger and enlarges, which is evidently beyond the human mind to grasp. To postulate (assume) having a place with no dimensions is significantly odd, or imagining things appear in and out of sight in a millisecond from nowhere, from nothingness, and disappear into nothingness, is extremely anomalous (unfamiliar, eccentric, unusual), as their whereabouts cannot be determined, and it only happens in the quantum world of subatomic particles.

The subatomic quantum particles have zero mass, which should mean not having any weight or heaviness. Fundamentally, quantum physics is based on subatomic particles that carry mass, but strangely enough, with zero mass. In other world they lack mass, as they have no heaviness, but they simultaneously carry mass. It would be wacky in our physical world for something to carry weight and not carry weight at the same time, and be in several places at the same time. It just would not make any sense. But they are normal occurrences in quantum realms. Quantum physics is today the strongest theory standing, and very reputable in the science of physics, which is based on uncertainty; there is no definite assessment in quantum physics, since it entirely depends on accidental events.

This is the reasoning behind most atheists' science, since they believe that the full-fledged, the integral nature of the worldly existence from infinitely minuscule (infinitesimal, diminutive, microscopic) to macro existence is based on quantum physics, in which quantum physics is comprised of, and related to, subatomic particles. And then they say, accidental events are the fundamental and the real nature of our material world. They further utter that, since quantum physics is the substratum, the ground for the physical world, and because quantum physics is based on accident, then we must conclude and be sensitized (aware) that the material world has also occurred accidently.

From what many scientists believe and say, we should interpret: the visible world, the tangible world, is created by the unseen realms, the immaterial world, from which it cannot be touched, experienced, cannot be seen, positioned, or even conceived. This should remind us of the meta-physical realms, in which holy sages, renowned philosophers, and many eminent and scholarly minded scientists, such as Ibn-Sinai, Galileo, Nicolaus Copernicus, Johannes Kepler, Francis Bacon, Sir Isaac Newton, Luis Pasteur, Blaise Pascal, Gottfried Leibniz, Werner Heisenberg, Marie Curie, and thousands of others, have explained the metaphysical realms, saying we are not as differentiated as we think. They have warned us of the world we do not see, the immaterial world, which apparently is the very exact reason we live, over and over through most of human history, and since what we do not see evidently controls and is affiliated with the world we see, the world we live in, and the entire universe. Why affiliated? Because if not, then the scientists, the physicists, and other inquisitive minds would not have been able to detect the world of subatomic particles, the quantum world, where utopias become real and further substantiated as we propel.

What they also are missing is interpreting the interactivities of the unseen world, the world of subatomic particles, as accident. Not giving it the probability of what we know as accidental, in which the meaning of an accident can often make sense in our world, might not mean accident in the imperceptible (undetectable, indiscernible) world, which should be better known as the "realms of magic." Where God can also laugh, when one thinks of manifesting a "theory of everything" that can perhaps be the answer to the mysteries of the universe.

The infinite power of God, which is beyond the human mind, is limitlessly diversified by nature, and is magnificent in creation, cannot be constrained in any one formula. We simply lack the ability to seek what is past our competency to delve into infinite a planetary system with trillions and trillions of galaxies, and trillions of universes, where we naturally are not able to dig into the boundless cosmos in trying to answer them with one formula known as the theory of everything.

Let's take a brief look at the Heisenberg uncertainty principle, which is a physical law that molds part of quantum mechanics. It basically says that the more accurate one measures the position of a particle, the less one learns about its exact motion (momentum of velocity and vice versa) in that instant. It is naturally difficult to comprehend the principle behind such an occurrence, but it apparently is harder to elucidate (explicate) it.

The Heisenberg uncertainty principle referencing quantum mechanics states that there is a fundamental limit to how well you can simultaneously know the position and momentum (where momentum is classical mass times velocity of a particle.)

The uncertainty principle, also known as the Heisenberg uncertainty principle or indeterminate principle, statement, articulated in 1972 by the German physicist Werner Heisenberg states that "the position and the velocity of an object cannot both be measured exactly, at the same time, even in theory." It also states that the exact position and momentum of an electron cannot be simultaneously determined. This is because electrons simply do not have a definite position and direction of motion at the same time.

Physicists often quote from T. H. White's epic novel _The Once and Future King_, where a society of ants declares, 'Everything not forbidden is compulsory.' In other words, if there isn't a basic principle of physics forbidding time travel, then time travel is necessarily a physical possibility. (The reason for this is the uncertainty principle. Unless something is forbidden, quantum effects and fluctuations will eventually make it possible if we wait long enough. Thus, unless there is a law forbidding it, it will eventually occur.) Michio Kaku, _Parallel Worlds: A Journey Through Creation, Higher Dimensions, and the Future of the Cosmos_

By now we should know that first there is no such thing as nothingness, or perfect vacuum, which should clearly question Professor Hawking saying in his 1988 book, entitled The History of Time, that the world was created from nothing. Also, in his book, he did not deny God. Then, in his

2010 book titled The Grand Design, he says that gravity is responsible for creation. Therefore, what he is saying is that because of gravity, the world was created from nothing.

The outstanding question that remains is: does gravity mean something, or does it mean nothing? If gravity means something, then the world is made of something, which clearly contradicts saying the world was made of nothing; and if gravity is not something, then gravity cannot be responsible for creating the world; unless perhaps the big bang created gravity. Or maybe gravity made the big bang possible? Which begs for asking the questions that if existence comes from nothing, is it matter that is the real reason for creation; is the big bang responsible for everything? Or is it gravity that made life possible? And on and on, in which such persistence for reaching nowhere land will hopelessly disappoint us all to the end of times.

The fact is that, unless we believe in an infinitely awakened consciousness and limitless cosmic force, which has eternally existed before the dawn of time and prior to any event, then humanity will never overcome being haunted by demonically spirited thoughts that eventually could drag us all into the cul-de-sac of callousness and irresponsibility. There, no just and constructive judgement can ever be mustered, for a convincing argument in imperative philosophical and scientific issues that could ill-effect mankind for the worse, because the repercussions of a godless society are as baffling and meaningless as believing in idolatrous icons.

Quantum physics thus reveals a basic oneness of the universe.

–Erwin Schrodinger

WHAT ARE WE?

Our daily engagement in having a financial life is as demanding as it is time-consuming; because of this, most people are numb toward exploring what we are, or perhaps do not even care to reference it as important at all. This is strikingly sad. Unless we can correctly assess the answer to what we are, the subtle captivity inherent in the lack of such knowledge will negatively affect our individual and social interactions and welfare, regardless of how advanced we seem to be in our modern lifestyle; the negative repercussions will eventually impact us all.

Historically, there are two major viewpoints on this rather intricate question. One is the materialistic view, which holds that humans are physical, behaviorist beings that act mechanically in response to external stimuli, experiencing a robotic-like reaction to environmental processes.

This view leaves no room for closeness to God, spiritual training, or any soul-searching activities. Science is materially based, and looks at the world objectively; it cannot explain it subjectively, and cannot understand the way innate forces operate. Materialists are trying to locate the center of the awareness, not realizing that cosmic awareness is predominant and is magically experienced through many forms and shapes; animals, plants, humans, planets, stars and galaxies, through the billions of universes, and so on.

What really matters is how we express it. Humans express consciousness dynamically, and are at the pinnacle of this awakened chain. The unexplained epiphany happens when the essence of the phenomenal world is not matter, but consciousness. When thoughts and the awakening mind elevate a few degrees. It is then what we knew as a miracle becomes reality. Cosmic energy makes our cognition and experiences possible.

On the other extreme, we have idealists who accept and proclaim the physical world does not exist, everything is just perception, and the material world is nothing more than our imagination.

Which answer we grasp over the other, either materialist or idealist, affects the way we think and how we respond to sometimes very delicate matters that we might face in our lives.

From a mechanical and reductionist perspective, man is perceived as a reduced entity; we are being lowered in status to resemble hardware and machinery, thus are better qualified in our robotic programming to deal with environmental changes. That, I say, is a rather senseless indoctrination, short-sighted in definition of man's attributes and a deadened evolution of a human being's characters.

Let's give the materialist view the benefit of the doubt. If so, should we remove the idea of having a programmer or not? If not, are we all programed the same and therefore must react uniformly to external stimuli? And if yes, what are the differences, if any, that distinguish us from lower species of animals that behave homogeneously by instinct? Which then means that any other human attributes and characteristics should not be immune to external changes or counted as intrinsically worthy, other than being solely behavioristic and instinctual. Either way, there must be an innately animated force that is conscious and sensitive to outside changes causing us to respond accordingly. There is also the need for some proprietor of awakening power in the animal kingdom to spur millions of them into survival of the fittest behaviorism, propelling beasts with brute strength to retaliate being haunted by humans who savagely kill their victims by overpowering them, assisted by camouflage and stealthy maneuverability. Which by the way, would become a recipe for disaster to follow if we were to become a disciple of atheistic views and hence regarded as "mechanically" oriented entities.

You might contest that the survival of the fittest mentality and belief is accepted as truth by many godly societies. To speak to that, I can reassure you we are dealing with hypocrisy in action by many, where self-centeredness and greed have taken over. The effects of this are worse than the work of any honest atheist or materialistic individual. The question that remains is: do human beings have intrinsic values? Do animals have intrinsic values and experience feelings and emotion deeply, as humans do?

When plants react to external stimuli like rain, sunshine, fertilizers, proper gardening; when they bear fruits with nutritional value and eventually dry out and die, are they also behaviorist, since beings react to outward catalysts, including humans? But it sure does not mean we are intrinsically barren, as we are far from it.

When you evaluate people from a mechanical point of view and deplete them of feelings and emotions, do they have the right, for example, to seek justice and react by taking revenge if one's innocent family is slaughtered by criminals? And if yes, then what exactly is it that pushes one to want revenge? Finally, do animals feel and react the same way towards such injustice when their kind is beheaded for dinner?

When one covers a ticking bomb and explodes to pieces, saving others from getting killed, is it the outside stimuli forcing one to sacrifice his or her life to such an extent, or is it because of intrinsic values?

If it is because of external stimuli, why would everyone present not be inclined to perform such extreme self-sacrifice? Or when one pulls his finger so fast from a burning-hot stove, reacting quickly to an outward incident so that one does not get burned, as compared to when someone jumps to his or her death trying to save a child's life, not to get killed by an oncoming bus? Should these two reactions to external stimuli be considered the same, and if not, what causes the extent of such sacrifice inherent to the latter one? Do all people react the same to fear of punishment, rewards, death, worries, justice, revenge, self-sacrifice, excitement, love, beauty, ambition, risk-taking, courage, hunger, wealth, poverty, loyalty, caring, kindness, compassion, philanthropy, benevolence, in giving and generosity, intuition, IQ and intelligence, insightfulness, wisdom, greed, uprising, or when they are discriminated against?

Are the reactions exclusive to each person and situation, or common to all of us? If not common, why not? I thought we as members of the human species should react the same to particular occurrences, since we are all mechanically labelled and descended to behave instinctually. How about when a soldier volunteers to be sent to the front line at a time of war—is it the same motivation as someone who spies for the enemy, no matter how many innocent lives are endangered or are wasted?

Do our emotions and feelings, our thoughts, imaginations, and dreams, our laughter and joy, pain and anguish, the language in which we communicate, and the sacrifices we make have weight, affect chemical composition, or occupy space? If yes, I thought only what carries weight, has chemical composition, and occupies space is manifested and bound to as materialistically real—as compared to agenda which are not manifested the same and are considered as superficially idealistic.

Look, there are intrinsic human values that are explored and put to work by heavenly characters every day and many times over that stem from human compassion and caring, from love and devotion, from loyalty and sacrifice, from dignity and honesty, from passion and longing for justice.

If some hard-headed ideologue behaviorist wants to turn a blind eye to blundering (error, lapse) and prove a miracle-like situation real, then well-known wisdom should apply; if it looks like a duck, swims like a duck, and quacks like a duck, then it is probably a duck. And if we are behaviorists who should mechanically react to environmental changes and automatically respond the same to circumstances facing us, why would anyone need to think or seek solutions to one's problems? We shouldn't have to, since we are supposedly programed to act by instinct, collectively interacting in a herd-like manner to address any auspicious or dire circumstances.

We ought to cling to the core of humanity, which contains the remnants of stardust as recently claimed by cosmic scholars, physicists, and space scientists. Since humanity should identify with people's pain and suffering, with their hunger and displacement from their abode and habitat, from natural tragedies that might have faced them, it should not let them die in vain. It takes time to discard "junk knowledge," ill-received information deliberately instilled in people's heads for the benefit of the few that sadly have become blinded with love of money, and numb to human compassion.

Their incriminating behavior forces the survival of the fittest mentality on desperate masses of people, making it a cutthroat society rather than creating a culture of cooperation. A true culture of compassion has proven to be immensely positive and very productive in bringing people closer together; this would certainly make a huge difference in improving people's lives, their prosperity, and in honoring God.

Let us capitalize on what in heaven's name we are all about. We are about light, we are about love, we are about healing. Stop brewing evil in the name of God, and in the name mankind, misleading them to believe they are cursed and perhaps do not deserve to live. Because you have appropriated and accumulated so much wealth, then you have been blessed and ought to have a clear conscience—this is far from the truth.

Your misconduct is exactly why atheists and behaviorists, agnostics and the like, are emboldening to doubt God. Because of the consequences of your misdeeds, mankind is ignorant enough to hold God responsible for human misery and their pain and suffering. The all-rounded patriarchal system compounded with irreparable ills should be stopped, which has yoked and damaged millions for the worse, if not billions of whom you find inferior, and not up to your discriminatory standard.

When Jesus was asked by his disciples, "Where do we come from?" he said, "We come from light." Contemporary scientists, with all of their might, scientific research, and magnificent telescopes, are now attesting to what Jesus said more than two thousand years ago.

The bottom line is that we are sacred beings, but unless we have the freedom to experience, to keep the good, repel bad and evil, we cannot progress as efficiently as possible. And without experimentation, no dynamic improvement should be expected.

"No man's knowledge here can go beyond his experience"

– John Locke

We should also know, where there is no democracy and human rights, people's happiness will be hampered.

What Immanuel Kant said becomes a reality, especially in dictatorial countries: "Happiness is not an ideal of reason but of imagination."

"God is not willing to do everything, and thus take away our free will and that share of glory which belongs to us"

– Niccole Machiavelli

"Liberty consists in doing what one desires"

– John Stuart Mill

17

WHY BELIEVE IN GOD?

Things alter for the worse spontaneously, if they be not altered for the better designedly.

– <u>Sir Francis Bacon</u>

The most imperative protectoral move you can ever take is to believe in and seek God. In a consumer-oriented society that is intensely materially based, profit is becoming the sole purpose and is replacing God. It is as if God exists today only as an empty shell with no kernel.

It is more urgent than ever to truly and sincerely call upon the omnipotent, omnipresent God and seek to know him with all your might. The conventional method of reaching God, as practiced by some charlatans, is nothing more than a joke; it is only about getting more dollars in their pockets. This form of practice uses scare tactics and sleazy maneuvers to fool and undermine people's normal rational thought.

This happens even though we live in the twenty-first century, and most people and civilized nations have become quite sophisticated, naturally questioning such phony religious practices. God does not deserve this kind of treatment, and neither do his true followers. Yet we see many instances of those who preach such a wrong message about God—and they should, in this writer's opinion, be dealt no mercy.

When you are spiritually broken and in need of spiritual shelter and help, and you seek refuge with those who claim to be men and women of God, and then receive nothing but trouble, it would take a strong, sane mind not to curse and deny God. We should discern that such false prophets are just more hypocrites that live among us. Their corrupt deeds spiritually kill and maim people's spirit, which has no remedy other than the true God. He is not the cause of human misery.

Rather, the causes are in large part from those who bludgeon others in the name of God. Never before has the existence of God been so well-substantiated, with so much hardcore support and proof that is heavily backed with reason and philosophical and scientific knowledge. Yet so many are becoming remote islands, getting further and further away from the vicinity of their Maker, no longer tethered to or encompassed within his territory. People of high moral fiber are asking why so many nations, peaked in education and immersed in civility of mind and manner, have such rampant and pandemic levels of crime and wrongdoing. Catastrophes are everywhere, as we are bombarded on all sides by disasters, wars, and hunger that are void of tranquility, serenity, and security of mind.

You need to question, why should a child die because of an untreated infected tooth, enduring it for so long, if his parents are unable to buy proper medical care? You should object when people are forced to sell their kidneys because they are financially pushed to the limit and exhausted from having the bare minimum to survive. You should object when so many commit suicide because they are fired and out of job, not being able to find proper vocation to sustain their family's livelihood.

And so many other tragic ordeals that happen because of extreme income disparity in which the real culprits extenuate (make a crime, or a mistake seem less serious or deserving of blame) misallocation of resources and ignore its devastating effects. In actuality, inordinate (exorbitant, extreme) income inequality is the real reason behind so much pain and agony.

You should ask why so many individuals insanely go on shooting sprees, often killing twenty, thirty, fifty, and more innocent bystanders in common places, even at places of worship, because of easy accessibility to guns and military-style machine guns, etc. These and hundreds of other justifying questions should be asked with honest intention, done in good faith, and through purity of heart to fix what is long overdue in many broken sociocultural, socioeconomic nations, to aim at preventing societal maladies (ailments) with lingering psychological effects and spiritual numbness hatching so much violence beyond repair. Caring to become part of the solution and collectively trying to remedy the problems facing mankind are the first steps toward believing in God.

Every day our livelihood is questioned and hanging by a thread. In such an environment, the lower self is praised so much that it cannot be changed without God's help.

The principle of causality states that if there is no intelligence in the design and the effect, there could not be intelligence in the cause. Therefore, if there is intelligence in man, there must be—not should be— must be intelligence in man's cause. It is of solidified reason that a being must exist as some form of mass in space and time. No creator can be part of what was created or within it. God, our Maker, does not visibly exist in created space, matter, or time as we know and perceive them.

Still, some theorists ignorantly inquire, "Where is God? Show him to me," or, "I went to space and did not see God anywhere."

We are not the products of chance; we are intelligently designed. A principle of modern science emerged in 1980 called the anthropic principle, the basic thrust of which is that human existence by accident or chance is not valid. Believing otherwise invalidates all laws of chemistry, all laws of conservation, angular momentum, and every other scientific law, such as physics, conservation of electric charges, and so on. To believe that matter is uncaused is to believe against and discard all the known laws and principles of science. Dealing with conservation of matter and energy would be nothing but an obtuse, insane approach to reason. Unless directed by some being endowed with knowledge and intelligence, whatever lacks intelligence cannot intentionally move towards an end. As the arrow that is shot to its mark by the archer, anything worth living has a purpose and is here to accomplish its goal and objective.

These facts can be seen throughout nature. The whole is made up of the parts, and if the parts have destiny and purpose, then logic dictates that the whole that comprises these parts also has a destiny and purpose.

To say we come from nowhere and we are going nowhere—that this is all just an accident—simply does not add up and is both wrong and contradictory.

Even the famous phrase "the survival of the fittest" presupposes the arrival of the fit. If Darwinists wish to maintain this purely biological theory, that the entire vast order around us is the result of random chance and random changes, then they are also saying that nothing of any empirical evidence can ever be confirmed, and no empirical science can be demonstrated.

Thomas Aquinas argued for God being the "Unmoved Mover." We know that there is motion in the world, and it follows that whatever is in motion has been moved by something else. This other thing, in turn, must have been moved by something, and so on. To avoid regression, we must posit a first and a prime mover that is beyond our space, matter, and time. That ultimate, prime, or unmoved Mover is our God. The late Steven Hawking, arguably today's most famous physicist, did not believe in a God at the end of his life, although he did earlier on.[1]

Yet he claimed, ironically, that the unseen force of gravity is what keeps life and the universe grounded and is also the root cause of existence. For those who do not have to see God to believe in him, gravity is merely an unseen force in the world that is subject to God's power, as are all the other unseen forces in the world, such as electromagnetic, atomic energy, and so on. One has to wonder why it is so difficult for Hawking to see the glory of the unseen God as the root cause of the infinite complexity of existence and the obviously intelligent design of the universe.

With all due respect to Professor Hawking, his is nothing but a vaingloriously (arrogance, vanity) prosaic (humdrum, ordinary) statement, uttered by a fallible man who was willfully blind to the obvious on all sides, as well as both macro- and micro-realities, both of which are beyond human perception. Only God provides the best explanation for DNA codes contained in and controlling the design and function of life on earth. Only God provides the best explanation for the absolute complexity inherent in every element of the universe, including cosmological, planetary, chemical, biological, physical, atomic, natural, electromagnetic, and gravity forces, all interconnected with utmost precision and balance to be optimal to support human life.

The impossible alternative is that every one of our highly complex inventions, such as binary code, sophisticated and powerful computers,

---

[1] Jamie Ducharme, "Stephen Hawking was an atheist. Here's what he said about God, Heaven and his own death." Time.com, March 14, 2018, accessed November 3, 2018, http://time.com/5199149/stephen-hawking-death-god-atheist/

and wireless and digital technology, occurred without any programming, testing, debugging, or planning. This impossible alternative, called the theory of random chance, holds that our modern engineering marvels are not the result of intelligent design but simply fell into place accidently, and it is all without purpose or meaning but simply exists infinitely as it always has, meandering aimlessly and vacuously (lack of intelligence, empty, void, no meaning.)

However illogical, improbable, and impossible, many have subscribed to this theory, despite the cognitive dissonance that inert, random matter is neither self-perpetuating (lengthening, prolonging), nor self-aware, nor capable of creating intelligence, purpose, or meaning. While it is true that all the phenomenological and biological systems could not and did not take a huge and unseen leap from simple, to complex, and to maturity, they are under the influence of and are being conducted with intentional, gradual effort and purpose.

Everything is part of a guided process and forward-looking instruction. One can only produce nature and invent science from an orderly cosmos and scientific blueprint; one can only create human complexity from a discipline-coded and superior source of life. Nothing orderly and disciplined, such as the theory of relativity or other imperative scientific laws and principles, could have come from a disorderly, chaotic, randomized, universe.

If physics is the heart and the soul of science, as physicists and scientists claim, then they are more aware than anyone that mathematics—the ultimate in logic and order—is the heart and soul of physics.

It is a vital principle that applied mathematics reasoning and logic produces harmony. It is a no-brainer that this could not and does not happen randomly but rather by intelligent design. It is only another baby step of inference that the universe, with such a conscious, infinite magnitude in intelligence, a disciplined Creator not only brought order, balance, beauty, harmony, logic, and endless complexity into being, but also has an eternal purpose and meaning for human existence. God's intelligent design is viable and enduring, which otherwise would have been extinguished in the very preliminary stages of its existence.

"It is undesirable to believe a proposition when there is no ground whatever for supposing it true"

– <u>Bertrand Russell</u>

"There is only one good, knowledge, and one evil, ignorance"

– <u>Socrates</u>

"If God did not exist, it would be necessary to invent Him"

– <u>Voltaire</u>

SOME METAPHYSICAL CONCERNS

When something changes or transforms, and after transformation takes place, is it necessarily the same thing, is its identity maintained?

Can consciousness (or ideas, or soul) exist without the body? Is there anything other than physical reality?

Does everything happen for a reason? Should we believe in being predetermined? Is there free will? Is there a cause behind everything that happens? And so on. It is not far from wisdom to believe that existence is causal, but then some believe existence has come about from nothing.

Philosophy begins with curiosity and wondering why things are the way they are, so the inquisitive mind has historically wondered what constitutes the basic stuff of the universe; why and how this basic resource progressed into the diverse forms we experience, and how it arrived to be. Those questions, and other related puzzling inquiries of existence on metaphysical dimensions, is the subject of our concern.

First, why is there anything at all, or something at all? This question becomes clearer when put in comparative form; why is there something rather than nothing? Some doubt whether we can ask this question because there being nothing is not an option. "What exactly is nothing at all? What would nothing be?" We analogize nothing with the idea of empty space, in which we can conceptualize nothing. Why do things exist now or at any given point?

This is the inquiry that Thomas Aquinas was interested in, not in a beginning cause but in a sustaining cause, for he believed that the universe could be eternal—although he accepted it on the basis of revelation that it was not eternal. He manifested his cosmological arguments around the question of what sustains things in the universe in their existence.

24

In the apparent world, cause and effect play a scientifically convincing and practical role, in which denial of causal relationship should mean futility in the assessment of any sensible technological endeavor. In the realms of cause and effect, Newton's laws of motion are still the proprietor and pioneer of so many reliable experimental accomplishments, but it seems they become irrelevant in the subatomic domain, the quantum world.

Quantum physics maneuvers in search of scientific breakthroughs to manifest rationale in the sphere of the unseen, as reasoning power changes course and spurs scientists to adjust to new laws that need to epitomize different criteria, motivating physicists and scholarly minded people in related fields to identify with revolutionary concepts in the invisible environment.

Even cutting-edge technology, such as the most advanced magnifiers and complex telescopes, have a difficult time making sense of intricacies of the imperceptible (hidden, inconspicuous) world where subatomic particles dance with much different rhythm. It seems that the laws of physics, mathematics, and applied mechanics are unable to substantiate reliable answers from the infinite dancing subatomic particles.

Scientists are rendered helpless to calculate homeostasis (equilibrium, balance) in particles smaller than the atom; it is the world of quantum physics, quarks, string theory, and beyond that has bewildered the magnificent minds of our time.

In particle physics, the notion of a particle is one of several ideas handed down from <u>classical physics</u>. But it also cerebrates (cogitates, meditates, reflects) the modern understanding that at the <u>quantum</u> level, <u>matter</u> and <u>energy</u> act very differently from what much of everyday experience would guide us to expect.

The new elementary particles, "quarks," have replaced protons, neutrons, and electrons as the fundamental particles of the universe.

> "In quantum physics, the study of material at the subatomic level, you get down to the tiniest levels. When they take these subatomic particles, put them in particle accelerators and collide them, quantum physicists discover

there's nothing there. There's no one home -no ghost in
the machine" (Dr. Wayne Dyer)

The Greeks believed the atom was the smallest thing in the universe;
they accepted that the atom was not divisible any more. Modern science has
since smashed that assumption to pieces, as in the past century physicists
have discovered hundreds of particles more diminutive (minuscule, tiny)
than an atom. These subatomic, indivisible units are called fundamental,
or primal, particles. For example, matter is composed of molecules that are
made up of atoms that are made up of protons, neutrons, and electrons.

While protons and neutrons can be further split into fundamental
particles known as quarks and gluons, electrons are themselves
fundamental—at least for now. As physicists and astrophysicists further
sharpen their knowledge of the universe and deploy more powerful
technologies, they will probably discover how to deal with the unseen
world reliably and to formulate transcendent concepts (ideas) that presently
might seem utopian. They could then present revolutionary scales in our
comprehension of how things actually work in the sub-realms of existence.

Fundamental particles of both matter and antimatter (in the form of
antiparticles) exist.

Corresponding to most kinds of particles, there is an associated
antimatter antiparticle with the same mass and opposite charge (including
electric charge). For example, the antiparticle of the electron is the
positively charged positron, which is produced naturally in certain types
of radioactive decay. Likewise, photons mediate electromagnetic force,
gluons mediate strong force.

> "Scientists currently believe that the tiniest particles are
> in the form of vibrating strings associated with the world
> of the unseen that sustains us." String theory has the
> potential to show that all of the wondrous happenings in
> the universe -from the frantic dance of subatomic quarks
> to the stately waltz of orbiting binary stars; from the
> primordial fireball of the big bang to the majestic swirl of
> heavenly galaxies -are reflections of one, grand physical
> principle, one master equation. Brian Greene

"Just as our nervous system and senses are applicable to the visible world, then it is the infinite potentiality of our brain in which we should thrive for to one day have access to ultimate reasoning power that should clearly resonate with the intricacies of the unseen world."

"We need a theory that goes before the Big Bang, and that's String Theory. String Theory says that perhaps two universes collided to create our universe, or maybe our universe is butted from another universe leaving an umbilical cord. Well, that umbilical cord is called a wormhole." Michio Kaku

If we do get a quantum theory of space-time, it should answer some of the deepest philosophical questions that we have, like what happened before the big bang? Michio Kaku

Professor Michio Kaku, professor of theoretical physics and the co-founder of string field theory, states that the latest version of string theory is called "M theory" (M for membrane), so we now realize that strings can coexist with membranes. So the subatomic particles we see in nature, the quarks, the electrons, are nothing but musical notes on a tiny vibrating string. What is physics? Physics is nothing but the laws of harmony that you can write on vibrating strings. What is chemistry? Chemistry is nothing but the melodies that you can play on interacting vibrating strings.

What is the universe? The universe is a symphony of vibrating strings. And then what is the mind of God that Albert Einstein eloquently wrote about in the last thirty years of his life? We now for the first time in history have a candidate for the mind of God. It is cosmic music resonating in eleven-dimensional hyperspace.

So first of all, we are nothing but cosmic music played out on vibrating strings, a membrane obeying the laws of physics, which are nothing but the laws of harmony on vibrating strings. But why eleven dimensions? It turns out that if you write theory in fifteen, seventeen, or eighteen dimensions, the theory is not stable. It caves in and has anomalies; it has singularity.

It turns out that mathematics itself prefers the universe to be in eleven dimensions. Now some people have toyed with twelve-dimensional theory. A physicist at Harvard University has shown that twelve dimensions actually looks very similar to eleven dimensions, except it has two times, double times, rather than one singular time parameter.

What would it be like to live in a universe with double time? If you walked into a room you would see people frozen in a different time than yours, since you beat with a different clock, yet the clocks are running perpendicular to each other. That is called the F theory, "F" standing for the Father of all theories. It seems M theory in eleven dimension is the Mother of all string theories, since it works perfectly well in other dimensions.

Beyond eleven, we have problems with stability; the theories are not stable, and they have deviations from the norm. They have singularity that kills an ordinary theory, so the laws of mathematics themselves force you into an eleven-dimensional theory. Also, because this is the theory of everything, there is more room in higher dimensions to put all the forces of gravity, electromagnetics, and nuclear forces together, where the four-dimensional space is not big enough to accommodate them all. When you expand into eleven dimensions, bingo, everything works well.

Currently, cosmologists claim that the fabric of space and time based on Einstein's relativity theory has culminated in "gravitational wave theory," which might be the answer to how space and time originated. The collision of two black holes approximately 1.3 billion years ago—a colossally powerful incident detected the first time recently by scientists—resulted in gravitational waves that created a ripple across space and time. This was initially hypothesized by Albert Einstein a century ago when he plugged the idea of space and time curvature into curiously minded scientists in related fields. Hence, we should expect the impossible, since planet Earth is only a tiny cell in the body of the cosmos, leaving an infinite number of other planetary cells and universes still to be explored.

Despite scientists' grand attempt in related fields for answers in the unseen world, they only become more puzzling and elusive, making belief in the world of magic more credible. It is the world of the impalpable (undetected, intangible) that has actually made what is seen possible. A world that human senses cannot detect, and fooling some people to crudely say that the invisible world does not exist. It should remind us of the big bang theory, where many also unreasonably claim that it popped out of nowhere.

The big bang, "The role played by time at the beginning of the universe is, I believe, the final key to removing the need for a Grand Designer, and revealing how the universe created itself. ... Time itself must come to a stop. You can't get to a time before the big bang, because there was no time before the big bang.

(We have finally found something that does not have a cause because there was no time for a cause to exist in. For me this means there is no possibility of a creator because there is no time for a creator to have existed. Since time itself began at the moment of the big bang, it was an event that could not have been caused or created by anyone or anything. ... So when people ask me if a god created the universe, I tell them the question itself makes no sense. Time didn't exist before the big bang, so there is no time for God to make the universe in.

It's like asking for directions to the edge of the Earth. The Earth is a sphere. It does not have an edge, so looking for it is a futile exercise." It seems "timeless" does not exist in Mr. Hawking's lexicon since he does not realize the "Grand designer" as he puts it is timeless.)

Stephen Hawking

Then Mr. Hawking carries on to say, "If the rate of expansion one second after the big bang had been smaller by even one part in a hundred thousand million-million, it would have re-collapsed before it reached its present size. On the other hand, if it had been greater by a part in a million, the universe would have expanded too rapidly for stars and planets to form."

Ironically, what Mr. Hawking says is a clear testimony to phenomenal intelligent design, mighty supervision, order, discipline, decisiveness, absolute precision, objectivity, management, and purpose, which it seems are not included in Professor Hawking's dictionary. He says if the rate of expansion one second after the big bang had been smaller by even one part in a hundred thousand million-million, it would have re-collapsed before it reached its present size. On the other hand, if it had been greater by a part in a million, the universe would have expanded too rapidly for stars and planets to form."

Mr. Hawking attributes the cause to nothingness, where no cause or time existed, and then abracadabra boom, suddenly primordial (time worn, primeval) existence appeared, which should remind anyone of magic, where miracles can happen, but then again, miracles are also God's attribute. Think about it: out of nowhere, with no cause, no space and no time, without a promulgator, and no creator, things can happen. This type of reasoning could send anyone for psychiatric evaluation, at least in our modern industrialized world. Alarmingly enough, unwarranted thoughts can become normality and eventually the law.

The big bang is now a dominant scientific fact where certain prominent scientists claim there were no activities before the big bang—meaning no matter, no motion, no time or space, just the void, and bear in mind that matter, motion, time, and space go hand in hand and operate in concert.

This should again affirm the view that life was produced from nothing. But then what we are incompetent to figure out is—what should be counted as magic or a miracle? This is obviously beyond our comprehension because as humans, our senses and nervous systems cannot comprehend miracles or deal with them in the name of science.

But reason still questions: did the big bang just present itself out of the blue, from nowhere? If yes, then that is magic, since no matter, no motion, no time, space, or energy could have ever existed before the big bang. To accept this is to believe that cause and effect as we know it in our physical world was not in existence then. Not accepting a prime mover in our regression analysis can go forever unless a prime mover for all moves is manifested indisputably.

If we do not accept an eternal God for the reason behind the sudden occurrence of the big bang, then we need to accept gradual movement and steady accumulation of energy and matter with an unsurpassed degree of lava and heat so focused that potentiated singularity and a very colossal explosion became a turning point in causing the big bang.

This, by the way, would have led to a chaotic and unorderly world. That is what any explosion must do, rather than implementing an utter miracle like a fabulously designed, majestically disciplined and displayed universe. I am not hesitant to say that the incremental build-up of matter and sharp concentration of molten (melted by heat) lava, explosive material, and gasses is more favorable and attuned with scientific communities than an enormous eruption taking place out of nowhere.

But if a gradual accumulation of matter was the case, matter is accompanied with motion, and motion is associated with time and space. They must have existed before the humongous explosion, and they must have been the preliminary requirements for what we know as the big bang because where there is matter exists motion, and where there is motion exists space and time.

We are often left with no idea but to believe nothingness should mean no activity of any sort. But we ought not to be remiss (thoughtless, heedless, lax) in saying that the so-called void should mean nothingness, which on the contrary, nothingness is the womb impregnated with all there is, and all there ever will be, patiently waiting to be sought for generating more miracles.

WHERE DO WE COME FROM?

Everything that exists is born for no reason, carries on
living through weakness, and dies by accident"

– <u>Jean-Paul Sartre</u>

This saying above by Jean-Paul Sartre should leave mankind with no hope,
and frankly, vulnerable to suicide, and host of other violent behaviors.

What is consciousness?
What is existence?
What is the universe made of?

Gospel of Thomas Saying 50
<u>Previous</u> -<u>Gospel of Thomas Home</u> -<u>Next</u>
This <u>Gospel of Thomas Commentary</u> is part of the <u>Gospel of Thomas</u>
page at <u>Early Christian Writings</u>.

Nag Hammad Coptic Text

50. (1) ΠΕΧΕ ΙС ΧΕ ΕΥϢΑΝΧΟΟС ΝΗΤΝ ΧΕ ΝΤΑΤΕΤΝϢωΠΕ
ΕΒΟλ ΤωΝ ΧΟΟС ΝΑΥ ΧΕ ΝΤΑΝΕΙ ΕΒΟλ 2Μ ΠΟΥΟΕΙΝ ΠΜΑ
ΕΝΤΑΠΟΥΟΕΙΝ ϢωΠΕ ΜΜΑΥ ΕΒΟλ 2ΙΤΟΟΤϤ ΟΥΑΑΤϤ ΑϤω2(Ε
ΕΡΑΤϤ) ΑΥω ΑϤΟΥωΝ2 Ε(Β)Ολ 2Ν ΤΟΥ2ΙΚωΝ (2) ΕΥϢΑΧΟΟС
ΝΗΤΝ ΧΕ ΝΤωΤΝ ΠΕ ΧΟΟС ΧΕ ΑΝΟΝ ΝΕϤϢΗΡΕ ΑΥω ΑΝΟΝ
ΝСωΤΠ ΜΠΕΙωΤ ΕΤΟΝ2 (3) ΕΥϢΑΝΧΝΕ ΤΗΥΤΝ ΧΕ ΟΥ ΠΕ
ΠΜΑΕΙΝ ΜΠΕΤΝΕΙωΤ ΕΤ2Ν ΘΗΥΤΝ ΧΟΟС ΕΡΟΟΥ ΧΕ ΟΥΚΙΜ ΠΕ
ΜΝ ΟΥΑΝΑΠΑΥСΙС

BLATZ

(50) Jesus said: If they say to you: Whence have you come? say to them: We have come from the light, the place where the light came into being of itself. It [established itself], and it revealed itself in their image. If they say to you: Who are you? say: We are his sons, and we are the elect of the living Father. If they ask you: What is the sign of your Father in you? say to them: It is movement and rest.

LAYTON

(50) Jesus said, "If they say to you (plur.), 'Where are you from?' say to them, 'It is from light that we have come -from the place where light, of its own accord alone, came into existence and [stood at rest]. And it has been shown forth in their image.' If they say to you, 'Is it you?' say 'We are its offspring, and we are the chosen of the living father.' If they ask you, 'What is the sign of your father within you?' say to them, 'movement and repose.' and

What we now hear from the most prominent scientists at the most advanced laboratories is that we are made of stardust. For many years, advocators of science have believed that human-beings are made of stardust, and presently, a fresh survey

DORESSE

55 [50]. Jesus says: "If people ask you: 'Where have you come from?' tell them: 'We have come from the Light, from the place where the Light is produced [. . .] outside itself <or: of itself?>. It [. . .] until they show (?) [. . .] their image.' If someone says to you: 'What are you?' say: 'We are the sons and we are the elect of the living Father.' If <people> ask you: 'What sign of your Father is in you?' tell them: 'It is a movement and a "rest."'"

of more than 170,000
stars exhibit how
true the old platitude
(cliché, buzzword)
is: they have realized
that: humans and
their galaxy have
approximately 97-98
percent of the same
sort of atoms, and the
elements of life seem
to be more prevalent
directed at the
galaxy's center, the
research found.
The imperative
components for life
on Earth, frequently
known as the
building blocks of
life, can be abridged
as CHNOPS: carbon,
hydrogen, nitrogen,
oxygen, phosphorus,
and sulfur. For
the first time,
many astronomers
have categorized
plenty of these
factors (elements)
in a monumental
embodiment of stars.

The astronomers
ranked each element's
abundance via a
method known
as chromatic
(spectroscopy); each
feature (element) vents
multifarious (unequal,
unlike) wavelengths
of light from within
a star, and they size
the depth of the dark
and bright patches in
each star's light gamut
(spectrum, range) to
decide what it was
made of.

Abstract questions of who are we? Where do we come from? Why are we here? What happens after we expire? What is existence? What is consciousness? and so on, historically have seen many views these questions, but the contemporary scientific approach by many scholarly minded scientists and prominent philosophers is that "our bodies are made of remnants of stars and massive explosions into galaxies," according to astrophysicist <u>Karel Schrijver of the Lockheed Martin Solar and Astrophysics</u> Laboratory and his wife, professor of pathology at Stanford University in their new book titled Living with Stars, how the human body is connected to the life cycles of the Earth, the planets, and the stars.

They believe that everything we are, and everything in the universe and Earth originated from stardust, and it continually floats through us even today. It directly connects us to the universe, rebuilds our bodies over and over again over our lifetimes.

The six most common elements of life on Earth (including more than 97 percent of the mass of a human body) are carbon, hydrogen, nitrogen, oxygen, Sulphur, and phosphorus. Those same elements are abundant at the center of our Milky Way galaxy.

Credit: Dana Berry/Skyworks Digital Inc.; SDSS collaboration.

The proportion of each element of life differed depending on the region of the galaxy in which it was found. For example, the sun resides on the outskirts of one of the Milky Way's spiral arms. Stars on the outskirts of the galaxy have fewer heavy elements required for life's building blocks, such as oxygen, than those in more central regions of the galaxy.

"It's a great human-interest story that we are now able to map the abundance of all of the major elements found in the human body across hundreds of thousands of stars in our Milky Way," Jennifer Johnson, the science team chair of the SDSS-III APOGEE survey and a professor at Ohio State University said in the statement. "This allows us to place constraints on when and where in our galaxy life had the required elements to evolve, a sort of 'temporal galactic habitable zone.'"

Consciousness is infinite energy, an awakened source, extremely resourceful, that is non-local, which means universal. Thoughts, ideas, insight, imaginations, dreams, creativity, ingenuity, feelings and emotions, mindfulness, space, time, qualia (the internal and subjective component of sense perceptions, arising from stimulation of the senses by phenomena), etc., are all interconnected within consciousness.

It is not tangible. All things maneuver within consciousness. It is the super glue holding what is animated, or not, what is instinctual or not, those with mind, or not. The entire existence is contained within consciousness. It is the very fundamental foundation to all there was, all there is, and what will ever be, as only the effects of consciousness are seen, as no experiment is ever possible without consciousness.

The power of semantics (related to the meaning of words and phrases) is connected to consciousness, since things do not exist if one is not aware of them.

It seems consciousness is the common denominator for the entire existence, and unless humanity comes into accord with this extremely potent force, no viable explanation by modern science can actually take place for explaining what is driving our universe.

For instance, the two major scientific revolutions of modern physics are first Albert Einstein's theory of relativity.

In the equation, the increased relativistic mass (m) of a body times the speed of light squared (c2) is equal to the kinetic energy (E) of that body.

E = mc2 Proof of Albert Einstein's special-relativity equation E = mc2, it means that mass and energy are relative, they are interchangeable, as they are not fixed.

The second theory says that space and time are relative; they are interchangeable and not fixed, they are equivalent. The formula is as follows: s2= -t2-c2 where space, time, matter, and energy are not absolute.

The actual physical reality of the world, and the experiences that we acquire from out there, what appears in our consciousness from maneuvering in the physical world are fundamentally different; they are not the same.

What we see, hear, taste, touch, and smell are just the illusion of the reality. the new paradigm is shifted in the assumption that CONSCIOUSNESS is the premier merit (capital) of reality.

Consciousness is prioritized for two reasons; first, it is potentiated for infinite experimentation, which is proffered (available) in all things. Secondly, because we do not directly experience the external world, what we grasp are the contents of consciousness, not to exclude our emotions, feelings, thoughts, and perceptions, and all the sensations that originate in our mind.

Immanuel Kant, the German philosopher, made a very clear distinction between the forms that appeared in the mind, known as "phenomenon," meaning that which appears to be, and the world that produced our perception of things and activities, known as "noumenon," meaning that which is grasped, apprehended, or detained. Kant emphasized, and insisted on phenomenon, where noumenon permanently stays beyond our knowing.

Many philosophers and prominent thinkers have insisted on the idealism theory saying that only the mind and mental contents exists.

A century ago, British philosopher John Locke argued that all knowledge is based on perceptions, caused by external objects acting on the senses. But Locke thought that perception was passive, the mind simply reflecting the images received by the senses.

Kant proposed that the mind is an active attendee in the process, constantly shaping our experience of the world. Reality, he thought, is something we each build for ourselves.

For Berkeley, the theologian bishop, he denied anything existing apart from our perception, that only mind and mental contents exist. His doctoring is generally associated and identified with "immaterialism," the doctrine that believes material things simply do not exist since they have no reality except as mental perceptions.

The difficult question for George Berkeley is that what happens to the world when no one is perceiving it. But Kant less radically believed there is a fundamental reality, but is never known directly; all that we can comprehend is the way objects appear in our mind. Through our senses: sight, hearing, smell, taste, touch, we experience the external world. Then our brain brilliantly, in a split second, takes all of these images received, and without us noticing, puts the entire data together and presents its own picture of the so-called reality from what is out there.

For instance, when we look at a plant, the light reflected from the plant shapes an image of the plant on our retina. Then, the photo-sensitive cells in the retina release electrons, setting off electro-chemical impulses that travel through the optic nerve to the visual cortex of our brain. The data endures a complicated procedure that then discerns patterns, colors, motion, and shapes, which the brain puts together as information received into cohesive position and makes its own version of the outside world. Eventually, an image of the plant shows up in our consciousness. The issue of concern is that how neural activities bring about conscious experience is an extremely difficult question to answer, since we have no idea how an image appears in our mind since it does occur, as we have the conscious experience of seeing a plant.

Conscious exposure on one hand generates an abysmally enigmatic circumstance. On the other hand, a fairly able-bodied world of materialism must be for real so that we can explain how it is that conscious events relate and interact with non-conscious physical incidents, and why we are not able to describe how physical phenomena gives rise to conscious experience. An ever present and ubiquitous consciousness can play a significant role in relatively clarifying most of the events taking place in our world. The irony is that we endure the body-mind experience, but cannot materialize consciousness, and it's not possible to describe dilemmas of phenomenal experience denoting physical realization. It seems consciousness is going to remain a mystery in the near future, or within the realm of infinity.

Images in the Mind

Parallel activities happen with the other human senses. The strings of a vibrating violin constitute pressure waves in the air. These waves stir up tiny hairs inside the inner ear, which then send electrical impulses to our brain. The same with vision; data received are analyzed and cleverly assembled, activating our experience for hearing music. For smelling, chemical molecules originating from the skin of a rose trigger receptors in the nose, leading to the experience of smelling a rose. And similarly, cells in the skin forward messages to the brain that guide to experiences of touch, pressure, texture, grain, and affection.

In short, all that I perceive—all that I see, hear, taste, touch and smell—has been reconstructed from sensory data. I think I am perceiving the world around me, but all that I am directly aware of are the colors, shapes, sounds, and smells that appear in the mind.

> "Every man's world picture is and always remains a construct of his mind, and cannot be proved to have any other existence." Erwin Schrödinger

Our perception of the world has the very convincing appearance of being "out there" around us, but it is no more "out there" than are our nightly dreams. In our dreams we are aware of sights, sounds, and sensations happening around us. We are aware of our bodies. We think and reason. We feel fear, anger, pleasure, and love. We experience other people as separate individuals, speaking and interacting with us. The dream appears to be happening "out there" in the world around us. Only when we awaken do we realize that it was all just a dream—a creation in the mind.

When we say, "it was all just a dream," we are referring to the fact that the experience was not based on physical reality. It was created from memories, hopes, fears, and other factors. In the waking state, our image of the world is based on sensory information drawn from our physical surroundings. This gives our waking experience a consistency and sense of reality not found in dreams. But the truth is, it is as much a creation of our minds as are our dreams (Erwin Schrödinger).

Therefore, all we know is what actually stems out of experience. We become in tune with the picture the brain draws, in which the brain maneuvers so rapidly that we cannot know what took place. For instance, the color green; in realty, there is no color green out there. When light of certain frequency is reflected from the physical world, which then is experienced in our mind, or consciousness, call it as you wish, we then see the color green. Colors are seen in particular shades after they are dealt with, or manipulated by, the brain. Colors are not in the material world; they are only wavelength and reflections. Colors are utterly the products of our mind. It is believed that consciousness is the field of all possibilities; in other words, consciousness makes anything possible. It is the foundation of our experience. "Everything that is experienced is perceived by mind, made by mind, and ruled by mind" (Buddha).

The Greek philosopher Demetrious, 400 BC, was the first person who used the term atom, meaning indivisible.

Demetrious thought that if one takes a piece of matter and divides it, and continues to do so, one will consequently arrive to a point where one could not divide it any more. This fundamental unit was what Democritus called an atom. He believed all matters consist of atoms; atoms are bits of matter too extremely small to be seen. There is an empty space between atoms. Atoms are solid, as they have no internal structure. Atoms of various substances are different in size, form, and weight.

Then, approximately one hundred years later, scientists discovered the atom is made of subatomic particles, which recently modern science found out those particles do not exist, they are just potentials for our experiences, as consciousness there, or better said: there is not a thing there.

"Matter as we know it, exist only in our mind" (Max Plank).

It seems the tables have turned, and contrary to calling idealists superstitious, it is clear that the materialistic view has scientifically been proven wrong, but no one has the guts to admit that matter as we know it does not exist, and everything that we call matter comes from something that is not materially based. Most contemporary scientists, and noticeably philosophers, now believe the essential nature of the universe is not physical. They also say that nature is a discontinuation, where there are gaps, suggesting on-and-off events.

Deepak Chopra said: "There is a field of possibilities, a field of pure potentialities, if not God, call it what you want. The immense potentiality of all that was, and all that is, and all there will be, if not God, then what?"

Science says there exists a field of non-local correlation, since everything is connected to everything else; there is a field of creativity, there are quantum leaps of opportunities promising miracles, and rightly so. It has now more than ever become clear that we are an undeniable part of the universal consciousness.

Rumi, the great Persian philosopher and poet, said: "You are not just a drop of the ocean, you are the mighty ocean in the drop." It is so surprising that our feelings, emotions, hopes, dreams, imaginations, thoughtfulness, insight, free will, freedom, often creativity like miracles, and millions of other things are done through our "neurons" that we cannot see. But then, some callously minded individuals are still denying an omnipotent God, that is beyond space, time, and infinitely so big to be detected by human nervous system. Not reckoning with such infinity enlightening and intelligent force, is extremely unscientific, and non-philosophical, in which science and philosophy are potently equipped to answer most of "whys" and "how's" of the world.

Einstein added that "Science without religion is lame, and religion without science is blind."

Steven Hawking said, "It would be very difficult to explain why the universe would have begun in just this way, except as the act of God who created beings like us."

Double slit experiment

One of the most noticeable experiments in physics is the double slit experiment. It uniquely shows that the strange behavior of the little particles of matter also have something of a wave position. The experiment manifests that every act of observing a particle has a dramatic effect on its observer. It shows that what we know as particles, such as electrons, exhibit both combined characteristics of particles and characteristics of waves. That's the illustrious wave particle duality of quantum mechanics.

It denotes that the act of observing, of measuring, a quantum system has a deep effect on the system. Strangely enough, as if the particles knew they are being looked at, they manage not to get caught in the performance of bizarre quantum pranks. The question of exactly how that happens constitutes the measurement problem of quantum mechanics. The double slit experiment reveals the principle limitation of the observer's ability to foresee the experiment's result. Richard Feyman called it "a phenomenon which is impossible to explain in any classical way, and which has in it the heart of quantum mechanics in reality, it contains the only mystery of quantum mechanics.

- ❖ "Everything we call real is made of things that cannot be regarded as real" (Niels Bohr).
- ❖ "Those who are not shocked when they first come across quantum theory cannot possibly have understood it" (Niels Bohr).
- ❖ "If you are not completely confused by quantum mechanics, you do not understand it" (John Wheeler).
- ❖ "If [quantum theory] is correct, it signifies the end of physics as a science" (Albert Einstein).
- ❖ "I do not like [quantum mechanics], and I am sorry I ever had anything to do with it" (Erwin Schrödinger).
- ❖ "Quantum mechanics makes absolutely no sense" (Roger Penrose).
- ❖ "It is safe to say that nobody understands quantum mechanics" (Richard Feynman).

And, in a little more detail, from Richard Feynman:

I am going to tell you what nature behaves like. If you will simply admit that maybe she does behave like this, you will find her a delightful, entrancing thing. Do not keep saying to yourself, if you can possibly avoid it, 'but how can it be like that?' because you will get 'down the drain,' into a blind alley from which nobody has yet escaped. Nobody knows how it can be like that.

Here's a rather more optimistic,

In two slit interferences, quantum mechanics cannot determine which slit the electron went through."

GOD, MAN, AND THE UNIVERSE

This statement reflects not the poverty of quantum mechanics, but its richness.

In classical mechanics, an electron must have a position — it must pass through one slit or the other.

In quantum mechanics an electron might have a position, but there is an infinitely rich variety of other possibilities as well.

It is no failure of our instruments that they cannot measure what does not exist.

The observe effect.

Observer effect may refer to the Hawthorne effect, a form of reactivity in which subjects modify an aspect of their behavior in response to their knowing that they are being studied. Same goes for the "Heisenbug" effect of computer programming, where a software bug seems to disappear or alter its behavior when one attempts to study it.

What is the Heisenberg effect?

In quantum mechanics, the uncertainty principle (also known as Heisenberg's uncertainty principle) is any of a variety of mathematical inequalities asserting a fundamental limit to the precision with which certain pairs of physical properties of a particle, known as complementary variables, such as position x and ...

Do particles behave differently when observed?

When a quantum "observer" is watching, quantum mechanics states that particles can also behave as waves. In other words, when under observation, electrons are being "forced" to behave like particles and not like waves. Thus the mere act of observation affects the experimental findings.

What is Heisenberg most known for?

He developed new theories in quantum mechanics about the behavior of electrons that agreed with the results of previous experiments. Heisenberg is most famous for his "uncertainty principle," which explains the impossibility of knowing exactly where something is and how fast it is moving.

In science, the term observer effect means that the act of observing will influence the phenomenon being observed. For example, for us to "see" an electron, a photon must first interact with it, and this interaction will change the path of that electron.

The Heisenberg uncertainty principle states that it is impossible to know simultaneously the exact position and momentum of a particle. That is, the more exactly the position is determined, the less known the momentum, and vice versa. This principle is not a statement about the limits of technology, but a fundamental limit on what can be known about a particle at any given moment. This uncertainty arises because the act of measuring affects the object being measured. The only way to measure the position of something is using light, but, on the subatomic scale, the interaction of the light with the object inevitably changes the object's position and its direction of travel.

With the advent of new technology modern science is able to dig deeper into the mysteries of universe. It is no brainer as it is now very clear, what is taking place in the unseen world is drastically different from what for so long had occupied the classical physicist's mind stating, what we see, is what we get. where modern science has proved many people wrong saying that: what you see is not what you get. And it is the unseen world which rules the physical world. Now more than ever the evidence of a magnificent creator is much more apparent to scientific community. Since prominent physicists, philosophers and scholarly minded individuals are now aware of quantum consciousness.

The views on new paradigm shift from a world known as objectively real which existed as a separate entity, and not connected to us has altered toward creationism. The question is if there is a God behind the existence? And the quantum world says yes, if not, how could quantum physic describe possibilities which can substantiate actual experience of events taking place in our world. None locality, cosmic awareness, and downward causation are the properties of consciousness, where no matter can behave non-local, since the quantum soup is entirely about energy oriented information and awareness. One cannot model life based on reductionists mentality, where life can be simulated in laboratory and become jubilated just because some short sighted scientists are able to manage a self-replicating molecule. One cannot reproduce life from a self-replicating molecule. "Life can only be produced from a down-ward causation." (Amit Go swami)

Paul Davis said, "The secret of life won't be cooked up in a chemistry lab."

Paul Davies

Life's origins may only be explained through a study of its unique management of information.

"Even the simplest bacterium is incomparably more complicated than any chemical brew ever studied."

The origin of life is one of the great outstanding mysteries of science. How did a non-living mixture of molecules transform themselves into a living organism? What sort of mechanism might be responsible?

A century and a half ago, Charles Darwin produced a convincing explanation for how life on Earth evolved from simple microbes to the complexity of the biosphere today, but he pointedly left out how life got started in the first place. "One might as well speculate about the origin of matter," he quipped. But that did not stop generations of scientists from investigating the puzzle.

The problem is, whatever took place happened billions of years ago, and all traces long ago vanished—indeed, we may never have a blow-by-blow account of the process. Nevertheless, we may still be able to answer the simpler question of whether life's origin was a freak series of events that happened only once, or an almost inevitable outcome of intrinsically life-friendly laws. On that answer hinges the question of whether we are alone in the universe or whether our galaxy and others are teeming with life.

Most research into life's murky origin has been carried out by chemists. They've tried a variety of approaches in their attempts to recreate the first steps on the road to life, but little progress has been made. Perhaps that is no surprise, given life's stupendous complexity. Even the simplest bacterium is incomparably more complicated than any chemical brew ever studied.

But a more fundamental obstacle stands in the way of attempts to cook up life in the chemistry lab. The language of chemistry simply does not mesh with that of biology. Chemistry is about substances and how they react, whereas biology appeals to concepts such as information and organization. Informational narratives permeate biology. DNA is described as a genetic database, containing instructions on how to build an organism. The genetic code has to be transcribed and translated before it can act. If we cast the problem of life's origin in computer jargon, attempts at chemical synthesis focus exclusively on the hardware, the chemical substrate of life, but ignore the software, the informational aspect. To explain how life began, we need to understand how its unique management of information came about.

In the 1940s, the mathematician John von Neumann compared life to a mechanical constructor and set out the logical structure required for a self-reproducing automaton to replicate both its hardware and software. But Von Neumann's analysis remained a theoretical curiosity. Now a new perspective has emerged from the work of engineers, mathematicians, and computer scientists, studying the way in which information flows through complex systems, such as communication networks with feedback loops, logic modules, and control processes. What is clear from their work is that the dynamics of information flow displays generic features that are independent of the specific hardware supporting the information.

Information theory has been extensively applied to biological systems at many levels from genomes to ecosystems, but rarely to the problem of how life actually began.

Doing so opens up an entirely new perspective on the problem. Rather than the answer being buried in some baffling chemical transformation, the key to life's origin lies instead with a transformation in the organization of information flow. Paul Davis. When an atom is broken down, quarks and electrons are discovered. Within these founded particles subsist pure energy that cannot be physically measured. Quantum science has concocted this energy as its exclusive intelligence, which replies with no common sense approach. Quantum physics knows that everything in our universe is managed with the same note through a grand, unified, indestructible force. But human curiosity does not stop there.

We question: what is existence? What is consciousness? What is our awareness of the universe, or the existence? We cannot be certain of any answer that has been rendered so far. What we know is the universe exists, and also we are aware that we exist." But both knowings are contextually puzzling. Scientists tell us that about 74 percent of the universe is made of dark energy, and also made of 22 percent of dark matter, of which only 4 percent is visible matter.

What is dark energy? What is dark matter according to Hubble site discoveries?

So what is dark energy? Well, the simple answer is that we don't know. It seems to contradict many of our understandings about the way the universe works.

We all know that light waves, also called radiation, carry energy. You feel that energy the moment you step outside on a hot summer day.

Einstein's famous equation, $E = mc2$, teaches us that matter and energy are interchangeable; merely different forms of the same thing. We have a giant example of that in our sky: The Sun. The Sun is powered by the conversion of mass to energy.

Something from nothing.

Could dark energy show a link between the physics of the very small and the physics of the large? Energy is supposed to have a source—either matter or radiation. The notion here is that space, even when devoid of all matter and radiation, has a residual energy. That "energy of space," when considered on a cosmic scale, leads to a force that increases the expansion of the universe.

Perhaps dark energy results from weird behavior on scales smaller than atoms. The physics of the very small, called quantum mechanics, allows energy and matter to appear out of nothingness, although only for the tiniest instant. The constant brief appearance and disappearance of matter could be giving energy to otherwise empty space.

It could be that dark energy creates a new, fundamental force in the universe, something that only starts to show an effect when the universe reaches a certain size. Scientific theories allow for the possibility of such forces. The force might even be temporary, causing the universe to accelerate for some billions of years before it weakens and essentially disappears.

Or perhaps the answer lies within another long-standing unsolved problem, how to reconcile the physics of the large with the physics of the very small. Einstein's theory of gravity, called general relativity, can explain everything from the movements of planets to the physics of black holes, but it simply doesn't seem to apply on the scale of the particles that make up atoms. To predict how particles will behave, we need the theory of quantum mechanics. Quantum mechanics explains the way particles function, but it simply doesn't apply on any scale larger than an atom. The elusive solution for combining the two theories might yield a natural explanation for dark energy.

Stranger and Stranger

Most of the universe seems to consist of nothing we can see. Dark energy and dark matter, detectable only because of their effect on the visible matter around them, make up most of the universe. Illustrated by Hubble site discovery.

It seems rather odd that we have no solid concept about what makes up 74 percent of the universe. It's as we had pioneered all the land on planet Earth and not ever in all our search found an ocean. But currently that we've grasped sight of the waves, we want to conceive what this colossal, peculiar and potent entity really is.

The idiosyncrasy (peculiarity, eccentricity, strangeness, quirkiness) of dark energy is exciting. It indicates to scientists that there is a discrepancy in our understanding that requires to be addressed, signaling the way toward an unexplored territory of physics. We see the cite (evidence) that the cosmos may be arranged enormously different than we previously thought. Dark energy both signals that we still have a great deal to cultivate, and warns us that we stand ready for another great hop in our comprehension of the universe.

We are aware of this: Since space is prevalent, this dark energy force is ubiquitous, and its outcome multiplies as space grows. Comparably, gravity's force is mightier when things are close together and tenuous (weak), when they are far apart. Because gravity is becoming weaker with the augmentation(enlargement) of space.

Therefore, some of the questions modern science has not been able to answer are: What is the universe? What is existence? Are they separate? What is consciousness? What is our awareness of consciousness? What is our awareness of existence? And so on. What we supposedly know is that the universe exists, and we are aware that we exist, even though we do not know where we come from and we do not know who we are, why we are here, and where we are heading.

Scientists tell us that 74 percent of the universe is arcane (mystic) force called dark energy, which Einstein pointed out as "cosmological constant" so scientists think it is the cause for expanding the universe quicker than the speed of light. It seems that galaxies move apart from each other, and as the speed of the movement of galaxies from each other increases more and more, spaces are split and further expand. Scientists believe that the "cosmic horizon" of outer space is presently forty-seven to forty-eight billion years away from where we are. Scientists also tell us that the remaining stuff, the 22 percent that is called dark matter is not atomic, which means it doesn't reflect light; it can neither emit nor absorb light. But it holds entire galaxies through the gravitational force; it is just not possible to interact with it.

Hence, 74 percent of the universe is dark energy, and 22 percent dark matter, which leaves 4 percent of atomic force. And then science reveals that 99 percent of this said 4 percent atomic force is hydrogen and helium that hasn't yet formed into stars. The remaining effect is .01 percent, which is apparently the visible universe from which 99 percent of .01 percent is not seen, which is intergalactic interstellar dust. Then figure that billions and billions of galaxies within galaxies, each with billions and billions of planets forming indefinite universes are constituted only within .01 percent that is atomic. This evidences what we so far comprehend and depend on, hoping the gravitational forces do not collapse for guarantying what exists, not to exclude humanity.

Scientists have realized that atoms are particles, particles are waves, and waves are possibilities that exist in what we know as nothingness. Therefore, past the emergence of molecules, when science arrives at the subatomic realms and then beyond, what they see is nothing; but then again, if the nature of our existence is nothing, where is consciousness? And what is consciousness? What is the biological nature of consciousness, if any? Starting with self, we cannot locate any one, any ghost or any shadow inside, no matter how advanced our magnifiers are or how sophisticated our scientific tools are, such as MRI, CT scan, laser beams, or x-rays machines, and using any other advanced radiation machine to detect the observing-self is just not possible. It seems the observer is delusional, since we cannot find who is doing the hundreds, if not thousands, of things that we daily do, but no one is to be found within us, or inside our brain. No matter how deep we look into every cell, every neuron, or any other part of our body, it is not going to happen. It is all about feelings, all about sensation. If we can feel our presence, feel our breath, our thoughts, that must be the observing self. And if we can feel the universe, that is what supposedly exists; which the sages, and scholarly minded people say has always existed beyond space and time.

Now how true that is, it is one's prerogative to convincingly accept or reject.

The observing self is not about thoughts, emotions, and feelings, but more an awareness entity. One knows when thinking and feeling because there is an awareness, but can we make sense of being aware? Yes, only by noticing the effects of being aware of self and the atmosphere around us. We change due to the human emotional roller coaster, due growing up, and as we mature, we often have to take a variety of positions in life. As our thoughts and feelings change, we deal with different roles in our lives. But the observing self does not alter; it seems the observing self does not change, but sees and experiences.

It makes you aware of your conduct, which is the result of your thinking self, your emotional self, your cultural self. The observing self does not judge, does not take responsibly, does not produce any thoughts. It surreptitiously observes without being seen. The wise, the saints, gurus, and the godly philosophers of the world have been insisting on a cognized universe all along, even before there ever was a brain or a body created, before you and I and everyone else started with a single cell, then multiplied, and replicated fifty times, arriving at about three trillion cells or more, making what we know as humans. Cosmic consciousness has always been the layout for existence in our world and is the reason we can experience and feel our identity, and have a sense of administrative control over the mind. Consciousness is the potential for experiencing our awareness of existence, and is prior to subject/object split.

Top of Form

Quantum physic is in line with the philosophy of science. It states that there is no actual world of electrons, photons, quarks, or any other subatomic entity that we might encounter in the future. There is only delineation (description) of the world that uses these terms and it works in explaining what one observes.

The traditional scientific inquiry, basically the "Newtonian world," is to learn about things as if they exist independently of the observer. It works well in the visible world where cause and effect, time and space, seem to be the nervous system of scientific experimentation—until we are faced with studying the quantum world of the very small. It is here, where the traditional ideas of causality, time, and space breakdown, where the observer's effect or consciousness plays a conspicuous (remarkable, prominent) role.

It is by way of observation that the quantum world arrives. Before observation, the quantum realm exists for mathematical assessments, acknowledged as probability waves. Once an observation happens, this situation collapses into something that can only be known in quantum terms. When one has the experience, one then perceives and gets into cognitive mode, where personal interactivity materializes looking at the universe. It is then the subject/object split substantiates.

The dynamics behind such subject/object split is of significance, since no one knows why and how should such transition takes place, giving the observer an illusion of the external world. The outside world impacts our senses; we become aware of our environment via the nervous system and our brain. We experience and become familiar with our surroundings. Yes, and as we experience, perceive, and analyze, the subject/object split occurs. This entire interchangeability happens with infinite speed, and so quick that no transformation of the subject/object split is ever noticed either by the naked eye or other senses, only to remind us of magic.

What so far is known is that our experiences, our creations, sketches, observations, and all that we are involved with, happens in consciousness, but there is no scientific corroboration (verification) of consciousness, since it cannot be seen by our senses, it can only be felt via awareness; for instance, one being conscious of oneself in one's mind. Consciousness observes, measures, evaluates; it verifies, but it cannot be observed or measured. All of scientific confirmation of consciousness is deduced. It is based on inference, which means a guess or opinion that comes from information that one has. The sole linear experience of consciousness is self-awareness within awareness.

Bear in mind that electrons and other subatomic entities are remarkably diminutive (infinitesimal, tiny), and they also have extremely low mass. They move extremely fast, and due to the Heisenberg uncertainty principle, their precise position is absolutely undetectable. We can solely approximate their position to within a confident uncertainty. Hence, not being able to know the exact position renders it impossible to watch them. With a mass so low, even the smallest interplay (synergy, interaction) with them by another electron or photon will send them flying off so that no one can observe them, and we're now left with a worse understanding of their EXACT location.

Due to the Heisenberg uncertainty principle (HUP), it is impossible to exactly locate electrons and quarks and other subatomic particles. Scientists only know where electrons are likely to be, but never where they actually are positioned. Electrons can exist in multistate, at the same time—things are extremely strange at the quantum level.

Bear in mind that the internet, laser beam, broadband, GPS, computer, fiber optic, are all the result of quantum theory. And yes, it is counterintuitive, but it is what it is. It is difficult to believe the activities at the atomic level. They use electron cloud models of atoms as a probability field to recognize their whereabouts. No one, including physicists, scientists, or anyone else, has seen a subatomic particle.

As Deepak Chopra says, there is no such thing as particle, it is space time event into consciousness. Therefore, in answering who are we? Again as Deepak Chopra says, "We are qualia matrix/ a continuum of probabilities in transcendent infinite field of possibilities." Deepak also believes we are luminous stardust with self-awareness.

UNREALISTIC SCIENTIFIC BELIEFS

Science is based on the observation of facts and measurements. This renders many scientists to posit that science is the most reliable way of knowing the truth. What is misunderstood is that the empirical analogy driven from direct observation, or what we know as a description of empirical facts, are basically descriptions of modes of human perception formed by the human nervous system and not through an assessment of reality. What occurs in each and every scientific endeavor happens after subject/object split. Therefore, there is no such thing as non-duality, it simply cannot be obtained. There is no observer-sovereign or self-governed reality.

What exists before the subject/object split is called qualia, which is defined as "the internal and subjective component of sense perceptions, arising from stimulation of the senses by phenomena." Qualia as a capable matrix subsists in marrow (core) consciousness before the subject/object split. Qualia's ghostly characteristics are sensation, images, feelings, thoughts, and emotions.

Heisenberg said, "What is observed is not nature itself, but nature exposed to our method of questioning."

And John Wheeler said, "Every particle, every field of force even the space time continuum itself-derives its function, its meaning, its very existence, entirely from apparatus elicited, concepts to questions we ask-this is a participatory universe."

Observation, scientific outcomes, comprehension, awareness, theories, space, time, events, and what we as human beings can meaningfully grasp, entire worldly activities and beyond, are all in the consciousness. Whatever we perceive, and what is hidden in the womb of nature waiting to be discovered and born, are the offspring of consciousness. Without mindful awareness, no theories can be coagulated. Without consciousness, no experience is ever possible. It has always been there with no interruption.

And as Deepak Chopra said, "Science cannot explain consciousness, but consciousness can conceive and construct the scientific method. How do we get the body experience even though we are not in the body?"

Our experiences of reality occur after subject/object split. Other organisms do not share the same experience as their reality. Hence, perceptual experiences differ as different species' (genus, breed, phylum) representation of mode of observation are varied. Relative to humans, spiders see ultraviolet and green; honey bees see ultraviolet, blue, and yellow. Reptiles see some colors and infrared. Birds see five to seven colors, mammals (cats and dogs) see two colors, but weakly. Most fish also see two colors. Rabbits and rats see two colors, blue and green. Squirrels see blue and yellow. Primates (apes and chimps, African monkeys) see as humans. Bats utilize echolocation to maneuver and find food in the dark. To echolocate, bats send out sound waves from their mouth or nose. When the sound waves impact an object, they generate echoes. The echo bounces off the object and returns to the bat's ear.

Chameleons have a distinguishing visual system that empowers them to observe their atmosphere in almost 360 degrees (180 degrees horizontally and +/-90 degrees vertically). They activate it in two ways. The first is with anatomical specializations that enable the eyes to spin freely. The next is the chameleon's ability to switch between monocular and binocular vision, meaning they can see objects with either eye independently, or with both eyes at the same time. The chameleon's eyeball works on different axes.

Dolphins have expanded the ability to utilize echo-location, often known as sonar, to assist them in observing better underwater. Scientists believe this competency probably evolved gradually over time. Echolocation permits dolphins to "see" by interpreting the echoes of sound waves that bounce off of objects near them in time.

The awkwardness for physicists, and many scientists, occurs in the world of quantum mechanics, where seeing means conscious observation, denoting that consciousness and the quantum world are inseparable. It seems that quantum activities and consciousness can never be quantifiable, materialized as thoughts, or arrived at as an object of thought.

The Buddhist states this unknowability by saying, "You can't bite your own teeth and can't taste your own tongue." And in the Bible, in Exodus 33:20, it is expressed by God telling Moses, "You cannot see my face, for no one can see me and live."

Nagarjuna said, "There is no runner beside the action of running and that outside of running there is no runner."

It would be easier for a scientist to meditate on the interaction of things, seeing the world not separately but as a unit, and not to cultivate the thing in itself. Scientists would agree there are no such things as persistence subatomic particles, and comparatively, a Buddhist would believe there is no persistent self. Neither scientist nor Buddhists contextually negate facts; they are not nihilist (atheists). Both scientists and Buddhists say it is a world of interactivities, where not much can be said on consciousness and the fundamental stuff of the universe.

But we need to think in quantum terms, since observation seems to be the essence of what we can drive at. Since particles move or run from point A to point B and when the observation is halted, both runner and the running cease to exist, as the particles return in manifesting probabilities, as they do not persist in time.

Scientists also need to know that all natural phenomena are governed by a vital life force outside the realm of physical and chemical laws. To believe that all natural phenomena, including the process of life, are governed by physical and chemical laws is not savvy, since any physical or chemical mechanism would prove futile if exhausted of the universal vital life force.

The fact is we live in an awakened, orderly universe, which is why any scientific formula, not excluding physical and chemical agendas or other scientific endeavors, respond to mathematics, geometry, and so on, which are the nucleus of most scientific research. Otherwise, no precise scientific discovery can be materialized in our laboratories. If not so, then no adequate assessment can ever be achieved, and no proper laws can be invented. We should expect going haywire in a DISORDERLY and CHAOTIC universe where no proper rules can be obtained, as law and order make no sense and issues such as discipline, meaning, responsibility, logic, objectivity, preciseness in conclusion, expectation, and hope, are out of the window.

"Subatomic particles do not exist but rather show 'tendencies to exist', and atomic events do not occur with certainty at definite times and in definite ways, but rather show 'tendencies to occur'" (Fritjof Capra).

SOUL HUNTERS: THE ENEMIES OF GOD

"The function of prayer is not to influence God, but rather to change the nature of the one who prays"

– <u>Soren Kierkegaard</u>

"I would never die for my beliefs because I might be wrong"

– Bertrand Russell

In a perilous world, the sacred Baha'i house of worship (Baha'is), chaitya/ Buddhist temples/monastery (abbots, lamas, monks, Buddhists), church buildings, particularity Catholic nuns and priests, the Hof (Germanic pagans), Hindu temple (puja), synagogue (rabbi), mosque (sheikh, mullahs), and other organized sanctuaries are meant for people to assemble and venerate God. People seek refuge in them for repenting of their sins and to rescue their souls from the toxically cultured world, but often with no avail, as to the contrary, many of these revered places of worship are so sadly abusive, often by the officeholders, men and women of the so-called godly obedient, in which some trustees have become the very menace that we should be warned against.

It seems the offenders, the men and women of God, set up booby traps triggered by the believers visiting certain inappropriate places of worship where the naïvely minded flock to their moral and spiritual death, as if they have surrendered to satanic rituals, taking away the decency of what

57

they stand for, and for most victims, permanently depriving them of the God they once believed in.

Many holy predators who preach the almighty God annihilate what we believe and hope for by taking advantage of the innocents, as the culprits, and the so-called priests, nuns, sheikhs, mullahs, rabbis, abbots, and other supposed saints, inappropriately infringe and prey on, killing the very religious spirit of their helpless victims as they impose on the target's sovereignty, sabotaging believers' souls.

They wickedly dehumanize their victims through rape and molestation and by other demonic misconducts. They veil themselves behind God to cover their beastly behaviors to get away scot-free. Then, rest assured, millions would doubt God when aware of such atrocities done by allegedly (erroneous testimony, supposedly, purportedly) religious role models and teachers of faith. And also, they have so naively downsized the scope of the infinite God to their likings, for satisfying their own selfish and wacky (ludicrous) agendas, aiming at filling up their pocket for the wrong reasons.

They have no brain malleability (plasticity), and without vast brain intelligence, as they manufacture a manmade God to fit their own agendas they are shortsighted and mentally incompetent to contrive reason for proving God.

The so-called theoreticians of faith are not able to separate facts from fiction and to substantiate logic from what is obsolete and does not make any sense. These hocus-pocus activities are happening in the twenty-first century, which is meant to be the era of civility of mind and manner and the age of the enlightenment.

They hence misdirect the populace and embolden some to question the existence of the all-powerful God. And further, because of the inability and abusive character of the agents to whom they so wrongly represent God, it leads in making the believer's position questionable and exacerbates the non-believer's views on God. Criteria, as such, should remind us of how shallow so many people's beliefs are in knowing God, and as Friedrich Nietzsche said, "God is dead, and we have killed him."

Humanity ought to become awakened to the infinitely resourceful God, the true God, the most loving, the omnipotent, the omni-present God that is by nature infinitely compassionate; a God that does not in any way call for protection by the religious extremists and terrorists who kill and maim innocent people.

They believe in the very same God, just with a different name or disparate (distinct) denomination; a God that can be felt in hearing our prayers and pleas, since the glorious Almighty has endowed humanity with senses and thought frequencies enabling us to maneuver in a conscientiously based universe.

Not a thing can ever go unnoticed; cosmic frequencies are ubiquitously aware and in tune with all that happens in our mind and zealously (relentlessly) grasps what is precisely taking place in the so-called physical world.

NOTHINGNESS

A universe that came from nothing in the big bang will disappear into nothing at the big crunch. Its glorious few zillion years of existence not even a memory.

–Paul Davies

First, why is there anything at all, or something at all? This question becomes clearer when put in comparative form: why is there something rather than nothing? Some doubt whether we can ask this question because there being nothing is not an option. "What exactly is nothing? What would nothing be?" We analogize nothing with the idea of empty space, in which we can conceptualize nothing.

> "The body is made up of atoms and subatomic particles that are moving at lightning speed around huge empty spaces and the body gives off fluctuations of energy and information in a huge void, so essentially your body is proportionately as void as intergalactic space, made out of nothing, but the nothing is actually the source of information and energy" (Deepak Chopra).

We ponder on this contentious issue whether things are created from something, or perhaps are made out of nothing. But then, the proper question should be addressed as: Is nothingness impregnated with an infinite number of things or not? And if not, then existence, and quintillions of scientific discoveries which scientists and scholars have divulged and employed, should mean fiction, and no more.

Our inventions have stemmed from nothingness and been transmitted into actuality from the unknown, in which we either have already concocted, or hope to excogitate (devise, design), in the future. And if yes, then we should tirelessly dig into nothingness to further get closer to the truth, and not let what is explicitly clear become a conundrum of a scientific and philosophical argument.

If our notion of space is as a particular type of relation between objects, the removal of all objects (everything) should leave nothing, including their interactions. We can easily be misled by the language of there being nothing at all, leading to the notion that nothing has no being or existence. Nothing might be a harbinger to the big bang. But this idea is also a misconception—though one widely held by many who believe the universe came about out of nothingness, for instance an Archimedean (void) variation (fluctuation.)

A vacuum oscillation is itself not nothing "but is a sea of prowess (conscious aptitude) energy endowed with vibrant structure and subject to imperative physical laws." Further, if nothingness in the void should mean "nothing," then there wouldn't be any possible state of affairs. But this could not be, since from "nothingness" is the actuality from which things come about.

Let's further delve into nothingness in which some of the so-called scientific community believe: it all came out of nothing, where nothingness is perhaps the suspect and from which life has originated.

We are conducive to perceiving and defining nothingness according to available human resources and competency. The term nothingness can be alarmingly deceptive, since what we know as nothing is actually everything. But since nothingness is incomprehensible to us at certain times, not discovering and realizing how, when, where, or by whom, nothing is going to give birth to our next scientific breakthroughs. Then we are deluded into believing nothingness as literally meaning immaterial and barren to us, which is based on our limited senses.

The consensus should be in accepting nothingness as the holy grail of creativity, and where the real potential lays for things we persist on to decode and eventually conquer. And if not, then we have acted shortsightedly in all of which we have discovered and hope to invent. We are faced with no choice but to delve into the reality of nothing and realize there is no such thing as a void.

Hence, it would make sense to switch and replace the word nothingness for the words the unknown. An advanced space digger telescope can reveal a world of magic to the eye, where human senses can only dream about, and certainly see as absence of matter and emptiness without a colossal scientific magnifier.

And if the most advanced telescope available to man could only ascertain some of the facts, then this should only mean we must strive for even better technology to make human dreams reality and closer than expected.

To say life came out of nothing is honestly an insult to reason, since literally it would mean God is in charge of the womb of what we know and grant as emptiness, which in contrary is filled with propitious (auspicious, favorable, benevolent) prospects that gave birth to all there is and all of which there will ever be.

Through the eyes of quantum physics, which represents the world of the unseen, renowned physicist Niels Bohr says (and many of his colleagues accept), "Atomic uncertainty is truly intrinsic to nature: the rules of clock might apply to familiar objects such as snooker balls, but when it comes to atoms and quarks, string theory, and other subatomic particles, the rules are those of roulette." Many scientists believe these subatomic particles are being thrown around by an unseen ocean of microscopic forces.

It is therefore apparent that we must adhere to the bounds of our senses to acquaint and comply with the world outside of us. As humans, we cannot reconnaissance with what is beyond our ability and knowledge to decipher. This should not mean that there is no magic in the air, or perhaps we need to quit searching for miracles. The history of evolution should validate the human mind that progresses into dynamic stages of enlightenment where boundaries are graciously torn and miracle-like discoveries become norms.

Bear in mind that one of the basic concepts in new Existentialism is nothingness. It includes the whole being, and being comes out of nothingness. According to this philosophy, being and nothingness are the same. The latter causes fear, and the former causes amazement. Fear is event-based on discovery in which man sees all existents standing on the basis of non-existence.

Our curiosity into the realms of speculation and probabilities is fostered and potentially backed up by hidden agenda conveyed into the unknown, ready to be exploited and burst into reality. Of course it is inclined to action by passion, human drive, time consumed, and keen enough to feel and detect the maturity and the magnificent moment of delivery. That is encouraged with hope, perseverance, and bearing hardship through many trials and errors; and then occasionally bull's-eyed into stepping stones for other miracle-like disclosures and sometimes a huge leap into successful challenges where our struggle in bettering human life pays off generously.

Paul Davies argues that one need not appeal to God to account for the big bang. Its cause, he suggests, is found within the cosmic system itself. Originally a vacuum lacking space-time dimensions, the universe "found itself in an excited vacuum state," a "ferment of quantum activity, teeming (producing) with virtual particles and full of complex interactions" (Davies 1984 191–2), which, subject to a cosmic repulsive force, resulted in an immense increase in energy. Subsequent explosions from this collapsing vacuum released the energy in this vacuum, reinvigorating the cosmic inflation and setting the scenario for the subsequent expansion of the universe.

But what is the origin of this increase in energy that eventually made the big bang possible? Davies's response is that the law of conservation of energy (that the total quantity of energy in the universe remains fixed despite transfer from one form to another), which now applies to our universe, did not apply to the initial expansion.

Cosmic repulsion in the vacuum caused the energy to increase from zero to an enormous amount. This great explosion released energy, from which all matter emerged.

Consequently, he contends, since the conclusion of the kalām argument is false, one of the premises of the argument—in all likelihood, the first—is false. Craig responds that if the vacuum has energy, the question arises concerning the origin of the vacuum and its energy. Merely pushing the question of the beginning of the universe back to some primordial quantum vacuum (nothingness) does not escape the question of what brought this vacuum laden with energy into existence.

A quantum vacuum is not nothing (as in Newtonian physics), but is a sea of continually forming and dissolving particles that borrow energy from the vacuum for their brief existence. A vacuum is thus far from nothing, and vacuum fluctuations do not constitute an exception to the principle enunciated in premise 1 (Craig, in Craig and Smith 1993: 143–4). Hence, he concludes, the appeal to a vacuum as the initial state is misleading.

Further, if the universe has a beginning, what is the cause of that beginning? This is the question that is addressed by the Avicenna's kalām cosmological argument, given its essence that everything that begins to exist has a cause.

Some are under the wrong impression that their kind of visage (image) and bounded interpretation of the so-called nothingness has no cause. But then the renowned British theoretical physicist Stephen Hawking says God did not create the universe, gravity did, and the big bang was an unavoidable consequence of the laws of physics.

In his book The Grand Design, Professor Hawking gets overexcited with pride, just human nature, as our good professor writes: "Because there is a law such as gravity, the universe can and will create itself from nothing. Spontaneous creation is the reason there is something rather than nothing, why the universe exists, why we exist. It is not necessary to invoke God to light the blue touch paper and set the universe going."

The first and foremost question should be, by gravity, does Mr. Hawking mean an energy-driven entity that is propelled by an energy-driven universe that also motivates electromagnetic forces and manifests light and heavy atomic forces; also associates with infinite numbers of other imperative phenomenon necessary to operate constructively for arriving at its objectives, orchestrated by the mind of God? Or does he mean gravity should replace God and for humanity to revere gravity as the reason for our existence?

If the latter, then it cannot be overlooked by any savvy and healthy mind to question how an unintelligent entity without any purpose-driven consciousness, absolutely without will and determination, utterly lacking common sense, could create and sustain a colossally intelligent and rational-minded environment and a magnificent cosmos fueled by order, while superbly managing to reach its destiny.

No sarcasm is intended, but I wonder if Professor's Hawking's findings should remind humanity of the dark ages when the so-called apostles encouraged people to believe and worship gods made of a variety of manufactured materials as the real cause for their demise and happiness. There is a classic saying, "Tragedy plus time equals comedy." Mark Twain wrote, "It's easier to fool people than to convince them they have been fooled."

Chew on this, and see if reason can digest such a callous matter; Mr. Hawking was somehow contaminated with many dreams believing that about fourteen billion years ago (when life roughly began, so say scientists), gravity created itself from nothing. One needs to question if must-have resources (crucial ingredients, the primordial soup) could have played a definite and significant role prior to either creating the first bio-cell or in dealing with prerequisite atmosphere for giving birth to the force of gravity. Millions, if not billons, of variables must be assumed as constant and utterly of no use but for gravity to pop out of nowhere to perhaps give some credibility to Mr. Hawking's insight.

Professor Hawking behaved just like another "reductionist," Blaise Pascal, who said that somehow we live in a bubble where laws of our universe can be reduced in manifesting gravity as the actual reason for the entire existence.

"All things have sprung from nothing and are borne toward infinity. Who can follow out astonishment career, the author of these wonders and he alone comprehend them" (Blaise Pascal).

In the remainder of How the Universe Got Its Spots, which is unbearably beautiful in both intellectual elegance and stylistic splendor, Levin goes on to explore questions of quantum relativity and free will, death and black holes, space time and Wonderland, and more. Complement it with Levin on science, free will, and the human spirit, then revisit Alan Lightman on how dark energy explains why we exist and treat yourself to this poetic primer on the universe written in the 1,000 most common words in the English language.

INFINITY

The skeptics refer to infinity as if there is actually such a decisive number as infinity active in mathematical realms, not realizing it is just a figure of speech since an integer, or fractional tally (count) as infinity does not exist in any true sense, and hence one should further investigate boundlessness. But some people still argue there is no beginning, nor is there an end.

Some argue there is neither a beginning nor an end to existence.

Al-Ghāzāli (1058–1111) argued that everything that begins to exist requires a cause of its beginning. The world is composed of temporal phenomena preceded by other temporally ordered phenomena. Since such a series of temporal phenomena cannot continue to infinity because an actual infinite is impossible, the world must have had a beginning and a cause of its existence; namely, God (Craig 1979 part 1).

Let's further discuss infinity. Craig concluded that an actual infinite cannot exist.

A beginning less temporal series of events is an actual infinite.

Therefore, a beginning less temporal series of events cannot exist.

The incorrect assumption, and the main suspect, is the subject of infinity.

And Max Tegmark, on the subject of infinity, wrote that infinity is a beautiful concept—and is also ruining physics. Infinity doesn't exist; the impossibility of an actual infinite.

A rubber band can't be stretched indefinitely because although it seems smooth and continuous, that's merely a convenient approximation. It's really made of atoms, and if you stretch it too far, it snaps. If we similarly retire the idea that space itself is an infinitely stretchy continuum, then a big snap of sorts stops inflation from producing an infinitely big space and the measure problem goes away. Without the infinitely small, inflation can't make the infinitely big, so you get rid of both infinities in one fell swoop—together with many other problems plaguing modern physics, such as infinitely dense black hole singularities and infinities popping up when we try to quantize gravity.

In the past, many venerable mathematicians were skeptical of infinity and the continuum. The legendary Carl Friedrich Gauss denied that anything infinite really exists, saying, "Infinity is merely a way of speaking," and, "I protest against the use of infinite magnitude as something completed, which is never permissible in mathematics." In the past century, however, infinity has become mathematically mainstream, and most physicists and mathematicians have become so enamored with infinity that they rarely question it. Why? Basically, because infinity is an extremely convenient approximation for which we haven't discovered convenient alternatives.

Consider, for example, the air in front of you. Keeping track of the positions and speeds of octillions of atoms would be hopelessly complicated. But if you ignore the fact that air is made of atoms and instead approximate it as a continuum—a smooth substance that has a density, pressure, and velocity at each point—you'll find that this idealized air obeys a beautifully simple equation explaining almost everything we care about: how to build airplanes, how we hear them with sound waves, how to make weather forecasts, and so forth. Yet despite all that convenience, air, of course, isn't truly continuous. I think it's the same way for space, time, and all the other building blocks of our physical world. He carries on to say that We Don't Need the Infinite.

Let's face it: Despite their seductive allure, we have no direct observational evidence for either the infinitely big or the infinitely small. We speak of infinite volumes with infinitely many planets, but our observable universe contains only about 1,089 objects (mostly photons). If space is a true continuum, then to describe even something as simple as the distance between two points requires an infinite amount of information, specified by a number with infinitely many decimal places. In practice, we physicists have never managed to measure anything to more than about seventeen decimal places. Yet real numbers, with their infinitely many decimals, have infested almost every nook and cranny of physics, from the strengths of electromagnetic fields to the wave functions of quantum mechanics. We describe even a single bit of quantum information (qubit) using two real numbers involving infinitely many decimals.

Not only do we lack evidence for the infinite, but we don't need the infinite to do physics. Our best computer simulations, accurately describing everything from the formation of galaxies to tomorrow's weather to the masses of elementary particles, use only finite computer resources by treating everything as finite. So if we can do without infinity to figure out what happens next, surely nature can, too—in a way that's more deep and elegant than the hacks we use for our computer simulations.

Our challenge as physicists is to discover this elegant way and the infinity-free equations describing it—the true laws of physics. To start this search in earnest, we need to question infinity. I'm betting that we also need to let go of it; infinity doesn't exist.

Famous mathematicians such as L. E. J. Brouwer, Per Martin-Löf, Errett Bishop, Ludwig Wittgenstein, Henri Poincare, Carl Friedrich Gauss and Leopold Kronecker didn't believe infinity existed. Many others, such as Bertrand Russell, doubted the existence of infinity in various forms and fought against the axioms of the mainstream mathematical community that were in flux at that time.

The most compelling argument to admit that infinity does exist comes from the Axioms (a fundamental rule, doctrine) of Mathematics, namely the Axiom of Infinity, which in plain English states: "Mathematical objects infinite in size, exist." Many prominent scientists and scholarly minded mathematicians believe no infinity should exist in the axiom of mathematics, or physics, which tightly depends on mathematics to present savvy results of their work.

And I say that mathematics, physics, and kindred (cognate, related) scientific experiences must deal with real numbers and are derived from a true state of being; which, by the way, can only be obtained from a disciplined universe for reaching reliable findings, since no scientific theory of any kind can be formulated in a chaotic world without orderly conduct. Further, infinity is nothing more than an assumption, where mathematics and related fields must eventually give in to finite assessment for a trustworthy conclusion. In the physical world, it would be hilarious to believe in an effect without a cause, since any serious scientific research must cultivate the beginning and the asymptotic (end) result for their research, where no open-ended outcome, or infinity-related concept, can be convincing.

Astrophysicist Janna Levin on free will and whether the universe is infinite or finite, in letters to her mother, writes,

"The simpler the insight, the more profound the conclusion."

By Maria Popova

In 1998, while on the cusp of becoming one of the most Significant theoretical cosmologists of our time, mathematician-turned-astrophysicist Janna Levin left her post at Berkeley and moved across the Atlantic for a prestigious position at Cambridge University. During the year and a half there, she had the time and space to contemplate the question that would eventually become the epicenter of her career—whether the universe is infinite or finite. What began as a series of letters to her mother, Sandy, eventually became an unusual diary of Levin's "social exile as a roaming scientist," and was finally published as How the Universe Got Its Spots: Diary of a Finite Time in a Finite Space (public library)— a most unusual and absorbing account of the paradoxes of finitude.

"I'm writing to you because I know you're curious but afraid to ask," Levin offers in the opening letter— a "you" that instantly becomes as much her mother as the person Virginia Woolf memorably termed "the common reader." From there, she springboards into remarkably intelligent yet inviting explorations of some of the biggest questions that the universe poses—questions most of us contemplate, sometimes consciously but mostly not, just by virtue of being sentient participants in the chaos and enchantment of existence.

A 1617 depiction of the notion of non-space, long before the concept of vacuum existed, found in Michael Benson's book Cosmographic, is a visual history of understanding the universe.

In an entry from September 3, 1998, Levin fleshes out her ideas on infinity and writes with exquisite Sagan-esque sensitivity to the poetics of science:

For a long time, I believed the universe was infinite. Which is to say, I just never questioned this assumption that the universe was infinite. But if I had given the question more attention, maybe I would have realized sooner. The universe is the three-dimensional space we live in and the time we watch pass on our clocks. It is our north and south, our east and west, our up and down. Our past and future. As far as the eye can see there appears to be no bound to our three spatial dimensions and we have no expectation for an end to time. The universe is inhabited by giant clusters of galaxies, each galaxy a conglomerate of a billion or a trillion stars.

The Milky Way, our galaxy, has an unfathomably dense core of millions of stars with beautiful arms, a skeleton of stars, spiraling out from this core. The earth lives out in the sparsely populated arms orbiting the sun, an ordinary star, with our planetary companions. Our humble solar system. Here we are. A small planet, an ordinary star, a huge cosmos. But we're alive and we're sentient. Pooling our efforts and passing our secrets from generation to generation, we've lifted ourselves off this blue and green water-soaked rock to throw our vision far beyond the limitations of our eyes.

The universe is full of galaxies and their stars. Probably, hopefully, there is other life out there and background light and maybe some ripples in space. There are bright objects and dark objects. Things we can see and things we can't. Things we know about and things we don't. All of it. This glut of ingredients could carry on in every direction forever. Never ending. Just when you think you've seen the last of them, there's another galaxy and beyond that one another infinite number of galaxies.

Illustration from Thomas Wright's visionary 1750 treatise 'An Original Theory,' found in Michael Benson's book Cosmographic, a visual history of understanding the universe

But having painted this bewitching backdrop for our intuitive beliefs, Levin sublimates the poet to the scientist, pointing out that however alluring these intuitions may feel, they are nonetheless ungrounded in empirical fact:

No infinity has ever been observed in nature. Nor is infinity tolerated in a scientific theory—except we keep assuming the universe itself is infinite.

It wouldn't be so bad if Einstein hadn't taught us better. And here the ideas collide, so I'll just pour them out unfiltered. Space is not just an abstract notion but a mutable, evolving field. It can begin and end, be born and die. Space is curved, it is a geometry, and our experience of gravity, the pull of the earth and our orbit around the sun, is just a free fall along the curves in space. From this huge insight people realized the universe must be expanding. The space between the galaxies is actually stretching even if the galaxies themselves were otherwise to stay put. The universe is growing, aging. And if it's expanding today, it must have been smaller once, in the sense that everything was once closer together, so close that everything was on top of each other, essentially in the same place, and before that it must not have been at all.

The universe had a beginning. There was once nothing and now there is something. What sways me even more, if an ultimate theory of everything is found, a theory beyond Einstein's, then gravity and matter and energy are all ultimately different expressions of the same thing. We're all intrinsically of the same substance. The fabric of the universe is just a coherent weave from the same threads that make our bodies. How much more absurd it becomes to believe that the universe, space and time could possibly be infinite when all of us are finite.

A decade and a half later, Alan Light man would come to write with a similar scientific poeticism about why we long for permanence in a universe defined by constant change. But however poetic the premise, Levin brings a mathematician's precision to her "reasons for believing the universe is finite, unpopular as they are in some scientific crowds."

In another entry twelve days later, she writes:

Infinity is a demented concept...

Infinity is a limit and is not a proper number. No matter how big a number you think of, I can add 1 to it and make it that much bigger. The number of numbers is infinite. I could never recite the infinite numbers, since I only have a finite lifetime. But I can imagine it as a hypothetical possibility, as the inevitable limit of a never-ending sequence. The limit goes the other way, too, since I can consider the infinitely small, the infinitesimal. No matter how small you try to divide the number 1, I can divide it smaller still. While I could again imagine doing this forever, I can never do this in practice. But I can understand infinity abstractly and so accept it for what it is.

Pointing out that all titans of science — including Galileo, Aristotle, and Cantor — were besotted with the notion of infinity at some point, "each visiting the idea for a time and then abandoning the pursuit," Levin notes that we can neither accept nor dismiss infinity on the basis of popular opinion alone.

In early October, she writes:

Where in the hierarchy of infinity would an infinite universe lie? An infinite universe can host an infinite amount of stuff and an infinite number of events. An infinite number of planets. An infinite number of people on those planets. Surely there must be another planet so very nearly like the earth as to be indistinguishable, in fact an infinite number of them, each with a variety of inhabitants, an infinite number of which must be infinitely close to this set of inhabitants. Another you, another me. Or there'd be another you out there with a slightly different life and a different set of siblings, parents, and offspring. This is hard to believe. Is it arrogance or logic that makes me believe this is wrong? There's just one me, one you. The universe cannot be infinite.

I welcome the infinite in mathematics, where … it is not absurd nor demented. But I'd be pretty shaken to find the infinite in nature. I don't feel robbed living my days in the physical with its tender admission of the finite. I still get to live with the infinite possibilities of mathematics, if only in my head.

Illustration by Lisbeth Zwerger for 'Alice in Wonderland.' Click image for more.

Understanding the infinite—both as a mathematical possibility and an impossibility of the physical universe—might be more a matter of coming to terms with infinite simplicity than with infinite complexity.

Characteristics of matter.

There are basically three kinds of characteristics of matter.

Some nonbelievers relate to matter as the real cause for existence, and do not accept any idea-driven spirit or energy-oriented life creation or design to ever be possible, as if matter is not energy-driven. Regardless of what state matter is in, solid, liquid or gas, all matter is energy-driven.

Therefore, one should research the quality and the essence of matter not only in the physical world, but certainly excavate (dig, burrow, and root) into the subatomic realm.

> "In all my research I have never come across matter. To me the term matter implies a bundle of energy which is given form by an intelligent spirit" (Max Planck).

Matter is made up of atoms. Depending on the sort of matter, the characteristics may differ. Solids have certain shape and volume but cannot be pressed. Likewise, liquids have definite volume but no distinct shape. Liquids cannot be compressed either. Gases are made up of random atoms with very high energy and have neither definite shape or volume. But gases can be compressed. Hence, it depends on which type of matter is available and what kind of characteristics are needed for an exclusive purpose.

Atoms possess weight, mass, volume, and density. All atoms unstoppably move. The more energy that is applied to a group of atoms, the more they move.

Atoms in a lower energetic state do not move much; they stay in place and palpitate (pulsate, vibrate.) Atoms in such a position make solid matter. Solids consist of fixed mass, weight, density, and volume.

Mass is the body (quantity) of matter in any object, while weight is the pull of gravity on the mass of that object. Volume is a measure of how much is physically there, and of space the object occupies or captures, while density is a description of how the mass takes up that space. Objects with higher solidity (density) have a lot of mass in a small amount of space.

Atoms that are more energetic and, hence, move more freely, are in a liquid state. Liquids also have a fixed mass, weight, volume, and density. Particles in a liquid can flow freely past one another rather than being stuck in a single position. While solids do not change shape easily, liquids can conform instantly to the shape of their container. Atoms in elevated energetic state (e.g., gases), can not only alter their shape, but also their volume, because the particles have sufficient energy to extensively separate from one another while flowing.

However, scientists have learned that atoms are not the smallest particles in nature. Despite their microscopic size, a number of much smaller particles exist, known as subatomic particles. In reality, it is these subatomic particles that form the building blocks of our world, like protons, neutrons, electrons, and quarks, or destroy it, such as alpha and beta particles. And since quantum physic deals with the world of subatomic particles and with much smaller units, like quartz, can better attest to the fact that no tangible substances are manifested in a state, as they notice the effect of energy-driven environment where frequencies are pulsating.

What the human eye sees as matter is actually energy-driven entities, since various kinds of matter are made of atoms, and atoms in liquid and gases are constantly in motion, imbued with high energy. Atoms in solid matter are in a low energy state; they stay in one place and pulsate. Hence, matter cannot be the reason behind creating life, since atoms in matter are constantly moving. Matter is unstable and in transition; matter is destructible. No matter is ever permanent.

> "All matter originates and exists only by virtue of a force...
> We must assume behind this force the existence of a
> conscious and intelligent Mind. This Mind is the matrix
> of all matter" (Max Planck).

Perhaps Professor Hawking saw matter-like substances as not energy-driven, which would be very odd. Then, the question should be how dubious, irrational, amply questionable, unintelligent, insensible, unconscionable, volatile (inconsistent), and perishable matter could create life-bearing intelligence in some state, manifesting extreme "knowledge" beyond belief.

Professor Hawking believed gravity is responsible for creating existence.

"In Stephen Hawking's new book The Grand Design, he says that because of the law of gravity, the universe can and will create itself out of nothing. But isn't that gravity being a module (subroutine, function) of mass, as per Einstein. How can one have gravity before mass and therefore how can gravity explain mass?"

Dr. Kaku: In Stephen's new book, he says that the Theory of Everything that Einstein spent 30 years of his life chasing, is known as string theory (or its latest incarnation, M-theory).

In string theory, we have a multiverse of universes. Think of our universe as the surface of a soap bubble, which is expanding. We live on the skin of this bubble. But string theory predicts that there should be other bubbles out there, which can collide with other bubbles or even sprout or bud baby bubbles, as in a bubble bath.

But how can an entire universe come out of nothing? This apparently violates the conservation of matter and energy. But there is a simple answer.

Matter, of course, has positive energy. But gravity has negative energy. (For example, you have to add energy to the earth in order to tear it away from the sun. Once separated far from the solar system, the earth then has zero gravitational energy. But this means that the original solar system had negative energy.)

If you do the math, you find out that the sum total of matter in the universe can cancel against the sum total of negative gravitational energy, yielding a universe with zero (or close to zero) net matter/energy. So, in some sense, universes are for free. It does not take net matter and energy to create entire universes. In this way, in the bubble bath, bubbles can collide, create baby bubbles, or simple pop into existence from nothing.

This gives us a startling picture of the big bang, that our universe was born perhaps from the collision of two universes (the big splat theory), or sprouted from a parent universe, or simply popped into existence out of nothing. So universes are being created all the time. (But Hawking goes one step farther and says that therefore here is no need of God, since God is not necessary to create the universe. I wouldn't go that far.

"Because there is a law such as gravity, the universe can and will create itself from nothing," he writes. "Spontaneous creation is the reason there is something rather than nothing, why the universe exists, why we exist."

"It is not necessary to invoke God to light the blue touch paper and set the universe going."

In the forthcoming book, published on 9 September, Hawking says that M-theory, a form of string theory, will achieve this goal: "M-theory is the unified theory Einstein was hoping to find," he theorizes.

"The fact that we human beings – who are ourselves mere collections of fundamental particles of nature – have been able to come this close to an understanding of the laws governing us and our universe is a great triumph."

Hawking says the first blow to Newton's belief that the universe could not have arisen from chaos was the observation in 1992 of a planet orbiting a star other than our Sun. "That makes the coincidences of our planetary conditions – the single sun, the lucky combination of Earth-sun distance and solar mass – far less remarkable, and far less compelling as evidence that the Earth was carefully designed just to please us human beings," he writes.

Hawking had previously appeared to accept the role of God in the creation of the universe. Writing in his bestseller A Brief History of Time in 1988, he said: "If we discover a complete theory, it would be the ultimate triumph of human reason – for then we should know the mind of God."

As essential as gravity is, just like other fundamental forces in nature, like electromagnetic, strong and weak atomic forces are derivatives and all are the reflection of the majestic power of God which, perhaps because of gravity, as Hawking puts it, "the universe can create itself from nothing." But it is the magnificent maestro (the majestically eminent) and undeniably superb programmer of the entire cosmos and beyond that manipulates and controls everything with awesome order and discipline more than anyone can imagine.

And of course, we mustn't exclude these imperative energy-driven forces, such as gravity, strong and weak atomic forces, along with electromagnetic forces, as they play a remarkable role to prevent nature from falling apart.

> "As a man who has devoted his whole life to many research about atoms this much: There is no matter as such. All matter originates and exists only by virtue of a force which brings the particle of an atom to vibration and holds this most minute solar system of the atom together. We must assume behind this force the existence of a conscious and intelligent mind. This mind is the matrix of all matter" (Max Planck).

Nothing Is Solid & Everything Is Energy – Scientists Explain the World of Quantum Physics

This is what the most prominent scientists are saying about an energy-driven universe.

It is presently clear that the world of quantum physics is an uncanny (spooky, unearthly) one. It sheds light on the truth about our world in ways that were not known before, since it disputes the contemporary scaffold (supporting structure) of customary lore (learning, information, knowledge.) This is what Niels Bohr, a multiple Nobel Prize-winning Danish physicist, who has made a meaningful bequest (endowment) to comprehending quantum theory and atomic structure, is saying quote "if quantum mechanics hasn't profoundly shocked you, you haven't understood it yet. Everything we call real is made of things that cannot be regarded as real." The bottom line is that: all of which we have thought about so far as our material world, is absolutely not material, and in the true sense is far from what we grasp as the physical world.

At the beginning of the nineteenth century, physicist's sought into the connection between the structure of matter and the energy. Further, the understanding that a physical, Newtonian world which regarded matter as the kernel of science was dropped; the scientific community realized that matter is nothing but an illusion, as they concluded that everything in our universe is made out of energy. "Despite the unrivaled empirical success of quantum theory, the very suggestion that it may be literally true as a description of nature is still greeted with cynicism, incomprehension and even anger" (T. Folger, "Quantum Shmantum," Discover 22:37-43, 2001).

Quantum physicists contrived that physical atoms are made up the mass of spinning air, liquid, etc., that pulls things into its center known as turbulence, vortices or whirlpool. The energy that are constantly spinning and vibrating, each one glimmering exclusively unique energy signature. Hence, if we see ourselves and figure out what we are, we are in reality made of vibrating energy beaming our own unique energy perception. This is fact, and is what quantum physics has consecutively revealed to us, again and again. We are much more than what we see ourselves to be. We should start to see ourselves in the manner of light and vibrating immortal souls, temporary inhibited by mortal bodies.

If one watches the composition of an atom through a microscope one would observe a small, undetectable, tornado-like vortex (whirlpool) with a boundlessly small energy vortices known as quarks and photons, which they make up the structure of the atom. And if one further focuses in closer and closer on the edifice of the atom, one would see nothing; one would see a physical void. Informing us that the atom has no physical structure, we have no physical structure, as physical things, in fact, don't have any physical building! As strange as it is, but it is now authenticated that atoms are made out of invisible energy, not tactile (palpable, tangible) matter. "get over it, and accept the inarguable conclusion, the universe is immaterial-mental and spiritual" (Professor of Physics and Astronomy at Johns Hopkins University Richard Conn Henry, The Mental Universe).

It's quite puzzling, isn't it? Our experience state that our reality is constructed of physical material things, and that we live in an independently existing, an objective one. The idea that the universe is not a symposium (conclave, assembly) of physical parts, as argued by Newtonian physics, and alternatively comes from a holistic participatory of immaterial energy waves, stemming from the work of Albert Einstein, Max Planck, and Werner Heisenberg, among other scholarly minded scientists and philosophers.

The Role of Consciousness in Quantum Mechanics

What does it mean that our physical material reality isn't really physical at all? It could mean a number of things, and concepts such as this cannot be explored if scientists remain within the boundaries of the only perceived world existing; the world we see. As Nikola Tesla supposedly said, "The day science begins to study non-physical phenomena, it will make more progress in one decade than in all the previous centuries of its existence."

Fortunately, many scientists have already taken the leap and have already questioned the meaning and implications of what we've discovered with quantum physics. One of these potential revelations is that the observer creates the reality.

As observers, we are personally involved with the creation of our own reality. Physicists are being forced to admit that the universe is a "mental" construction. Pioneering physicist Sir James Jeans wrote: "The stream of knowledge is heading toward a non-mechanical reality; the universe begins to look more like a great thought than like a great machine. Mind no longer appears to be an accidental intruder into the realm of matter, we ought to rather hail it as the creator and governor of the realm of matter (R. C. Henry, "The Mental Universe"; Nature 436:29, 2005).

One great example that illustrates the role of consciousness within the physical material world (which we know not to be so physical) is the double slit experiment. This experiment has been used multiple times to explore the role of consciousness in shaping the nature of physical reality.

A double-slit optical system was used to test the possible role of consciousness in the collapse of the quantum wave-function. The ratio of the interference pattern's double-slit spectral power to its single-slit spectral power was predicted to decrease when attention was focused toward the double-slit as compared to away from it. The study found that factors associated with consciousness, such as meditation, experience, electro-cortical markers of focused attention and psychological factors such as openness and absorption, significantly correlated in predicted ways with perturbations in the double-slit interference pattern. There are many scientific studies that prove consciousness can effect and change our physical material world.

What's The Significance?

The significance of this information is for us to wake up and realize that we are all energy, radiating our own unique energy signature. Feelings, thoughts, and emotions play a vital role; quantum physics helps us see the significance of how we all feel. If all of us are in a peaceful, loving state inside, it will no doubt impact the external world around us and influence how others feel as well.

> "If you want to know the secrets of the universe, think in terms of energy, frequency and vibration." – Nikola Tesla.

Studies have shown that positive emotions and operating from a place of peace within oneself can lead to a very different experience for the person emitting those emotions and for those around them. At our subatomic level, does the vibrational frequency change the manifestation of physical reality? If so, in what way? We know that when an atom changes its state, it absorbs or emits electromagnetic frequencies, which are responsible for changing its state. Do different states of emotion, perception, and feelings result in different electromagnetic frequencies? Yes! This has been proven.

Random chance:

> "Quantum mechanics is certainly imposing. But an inner voice tells me that it is not yet the real thing. The theory says a lot, but does not really bring us any closer to the secret of the 'old one.' I, at any rate, am convinced that He does not throw dice." Albert Einstein

Einstein is so right; God does not throw dice. As far as progression in quantum physics, the world has come a long way since Einstein.

We are what we learn. But the essence of who we are, and what we do, all that exists, is what the Chinese call "chi," which is the fuel that drives what we know as life.

GRAVITY

How vital is gravity really? Well let's put it this way: life would not be possible without it. An average person perhaps does not think about gravity as a physicist or any other related professional does, yet gravity affects us all, and because of gravity, we do not fly up into space when we feel like jumping up. It is gravity that pulls us down; hence, we fall down and not up. And gravity is why objects crash down to the floor. This mysterious force is the reason we are bound to Earth, enabling us to live as we do.

No one can honestly claim where this mysterious force comes from except that without it, life would not be possible. We discern from Isaac Newton's gravitation law that objects in the universe exert a force of attraction on each other. This interconnectivity is based on the mass of any two objects and the distance between them. The greater the mass of the two objects and the closer the distance between them, the more powerful the pull of the gravitational forces they impose on each other.

We also know that gravity can work in a complicated system with several objects. For instance, in our own solar system, not only does the Sun influence gravity on all the planets, holding them in their orbits, but reciprocally, each planet exerts a force of gravity on the Sun, as well as all the other planets with varying degrees based on the mass and distance between the bodies. This not only includes our solar system, but is also true for beyond just our solar system. The fact is that every object with mass in the universe pulls every other object that has mass—again, the attractions have varying degrees based on mass and distance.

In the theory of relativity, Albert Einstein described how gravity is more than just a force: it is a curvature in the space-time continuum. That sounds like science fiction, but simply put, the mass of an object makes the space around it bend and curve. This is often shown as a heavy ball sitting on a rubber sheet, and other smaller balls fall in towards the heavier object because the rubber sheet is warped from the heavy ball's weight. In actuality, we can't directly see curvature of the space, but we can discover it in the motions of objects. Any object caught in another celestial body's gravity is affected, since the space it is moving through is bent or curved toward the object.

A phenomenon known as "gravitational lensing" can enable us to detect the effects of gravity on light. A large galaxy or cluster of them can also cause an otherwise straight beam of light to curve, circling it, creating a lensing effect.

This is what scientists are saying: "But these effects – where there are basically curves, hills and valleys in space — occur for reasons we can't fully really explain. Besides being a characteristic of space, gravity is also a force (but it is the weakest of the four forces), and it might be a particle, too. Some scientists have proposed particles called gravitons cause objects to be attracted to one another. But gravitons have never actually been observed. Another idea is that gravitational waves are generated when an object is accelerated by an external force, but these waves have never been directly detected, either."

The scientist further acclaim that

"Our understanding of gravity breaks down at both the very small and the very big: at the level of atoms and molecules, gravity just stops working. And we can't describe the insides of black holes and the moment of the big bang without the math completely falling apart. The problem is that our understanding of both particle physics and the geometry of gravity is incomplete."

"Having gone from basically philosophical understandings of why things fall to mathematical descriptions of how things accelerate down inclines from Galileo, to Kepler's equations describing planetary motion to Newton's formulation of the Laws of Physics, to Einstein's formulations of relativity, we've been building and building a more comprehensive view of gravity. But we're still not complete," said Dr. Pamela Gay. "We know that there still needs to be some way to unite quantum mechanics and gravity and actually be able to write down equations that describe the centers of black holes and the earliest moments of the Universe. But we're not there yet."

ORDER AND MATHEMATICS

Order plays an extremely vital role in our lives, without which, we simply wouldn't be able to reach our objectives and would become vulnerable to chaotic atmosphere. Scientists, mathematicians, innovative minds, and other scholarly oriented inventors who create premier discoveries know that the nucleus of most scientific novelties (something new, invention) and technological undertakings is mathematics. And that mathematics undeniably dictates order, without which, no accurate assessment is ever possible.

Walter Bradley said, "An orderly universe is described by mathematics." And Heraclitus said, "There is a stability in the Universe because of the orderly and balanced process of change, the same measure coming out as going in, as if reality were a huge fire that inhaled and exhaled equal amounts."

A disorderly universe with muddled (disorganized) conduct, without any disciplinary measures and in acting lawlessly random, cannot be measured or correctly assessed to produce reliably precise results for dependable scientific discoveries.

This should make those who believe we are the product of random chance, the result of a helter-skelter universe, to think twice and know the only alternative to an intelligently designed and orderly universe is to accept being blindly propelled with no purpose, and to ignore that "no genius and bright product can ever be produced by obtuse, dull and ingenious force."

We ought to be reminded of this ingeniously potent force that has flawlessly directed towards its destiny for more than fourteen billion years, and perhaps for trillions of years to come; call it God, Allah, the Creator, or whatever you wish.

The conscientious universe is robustly alive. It is active in its ever evolutionary track for ever so long; otherwise, it would have been extinguished and exterminated in its very preliminary stages, and not lasting as long as it has. It is still heralding, without any hesitation or in every maneuvering hasty, exercising and exhibiting the very essence of existence and balance with awesome power and might.

Nicolas Copernicus wrote: "The universe has been wrought (carefully formed, shaped) for us by a supremely good and orderly creator."

The universe had a beginning

We should clear our mind from insensible views deficient of reasoning power, in this case, specifying if our extremely complex universe had a beginning or not. It is rather difficult to renounce years of cultural conditioning that we are still mulling (pondering, cogitating), often without any merit. It is not easy for millions to discard such idea that "in the beginning, God created heaven and earth," and so no. Yes, of course an intelligent designer is responsible for creating our universe, and not excluding the entire cosmos. But it ought not to be stated as grossly as acknowledged without the merit it so justly deserves.

Many schools of thought have traditionally assumed that the universe had no origin, and some believed otherwise.

Abrahamian's faith of Judaism, Christianity, and Islam also believed in a beginning and the end. Hence, the burden of proof can become as meandering and puzzling as the subject matter itself, if one is not clairvoyant (able to see beyond the range of ordinary perception) and enlightened enough to defend the truth as thoroughly as possible.

In primeval times, the ancients either fatuously (foolishly, inanely) or wisely believed that gods made the universe out of eternal mushy water that had been there forever. And from Plato to Einstein, the scientific view was that our universe has simply existed before anything else, therefore lessening the burden of scientific proof on the origin of the universe, since paranormal was rather cumbersome for relative understanding and not attuned with time parameter.

In his book Show Me God, George Smoot (head of the NASA COBE satellite team that discovered cosmic "seeds") says, "Until the late 1910s, humans were as ignorant of cosmic origins as they had ever been. Those who didn't take Genesis (birth, inception, and onset) literally had no reason to believe there had been a beginning."

Adduce (notes, evidence, invoke) for a beginning

Einstein's general theory of relativity declared the universe's expansion. Expansion marked a beginning, and a beginning implied a Beginner.

The evidence became undeniable, however, when Edwin Powell Hubble utilized the largest telescope of his time to display that all the galaxies are precipitately (impetuously, rushing) going away from us, and in which there was an exact, linear relationship between the galaxies' distance and their velocity, as Einstein's equations foresaw.

Profusion (abundance, wealth) of Helium.

Later scientific findings carried on to strengthen the big bang concept, as Fred Hoyle humorously first called it. While Hoyle was insisting on proving his "steady state theory of an everlasting universe," he instead validates that only an incredibly hot, condensed origin for the universe could elucidate (explain, clarify) the reason for the plentifullness of helium in the universe.

An external job

The great quest of science is to find the cause for every effect. But as we trace the cause-effect chain back through time, we come to a scientifically perplexing moment at the beginning where cause-effect relationships simply stop. This denotes the theory of creation out of nothing, the emergence out of nothing, a universe that is theological and correlated with monism religions (Judaism, Christianity, and Islam), since they all teach creation ex nihilo (creation out of nothing).

As Einstein stated: space, time, and matter are inextricably interconnected. The development of the universe is not because of galaxies whirling out into a larger void, but of space itself elongating and carrying galaxies along for the ride. This means that if our journey toward the end of time ends with disappearance of matter, then time and space must disappear too. Logic tells us that causes must precede their effects. So what reasoning other than the cause of our universe being placed outside of it is there, when there is no time before the beginning?

This God could not be contained by the universe. King Solomon prayed: "The heavens, even the highest heaven, cannot contain you. How much less this temple I have built!" (1 Kings 8:27 (link is external)). Naturally, the idea of monist varied much from the image of physical gods accepted by ancients, where so many gods were worshiped, not excluding the ocean gods, earth gods, sky gods, sun gods, moon gods, star gods, animal-headed gods, and many goddesses, etc.

Monism is theology that delves into metaphysical views, where there are no decisive divisions other than a unified set of laws underlining God and nature. This is in contrast to dualism, which believes that there are two kinds of essences, and from pluralism, which maintains there are many kinds of meaning and materials.

The word monism is based on the idea of "monad," derived from the Greek monos, which means "single with having no subcategory, or any division. Monism is subject to different contexts within metaphysics, God, epistemology (distinguishes justified beliefs from opinion), morality and ethics, philosophy of the mind and existence, and so on.

But it always means oneness contesting dualism in body and soul, in matter and spirit (an energy-driven concept), object and subject, matter and force, where monism refutes and denies any distinction and persists on conceptual unity in a higher realm. The attempt is to eliminate the dichotomy (bisection, cutting in two, halving) of body and mind.

And today, if science points to a Creator who must be separate from the physical universe, then pantheistic ideas of God appear to be as misconstrued as polytheistic ones. The Eastern notion of a Star Wars God, a God who is a mere "Force" that is one with or part of the universe, is seriously challenged by modern cosmology.

A Creator outside of time

Nothing that is confined to time could have created the cosmos. The Creator must have existed before the beginning of time, and from a God perspective, God exists in our past, present, and future simultaneously.

Some have accepted a beginning, but they have described it as a random event, drafting a similarity between the origin of the universe and quantum events. Quantum theory states that even though space seems to be empty, in reality it is filled with virtual particle pairs that appear and fluctuate for extremely short periods of time. Our universe might have come into being via such a quantum vibration.

Fred Hoyle states, "The physical properties of the vacuum would still be needed and this would be something." The space in our universe is called a "false vacuum" since in actuality, it has properties that make it much more than nothingness—it is not an empty space as we assess it.

Besides, what we grasp as empty space stems from our limited senses that are only applicable to the visible world. Unless we're utilizing sophisticated telescopes and an up-to-date magnifier, we would be completely estranged from subatomic life and the quantum world.

Physicist Robert Gange states that relating to quantum physics, any universe that lasts for more than a Planck time (10-43 seconds) demands more than an arbitrary notion and a chance to describe it. Gange believes that quantum physics refers not only to an outside sustainer, but also to an outside initiator.

Physicists say that our universe is an astonishingly fine-tuned environment, and they are very interested to know how it happened to be this way.

Most scientists agree on the critical density of the universe; that it expands at a precise rate, just right for the building of galaxies, rather than ending in a premature collapse or a too-quick scattering (dispersion, refraction) and must have a flawless conductor. Physicists assent that the augmentation rate at the beginning had to be fine-tuned to one part in 10 to the 60th power; that's 1 with 60 zeros after it, a level of accuracy that they call "insane."

Stephen Hawking referred to this critical balance when he said, "The odds against a universe like ours emerging out of something like the big bang are enormous." Hawking also acknowledged the ratio between the masses of the proton and the electron as one of many critical numbers precisely met in nature. "The remarkable fact," he said, "is that the values of these numbers seem to have been very finely adjusted to make possible the development of life."

An incredible fine-tuning for life's advantage challenges natural explanation. After British astrophysicist Fred Hoyle calculated the probabilities that carbon would have exactly the same resonance by accident, he claimed that his atheism was greatly shaken, adding, "A common sense interpretation of the facts suggests that a super intellect has monkeyed with physics."

Fine-tuning undeniably pertains to each of nature's four fundamental forces that are so precisely harmonized that the ratios between them cannot differ without crushing the possibility of life. If the strong nuclear force were slightly weaker, the universe would only end up with hydrogen; if a nuance (slight degree) stronger, the universe would be depleted of hydrogen (and, of course, without stars). Stronger or weaker electromagnetic forces or a different value for the gravitational constant would also end in a universe with no stars.

Physicist Edward Kolb of the Fermi National Accelerator Laboratory stated, "It turns out that 'constants of nature,' such as the strength of gravity, have exactly the values that allow stars and planets to form .... The universe, it seems, is fine-tuned to let life and consciousness flower." Science, he declares, may never be capable of telling us why this is the case. The breathtaking convergence of quantum mechanics theory, microscopic world theory, general relativity, elementary particle theory, our theory of the universe as a whole in which the ideas involved, are speculative. This area of research is still an interesting brawl where the power of imagination is as imperative as careful calculation and surveillance.

Quantum mechanics is the most principled theory about the microscopic world. This precise, mighty, profound, and most attractive theory educates us that the world of the tiny is extremely varied from the world of our day-to-day experience. One remarkable difference is that infinitesimal (tiny, microscopic) things have opaque (vague, obscure) properties.

The Heisenberg uncertainty principle illustrates this shadowy situation by declaring that one cannot modulate (harmonize, attune) and measure a particle's position and speed at the same time as accurately as one desires. To size one very solicitously (carefully) will dislocate the measurement of the other, which disappoints the lector (reader), with the result that the particle has a specific position and velocity, but scientists are unable to measure it.

A more truthful statement of the fact denotes the uncertainty principle presents that a particle does not have a particular situation or velocity. The scientific measuring shows that scientist and the particle coincidently (collectively) generate unclear position or velocity.

It seems magic is truly orchestrating the invisible world of subatomic particles, as scientists name nothingness the vacuum and where the vacuum has ghostly properties. They admit particles and antiparticle spring into existence and disappear again. The physicists attest they must act so fast because they cannot directly see them, and because they are invisible, they call it a vacuum. By now, the scientists know that the quantum things appear and vanish, pop in and out of existence.

General relativity is the most Grass-Rooty theory concerning the whole universe; about gravitation, and about space and time. Einstein reminded us that these things inextricably entwine. Even though general relativity is not a quantum theory, scientists believe that every theory at its foundation has to be a quantum theory.

ENTROPY

The second law of thermodynamics (physics that deals with the mechanical action or relation of heat, electromagnetism, microphysics, mechanics, and quantum mechanics) states that the amount of energy in a system that is available to work is dwindling (diminishing.) Entropy rises as available energy lessens, which interprets that the innate proclivity (inclination) of things is to move toward chaos, not order, and accessible energy needed for moiling (working) is lost as heat in the process. Asymptotically (eventually, ultimately) the universe will run down, and everything will end because all the energy that is available will be more or less evenly allotted (allocated, distributed) so no work can be fulfilled and life can no longer exist.

This is how all things are naturally going to end up. Every living entity will eventually die, and nonliving things wear out and become destroyed. But the universe is not endlessly old because the universe is operating feasibly and without disturbance. The universe would have been exhausted of usable energy if the universe were infinitely old. An infinite universe with no beginning essentially would require infinite usable energy, which, according to the laws of entropy, is not possible. Therefore, the universe must have a beginning. And because the universe had a beginning, it cannot be of infinite size.

Because motion, time, and space are undeniably interweaved, it would demand an infinite amount of time to become infinite in size. Since the universe had a beginning, it couldn't have had an endless amount of time to expand; hence, it is finite in size. No endless regression events are possible, since that would mean the universe was infinitely old. And again, if the universe is already in a state of unusable energy, then it would have been infinitely old, which is not the case.

If any regression analysis has to stop at some certain point, any mathematical or any math-derivative agendas need to start with a beginning and sensibly calculate the progression until the end to have a reliable result. Any event, for that matter, must have an initial position and then an expiration date. I wonder why regression events that must have stopped at some infancy point for the universe to initiate should be difficult to comprehend in which reasoning at that specific point beyond space and time certainly demands an UNCAUSED CAUSE, the omnipotent and the omnipresent God.

One might still say that is supernatural to believe in an uncaused cause. But then again, one should ask oneself, if the subatomic particles at the quantum level cannot be tested, since they too quickly appear and disappear, it seems the particles are being influenced as soon as the examiner physicist, or any related quantum scientist, tries to calculate the event. If that is not supernatural, I do not know what it is. Because in the natural world at the Newtonian level, and the visible world everything can be tested, examined, and derived with an adequate result.

We should not forget that the human nervous system can only relate to vibrating frequencies of the visible world, as many individuals so strangely deny what they cannot not fathom. It should resonate to the inquisitive mind that the uncaused cause of the universe has to be infinitely bigger in size and span than the universe that it caused into existence. Other than that, we have the uncaused cause manifesting into existence something greater than or equivalent to itself.

Any entity or event that is inseparable from the universe cannot create itself into existence, because anything that is natural to the universe is part of it. This is not as uncanny as some people may think, since there must be an uncaused cause outside of space and time that has brought life into being, but certainly not subjected to the laws of the universe.

Pascal's wager is an argument in philosophy devised by the seventeenth-century French philosopher, mathematician, and physicist Blaise Pascal (1623–62).[1] It posits that humans bet with their lives that God either exists or does not.

Pascal argues that a rational person should live as though God exists and seek to believe in God. If God does not actually exist, such a person will have only a finite loss (some pleasures, luxury, etc.), whereas they stand to receive infinite gains (as represented by eternity in Heaven) and avoid infinite losses (eternity in Hell).

DEMOCRACY AND JUSTICE

People do not have to die to live, struggling for employment, food, shelter, fighting for the very basic necessities of life to keep them afloat, as billions are horrified as they face devastating condition just to survive. This is not how living should be. There are serious flaws in the allocation of resources and grave wrongdoing in how humanity needs to be treated. Since it seems justice is managed via force and by the power of gun, I wonder if God has anything to do with it?

The voices of justice must resonate with friend and foe; it must awaken the ignorant and the cruel. It is mandatory, and utterly not optional for the deprived and the righteous to be heard. In a democratic society, justice, heard loud and clear, not suffocated, is the only tool available that can expose and chastise the evils of the uncivilized, and the callous behaviors of the reprobate (a person who behaves in a morally wrong way.) As Reinhold Niebuhr says, "Man's capacity for justice makes democracy possible, but man's inclination to injustice makes democracy necessary."

It is of moral imperative to deny an oligarchical democracy, where the rest are tricked into believing they live in a democratic state and they do not. People must demand constructive change to prevent further corporate takeover, since corporate imperialists have no loyalty to either people or the state of the republic.

We are not delusional when we hear a painstaking cry for help—or are we? That is when we lose courage and behave with numb indifference to inequities for the wrong reasons, which keeps so many acting sub-human and away from doing what is right. And as Benjamin Franklin said, "Justice will not be served until those who are unaffected are as outraged as those who are."

Justice must be done in a timely manner to prevent genocide. Fair play must halt displacement of inhabitants from their homeland and stop further devastation in global warming, where a toxic and destructive atmosphere is literally killing human-beings for the sake of greed and hoarding money. Global policies must become in tune with movements already implemented towards one nation under God, since revolutionized technology and speed-of-light communication is making phrases such as this by Marshal McLuhan undeniably true: the world that has been "shrunk" by modern advances in communications. McLuhan likened the vast network of communications systems to one extended central nervous system, ultimately linking everyone in the world.

It is so undeniably true that dynamic communications, and the so fluent socio-cultural, socio-economic, and international political interactivities, cannot be obstructed by the walls of nationalism and prejudices anymore. It is quite difficult to turn conscionable people into robots, as if they ought to be controlled by remotes, striving to keep so many silent to undergo mental and spiritual sabotage.

It is time to wake up and notice the decisive difference in shifting priorities awaiting mankind. As Martin Luther King Jr. said, "An injustice anywhere is a threat everywhere." Globally, atrocious behavior must be noticed and dealt with.

WORK AND PRODUCTIVITY

Acting accordingly productive is the gist of living. Any consciously intelligent member of society should know that idleness and shirking can make one's sovereign position weak and vulnerable to dependency on others. There is no guaranty that wrong and morbid behavior is requested from the needy to satisfy the provider's demand. In exchange for receiving funds, as willful solicitation is often expected in return, an unproductive and jobless individual can be open to all sorts of vileness just to maintain one's basic needs for survival.

Managing short-term budgeting, and planning long-term financial activities—saving, wisely overseeing, and controlling one's financial status—are the keys for staying economically independent. The capitalist economy is systematic and very disciplined; it is cruel, and does not budge to any incompetency or sluggishness. Karma believes "what goes around, comes around," and this is true in every literal sense in dealing with balancing one's income and expenditures.

Once the victim of a monetary system and vile bankruptcy, there are no immunities but awaiting the tragic consequences of homelessness and dependency on other financially able bodies to either help, or not.

This scenario is not only true on an individual basis, but also ominous when exercised on a larger scale, when people are collectively unemployed. An unproductive nation redundantly looks for philanthropy from other powerful and productive nations, and their mercy.

Behaving lazily and not being productively active, not managing time, and in acting nonchalant, easily quitting, and not challenging the odds, or acting incompetent and not persevering enough to fight back against tough times will surely invite a systematically dire culture of creeping normalcy where the inhabitant's destructive behavior can become the norm. Concentrate all your thoughts upon the work at hand. The sun's rays do not burn until brought to a focus (Alexander Graham Bell).

When losing golden opportunities and repeatedly making wrong decisions, one can lose self-confidence and the value of independency, and end up hoping for survival. Productivity is not accidental. It is certainly the result of a commitment to excellence and hard work, savvy thoughts, bright planning, and concentrated effort in which one can muster magnificent creativity. But we ought to realize it is faulty to measure productivity checking one's BlackBerry over dinner and in obsessive behaviors with one's gadgets.

THE SUBCONSCIOUS MIND

As the science of psychology and psychiatric behaviors advances, we become even more consciously alert. Your subconscious mind is a second, hidden mind that exists within you. It does translate and acts upon the predominating thoughts that reside within the conscious mind. It objectifies circumstances and positions and identifies with the images that impact us from within.

Perceive your subliminal mind as tremendously fertile soil, an infinite agricultural ground that produces any seed you plant in it. One's habits, beliefs, and thoughts are implanted, and seeds are constantly sown till the day one expires. Just as grape seeds generate grapes, and walnut seeds produce walnuts, lemon seeds generate lemons, and wheat seeds produce wheat, the nature of your thoughts will affect you without you even being aware. You will reap what you sow; this is a fact.

It is also known that we are the products of our environment. So, it makes much sense to establish a constructive atmosphere and productive upbringing not to jeopardize our position where toxic thoughts and misconducts are cultured and normalized. It is also hugely important to educate people, since we play the role of gardeners, which for most should mean we are responsible for planting wisely so that all kind of seeds are not manifested into our subconscious mind.

As gardeners that tend to the soil of our unconscious mind, we need to meditate on what enters into our mind; as they say, garbage in, garbage out. The subliminal doesn't prejudice, judge, delete, or censor. It will stress success, plenty, and good health just as simply as shortcomings, scarcity, defeat, ill health, distress, and misfortunes do. Your subconscious mind imprints what is marked with feeling and repetition, whether these thoughts are positive or negative. It does not assess things as your conscious mind does.

This is why it is very crucial to know what you are thinking. Your subconscious mind is subjective. It does not think or reason on its own. It solely takes orders it captures from the conscious mind. It is fertile ground in which the seeds of our thoughts germinate and are cultivated. Your conscious mind commands, and your subconscious mind obeys. One has the prerogatives and should be able to wisely choose, especially if one has the blessing of having a decent environment and the opportunity of a good and prosperous upbringing.

Synchronicity

Once you understand that your subconscious will bring you what you need or desire, and you begin working daily to project thoughts and images of what you want, seeming chance events will start happening to you. To the untrained mind, synchronicity appears to be coincidence or luck, but it is neither. It is simply the operation of the forces you have set into motion with your thoughts. This powerful inner collaborator, working with your conscious mind, will bring to you the people and circumstances you require to achieve your goals.

We are all part of the greater whole.

Modern physics sees the universe as a vast, inseparable web of dynamic activity. Not only is the universe alive and constantly changing, but everything in the universe affects everything else. At its most primary level, the universe seems to be whole and undifferentiated, a fathomless sea of energy that permeates every object and every act. It is all one. Scientists are now confirming what mystics and seers have been telling us for thousands of years: we are not separate from, but part of, one greater whole.

We now know that everything in the universe is made up of energy. Everything from the items in your home, to the events that happen to you, and even our thoughts, are made up of vibrations of energy. This means our thoughts are made of the exact same substance as the building blocks of the universe. Knowing this, we can use it to our advantage.

In the past, it might have seemed unbelievable that we could create our reality through this process. But now we know how to do it, and why it works. Since our thoughts are energy, it only makes sense that repeated images, affirmations, deeply held beliefs, fears, dreams, and desires would have an effect on our own reality by vibrating within the larger fabric of reality. In fact, if we are all linked, how could it be otherwise?

The subconscious mind is something that has a huge effect on every action, but is constantly overlooked. Instead, the focus is often on our conscious mind, which contains the critical thought function of our brains. The subconscious is the powerful layer underneath. It encompasses the awareness of all things the conscious mind cannot recognize. Once the subconscious is tapped into, this remarkable part of the brain plays many different roles in your everyday life.

The Memory Bank

Your subconscious mind is similar to a huge memory bank. Its faculty (capability, competency) is virtually (almost entirely, pretty well) unlimited. It perennially (infinitely) stores everything that ever occurs to you. By the time you reach the age of 21, you've already permanently stored more than one hundred times the contents of the entire Encyclopedia Britannica. Under hypnosis, older people can often remember, with perfect lucidity, events from sixty years before. Your unconscious memory is just about perfect. It is your conscious memory that is suspect.

The function of your subconscious mind is to store and retrieve data. Its objective is to make certain that you respond precisely the way you are programmed. Your subconscious mind makes whatever you utter and do fit a pattern consistent with your self-thought. It is your "Master Program."

The Obedient Servant

Your subconscious mind is subjective. It does not think or reason independently. It merely obeys the commands it perceives from your conscious mind. Your conscious mind can be thought of as the gardener planting seeds. Your subconscious mind can be thought of as the garden, or fertile soil, in which the seeds germinate. Your conscious mind orders and your subconscious mind obeys. Your subconscious mind is an unquestioning servant. It works 24/7 to make your behavior fit a pattern coherent with your emotionalized thoughts, desires, and hopes.

Your subconscious mind cultivates either blossoming flowers or a wasteland of weeds in the nursery (botanical garden) of your life. Whichever you plant is based on the mental equivalents you create.

The Preserver of Balance

Your subconscious mind has what is called a homeostatic impulse. It keeps your body temperature at 98.6 degrees Fahrenheit. It keeps you breathing regularly and keeps your heart beating at a certain rate.

Your autonomic nervous system maintains a balance among the hundreds of chemicals in your billions of cells. Your entire physical machine functions in complete harmony—most of the time.

Your subconscious mind also practices homeostasis in your mental realm. It keeps you thinking and acting in a manner consistent with what you have done and said in the past.

The Comfort Zone

All your habits of thinking and acting are stored in your subconscious mind. It has memorized all your comfort zones and it works to keep you in them.

Your subconscious mind makes you feel emotionally and physically uncomfortable whenever you attempt to do anything new or different. It goes against changing any of your already set patterns of behavior.

You can feel your subconscious pulling you back toward your comfort zone each time you try something new and challenging. Even thinking about doing something different from what you're accustomed to will cause you feel tense and uneasy.

One of the biggest habits of successful people is always stretching themselves or pushing themselves out of their comfort zones. They know that smugness (self-satisfaction, complacency) is the great enemy of creativity and future possibilities.

MODERNISM VS. TRADITIONALISM

Humanity is facing a fundamental and often difficult matter that has permeated into every aspect of our lives, and apparently with little competency to resolve. Modernism is facing off to overcome traditionalism, which is making life convoluted (twisty, winding) and difficult. Global inhabitants, particularly developing countries, are caught between decisive transition from traditionalism to modernism, not because they want to, but because they have to.

It is the almost daily advances in technology that have increased information and knowledge that has resulted in modernism, and dynamic worldly communication encompassing cultural, social, economic, and scientific discoveries make it a blessing.

But it's also discouraging, since the old beliefs and new trends of thought do routinely clash, and sometimes for the worst. Like giving birth to religious extremism, terrorism, and enacting dictatorial regimes that hinder modernity for maintaining the status quo to halt progress.

Advances in technology and science are inevitable. It is the womb of nature that is impregnated with piercing ideas and faithful inventions sought by miraculous minds relentlessly endeavoring and searching for new discoveries that are inundated (overwhelming) and revolutionizing contemporary status to enhance human lives, and in making further advances to modernize our position for better living.

We dig into the unknown looking for answers, searching to satisfy our curiosity, hoping for the pursuit of happiness, to quench our thirst for mindboggling questions such as why are we here, where did we come from, and where are we going? What is our purpose for living, and is there a God? And if yes to this last question, why so much pain and suffering?

There are hundreds if not thousands of other imperative inquiries that are basically interrelated with historical human science (anthropology, biology, medicine, sociology, astrology, space, ecology, etc.), digging into cultural morality, spiritual, philosophical, and scientific inquisitions, and more. They substantiate direction and hope to fulfill generations' urges for good living that might one day make millions of enigmatic positions and unanswered questionings transparent and amazingly clear.

It shouldn't be a hesitancy in knowing that freedom, democracy, liberty, human rights, and the pursuit of happiness are keys to creating a flourishing atmosphere promising human progress. They need to be incited and free from limitation, dictatorial anxiety, and a policing environment.

The culprits are inclined to unwaveringly safeguard unabsorbent and unnecessary traditions, as they are not in accord with time parameters and modernism, since they often carry dark ages mentality that impedes greatness into the future.

But modernism should certainly be accompanied by making big attempts to inspire citizens' progressive attitude to gain knowledge and to maintain social security for better living.

It's time for free education, free medical care, free housing, and free transportation, and most definitely employment for everyone so that people can be relatively free of stressful financial uncertainties which make millions bereft (barren, utterly lacking) of the ability to devote time and energy to magnify production and become a better member of society.

It is savvy to realize that some schools of thought and socioeconomic, socio-cultural entities are by nature more advanced than others.

For instance, institutions that practice social-democratic systems and prioritize social security first and then manifest democracy, like Scandinavian societies, such as Denmark, Finland Norway, Sweden, Iceland, and to some degree Germany and France, Canada, and others that are social democracies. They are countries that value equality, trust, and public welfare services, as they are well-adjusted for furthering human accomplishments and civility of mind and manner. They are adequately positioned, as they first attend to basic human needs and then value democracy, as freedom should be considered a sacred and inseparable part of humanity, but not abused.

Freedom and good behavior do complement each other, and one without the other invites a crime-infested society, often with nasty outcomes. Democracy first, and then social security second, has unleashed so much violence and inexorable (uninviting, austere, harsh) individualism, truly actuating survival of the fittest behavior and everyone to his own attitude, resulting in impetuous (marked by force and violence action, impulsive) decision-making and defaults that make it almost impossible to give meaning to peaceful coexistence and human rights.

It is noteworthy to know this system of democracy-social, which most capitalist systems practice, has unleashed excitement in violence and often destructive actions that encourage smell-blood conduct that is for sure provoked by Hollywood and more recently, politics. Bollywood, savagely digital video games, deadly sports and competitions, and other "entertainment" fallacies have globally caused havoc, especially among younger generations that are extremely chaotic, criminal, and inhumane.

It seems they are people with no conscience, and I am afraid so-called professionals deliberately promote criminal behaviors, endorsing destructive programs and extremely violent movies and distasteful television agendas, satellites, and other mischievous social medias that are utterly barbaric.

"Because one cannot exercise true democracy in a violent society." If one is bereft in training and education, and not able to experience a civil society, one is much more inclined to act immorally and criminally when unemployed and hungry, when one's loved one is sick or terminally ill without having access to professional medical help, or without housing assistance, where so many have to end up living on the street and homeless.

I believe those institutions that practice democratic-social rather than socio-democratic are literally facing agendas that are backward, and not in favor of the majority of their citizens—but they are making living extremely luxurious for the very few, which gravitates towards lopsidedness in almost every aspect of our lives since perhaps they inadvertently are encouraging a menacing atmosphere that most definitely demands a police state.

I am afraid democracy-social has also caused a serious dilemma, especially in developing nations, since they are often faced with dictatorial governments and fascist regimes that do not believe in fair allocation of resources, resulting in extreme income inequality, while the ruling elites also reject freedom and democracy, and even if they exhibit some, it is definitely cosmetic, and not at all authentic.

RESPECT, RETURN THE FAVOR

Yes, it is true that some individuals might behave kinder than others, tolerate undesirable conduct, and perhaps insightfully bear inconsiderate actions. Even put up with impetuous, cruel, and hasty behavior. Whatever the case may be, the point is that we all have a boiling point that will sooner or later erupt if we are pushed to our limits.

Many take acts of love and kindness for granted, giving no thanks and without returning the favor. When one is continuously sacrificing and is constantly there to give so much of oneself, but not being appreciated, it will gradually but surely influence one's subconscious mind, which can eventually surface, making the caregiver exhibit harsh retaliation in one way or another.

Expecting nothing in return is because of one's devotion, act of kindness, and goodness of heart that should not be taken advantage of. When one is careless for so long towards one's benefactor, and retorts (to say in reply) nonchalantly, one can unexpectedly face violence from the very same person that has ceaselessly assisted him or her in their time of need.

When it comes to human emotions, time is of the essence; true feelings and emotions do not occur abruptly. They gradually mature and progress; they can be subtle, and not alerting.

If others are neither emotionally intelligent nor sensitive enough to appreciate one's ceaseless support and good deeds, or perhaps are acting with complicity or not wanting to reciprocate, then be smart and terminate the unjustified one-way relationship before it erupts like a volcano, making damage beyond repair.

For instance, in a marriage where the marital covenant is at stake, both parties need to sincerely comply by the rules of marriage that encourage the couples to appreciate each other and to sacrifice within their means for keeping the sanctity of the marriage intact.

We ought to be reminded that no matter how much one is in love or is willing to sacrifice, if the significant other cannot mutually favor and render sincere love in return, then in the name of good will and decency, one should not persist in taking advantage of the significant other; it will sooner or later backfire.

If not able to constructively deal with one's egotistical conduct, then bail out softly before resentment can brew to a point of no return with irreparable damage. Remember, even a mother's unconditional love has its limit.

It is of paramount importance that you always return the favor. We sometimes might not be able to respond financially, but it is always possible to render kindness, either with words or actions. Many of us take things for granted, forgetting that no matter how much of a saint one really is, or how much of a good character one might be, we are not perfect. What I mean is, we all do have a threshold, a breaking point that can cause anyone to behave adversely and in negative ways. One should try to overcome one's selfishness and believe in the decency of a fair give-and-take relationship where compassion, balance, and appreciation is truly served.

"We are what we repeatedly do. Excellence, then, is not an act, but a habit" – Aristotle

The secret is to do what is mindful and virtuous, where bad habits cannot eventually tear us apart.

CREEPILY MANEUVERING

When people are kept illiterate by design, they easily succumb to fallacies of the ruling system as they acquiesce (submit, give in) to dishonest politicians that are in cahoots with business elites determined to preserve the status quo. Prerogative gentries (privileged class) are entitled to receive the best, while the underprivileged and financially repressed are restlessly engaged in an unbearable lifestyle, worrying about their next meal and a roof over their head, and how to deal with irreparable health problems they encounter.

That is exactly why no weight is put on the miracle of learning for the deprived by the powerful, coupled with keeping people busy with a difficult life, which results in ill conditioning for the poor and jeopardizes their position, making it impossible for them to grow, despite much insane positivism and obsolete affirmations that supposedly are meant to motivate the hopeless and help the destitute.

The suppressors are well aware that literacy, knowledge, and information awakens people to question more and ask why. In which all answer should apparently lead to bizarre sociocultural and socioeconomic plans meant to cultivate the worst in people and to bind them to the psychology of work while facilitating millions with the conditional techniques to make them one-track-minded in maximizing productions for the rich elites and to act docile (amenable, obedient) and robot-like in taking orders.

It should remind one of Pacific salmon, which are motivated to lay their eggs and are determined to breed after an arduous journey struggling upstream, which makes them exhausted. And sometimes amid the ferocious storm, that is the very reason for their death.

And if they are not caught by fishermen and other predators, like bears and eagles, or do not get trapped behind dams and large waterfalls before breeding, they are very lucky, since so many cannot make it to fulfill their mission, what they are destined to do.

NATURE OR NURTURE?

Which one of these is the responsible party: our genes or our environment?

Is it our genes and our biology that is responsible for our behavior and who we really are? Or could it be the environment and the way we are raised that is the main and decisive factor in how we are shaped?

Genes are defined as "a specific sequence of nucleotides in DNA or RNA (messengers) that is located on a chromosome which is the functional unit of inheritance controlling the transmission and expression of one or more traits by specifying the structure or a particular polypeptide and especially a protein or controlling the function of other genetic material."

In layman terms, we can say that nature is the bottom line, and the very reason for our behavior. It is a deterministic factor to the code of codes and how we are driven to be, because we are predisposition, preprogrammed, and there is nothing that we can do about it. Therefore, we are predestined to be who we really are. Or is it the environment and how we are nurtured and fostered that plays the real decisive factor, and a huge role in identifying who we really are that shapes our true personality and character?

Scholars of biology, philosophy, the environment, anthropology, sociology, psychology, neurology, psychiatry, nutrition, physiology, economy, and many other social, cultural, mental, and behavioral sciences have wrestled with this perplexing human issue for many years now. The overall assessment and the truth behind this very crucial point is that "it is virtually not possible to understand and to comprehend how human biology would be able to function outside of the context of the environment."

To believe genes are things that cannot be changed, since they are rooted in our very biology and they are to determine our fate and manifest what kind of personality we become, is a very detrimental and hazardous view that has polluted many people's minds, leaving horrifying side effects and is an extremely irresponsible way to deal with this crucial human quandary (dilemma).

Obviously, believing in the gene argument and the hypothesis as being the only fateful factor in shaping our behavior and character, and in denoting who we really are, permits the luxury—and the irresponsibility—of not adequately dealing with this damaging idea. To leave out the historical, environmental, social, political, economic, and many other variables and educational factors that are responsible in shaping our personalities, our behavioral mishaps, or good characters, is to unjustly deny anyone his or her true potentiated identity for the better, as most probably so many deprived individuals could become much more progressive and improved people if they were not exhausted from living in an improper atmosphere and depleted from decisive educational agendas that could spur and motivate millions toward the right direction.

Tell me if violent Hollywood movies and violent video games and so many other electronic conditioning gadgets are not deliberately designed and programed to shape people's minds and to emotionally disconnect people and cultures, which certainly brainwash future generation to become zombie-like, as many do the most inhuman behaviors, regardless of what type of genes or traits they carry or have been born with. Would we still be in this violently messy society as we literally are, where, for example, so many mass shootings occur in schools, high schools, colleges and universities, killing and injuring innocent people? And ironically, these centers are designed to literate students for the best they can be. Or other mass shootings that redundantly happen in public gatherings, shopping malls, and many entertainment places, where people are supposed to unwind and relax from exhaustive daily workloads and have a good time. Hundreds of other crime-infested neighborhoods are dealt with as remote islands, where no hope for recovery and improvement is ever mustered to prevent or mitigate further atrocities relating to social and economic disasters.

Tell me if hate-mongering movies, and the most distasteful sexual programs and scenarios, have anything to do with our thoughts and conduct as human beings, as the human brain cannot tell the difference, particularly for the most naïve (ingenious mind, deficient in worldly wisdom), and perhaps mentally disturbed, between films onscreen and films playing in the mind.

And yes, of course it is good to pray for peace, health, happiness, liberty, human rights, and justice for all. for the sake of goodness, and for the love of God, let's not turn a blind eye and play these utterly double-standard and misleading games on people's psyches, taking them for fools. That would eventually lure them into the corner to give in to these subtle and creeping misdeeds. I am sure you, the culprits, know that living is easy with eyes closed. For the love of God, open your eyes! Humanity is on the verge of annihilation because of your greed for wealth and power.

Promoting a genetically predispositioned argument and predestined nature as an absolute, and expecting no progress in genetically programmed human beings, is a diabolical and premeditate folly that gives a green light to those who justify their lies and deplorable acts in any society. It should remind us of eugenics, where the idea was to create an environment where variables were to be controlled for the production of good offspring, to improve and control such variables as health, beauty, intelligence, aptitude, strength, and other outstanding and desirable factors that would have been complimentary to their prejudiced and discriminatory notions.

I say discriminatory because there are enough resources to gratify every born child with the best possible outcome.

ESSENTIALLY REQUIRED

Do not be fooled into acting foolishly arrogant or in behaving cocky and irrational. These inept behaviors do not comply with the spirit of goodness and what is right. Use your mental, spiritual, moral, physical strength, and your financial strength to progressively leverage and extend help to the deprived and those in need, the destitute. Acting otherwise will put you in a stranglehold to one day suffocate you.

Being blessed and endowed with so much wealth, prosperity, and power is a premeditated and predestined trust in you, expecting you to be fair in the just allocation of resources and not to bondage mankind. It is all about making it or breaking it. Remember, nothing is meant to be with no purpose; it is a universe amazingly well-designed, superbly constructed to reach its objective and goals.

We are lucky to be part of it, at this particularly wonderful phase; given a choice and the freedom to be constructive or to behave destructively, to annihilate it all. And since it is no longer a hypothesis but a fact that the weapons of mass destruction are now as real as wisdom is beyond value.

IF I WAS GOD

I am glad that God is God, and I am not, as God is a God of infinite patience, the most compassionate with infinite forgiveness, infinite resourcefulness, infinite justice, infinite effluence of good, the most benevolence, the most merciful, infinitely prevalent, infinitely graceful, the Proprietor of all there is, the most graceful, the Fiduciary of time, space, and beyond.

I say the most patient because no one but God can tolerate the evils of man. And yes, survival of the fittest is very much alive in the animal kingdom, as beasts kill and devour beasts, as by nature they are baneful (harmful) serving their instinct (non-taught, biological capabilities) to survive. It is a jungle out there, but so is here, a crime-ridden atmosphere; only with one difference. What the beasts go through is mandatory, while so many of us choose harmful behaviors and violence although they are not compulsory, but optional.

Then again, the so-called "animal man" with some instinctual traits is confident with mind power and created with a brain that is potentiated to one-day reach the entire universe. Man is credited with intelligence, goodwill, consciousness, and as one is entrusted with wisdom, self-awareness, sacred feelings, righteous emotions, and is also a moral being with the likelihood of acting in the image of God. That is why the "animal man," with some instincts, is as well-named a human-being.

One ought to acknowledge and know that man's instinctual conduct for living is to stay alive for manifesting its heavenly qualities, to produce good deeds, to work hard and shine, to ascend and be the best that one can be. To sacrifice when one hears a cry for help, and to negate the unjust, to encourage happiness and discourage sadness, to be considered, to tolerate others, and assist the less fortunate, to denounce fascism, to believe in freedom, democracy, dignity, and human rights. To let freedom of thought, freedom of speech, freedom of expression, freedom of religion, and freedom of assembly thrive. To believe in collective cooperation, to believe in a world with no boundaries and walls, to practice in good faith, to live and let live; otherwise, why should anyone be different than a beast?

I am sure the all-knowing God has taken those reverence merits (values) into account when God created human beings, and perhaps God has taken those profound properties in man for granted. But God is being betrayed in return, and with no sign of remorse from mankind that it is doing the infinite wrong. I wish humans would have not been entrusted with ultimate generosity and kindness, and had not been taken for granted to act in his image.

I wish human creatures were born with intelligence, and not a clean slate at birth. I wish we were wise and knew enough from the day we were born, from the very beginning, to discern right from wrong so that perhaps infinite wrongs and perpetuated crimes could have been avoided or relatively mitigated. But that would have been against the evolutionary nature of the entire universe, which is gradually perfected and awakened, as everything is bound to incrementally advance, reaching its potentiated trace and maturity. So basically that thought is futile and out of the question.

The other alternative is to be born with a thumb-like horn, realizing that unless one would wise up as one grows and perseveres to ripen to the height of humanity in acquiring education, knowledge, integrity, wisdom, intelligence, empathy, caring, hard work, sacrifice, and being a productive member of society, then one's horn would not diminish as one grows, but it would get larger. Which of course would raise a red flag for the rest as a clear sign to watch out and be aware of the beast-like personality that one carries.

This not only motivates the horn-bearer to diligently try for bettering oneself so that one's horn would eventually vanish, as one can gradually become the best that one can be, since no one likes to become finger-pointed and shunned regardless of one's gender and ethnicity or any other personal trait; but warns those improved, the wise and civilized, to keep away from troubling souls. To stay away from those impregnated with stupidity and violence as signified by the height of their horn, aiming at correcting a violent society infested with offenders.

It could be that atrocities occur because not every victim is an expert psychologist, psychiatrist, or a professional sociologist, to relatively detect insane characters, to perhaps avoid trouble, and certainly before is too late.

This alternative also has its flaws, because it cannot work in uncivilized nations where no commitments are made to grassroots change of the backward conditions, where people's pride is suffocated and no funds are available for training, skill, and education, and the entire society is dominated by illiteracy, where the power of force, hypocrisy, and violence is the key to advancement, and it can be a blessing to have a long horn and rough attitude to overpower others. This is where behaving inhumanely and approaching the peak of savagery for one's own interest and pleasure is the key to success. Furthermore, it would take away the dignity from the one born with horn, as it simulates and lowers a human's position to beasts.

The other option would be to professionally (exhibiting conscientious and ethical standard) facilitate newborns in highly standard centers for the first three to four years of their lives, which are extremely crucial in shaping their personality, accommodated by the state for upgrading the children with the most viable learning assistance through every decisive educational training and health field study possible, to the expected result. It is also extremely imperative that children have access to parental love while under professional care, to avoid negative emotional side effects that are bound to occur if babies are deprived of parental love.

This scenario demands skillful devotees that are willing to exercise every humane ingredient possible to also boost the motherly love and parental care that any child needs to prosper, which seems a bit utopian, because it is bound to time and very far in the future, when people are advanced in their thoughts and the overall society has the emotional intelligence to accept the visionary expression, "From each according to his ability, to each according to his needs," a slogan popularized by Karl Marx in his 1875 Critique of the Gotha Program. The principle refers to free access and distribution of goods, capital, and services.

After all is said and done, not only are we the product of our genes, but also the product of our environment, in which a productive atmosphere demands constructive plans, and certainly adequate funding to properly spend on decisive matters, not to exclude professional and adept management to oversee the upbringing of the children, especially in poverty-stricken areas where people are much more at risk for destructive behaviors, where there is no light at the end of the tunnel.

I am afraid it has become a testosterone-driven world where aggression, bullying, and brute force works, as no civility of mind and manner matters, as millions are taking advantage of God's blessing and infinite patience as he watches the devil's work in most of us, but still renders a chance until judgment day or punishes the culprits without letting the transgressor (violator) connect the crime that one commits to one's later punishment while living.

We should realize that God has ushered the way and has endowed humanity with a mind, a brain that can think and create miracles, a will to freely choose and ask why, and a spirit to challenge the unjust. While knowing that God's interference in any and all that we choose to do should contradict free will and is despotic, that is why it is left up to the victims to fight back and constantly pressure the evils of our time and say no to the unfair and unethical practices of the few, curse like mighty and belligerent souls.

It is critically vital to question the empire of wealth and influence, the rich elites, that have unfairly accumulated the entire wealth of the globe, since modern moguls have denied opportunity to billions and have decided to let their horns grow and ram into all that is just, violating the basic principle of humanity, which is to not let innocent people die for the sake of accumulating enormous wealth in the hands of the few.

The key is fair allocation of resources, where a family-oriented society would be competent enough to adequately survive and not become so stressed-out and pressured to go through unbearable family violence, to become dispersed and broken into a single family parenthood, or utterly destroyed, which the end result would be a chaotic society having rampant crimes without the possibility of an argument or evidence in affirmation.

And for the after-death reward, or demise, reason should dictate those guilty as charged, or those with good deeds won't burn in Hell or drink wine in Heaven, but inevitably ought to expect either grace or ills of some sort, other than being incinerated in Pandemonium (the capital of Hell) or land in the vicinity of milk and honey, surrounded by beautiful girls and handsome men, accompanied by soothing music, breathtaking dancers, along with exotic birds surrounded in a majestic atmosphere.

Logic dictates that justice should be accordingly swift, and within precise measure. And of course, the expression that says "innocent until proven guilty" is out of the question, since the ever-present God already knows the accused and can utterly identify the perpetrator. Other than that, fear of Hell and Heaven, in all honesty, seems bogus and beyond my mind, as it is denied to those charlatans that blindly claim they have talked to the Almighty and know of the judgement day. They naively claim they are aware of the punishment mechanisms God carries to chastise us in Hell, or prize us in Paradise.

One thing that I am certain of is: what comes around, goes around, as a multiplier of castigations (punishment) should face those exploiters in which their demonic conduct wrongly effects so many innocent human beings that burns them like wildfire as they are boycotted from having the least opportunity in this lifetime. I also know, and so should you, we were born from dust, and to dust we shall return, and should excitingly await our soul to depart to higher realms for a new beginning, perhaps a being not inhibited with imperfections, but a higher spirit in a higher realm.

We all should expect some type of positive or negative response after death. It is infinitely far from reasoning and savviness of mind to accept vanity in a universe that not a single cause is without its merit, since everything is so precisely calculated. The irrefutable fact is that what we do not see controls what we see, and also oversees human conduct.

In entropy there is a principle that says: unless there is a greater control over a process, either a complex chemical reaction or anything else, the process generates chaos; and as big as our universe is, it certainly demands a higher force to control and keep the universe, the entire cosmos and beyond, orderly; which should warn us that there is judicious and epiphenomenon (indirect) control in everything.

IT IS NOT WHAT IT IS

Life goes on, and perplexingly enough, we often disappointedly wonder, and justly so question, why thousands of unfair, gloomy, and painstaking situations are materialized, and are kept vague, not identifying the actual source of suffering for so many, making the inquisitors believe "it is what it is" and this is how living works while controlling people's minds by the very advanced technology of thoughts and startling (staggering, astonishing) psychological and psychiatric maneuvers.

These are well-executed through dubious media and bogus delivery instruments of greed and immorality to preserve the status quo for the handful of bloodthirsty corporate sharks, since the perpetrators relentlessly fuel their oligopoly system by spilling millions of the innocents' blood without mercy. The corporate media, through never-ending electronic illusions, merges fact and fiction until it is perceived indiscernible and not clear, entrapping people's minds into believing the worst.

In the meanwhile, the victims are busy fighting manufactured racial and ethnic tension, struggling with an extreme disparaging social and economically classified society, and with the very troubling income inequality. They're also impacted by a toxic ecological system, putting up with violence inside our borders and outside, and bearing the devastating consequences of unjust, and unfair competition that is the gist of a free enterprise system.

The invisible hand of the market is to balance supply and demand, but only a few have monopolized the world economy by humongous trusts, cartels, bank holding companies, and through global financial intuitions where domestic and small businesses, middle, and the working class do not stand a chance to thrive.

People are not even immune from consuming basic food to stay alive, since billions can utterly not afford organic and wholesome produce and meat, so they have no choice but to eat poisonous junk foods that are infested with chemicals and preservatives and a host of other malignant agents deemed to kill consumers for the sake of generating billions of dollars of profit for the empires of wealth and power.

It seems the air, food, and water are purposely infected, surreptitiously planned to exterminate inhabitants of the overpopulated world, also causing thousands of other atrocious conducts done by the global corporates without any impunity. It should remind one of the expression that says "pick your poison"; either die from hunger, or die from taking food that is supposed to nourish people.

Transnational corporations and their cronies brainwash so many that it is normal to put up with this globally caused hell, and it is ok to live at your own risk with a pandemic-oriented culture of insanity causing humanity irrefutable troubles; after all, so they say, this is the price we pay for our freedom, as they muddy sacred words such as human rights, liberty, and the pursuit of happiness, literally done under a capitalist culture that ironically tries to export freedom and democracy. Civilized and proud nations need to rethink new ways to catapult beliefs that have quick-sanded so many hardworking people without any hope for recovery. Progressive mechanisms of governing can replace the outdated approach to many of a nation's irresolvable dilemmas and gridlocks. The truth is that it is not what it is, and I wonder if God has anything to do with it.

EVOLUTION VS. REVOLUTION

According to the dictionary, some of the definitions for revolution are A) a sudden, radical, or complete change. B) a fundamental change in political organization, the overthrow or renunciation of one government or ruler and substitution of another by the governed. C) activity or movement designed to effect fundamental changes in the socio-economic situation. D) a fundamental change in the way of thinking about or visualizing something, a change of paradigm. E) a changeover in use of preference, or technology of thoughts.

Revolution also means: the action by celestial body of going around in an orbit or elliptical course; also apparent movement of such a body round the earth. The time, taken by a celestial body to make a complete round in its orbit, the rotation of a celestial body on its axis: completion a course (as of years); the period made by the regular succession of a measure of time or by a succession of similar events, motion of any figure about a center or axis.

Evolution, according to the dictionary, means a process of change in a certain direction: Unfolding, the action or an instance of forming and giving something off: Emission, furthermore, a process of continuous change from a lower, simpler, or worse to a higher, more complex, or better state: Growth. A process of gradual and relatively peaceful social, political, and economic advance, the process of working out or developing, something evolved.

Human beings, by nature, are bound to what their genes are made of and influenced by the environment they live and are raised in. Relatively speaking, there are basically four scenarios that can impact our wellbeing or demise; as in good judgement one cannot say that genes and DNA are the sole reason to who we really are and the only cause for people's character buildup.

Many inherit excellent and healthy genes that significantly affect their physical, emotional, and mental attributes, as they are endowed with intelligence, high IQs, compassion, and other decisive humanly factors. And the environment they are born to is also constructively productive and magnificently fruitful, where negative variables often stand no chance to detour someone's promising fate and enhanced position.

Then, we have those with good genetic characters and attractive human properties, but they are, I am afraid, born into an environment that is not suitable for anyone's upbringing, which can most definitely affect their personality and significantly reduce their ability for success, preventing what great deeds they could have probably accomplish.

The third situation is when one is born chromosomally disadvantaged, but are fortunate to be born into an impeccable (flawless), witty environment with tremendous opportunity to grow.

The fourth condition is the worst, when one is born with unfavorable genes, chromosomes that are not auspiciously oriented (a specific sequences of nucleotides), and born into a destructive and unpleasant atmosphere as well, which is cause for one's ugly fate, as they can have a gloomy multiplier effect on one's life.

Sadly, millions globally suffer from grave income inequality and are stricken with utter poverty, which denies them any opportunity to progress since the monetary system persistently drives to widen the gap between the haves and the have nots. The system deepens social and economic gaps, alienating billions from each other and self, disassociating billions from a meaningful life.

It alienates us from family, from work; it removes so many from body, mind, and soul, ending in acting robot-like. We have become zombies, as if a supernatural power has entered billions to behave will-less, speechless, only capable of automatic movement directed at producing zillions for the rich elites and the corporate bosses; only to glorifying the gone-mad empires and for the actual wealth-producers, to be humiliated and discarded when out of use. The system so cleverly manages such atrocities by linking it to our fate, and subtly enculturing that it is how God's plans work. Imagine what can culminate if the environment is fundamentally altered for the better, where the atmosphere is not as toxic as it is designed to be and everyone gets a chance to grow no matter what genes one carries.

The corporate capitalists and the oligopoly system of ruling that comprises roughly 5 percent of the Earth's population hold and control more than 90 percent of the international resources and the entire wealth of nations without any mercy. Humongous private enterprises rule governments and the world by force and through evasive, clandestine, and not so legitimate conduct that is so puzzling it should certainly raise eyebrows.

Evolution relates to the historical development of a biological group (as a race or species): phylogeny, development of a new biological group, speciation, a theory that the various types of animals and plants have their origin in other preexisting types and that the distinguishable differences are due to modifications in successive generations; the extraction of a mathematical root, a process in which the whole universe is a progression of interrelated phenomena. Both revolution and evolution have historical trademarks, and the footprints for either evolution or revolution can be traced from millions of years ago.

The truth is that evolution, in its real sense, encompasses time, steady transition, and requires maturity, where no revolution is possible without evolutionary process for reaching animated revolt.

To be specific, sociopolitical and socioeconomic changes definitely demand a cultural revolution that is bound to gradually gain knowledge and information, where the overall society would be ripened enough and ready to tolerate the explosive nature of the revolution, to acknowledge and align themselves to the new condition, since decisive issues are expected to proactively be gauged with a different yardstick, to become as promising and helpful as possible to quench people's thirst for gaining dynamic results.

The evolutionary process is basically continuous, where the incremental changes constantly happen and gradually resume the higher stages of development. No existence or any phenomena can escape this scientifically natural and realistic fact, since its reality is ingrained in the very nature of the universe itself. The footprint of evolution is prevalent and can historically be traced where it is deemed necessary.

Every nuance of natural and social sciences, and in what we see and known as the tangible world, needs to deal with the evolutionary process of things—unless we want to believe in the world of magic, where superstition can rule us and things burst out of nowhere. Socioeconomic, sociopolitical, and cultural manifestations of events are no exception to the evolutionary facts, and ought to be taken seriously and heavily valued.

No matter what stages of evolutionary process we are in, taken from the dark ages to contemporary societies, there will always be the exploiters and their victims. Name any system you wish, no perfect society is ever going to materialize to forcefully but effectively deal with unjustified and unfair situations of mankind since the mechanism of greed, self-interest, and thirst for power can undeniably mushroom in any so-called progressive situation. This can prevent accessing an ideal utopian environment. The good news is that relatively speaking, gradual evolutionary changes for the better are often possible, which definitely calls for relentless objections and criticism of the governing bodies and the crooks in charge through intelligently constructive means and by constantly holding authority's feet to the fire, demanding fair play.

It is very crucial to know that fundamental requirements for a civil society are literacy, higher education, information, wisdom, preserving knowledge, insightful leadership, modernization, up-to-date infrastructure, training and skills, and the most imperative, money well spent on these decisive issues that are all key ingredients for any talented society to demand an ideal prospective for better living.

An educated and informed society can significantly disrupt the culprit's peace of mind and disturb their tranquility, where the powerful elites must not be unleashed to abuse their power that is rendered to them by the people. The governed should take the livelihood away from the public enemies that intend to keep the master-slave relationship intact.

Bear in mind, when we historically refer to social and political revolutions, we are reminded of bloodshed and huge sacrifices without much improved change—often, changes for the worse. What is gained from most revolutions are temporary excitement and rabblerousing, where violence is inevitable, since most of failed revolutions would have been successful if only they could have occurred in a timely manner, as thoughtfulness and socio-cultural progress in any nation is of utmost importance.

WHERE IS GOD?

God is the silent voice within you, behind every nuance of existence. God is beyond the infinite universe; God is not matter, as positivism doctrine and other beliefs as such so naively utter, "I must see God to believe it." God is the silent pulsation and the rhythmic throbbing you experience, making you feel alive. God is the unseen thoughts and invisible memories one cannot see, but experiences the effects of, and is literally impossible to live without. God is in every breath you take to keep you animated.

God is the oxygen circulating through your body; God is your faith. God is your good conscience, your kind behavior. God is the cosmic energy that permeates all beings and percolates everything in existence. If God could be seen, then God would have descended to our physical level. God is the infinite Spirit beyond the mind of the universe, and we are so lucky to be the proprietor of a single drop of this holy soul.

One feels God when being enlightened, considered, compassionate, and when in love; you sense God when you empathize and feel pity for others in need. It is when one is strengthened with faith and acts hopeful despite difficulties, and self-sacrifices, forgives, and believes in piety and patience. One feels the presence of God when one is philanthropically active, and notices God when one passionately tries to save lives.

Your ingenuity, intelligence, and talent, your dreams and desires, seeking truth, fighting for freedom, democracy, equity, justice, and peace, are all reflections of God within you. It is only then that you feel God as one sees no choice but to practice one's higher self, where the spirit of goodness directs you to do no evil and become pleasantly righteous in all that you do. It is when you are in a realm engulfed with the spirit of the almighty God, the omnipotent, omniscient, and omnipresent Father, that you are accorded with infinite silence of the almighty God within you.

Do not fall into the trap in the world of the blind leading the blind, as some people stand their dogmatic ground like an empty walnut shell with no kernel and claim: why believe in something one cannot see? This pushes them to the brink of behaving in a delusional way in their belief and deprived of any adequate reasoning; it makes them obscure and despondent. They do not realize that "ideas are the origin and cause to all matters, since thought are energy driven, and because matter disappears, as matter is never stable to rely on."

Some so unduly try to mimic and build artificial human brains in laboratories, practically a vain attempt, not knowing their effort will be futile. Our human brain comes with a super complex software called the mind that is inseparable from the cosmic programming potentiated to conquer the universe, and is linked to cosmic energy that has rendered sanctuary to mankind and enabled humanity to reach the heavens above.

It is an EXTRATERRESTRIAL and a metaphysical domain that rejects making brain hardware manufactured by mortals that is beyond our limited senses. It is the world of unseen that surreptitiously maneuvers, the quantum world, the world of string theory, and the world of subatomic particles, where even the most complex telescopes and advanced magnifiers are not as efficient as they need to be to reveal the magic that lies in the heavens above, as its magnanimity should be appreciated.

The prevalent sacred energy, the electromagnetic forces, the gravity, and the small and big atomic forces that are so potent and not visible, which we take for granted, are the work of the unseen energy that fuels everything we do via internet, cells, digital gadgets, computers, TV and satellite, radar, and so many other things such as x-rays, scans, MRI, and other medical technology that is influenced by the undetected energy, making our living healthier and much easier.

It is all about the unperceived world that orchestrates and rules the world we see; it is all about the almighty God, that some credulously choose not to see.

"Rejoice with those who rejoice" is paired with "mourn with those who mourn" in Rom. 12:15. Even more interesting is what follows in v.16, "Live in harmony with one another. Do not be proud ... Do not be conceited ...

Be careful to do what is right in the eyes of everyone" (v. 17) ... "If it is possible, as far as it depends on you, live at peace with everyone" (v. 18).

Atheists, infinity, and evolution

Referencing atheists' claims on evolutionary perspectives, it shouldn't be odd to identify with motion and grasp the meaning of any evolutionary work, defined as "a process of change in a certain direction as also applicable to Darwinian account of the origin of species." We then should know that evolution and motion are correlated, and evolution without motion will literally lose its significance and conceptualized meaning.

No evolutionary process can be defined without a starting point, a departure that can lead to its destiny, or a task well done and completed.

If so, it is only common sense to know the first requirement for motion is to have an origin, a starting point; infinity translates as having no inception and without an end. As so many nonbelievers adamantly believe in evolution as a scientific fact, it should only serve them futilely, since they cannot learn that evolution must have a beginning and an expiration date, where a complete course of event is substantiated, no matter how long the duration or the complexity of the situation.

It is a conflict of interest with huge discrepancy to believe in evolution and in the meantime accept infinity and a life with no origin, because an infinite existence cannot objectify an end and should only mean having no purpose; otherwise, if rational, we should expect life with having a start and an end.

And if the message is to understand evolution based on matter, then we must understand that where there is matter, there is motion, and where there is motion, then time and space are certainly involved. If so, then having an origin, a departing point, and in reaching a designated destiny for objectifying a purposeful deed is not far from reason, as it should make much sense. No sensible analogies can occur in believing otherwise.

GLOBALIZATION AND THE
DISHARMONY OF THOUGHTS

In our contemporary world, even the farthest dwellers of the planet are unquestionably affected by global political, cultural, and financial interactivities, where the conglomerate (cartel, trust, consortium) news media is leveraged to influence so many through modern telecommunication and technological innovations.

Today's generation possess advanced industries that can unfold superb thoughts and brilliant activities. We are able to disclose helpful breakthroughs and information via dynamic ways of communication. Technology has made the globe much smaller, as billions of people can share and enjoy the exchange of ideas, access plenty of information, become enlightened on vital issues, and learn about other cultures. Education can certainly play a key role in differentiating fact from fiction, to identify with progressive ways of life, and to speed up partaking with those who truly value freedom and human rights.

It is a blessing that many social media empower people to discern lethal ideologies from constructive outlooks and enable us to distinguish dark ages thoughts from revolutionary concepts that are potentiated with robust plans and animated programs to make a better world possible. Further education gives meaning to the expression that "knowledge is power" because related socio-cultural cognizance should certainly make us aware of taking sides with those who value humanity and what it stands for, rather than blindly aligning with static beliefs and backward traditions that literally squander so many lives as we speak. With astonishing headways in science and great technological novelties (inventions), enormous military and puissant (powerful) policing, along with massive accumulation of wealth and influence beyond anyone's imagination, the wealthy empires can positively resolve many prolonged iniquitous (sinister) sagas beholding humanity. Imperial corporations can halt consolidated attacks from fiendish (perversely diabolical) Jihads and put an end to the prolonged purgatory state of mind that has disturbed world peace and tranquility. So many diversified groups and guilds have yielded to subtle fear, from small-scale business meetings to large enterprise assemblies.

People worry in every important gathering and affluent community, in government entities, even at places of worship, in national and international airports, as millions of innocent travelers become nervous not knowing where terrorists have designated their next targets, and when or how terrorists are going to strike again and again, blasting themselves off and exploding other harmless human beings to pieces.

They can stop religious extremist's sporadic attacks and their fragmented inhumane terrorist behaviors at will. The mighty powerful are illusions that ordinary people who, unlike the super-rich, have no protection against sinful terrorism, and other wicked misconduct can live in a bubble impervious from harms, since the powerful elites act so indifferently to people's sufferings and very fragile situations they endure. Many believe that wars give birth to advance civilizations, which fools them into spreading their wings too far, where they do not belong, and the very reason to losing it all.

Albert Einstein said, "The pioneers of a warless world are the [youth] who refuse military Service." Charles Sumner noted, "Give me the money that has been spent in war and I will clothe every man, woman, and child in an attire of which kings and queens will be proud. I will build a schoolhouse in every valley over the whole earth. I will crown every hillside with a place of worship consecrated to Peace."

And Eve Merria so eloquently said, "I dream of giving birth to a child who will ask, Mother, what is war?"

President Thomas Jefferson said, I recoil with horror at the ferociousness of man. Will nations never devise a more rational umpire of differences than force? Are there no means of coercing injustice more gratifying to our nature than a waste of the blood of thousands and of the labor of millions of our fellow creatures?

CAPITALISTS AND CULTURE

The effect of capitalists' transgressions is so structurally designed that has fundamentally influence on our way of life, where our thought process has deliberately been molded to accept our own demise without noticing the culprit's surreptitious behaviors and ugly intent. The significance of capitalists' cultural and social interactions epitomizes class differentiation, since its fundamental belief system is blatantly biased but intricately formatted in the fabric of many societies without its horrifying maneuvers being identified and clearly detected. And because of the corporate capitalists dominating the economic and political system, basic liberty and human rights are already being eroded, which can further lead to a fascist and dictatorial state of governing to further uphold the exploitive and backward system intact.

It is a shame seeing too often that wealth and money, prestige, influence, rank, and fame, dictate morality, virtues, dignity, integrity, etiquette, manners, and other humane principles; since even believing in God is washed out and has become an inseparable part of propaganda and spiritual offense. Every word is carefully tailored, and what is grasped as right or wrong is meant to prolong the nature of the beast and to conserve the status quo, as the entire culture is set up to save the rich oligopolistic regime at any cost while constraining progressive thought.

Its settings and cultural layout are overwhelmingly poisoned, but they are acknowledged as norms and are fluently communicated among the ordinary man's belief system that has adversely effected so many for the wrong reasons. People subconsciously relate to cultural linguists and are entrapped in a host of premeditated agendas planned to keep them apart and under control.

For instance, when deprived, and the working class are not sexually monogamous, they sure are demonized as whores and finger-pointed to as misfits and prostitutes, but when the super-rich are promiscuous and sexually active they are known as celebrities, titled as the rich and the famous. We ought to know better since the superbly rich are God's chosen people, with luck, that are blessed with prosperity and extreme fortune. And when tycoons forfeit billions, they are the victims of an economy gone bad, and hence need to be saved by taxpayers' hard-earned money. But when a nobody, an ordinary dude, diligently tries but cannot find job, again due to an economy that is gone wrong, and takes a loaf of bread, or cannot pay his bills, then he is a thief, an outcast that must be sternly punished and incarcerated. And if anyone dares to complain, they are then labeled with being "a rebel with no cause," or lazy, a vagabond (hobo, derelict, bum, drifter), and is slapped with being a failure and a non-productive member of society.

Is it not obvious that the making of financially destitute people, which by the way, count for extremely large numbers, should constitute a toxic environment that can certainly feed into producing wretched and hostile members of society. Many not only are a threat to themselves but to others, since they are exhausted from having the basic training and education to equip them enough for a better future.

The poor have to live on everyday prayers to survive, since the system has made sure the working and the middle class are insecure so that the corporate rich can play with people's fate and keep them as vulnerable as possible, leaving them no choice but to obey the capitalist bosses for their minimal subsistence. And because the deprived masses, the indigents, are unsafe and not adequately guarded against life's financial, social, and political hazards, many are bound to risk their shady position doing wrong for making the bare minimum to function. Then, of course, they have to bear the utmost of punishments, and with no professional help available to represent them justly, they may pay with losing their lives or facing a long imprisonment time.

On the other hand, when the super-rich risk in doing wrong and they get caught, there are always topnotch lawyers and other decisive avenues available to free them with only a slap on the hand. This reminds us that when justice is trampled, humanity shall mean nothing other than beastly conduct. It is time to deny the expression that says "it is what it is" because accepting it is what it is will denote the spirit of a nation, and who we really are as moral and civilized inhabitants. There is a saying that if you have integrity, nothing else matters; and if you don't have integrity, nothing else matters. people should not let the system take away their integrity, which is the essence of one acting as a human being.

It is not a lie that extreme income inequality, class differentiation, stark poverty, social and economic insecurity, nationalism, wars of aggression, ethnic cleansing, genocides, forced migration, overpopulation, misallocation of resources, unemployment, inflation, recession, economic depression, stagnation, deceptive economic practices, unfair and wrongful competition, monopoly, policing the world, race for atomic and other horrific weapons, climate change, extremism, toxic food industries, conspiratorial pharmaceutical corporations, financial industrial complex and corporate hegemony, jihadists, Armageddon nonsense, religious enmity and other faith-based encounters, homemade and international terrorism, fear, distress and anxiety, cause high statistical-oriented violence.

Parochialism (radicalism, sectarian), individualism, apartheid (economic and political discrimination), racism, prejudice behaviors, sexism, gender inequality, xenophobia, misogyny, family violence, troubling addictions, prostitution, sex, drugs, alcoholism, homicide, suicide, loneliness, homelessness, unheard of mental and physical illnesses, illiteracy, bankruptcy, and a host of other ills have so sadly become the fate of humanity. They are the hallmarks of the capitalist system that values money over human lives and dignity, as so many malefactions (evil deeds, crime) are conducive to its culture and malignant nature of this ferocious system.

These cruel and bitter situations urgently call for a dynamic and constructive response to make a better world possible, because positive changes should significantly affect the status quo to avoid global destruction that can potentiate everyone's demise, since its troubling signs should already be crystal clear for every enlightened and inquisitive mind to further cultivate the next progressive socioeconomic stages in the most advanced and civilized nations and to gradually permeate and trickle down into developing countries, because we all certainly are in this mess together.

EMOTIONAL DISCORD

Anger and fear are very challenging issues for us all. We resort to our animal nature when we are angry. We also become anxious, nervous, and worried when fearful. It is not an easy task to control these very damaging emotions. Anger can build up gradually if things do not go our way, or with having a one-track mind acting dogmatic and opinionated. A variety of reasons could stir up an outburst and make us do the unthinkable.

To name a few: ignorance, jealousy, greed, selfishness, or feeling resentment towards others when one is financially deprived. And the inferiority complex that is felt when one sees those with superiority complex rules the day.

Often feelings of being alienated, having negative thoughts and emotions, a sense of being a nobody despite hard work and extreme effort that one makes to reach one's objectives, but one is not even able to make a decent living for oneself and loved ones can surely have an adverse effect on many people. These troubling situations can ruin our health, and our social and spiritual wellbeing. Sometimes they're so destructive they need immediate medical and psychological attention.

We can become frustrated and distressed when we are unable to correctly assess our financial position, and miscalculate the actual capacity for undertaking an endeavor that becomes almost impossible to successfully manage. And when lacking crucial resources imperative to finish the task can fail us, it surely then makes one the victim of tremendous pressure and causes too much stress. A troubled marriage and a host of related issues with family violence can utterly destroy our peace and tranquility, no matter how rich or poor one really is. And when in fear, we can panic and become distressed and behave strangely, especially when one's life or loved one's life is threatened. Our fear can also be economically based when we lose jobs, as our livelihood becomes threatened and we no longer have the means to comfortably support ourselves.

Bear in mind also that we live in a crime-infested society forcing us to constantly be watchful, and in fear of losing our lives or in getting maimed, which can deny us the basic serenity of mind, depriving citizens from having peace and making so many vulnerable to anxiety and nervous breakdown. We have been preyed on in the most civilized nations by wealthy, influential, and powerful elites, since they utterly control viable resources where they mismanage funds for their own livelihood but render citizens with wrong information and deprive so many from having basic knowledge and training. As millions cannot afford proper education, they are left out from improving their miserable condition. People are so engaged in making a living it has forced them not to care for what is actually taking place, and therefore not participating to stop troubles facing them, which sometimes affect the ordinary man the most.

To resolve our conflicts in a truly civilized manner, not letting violence get the best of us, we need to know that we are the product of our environment. Practically and diligently, try to bring about a dynamic and a do-good culture. We need to encourage humanity that seems it is forgotten, to persist on the welfare of the majority and all the people; we should not let the powerful elites furnish an environment conducive only to their interest. We cannot expect those that are cocooned in so much comfort and possess extreme fortune and fame to give a damn about others in need.

Until troubles reach us all with no mercy or a way to escape it, knowing divided we fall, our ignorance will clear the way to be easily conquered. We should have the audacity to challenge norms and our cultural limitations, to become globally savvy, and enlightened, and possessing a fine personality to accept everyone with no prejudices, and as a first-class citizen of the world. We should not believe in boundaries, and actively interact with other nations and cultures. Not acting in vengeance, either in our private and family lives or in our social life, but in a peaceful manner acting wisely. We should be able to control and to manage our emotions, particularly our anger and our fears.

Wise people persist on reaching a stage where no violence of any sort could take place. That is possible only if we invest more in our brain to raise our knowledge and information for collective bargaining and everyone's livelihood, and not in manipulating others by their lack of education and through fear and anxiety keep people divided and colonize them for taking their valuable resources, annexing (sequestering, taking by force, expropriate, usurp) what belongs to them.

DOES THE SOUL EXIST?

Recent scientific theory notices life's spiritual parameter. This refers to the reality of the soul, among many other affiliated and vital issues in our lives. Religions relentlessly remind us about its existence, questioning how do we know if souls really exist? A series of new scientific experiments shed light on this primordial <u>spiritual</u> question.

The question of the soul is raised with the idea of a future life and our belief in the next realm of existence. It is an animated and subtle issue that permeates our thought; it cannot be reflected upon via scientific analysis, which since has created skeptics that misunderstand such potent energy. The enlightened are relentlessly curious, wanting to know about its manifestation independent from our physical body. The human soul, like our mind, is not visible, and is as important if not exceedingly more tempting to evoke our curiosity. Our mind, although not perceived through tactile sense, does play a very significant role in our mental and cognitive activities. Only the effects are known, and the evidence is substantiated in our undertaking of tasks.

Yet, some physicists and scientists cannot fathom or accord insightfully with a spiritual dimension of life. Mr. Steven Hawking stated, "We're just the action of carbon and proteins which protein is made of amino-acid that is the building block in our life. And when amino-acid, and other molecules such as salt and water are mixed the soup responsible for creating life happens. He further stated we can make life with lifeless molecules, since a molecule began to replicate itself from the raw material of nature.

Mr. Hawking goes on to say that we are a wonderful biological machine produced through biological evolution, in which evolution is a process that is powerful enough to produce a species from previous species, as the strongest of them all will survive a process called the survival of the fittest, which in the long run will morph into other species, and that is how life began. Mr. Hawking carries on to say life is a process of chain reaction inside a wonderful biological machine that can infinitely carry on if some grave disaster does not happen, as DNA can replicate itself, where amino acid and other molecules can actually assemble themselves. Mr. Hawking and others explain that we live a while and die . . . and the universe? It too has no purpose with no meaning. He goes on to utter that it is all planned and worked out with no need for spirit. The irony is planned by who, if the plan has already been laid out?

One should respect the scientific analogy that Mr. Hawking and others are pondering on, but in the meanwhile, let's not forget they are only indicating a viable mechanical process taking place in nature that is exhausted of any dynamic life force, which does not explain the impetus behind, as he puts it, the "wonderful biological machine." Mr. Hawking seemed not to know so obviously that nothing cannot create something.

And let's assume that life began about four billion years ago, starting with a single cell that replicated itself and became what we currently are through the intricacies of the evolutionary process. Then the question is how their claim could ever be validated if the precise raw material and the careful conditional environment that could have been comprised of millions of variables, if not billons, would have not been present, since I am certain that life did not originate in a bubble.

How could such evolutionary advancement ever take place or be accredited with the absence of a very potent and intelligent energy source, and occur without a sacred spirit or a ubiquitous soul? If so, seeing a dead man walking in a science fiction movie should not raise any eyebrow and be seen as fact. Overwhelming scientific discoveries are literally available that attest to cosmic energy that is clearly shown in an infinite number of species, making life in its entirety possible.

I am afraid Mr. Hawking acquainted the cause of such astonishing animated energy to the force of gravity, which he thought is responsible for all there is, But then, we can only wish it would have been that easy to extrapolate a definite conclusion on an unanimated thing to represent vigorous life-bearing reality, since it should alert us not to expand on emblematic lab work experiments and avoid stretching them as authenticated facts.

For such a puzzling and complexly intelligent entity as the cause of life, a phenomenon full of vigor with infinite intricacies is clearly beyond anyone's imagination to empirically identify with. Mr. Hawking's findings should only be delivered as hypothesis, and no further than speculation.

A new theory of everything demands an insightfully convincing theory rather than a materialistic model that denies the tutelage of the enigmatic soul that can only denote unripe knowledge and yet callous wisdom in acknowledging truth. Neuroscience, I am afraid, is constrained only to lab work as it tries to decode the material brain but is distracted from realizing the intricacy of the definitive human mind and insightfully exhausted from knowing the transcendent soul.

Scientific views have deselected the soul as an object of human belief and reduced it to a psychological idea that forms our cognition from the perceptible natural world. This believes delivery of "life" and "death" are no more than the common notion of "biological life" and "biological death."

The active assumption is simply that the laws of chemistry and physics, and all that exists, are just dust orbiting the core of the universe. This unreasonably equates the energy-driven cosmos as lifeless, which is contrary to the colloquial scientific view that everything is purposefully programed to collectively fulfill its destiny. Nature and bio-centric agendas are energy-driven and cooperatively spearheaded to fulfill its destiny.

The physical world relates to our limited senses, and constraints of the human nervous system, which has led many in making serious flaws for assessing the reality of our lives. This should remind us of great spiritual thinkers and philosophers who tirelessly pursued to find the link between the human mind and the conscious universe, and often with much more convincing outcomes than what science has to say.

It is no longer dubious that consciousness is the core of the animated, and makes sense on the reality of the cosmos. Even though the contemporary scientific paradigm is based on the credence that the world has an objective observer-independent existence, real trial suggests antithetical, since a great number think life is just the activity of atoms and particles that spin around for a while and then dissipate into nothingness. But if we add life force to the equation, we can elaborate on some of the major puzzles of science, including the uncertainty principle, the wrangling and tweaking (enhancement) of the laws that shape our universe.

Let's contemplate on the famous "two-slit experiment," and the observer effect phenomenon. Since it elaborates on when one watches a particle enter through the holes, it maneuvers like a bullet, passing through one slit or the other. But when no one observes the particle, it exhibits the action of a wave and can pass through both slits simultaneously. Likewise, experiments tell us that undetected particles exist only as waves of probability, as the great Nobel laureate Max Born proved in 1926. They're statistical predictions—nothing but a likely consequence. Until observed, they have no real existence; they only do when the mind sets the framework in place, and they can be thought of as having duration or a position in space. Experiments make it unavoidably clear that even mere knowledge in the experimenter's mind is good enough to flip-flop possibility to reality. Many scientists believe the observer-dependent behavior not only is applicable in the subatomic world, but showed that "quantum strange" also happens in the human-scale world.

In referencing whether humans and other living creatures actually have souls, over two hundred years ago Kant pointed out:

Everything we experience – including all the colors, sensations and objects we perceive – are nothing but representations in our mind. Space and time are simply the mind's tools for putting it all together.

Will Durant wrote: "The hope of another life gives us courage to meet our own death, and to bear with the death of our loved ones; we are twice armed if we fight with <u>faith</u>."

We should be reminded that the human mind and soul are not visible and materially oriented, but the effects are known and can be experienced, since without having a "sound mind," a worthy living is not possible. Our mind is also believed to be a derivative of our physical brain. If so, why should the human soul that is irrefutably ingratiated with our powerful emotions and feelings be any different from a non-visible mind?

And why are scientists and other scholarly minded individuals not able to verify and identify the real substance behind referencing human thoughts and the essence of our ideas and where they come from? They bombard us every second, and no one has an inkling on how ideas are manufactured or formed and what they are made of, and consciousness is nowhere to be found in our brain, since the most prominent scientists do not have the slightest clue where consciousness is located in our brain.

The answer is that consciousness is non-local; it is universally vast, prevalent in every fiber of existence, either animated or not, where unanimated matter is only coagulated condense energy that pulsates at a lower rate, and not as actively vibrating as animated entities that throb at a higher grade.

Perhaps scientists expect to find the human soul in laboratories. I believe there should not be any ambiguity in the by-productivity of human soul, because we need to ask: who or what is it that cries when unhappy and pressured? What and who is it that laughs with joy when happy and vibrant? What and who is it that hopes and desires; gets nervous, panics, becomes frightened and desperately seeks to be free, is in search of progress, and diligently tries to be somebody? Acts heartened and captivatingly courageous for the right reasons? The human soul.

What becomes sad when it faces injustice? Feels pity and becomes depressed when others are in need of food and shelter? What feels stranded, frustrated, and lost when deprived of love, like a dead man walking? What envies? What is rejuvenated when in love, wanting to conquer the world? What jumps to its death to save an innocent life? What hates to be alone and can get alarmingly belligerent and dangerous? What acts manic and behaves insanely? What acts wisely, seeks logic, acts greedy, acts cool, has purpose, seeks happiness, attracts love and repulses fear, adores to be praised, and seeks human rights and freedom, and wants to belong? The human soul.

The human soul reasons; it chooses, gets curious, is judgmental, has willpower, manifests consciousness, conveys intelligence and constitutes the most strengthened forces to challenge nature. It perseveres and to breed, and wants to make sure of life continuum for others to come and the next generation to be. It is like being hypnotized and programmed without our consent and interference; it seems it is on autopilot as it is preprogramed and predestined.

It might sound farfetched, but we should keep digging until one day, humanity can perhaps catch up with its soul-searching idea where spiritual endeavors and undertaking are prioritized, rather than our quest for so much materialism and pride. And also because we are geared into putting up with so much egregious disparity, taking our very soul hostage, trying to make a living just to survive, leaving no time for any soul-searching. Our spirit belongs to higher dimensions; we should realize that and let it connect to the infinite power of the universe, where it belongs.

If so, it is only then when humanity can reach its true essence. But this is not an easy task, because our mind and spirit are caged and fettered to fit the present standard of living, which is caught in the web of uncertainty and materialism. It sure makes it difficult to quench our thirst for seeking true love and let our soul evolve into aesthetic living to objectify happiness; to enrich the way we live, which can potentiate the image of God in man and for humanity to reach higher realms, if given a chance.

Floating man, flying man or man suspended in air by Avicenna (Ibn Sina, d. 1037) refers to the existence of the soul. The argument is used to argue for the knowledge by presence. The argument is that the subject is suspended in midair in which he can reflect on his own without any help from sense perception and is deprived of assistance from any material body.

According to Avicenna, we cannot deny the consciousness of the self. His argument is as follows: Let's imagine a fully developed and perfectly shaped person, but with his vision disguised from perceiving all external objects—suspended in the air, and not protected by any perceptible current of the air that supports him. His limbs are apart and kept out of contact with one another so they do not feel each other. Then let the subject consider whether he would confirm the existence of his self. Avicenna argues that the "floating man" would ratify (approve) his own existence, although not affirming the reality of any of his limbs or his bowels, inner organs, kidney, heart, or brain, or any external thing. That indeed, he would affirm the existence of this self. Ibn Sina believes that inner awareness is utterly independent of sensory experiences.

This argument depends on a contemplative thought experiment. We have to imagine a man who, by accident, arrives into existence cultivated (developed) and fully formed, depleted of having any relation with sensory experience of the world or of his own body to ameliorate (make better), making him aware of his position. There is utterly no physical contact with the outer world. According to Avicenna, this subject is, however, essentially conscious of himself. His argument is that the self is not coherently (consistently) a substance, and there is no subjectivity, as Avicenna tries to prove the existence of the soul, or "Nafs." That is completely independent of sensory interactivities.

Descartes's Cogito and Avicenna's Floating Man

Before the French philosopher <u>Descartes</u> (1596–1650) referred to the existence of the conscious self as a cusp (turning point) point in epistemology, utilizing the phrase "<u>Cogito ergo sum</u>," the eleventh-century Tajik-Persian philosopher <u>Avicenna</u> had pointed out the existence of consciousness in the flying man argument. Thus, long before Descartes, Avicenna had accomplished an argument for the existence of <u>knowledge by presence</u> without necessitating for the existence of the body.

Both Avicenna and Descartes accepted that the soul and self are something other than sense data. Also, Avicenna believed that there is logically no relationship between the self and the body. He believed there is no logical dependency between them. We live in two worlds; the physical world, which the human body must respond to for survival, and the immaterial realm, in which our mind, the subconscious, and if you prefer the spirit or the soul, maneuvers, as only the effects are seen as our thoughts and ideas materialize, often creating physical wonders where matter substantiates.

Criticism

Adamson says, "The weakness in the argument is that, even if the flying man would be self-aware, the thought experiment does not prove that the soul is something distinct from the body. One could argue that the self-awareness is seated in the brain. In this case, in being self-aware the flying man is only aware because of his brain that is doing the experiencing, not because of a distinct soul. He just doesn't realize that the self-awareness is a property of his nervous system."

Mr. Adamson misses that what we know as the nervous system, is the "self," which is the property of consciousness. One should be savvy-minded enough to know: The nervous system is the consciously oriented self, since the apparatus of the nervous system is not seen, only the effects are noticed.

INCORPOREAL GOD

"Is man merely a mistake of God's? Or God merely a mistake of man's?"

– Friedrich Nietzsche

And I say, neither, since what has sought God is so far shallow; and what has assessed man is not adequate.

> Not knowing the whole truth. No one can claim if either one has made a mistake or not. "I can control my passions and emotions if I can understand their nature"

– <u>Spinoza</u>

We live in an age of information and intelligence, an era that defies superstition and hocus-pocus maneuvers that are based on lies and charlatanism. If a rational dialogue is intended, subjects like incorporeal (having no material body or form) God, existence, consciousness, mind, subliminal mind (unconscious mind), morality, spiritualty, philosophy, science, the universe, cosmos, soul, metaphysics, and the like, should not be toyed with. Also, issues such as monetary and fiscal policies, extreme income inequality, racism and apartheid behavior, neo-colonialism (the economic and political policies by which great power indirectly maintain or extend its influence over other areas or people), feminism, corporate capitalists, climate change, wars of aggression, and threat of atomic war, should constructively be dealt with. This list is definitely not to undermine vital social issues like gun control, police brutality, human trafficking, immigration, unscrupulously powerful lobbyists, abortion, violence, drugs, police brutality, single parenthood, prostitution, pedophilia, unjustified incarceration, capital punishment, overpopulation, and so forth that are in need of urgent attention.

Such subjects are complex and can often be vulnerable to ambiguity and shortsightedness. This should alert one to avoid being derailed from what makes sense and is wise, and to dispose of what lacks logic, or is vain and does not make sense.

The subject of existence and God urge meditative minds, as they are intricate by nature and are solely possible through the recognition of circumstantial evidence. They can be astonishing when they are knowledgeably discerned through inference and with clear-sightedness.

Anyone in their right mind should not claim seeing God or physically speaking to God, because the almighty God is not limited in space and time as we mortals are, and since no messages fall from the sky and/or from an incorporeal God above except snow, rain, drizzle, and perhaps asteroids (planetary bodies) that every billion years or so strike planet Earth with devastating effect. That is why dinosaurs vanished, and meteorites (comets, falling star, fireball, meteor) reach the surface of Earth without being completely vaporized.

What prophets of God can claim are they offer mind-bending revelations and genius, are superbly intelligent, magnificently talented, with amazing wisdom and creativity, since prophets possess incredible IQ that was bestowed upon them to lead humanity to the light at the end of the tunnel, helping them with meaning to get out of the dark ages, and often from desperate and chaotic situations? Prophets were sages that so wisely paid attention to circumstantial evidence of what our universe divulged that at the twenty-first century it's what quantum mechanics has discovered to talk about the world of the unseen.

Quantum physics and the realm of the subatomic particles sees the universe not as a pharmaceutical entity, as Newtonian physicists or as atheist scientists have thought of, solely acknowledging the physical world. Instead, the universe is imbued with spirit, the invisible energy that manages what we see, where matter is inconspicuously vibrating as condensed energy. So we ought to know we are an inseparable part of this infinitely vast universe where the sky is not the limit. Making the expression of you are what you believe very true, where reprogramming one's thoughts is the key to changing one's life. Popsugar: "If an egg is broken by an outside force life ends. If an egg is broken by an inside force, then life begins. Great things always begin from inside." And that inside force is what absolutely controls and manages life in its entirety.

The [invisible] field is what solely manages the visible world.

Albert Einstein said: "The [invisible] Field is the Sole Governing Agency of the Particle." We are often baffled by phenomena and the state of affairs in our life, desperately wanting to alter our destiny. We desire to get all we wish out of life. But the fact is, the way we counter our environmental stimuli determines our fate. Our shortcomings are within. Wonderful and positive things in our life occur when this limitation is broken by the unseen field of energy within us.

Beneath what is deciphered as thoughts, mindfulness, conscious, subconscious, spirit, and soul are but subtle energy that drives us to be who we are. Most of all, it is the subconscious mind that is mostly responsible for how one reacts to the outside world, from which our nervous system and senses of seeing, hearing, tasting, smelling, and touching receive stimuli and capture information. Our conscious mind can be credited with logical manifestation and having 5 to 10 percent decisiveness in how we respond to the external environment.

Seemingly, every cell in one's body is affected by every single perception that one has, as if billions of cells do have their own central processing unit in which they all so amazingly work with extreme discipline and cooperation, comprising a very intricate system. Being an integrated part of the universal energy, the human brain acts as a mediator, or a transmitter, which proclaims vibrations, leadership, and path to one's cells. But then who is behind one's choosing the stations that are in tune with millions of everyday broadcasting thoughts?

It is not a mystery anymore that just thinking about something makes our brain release chemical neurotransmitter messengers that communicate with our nervous system and even part of itself.

This makes the role of neurotransmitters extremely essential, since they control our happiness, sadness, or being stressed, as well as digestion and other hormonal bodily functions.

Interestingly enough, we ought to know even our base energy-oriented thoughts are very relevant to "epigenetics." It is now scientifically proved that our environment, and how we interpret the occurrences in our lives, and how we respond to them, directly impacts the behaviors of our genes. They control biology, as it is not so much about self-actuating genes, as it was thought before. Genes can turn themselves off and on to decisively influence our personality and who we really are. The headway in biology realizes that when we change the way we think and alter our perceptions or beliefs, we relate entirely different messages to our cells and can reprogram and revamp cells' meaning and their expression. It is believed that each and every cell in our body is replaced approximately every two months. So, one can reprogram downbeat (bearish) cells to be more positive and optimistic, hence changing your life for a more constructive and better life.

Hence, it is absolutely imperative for parents, and those responsible for upbringing children, to be accommodative, as they need to provide a decent and productive atmosphere so that the children can benefit. It is scientifically proven that children from age 0-7 will record everything that happens around them in their subconscious mind; and they will behave what they have recorded, affecting themselves and consequently, the society in which they are living. A great majority of our perceptions are hidden below, but directly involved in what we do, since our subconscious mind is extremely attentive from age 0-7 in our thoughts, perceptions, and visual images that we have encountered, as well as beliefs, habits and emotions, what we value, our protective reactions, and everything that we experience around us.

Comparably, our conscious mind takes part in producing thoughts and in choosing which route to take, as the conscious mind proactively decides and controls what to do. Unlike the subconscious mind that has a mind of its own. Therefore, if one wants to alter what one is dealing with, one must change the present perception that he or she is experiencing, and rather believes in.

When our senses receive a signal, they immediately respond and send the message to our brain to process and respond to the situation. It is noteworthy to know that the conscious mind deals with logic and what makes sense. But the desires of the conscious mind have to be in line with the belief system and the values, since it is overpowered by the subconscious mind. The conscious mind makes decisions and forwards orders to the subconscious mind. The subconscious will carry out the directive-oriented position based on what is programmed, not essentially based on what one is requesting.

There are some energy-based dynamics you can reprogram your belief system with, like active meditation, visualization, positive self-talk, affirmations, and adamantly trying to delete the past experiences and flashbacks, not reminding oneself of the past episodes to prevent reoccurrences. Repetition of an affirmation over time alters the neural pathways in your brain to generate new belief, since a fresh network of neurons can be created to manifest a new paradigm shift and manifest a refreshing landscape of thoughts.

It is not nonsense to visualize and focus on mental images in your mind's eye that enable you to make your dreams come true, reach your objectives, and for making your mental images become physical reality. Positive self-talk, meditation, repetition, being receptive, and aligning oneself to actually living your dreams and making your mind a fertile ground for implanting seeds, soaking words and images deep into your sub-conscious mind, will eventually flourish and bear fruit of making your desires a reality. It is all about the incorporeal God that is formless, a superbly magnificent energy, literally so prevalent that oversees everything in existence and knows precisely who we are.

CULTURE OF WARS

"The brave man is he who overcomes not only his enemies but his pleasures"

– <u>Democritus</u>

And I say, if so, then no enemies are manufactured to overcome.

"Good and evil, reward and punishment, are the only motives to a rational creature"

– <u>John Locke</u>

As <u>Voltaire</u> says, "It is forbidden to kill; therefore, all murderers are punished unless they kill in large numbers and to the sound of trumpets."

We should take inventory and correct our character flaws in order to resist straying from righteous conduct and become impervious to sinful temptation and wrongdoing.

There is a sacredness of belonging to the human race. We must stop walking sideways along the thick walls of cultural and habitual ignorance that have caused so much tyranny and misdeeds that if persisted upon, will eventually destroy us all.

Many nations are victimized by the culture of war, since culprits must relentlessly manufacture and find sickening reasons to infringe upon a vulnerable nation's affairs and sovereignty to justify wars of aggression. Corporations' piercing power and influence have dominated our thinking pattern for the worse, which has negatively affected the way we live.

Wrongdoings in national and global affairs have mutated like a vicious virus, dominating the way we live, creating havoc that has horrifically affected billions of innocent people. "All war is a symptom of man's failure as a thinking animal," as John Steinbeck so aptly put it.

Ordinary men are not immune to insidious maneuvers furtively executed to make noticeable differences in race, religion, nationality, creed, sexism, creating class war, and in widening income inequality gaps. They have managed to sow seeds of animosity for engendering divisive behaviors to cover up the innate problems and troubling nature of the capitalist economic system.

Relative social stability goes haywire in the midst of troubling times when depression leaves the system in economic paralysis and political gridlock, since there is no way out of its misery and stalemated position except thorough global violence and socio-cultural belligerency. As Mahatma Gandhi noted, "What difference does it make to the dead, the orphans and the homeless, whether the mad destruction is wrought under the name of totalitarianism or in the holy name of liberty or democracy?"

Their conspiracies refute solidarity, encouraging mayhem against fundamentally decisive forces for making a better world, opposing the people, where oligarchical democracy is manifested. Others are illusions about freedom, liberty, and the pursuit of happiness for mankind. This ironically paves the way for a dark ages mentality and activating backward schools of thought that can lead to cultural catastrophe. "Never think that war, no matter how necessary, nor how justified, is not a crime," are the wise words of Ernest Hemingway.

Corporate capitalists claim morality in their legal, social, and business charters. They claim ethics, good faith, and dignity, loyalty and human rights in their establishment protocols. They claim freedom and democracy; they hypocritically seek justice, social welfare, pretending no discrimination or prejudice of any sort, claiming liberty and the pursuit of happiness for everyone. Yet they hypocritically shroud the demons inside to cover up their wicked and inhumane behaviors.

They operate under false pretenses based on lies to further accomplish their objectives for monetary gain, where they willfully distort facts and vicariously execute them via others with revolting intent to cause malice and harm to those who do not conform to the insane and preposterous games they play to provoke troubles.

We must awaken to the culture of fear and manufactured wars that relentlessly solicit the ordinary citizen's vote to engage in neo-colonist conduct and ruthless behaviors for annexing valuable resources from defenseless inhabitants, forcing displacement and illegal migration of the helpless people to nowhere lands. "The world will not be destroyed by those who do evil, but by those who watch them without doing anything," is an apt Albert Einstein quote we need to heed.

They feed on the name of the republic while outsourcing jobs and all the resources available to them, destroying communities. They know no boundaries; multinational corporations act like a magnet towards cheap labor and raw material to exploit and plunder unprotected natural resources. And wherever they are tax exempt, they are free from any legal or financial obligation to compensate for the environmental mess and horrific illness they have cause for so many indigenous and innocent inhabitants.

They have forced the relocation of millions of people because of global warming and rising sea levels, acid rain, fossil fuel and carbon monoxide emission, as well as radioactive byproducts and toxic mine waste. Toxic dust in the polluted air and contaminated water and land which the indigenous live on and must cultivate for their very subsistence cause illness and death. Diminishing ozone layers because of air assault by many global chemical and gas producing companies has caused grave and immediate danger to human health, creating many problems, especially skin cancer.

"Man is born free, but is everywhere in chains"

– Jean-Jacques Rousseau.

We are not shielded against the sun's ultraviolet rays, and too many dangerous chemicals and gases have damaged and depleted the ozone to the stratosphere, making it a huge hazard against humanity.

They have shamelessly left no sanctuary or any livelihood for people to unwind and seek immunity from so many hazardous agents, and so much of greenhouse gas emissions and its dire effect without any remorse.

Destroying people's health and livelihood through food products immersed with antibiotics, preservatives, MSG, trans fat, glutens, saturated fat, and filled with artificial coloring, preservatives, saturated with chemical and hormonal agents, bleaching flour and sugar, and numerous other food products with a killer agent known as Azodi Carbona mide, sweeteners, and carbonated drinks.

They have taken over the government and conned the public with brazen lies of financial losses, asking the government to bail them out of their economic recession and desperately failed monetary situation with taxpayers' hard-earned money. What these demonic entities sow for profit, people must reap with illness and homelessness.

They unilaterally improvise demonic plans, concocting conspiracies to go to war as corporate media and other corporate lackeys manufacture consent, undermine people's intelligence, and betray inhabitants' trust by deceptive practiced acts, and in bad faith, as the corporate dynasty fabricates and conditions masses of people into irrational exuberance to wage wars of aggression on innocent nations, just because corporate capitalists are rich and have the resources to decimate people, creating bloodbaths, carnage, and forced exodus, and all for hegemonies and territorial schemes but in the name of exporting freedom, democracy, liberty, and human rights through self-made enforceable laws.

And yet, they have hijacked God to shroud the demons inside, to cover up their wicked and inhumane behavior. They operate under false pretenses, based on fibs to further accomplish their objectives for monetary gain, where they willfully distort facts and vicariously execute them with sickening intent to cause malice and harm to whomever is not a conformist to the insane and preposterous game, which they play to provoke and stir troubles ruthlessly and with no clemency at all. For them it is as easy to benefit through creating havoc as it is to catch fish in muddy water. Someone tell me, where is the conscience in that, and where does this patrimonial claim of morality "in God we trust" fit?

This ugly criterion can lead to extremism, which can lead to Hitler-type fascism, since there are already plenty of indicators supporting that. The irony is they govern in the name of the republic, and then, everything public is demeaned and not prestigious, and even bad, including our public schools and public transportation. But everything private is sacred, making them the pillars of society.

Seeing anything public look like an omen against many, with no viable choice, we need to reckon with pluralism and in the meanwhile, we should also give validity to our private life. But let's not become victimized and subservient to the rule of corporate privatization, which is meant to cause ill deeds, taking advantage of isolating people by creepily coaching them through their effective propaganda machines, making them become self-centered and act like remote islands towards each other.

We need to give meaning to human society since by nature, collective activities are the kernel of who we are. Let's not become obsessed with self in a world where no one can survive alone. We should act introspectively and cogitate (think deep), making a choice of a life to co-inspire with each other, as the universe co-inspires with us. We need to realize while progress is the key to human success, it should not take over humankind. We ought to know how cultural agendas and beliefs impact our wellbeing and health, which can in turn influence our mind and thoughts, and therefore affect our physical body for either worse or better. We must treat one another with humane behavior, not acting vicious and indifferent towards others. And stop being disoriented because of mass propaganda and through bombardment of baseless conditioning aimed at keeping us apart while they celebrate our being divided, while they enjoy every minute of their life at people's horrifying expense.

We ought to realize that profound anxiety is the impetus behind our greed. Fear is purposefully played to dominate our life and our degrading social order. They exert fear to dominate and control this inhumane social order. Extreme separation is hurting us all and is an ace in their hand, playing us every which way they want. Humanity has got to understand that the explosion of the concentration of wealth has resulted in our separation, implementing devastating class differentiation, which has caused an upsurge in inequality, raising the potential for a bloody encounter. To avoid violence in its true sense and on a massive scale, we should preemptively strike the culprit of individualism and work towards our collectivism and break through this concrete wall of inequalities, since the resources that are bound for human survival are unconsciously and immorally allocated. It has created a huge financial gap between the haves and the have nots. We need to pay attention and return to our "oneness," witnessed by our biological birth to our very death and to whom and what we return to.

We need to truly understand that we are the byproduct of a cosmic consciousness, giving us the freedom and the liberty to behave as an inseparable part of this awakened force. Not to abuse our freedom and our will, and not to choose evil over goodness. We need to comprehend that we are not self-made, we are not our own property, we are the property of our Creator, and sustained through our beloved God.

It is crucial to understand that human beings are sacred and must not murder anyone or make them perish by the millions via genocide. We must not abuse them. Must not rape them and lie to them, must not infringe on anyone's sovereignty, and must not belittle humanity in any way, because in doing so, you are hence insulting our almighty Creator, abusing God's property and belongings. Our life is a gift; our sustenance through sacred Mother Nature is also a gift. Can anyone in their right mind not think that when people have difficulty breathing the air, cannot drink the water or grow crops to eat because they are contaminated and polluted by multinational corporations, energy and chemical companies, that this is also terrorism? Can anyone in their right mind not think that when people become so cornered and desperate with having nothing to lose, when they see their loved ones perish right in front of their eyes because of hunger and sickness and disease caused by the very species called human corporate, should they not react violently?

This entire human tragedy is caused because only a few powerful 1 percent of the global society wants to keep the status quo, where they hold 70 to 80 percent of the resources, just to have their way, because of greed and because they are totally disconnected from the rest of humanity that live in pain and with agony. They make their decision solely based on profit maximization and what is best for their major stockholders at people's expenses, and have the policing power to enforce it and the media to back them up. That is why many religions insist on "thou shall not kill," "thou shall not rape," "thou shall not lie," "thou shall not steal," and so forth, because when one does, one is messing with God, since no one is self-creator; no one is self-made.

When one knowingly depletes helpless people of their rights and confiscates the very means of their subsistence, that is stealing. And when they die because of so many maladies and hunger, that is murder. And when they are forced to relocate over and over because of turning their livelihood to a horrific situation, that is raiding and looting. And when you pay handsomely to the media to back you up and do the coverup, that is lying. And when you order to imprison and detain and torture innocent people, that is raping people of their rights. This model and economic system that so unethically and inhumanely upholds corporate capitalism exploits and annihilates all that is in its path. It has declared war on God, and God's belongings, humanity and nature. People are God's belongings. They are sacred. The nature that sustains them is sacred. One must not mess with that.

We need to face the reality of the emergence of new thoughts and to identify with the paradigm shift to break through the ills of individualism and push to cultivate a real social and economic renaissance, where collective bargaining and happiness could mean something, and not just be a fad.

Our vision for a good future can be structured at the grassroots level, where happiness is no longer a phantom but a fundamental truth and a sincere expedition into capturing a new life and a better living for all of humanity. But then, to reach true success in our life we need visionaries that are not selfish in their sight to maximize profit and to benefit themselves alone at the expense of others. We must have passion to follow through, and we need an environment supportive of dreamers and for visionaries to have the liberty to act, since for new ideas and creativity to flourish they should be induced and encouraged, not inhibited. We must have an atmosphere that honors freedom of thought, freedom of press, freedom of speech, freedom of assembly, freedom of privacy, freedom of expression, freedom of religion and worship, and freedom of interactions.

It is utterly important to have an atmosphere free of any kind of prejudice and bigotry that can motivate people to participate in daring challenges to overcome their shortcomings and to be the best they can be. As Spinoza said, "Freedom is absolutely necessary for the progress in science and liberal arts."

And I attest that "freedom and democracy is fundamental to the very core of our existence and happiness, it rejuvenates and makes intellectual properties to flourish." We ought to remember those successful visionaries must have had the passion to execute every inch of their plan with the intent to win, and sometimes despite the insurmountable challenges facing them, they have overcome all the hurdles in their life, no matter how difficult the setting. Joseph Campbell said, "<u>Opportunities to find deeper powers within ourselves come when life seems most challenging.</u>"

He also said, "<u>It is by going down into the abyss that we recover the treasures of life. Where you stumble, there lies your treasure.</u>"

We ought to know when we do not discover our vision, and do not care to locate what we are good for and passionate about, then others will set our vision for us, and I am afraid not to the best of our interest, but theirs, in which we become a vehicle to help them reach their goal. With that said, should our purpose in life and where we stand matter in alleviating others' pain and suffering or not? And if yes, it is vital to truly understand the nature of our existence and why we are here. And why have intelligence if it is not put to good use? We ought to make a difference for the better in the world and persevere to reach our goal despite perhaps facing significant and dramatic challenges in reaching our objectives. We must understand how easy it is to become baffled about God and consciousness in today's materialistically intense society.

This cannot be done unless we explore who we really are as human beings and restore time to meditate on our inner self and perhaps truly connect with God and with nature, and to resist wrongful temptation. We are the heightened state of awareness, trusted with not having to manifest destruction and in not doing wrong. We are an inseparable part of nature, which does not operate hastily but works its way up gradually and with patience. The reason behind our stressful and chaotic life is that we have senselessly prioritized hoarding wealth and quantified living over the quality of life with no limit. We need to take time, as precious as time is, to delve into the very core of our being and to contemplate and savor the goodness of life in its generous offering. We are too absorbed with the culture of entitlement and with the celebrity culture and Hollywood-style action movies, through which we understand the rest of the world. We are into believe that change is to come through government and not via bottom up, but from top to bottom.

We are indoctrinated into nationalism and patriotism just for backing the super-rich up, and just in case their trillions of dollars of outsourcing jobs and resources goes raw, and perhaps they'll have to redeem it via wars and military intervention. Or when they target to extort many nation's natural resources, needing military backup to a point of genocide and making innocent people perish so they can become richer, to tighten the yoke even more around our neck and force us with more austerity.

We are trained into believing everyone is entitled to his or her own. We have evolved into a culture of indifference, where no crime is too big to shock us anymore. We just brush it off as, it is not going to happen to me or to any of my loved ones, and how quickly we forget about the ever present violence. We need to open our neuropaths by repeating compassion through empathy and kindness, to connect to others with love and understanding, letting them know of the serious problem caused by a corporation facing us all.

And finally we must realize when we are not aware, or behave indifferently, we vote to be further enslaved. We need to question more and practice activism to find constructive solutions. We need to uphold morality and righteousness, and continue to dig into the spirit of the whys of the issues from philosophical aspects, as well as the hows of matters from scientific perspectives.

We need to investigate the unjustified allocation of resources. We should give validity to our private life, but not to become victimized by a system of utter individualism where the colossally wealthy can hold onto unimaginable resources to enslave billions of people, as the victims of poverty gradually perish, as they survive on bare minimum with no hope for financial recovery. We know there are other dynamic economic systems that aim at maximizing workers' welfare and enhance people's livelihood.

VISIONARIES AND THE MIRACULOUS UNIVERSE

So many visionaries harnessed nature through zealous leaps, from discovering fire from the times living in caves to an agricultural environment, and inventing tools which peaked in the industrial revolution, reaching the nuclear and electronic age, and to the present age of quantum physics. It seems quantum computation is the next big thing in advancing humanity, transforming our lives from the digital era to the quantum level.

The quantum revolution has already augmented human intelligence through the explanation of the structure of matter, discovering the energy nature of matter, also understanding molecular biology, radiation, lasers, semiconductors, transistors and its derivatives, nuclear reactions, telecoms, nanotechnology, why the sun shines with fusion reaction, and so forth.

It is deservingly just to respect utopians behind scientific discoveries in our universe, but also understand there will always be mysticism in our world; inquiring scientific and scholarly minds are set to demystify them. There are still many intriguing subjects to remain puzzling and outside the scientific realm, and for humans' competency to answer.

Perhaps collective wisdom and philosophy could offer some convincing argument. In his book Computing the Universe, Seth Lloyd describes, "how the simple right atoms bumping into just the right other atoms can effect everything, all interactions between particles in the universe convey not only energy but also information- in other words particles not only collide, they compute."

He carries on to say, "The dance of matter and light had the power to produce our universe and everything in it." Lloyd also acknowledges the universe computes itself and says, "As computation proceeds, reality unfolds."

From this type of cognition, we can culminate that we are the derivatives and the production of energy, consciousness, motion, and matter contacting matter—a huge cosmic dance in its actual sense of comprehension.

In much of what Lloyds believe, also John Wheeler related, thinking about the universe, he explained, "Everything it-every particle, every field of force, even the space and time continuum itself derives its function, its meaning and its very existence entirely from binary choices and bits. What we call reality arises from the posing of yes or no questions."

In other words, Wheeler was suggesting, "The things that make the universe and life, what they 'are' are really information, little specks of polarity. Everything boils down to opposites." Pluses and minuses, male and female, on and off. If what Wheeler sees as the particles of the universe are similar to computer bits of information, and Lloyd states, "The universe is a quantum computer," then they are suggesting that we are living in a simulated reality. If so: Who is the programmer that initiated our cosmic and universe computer simulation?

Can we accept the cosmic architect as the designer replacing God? When did this cosmic computer begin its activity, and how long has it been there? What about when we die; do we just leave our virtual reality and go on to live in another realm outside of our present world and experiences?

Where is the central processing unit in this simulation computer? Is it our brain, or does our brain act as a mediator to link us to the supercomputer mainframe and the cosmic consciousness beyond its limitation? Our simulation of the world and us as its coherent might be begging for an access code that perhaps can help humanity in a far future to upgrade and to upscale programs of life for peace, healing of incurable diseases, finding happiness, and remedying natural disasters. And perhaps rewire the human nervous system and correct other human impasses through conscious binary effect, just as we code the internet connection and word processors.

It is a miracle to historically notice the simultaneousness of a new idea and the technology to deliver it are so coherent that happen when all the ingredients, including the right mathematical formulas and the right experiments, arrive precisely when we need them to connect the pieces of the puzzle to make a new paradigm shift and have a very useful entity for humanity to propel and progress even further and in having a better life.

ENTROPY, AND THE ORIGIN OF UNIVERSE

The dictionary defines the word entropy, which finds its roots in the Greek entropia, as "a turning toward" or "transformation." The word was used to describe the measurement of disorder by the German physicist Rudolph Clausius and appeared in English in 1868. A common example of entropy is that of ice melting in water. The resulting change from formed to free, from ordered to disordered increases the entropy.

Also entropy is known as: a measure of the unavailable energy in a closed thermodynamic system that is also considered to be a measure of the system's disorder which is the property of the system's state and that varies directly with any reversible change in heat in the system, and inversely with the temperature of the system, the degree of disorder or uncertainty in a system.

The degradation of matter and energy in the universe to an ultimate state of inert (inactive, lacking vigor or vitality) uniformity.

The idea of entropy comes from a principle of thermodynamics dealing with energy. It usually refers to the idea that everything in the universe eventually moves from order to disorder, and entropy is the measurement of that change.

1. a thermodynamic quantity representing the unavailability of a system's thermal energy for conversion into mechanical work, often interpreted as the degree of disorder or randomness in the system.
2. lack of order or predictability; gradual decline into disorder.

If energy is high, the randomness and chaos are absolutely present, which indicates a good reason that entropy departs from chance. It must certainly be applicable to life made on planet Earth, so intelligently created, and which is superbly orderly and disciplined, which makes it very far and contrary to being chaotic and disorderly, as it literally is very suitable for human, animal, and plant life, maneuvering in a magnificent low entropy state of being. Wherever we see low entropy in our world, it stipulates hypothetical evidence that intelligence, energy, and design have been put into it, and perhaps what applies to the human world apply to the entire cosmos.

Maybe the universe itself required the input of intelligence, energy, and design from the outside to make it "human-ready." As Stephen Hawking once beautifully put in his book, A Brief History of Time, "What is it that breathes fire into the equations and makes a universe for them to describe? "Be hold that a physicist's equations will never directly make anything; they're maps, not territory. They rationally describe possible structures or entropy states. An equation may provide a description of something that actually is. But an equation doesn't turn "water into sugar cane juice," or nothing into something.

Hence, Mr. Hawking's question still remains. Who or what made the equations of our human-habitable universe that breathes fire into the equation, and evolves into matter, then carbon-based flesh, then minds?

Mr. Paul Davis wrote in his book, God the new Physics, that a mathematical investigation shows that order is exponentially sensitive to rearrangements. That is to say, the probability of a random choice leading to an ordered state declines exponentially with the degree of negative entropy. An exponential relation is characterized by its rapid rate of growth (or decline). For example, a population that grows exponentially doubles its size in a fixed interval of time: 1, 2, 4, 8, 16, 32…

The exponential factor implies that the odds against randomly generating order increase astronomically.

For example, the probability of a liter of air rushing spontaneously to one end of a box is of the order 10 to the power 1o to the power 20 simultaneously, which stands for one followed by 100,000,000,000,000,000,000 zeros. Translated into a cosmological context, the conundrum is this. If the universe is simply an accident, the odds against it containing any appreciable order is ludicrously small." Witnessing creation should be a good enough reason to believe in a supreme being and a divine creator, an absolutely sovereign being who is devoid of any anthropomorphic qualities, beyond space and time. The cosmological argument is an argument for the existence of God that says that God is the First Cause that created the universe (source: Wikipedia).

It's also known as the argument from first cause, the causal argument, or the argument from existence. The argument below is a variant of the cosmological argument, which states: Something outside the universe has always existed.

And I say that nothing cannot create something, at least in a material world, and if quantum physics believes it does, as the physicists believe it can occur in subatomic realms, then that is miracle. There must be a programmer, cosmic energy, conscious-able universe, intelligence, order, purpose, destiny, finite beginning with finite end, responsibility and discipline, space, motion, time, intention, not accidental, with and no chance, no randomness, no probabilities, precursor environmental catalyst, complexity of the structure of living organism, willfulness, dynamism, and not mechanical. These are birds of the same feather, which flock together. Matter is all vibrating oriented energy and conveys all the above although not visible to the naked eye.

Abiogenesis, or the origin of life, is defined as: the natural process through which life originates from non-living matter, but from organic blend, where the change from non-living to living entities was a gradual process of increasing complexity, and not instantaneous. It believes the earliest familiar life-forms on planet Earth were fossilized microorganisms that may have existed as early as four billion years ago, and not long after the Earth's formation about 4.5 billion years ago. Life was harmonized through carbon and water, and construed based on lipids (fatty cell walls), carbohydrates (sugar, cellulose), amino acids (protein metabolism), and nucleic acids (self-replicating DNA, RNA).

Scientists sought their research via paleontology, astrobiology, biochemistry, molecular biology, and scrutinizing fossils digging into geology, etc., trying to determine how pre-life chemical activities initiated life. They believe life arose under conditions that are noticeably different from those on Earth today. The biochemistry of life may have begun shortly after the big bang, 13.8 billion years ago, they say, during a habitable epoch when the age of the universe was only 10 to 17 million years. The panspermia hypothesis suggests that, "microscopic life was distributed to the early Earth by space dust, meteoroids, asteroids and other small Solar System bodies and that life may exist throughout the universe, The panspermia hypothesis proposes that life originated outside the Earth, but does not definitively explain its origin."

The classic 1952 Miller–Urey experiment and similar research demonstrated that, "Most amino acids, the chemical constituents of the proteins used in all living organisms, can be synthesized from inorganic compounds under conditions intended to replicate those of the early Earth. Scientists have proposed various external sources of energy that may have triggered these reactions, including lightning and radiation. Other approaches ('metabolism-first' hypotheses) focus on understanding how catalysis in chemical systems on the early Earth might have provided the precursor molecules necessary for self-replication. Complex organic molecules occur in the Solar System and in interstellar space, and these molecules may have provided starting material for the development of life on Earth."

The troubles kick in when some behave ambiguously and act irresponsibly, throwing in ideological doctoring's that are shallow and depleted of reason. They render insightfulness with grief, because these mal deeds affect many callow minds, as they leave their ill-footprint behind and sometimes with horrific consequences to tragically burden the society in its entirety, as they give mixed signals.

In Charles Darwin's book On the Origin of Species, he wrote: "The exquisite organization of living creatures seems to offer the best possible demonstration of a supernatural designer, yet the evidence of biology and geology provides an adequate explanation for the extraordinary characteristic of biological organism." That is why the proponents of God's existence are pulling their hair, and emphasize the role of a supernatural programmer, programming extraordinary design, not only in biological matter, but in all that exists. He believes in evolution of biological "order" by mutation and natural selection.

Were Mr. Darwin and the like hallucinating when they talked about order? Did they not know "order" is followed by intelligence and consciousness, without which no experience is ever possible? And with responsibility, and a sense of purpose, a role of a live and genius operator that must act magnificently talented and orderly to design such a glorified universe, and absolutely not accidental.

Then we have Mr. Hawking saying oh no, gravity is responsible for our being and the life on planet Earth, and Mr. Marx saying oh no, it is economics which is the spine to our way of life. And Freud's pushing on human sexual behavior, and sees a huge importance in that. Freud even suggests that "God concepts are projection of one's father." And others, like John Paul Sartre, throw in existentialism and seeing (anthropomorphic) the role of human beings attributed as the principle which should rule, along with many other so-called doctorings, lowering his Godhood to believing in fire, manmade statutes, the sun, the moon, the oceans, and nature itself.

Pantheism is very old, even older than Buddhism, which put emphasis on transcendent qualities such as compassion., Most Taoists are pantheists, as are many Chinese, Japanese, and Western Buddhists, deep ecologists, pagans, animists, followers of many native religions, and many Unitarian Universalists.

The central philosophical scriptures of Hinduism are pantheistic. Many atheists and humanists could be pantheist, because of their deep respect for nature and counting it as sacred. Scientific or natural pantheism is a new way of belief for pantheism that deeply reveres the universe and sees nature as sacred, and happily accepts and regards life as the essence of living and body and Earth, but does not believe in any supernatural deities, entities, or supreme beings.

The Shinto religion ("the way of the Kami") is the name of the formal state religion of Japan that was first used in the sixth century CE. Shinto has no founder, no official sacred texts, and no formalized system of doctrine.

Shintoism and Japanese culture, attitudes, and sensitivity are compatible, creating a distinct Japanese consciousness. Belief in kami— sacred or divine beings, although also understood to be spiritual essences— is one of the foundations of Shinto. Shinto understands that the kami not only exist as spiritual beings, but also in nature; they believe kami exists within mountains, trees, rivers, and even geographical regions. In this sense, the kami are not like the all-powerful divine beings found in Western religion, but the abstract creative forces in nature.

Because of the kami (divinity and sacred spirit), the understanding is that the Shinto followers are supposed to live in harmony and peaceful coexistence with both nature and other human beings. This has made it possible for the Shinto religion to exist in harmony with other religious traditions.

Natural deities, supernatural deities, worshiping multiple gods or goddess, monotheism, polytheism, and so many other faiths were addressed in search of God. A deity of good versus evil of equal power by Manichaeism and Zoroastrianism is documented from many years ago. Most Hindus are polytheistic or monotheistic, but relaxed enough to believe in and pray to many gods. Pascal Boyer says, "While there is a wide array of supernatural concepts found around the world, in general supernatural beings tend to behave much like people, the construction of gods, and spirit like person (anthropomorphism), is the oldest characteristic." In the same account, Emile Durkheim was one of the earliest to suggest that "God represent an extension of human social like to include supernatural beings." Psychologist Matt Rossano contends that, "When human beings living in a large group, they may have created Gods as a means of enforcing morality. In small groups morality can be enforced by social forces such as gossip or reputation."

However, it is believed that to enforce morality in a much larger population is harder than in a small group. He also indicates that by including ever watchful gods and spirits, humans discovered an effective strategy for restraining selfishness and in building more cooperative groups. More recently, "Neuro-Theology," a term that was used by Aldous Huxley that studies religious experiences of gods and spirit, digs into the interconnectedness of humans and religion in terms of cognitive neuroscience.

So searching for God is not new; it has carried its track through the entire human history. Some contemplate God as self-reflection and see the Almighty through many other entities, which has rendered humanity with innumerous distorted perceptions of God. The essence of this whole confusion has always been the absence of the beloved through so many distractions, causing sheer abandonment of the truth.

Not noticing that God is the measure of our pain and suffering the further we are from our beloved God, the more fear, loneliness, anxiety, and meaninglessness we encounter. Any cultural novelty should address that, and make people aware of this infinite urge for belonging and to answer our human yearning to know who we are, and where did we come from, why are we here, where are we going to, and so forth. Not through visualization, but via searching souls seeking the divine. And seeking God by visualization alone most definitely makes us mechanical and a reductionist that can never bring about the infinite vastness and the magnificence of the work of God. Referencing Isaac Newton, he said, "Whence arises all that order and beauty we see in the world?" And because we are not our own property, since we did not create ourselves, but realizing that we are a gift, life is a gift bestowed upon us, this alone should change everything. Someone once said, "We are all part of a global lineage of remembrance."

Recognizing our nothingness and our belongingness to the divine, our hearts should be the receptacle of the divine, not saturated with vain and superficial needs. We must truly seek God, not through intellect, but by intuition, wisdom, and faith, where wisdom should mean the search for meaning, where rationality is sought, and where reason should prevail. Joseph Campbell put it this way, "God is a metaphor for that which transcends all levels of intellectual thought. It's as simple as that."

When Prophet Mohammed was asked by an Arab Bedouin, how can I know there is a God? He simply told him: when you see camel dung, you should decipher that a camel was here, and when you see footprints on sands, common sense should tell you a passerby, a human being was here. In seeing the undescribed beauty and the magnificent creation of the sun, the moon, the stars, and the entire life should resonate with you and to acknowledge the derivatives and the undeniable circumstantial evidence of the almighty God.

William Paley wrote in his book Natural Theology that in crossing a heath (a tract of wasteland) suppose I pitched my foot against a stone, and were asked how the stone came to be there: I might possibly answer, that, for anything I knew to the contrary, it had lain there forever; nor would it, perhaps, be very easy to show the absurdity of this answer. But suppose I found a watch upon the ground, and it should be inquired how the watch happened to be there in that place. I should hardly think of the answer I had given before-that, for anything I knew, the watch might always have been there.

"Yet why should not this answer serve for the watch as well as for the stone? The intricate and delicate organization of a watch, with its components dovetailing (to fit skillfully to form a whole, to fit together accurately), is overwhelming evidence for design. Someone who never seen a watch before would conclude that this mechanism was devised by an intelligent person for a purpose."

Mr. Paley went on to say that the universe is similar to a watch in its intricacy and organization, but within a much greater scale. Hence there must be a cosmic designer that has made the world the way it is, and surely for a purpose. It should behold us that the contrivances (concoct, discover, design, excogitate) of the universe does exponentially exceed the contrivances of any art or mechanical device made by man, in terms of its complexity, its purpose, and its subtlety, action, keen hood, and curiosity.

Aquinas said, "An ordered ness of action to an end is observed in all bodies obeying natural laws, even when they lack awareness, which shows they truly tend to a goal, and do not merely hit it by accident." Scientific evidence shows us that the universe hasn't always existed. Here are some of the evidences that support that the universe had begun at a certain point of time.

The Second Law of Thermodynamics says that the amount of spendable energy in an encapsulated and closed system, like in the situation of the universe, is decreasing. In other words, the amount of usable energy will die out, just like the batteries die in any electronic equipment operating with a battery. If our universe, which is a closed system, is in fact running out of energy, then the universe can't be eternal because a finite amount of energy could never have brought the universe through the infinity of time. Hence, it does not make sense to accept an argument that believes in no beginning with no end.

2. The Universe is Expanding

In 1929, Edwin Hubble made a discovery that our universe is expanding. Once scientists realized that the universe was expanding, they then understood the universe would have been smaller in the past. At some point, the entire universe would have been a single point. This point is what many people refer to as the big bang, which is the designated point when our universe began to exist.

3. The Cosmic Background Radiation

Physics.org explains the Cosmic Background Radiation as, "The left-over heat from the fireball of the big bang in which estimates the Universe was born about 13.7 billion years ago." All of science and common sense teaches that life, the world, and the universe is "running down." Thermodynamics teaches that the universe has a fixed amount of energy (taking into account that all mass translates into energy), since the entire system is propelling from a state of higher order to a more disordered state. Eventually, it will reach and enter into a motionless state of complete disorder. We ought to know that all and everything dilapidates; machines rust and wither away, people grow old and die, the birds and the bees, plants and trees, all shrivel and terminate. So do the stars, galaxies and so forth; they burn out, etc.

If matter has always existed, and it always strays off course and divagates to a more disorderly state, then why has the universe not "run down"? It would have already expired, and we would not be here. Our very existence disproves the plausibility of this alternative. The very fact that it is running down demands that it must have had a beginning. The most powerful evidence is the very world that surrounds us. Apostle Paul also spoke of this.

> "For since the creation of the world His invisible attributes
> are clearly seen, being understood by the things that are
> made, even His eternal power and Godhead, so that they
> are without excuse" (Romans 1:20).

This creation informs us of God's existence, but it also exhibits his great and eternal power that is part of his divine nature as member of the Godhead. Through what is visible and the seen world, we are able to see something of these otherwise invisible attributes. Even though it cannot be scientifically proven, the evidence is so compelling that if one fails to realize and acknowledge his Creator, he is left without excuse.

While the age of the Earth is assumed by scientists, most do agree that the Cosmic Setting Radiation does point to a finite universe that has a specific age. Therefore, the cosmological argument on God, summarizes that something exists (the universe), which has not always existed. Hence something outside the universe must have always existed, which did create the universe. Nothing cannot create something, at least in our physical world.

Therefore, to avoid cause regression analysis to infinity, where something is to have caused something else, it must at one point have stopped, which did not have a cause, giving into the cause of all causes to prevent regressing to infinity. Something must have always existed in order to cause the universe into existence.

However, the cosmological argument states that "everything that came into existence must have a cause. God didn't come into existence, He always was, is, and will forever be. The cosmological argument refers to the first cause of the universe as someone that has always existed.

If we open-mindedly look at our universe, we can then discern that our God is self-existent, and must be: timeless, non-spatial, and not matter-like; omnipotent, omniscient, and omnipresent, with infinite power and infinitely intelligent, since he has created a flawless universe and the vast cosmos with enormous precision and with awesome ability, turning a state of nothingness into the amazing phenomenon of the time-space universe.

In Stephen Hawking's book The Grand Design, Hawking writes, "Because there is a law of gravity, the universe can and will create itself out of nothing." Both Hawking and Lawrence Krauss suggest that it is theoretically possible for the universe to have come from nothingness, using M-theory, string theory, and quantum mechanics to replace gravity, with God as being the Creator. But evidently there are major shortcomings to M-theory, and there are a number of prominent physicists who point out these mistakes:

1. M-theory requires the law of gravity, and gravity is not "nothing." It's "something. Nothing is no-thing; it's the state of non-existence. One can be certain that gravity isn't nothing, it's something. When physicists talk about nothing, they are talking about a quantum vacuum. But there's

a problem. A quantum vacuum is not nothing, since the quantum vacuum has the attributes and the properties of something.

Referencing that "God has made human being in his own image," Mansour al-Hallaj, the Persian philosopher of the eleventh century, said, I saw my Lord with the eye of my heart.

> He said, "Who are you?" I said, "I am you."
> You are He who fills all place
> But place does not know where you are.
> In my subsistence is my annihilation;
> in my annihilation, I remain you.

It is now scientifically substantiated that the world we see and experience is actually made of molecules, and molecules are comprised of atoms, and atoms are made of subatomic particles like protons and electrons that according to scholarly minded physicists, are 99.99999 percent empty space and electrical spin.

Physicists tell us atoms are made of particles, and particles are waves, and waves are possibilities, where these possibilities exist in nothing. By today's findings, the tiniest of them all are quarks, which in turn are part of a superstring field that comports frequencies and vibrating strings, which make the actual particles relating to the nature of their vibration. Bottom line is, the astrophysicists tell us when they search beyond molecules with the most sophisticated telescopes into the microscopic realm and subatomic cloud, they are unable to find anything. Hence, many of them conclude we come from nothing.

Forgetting that nothingness is the source of all that has existed and is impregnated with all there will ever be, humanity should expect the infinite possibilities from nothingness. We ought to study the microscopic realm and the unseen world of the subatomic world through our third eye, and with mindfulness, and to welcome these amazing matrixes and discern them fully in our contemporary age.

Neil Bohr, the Nobel Prize-winning father of quantum mechanics, said, "Everything we call real is made of things that cannot be regarded as real. In quantum mechanics hasn't profoundly shocked you yet, you don't understand it well enough." We are active in a world of physical objects,

167

but this is how our brain accords and translates captured sensory data and information. From the tiniest and at the largest scale of nature and the way we interact with our world, this physical reality is not in existence.

Mr. Bohr believed the constituents of matter have absolutely no physical structure. He continues to address the idea of reality, which he believes is a cosmic concoction of non-localized energy and empty space. He carries on to say, "It becomes clear that our thoughts and the signals they register in the brain also have these same properties at their smallest level. Our thoughts are also an activity of the universe, and all activities take place within the same quantum realm prior to manifesting in physical reality."

Referencing objectivity and subjectivity, scientists keep them apart, to only reflect on external and the material world as they sever and isolate subjectivity in assessing their findings from the external world to objectify their results. They have no clue why subjective experiences exist at all, and why there is intelligence, and why sentiment evolves. We should awaken to the fact that consciousness and reality are not separate, as many scientists want us to believe. Many prominent physicists accept that there is no way to explain how something as material as chemical and physical processes can give rise to something as immaterial as experience.

The sudden realization happens when the essence of the remarkable world is conscious and not matter. It so happens that when our mindfulness is elevated and our consciousness is raised, we look at the world differently. It is because of cosmic energy (consciousness) that connects and makes our cognition ability and experiences possible. Deepak Chopra summarizes consciousness:

"As subjectivity/awareness, the ability to experience or feel having a sense of self-hood, and the executive control of the mind, and in Vedanta, consciousness is the potential for experience, consciousness is beings or existence, and it is prior to subject/object split, consciousness is the ground of existence, Sat-Chit-Ananda."

Deepak Chopra carries on to say, "Science depends on the experiences of the external world which is the perceptual reality, but not the fundamental reality." Perceptual realities are the description of the mode of observation; in other words, different species see the world differently. Reality is the species-specific description of the mode and the culture of observation.

Indicating science, Deepak says, "As systematic enterprise that builds on and organizes knowledge in the form of testable explanation and prediction about the universe, science is based on loop of observation theory experimentation and validation, science is based on facts, science relies on empirical measurement, it quantifies, unusually in terms of unit of mass, energy, velocity, and position, science is the objective truth."

Professor of theoretical physics Amit Gozwami indicates some principles on quantum mechanics. He expresses his finding's first as wave-function. Saying a quantum object can simultaneously be at many places, like an electron, which can be seen at different places at the same time. It can be sized in space as a wave, known as the wave property. Secondly is the discontinuity, a quantum object disappears at one point and appears elsewhere without having ever being notice to depart and travel the intermediate space, it is known as quantum jump, it basically teleports. Then, is what professor Amit calls Action-At- Distance, when a quantum object is seen, at the same time predisposes its interdependent twin object, regardless of the distance. Anything that happens to the electron, he says, the exact same or the opposite will occur to the proton. It is believed that Einstein named this "spooky" action at a distance. Then is the observer effect.

Which says a quantum object cannot be detected in ordinary space-time until we can notice it as a particle. It adheres to the fact that the quantum object can infinitely subsist as a non-local wave until is being directly noticed. Consciousness literally breaks apart the wave-function of a particle as soon as is observed. And insinuates that: if not consciously observed, it would physically stay un-seen in an opposition of potentiality. Hence observation not only produces the consequences but also shifts what needs to be measured. This rather bizarre posit (axiom, presumption, hypothesis) of quantum theory, which has long intrigued physicists and renowned philosophers alike, says that by the very act of watching, the observer affects the observed reality. This was validated in what is recorded as the double-slit experiment, as the presence of a conscious observer altered the action of an electron from a wave state to a particle state, which is familiarized as the observer effect, and entirely shakes what we presume to be the fact about the physical world. The findings of this experiment were published in the peer-reviewed journal Nature, in which the scientists summarized saying, "The introduction of a which-path (welcher Weg) detector for determining the actual path taken by the particle inevitably involved coupling the particle to a measuring environment, which in turn results in DE phasing (suppression of interference)." What is literally saying interprets that: the measurement system used to notice the activity of the particle affected the action of that particle.

> "[T]he atoms or elementary particles themselves are not real; they form a world of potentialities or possibilities rather than one of things or facts."

> — Werner Heisenberg

> "Not only does God play dice but... he sometimes throws them where they cannot be seen."

> — Stephen Hawking

The double-slit experiment repeated

As scientist Dr. Dean Radin said in a paper replicating the double-slit experiment, "We compel the electron to assume a definite position. We ourselves produce the results of the measurement." Now, a common response to this is, "It's not us who is measuring the electron, it's the machine that is doing the observation." A machine is simply an extension of our consciousness. This is like saying, "It's not me who is observing the boat way across the lake, it is the binoculars." The machine does not itself observe anything any more than a computer that interprets sound waves can "listen" to a song.

This has led some scientists to speculate that without consciousness, the universe would exist indeterminately as a sea of quantum potentiality. In other words, physical reality cannot first exist without subjectivity. Without consciousness, there is no physical matter. This is known as the Participatory Anthropic Principle, and was first proposed by physicist Dr. John Wheeler.

Essentially, any possible universe that we can imagine that it does not have conscious observers in it can be ruled out immediately. Consciousness is therefore the ground of being, and must have existed prior to the physical universe. Consciousness literally creates the physical world.

These findings provide huge implications regarding how we can understand our interconnectedness with the external world. "We create our reality" is used to refer to the fact that our thoughts create the perspective we have of the world, but we now have a more concrete and literal understanding of this phrase. We actually give rise to the physical universe with our subjectivity.

"I regard consciousness as fundamental. I regard matter as derivative from consciousness. We cannot get behind consciousness. Everything that we talk about, everything that we regard as existing, postulates consciousness." – Max Planck, Nobel Prize winning originator of quantum theory, as quoted in The Observer (25 January 1931). The bottom line in the world of quantum physics is that physical objects can lodge and occupy several different states simultaneously, which is related to abnormal situations of parallel worlds. Particles subatomically and at microscopic level show up in many places at the same time, denoting them by scientists as "superposition," where a single electron can be found in many places playing many possibilities, where a single particle uses all the possible progression or a line of development resembling a trajectory to travel from point A to B, and so forth, and not limited to one single progression or trajectory.

Scientists now believe quantum computation is necessary to perform and compute the collaboration that occurs among parallel universes at microscopic scales, since it needs to search through the enormous landscape of possibilities, to explore many directions, perhaps within millions of parallel universes at the same time. Scientists believe physical systems can maneuver with all the possibilities available to them at the same time, where those possibilities can converse and interact together, miracles are in the making beyond our imagination and wildest dreams.

They also tell us that we do not see objects as they are, we see them as we are. And the way our brain is set up and our DNA is structured, not a single person is going to ever show up like any one of us in millions of years before we existed, or in millions of years to come after we are gone.

The scientist and astrophysicist claim 70 percent of our universe is made of dark energy, and also claim that millions of galaxies are drifting apart travelling at more than the speed of light as they drop into the unknown. And 25 percent is made of dark matter, which means it is not visible and does not reflect light, give off, or suck up light, therefore known by the scientific community as not atomic. The scientists address their findings as 99.9 percent of the universe is made of hydrogen and helium that has not shaped into stars, and also tell us only 0.1 percent of 1 percent is visible because the rest of it is not atomic. And what they conclude is we are depending on this 0.1 percent of the 1 percent that is atomic, and perhaps we are made of that. And if the gravitational forces of galaxies in dark energy collapse, we would not be here.

Perhaps it is good enough reason for astrophysicist Mr. Hawking to conclude that an inanimate force of gravity is the cause of everything and has replaced God in his mind. I wonder if we could have ever formulated any practical scientific theory if science was to decide on o.1 percent of 1 percent from a total of the 100 percent unknown in question, which was assumed and undertaken to be experience on. Mr. Hawking is limited to planet Earth from an apparently infinite number of planets, trillions of galaxies, and billions of universes, which should make his findings very limited and not credible at all.

Let's check into related and peripheral issues, where they are a preponderance and play an enormous role in our life. We'll delve into the subject of spirit and consciousness and also look into matter, which science feeds on and believes in the doctrine of materialism referencing having no mind, no spirit. Scientists accept nature as mechanically oriented, having no awakening concept or any consciousness. They see and analyze our world as machine-like; conveying sets of fixed rules so it will be easier for scientists to adequately assess findings, and hence, for scientists to draw their conclusions while avoiding too many variables and elusive changes without interference. They forget this wonderful structure and beautifully designed world, richly textured, is just an illusion, and all of it takes place in our brain. Scientists view events as empirically as they actually experience them, and they quantify their findings, since they factor in human perception utilizing the human nervous system and consciousness. Since they cannot measure or mathematically quantify consciousness, they are also not able to directly observe conscious energy, so they throw the baby out with the bathwater and claim perhaps none exists.

On the other hand, the world of business is also preoccupied and contemplates on wealth creation, and capitalist ideology encompasses a broad cultural spectrum which leads to the world of materialism as investors adamantly pursue consumer-oriented environments. It seems customers are mesmerized with possessing a life of luxury at any cost and behaving skeptically towards non-material thoughts, but are obsessed with wealth-creating ideas over any spiritual endeavors. Too many people are driven to believe and are encouraged by material philosophy over spiritualism.

CYBERSPACE

As imperative as technology is for modernized living and in making further progress, we should not lose sight of what makes us human.

Unfettered freedom, impulsive behaviors, disinhibiting activities in the cyberworld ought to be alarming.

A cyber-psyche can bring trouble, where an extreme cyber realm can invite apocalypse (disaster), where loss of identity is surprisingly relevant, as if those exorbitantly (unduly, excessively) engaged have no soul.

Questions such as who are we, and who are we becoming in the cyber world, would not be out of line, and actually should be inspiring for alerting industrialized nations to avoid a chaotic atmosphere where turning into mechanical humans can become quite harmful.

In cyberspace, anonymity is fostered, making us vulnerable to exploitation, cheating, insensitivity, deception, irresponsibility, social brutality, and inflammatory and impulsive behaviors.

The culture of cyberspace can well become an underground for criminal activities and illicitly ubiquitous maneuvers, where evaluating mates and appraising cyber companions is visceral. Not actually knowing who we are dealing with, since one lacks daily face-to-face experience and instinct in evaluating and appraising mates can safeguard cyber predators to victimize others, and often with impunity.

The issue is of concern, since online conduct has become socially acceptable, where harmful behaviors are changing fundamental human relationships, where an array of misconduct is not funny or silly anymore but compulsive, threatening, hyper-stimulating, addictive, and potentially dangerous.

It seems the law and forensic perspective can be of little help, what with lack of regulation, privacy, accountability, and naïveté (inexperience, callowness), proclivity, disguising, and other insidious behaviors where the end justifies the means for the malefactors (criminals, culprits) for feeding their wrongful and addictive behaviors, while often harming the innocents, where so many can be emotionally impaired for life.

Not to forget that cyberwarfare is already of tremendous concern in the use or targeting in a battlespace linking computers and online networks and control systems, where operational cyberattacks, espionage, sabotage, hacking, and other menacing cyber offensives can most definitely disrupt our daily living for the worse.

INTROVERTS VS. EXTROVERTS

Extrovert personalities are much more common in freedom-oriented societies, since Western culture is basically synonymous with democracy and human rights, leaving not much space for one to easily become finger-pointed or blamed for behaving outside the traditions, They can say what they want without persecution, contrary to dictatorial countries, where introvert behaviors are as common, as even defending one's right is prohibited, as freedom of speech, freedom of press, freedom of assembly, and even freedom of religion is prohibited. In feudal agrarian cultures, dictatorial behavior is frequently exercised. They are the products of fear and illiteracy, where open-mindedness is punished, where lack of education does barely question if perhaps the entire cultural setup is wrong, where one does not have to become brainwashed to either kill or be killed for one's beliefs.

> "I would never die for my beliefs because I might be wrong"
>
> – Bertrand Russell

It is a pick your poison scenario, since dictatorial cultures are geared to low socio-cultural stimulation, without a robust economy, which often produces introverts, where they normally shy away from others, especially the opposite gender. And since the overall society is tilted towards a lower social arousal, and not diversified in economic stimuli, inhibiting excitement in socio-economic productivity; and since unisex activities are not the norm, as males and females cannot freely intermingle without legally being engaged or married, as sexism is definitely alive, where women are biased against in finding jobs and discouraged from pursuing higher education, and so on.

On the other hand, some extroverts can exaggerate in behaving fearless, enacting mal-mannerism, where sometimes reverence is lost, or when no value boundaries are set in dealing with others, as if rationale should not be of an essence, exhibiting an aggressively intrepid (dauntless, bold) attitude. And because Western socio-cultural and socio-economic criterions produce independence, since comparatively the employment rate in socio-agrarian nations, known as developing countries, is much lower than industrial-oriented societies with a much higher rate of employment, this potentiates the younger generations to influence the rules, rebel, and even change the cultural settings.

Extreme chivalrousness, shying away, irrationally hiding personal agendas, not sharing one's problems for seeking help are usually common when introverts are forced to live within the family rules, also facing social dilemmas, and confronting economic hurdles. There are often single breadwinners responsible for their family's well-being, as many developing countries lack providing enough jobs to adequately fulfill employment for so many that are competent to work, but cannot find vocation. The cultural settings often demand respect, especially in a strict disciplinary atmosphere. And since maneuvering within traditional dilemmas can often be misunderstood, leaving gaps in people's participatory and communicative discourse, as they often could not freely say what they mean or do what they say, mixed signals are quite common in dealing with sex, love, and of course, sexual orientation.

The truth is that we heal when we connect. We can adjust better and make progress in an open-minded society. It is human nature wanting to belong. Being honest about how we feel can heal us; it can expedite to remedy the problems. We are more resilient, and often more courageous when in groups. Collaboration is the key to success, especially within the global scale; good foreign policy and cooperation can identify with prolonging existence in this rather fragile worldly social and economic atmosphere. A constructive extrovertist's attitude can be a blessing, when people can freely speak their mind and professionally communicate in decisive matters to bring peace and happiness to all, because everyone should matter.

In a closed circuit environment, people do fear social judgements, which forces so many to mind and worry about what other people think of them. That is not encouraged in open societies. This is not to say there are no introverts in advanced societies, of course they are; but within lower rates, since free cultures relatively do not foment being excessively worried about other people's opinions or care what others think of them.

Overall, introverts prefer quiet settings; they shy away from the crowd, which can be difficult to deal with in school or in any other group activity, place, and social gathering where classmates, teachers, and grownups can make remarks about those quiet children and silent participants.

Generally speaking, we get more introverted as we grow older. Many elders have less interest in making friends; perhaps not needing to be praised, domineering, and not carrying a Napoleon syndrome attitude. People become more reclusive as they get older. It may be low testosterone, inducing less energy, and since much of our needs diminish in finding mates, finding jobs, finding new friends, sometimes not even eager enough to locate family members, peers, colleagues, and old lovers, there is just less incentive for conquering the world.

In advanced and industrial nations, technology, information, media, and market dynamics are catalysts for motivating people into upper mobility and in changing their lives for the better. This even influences the introvert, especially the youth, to become part of the excitement, to engage in a free market society where the inhabitants forgo cultural and social taboos, which leaves fewer obstacles to improve self. Whereas comparatively feudally agricultural oriented nations convey plenty of forbidden issues, or the so-called "out-of-bounds matters" as they play as brick walls, literally prohibiting individual and social progress. It becomes exponentially difficult when imperial governments hire terrorist states to ambush their own nation into poverty and silence, where crying out loud, complaining, and any criticism is punished, forcing so many into acting introverts and minding your own business mannerisms.

In many underachieving nations, tribal mentality still rules, where they lack social, political, and economic dynamics to authenticate true democracy and human rights. It is unlikely for minority groups to dominate the socio-political and socioeconomic agendas, as they are disfranchised, and as most bear prejudice, racial hurdles prevent them from reaching upper-mobility status.

It is also so sad that nepotism (the practice among those with power and influence of favoring relatives or friends, especially by giving them jobs, and endorsing individuals that have been recommended by other powerful colleagues) is very much alive in many third world countries, and even the United States under the Trump administration. They get preferential treatment, the old boy network, and looking after one's own. Acting biased and partially towards others is often exercised by the elites and the influential authorities. No transparency is ever allowed, keeping the citizens in the dark; no one dares to question the authorities and/or criticize the culprits in charge. Being outspoken can be dangerous, where the introvert behaviors and in keeping quiet is a blessing that might help one to stay alive.

Either way, extrovert traits are valued over introvert customs and behaviors where socio-cultural and socioeconomic dynamics can play a magnificent role in awakening billions and in goading introverts that we have already arrived into the twenty-first century, which requires a very competitive atmosphere where quality characters are demanded for success. It is imperative to know that solitude and a meditative mind should help in brainstorming to manifest creativity, open-mindedness, and passion for reaching for the stars, which sure can help one to become marketable and engage in communicating with other inquisitive minds, not become a remote island. And since many successful businesses look for extrovertly intelligent persons with good attitudes to maximize profit, employers seek extroverts with good quality for better productivity.

THE AMAZING HUMAN BRAIN

Can you imagine that everything in existence is perfunctory (lacking in interest or enthusiasm, just mechanical), operating as machines? If so, why not label and call it the planet of robots, where there are no goal-oriented organisms, only a mechanical world of machines. That is how our brain seems to be.

Let's assume we are robots, and nothing shorter than assimilated computers. If so, it would be unwise to imagine a digital world without software, lacking an absolutely powerful script writer, a competent programmer, in which trillions of species convey DNA and are so meticulously designed, an absolute miracle, since every single species, including humans, is assigned with an identity that is uniquely different than others, and for practical purposes. Precise blueprints of who, and what we are, so exquisitely planned that should put any inquisitive mind in awe.

We need to be reminded that a gene is part of DNA, which carries an individual's genetic information relating to one's characteristics. As informative as DNA is, it is callous not to see the urgency of a magnificent designer in manifesting entities as complicated as DNA and genes, demanding a breathtakingly animated being, and in understanding that matter and energy cannot produce data, lacking an intelligent designer. DNA is a map for the amplification of the living organism.

Some assume a pool of chemicals can perhaps form a living cell, or perhaps a primordial bacterium of some kind is responsible for DNA. Not fathoming that even the simplest life form requires a highly complex message with some 500,000 DNA characters. DNA is written with a combination of four chemicals: adenine, thymine, cytosine, and guanine, which scientists abbreviate as A, T, C, and G. Those are the letters of the DNA alphabet that encode all information necessary for life. In the simplest microorganisms, it takes 500,000 letters to produce a living organism.

Researchers, biologists, neurologists, and those active in genetics and related fields, medicine and anthropologists, believe there are five hundred thousand A's, or C's, or T's, or G's in a human being. It takes three billion (3,000,000,000) of those letters to manifest a copy of you, and there is one of those three-billion-letter messages inside every cell in everyone's body. Wouldn't it be insane to posit the cause to an inanimate, unintelligent matter, where such a magnificent task as DNA could take place by chance, and to occur in the realm of probabilities?

Many scientists take the human brain as having no conscious. They believe that our thoughts, memories, our vision, imaginations, our dreams, ideologies, values, interest, compromise, compliance, dignity, emotion, insensitivity, cruelty, and feelings of fear, shame, sadness, despondency, grief and sorrow, pain and suffering, willingness, courage, accountability, happiness, ecstasy, joy and longing for love, depression, transfiguration (metamorphosis, spiritual change, exalting, glorifying), deity, our sense of purpose, our intuition, pride, wit, talent, reasoning power, intelligence, ingenious, ingenuity, generosity, wisdom, aspiration, hopes and desires, inspiration, dialogue, patience, behaving hastily, diplomacy, satisfaction, courage, gratitude, gratefulness, affability, our love and empathy, apathy, ill feelings and brutality, hatred, tension, animosity, scorn, feeling of disdain, positive attitude, optimism, pessimism, rejection, loneliness, sexual temptation, reluctance, acting desperate, ire (rage anger), worry, revenge, offense, defense, homicidal, suicidal, feeling of regret, preserved, feeling of guilt, betrayal, mistakes, humiliation, resentment and despair, ineffable (taboo-like, indescribable), competitiveness, sacrifice, loyalty, devotion, sympathy, caring, longing for justice, fairness, rivalry and cooperation, ambition, withdrawal and shying away, introvert, extrovert, playfulness, domineering attitude, laid-back and laziness, persistence, perseverance, jealousy, eagerness, our sense of solitary, reclusiveness, feeling of resentment, meanness, blame, optimism, bliss, trust, pride, ego, selfishness, vision, righteousness, passion, obsession, captivation, compassion, transcendence, responsibility, meditativeness, focusing, confidence, intuitiveness, engaging, creativity, our sense of comprehension and resonance, despondency, revelation, reverence, serenity, affinity, gratitude, understanding, our sense of wonder, peace and tranquility, puzzled, abstract (general, not specific), exclusiveness, acceptance, forgiveness, anxiety and stress, clarity, rationality, our beliefs, craving, aggressiveness, satisfaction, trustworthiness, defiance, temptation and desires, our sense of neutrality, our sense of affiliation, belonging, faith, and so forth, are only supposed to be the byproducts of a mechanical brain that is fueled through electro-chemical charges, and is because of some chemical reaction.

The question is, how would our brain know what sort of hormone or electrical impulse should generate to manifest a particular thought, or designated feeling? And how does a human brain activate billions of neurons, where trillions of synapses spark to make us think and function the way we do; often so brilliantly, which should make one believe in magic, intuition, revelation, telepathy, and the like? It makes one overwhelmed by the rush of verve (mental strength), leaving little doubt that our human mind is of cosmic energy, where the presence of God is felt.

Do we really know the mechanics and the process in which hormonal secretion happens, and why? And how would our brain know and distinguish the joy hormones from the sad hormones? And why not exude exhilarating feel-good hormones when we are in pain? If done erroneously, mixed signals should be expected with a confused central processing unit. And why not emit sad hormones when we are really happy and vigorous?

Our brain reacts to the outside stimuli through electrochemical activities. It produces the precise amount of joy hormone in a peaceful and serene atmosphere, as well as generating the exact scale of agonizing and distressful hormone when in hostile and frustrating situations.

The question is, how would our brain know what kind of hormone to release for specific situations, and what quantity of variety of hormones available should exactly be produced to fit different scenarios and not go haywire, where excreting out of balance hormones can mean irreparable damage?

If our senses are responsible for us behaving as humans, senses are not of matter, and if it is our brain, the brain is also energy-oriented, with great ability of relating to formlessly ubiquitous cosmic energy, literally mindful, and magnificently aware, which reverberates (echoes) to the outside world.

The nervous system is impacted by our senses; what mechanism actually takes place for our brain to activate messages to the rest of our body for complying to the outside world?

What really triggers a lump of fatty tissue with trillions of microscopic nerves, blood vessels, capillaries, neurons, and synopsis, where they connect with no flaws, to create consciousness, manufacture thoughts, build experiences, derive messages, keep memories . . . and why? And why convey intent and intelligence?

Quantum physics has enlightened us in subatomic realms, where the world of string theory, invisible quarks, and vibrating waves actively maneuver, as their operational frequencies are as intricate and way beyond our human senses to reckon with.

Our thoughts, feelings, and emotions, the human nervous system, and the entire planetary life, sensations, intelligence, and mindfulness, are played at different frequencies that are quite different from the frequencies played in the invisible world of subatomic particles. The wave parameters in the unseen realm sing a much different song, limiting us to make evidence of the cause, but to see the effects.

What we invent and magically create are the byproducts of a thought and ingenious ideas, often brilliantly imaginative like building shuttles, conquering other planets, playing Mozart, curing the deadliest of diseases, or when one perishes or is glorified in the name of love. We are not apart from the very imperative forces of our universe, and although they are invisible, they play an extremely essential role in nature.

The five forces of nature as they sustain our universe are:

Gravity, which pulls and pushes on energy and momentum, also based on Einstein, who generalized Newton's idea saying gravity pulls on mass, as the gravitational field holds planets, stars, and entire planetary system and galaxies together.

Electromagnetism, which includes both electric and magnetic forces, pull and push on particles that convey electric charge, and keep atoms together. Electromagnetism is linked with electric and magnetic fields, and also with the particle of light, known as the photon.

The Strong Atomic (Nuclear) Force, a force that pulls and pushes on quarks, anti-quarks, and gluons, also holds protons and neutrons together; a remnant version of this force keeps atomic nuclei together. The strong atomic force is associated with the fields and particles known as gluons.

The Weak Nuclear Force (a force that affects most particles but is too weak to hold them together; its main effect is to cause many types of particles to dilapidate (decay) to other particles, and to let production and observation of neutrinos. The weak nuclear force is related to the fields and particles called "W" and "Z."

The Higgs Force, an extremely weak force, not currently observed, but expected to be present, the Higgs force is affiliated with the Higgs field and particle.

The above five forces of nature play decisive roles to maintain, balance, and prolong life. Our mind, spirt, or soul, call it as you wish, can respond to the awakened forces of the universe. That is exactly why we can identify with the unseen energy oriented in cyberspace, internet, cell phones, GPS, and medical diagnostic equipment, not to exclude diagnostic imaging machines (i.e. ultrasound, MRI, PET, and CT scanners), and x-ray machines, infusion pumps, medical lasers and LASIK surgical machines, etc.

It seems that everything happens in our brain. Not only is the human brain the most complex part of the human body, but it is known to be the most intricate entity in the universe. Our brain is the center of consciousness; it controls the entire voluntary and involuntary movement and other bodily functions. The brain dialogues with each part of our body via the nervous system, in which it carries electrochemical signals to execute orders received from the central processing unit.

An adult human brain is about three pounds. This jelly-like matter interrelates our mind to cosmic consciousness. The universe is fueled by this ever present cosmic life which our mind is an inseparable part of, and without life, couldn't be possible.

Our senses are impacted by the real world, interpreted by the brain into making sense. It is acknowledged that our conscious experience of events is actually delayed, giving the brain milliseconds to sort and synchronize the information, match it, package it, and deliver it.

Neuroscientists also credit that when our brain receives data with cross references of sight, sound, touch, hearing, and smell, they move together to make different tasks possible for each varied sensory information received by our brain.

It takes a delay gap to process and deliver it for us, and then reflect. It is also scientifically known that even if we are deprived of the outside world, our brain depicts its own reality related to its internal model, since there is already a model existing in our brain.

Our brain is the closest thing to gamut (range, spectrum) of electromagnetic radiation, x-rays, ultrasound, MRI, gamma rays, radio waves, air compression waves, and electrochemical signals, which also makes all sensory perception possible relevant to our dreams, feelings, memories, intelligence, our desires, emotions, and retro diction events (information or ideas to infer past events or states of affair), and so forth.

Our brain is pertinent to what we perceive, as our mindfulness literally relates to experiences of the moments in our life. Have you not noticed how time flies when in love, how time passes so quickly and elated when we are engulfed with joy and pleasure?

And amazingly enough, when fear is induced, or a bad accident of some kind occurs, it feels like eternity, like time is moving in slow motion. We now understand that from cradle to grave, human beings are networks in progress. We are not fixed entities, since our neurons continuously alter, showing the human brain's plasticity because of creating new and fresh neurons, especially for studiously inquisitive minds.

Diversifying and mental challenges, gaining knowledge and experience, and for exercising our mind through posterior hippocampus potentiates the brain for getting physically bigger.

The longer and the more mind challenges and learning new thing with years of practice, the more we should expect for our brain to enlarge in certain areas. It is also believed our brain secretly controls all that we do, even that which is hidden and not revealed to us.

It is interesting to notice many newborn animals are ready to encounter the challenges they face when they are born, since they are already instinctually programmed before being born. Humans take the longest time span among other species to competently manage their environment and the world around them. They can be conditioned to fit, and become compatible with their surroundings.

We can grow, learn, and progress through experience, and we can adapt accordingly. The hidden agendas to our human brain are in the connection of millions of new neurons as they flourish as we take new learnings and become skilled in accomplishing new tasks. The secret is not in the number of cells, because they seem to be the same in their number in young and old people.

Our early learning, even before two to three years of age, is very crucial, as it will play a critical role for the rest of our life. Not engaging our brain in mental activities and in experiencing fresh ideas can dramatically shift our memory perception for the worse, and make us lose our cognitive ability. The human brain can be compromised if left with no access to mental strength, leading to lack of vigor and recollection problems.

When faced with a critical situation, amygdales located in the temporal part of our brain activate and play a huge role in our response to emotion and fear. Amygdala is almond-shaped and is situated within the temporal lobe of brain. it is engaged in emotions and motivation specific to our survival. Amygdala processes feelings of fear, pleasure, and joy, and is also responsible for memory storage in different parts of the brain. It is also understood that determination is based on how big an emotional response an event invokes.

Amygdala is automatically connected with fear and anxiety and hormonal excretion. When we become startled and fearful of an unexpected and a bitter sound, the amygdala heightens our perception of the sound, which causes us to react with a fight-or-flight response. And this response activates the sympathetic branch of the peripheral nervous system, which causes accelerated heart rate, dilated pupils, increase in blood flow to muscles, increase in metabolism rate, and sometimes showing the victim with a pale face, since blood accumulates in our limbic system from other parts of our body for better maneuverability in fight-or-flight response.

Amygdala is also involved with memory, hormonal secretion, emotional responses, arousal, and automatic response to fear. It is located deep within the temporal lobes, median to hypothalamus, and right next to hippocampus. The amygdala gets sensory news from the thalamus and from the cerebral cortex.

The thalamus is also a limbic system structure, and it links areas of the cerebral cortex that are involved in sensory perception and movement with other parts of the brain and spinal cord that also have a role in sensation (conveying nerve impulses from sense organs to the nerve centers) and movement. The cerebral cortex processes sensory information captured from vision, hearing, touch, and other senses, and is engaged in decision-making, problem-solving, and planning.

It is through our sense of vision, hearing, touch, smell, and taste that we connect and respond to the environmental changes around us and with each other. Various environmental activities impact our senses, which are then captured by our nervous system to be assigned to many different parts of our brain accordingly, making specific parts of our brain respond to a variety of incoming messages, which we are then instructed to fulfill the tiniest or a major function.

Trillions of brain cells and capillaries, one hundred billion neurons and trillions of synopsis, quadrillions of interactions and more are constantly at work to make what and who we are. No one can claim to have seen the mechanics of how our senses record and reflect upon environmental activities, which are then sent to different parts of our brain via our nervous system.

It is wondrous how messages are laser-precise and directed to specific parts of our brain, then the brain orders our body to react in accord with the incoming messages. It should not be surprising to call them senses, since we cannot materialize any of them, if not of spirit, then, why call them senses? Our senses, the nervous system, and our mind are energy-oriented and derivatives of the cosmic energy field.

Messages retrieved and commands sent from the brain to our nervous system are not received by insensitive tissues, deadened nerve cells, and a network of irresponsive arteries, capillaries, bones, and muscles, etc. And yes, our brain commands messages back to the nervous system for us to execute them, but then again which us, who is the operator, who is behind I, or behind any of us? Is it the one hiding behind our brain, the subconscious mind, or the one perhaps hiding behind the physical body, within our spirit and into our soul, or the operator is probably the soul, ruling over us, but where?

Whom are we actually addressing these massages to? Who is really running the show? Is it our brain that is self-governed that is responsible for all of what is happening?

Surgeons work on physical bodies (patients) to operate on, utilizing sharp knives and scalpels, and physicists, chemists, biologists, and so on, need laboratories for experiencing on actual matters. It habituates them to developing a one-track mindedness, which makes them so anxious looking for results that necessitate actual findings. They forgo the reality of mind over matter, acting negligent of the higher realms. They wave to denote the ever present soul and the ubiquitous spirit.

Most scientists persist on having viable results, not for the convenience of their undertakings, but because of the plausible and confirmed results they are looking for. Most scientists are reluctant about the unseen world that lurks behind all and everything we do. They make the material world prominent without paying attention to the elephant in the room, the spirit of things, which makes it misleading.

The average human brain contains approximately100 billion neurons (nerve cells) that are the core component of our nervous system, and our brain enables transmitting information by electrochemical signaling. Our brain sends a great deal of electrical impulses to other neurons, which makes our perception of reality possible.

With millions of neuroglia (or glial cells) to support and protect the neurons, each neuron may be connected to up to 10,000 other neurons, passing signals to each other, constituting a network of as many as 1,000 trillion synaptic connections, since every spark executes a thought for processing. That is believed to be about an average of four to five thousand thoughts taking place within each hour; you do the math. Similarly, by some measure, scientists equate our brain to a computer that renders a 1 trillion bit per second processor.

Bear in mind, the estimates on the human brain's memory capacity vary wildly from 1 to 1,000 terabytes (for comparing our brain terabits with the 19 million volumes in the US Library of Congress, which only represents about 10 terabytes of data). Each terabyte is 1,024 gigabytes, or 1,099,511,627,776 bytes, one trillion bytes.

The information process within the brain occurs during the processes of memory <u>encoding</u> and <u>retrieval</u>. It happens when the brain utilizes a combination of chemicals and electricity. It is a very complicated process that involves a variety of interconnected steps, intricately designed.

Every neuron keeps a voltage gradient (grade, slope, inclination) across its membrane (plasma, nucleus) due to metabolically driven differences in ions of sodium, potassium, chloride, and calcium within the cell, each of which has a different charge. If the voltage changes significantly, then an electrochemical pulse called an action potential, or nerve impulse, is generated. This electrical activity can be measured and displayed as a wave form called brain wave, or brain rhythm.

A typical neuron generates a soma (the bulging, stretched into a more rounded shape cell body that contains the cell nucleus), dendrites (long, feathery filaments connected to the cell body in a complex branching "dendritic tree"), and a single axon (a special, extra-long, branched cellular filament, which may be thousands of times the length of the soma).

Unlike other body cells, most neurons in the human brain are only able to divide to make new cells (a process known as neurogenesis) during fetal processes and for a few months after birth. Brain cells may grow in size until the age of about eighteen years old, but they are essentially designed to last for a lifetime.

Surprisingly enough, the only area of the brain where neurogenesis (the birth, the origin of neurons) has been shown to continue throughout life is the hippocampus, an area vital to memory encoding and storage. Deepak Chopra said, "<u>Our minds influence the key activity of the brain, which then influences everything; perception, cognition, thoughts and feelings, personal relationships; they're all a projection of you.</u>" Our sensory and neuron networks are bound to exclusive frequency, and experience our world within the possibilities of those vibrations. And when information is received by our brain, then our brain alters and interprets those incoming signals according to its potential and active cells available for percentage usage, which makes our perception of reality possible.

The Gospel of Thomas talks about how beliefs are so powerful, when referring to Jesus saying how the union of thought and emotion can literally alter our reality. "When you make the two one, thought and emotion," he begins, "you will become the son of man, and when you say mountain move away, it will move away."

This so-called empirical realty is based on mode of observation, which varies in many species of animals, since their perception of reality is very different from one another, including us. For example, snakes see through infrared, and dogs have great sense of smell, and honey bees see through ultraviolet, whales and dolphin operate with ultrasound and through echo location, so does the bat. How a chameleon sees the world and operates on several vision axes is much different than us; insects having many eyes see the world entirely different.

Dr. Andrew Jackson, from Trinity College, Dublin, who led the study, said, "A lot of researchers have looked at this in different animals by measuring their perception of flickering light.

"Some can perceive quite a fast flicker and others much slower, so that a flickering light looks like a blur.

"Interestingly, there's a large difference between big and small species. Animals smaller than us see the world in slow-motion. It seems to be almost a fact of life.

"Our focus was on vertebrates, but if you look at flies, they can perceive light flickering up to four times faster than we can.

"You can imagine a fly literally seeing everything in slow motion.

"The effect may also account for the way time seems to speed up as we get older," Dr. Jackson said.

This is why animals notice natural hazards a bit sooner than humans. When we see the sky as blue, it is not what other species see as blue. The significant issue is that dissimilar species with different nervous system operate at different frequency rates and since they resonate with the outside world unequally, they do as they are wired.

Hence, how millions of species functions depends on the specific description, with the mode of observation and culture in which they maneuver. This signifies that perceptual reality is not actual and fundamental reality; it is through our brain and nervous system that our world is shaped, a world that scientists tell us is odorless, tasteless, sightless, and so on.

When scientists claim realism and objectivity, they do not consider the subjectivity of consciousness, since they cannot prove its existence.

Some scientists imply take "the observer" as hallucination, and if so, and the observer is an illusion, then the observed should also be an illusion, since logic tells us illusion creates illusion, and cannot make reality form delusion. Either the observer is an illusion, which does not comply with our very nature, or it is outside space and time as we know it.

How can we imagine, how can we formulate theories, how can we constitute design in our consciousness, how can we manifest beauty, aesthetics, art, poetry, love, and grasp the meaning of any non-matter entity at all? Where are observations made, if not in our very conscious?

Our brain processes wondrous amounts of information. It captivates colors for the eye to see, the temperature around us, the amount of pressure we feel, the sound, even the dryness of our mouth. It holds and resonates with our emotions, thoughts and feelings, our memories. It simultaneously keeps track of our bodily functions, including breathing, eye and eyelid movements, hunger, blood circulation, and so forth.

Our brain processes a million messages a second, while it weighs in all of these data, and filters and discards the unimportant ones. This screening operation lets you concentrate efficiently in the world. It carries intelligence; it reasons, it dreams, generates feelings, and meditates on taking action as it interacts with its environment and with other people. Imagine many parts of the entire brain, each with a very complex and crucial task, playing in a mechanically oriented atmosphere with no dynamics, and without a competent programmer or an omnipotent planner.

I wonder how this amazing organ behaves so marvelously as a control center by receiving, translating, and directing sensory information throughout the entire human body. Our central nervous system includes the brain and spinal cord. There are three major branches that comprise our human brain. They are the forebrain, the midbrain, and the hindbrain (the lower part of the brainstem, the posterior of the three primary divisions of the developing vertebrate brain). Each and every division of our brain does exactly what it is known for and specified to do. But then again, how does the same material brain recognize the particular task assigned to each and every part of it with an awesome awareness and discipline?

The intricacy and the anatomy of human brain and its subcategories are imperative. The forebrain is responsible for a variety of routines, not to exclude receiving and processing sensory information, thinking, perceiving, generating and understanding language, and controlling motor activities.

There are two major parts of forebrain, which are known as the diencephalon and the telencephalon. The diencephalon includes the thalamus and hypothalamus, which are both responsible for such deeds as motor control, relaying sensory information to other parts, and controlling autonomic functions. The telencephalon holds the largest part of the brain, the cerebrum. Most of the actual information processing in the brain takes place in the cerebral cortex.

The midbrain and the hindbrain collectively comprise the structure of brainstem. The midbrain is the portion of the brainstem that links the posterior, also recognized as hindbrain and the forebrain. This region of the brain is active in visual and auditory responses, as well as motor function.

The hindbrain extends from the spinal cord and is composed of the metencephalon and myelencephalon. The myelencephalon, or "afterbrain," is the most posterior region of the embryonic hindbrain, from which the medulla oblongata develops.

The metencephalon contains structures such as the pons and cerebellum. These regions assist in maintaining balance and equilibrium, movement coordination, and the conduction of sensory information. The my.elen.ceph.alon is the posterior part of the developing vertebrate hindbrain or the corresponding part of the adult brain composed of the medulla oblongata, which is responsible for controlling such autonomic functions as breathing, heart rate, and digestion.

Other vital parts of the brain contain various structures that have a multitude of functions. Below is a list of major structures of the brain and some of their functions.

Basal Ganglia: Involved in cognition and voluntary movement. Diseases related to damages of this area are Parkinson's and Huntington's.

Brainstem: Relays information between the peripheral nerves and spinal cord to the upper parts of the brain. Consists of the midbrain, medulla oblongata, and the pons.

Broca's Area: Speech production, understanding language.

Central Sulcus (Fissure of Rolando): Deep groove that separates the parietal and frontal lobes.

Cerebellum: Controls movement coordination. Maintains balance and equilibrium.

Cerebral Cortex: Outer portion (1.5mm to 5mm) of the cerebrum. Receives and processes sensory information.

Divided into cerebral cortex lobes.

Cerebral Cortex Lobes:

Frontal Lobes: involved with decision-making, problem solving, and planning.

Occipital Lobes: involved with vision and color recognition.

Parietal Lobes: receives and processes sensory information.

Temporal Lobes : involved with emotional responses, memory, and speech.

Cerebrum: Largest portion of the brain. Consists of folded bulges called gyri that create deep furrows.

Corpus Callosum: Thick band of fibers that connect the left and right brain hemispheres.

Cranial Nerves: Twelve pairs of nerves that originate in the brain, exit the skull, and lead to the head, neck, and torso.

Fissure of Sylvius (Lateral Sulcus): Deep groove that separates the parietal and temporal lobes.

Limbic System Structures:

Amygdala: involved in emotional responses, hormonal secretions, and memory.

Cingulate Gyrus: a fold in the brain involved with sensory input concerning emotions and the regulation of aggressive behavior.

Fornix: an arching, fibrous band of nerve fibers that connect the hippocampus to the hypothalamus.

Hippocampus: forwards memories out to the designated part of the cerebral hemisphere to be stored for long-term and retrieves them when necessary.

Hypothalamus: directs a multitude of important functions, such as body temperature, hunger, and homeostasis.

Olfactory Cortex: Receives sensory information from the olfactory bulb and is involved in the identification of odors.

Thalamus: Mass of gray matter cells that arranges sensory signals to and from the spinal cord and the cerebrum.

Medulla Oblongata: Lower part of the brainstem that assists in controlling autonomic functions.

Meninges: Membranes that deal with and protect the brain and spinal cord.

Olfactory Bulb: Bulb-shaped end of the olfactory lobe, activates the sense of smell.

Pineal Gland: Endocrine gland involved in biological rhythms. Secretes the hormone melatonin.

Pituitary Gland: Endocrine gland involved in homeostasis, regulates other endocrine glands.

Pons: Arranges sensory information between the cerebrum and cerebellum.

Reticular Formation: Nerve fibers located inside the brainstem that regulate awareness and sleep.

Substantia nigra: Helps to control voluntary movement and regulates mood.

Tectum: The dorsal region of the mesencephalon (midbrain).

Teg.men.tum: The ventral region of the mesencephalon (midbrain).

Ventricular System: links system of internal brain cavities filled with cerebrospinal fluid.

Aqueduct of Sylvius: canal that is situated between the third ventricle and the fourth ventricle.

Choroid: generates cerebrospinal fluid.

Fourth Ventricle: canal that passes between the pons, medulla oblongata, and the cerebellum.

Lateral Ventricle: largest of the ventricles and situated in both brain hemispheres.

Third Ventricle: makes a pathway for cerebrospinal fluid to flow through.

Wernicke's area: This area of the brain assists with spoken language and how it is understood.

To summarize some of the activities of human brain, a marvel of a creation where genius and miracles are discovered.

Our human brain is the central organ of the <u>nervous system</u>, located in a thick, bony skull that relatively protects it from damage that might occur. It is similar to and has the same general build as the brains of other <u>mammals</u>, but with a much more highly developed <u>cerebral cortex</u> than any other animal. This has led to the evolutionary success of widespread supremacy of the human species across the planet.

Larger beasts, such as whales, sharks, crocodiles, and elephants, have larger brains, but when sized and measured using the cephalization ratio, which compensates for human body size, the quotient for our brain is almost twice as large as that of some dolphins, and three times as large as that of a <u>chimpanzee</u>.

Much of the increase in size comes from the cerebral cortex, especially the <u>frontal lobes</u>, which are associated with the thinking brain, <u>executive functions</u>, such as having a choice, with having will, taking risk, <u>self-control</u>, <u>planning</u>, <u>reasoning</u>, and in general, <u>abstract thought</u>. The portion of the cerebral cortex related to vision and the <u>visual cortex</u> is also greater than other animals, and enlarged in humans.

<u>One hundred captivating facts about the human brain</u> gathered by scientists and medical society in their scholarly rendered research. The human brain has bewildered and puzzled masses of people throughout history. Some scholars, scientists, and medical authorities have spent their whole lives trying to figure out how the brain works.

It should not be of any surprise why curious minds enjoy learning facts about this astonishing organ in the human body. Below, you will find 100 facts about the brain, including how it maneuvers, how it expatiates (to explain by setting forth in careful and often elaborate detail), what it controls, how it affects sleep, dreams, emotions, and the power of our memory and the way we think. Furthermore, let's debunk some of the brain misconception myths that people accept as gospel truth.

Physical make up and attributes of the human brain.

Weight. The weight of the human brain is about three pounds.

Cerebrum. The cerebrum is the largest part of the brain and makes up 85 percent of the brain's weight.

Skin. Your skin weighs twice as much as your brain.

Gray matter. The brain's gray matter is made up of neurons, which gather and transmit signals.

White matter. The white matter is made up of dendrites and axons, which create the network by which neurons send their signals.

Gray and white. Your brain is 60 percent white matter and 40 percent gray matter.

Water. The brain is made up of about 75 percent water.

Neurons. Your brain consists of about 100 billion neurons.

Synapses. There are anywhere from 1,000 to 10,000 synapses for each neuron.

No pain. There are no pain receptors in the brain, so the brain can feel no pain.

Largest brain. While an elephant's brain is physically larger than a human brain, the human brain is 2 percent of total body weight compared to 0.15 percent of an elephant's brain, meaning humans have the largest brain to body size.

Blood vessels. There are 100,000 miles of blood vessels in the brain.

Fat. The human brain is the fattest organ in the body and may consists of at least 60 percent fat.

The Developing Brain. Starting from within the womb, fetal brain development begins the amazing journey that leads to a well-developed brain at birth that continues to grow for 18 more years.

Neurons. Neurons develop at the rate of 250,000 neurons per minute during early pregnancy.

Size at birth. At birth, your brain was almost the same size as an adult brain and contained most of the brain cells for your whole life.

Newborn's growth. A newborn baby's brain grows about three times its size in the first year.

Stopped growing. Your brain stopped growing at age 18.

Cerebral cortex. The cerebral cortex grows thicker as you learn to use it.

Stimulation. A stimulating environment for a child can make the difference between a 25 percent greater ability to learn and 25 percent less in an environment with little stimulation.

New neurons. Humans continue to <u>make new neurons</u> throughout life in response to mental activity.

Read aloud. Reading aloud and talking often to a young child promotes brain development.

Emotions. The capacity for such emotions as joy, happiness, fear, and shyness are already developed at birth. The specific type of nurturing a child receives shapes how these emotions are developed.

First sense. The <u>first sense to develop</u> while in utero is the sense of touch. The lips and cheeks can experience touch at about 8 weeks and the rest of the body around 12 weeks.

Bilingual brains. Children who learn two languages before the age of five <u>alter the brain structure</u>, and as adults have a much denser gray matter.

Child abuse and the brain. Studies have shown that child abuse can <u>inhibit development of the brain</u> and can permanently affect brain development.

Brain Function. From the invisible workings of the brain to more visible responses, such as yawns or intelligence, expose how the brain works with these facts.

Oxygen. Your brain uses 20 percent of the total oxygen in your body.

Blood. As with oxygen, your brain uses 20 percent of the blood circulating in your body.

Unconsciousness. If your brain loses blood for 8 to 10 seconds, you will lose consciousness.

Speed. Information can be processed as slowly as 0.5 meters/sec or <u>as fast as 120 meters/sec</u> (about 268 miles/hr.).

Wattage. While awake, your brain generates <u>between 10 and 23 watts</u> of power—or enough energy to power a light bulb.

Yawns. It is thought that a yawn works to send more oxygen to the brain, therefore working to <u>cool it down</u> and wake it up.

Neo cortex. The neo cortex makes up about 76 percent of the human brain and is responsible for language and consciousness. The human neo cortex is much larger than in animals.

10 percent. The old adage of humans only using 10 percent of their brain is <u>not true</u>. Every part of the brain has a known function.

Brain death. The brain can live for 4 to 6 minutes without oxygen, and then it begins to die. No oxygen for 5 to 10 minutes will result in permanent brain damage.

Highest temperature. The next time you get a fever, keep in mind that the highest human body temperature ever recorded was 115.7 degrees–and the man survived.

Stress. Excessive stress has shown to alter brain cells, brain structure, and brain function.

Love hormones and autism. Oxytocin, one of the hormones responsible for triggering feelings of love in the brain, has shown some benefits in helping control repetitive behaviors in those with autism.

Food and intelligence. A study of one million students in New York showed that students who ate lunches that did not include artificial flavors, preservatives, and dyes did 14 percent better on IQ tests than students who ate lunches with these additives.

Seafood. In the March 2003 edition of Discover magazine, a report describes how people in a 7-year study who ate seafood at least one time every week had a 30 percent lower occurrence of dementia.

Psychology of the Brain. From tickling to tasting to decision-making, find out how the brain affects what you experience.

Tickles. You can't tickle yourself because your brain distinguishes between unexpected external touch and your own touch.

Imaginary playmates. A study from Australia showed that children with imaginary playmates between the ages of 3 and 9 tended to be first-born children.

Reading faces. Without any words, you may be able to determine if someone is in a good mood, is feeling sad, or is angry, just by reading the face. A small area in the brain called the amygdala is responsible for your ability to read someone else's face for clues to how they are feeling.

Ringing in the ears. For years, medical professionals believed that tinnitus was due to a function within the mechanics of the ear, but newer evidence shows that it is actually a function of the brain.

Pain and gender. Scientists have discovered that men and women's brains react differently to pain, which explains why they may perceive or discuss pain differently.

Supertasters. There is a class of people known as <u>supertasters</u> who not only have more taste buds on the tongue, but whose brain is more sensitive to the tastes of foods and drinks. In fact, they can detect some flavors that others cannot.

Cold. Some people are much more sensitive to cold and actually feel pain associated with cold. <u>Research</u> has shown that the reason is due to certain channels that send cold information to the brain.

Decision-making. Women tend to take longer to <u>make a decision</u>, but are more likely to stick with the decision, compared to men, who are more likely to change their mind after making a decision.

Exercise. <u>Some studies indicate</u> that while some people are naturally more active, others are naturally more inactive, which may explain why getting out and exercising is more difficult for some.

Boredom. <u>Boredom</u> is brought on by a lack of change of stimulation, is largely a function of perception, and is connected to the innate curiosity found in humans.

Physical illness. The connection between body and mind is a strong one. <u>One estimate</u> is that between 50-70 percent of visits to the doctor for physical ailments are attributed to psychological factors.

Sadness and shopping. <u>Researchers have discovered</u> that those experiencing the blues are more willing to spend more money in an attempt to alleviate their sadness.

Memory. Learn how scent, jet lag, and estrogen affect memory, plus plenty of other information, with these facts.

Jet lag. <u>Frequent jet lag</u> can impair your memory, probably due to the stress hormones released.

New connections. Every time you recall a memory or have a new thought, you are creating a new connection in your brain.

Create associations. Memory is formed by associations, so if you want help remembering things, <u>create associations</u> for yourself.

Scent and memory. Memories triggered by scent have a <u>stronger emotional connection</u>, therefore appear more intense than other memory triggers.

Anomia. Anomia is the technical word for tip-of-the-tongue syndrome when you can almost remember a word, but it just won't quite come to you.

Sleep. While you sleep at night may be the best time for your brain to consolidate all your memories from the day.

No sleep. It goes to follow…lack of sleep may actually hurt to create new memories.

World Champion. A world champion memorizer, Ben Pridmore memorized 96 historical events in 5 minutes and memorized a single, shuffled deck of cards in 26.28 seconds.

Estrogen and memory. Estrogen (found in both men and women) has been shown to promote better memory functions.

Insulin. Insulin works to regulate blood sugar in the body, but recently, scientists have discovered that its presence in the brain also helps promote memory.

Dreams and Sleep. The amazing world of dreams and what happens during sleep is a mystery rooted in the brain.

Everyone dreams. Just because you don't remember your dreams doesn't mean you don't dream. Everyone dreams!

Nightly average. Most people dream about 1-2 hours a night and have an average of 4-7 dreams each night.

Brain waves. Studies show that brain waves are more active while dreaming than when you are awake.

Lost dreams. Five minutes after a dream, half of the dream is forgotten. Ten minutes after a dream, over 90 percent is forgotten. Write down your dreams immediately if you want to remember them.

Blind people dream. Dreams are more than just visual images, and blind people do dream. Whether or not they dream in pictures depends on if they were born blind or lost their vision later.

Color or B&W. Some people (about 12 percent) dream only in black and white while others dream in color.

Virtually paralyzed. While you sleep, your body produces a hormone that may prevent you from acting out your dreams, leaving you virtually paralyzed.

Snoring. If you are snoring, you are not dreaming.

During a dream. If you are awakened during a dream, you are much more likely to remember the dream than if you slept until a full night's sleep.

Symbolism. As those who invest in dream dictionaries can attest, dreams almost never represent what they actually are. The unconscious mind strives to make connections with concepts you will understand, so dreams are largely symbolic representations.

Adenosine. Caffeine works to block naturally occurring adenosine in the body, creating alertness. Scientists have <u>recently discovered</u> this connection and learned that doing the opposite—boosting adenosine—can actually help promote more natural sleep patterns and help eliminate insomnia.

Dream showings. <u>Japanese researchers</u> have successfully developed a technology that can put thoughts on a screen and may soon be able to screen people's dreams.

Airplanes and headaches. <u>A study</u> showed a correlation between flying and headaches, and states that around 6 percent of people who fly get headaches brought on by the flight itself.

Juggling. Juggling has shown to change the brain in as little as seven days. <u>The study</u> indicates that learning new things helps the brain to change very quickly.

Disney and sleep. A study published in the journal Sleep Medicine describes how <u>Disney creators used real sleep disorders</u> in many of their animated pets.

Blinking. Each time we blink, our brain kicks in and <u>keeps things illuminated</u> so the whole world doesn't go dark each time we blink (about 20,000 times a day).

Laughing. Laughing at a joke is no simple task, as it requires <u>activity in five different areas</u> of the brain.

Yawns are contagious. Ever notice that you yawned after someone around you did? Scientists believe this may be a response to an <u>ancient social behavior</u> for communication that humans still have.

Brain Bank. Harvard maintains a <u>Brain Bank</u> where over 7,000 human brains are stored for research purposes.

Outer space. The lack of gravity in outer space affects the brain in several ways. <u>Scientists are studying how and why</u>, but you may want to hold off on your next trip to the moon.

Music. Music lessons have shown to considerably boost <u>brain organization and ability</u> in both children and adults.

Thoughts. The average number of thoughts that humans are believed to experience each day is 70,000.

Ambidexterity. Those who are left-handed or ambidextrous have a corpus collosum (the part of the brain that bridges the two halves) that is about 11 percent larger than those who are right-handed.

Brain tissue has a consistency that is very similar to tofu.

Our brain can generate twenty-five watts of power at any given time. It could power a light bulb.

During pregnancy, a woman's brain will shrink. It will take up to six months to regain its size.

When we are born, our brain is about the size it is now. That is one reason why babies have such large heads relative to their body.

Our brain is more active when we are sleeping.

Information can go in between parts of our brain at a speed of two hundred sixty miles per hour.

We have over one hundred thousand miles of axons in our brain. They could wrap around the Earth four times. Axon is a long and single nerve-cell process that conducts impulse away from the cell body.

Our brain does not have pain receptors. It cannot feel anything. That is why brain surgeon can perform brain surgery on a conscious patient.

One can survive only having one side of one's brain.

There are more than one hundred thousand chemical reactions happening in our brain every second.

Our brain will continue to develop until we are in our late forties.

Every day we have about seventy thousand thoughts.

Experts estimate that over a lifetime, the modern human brain retains up to quadrillion pieces of information. We have more brain cells when we are two years old than we will have at any other point in our life.

Our brain accounts for 2 percent of our mass, but uses 25 percent of our oxygen and energy. The human brain is the greatest wonder of creation. This little organ weighs only 1,500 grams but contains billions of nerve cells. Each nerve cell is joined to others by hundreds of little offshoots, and the exchange of information between them is quicker than the telephone exchange of a busy capital city.

The number of telephone links in one brain exceeds the number of stars in a galaxy. It would be more than 1,000,000,000,000! No computer or telephone exchange is in a position to store and swap so much information in such a small space as that occupied by the human brain. Most people talk casually about their little grey cells without ever taking hold of what happens inside them.

While you are reading these words, your brain is carrying out a vast number of highly complex functions. You are turning the pages with the most delicate movement of your muscles. The muscles in your eyes are adjusting so that you can see with equally sharp clarity in changing light conditions. Your retina is picking out the letters on the paper and reducing them to tiny points, which the optic nerve sends on in the form of an impulse code to the visual center, where the words are reassembled into a new picture.

If our brain should be mechanically defined, why would anyone need to be mindful of his or her environment? They ought to automatically take place. Further, should we not take psychogenesis and other psychiatrically related fields, or analytical psychology as a mockery and futile, since they delve into the origin and development of mental functions, traits, and states that investigate patients from cognitive health, sound-mindedness, abilities and perspectives? Psychiatrists, psychologists, neurologists, and so forth, evaluate individuals mentally and assess abnormalities of the brain in identifying specific mental illness in search of a cure. Is the world of unseen, the word of telepathy, dreams, imagination, and so on, just illusions?

Quantum consciousness rather than quantum physics is what gives birth to all that we know, and the unknown. What we perceive as nebulous (not clear) consciousness is what manages the void, where the womb of nothingness has delivered all that we know and is potentiated with miracles to be discovered. Our brain is linked to cosmic energy, through which our mind and thought processes function.

We are the byproducts of an awakened, thought-oriented entity where no senseless, unintelligent matter can ever be produced. You might ask, if so, then everyone should uniformly carry the same level of intelligence and consciousness, and perhaps think the same, since it is fed from the same source via our brain. "I do not feel obliged to believe that the same God who has endowed us with senses, reason, and intelligent has intended us to forgo their use" (Galileo Galilei).

With learning new things, acquiring information and knowledge, brain plasticity becomes possible, which makes more neurons and intensifies the connection with other neurons as it fires up more synopsis, leading to higher IQ and intelligence, arriving at a higher cognitive ability, and often dynamic thinking, just like a cell phone or a radio transmitter, a TV or a satellite dish that is a tool and a means which enable us communicate, but then the actual signal is provided from elsewhere. An intelligent person with an alert mind is similar to advanced cell phones that should make a difference in sound resonance, diversity in overall functions, and clarity of hearing and conversation. To have an intelligent brain is like having an advance Apple iPhone, which can make better connection acting as a smart intermediary.

Graham Hancock said, "I don't believe that consciousness is generated by the brain. I believe that the brain is more of a receiver of consciousness."

CONSCIOUSNESS

How would you define consciousness? What precisely is consciousness? One can become aware of something because of one's consciousness. Consciousness is the essence of existence that allows you to have an experience. Without consciousness, we cannot participate in anything personally at all. As birth is an experience, life, near death, and everything that is ever known to man is an experience, which if we lack consciousness, no experience is ever possible.

Crawling, walking, running, and exercising, are experiences. Falling in love, making love, liking, getting hungry, and becoming thirsty are all experiences. Learning a new language, hearing, listening, and talking to someone is an experience. Singing and having an accident are all experiences. Cleaning your room, yawning, napping, listening to music, fighting, making peace, making friends, giving birth, becoming sick, catching cold, worrying, feeling melancholy, dreaming, fear, depression, happiness, sadness, and so on, are all experiences.

The bottom line is, our lives are the sum total of our experiences. With the absence of memory and consciousness, no living and no experience is ever possible, since consciousness is the very foundation and the actual basis for having to experience anything. Consciousness and experience are a two-sided coin. Thus, without consciousness, experience cannot exist. We would have no intelligence, no mind, no memory, no thoughts, no emotions, no dreams and imagination, and no sensory perception of any kind.

Consciousness is absolutely crucial and extremely provisional for our existence, which, as intangible as it is, without it, we cannot truly live even in millionth of second. Yet there are those naïve souls that still emphasize the superiority of matter, and ignore the utter validity of energy-driven consciousness over matter-based agendas. Consciousness is cosmic; it is the source that does not change but miraculously feeds infinite variance phenomenon.

What electricity is to millions of lamps with various shapes and sizes, consciousness is to our diverse experiences that are enormously mutable. Consciousness is never interrupted; there is never a gap in consciousness. It is always there. Even when sleeping we can remember our dreams after we wake up, which signifies no gap in consciousness. Perhaps a bit of experimental memory lapse, but no interruption in consciousness, prevalence, continuity, and without change. The same is true with expanded consciousness. Consciousness is an infinite source. It is beyond what enlargement means to human beings.

It is our mind that can advance, and perhaps become more intelligent, wiser, because of the expansion in experience. Neurons, nerve cells, or brain cells are the fundamental component of the nervous system in general and the brain in particular. A neuron is an electrically charged cell that develops and offloads information by electrochemical signaling.

Neurons are not like other cells. They neither die off to be replaced by new ones, nor divide, and they can't normally be replaced after being lost, although there are a few exceptions. It is noteworthy to know that because our brain is malleable, our mind can be expanded and further grow intelligently. The average human brain has about 100 billion neurons (or nerve cells) and many more neuroglia (or glial cells) that serve to protect and support the neurons.

Behind every great mind lays a super energy-driven brain with dynamic features, just like a highly advanced satellite and up-to-date Apple cell phones that are utilized as they brilliantly communicate as the brain identifies and grasps cosmic energy and renders thoughts that are also energy driven to make sense of our world.

If our brain was anything less than an energy-based entity, it could not recognize and identify with an energy driven cosmic, the higher memory capacity, the higher terabytes where more neurons firing means higher intelligence with raised IQ. It is imperative to know that consciousness is not limited to any boundaries. It is not confined. It is boundless in its nature, and contrary to space, it has no outer edge. The vibrating frequencies of our mind to comprehend are limited, which are not the limits of consciousness.

Further, no scientist has ever located consciousness anywhere within the brain, which has incited them to believe consciousness as an epiphenomenon (spin-off, by-product) of existence. Logic dictates that what is boundless is everywhere; it is not contained within any perimeter to be found in a specific place.

It is natural to think that we have an apart consciousness because of individual experiences. We are under the impression that consciousness is located in our brain, or someplace within our nervous system which the body carries everywhere we go. Believing that consciousness is generated by the human brain is delusional, and as egotistical and anthropocentric (human-centered) as it can be. This paradigm shift is to know that consciousness is not within us; we are within the consciousness.

The point should gravitate towards knowing that everything thing is utterly energy-driven, constructively managed and disciplined to produce goodness. And because we are also an undeniable part of nature with a conscience, we need to identify with virtues and positive energy to constructively generate moral excellence. Other than that, our efforts will be repudiated and eventually haunt us for worse; since doing right is structured within the entire universe and not excluding human beings. The essence of living is to do right, and believe that without good conscience, no good experience can ever be possible. We are not exempt from the infinitely creative and immensely resourceful nature, and we need to properly converge and run along the same lines.

Many scientists see nature as aimless, where evolution is objectified with no purpose. This should mean no beginning or an end, making it a hypocritical (charade, farce) thought, and far from reason. They simply choose not to see the reality of matter, the reality of motion and time which are intertwined, and one cannot exist without the other. Evolution means a gradual moving forward, and any evolutionary motion must convey purpose. What I mean is: wherever there is matter, exists motion, and where there is motion, exists time, and where there are motion and time, there must be purpose.

There are many controversial subjects dealing with the context of God and science. Inquiring minds want to delve into knowing if matter and science are the root cause of all there is, or is it God that is sovereign and in control. And there are millions, if not billions, of pious and curious characters that postulate (hypothesis, suppose, assume, posit) and ruminate (to think deeply, to ponder) trying to reach positive gain in discerning the reality of life deemed to our Creator, or perhaps atheists interested in knowing if matter and science are the anchor to everything.

And those who fanatically believe in grotesque (unheard-of, bizarre) concepts referencing life and existence without inference, they are depleted of any puissant (powerful) and convincing arguments. Either way, there is no doubt that science or technology has transferred humanity from the clenches of ignorance and has protected us from dark ages and inquisition-like atmosphere to modern times.

Our safety and security has tremendously been improved and positively shifted. We have progressed gradually but surely to an advanced era where miracle-like discoveries are employed and give humanity encouragement and impetus to conquer what seems to be the impossible, and to hope for the best which is yet to come in contemporary times.

Science and technology have made it literally practical to access brilliant ways of communication via the internet, Twitter, Facebook, Skype, blogging, cell phones, fax, satellites, and many other advanced intermediaries and digital entities. They have immensely affected and played a catalyst in positively shaping our life, and have made it possible to know the world in dynamic ways, where decisive changes take place and resonate where most applicable. Technology has made our life easier and more productive and promising.

There is no doubt that science has mitigated trepidation (fear, dreadfulness) and human superstition from the unknown. And also through which the mastery to our planet is appreciated and still propelling. With that said, we should not give all the credit to such tasks as science, no matter how advanced we are in our scientific endeavors or with having cutting edge technology in producing creative products available to us. "The more I study science the more I believe in God" (Albert Einstein).

And yet, science cannot tell us why we should be good. Science cannot tell us who are we, and where we came from, and why we are here, or where are we headed. Is existence real? Why did life come about? What is the meaning of life? Is self-awareness and knowing of the world around us real? Or does everything just happen in our brain and our reality is just an illusion?

And what is consciousness? Where does our consciousness and awareness come from? And is there life after death? How and why do we experience things, and why intelligence? Furthermore, why can't the most scholarly and scientific-minded of all times even collectively simulate a human brain having the same characteristic and attributes? Scientists awaken us to the uncharted territories and possibilities, like if we did not have to die, perhaps live up to an average age of three to four hundred years, or to experience parallel universes, and so forth.

To manifest a much more innovative brain, which has already led us from the hunter and gatherer environment to present position, where conquering other planets is the norm, neuroscientists tell us no region of the brain works in separation from other parts of brain, as they all work in concert and in interconnectivity with each other.

They state that our senses of seeing, sound, smell, taste, touch turn into electrical signals and then are directed to our brain, and our brain makes meaning out of those incoming electro signals. They continue to express at the beginning the signals are unintelligent, but our brain figures out a way to decode encrypted signals, making sense of them.

Mr. David Engleman, a contemporary neuroscientist, disclosed an exciting view, saying, "A new chapter in our life might be at the horizon where our brain flexibility can perhaps change our physical body. And that advanced robotic could very much influence our neurotic brain. Where technology can enhance our body through human fragility to human indestructibility."

Mr. David Engelman also elaborated on how the scientist can use liquid nitrogen to preserve people's brains, giving them a chance at life again after they die. This is a monumental leap of faith, where jaw-dropping endeavors can boldly claim beyond belief criterion like storing one's unique pathways and links to store memories. Every brain that stores a lifetime of wisdom information and experience is preserved, an option that scientists are trying to make sense of.

In a nutshell, what they are saying is, our mighty brain has the potential to make sense of the complicated stuff, where transparency of millions of signals sent to it become immediately clear and understood, which in return are made applicable to command our body to execute them in an orderly manner.

This gives rise to the idea that we can perhaps try to program the brain through biorobotic engineering and computer-like simulation, where extraordinary tasks can be sent to our brain via electrochemical signals, which at first might seem vague and unintelligent to our brain, but it will soon decipher and decode any related message received, enabling us to conquer the next phase of human revolutionary endeavors. If so, it can land us in unimaginable places that presently seem and sound just like fiction, not reality.

There is a saying that if you cannot take the horse to the water, then take the water to the horse. Scientists are trying to externally influence the brain through biorobotics to access the other 90 percent of human brain that is not activated, which might supposedly be manifested in a distanced time. And since it is commonly believed that we are currently using only 7 to 10 percent of our brain, then obviously there should be 90 percent availability left to become exploited and explored into uncharted territories, completely unknown to man, expediting to opening up the brain's potentiality for the comfort and progress of humanity—I hope.

Mr. Engelman narrated, "If we can make a digital view of the brain, then we can run software on brain creating simulation on what the brain can do. This will be a colossal step in exploring some of the incredible potentiality of human brain in uncharted areas.

Pavel Osten and Troy Margrie, on mapping brain with a light microscope, wrote:

The beginning of the 21st century has seen a renaissance in light microscopy and anatomical tract tracing that together are rapidly advancing our understanding of the form and function of neuronal circuits. The introduction of instruments for automated imaging of whole mouse brains, new cell type–specific and trans-synaptic tracers, and computational methods for handling the whole-brain data sets has opened the door to neuroanatomical studies at an unprecedented scale.

We present an overview of the present state and future opportunities in charting long-range and local connectivity in the entire mouse brain and in linking brain circuits to function. Neuro scientist are trying to map out the entire brain circuitry and wiring that is to underpin all and the total work of the brain, with its memory, information and experiences, by magnifying each part of the human brain one hundred times or more. Scientists say a super organism is created when each segment of the brain works in concert as a complex colony.

Like the ants and the bees do, since an ant or a bee cannot serve its purpose if left alone, unless are able to work collectively and within the entire net-work, and with the whole system, and since a single bee or a single ant is lost, going in a circle, while a colony of ants or bees works just fine in reaching their objective. It is now certain that consciousness has to do with integrated circuitry and activity of the entire brain, and not to single out singular cell behavior.

The challenges that Mr. Engelman pointed out were: can we become a non-biological being where we can be digitally uploaded to the unthinkable, like living in a restructure of the past, or to practically make sense of parallel universes, or even stop death and dying, or simulating anything we wish to occur? Perhaps analogous to the fictional genie in the bottle, which if freed from the limited environment of the capped bottle, then even the entire world is not a limit.

Where the interconnectivity of our mind, our physical body, and the become, no simulation leveraged by bio robotics, or other automation reassembly can ever create human conscious, emotion and feeling in its authenticated form as we can experience as actual human beings. So you're made of detritus (pieces left from exploded stars); get over it. Or better yet, celebrate it. After all, what nobler thought can one cherish than that the universe lives within us all? Rene Descartes said it more plausibly when he stated, "How can we even know what we are experiencing is the reality."

CONSCIOUSNESS AND THE EMPTINESS

A mind can perhaps live in a computer machine, where mechanically it makes it possible to do gargantuan tasks, making the artificial intelligence possible beyond our dreams, where it can solve enigmatical issues and dynamically resolve beyond-belief problems, but not to ever be trusted in manifesting a truly innate human fulfilment. Our sense of consciousness and spirit is an extraordinary concept that cannot be simulated no matter how far we go in exploring our brain, since our brain is matter and a medium that links our energy-oriented mind to the cosmos.

With all of that said, the question again that will rise to surface is: who is this shadowy observer inside each and every one of us that thinks, feels, sees, hears, tastes, smells, is curious, has emotion and will with memory, can choose; imagine, desire, and hope, has intuition and is creative, has conscious with a subliminal entity working below the threshold of one's consciousness—but cannot be found with even the most sophisticated and scientifically advanced instruments.

And no matter how deeply and thoroughly we search into the tiniest of cells, neurons, or any other biological network, we cannot find anyone there. The question that remains is, are we not real? Are we all hallucinating or imagining things? Can illusion experience a real world, or is our world also an illusion? Or are we perhaps under some kind of spell that is meant to condemn us in not understanding more than what we are supposed to? If not, who is this ghostly observer within us that self-inspects without being detected and is not identified?

Tezin Gyatso, His Holiness the fourteenth Dalai Lama, explains,

We all have a valid, proper sense of self, or "I," but then we additionally have a misconception of that "I" as inherently existing. Under the sway of this delusion, we view the self as existing under its own power, established by way of its own nature, able to set itself up.

However, if there were such a separate I—self-established and existing in its own right—it should become clearer and clearer under the light of competent analysis as to whether it exists as either mind or body, or the collection of mind and body, or different from mind and body. In fact, the closer you look, the more it is not found. This turns out to be the case for everything, for all phenomena.

The fact that you cannot find them means that those phenomena do not exist under their own power; they are not self-established."

His holiness carries to say on the subject of emptiness and existence,

A consciousness that conceives of inherent existence does not have a valid foundation. A wise consciousness, grounded in reality, understands that living beings and other phenomena—minds, bodies, buildings, and so forth—do not inherently exist. This is the wisdom of emptiness.

Understanding reality exactly opposite to the misconception of inherent existence, wisdom gradually overcomes ignorance.

Remove the ignorance that misconceives phenomena to inherently exist and you prevent the generation of afflictive emotions like lust and hatred. Thus, in turn, suffering can also be removed. In addition, the wisdom of emptiness must be accompanied by a motivation of deep concern for others (and by the compassionate deeds it inspires) before it can remove the obstructions to omniscience, which are the predispositions for the false appearance of phenomena—even to sense consciousness—as if they inherently exist.

Therefore, full spiritual practice calls for cultivating wisdom in conjunction with great compassion and the intention to become enlightened, in which others are valued more than yourself. And further on the subjects of no self, emptiness, and if objects exist, His Holiness says,

Selflessness,

Both Buddhists and non-Buddhists practice meditation to achieve pleasure and get rid of pain, and in both Buddhist and non-Buddhist systems the self is a central object of scrutiny. Certain non-Buddhists who accept rebirth accept the transitory nature of mind and body, but they believe in a self that is permanent, changeless and unitary. Although Buddhist schools accept rebirth, they hold that there is no such solid self.

For Buddhists, the main topic of the training in wisdom is emptiness, or selflessness, which means the absence of a permanent, unitary and independent self or, more subtly, the absence of inherent existence either in living beings or in other phenomena.

The Two Truths

To understand selflessness, you need to understand that everything that exists is contained in two groups called the two truths: conventional and ultimate. The phenomena that we see and observe around us can go from good to bad, or bad to good, depending on various causes and conditions. Many phenomena cannot be said to be inherently good or bad; they are better or worse, tall or short, beautiful or ugly, only by comparison, not by way of their own nature. Their value is relative.

From this you can see that there is a discrepancy between the way things appear and how they actually are. For instance, something may—in terms of how it appears—look good, but, due to its inner nature being different, it can turn bad once it is affected by conditions. Food that looks so good in a restaurant may not sit so well in your stomach. This is a clear sign of a discrepancy between appearance and reality.

These phenomena themselves are called conventional truths: they are known by consciousness that goes no further than appearances. But the same objects have an inner mode of being, called an ultimate truth that allows for the changes brought about by conditions. A wise consciousness, not satisfied with mere appearances, analyzes to find whether objects inherently exist as they seem to do but discovers their absence of inherent existence. It finds an emptiness of inherent existence beyond appearances.

Empty of What? by His Holiness Tezin Gyatso

Emptiness, or selflessness, can only be understood if we first identify that of which phenomena are empty. Without understanding what is negated, you cannot understand its absence, emptiness.

You might think that emptiness means nothingness, but it does not. Merely from reading it is difficult to identify and understand the object of negation, what Buddhist texts speak of as true establishment or inherent existence. But over a period of time, when you add your own investigations to the reading, the faultiness of our usual way of seeing things will become clearer and clearer.

Buddha said many times that because all phenomena are dependently arisen, they are relative—their existence depends on other causes and conditions and depends on their own parts. A wooden table, for instance, does not exist independently; rather, it depends on a great many causes such as a tree, the carpenter who makes it, and so forth; it also depends upon its own parts. If a wooden table or any phenomenon really were not dependent—if it were established in its own right—then when you analyze it, its existence in its own right should become more obvious, but it does not.

This Buddhist reasoning is supported by science. Physicists today keep discovering finer and finer components of matter, yet they still cannot understand its ultimate nature. Understanding emptiness is even deeper. The more you look into how an ignorant consciousness conceives phenomena to exist, the more you find that phenomena do not exist that way. However, the more you look into what a wise consciousness understands, the more you gain affirmation in the absence of inherent existence.

Do Objects Exist?

We have established that when any phenomenon is sought through analysis, it cannot be found. So you may be wondering whether these phenomena exist at all. However, we know from direct experience that people and things cause pleasure and pain, and they can help and harm. Therefore, phenomena certainly do exist; the question is how? They do not exist in their own right, but only have an existence dependent upon many factors, including a consciousness that conceptualizes them. Once they exist but do not exist on their own, they necessarily exist in dependence upon conceptualization.

However, when phenomena appear to us, they do not at all appear as if they exist this way. Rather, they seem to be established in their own right, from the object's side, without depending upon a conceptualizing consciousness.

When training to develop wisdom, you are seeking through analysis to find the inherent existence of whatever object you are considering—yourself, another person, your body, your mind, or anything else. You are analyzing not the mere appearance but the inherent nature of the object. Thus it is not that you come to understand that the object does not exist; rather, you find that its inherent existence is unfounded. Analysis does not contradict the mere existence of the object. Phenomena do indeed exist, but not in the way we think they do. What is left after analysis is a dependently existent phenomenon. When, for example, you examine your own body, its inherent existence is negated, but what is left is a body dependent on four limbs, a trunk, and a head.

If Phenomena Are Empty, Can They Function?

Whenever we think about objects, do we mistakenly believe that they exist in their own right? No. We can conceive of phenomena in three different ways. Let us consider a tree. There is no denying that it appears to inherently exist, but: We could conceive of the tree as existing inherently, in its own right.

We could conceive of the tree as lacking inherent existence. We could conceive of the tree without thinking that it inherently exists or not. Why is science mute about many things of great concern, like the big bang, and why there was transformation of inanimate matter to animated matter? And why changes from plants to beasts, and eventually to the human animal. And as science states: The big bang explosion took place in a millennium of a second. If so, such an explosion must have made absolute destruction, rather than making a very intricate and orderly life such as ours possible.

And where in the world have you ever heard, or seen, that an unintelligent, lifeless substance, a spiritless matter of any kind, can give birth to such bright, skillful, and vivacious life like ours? With thousands of other sensible questions pending, science cannot come close to answering.

It should make one puzzled when a leading scientist like Mr. Steven Hawking addresses such important issues as time and believes the big bang and time originated simultaneously, and somehow the big bang gave birth to time, forgetting that leading physicists and scholarly minded scientists also adamantly believe that where there is matter, there is motion, where there is motion, there is space, and wherever there is space, there is time. And is it not fair to say evolution must have encompassed everything, including the big bang?

And because evolution occurs gradually within things, moving them to alter from simplest to more complex beings, then, if so, shouldn't we assess and conclude that time must have existed before the big bang, since the big bang also must be relevant to the gradual accumulation of matter, in which it must have reached its limit and apex before the big explosion?

You might say, even evolution started at the same time as the big bang. But then, to probe and follow reason with a sensible mind, shouldn't we agree on the accumulation and the gradual buildup of matter, like lava, which eventually became unimaginably hot that should have caused the big bang? I am sure no reliable scientist would attest to the big bang happening out of nowhere with the "abracadabra" incantation.

Either way, we need to know matter must have existed before the big bang, innately with motion and naturally driven with time. What does it take to convince humanity that there is an absolute power with unimaginable influence and order ruling everything there is and all of which there will ever be? And unless we believe in this literal ultimate power other than ours, in which human conduct and a moral compass should be directed to and evaluated with, we will be perplexed and ought to run into mental and spiritual confusion and into the unknown, where trouble is to perceive us.

Therefore, we should not behave maledicted (to speak evil), and not be spurred into behaving malevolently, but explore benediction (blessing, benevolence) and seek authenticity in our character when referencing the almighty Creator; and to convey honesty and goodness in our heart towards mankind with no prejudice or ill will.

Knowing that even the best of man's behavior is relative, no matter how righteous, we are bound to make mistakes, as we cannot be perfect by nature.

Hence, the omniscient and omnipresent God is the absolute power, which makes it possible for our relative and sometimes convoluted (twisted) mind to seek clear-sightedness, and through which we should be alerted with our behaviors. Believe in the world of the unseen, as you should reckon that it is the world that makes the world we experience possible. Behold in "what goes around, comes around." The problem starts when people cannot connect their wrongdoings with later punishment they receive in life. You might claim there are those who do wrong with no ill consequences. But that cannot be any further from the truth, since no one is in anybody's heart to truly know what pain and suffering they are wretchedly entangled with.

In reference to the world of the unseen, I should mention the world of planets, entire stellar system, galaxies, the universe, the world of the atom, photon, protons, neutrons, electrons, quarks, lepton, and the world of Higgs, and Higgs bosons, Higgs field, the world of wave links and frequencies, the world of the entire energy field. The world of quantum, the world of string theory and other subatomic particles, the world of electromagnetic forces, strong and weak atomic forces, the forces of gravity, the world on parallel but unseen universes, and so on.

I am sure there are many other unseen forces to be discovered in the near future by talented and curious-minded people. This should tell us it is definitely not all about what we are able to discern with our limited senses, but should very much be about the invisible world we cannot see. Deepak Chopra said, "Observation is made in conscious (awareness), theories are conceived in consciousness (awareness), science cannot explain consciousness, but consciousness can conceive and construct the scientific method, science itself is the off-spring and the product of consciousness."

It is important to see the role of consciousness in an UNseen world that makes our reality possible and expresses the visible world through our senses so that we can experience real living. Persian poet Jalal Adin Rumi, in the book I Have Passed Beyond all Thoughts by Craig Person, is quoted as saying,

Normally our minds are continuously stirred by perceptions, thoughts, and feelings, much as the ocean is constantly swept into waves by winds and currents.

This mental activity obscures the mind's true nature. But like an ocean the mind can settle down. It can become calm, quiet, and silent, while remaining awake. When it does, one experiences the mind's essential reality—unbounded pure consciousness. This inner field lies beyond thought and feeling, even beyond space and time.

Essentially, it takes open-mindedness and awareness to relate to delicate and complex matters, where events maneuver in the microscopic realm and beyond our senses to adapt to these magnificent happenings. Consciousness is a matrix that acts on a different level, but evidently is the operator of the unseen world and what it holds as intrinsic value and the essence of every phenomenon that the external and the extrinsic world experiences, including humans and what they relate to.

There is consciousness in everything, but different entities express consciousness differently. Of course, animals cannot relate to consciousness and direct it as we do, since consciousness is implanted in humans much deeper than in animals and plants, and is much more subjective to the human mind and spirit.

The world we recognize is generated in our mind through consciousness utilizing our brain. Cosmic conscious holds infinite potential that engulfs material phenomenon, which makes the world of matter secondary in cosmic existence. When we see the color green it is consciousness working through our senses and simultaneously with our nervous system to make the color green relevant to our eyes and visionary system.

We can see the color green as light reflect off the retina, which is defined by the dictionary as "the sensory membrane that lines the eye, is composed of several layers including one containing the rods and cones, and functions as the immediate instrument of vision by receiving the image formed by the lens and converting it into chemical and nervous signal which reach the brain by way of optic nerve." Evidently, a bundle of nerves goes to the back of our brain, known as the occipital lobe. The occipital lobe is the back part of the brain that is involved with vision, to make us see the color green.

Most of us see the color red the same, the color green the same, the color blue and white the same, and so forth, despite our retina or group of nerves involved and our brain not being exactly similar. It is the cosmic conscious imprinting on our brain to make these realities the same. Now imagine if we would all see colors and other objects differently; it would be a world so chaotic and impractical beyond anyone's imagination. If so, how would anyone be able to identify a thief, a murderer, a rapist, or anything at all, since witnesses would all give a much different description of the culprit, one seeing black, one seeing white, and the other seeing burgundy, or perhaps short, tall, fat, or skinny? This is also true with any other object.

And by the way, have you ever paid attention to the trillions and trillions of deletions done on your computers, cell phones, and other digital gadgets and electronic equipment? This is perhaps done every minute by billions of users, and have you asked yourself, where do these cleanups and expunging's go?

In 1927, many prominent physicists, including Albert Einstein, Bohr, Marie Curie, Schrodinger, Marconi, Werner Heisenberg, and others, gathered in Brussels, Belgium, to discuss consciousness and atomic war.

Albert Einstein was approached by the others, and was told that the mind of the researchers was affecting the conclusions of their experimental work, where it seems that the observer and the observed are in the same loop. The presence of the observer eventually destroys the information; disabling the researcher to substantiate any reliability in results while testing for consciousness.

Einstein could not believe that, since he thought this would violate all the scientific knowledge on mathematical models and behaviors. Later on he acknowledged and referenced this, saying, "Anyone who became seriously involved in the pursuit of science becomes convinced that there is a spirit making evidence in the laws of our universe much greater and undeniably superior than that of man." Max Plank, the father of quantum physics, also said, "All matters originated and existed only by the virtues of a force which we must assume behind this force there is an intelligent and conscious mind, this mind is the matrix of all matters . . . Science cannot explain consciousness, because the presence of the observer interfered with the result of every experience he is doing, since the observer happens to be part of the same loop; he would cause the collapse of the wave function, making a chaotic effect on the situation."

He defined the wave function in the mathematical structure as, "The waviness of the probabilities of events at quantum level." They all believed that the language of quantum communication is how the universe communicates through wave links with frequencies beyond what we can practically and visibly participate in, and via subatomic particles. They concluded that spirit is not a force like an electromagnetic force, or the strong and weak atomic forces, or the force of gravity. They believed spirit is consciousness.

They agreed collectively that consciousness was too potent, and if it ever got a chance to be fully administered and exercised, it could surely one day enter staller civilization and perhaps communicate with parallel universes. It is believed that our bio-consciousness has the ability to transfer information and communicate with the spirit of the universe. And since our collective consciousness can significantly influence our life for the better, if ever given a chance, we ought to act keenly to what science believes in. Scientists tell us that atoms are particles, and particles are waves, and waves are possibilities, where these possibilities exist in nothingness. Henceforth, nothingness should mean everything, including cosmic energy and awakened consciousness. In another words, nothingness is the potential for experiencing awareness and becoming conscious of the consciousness, which is the nervous system of our existence. Heisenberg said, "What we observe is not nature itself, but nature exposed to our method of questioning."

I believe it is the absolute and the omnipotent Creator that rules this whole being through the energy of consciousness. The good news is that humans are adamant they'll even further explore into the world of microcosms known as the "submicroscopic world." Prominent physicists and scientists tell us there are trillions of planets and galaxies, and billions and billions of universes beyond our imagination that should only comprise and count for .01 percent of what there is. The rest is dark energy and dark matter. They also say the universe is still expanding, since Hobble Edwin showed the distance galaxies are all moving away.

It should at least give us the clues, not to be cocky about the things we can understand, since there are an infinite number of things we still cannot fathom. Believe in the unseen almighty God, which could be the best self-defense ever known to man. And since we could not be far from being sadistic and mentally sick to truly claim believing in God and the heaven above, but still be wicket and cause evil. If one sincerely believes in God and can identify with our Creator of the heavens and the Earth, but still cause harm to others, then he or she should immediately seek treatment.

We need to understand that without holding high moral ground and prioritizing virtues in seeking compassionate thoughts and empathy, we will not reach tranquility in our life, and will be denied from having fidelity and trust with others. The gist of the matter should be about the energy that is prevalent in everyone and everything, not apart from the sanctified energy of the cosmos, which should not be abused. Every time we purposely and knowingly do wrong we are abusing the living sacred energy within, which is granted and empowered within us by the absolute power, the omniscient, and the omnipresent God. We are abusing our Creator.

Humanity is at a point where any demonic character can push a nuclear button and cause pandemonium and panic when rushing to judgment and being hasty with our decision to retaliate. They can desecrate life and leave our ashes behind. Many nations are now so advanced with their digital arsenals and diversified weaponry but they are not conscionable enough to scrutinize the consequences of their inhumane action.

Such frail behavior could release annihilation to whom it may concern and ensue the wrath of God on us, killing and destroying millions of innocent people without a morsel of regret on the culprit's part. But naïve and negligent enough not to comprehend when indicted because of one's wrongdoings by inescapable and justified laws of the universe and the heaven above, you are guilty as charged, and being easily acquitted won't be the case. In conclusion, I'd like to quote several prominent scientists and physicists referencing consciousness, our life and the universe.

Information is everything.

In the final decades of his life, the question that intrigued Wheeler most was: "Are life and mind irrelevant to the structure of the universe, or are they central to it?" He suggested that the nature of reality was revealed by the bizarre laws of quantum mechanics. According to the quantum theory, before the observation is made, a subatomic particle exists in several states, called a superposition (or, as Wheeler called it, a "smoky dragon"). Once the particle is observed, it instantaneously collapses into a single position.

Wheeler suggested that reality is created by observers and that "no phenomenon is a real phenomenon until it is an observed phenomenon."

He coined the term "Participatory Anthropic Principle" (PAP) from the Greek anthropos, or human. He went further to suggest that "we are participants in bringing into being not only the near and here, but the far away and long ago" (Ref. Radio Interview with Martin Red fern).

This claim was considered rather outlandish until his thought experiment, known as the delayed-choice experiment, was tested in a laboratory in 1984. This experiment was a variation on the famous double-slit experiment, in which the dual nature of light was exposed (depending on how the experiment was measured and observed, the light behaved like a particle, a photon, or like a wave).

Unlike the original double-slit experiment, in Wheeler's version, the method of detection was changed AFTER a photon had passed the double slit. The experiment showed that the path of the photon was not fixed until the physicists made their measurements. The results of this experiment, as well as another conducted in 2007, proved what Wheeler had always suspected—observers' consciousness is required to bring the universe into existence. This means that a pre-life Earth would have existed in an undetermined state, and a pre-life universe could only exist retroactively.

A universe FINE-TUNED for life

These conclusions led many scientists to speculate that the universe is fine-tuned for life. This is how Wheeler's Princeton colleague, Robert Dicke, explained the existence of our universe:

"If you want an observer around, and if you want life, you need heavy elements. To make heavy elements out of hydrogen, you need thermonuclear combustion. To have thermonuclear combustion, you need a time of cooking in a star of several billion years. In order to stretch out several billion years in its time dimension, the universe, according to general relativity, must be several years across in its space dimensions. So why is the universe as big as it is? Because we are here!" (Cosmic Search Vol. 1 No. 4)

Stephen Hawking has also noted: "The laws of science, as we know them at present, seem to have been very finely adjusted to make possible the development of life." Fred Hoyle, in his book Intelligent Universe, compares "the chance of obtaining even a single functioning protein by a chance combination of amino acids to a star system full of blind men solving Rubik's Cube simultaneously."

Physicist Andrei Linde of Stanford University adds: "The universe and the observer exist as a pair. I cannot imagine a consistent theory of the universe that ignores consciousness" (<u>Biocentrism: How Life and Consciousness are the Keys to Understanding the Universe</u>)

Wheeler, always an optimist, believed that one day we would have a clear understanding of the origin of the universe. He had "a sense of faith that it can be done." "Faith," he wrote, "is the number one element. It isn't something that spreads itself uniformly. Faith is concentrated in few people at particular times and places. If you can involve young people in an atmosphere of hope and faith, then I think they'll figure out how to get the answer."

CONCLUSION:

Wheeler died of pneumonia on April 13, 2008, at age 96. His whole life he searched for answers to philosophical questions about the origin of matter, the nature of information, and the universe. "We are no longer satisfied with insights into particles, or fields of force, or geometry, or even space and time," he wrote in 1981. "Today we demand of physics some understanding of existence itself" (The Voice of Genius: Conversations with Nobel Scientists and Other Luminaries)

> Let's hope that young scientists will continue to be encouraged by these words and will push the boundaries of human imagination beyond its limits, and maybe even find the elusive final theory – <u>a Theory of Everything</u>.

Keep up your contiguity (nearness) with science, philosophy, and educate yourself, and be of benefit to eager minds to a point of sacrifice. Enlightenment needs to become an epidemic.

> Words will push the boundaries of human imagination beyond its limits, and maybe even find the elusive final theory – <u>a Theory of Everything</u>.

BREEDING MERCENARIES' CULTURE / DARK MONEY

"All that is necessary for the triumph – of evil is that good men do nothing" mistakenly attributed to <u>Edmund Burke</u>.

Mercenaries are the most treacherous individuals known worldwide. They instigate demonic acts and work for mean-spirited people with a Mafia mentality. They know no boundaries in murdering people or assassinating the opposition, as they normally are experts in sabotage, espionage, and infiltration, disguise and deception. They kill and maim, and do the unthinkable without a conscience, just for the love of receiving a paycheck. Presently we have mercenaries in Africa, unemployed men throughout the Middle East, terrorists who are actually mercenaries as they ruthlessly slaughter innocents in the name of Allah (God) to obtain money for their own survival and the West's corporate armies hired for money.

The anonymity of so many evil-minded culprits behind hiring these assassins makes them immune to prosecution. They would become futile in their devilish conduct if they couldn't motivate others to do the work for them. They seduce and fund the hungry, accommodate the broken, the hopeless, the needy, and entice the hate fools and the greedy to accomplish their beastly and inhumane tasks. Mercenaries are the invisible hands of barbarism, and they do come in many shapes and forms. Other kinds of mercenaries are the lackeys of corporations. They come in the form of media, as they first bellow the bullhorn of propaganda, misleading the public, and softening the road for Godfathers of crime and their mischievous conduct in the name of profit. They accumulate more wealth fueled with spilled blood wherever they deem necessary. A new era of corporate exploiters and financial elites have so far managed to play as the neo-colonist to bribe and enslave high state officials, even presidents and prime ministers, to change the fate of less powerful nations for the worse with the stroke of a pen, often overpowering the majority vote of the citizens. Where people's democratically elected president is either assassinated or a coup-d'état is formed against them and they're removed from the office of presidency, dark money plays a huge role in their inhumane schemes.

They are anonymously powerful people behaving in anonymous ways to circumscribe the very laws that ensure our democracy, illegally shifting dark money (secret money) in campaign contributions to install who they want in public office. They are in cahoots with public officials who have sold people out. The concentrated financial influence of special interest in our politics is the elephant in the room of politics, when spending gargantuan amounts of money has blinded the public to not notice the problem our nation faces. The survival of American democracy is on the line if we choose not to act, since dark money lurks at the heart of our political crises.

History is loaded with conspiracies by government officials who colluded with powerful and the very influential people to change what people favored for the benefit of the few. Roman politicians paid mobs to riot on their behalf. It is extremely essential to understand the role of dark money in politics and its perennial (everlasting) menace to our democracy. Dark money is cash whose source is not known, and which is spent to alter political outcomes to favor the financial elites.

Dark money can be noticed as the underlying corruption from which our crises eventually arrive: the collapse of public trust in politics, the rise of demagogic anti-politics, losing faith in the system, assaults on the living world, public health and civic society. They clearly manifest that democracy is senseless without transparency. The tobacco industry, gun industry, fossil fuel, biotechnology, junk food companies, the pharmaceutical industry, petroleum industry, and so on, have influenced our democratic elections by contributing very large sums of money aimed at placing their favorite congressmen, senators, and even presidents into office. They manufacture false identities, bogus scientific controversies, and fake news, as the ultra-rich manipulate the media outlets and manage to buy the political systems with the help of their affiliated mercenaries and devoted goons.

"Total liberty for wolves is death to the lambs." —Isaiah Berlin

— Jane Mayer, <u>Dark Money: The Hidden History of the Billionaires Behind the Rise of the Radical Right</u>

Many believe that because of having the will to choose, and since we are able to think and make conscious decisions, then we should be immune to perils of bizarre conditioning and not so susceptible to being influenced and perforated by its ongoing lies and tricks that brainwashing conveys. But I am afraid that is not the case, as we are very vulnerable to the malicious conduct of brainwashing, and pay a heavy price for it, without even noticing its forcible inculcation: to instill or impress an idea on someone, so inculcation is the process of instilling or impressing ideas, beliefs.

The perpetrators' premeditated plans are subtly manufactured, as they carry no reliable information. They wittingly deliver fake news in bad faith as they hit consumers with humbugs to establish their morbid objectives. Corroborative (supporting, confirming) evidence is not quite easy to obtain, which is very sad and inhumane, and should remind us of tampering with mail, which is considered a federal offense.

They have convinced the populace to participate in their pernicious behavior and into augmenting their position. Media are immune to dissidence and meaningful complaints against them, by orchestrating people to get accustomed to junk information through hideous tactics, where false propaganda has become ill-intended and unfortunately the norm. Mass propaganda manipulates people's emotions and preys on citizens through demagoguery, which historically is proven to be more effective than reason, since it does efficiently move people towards the intended target and into accomplishing the culprit's wicked task, icing its forcible inculcation of belief (brainwashing) with lies and deception.

Joseph Pulitzer said, "A cynical, mercenary, demagogic press will in time produce a people as base as itself. They act profoundly undemocratic without the consent of people, as they implement covert missions with significant wrongdoings." And Henry A. Wallace said, "A fascist is one whose lust for money or power is combined with such an intensity of intolerance toward those of other races, parties, classes, religions, cultures, regions or nations as to make him ruthless in his use of deceit or violence to attain his ends."

We are faced with the worst kind of mercenaries: the religious mercenaries. For them, God is an excuse to reach their filthy objectives. Most are fake at heart and malignant in nature, since they behave hypocritically and aim at raping and murdering in the name of Allah (God). This should alert freedom-loving people to stay away from being dragged into the war of religion, because that is what they are after, the war of ideology, where doctrines of many denominations are to supposedly clash and eventually slaughter millions of innocents under the allegiance to and duty for one's faith.

These malefactors and the messengers of hate are ignorant enough not to realize humanity has reached the age of awakening, and will not be mouse-trapped into a medieval cultural of thinking and enslaved by their dirty schemes, since wise and conscionable people of the world are enlightened enough to side with democracy, liberty, and human rights and they will stand united to protect lives and the pursuit of happiness.

Without knowing who is who, so many live hypocritically. With boisterous living they exhibit a good front and behave meticulously in public, as they hide their growth negligence of God. They behave cryptically, and are estranged with morality and extinct from virtues. They forfeit the truth and arrogantly tell people what to think, and dictate to them how to behave in the name of God and goodness while they literally derail from what they profess and secretly incite ruinous and bizarre conduct. We need to look at the bigger picture, aimed at acting compassionately towards the entire humanity and not only for the faith-based group that we happen to belong to. We must insist on crumbling the walls of religious prejudice and racial hatred, and truly believe in one nation under God.

We are deliberately kept apart, living a sectarian lifestyle blinded with pride and self-centeredness. The potential for provocative and ill behaviors are constantly present so the preacher of resentments and disunity can live on manufactured vanity (narcissism), breeding a culture of ignorance and with people's financial support. Dalai Lama said, "There is no need for temples, no need for complicated philosophies. My brain and my heart are my temples; my philosophy is kindness." And Yehuda Berg wonderfully said it thus: "I do believe that the original sources of all religions should be taught, because with that we will find our similarities, not just our differences."

I believe that if Mohammed, Buddha, Jesus, and Moses all got together, they would be best of friends because the spiritual basis of all religions is something that builds unity. But that is not what the demons of our times ever consider and hope for. They don't want a better world, to make peace and unify under one God where sociocultural and socioeconomics would not and could not keep us so far apart. These mercenaries of evil disseminate fear and choke off the opposition, no matter how significant and justified the opposition are in their demand for a better life.

People should be aware of tyranny by the invisible hands of misfortune silently driven, presiding at the most vulnerable and heart-wrenching places. Media pipes in with rage and anger towards the target to win citizens' vote for the state and the corporations to break into all-out war with the less powerful nations, to devour people's natural resources, to confiscate their wealth, and all in the name of bringing freedom and democracy to them.

This bizarre and inhuman conduct is possible because indignant corporates are in cahoots with their cronies and puppets, as they confabulate (talk informally) in secret to mandate vicious plans against the innocents, as culprits' diabolical ideas affect millions for the worse—and apparently with no shame. The state and corporations implement sanctions, crippling trade embargos and militarism to decimate the designated prey, forcing displacement and homelessness and the exodus of natives from their homeland and into concentration camps. All aimed at annexing their resources for profiteering, making a deliberate mockery of democracy, character, virtues, and human rights.

this reminds us of colonialism phase two, strategized with devastating sanctions, modern weaponry, and complex tactical combat, where collateral damages include murdering innocent and godly people of faith. You might not believe in God, which you hypocritically claim and perhaps grasp in the privacy of your mind as not real, but fasten your seat belt, as you are to face a ride so tragic, with the curses of mishaps descending on you beyond anyone's imagination. The Almighty never misses his just and laser-precision punishing the perpetrator in the most unexpected places and times.

We ought to comprehend that "no leaf is to ever fall without the Almighty noticing it." One can perhaps be invincible and manage to hide one's hands from doing wrong, but rest assured, godly retribution in the name of Heaven and Earth is closer to you than the aorta of your neck. Common sense should foresee mitigated punishment from the Almighty if one is callow and sterile of intelligence and handicapped with no wisdom. But God help you when you knowingly cause such deliberate atrocities beyond belief.

Many tycoons and business biggies obnoxiously see themselves as the creators of affluence and consider other hardworking people—the real wealth-makers—as moochers. They do not realize that societies run by policing and capital punishment are those where fascism is constantly at work to chastise desperate people against their will and just demands for employment, food, and shelter. They keep people at their mercy, since they have expropriated all the resources and choose not to fix the root causes of the social and economic problems.

Corporate takeover by the elites has turned capitalist institutions into despotic regimes and plutocracies, where fair play and decent competition is denied and public welfare, humanism, and people's wellbeing is vilified. And because the inequality gap has sadly widened beyond belief, forgetting it is "we the people," as stated in the Constitution, that hold all the political power, not "we the corporations and the oligopolies." People delegate some of that power to the government of their choice to do their job in the name of God and the masses.

They have lost integrity in not keeping people's interest at heart. This should be the case before all hell breaks loose, and in the midst of panic and fear, some type of weird government will take over and endanger the essence of freedom and democracy that is the most sacrosanct entity known to man.

It is urgent that we wake up to access the core human values and become enlightened, where saving lives over profit is practiced. And to know when people's morale is lifted with the hope for a better future, it will motivate many to cooperate and attain vital agendas that everyone can identify with to accomplish them successfully and to reach their relative objectives. Entering into collective bargaining with decent conscience and in good faith, whether in our foreign policies or domestically, can benefit us all, and hence, everyone willing and able to work should not be denied such, thus becoming a productive member of society.

It is long overdue to call for redistribution of wealth and the need to lessen economic gaps so everyone can be sheltered with basic subsistence. Exercising genuine care for the needy should help to keep out hatred from our heart and perhaps shun belligerent encounters and crime-related tragedies where peace, safety, and tranquility of mind is restored. Holding onto 90 percent of resources by the few, while billions are fed dirt, and with no place to rest their head, is not freedom.

Freedom is only sacred when one's liberty does not infringe on others' sovereignty. Holding onto 90 percent of the resources by the few is declaring an economic war of aggression on humanity that is forfeiting people's right of existence and literally taking their freedom away. I believe this is even worse than conventional wars, since it causes gradual but sure destruction of a nation. Pope Francis said, "Human rights are not only violated by terrorism, repression or assassination, but also by unfair economic structures that creates huge inequalities." Pope Francis justly believes money should serve and not rule; so should any decent human being.

MIRACULOUSLY INTRIGUING PHENOMENA

Many wonders of the Milky Way universe and beyond are so enthralling, it strikes any inquisitive mind with awe. And yes, the ever present cosmic energy, or if you like, "quantum consciousness," as eternal as it seems to be, is influenced by our God, the infinite source of wisdom, with supernatural ability, flawlessly overseeing all there is and all that might ever exist. Bear in mind that mass energy as imperatively life-bearing it is not eternal. Scientists tell us it wears out, empowering reason to believe our mighty God is only eternal.

For instance, the Sun is 93,000,000 miles away from Earth, yet sunlight is our main source of energy. The sun is so fervent (flaming), the scorching heat at the core of our sun is 27,000,000 million degrees Fahrenheit. It gives more output energy in one second than mankind has generated since human existence.

The speed of light is 186,000 miles per second. If we travel at the speed of light going around the Earth, we can circle the Earth seven times per second. And remarkably enough, it will take 28 billion years or more to circle the universe at the speed of light. As the Bible tells us, God stretches out the heavens. It appears that the entire universe is stretching, as more than 100 billion galaxies, planets, nebula (groups of stars that are very far away), constellations, galaxies, cloud of gas or dust in space can sometimes be seen at night. And the stars in our universe are moving away from each other. Einstein shed light on some of the mysteries of our world with the well-known equation of $E = mc2$, where(E) is energy, (m) is mass or matter, and (c) is the speed of light. It is possible to turn mass into full-blown energy; if you expunge (annihilate) mass, it will produce energy, light, power, and sound, since there is incomprehensibly vast energy in all matter.

Bear in mind that even light and energy carry weight if scalable. Hence, one can convert mass into whole energy. It is fascinating to know that if the mass of an average-size tree could be changed into energy and possibly conserved, the power produced would be 45,000,000,000,000 KWH. Bear in mind that the USA yields 4,000,000,000,000 KWH of power annually. So if a single tree was converted into energy, and of course harnessed, the single tree would supply all of the USA with 10 years of electrical power.

The vast energy in a single grain of salt can electrically charge an entire household for several months. We are endowed with a universe potentiated with infinite energy. Some illuminating thoughts on the ingenuity of the design behind DNA, which contains a marvelous blueprint for all living things, where the intensity of information in a pinhead of DNA is nothing short of a miracle indeed. The amount of information conveyed in a pinhead volume of DNA will pile up books 500 times higher than from here on Earth to the moon.

DNA is very powerful information storage, written in codes as a linguistic system that can only come from an intelligent source. This denotes the impossibility of any matter-oriented entities giving rise to myriads of fascinating data, as matter is not insightfully driven to give imperative information. Scientists clearly know that DNA language can only be written in code by an intelligent source. DNA is three-dimensional molecules that are self-replicating and competent to make identical copies quickly and efficiently.

DNA are molecules that are self-correcting. There are special enzymes that can detect and correct replication errors on a minute-to-minute and second-to-second basis. The laws of information science say that information never originates by itself, it must come from an intelligent source. The information conveyed by DNA are transcendently enlightening, which should debunk any nomadic idea that an unintelligent matter devoid of any sense can create life.

Further insight on DNA molecules should convince anyone about the absurdity of the universe appearing by random chance. The DNA code informs; it programs a cell's behavior. All precepts, all advice, all instructions and plans come with volition and with having aims. Those who write teaching manuals do so with purpose. It should be enlightening to know that in every cell of our bodies there exists a very detailed instruction code, much like an infinitesimal (miniature) computer program. As you may be aware, a computer program is constructed of ones and zeros, like this: 110010101011000. The way they are arranged instructs the computer program what to do. The DNA code in each of our cells is very alike. It's made up of four chemicals that scholarly minded scientists abridge (shorten, abbreviate) as A, T, G, and C. These are suitably sequenced in the human cell like this: CGTGTGACTCGCTCCTGAT, and so on. There are three billion of these letters in every human cell!

As you can program your phone to alert you for specific reasons, DNA instructs the cell. DNA is a three-billion-lettered program telling the cell to comply in a certain way. It is a complete instruction manual. One needs to ask: how does this information program end up in each human cell? These are not just chemicals or formulas without intent, they are chemicals that instruct, coded in a very detailed way specifically how the person's body ought to develop.

Natural, biological, and physical reasons are absolutely lacking as an explanation when programmed information is involved. One simply wouldn't find instruction, exact information like this, without someone purposefully contriving (building) it.

Within each cell there is an area called the nucleus, which contains the all-important chromosomes. Chromosomes are microscopically small, rod-shaped structures that carry the genes. Within the chromosomes is an even smaller structure called DNA. This is the most important chemical substance in the human body—or in any other living thing. Increasing scientific revelation of DNA molecules has caused enormous problems for materialism.

DNA is a super-molecule that stores encrypted innate(hereditary) data. It coheres of two long tethers (cord) of chemical building blocks twined and put together. In humans, the strands of DNA are about two yards long, yet less than a trillionth of an inch in thickness.

In function, DNA is similar to a computer program on a floppy disk. It stores and relocates encoded information and tutelage. It is said that the DNA of a human being keeps enough facts and figures code to fill 1,000 books, each with 500 pages of tiny printed type. The DNA code generates a product much more complex than that of any computer. Surprisingly, this giant set of education fits comfortably within a single cell and routinely directs the formation of entire adult humans, initiating with just a single fertilized egg. Even the DNA of a bacterium is superbly complicated, which conveys at least three million units, all arranged in an extremely precise meaningful procession. The molecules that engulf DNA constitute an amazingly fabulous mechanism beyond belief - a truly microscopic prodigy (a miracle, marvel.)

The data is so tightly stored that the amount of DNA requisite (needful) to cipher (encode) the entire people living on planet earth would possibly fit into a space no bigger than an aspirin tablet!

Many scientists are persuaded that cells having such a complicated code and with such complex chemistry could never have come into existence by pure chance and with undirected chemistry. No matter how chemicals are vitiated (amalgamate, mix, blend), they do not engender DNA coils— or any intelligent code—at all. Only DNA propagate (multiply, spawn) DNA. Biology is the most powerful technology ever created. DNA is software, protein is hardware, cells are factories. Arvind Gupta

A couple of prominent scientists computed the aberrant (deviant, abnormal, odds) of life made by natural projection. They evaluated that there is less than 1 chance in 10 to the 40,000 power that life could have come from by disorderly trials. That's 10 to the 40,000 power, which is a 1 with 40,000 zeros after it! Why is natural selection not a random process? Evolution is not a random process. The innate variation on which natural selection acts may happen randomly, but natural selection by itself is not anarchic what so ever. The survival and procreation success of an individual is straightly connected to the ways its inherited traits behave in the context of its local environment.

Essentially Fodor & Piattelli-Palmarini are saying that "Darwin denies God as an agent but then gives Mother Nature all the qualities of God. That is, in a scientific book you might read on page 2 that God does not exist but then on page 5 you will see Mother Nature "choosing", "selecting", "deciding", "having wisdom", etc… It is simply a bait and switch,"

Life couldn't have had a random start. The problem is that there are about two thousand enzymes, and to fortuitously acquiring them all in a disorderly manner and disciplinary trial is solely one part in 10 to the

40,000power, an infinitely small possibility that could not be met even if the entire universe comported (tally, agreed, consist) of organic soup. If only one is not biased either by social acceptance or by a scientific training into the belief that life originated on the Earth. This simple math should convince any savvy individual, and utterly annihilates the idea of having no intelligent designer out of any judicious and decent court ruling.

Further, so many evolutionists act like they are irrelevant with the meaning of the word "selection." They keep saying "natural selection", which Selection according to any dictionary means (to pick, to choose, to select), if so, who is selecting, choosing by whom? Any sensible picking acquires intelligence, and intelligence demands savvy mind.

How can one gain some conception of the size of such a huge number? According to most Evolutionists, the universe is less than 30 billion years old—and there are fewer than 10 to the 18th power seconds in 30 billion years. So, even if nature could somehow have produced trillions of genetic code combinations every second for 30 billion years, the probabilities against producing the simplest one-celled animal by trial and error would still be inconceivably immense. In other words, probabilities greatly favor those that believe an intelligent designer was responsible for originating even the simplest DNA molecules.

Chemist Dr. Grebe notes, "That organic evolution could account for the complex forms of life in the past and the present has long since been abandoned by men who grasp the importance of the DNA genetic code."

Researcher and mathematician I. L Cohen adds, "At that moment, when the DNA/RNA system became understood, the debate between Evolutionists and Creationists should have come to a screeching halt. the implications of the DNA/RNA were obvious and clear. Mathematically speaking, based on probability concepts, there is no possibility that Evolution vs. the mechanism that created the approximately 6,000,000 species of plants and animals we recognize today."

Evolutionist Michael Denton stated, "The complexity of the simplest known type of cell is so great that it is impossible to accept that such an object could have been thrown together suddenly by some kind of freakish, vastly improbable, event. Such an occurrence would be indistinguishable from a miracle."

Famed researcher Sir Fred Hoyle is in agreement with Creationists on this point. He has reportedly said that supposing the first cell originated by chance is like believing a tornado sweeping through a junk yard might assemble a Boeing 747 from the materials therein.

It is important to note that the information written on DNA molecules is not produced by any known natural interaction of matter. Matter and molecules have no innate intelligence allowing self-organization into codes. There are no known physical laws that give molecules a natural tendency to arrange themselves into such coded structures. Like a computer disk, DNA has no intelligence. The complex, purposeful codes of this "master program" could have only originated outside itself. In the case of a computer program, the original codes were put there by an intelligent being, a programmer. Likewise, for DNA, it seems clear that intelligence must have come first, before the existence of DNA. Statistically, the odds are enormously in favor of that theory. DNA bears the marks of intelligent manufacture.

Dr. Wilder-Smith is an honored scientist who is certainly well-informed on modern biology and biochemistry. What is his considered opinion as to the source of the DNA codes found in each wondrous plant and animal? "An attempt to explain the formation of the genetic code from the chemical components of DNA. is comparable to the assumption that the text of a book originates from the paper molecules on which the sentences appear, and not from any external source of information. As a scientist, I am convinced that the pure chemistry of a cell is not enough to explain the workings of a cell, although the workings are chemical.

"The chemical workings of the cell are controlled by information which does not reside in the atoms and molecules of that cell. There is an author which transcends the material and the matter of which these strands are made. The author first of all conceived the information necessary to make a cell, then wrote it down, and then fixed it in a mechanism of reading it and realizing it in practice—so that the cell builds itself from the information."

One only need to look carefully at any living creature to gain some concept of their enormous complexity. If you have a pet, consider the complexities that must be involved—enabling that "package of matter" to move about, play, remember, show signs of affection, eat, and reproduce.

If that is not enough to boggle your mind, imagine being given the task of constructing a similar living pet from carbon, calcium, hydrogen, oxygen, etc.—the animal's basic constituent parts.

If you have ever held a beloved pet in your hands, completely limp and dead, you may have some comprehension of the helplessness of even the most intelligent and sophisticated scientist when it comes to the overwhelming problem of trying to create life.

In contrast, the natural world does not have the advantages people bring to the problem. In nature, there are only matter, energy, time, chance, and the physical laws—no guiding force, no purpose, and no goal.

Yet, even with all of modern man's accumulated knowledge, advanced tools, and experience, we are still absolutely overwhelmed at the complexities. This is despite the fact that we are certainly not starting from absolute zero in this problem, for there are millions of actual living examples of life to scrutinize.

We all begin with a single cell, then grow to more than 100 trillion cells, as each cell is an incredibly complicated nano-chemical machinery, with thousands of variations, and beyond anyone's imagination how each cell works. Cells come with a manufacturer's manual, referencing instructions of how each single part needs to operate.

Absolutism and relativism

Absolutism can mean different things in various situations. Prescribing value judgment would be difficult to comply with, for example, ethical decisions based on objective rules. It constitutes that some things are always right and some other things are always wrong. They are the same for all time, places, cultures, and people. A common example of Absolutism is Kantian Ethics, which is difficult to institute due to circumstances that arise in different situations.

People will do what they think is the right thing to do, since they are often influenced by their environment and because how people are brought up can sharply affect them in what they believe. One cannot expect universal civility of mind and manner, where morality could decisively count, since so many places are simply exhausted from having constructive means and the rudimentary ingredients to barely enlighten them with the most basic requirements for education and insightfulness.

To even make a relatively just society economically prosperous, with learning opportunity and training, proper education, good role models, wisdom, compassion, and awakened consciousness, it is required that consumers distinguish the intricacies between right and wrong, and to realize, as Plato puts it: "Goodness is its own virtue."

There are so many variables that can affect one's decision, starting with self-interest, greed, inferiority complex, desire, economic deprivation, lack of empathy, not having the right education and training, being deprived of analytical and reasoning skills, dignity and worth of the person, proper role models, peer pressure, wrongful environmental effects, and so on, which make one prone to irrational thinking and a static mindset. For instance, is it wrong or right to abort a living baby inside one's mother womb, where the mother desperately seeks abortion and pleads for her freedom to do so? This and many other dilemmas facing us often cannot be justly resolved.

For Kant, morality is only possible if free will exists. If deprived of being free, we would not be able to select which action to take. In which case, we could not be held responsible, since we are forced to do as we are told (in a positive or negative way) for our actions (we would be like programmed robots). But then again, we can be victimized by our own freedom of decision-making and by our own free will, if not having enough mind power and intelligence to manifest the right resolution. And morality can sometimes contradict rationality. This contradiction indicates that an act (or maxim) is immoral, no matter how desperate one's condition.

Like it is immoral to steal a loaf of bread when one's loved ones are almost perishing because of being hungry and homeless. Often it is not right to treat people the same due to circumstances that arise due to different situations. Put simply, not everyone can live by the same rule, because of wrong socioeconomic and sometimes immature sociocultural and callous sociopolitical agendas that have unjustifiable influence over all mentality in accepting extreme inequality in the allocation of resources. That is fundamentally wrong, since it can only happen where fear rules.

We all know that a hungry mob is an angry mob. No matter how anyone should persist on morality and the correct rule of conduct, deprived masses of people will mostly not budge. Some say it is the era of consciousness and we can constitute progressively oriented maxims to implement morality and perhaps reference flawless ethical rules and absolute dogmas. We are human beings and we are bound to make mistakes; no human mind is an exception to the rule.

Moral truths are subjective feelings about human conduct, which can never obtain the status of fact, as they are the result of ways of life and ideas that differ from culture to culture or person to person, depending on people's position and circumstances. We cannot make absolute moral rules where its dynamics could not be questioned. Man's commandments can be questioned; only God's references to morality and ethics need to be relied on and taken as absolute.

The bottom line is, we as human beings need to have references throughout our lives; call them rules, or laws and regulations, call them what you like. The point is, we must have reference points to make our interactivities practical and to make sense of what we are engaged in, and abide by the correct standard, since without make sense, mottos we would be lost. We can become reckless and perhaps chaotically exposed. For instance, when weighing something, you ought to have pound or kilogram as your reference point.

When measuring long distance, you need to reference mile or kilometer; when measuring height, you must reference foot, inches, meter, or centimeter, etc. When you measure volume, you need to reference gallon or liter; monetary units, dollars, pounds. Numbers, signs, colors, and thousands of other things can manifest references to help us manage our lives.

References give meaning to our lives. They bring order, enabling us to manage things. But it does not mean they cannot be changed and perhaps replaced. Referencing morality is not as easy, because human beings are complex beings, and difficult to deal with. Godly ways and ethical conduct cannot be as relaxed as we sometimes want them to be. Contrary to what Kantians believe, that one should be free to choose what one designates as being "ethical," this can bring disorder, since people and society's morals cannot homogeneously be agreed upon.

And for practical reasons, divine laws and "absolute maxim" cannot be compromised (e.g., thou shall not murder, thou shall not rape, thou shall not steal, thou shall not lie, no pedophilia, do not discriminate, and so on). These must be exercised to give meaning to the expression "live and let live," where empathy can avoid cruelty, and orderly conduct would prevent mayhem.

In comparison, relativism believes that nothing is intrinsically right or wrong. It can be influenced due to cultural and societal differences, since not every group, nation, or country should be run with the same stick. Relativism can alter due to historical events and modernization. What was perhaps true fifty or one hundred years ago might not hold water at the present time. Some traditions can even be counterintuitive and extremely backward, affecting everyone if still practiced.

"God is the absolute truth, there exists an absolute truth." Suppose we assert the negation of the statement, that is: there is no such thing as absolute truth. By making that assertion, we claim that the sentence: "There exists no absolute truth" is absolutely true. The statement is self-contradictory, so its negation, "There exists an absolute truth," is true.

But God, absolute divinity, must not be confused with mortals having utter power. No mortal, because of its nature in self-interest and greed, must be allowed to have absolute power. No mortal should be trusted with absolute morality, since human beings are definitely bound to make mistakes and cannot be an absolute role model. We all make mistakes and can sin in one way or another, but our wrongdoings are relative in their nature. Some are heavy players in behaving horrifically and inhumanely in doing felony crimes, and some perhaps engaged in petty crime. That is why we must have a just judiciary system to enforce due process of the law to accordingly render punishment. And there are those that are not noticed or caught when acting immorally, or perhaps made an unintentional mistake.

I believe when Kant talks about "Categorical Imperative" as a basis of morality by criticizing the golden rule is a bit of a stretch. Kant expects everyone to play as a universal role model; that is certainly a utopian idea, where fear of punishment makes a relative living possible. And since progressive behaviors are undeniably ingratiated with high consciousness through elaborate wisdom that we lack, not too many can abide by the rule of choosing what is "right" over what is "pleasing." That is what morality is, to choose right over wrong.

It is difficult, not to say that is impossible, for an individual's act per the short-term pleasure of the senses to be ignored, which can deliberately or unknowingly harm others and the environment. In the process, individuals are indirectly inflicting harm on themselves. What is good for self should be good for the universe; or what is good for the universe should be good for the individual as well.

This should remind one of the materialism and capitalism that might be pleasing to individuals in the short-term, but they are eventually harming the overall humanity by over-production and over-consumption. Choosing moderation in accumulation of wealth, and spirituality over materialism, is good for the individual as well as the universe.

Catholics believe that after death we wait in purgatory, a limbo state, before our fate is decided on for ending up either in the inferno or sent to Heaven. And I say millions are already experiencing hell; ask anyone with old age, who is weak, often sick, has no income, or is a single parent, widow, or homeless. Capitalists cannot in any way identify with social programming, where the needy could have realistic welfare, assistance for the elderly, disabled, and the working class after they are laid off or kicked out of the work force without benefits.

Rich elites are smoke-screened with conveniences and are confident with resolute influence and financial might. This has since overpowered their ethical behavior for the worse. They have caused irreparable damage to humanity and what they stand for by selfish ideas and how they so arrogantly refuse to attend to the suffering of the world around them. There is an expression that says: "Power tends to corrupt, and absolute power corrupts absolutely."

The rich elites are neither rational enough to insightfully commit to correcting the painful socioeconomics, the unjustifiable socio-politics, nor responsible enough to pay any attention to the global warming and the environmental disasters that are literally escalating as they accumulate so much wealth at the price of spilled blood. "Live simply that others may simply live" (Mahatma Gandhi).

A good reminder is that too much of anything can become lopsided, where moderation is ignored and too much power is in too few hands. This can exponentially hurt people for the worse; it's just human nature. No one should be allowed to have absolute might. It can eradicate the God within us. God's absence can bring out the demons to leave their footprint with destruction and demise, giving true meaning to the word hell, and in witnessing how the sanctity of God and the sovereignty of nature is dull-mindedly infringed upon.

They act nocturnally (diurnal, mainly active at night) and are surreptitious in their conduct, betraying the consumer's trust. This should put shame on the expression on our entire monetary system that says "in God we trust." As William Shakespeare put it, "What a terrible era in which idiots govern the blind."

POSITIVISM DOCTORING

Positivism says that all real knowledge permits proof, and that all authentic knowledge assumes that the only worthy knowledge is scientific. Thinkers such as Henri de Saint-Simon (1760–1825), Pierre-Simon Laplace (1749–1827) and Augusts Comte (1798–1857) believed that the scientific method, the circular dependence of theory and observation, must replace metaphysics in the history of thought. Émile Durkheim (1858–1917) reformulated sociological positivism as a foundation of social research.

Wilhelm Dilthey (1833–1911), in comparison, fought stringently against the thought that only explanations derived from science are valid. He reprised the argument, already found in Vico, that scientific explanations do not reach the inner nature of phenomena and it is humanistic knowledge that gives us insight into thoughts, feelings, and desires. Dilthey was in part influenced by the historicism of Leopold von Ranke (1795–1886).

Countering positivism

At the turn of the twentieth century, the first wave of German sociologists, including Max Weber and Georg Simmel, rejected that doctrine, thus founding the anti-positivist tradition in sociology. Later, anti-positivists and critical theorists have associated positivism with "scientism"; science as ideology.

Later in his career (1969), German theoretical physicist Werner Heisenberg, Nobel laureate for pioneering work in quantum mechanics, distanced himself from positivism by saying: "The positivists have a simple solution: the world must be divided into that which we can say clearly and the rest, which we had better pass over in silence. But can anyone conceive of a more pointless philosophy, seeing that what we can say clearly amounts to next to nothing? If we omitted, all that is unclear we would probably be left with completely uninteresting and trivial tautologies."

"Everything we call real is made of things that cannot be regarded as real" (Niels Bohr).

Everything that we see is ruled by what we do not see.

With the rate humanity is progressing, knowing about string theory and similar breakthrough theories, where scientists are digging into other dimensions, such as "eleven dimensions," befits their findings that can perhaps soon substantiate success. Miracle-like experiences as such wouldn't be a thing of the past, as with newer discoveries we can exponentially grow to one day see and kneel to God, giving us the heavenly chance to swirl into deep cosmos with pure joy and extreme delight, whence, with no doubt, we can feel and taste the infinitely glorious forces of the universe and be able to activate them at will.

To those that persist in thinking, I must see God to believe in God, the adequate question should start with self-cultivation, to know self-first. No disrespect, but not everyone can honestly digest the complexities of metaphysical subjects. When one says, "I love God," one must first know correct self-awareness, which is the key. Ralph Ellison, the invisible man, said: "When I discover who I am, I'll be free." Then perhaps one is to take on knowing God. And when one insists on denying God unless one can see God, he is stretching it not a bit, but a whole lot. "Wise men speak because they have something to say; fools because they have to say something" (Plato).

Forget that the most impressive and beautiful things cannot be seen, and not even tangible, they must be felt with the heart. Looking beyond our reach into a higher realm, looking for a physical God that is not inhibited within space and time, will certainly prove futile. We can only see the effects of our mind and our thoughts. We can only notice the reflection of our intelligence, IQ, talent, beauty, imagination, and thousands of other things that most definitely play gigantic roles in our lives that are not tangible and cannot be seen, but we certainly can notice the effects.

Just as our nervous system and senses are applicable to the visible world, it is the infinite potential of our brain we should strive for to one day have access to ultimate reasoning power. That should clearly resonate with the intricacies of the unseen world.

Can we ever see or feel our bones lengthen as they grow to make us taller? On average, sixteen to eighteen million magnificent thunderstorms occur each year, releasing adequate amounts of hydrogen and nitrogen to fertilize crops. This phenomenon is not seen by the naked eye, but it exists nonetheless. The vital energy activated in every animated being is not seen, and yet without it, no life is possible. There are millions if not billions of other undetected agendas that can practically make us or break us. They are not visualized or detected by the naked eye, but they exist.

We cannot see our memories that without life, becomes practically impossible; ask any Alzheimer's patient. Our pain and suffering, our anger and resentment, our happiness, our hopes and desires, our intentions, cannot be seen, only felt. We can only feel hunger and thirst; we can only feel when we are in love. We can see the utterance (expression) on people's faces, detect certain parts of brain change in response to stimuli, but their emotions are utterly intangible. We cannot see consciousness, despite numerous scientists trying their utmost effort to locate consciousness anywhere in the brain, but utterly with no success.

Atoms are the tiniest building blocks of matter and every other thing in an observatory universe such as ours, but they cannot be seen with the naked eye. Do you see thousands of pressure points pulsing throughout your body? No. But one can feel them. Do you see when your senses report to your brain and impact your nervous system, making it aware of certain tasks, which then your body respectively responds to accordingly?

Air, the oxygen we breathe, which ironically is what keeps us alive, cannot be seen, but felt.

Ultraviolet light is a type of electromagnetic wave that makes sunburn. They say bumblebees can see ultraviolet light, but humans cannot see it. The Hubble space telescope utilizes ultraviolet light to detect stars and galaxies in space.

We can see gravity's effects, but we cannot see it, as we cannot see light and heavy atomic forces, but the effect can absolutely be devastating. No electromagnetic force can be seen, but the effect of electromagnetics is very much alive.

Infrared, which emits heat, radiates infrared waves, for instance our body infrared, which is a sort of electromagnetic wave. We can see the brain and brain's chemical activities but our mind, memories, and thoughts are utterly intangible.

Quantum particles exist in the subatomic realm, which scientists tell us they pop in and out of for a split second, and can only be realized through electrostatic forces.

We can imagine the whole universe is out there, which can be seen partially by telescope. But we cannot know where it actually ends. It is mind-bending to think about our universe. But imagining the limit of the entire cosmos, if any, is not practical, at least in the present era.

Radioactivity is one sort of electromagnetic wave. Some are approximately one foot long to several miles in length. Electromagnetic frequencies transmit data and are utilized for radio, satellites, computers, and things of that nature.

Dark matter does not vent light or energy, yet it can be seen by mathematically calculating the motion of planets. Scientists tell us that about 80 percent of matter in the universe is made up of dark matter.

Anti-matter owns qualities that are antithetical (reverse, opposite) to regular matter. When matter and anti-matter collide, they both become destroyed. Scientists tell us they exist through the world's particle accelerators and other scientific methods.

Numbers are not seen, but in almost every imperative undertaking, we need to rely on numbers to manifest correct assessments. Our private finances and business affairs, and science-related endeavors, or any other vital undertaking, will practically go haywire without mathematics. Just because we cannot see what rules us, even on our earthy planet, does not mean they do not exist. I cannot reiterate (say again) it more that the world we do not see manages the world that we see.

Just as our nervous system and senses are applicable to the visible world, it is the infinite potential of our brain we should strive for to one day have access to ultimate reasoning power that should clearly resonate with the intricacies of the unseen world.

Can one see what literally keeps one alive? Can you see your jugular beating? Can you see your carotid arteries pulsating? Not unless you feel it with your fingers. Can you see your food digesting? Can you see the oxygen you breathe? Can you see your thoughts and memories? Can you see the urge to mate and to multiply? Can you see your cravings and desires?

Can you see thousands if not millions of acting hormones and enzymes where every thought and movement and every biochemical, bio-mechanical, biophysical activity has to happen for one to function properly and not in disarray? Can you see your mind, and can you see God? No. You feel most of them, and without them, we expire.

The vital energy activated in every animated being is not seen, and yet without it, no life is possible.

Our faith is not seen, but it is an inseparable part of our daily lives and a decisive factor in all that we undertake. For instance, we put our trust in the pilot's hand that airlifts the jumbo jet we are in, or the taxi driver who transports us home. Every time we drive and are behind the wheel we have faith and expect to reach our destiny, but our expectation is not seen or materialized. We take a leap of faith when we expect our parachute to open in midair as we jump out of a plane and then guide us to where we should land. A pregnant mother expects in good faith no complications during delivery, and impatiently expects to hold her healthy baby right after it is born. And when soldiers are placed on the front line of nasty wars and in devastating combat situations, they expect to return to their loved ones.

We expect to wake up every morning as we lay in bed and sleep at night. Millions of other faith-based beliefs and the over-arching concept of "in God we trust" are the impetuses and the moving forces we cannot deny or do without; such forces are not seen, and yet are the essence and irrefutable attributes to our lives.

Mr. Michio Kaku, professor of theoretical physics and the co-founder of string field theory, states:

The latest version of string theory is called "M theory" (M for membrane), so we now realize that strings can coexist with membranes. So the subatomic particles we see in nature, the quarks, the electrons, are nothing but musical notes on a tiny vibrating string. What is physics: physics is nothing but the laws of harmony that you can write on vibrating strings. What is chemistry? Chemistry is nothing but the melodies that you can play on interacting vibrating strings. What is the universe? The universe is a symphony of vibrating strings. And then what is the mind of God that Albert Einstein eloquently wrote about in the last thirty years of his life? We now for the first time in the history have a candidate for the mind of God. It is cosmic music resonating in eleven-dimensional hyperspace.

It is appropriate now to indicate a couple of mind-boggling situations where eventful design creation should perplex and amaze any savvy-oriented mind.

Reductionist vs Holism Positivism

I must see God to believe in God.

"Astronomers now find they have painted themselves into a corner because they have proven, by their own methods, that the world began abruptly in an act of creation to which you can trace the seeds of every star, every planet, every living thing in this cosmos and on the earth. And they have found that all this happened as a product of forces they cannot hope to discover…. That there are what I or anyone would call supernatural forces at work is now, I think, a scientifically proven fact." (Astronomer, physicist and founder of NASA's Goddard Institute of Space Studies Robert Jastrow).

Confucius said, "Real knowledge is to know the extent of one's ignorance." There is much truth in what Confucius said, which can probably help many not to behave conceitedly, at least as it evolves around our actions, and in what we take as truth, for one: we have lopsided belief in self so much, and I might add unreasonably emphatic in self-adequacy, that we have forgotten about who actually is in command.

THE BOTTOM LINE ON THE ORIGIN OF LIFE

During all recorded human history, there has never been a proven case of a living thing being generated from anything other than another living thing.

As yet, evolutionism has not made a scientifically credible explanation for the origin of such tremendous complexities as DNA, the human brain, and many other elements of the cosmos.

It is highly callous for materialists to say that all living things evolved into existence from nothing and without any conscientious instruction and with no scrupulous blueprint. Science has yet to discover how even one protein molecule could have truly come into existence by dull natural processes rather than dynamically guided energy-driven evolution.

There is not a scientific fact that life did (or ever could) have evolved into existence from non-living matter. Further, there is not even a slight evidence that spontaneous generation is possible.

Only DNA is known to produce DNA. No chemical interaction of molecules has even come close to producing this ultra-complex code that is so essential to all known life.

Posted July 22, 2012 Alan McDougall, the 1/1040, 000 probability actually refers to the chance of obtaining the required set of enzymes for the simplest living cell. How was this probability derived? We know that amino acids are the building blocks of enzymes, so what part of probability that you give is the chance of obtaining the required amino acids for those enzymes?

The researchers probably calculated the odds for a limited set of molecules to combine to the desired configurations. What they fail to take into account is that there are an exponential number of molecules performing exponential random combinations over billions of years. Some of which will combine to the desired configuration. Combine those together, and the odds shorten to the extent that it obviously becomes a certainty, judging by the fact that DNA, enzymes, et al. (together with further example of that sort) are extant (currently or actually existing).

On Sunday, July 22, 2012 at 2:42 PM, Joatmon said:

I would say that the odds against life evolving by chance is very large. This is evidenced by the fact that so far we haven't found any except here on earth.

I would say we haven't looked, and that we don't have many places to look. The only planets in the Sun's habitable zone are Venus, Earth, and Mars. There's a lot more to habitability than merely being in a star's habitable zone. Venus has too thick an atmosphere. Mars, too thin. Neither Venus nor Mars has an active plate tectonics (climatology, meteorology, geophysics, oceanography, seismology, geo chemistry) system. Mars might have been habitable long ago, and Mars does show some signs of having borne life long ago. It shows some signs that it still bears life right now. We do see life on the one planet that is habitable, and that life originated very shortly after conditions became hospitable for life. Judging from a sample size of one, maybe two (which is all we've got), it appears that primitive life is very likely to arise if conditions are right. That said, judging from a small sample size is always an iffy proposition. We need more data.

The theory of evolution discloses that life started, and evolution progresses by random chance. Yes, fortuitous (accident) hugely maneuvers in evolution, but this debate utterly disregards the principal role of natural selection which is contrary to chancy behaviors, and disorderly conducts.

Chance, in the form of mutations, brings about genetic volatility (variance), which is the basic material that natural selection has to work with to create what is necessary. Then, natural selection extricates (disentangle) definite variations. Those variations that render higher reproductive success to their holders (and chance makes sure that such beneficial mutations will be inescapable) are kept, and less successful variations are eliminated. When the atmosphere changes, or when organisms move to a different environment, different vacillations are chosen, eventually succession to different species. Harmful modifications normally expire out quickly, so they don't obtrude (impose, barge in) with the process of beneficial mutations amassing.

Nor is abiogenesis (the origin of the first life) merit to chance. Atoms and molecules arrange themselves not merely randomly, but due to their chemical properties. Complex molecules form spontaneously, and these complicated molecules can influence each other to make even more complex molecules. Once a molecule molds that is essentially self-replicating, natural selection will direct the formation of ever more efficacious (most effective) replicators. The initial self-replicating object didn't need to be as complicated as a new cell or even a strip of DNA. Some self-replicating molecules are actually not really all that complex.

A calculation of the probabilities of abiogenesis (the idea of impromptu origination of living organism straight from lifeless matter) is good-for-nothing, unless it accounts for the colossal range of starting materials that the first replicator perhaps has formed from, the chancy innumerable various forms that the first replicator might have held, and the fact that much of the construction of the replicating molecule would have been non-random to start with.

One ought to also realize that the theory of evolution doesn't rely on how the incipient (inaugural, first) life began.

In short, life does not evolve by chance alone, nor does the theory of evolution have anything to do with how life began. That's a completely different theory.

The universe functions by steady laws of nature. Why does it?

In the midst of global social, political, and economic mayhem, as the chaotic world threatens us all, there are so many dire gridlocks and uncertainties torturing humanity without mercy it makes man guilty as charged, not God.

But look at what we can depend on day after day: all the forces of the universe, not to exclude gravity, remain consistent. Imperative resources are produced to sustain and to keep us going. A hot cup of cocoa left on a kitchen counter will get cold. The earth rotates in the same 24 hours, and the speed of light doesn't alter—on Earth or in galaxies far from us. How is it that laws of nature never change? Why is the universe so orderly, and conducts so faithfully, refreshed after a deep and tranquil sleep for a day of hard work? And when a healthy baby is delivered after nature's time span of nine months has matured from one's mother womb, and so on.

"The most prominent philosophers and the greatest scientists have been impacted by how strange this is. There is no formal principle of reasoning necessity for a universe that obeys rules, let alone one that abide by the rules of mathematics. This consternation (amazement) springs from the acknowledgement that the universe doesn't have to act this way. It is easy to envisage (fancy, imagine) a universe in which conditions change unpredictably, and criterions modify from instant to instant, or even a universe in which things burst in, and pop out of existence."

Richard Feynman, a Nobel Prize winner for quantum electrodynamics, said, "Why nature is mathematical is a mystery... The fact that there are rules at all is a kind of miracle."

Why can't we feel Earth's spin, and other miracle-like phenomena?

We do not feel Earth's spin as it rotates ceaselessly because we're all moving with it, at the same constant speed. Earth rotates on its axis once in every 24-hour day. At Earth's equator, the speed of Earth's spin is about 1,000 miles per hour (1,600 kilometers per hour). The day and night come and go and carry us all along around and around in a lofty (formidable, grand) circle under the stars every second of the day, yet we don't feel Earth spinning. Why not? It's because utterly everything, including Earth's oceans and atmosphere, are spinning along with the Earth at the same constant speed. We'd feel the spin if unexpectedly the Earth stopped moving, which then would be a feeling similar to riding in a fast car and the driver suddenly slamming on the brakes! Why can't we feel Earth's spin?

Think about riding in a car or flying in a plane. When you're smoothly riding, you can feel as if you're not moving. An airbus jumbo jet or a Boeing jumbo jet flies at about 600 miles per hour (about 950-1,000 km per hour), or about half as fast as the Earth spins at its equator (lines of latitude and longitude.) But, while you're riding on that jet, close your eyes; it would seem to you as if you do not move at all. And when the flight attendant comes by and pours drinking water, or any of the beverages available (tea, coffee, hard liquor, or soft drink of any kind) into your cup, what you are drinking doesn't fly to the back of the plane.

That's because your drink, the cup you are drinking with, and you, are all moving at the same rate as the speed of the plane. Now meditate about what would occur if the car or plane wasn't moving at a constant rate, but instead speeding up and slowing down. But because they couldn't feel Earth move, they decoded this observation to give meaning that Earth was motionless and "the heavens" moved above us. It was the Greek scientist Aristarchus who initially proposed a heliocentric (Sun-centered) model of the universe hundreds of years BCE. The world's great thinkers upheld the idea of geocentric (Earth-centered) of the macrocosm for so many centuries.

It wasn't until the sixteenth century that the heliocentric model of the solar system, taking a particular body as central, began to be understood. While having some errors, Copernicus' model finally convinced the world that Earth spun on its axis beneath the stars and also moved in orbiting the sun. Bottom line: the reason we don't feel Earth spinning on its axis? It's because Earth rotates steadily and moves at a fixed rate in orbit around the Sun, carrying us all as passengers along with it. If that is not a miracle, I do not know what is.

The elaborateness of planet Earth indicates a purposeful designer who not only made our universe, but also sustains it as we speak. God's endless design can infinitely be manifested.

The Earth is perfectly sized. The Earth's size and corresponding gravity keeps a thin stratum (layer) of mostly nitrogen and oxygen gases stretching approximately 50 miles above the earth's surface. If Earth were smaller, an atmosphere would be impossible, like the planet Mercury. If Earth were bigger, its ambience (climate, atmosphere) would keep free hydrogen, like Jupiter. Earth is the only known planet furnished with an environment of the proper mixture of gases to nourish plants and animals, including human life.

Our planet Earth is situated the right distance from the Sun. Reckon the temperature swings we face, about -30 degrees to +120 degrees. If the Earth were any further distant from the Sun, we would all freeze to death. Any nearer and we would incinerate. Even a fractional volatility (vacillation) in the Earth's location to the Sun would make life on Earth just not possible. But the planet Earth maneuvers perfectly within desirable distance from the Sun while it spins around the Sun at a speed of virtually (almost) 67,000 mph. It is also rotating on its own axis, letting the entire surface of the Earth be properly cooled and warmed each day.

The moon is the perfect size, and within the exact distance from the Earth for its gravitational pull. The moon makes imperative ocean tides and movement so ocean waters do not stagnate, and yet our incredibly huge oceans are inhibited from spilling over across the global continents.

Water, as colorless, odorless, and without taste as it is, keeps every living thing alive. Plants, animals, and human beings consist mostly of water (about two-thirds of the human body is water). The distinguishing traits of water are specifically made for life.

Water can reach a boiling point and can be frozen; water allows us to live in an atmosphere of vacillating temperature changes and keeps our bodies a steady 98.6 degrees.

Water is a universal solvent. The liquidity of water means that different chemicals, minerals, and nutrients can be carried all over our bodies and permeate the smallest blood vessels.

Water is chemically neutral by nature, meaning it does not affect the makeup of the substance it carries. Water enables food digestion and helps nutrients, vitamins, and minerals to be absorbed and used by the body for creating energy.

Amazingly enough, water has a unique surface tension (tightness). Water in plants can flow upward against gravity, carrying life-giving water and nutrients to the uppermost of the tallest trees. Water freezes from the top down and floats, so that fish can carry on living in the winter. Oceans contain 96 percent to 97 percent of the Earth's water. There is a system designed on our planet Earth which purifies and cleans salt from water, and then dispenses it throughout the entire globe. The evanescence (evaporation) takes the ocean waters, leaving the salt, and forms clouds, which are then carried by the wind to distribute water over the land for vegetation, animals, and humans. It is a system of cleansing and supply that maintains life on this planet, a great recycling system.

The human brain concurrently (at the same time) projects an astonishing amount of information. Our brain discerns all the colors, the things we see, the temperature we feel around us, the pressure we feel against the floor, the sounds, the dryness of your mouth, even the texture of anything we feel. The brain holds and processes our sentiments and emotions, thoughts, the power of reasoning, and memories. Our brain simultaneously keeps track of the ongoing functions of our body, like breathing patterns, heat, eyelid movement, thirst, hunger, and the movement of the muscles in the entire body. It retrieves messages and renders order to other parts of our body.

The human brain develops more than a million messages a second. It weighs what is crucial of all this data, filtering out the unimportant items. This screening work permits one to focus and function effectively in our life. The brain acts differently than other organs. There is an intelligence to it; the ability to be logical, to generate feelings, to dream and devise, to take action, and connect to the environment and people.

The eye can perceive among seven to eight million colors. It has automatic focusing and manages an amazing 1.5 million messages at the same time.

Evolution insists on mutations and changes from and within existing organisms. Yet evolution alone does not fully clarify the source of the eye or the brain—and how in heaven's name did the start of living organisms happen from nonliving matter? The universe had a start—what caused it?

Scientists are now confident that our universe originated with an extremely colossal explosion of energy and light, which we know as the big bang. Everything that exists: the beginning of the universe, the start of space, and even the initial start of time itself, is due to the big bang effect.

Astrophysicist Robert Jastrow, a self-described agnostic, stated, "The seed of everything that has happened in the Universe was planted in that first instant; every star, every planet and every living creature in the Universe came into being as a result of events that were set in motion in the moment of the cosmic explosion. The Universe flashed into being, and we cannot find out what caused that to happen."

Steven Weinberg, a Nobel laureate in Physics (the recipient of honor or recognition for achievement in an art or science) said at the moment of this explosion, "the universe was about a hundred thousand million degrees Centigrade...and the universe was filled with light."

The most prominent scientists say that the universe has not always existed. It had a start. what caused that? They have no explanation for the sudden explosion of light and matter. THE BOTTOM LINE on the origin of life, unless one is to tie up evolution, which in some cases makes scientific sense, to the umbilical cord of the almighty God. It will become nothing less than a farce to believe the criteria the nonbelievers offer on how life incepted from nowhere, in random chance, and without a superbly intelligent source.

To further cultivate the agnostic's claim for an absentee of design and lack of a designer, any stable mind should ask: can any architect, draftsman, planner, builder, mechanic; chemical, electrical, electronic, computer, industrial, or construction engineer; or any other professional analyst ever substantiate a meaningful and mindful design without a reliable blueprint and masterfully composed schematic?

Imagine a world where anything and everything can be built, managed, sustained, and preserved without anyone lifting a finger. All activities of the world we live in would have no one to effectively think, and would be barren of anyone from spending time, not able to devote funds, skill, and energy to make them.

Imagine your dinner with a variety of food is served to you out of nowhere, and without a cook. Imagine the place you live, poof, appeared overnight, out of nowhere, without building materials, denied of helping hands, and without a crafty schemer, plotter, mason, or a builder. The thought of such a ludicrous (inept, absurd) claim is personally beyond my comprehension.

To believe in an existence without a cause, at least in the Newtonian's world of cause and effect, is derisive (false), and nothing short of a fairy-tale story that children might buy. But as they mature, they certainly laugh at their own naivety when they are reminded of folktales (myth driven saga) they once saw as truth.

The fact is that if this breathtaking universe and staggering (startling, mind-boggling) cosmos was built from nowhere, as most atheists claim, and out of nothing without a maker, then they should believe in the supernatural, which needs to signify a magical universe manipulated by an infinitely brilliant and enchanting designer.

We ought to bear in mind that every couple of centuries, billions come and go. The truth is that history can only identify with those who make history, great souls such as Moses, Jesus, Mohammad, Buddha, Socrates, Plato, Aristotle, Rumi, Omar Khayyam, Avicenna, Shakespeare, Firdausi, Sadie, Luther, St. Augustine, Descartes, Pascal, Rousseau, John Locke (the father of liberalism), Hobbes, Adam Smith, David Hume, Nietzsche, Bertrand Russell, Pasteur, Michael Angelo, Picasso, Immanuel Kant, AL Rahman al-Sufi (Azophi), Kepler, Galileo Galilei, Nicolas Copernicus, Newton, Edwin Hobble, Einstein, George Berkley, Voltaire, Hegel, Marx (may God bless his soul), and so on, through their miracle work, and in how they reached the essence of their geniuses. So should we identify with the work of God and God's majestic derivatives through "evolutionary creation." The point is that it is a drop of the infinite mind of God, which is sacredly implied within the mind of man in which divine messages are manifested. And since great minds are behind great ideas, it is what drives history and revolutionizes our world from the most primitive to the age of modernity, where civility of mind and manner is accordingly encouraged.

Many of the main principles and fundamental ideas underlining the structure of our contemporary world are barely 200 years old. Modern science depicting democracy and natural rights were all introduced by the enlightenment, a revolution of the intellect that seized Europe between 1600 and 1800, in which they challenged proven ways of dealing with reality.

Some contemporary scientists believe there are as many universes as there are refined sands on planet Earth. This should make one wonder, do physicists and scholarly minded scientists believe The Milky Way and the entire cosmos sprang out of nowhere from a single-celled organism and originated from planet Earth without any purpose, as explained in Darwin's theory of evolution where mutation and natural selection signify Darwin's survival of the fittest theory?

The Hubble telescope is the best instrument available for galaxy counting and estimation. The telescope, launched in 1990, initially estimated about two hundred billion galaxies, and still counting, for billions more as more advanced telescopes are expected to bring thrilling news as science progresses further.

The theory that says all species were created from a single-celled organism; did it also give birth to cosmic existence? Or was it perhaps extraterrestrial, and other planetary inhabitants which made life possible on planet Earth?

Or shall we believe the proponents of the big bang theory, like Professor Hawking and the like, that accept gravity is responsible for creating life as we know it?

Or did life perhaps appear on planet Earth from other universes and galaxies, brought about by extraterrestrials, or caused through any other means under the approval of God?

Meaning, order, discipline, purpose, objectives, beginning, the end, fate, destiny, responsibility, inspiration, dreams, imagination, commitments, sacrifice, good deeds, generosity, awesome precision and flawless management, moral conduct, intelligence, conscious mind, empathy, will power, compassion, relativism, absolutism, sustainability, fate, love, honor, devotion, decisiveness, beauty, good and evil, punishment, reward, and hundreds if not thousands of related sociocultural, ethical, legal, and judiciary concepts should put us on a very slippery road and ought to be redefined, not based on spirituality, justice, integrity, empathy, morality, or any other divine law, but depending on Darwin's survival of the fittest doctrine, where no criminal and atrocious behavior should honestly be condemned.

The strong needs to make the weak perish to survive, rather than cooperate and collectively challenge nature to further conquer the unknown for humanity's sake and comfort, to exercise "live and to let live mentality." Otherwise no genocide, wiping out nations through war of aggression, and via conventional weaponries, cluster bombs, biological and hydrogen bomb, should be damned. And let' not forget this type of toxic and cruel dogma (axiom, principle) has already done so much damage to humanity and is still counting.

And yes, since the key is wisdom, a tiny decimal in gradual brain cells aperture (opening) will result in billions of neurons to spark at trillions of synopses where they juncture to inspire apex creativity in mental and physical makeup to benefit humanity.

The incremental escalation in firing brain neurons eventually takes a positive leap in exalted endeavors, which should mean utter freedom from the clutches of ignorance, where the mind of God is truly signified and curiously discerned. We need to awaken to this undeniable fact that unless we prioritize education and pay more attention to learning and in gaining knowledge, we will be devoid of vital information that can shed light on decisive issues of our time where miracle-like events and beyond imagination breakthroughs become reality, setting the stage for the next paradigm shift in human glory.

Glittering stars become a dancing ground to celebrate the mind of man. In turn, mindfulness emanates wisdom where the power of reasoning should repel stupidity and the human beast is to be far-fetched and to substantiate collective attributes conducive to good deeds and virtuosity with aesthetic behaviors in making progressive task possible. Positive evolutionary perspectives can purport (convey) civil communication and constructive dialogues.

Our subconscious mind, which restores thought pattern and behaviors in a vast reservoir, can be tapped to build modern and revered character where barbaric and inhumane deeds are unanimously renounced.

This should awaken mankind to preserve the sanctity of higher self and strive to access the pinnacle of success in emergency accommodation for the acquisition of denoting education, proper employment, decent housing, and efficient medical programs, constituting genuine safety nets with no-nonsense financial plans for retirees and seniors.

Ethology (a branch of scientific knowledge dealing with human character and with its formation and evolution) can patent time parameter and accord with the era of human consciousness, promenading civility of mind and manner.

Make emergency accommodations not prerogatives or optional, but mandated wisdom to save lives and for people's well-being and prosperity, replacing violence with peace, justice, democracy, and human rights, where stoic actions are not encouraged, and sensitivity and compassion towards others' pain and suffering is positively addressed.

To feel responsible in relentlessly seeking practical resolution to ill criterion and on the actual causes for abysmal hurt (profound) which has forced many to lose hope and integrity in the face of degradation and misfortune, as defective products that are constantly disseminated to create restless atmosphere and anxiety as competent broker of fear and uncertainty structure institutionalized strategy to celebrate people's segregation and disunity with expensive Champaign and caviar.

They choose to manufacture hatred and through improvising vile insure the status quo and the fluidity of enslaving the wretchedly poor and destitute, where cerebral deficiencies and economic benevolence for some has solidified the concept of divide and rule, rendering masses of people incompetent to perceive the truth and not able to expose the prevalence of corporate madness, to unveil culture of falsehood and charlatanism, where God is toyed with to yoke dissidents in his name, as if the poor are reincarnated to live miserably and are condemn to be punished because of their character flaws and misdeeds in previous life.

This, by the way, justifies the Darwinism mentality through the survivor of fittest doctrine, and also pampers the extremist's ideology that says everything is fate-related, and is the God which is sentencing the helpless to tolerate what they deserve; either way, the rich elites are the beneficiary of such cultural nonsense and ill-diagnosed criterions.

The atheist's ideology is tenuous (weak) since its missing links and flaws are existentially too risky to depend on, where they meet with the infidel's extremism that cannot be trusted because of their backward mentality and brute behaviors towards other so-called nonbelievers. This leaves humanity with no choice but to align with cultures that are insightful and scintillating (stimulating, witty) on a metaphysical realm, where heavens are aspiring human souls and the cosmic spirit is permeated into each and every animated being. Exhibiting magic and wonder about the absolute power of the omniscient Creator should inspire humanity to cultivate further into the celestial kingdom and closer to the enchanting (majestic) nature of the universe.

Evidence for Creation › Evidence for God › Design and Purpose › God Caused Meaning

Humans have always wondered about the meaning of life...life has no higher purpose than to perpetuate the survival of DNA...life has no design, no purpose, no evil and no good, nothing but blind pitiless (cruel) indifference.1 —Richard Dawkins

Thermodynamics,

The laws of thermodynamics explain the connection between thermal energy, or heat, and other forms of energy, and how energy influences matter.

The First Law of Thermodynamics states that energy cannot be created or destroyed; the total quantity of energy in the universe stays the same.

The Second Law of Thermodynamics is about the quality of energy. It says that as energy is transformed, some of it is wasted. The Second Law also states that there is a natural tendency of any isolated system to deteriorate into a more disordered position.

Saibal Mitra, a professor of physics at Missouri State University, finds the Second Law to be the most interesting of the four laws of thermodynamics. "There are a number of ways to state the Second Law," he said. "At a very microscopic level, it simply says that if you have a system that is isolated, any natural process in that system progresses in the direction of increasing disorder, or entropy, of the system."

Many scientists believe that all processes result in an increase in entropy. Even when the order is increased in a specific location, for instance by the self-assembly of molecules to make a living organism; when one takes the total system including the environment into consideration, there is always a net increase in entropy. Also bear in mind that no isolated system of any kind, and without any guidance also exhausted of being superbly directed, call it life or anything that you wish, could possibly run its course for 4.54 billion years and not become entirely eradicated.

In the meanwhile, now the strongest of our ancestors have managed to get us to where we currently are, as Darwin's survival of the fittest theory states, which signifies the fittest of all creatures, including us people, have successfully managed to transfer their genes, and since we have steadily resin from ape to man.

Some anthropologist and other related fields believe we are here because the most conservative of us all did manage to stay alive to convey their genes, which contradicts Darwin's aggressive behaviors of the fittest. So many also question and say, "from monkey to man, from man to what?"

I am also wondering if evolution has graduated our predecessors from ape to man and progressively turned monkeys to human beings, why then are so many monkeys and apes still around? Perhaps evolution has cursed some of their forefathers, denying them the right of becoming full-fledged humans, and since has excluded them to benefits from what evolution has to offer. If yes, why? I am not being sarcastic, as these questions and millions other should pop into any sensible mind.

WE SURE ARE ALL IN A BUBBLE

Civil life requires civil manner; we cannot have a modern life with primitive behaviors. We must not let industrialization to iron out our mind and mold us into senseless, soulless, and cold machines depleted of humanistic characters, where cruelty can become the norm in absence of compassion and caring.

And as technology progresses and intensifies, it can influence us into acting "robot-like" which in all honesty plenty of alarming socio-cultural and socio-political, and socio-economical signs are activated as they already have infected our thoughts, and in how we see the world. Because often our collective action is so far off from decency in mind and manner and shifted away from what it manifests as correct paradigms in which if righteous deeds are applicable, they can free us from troublesome, toxic, and superfluous (non-essential, not necessary) environment, they can extricate humanity from acting inhumane. Which one should be reminded of the presence of God in everything that one does. And as Rumi the Persian poet, jurist, theologian, and mystic Sufi said:

If in thirst you drink water from a cup, you see God in it. Those who are not in love with God will see only their own faces in it All day I think about it, then at night, I say it. Where did I come from, and what am I supposed to be doing? I have no idea. My soul is from elsewhere, I'm sure of that, and I intend to end up there.

Your task is not to seek for love, but merely to seek and find all the barriers within yourself that you have built against it. Silence is an ocean. Speech is a river. Silence is the language of God, all else is a poor translation.

Out beyond ideas of wrongdoing and right doing, there is a field. I will meet you there. The breeze at dawn has secrets to tell you; don't go back to sleep. You must ask for what you really want; don't go back to sleep. People are going back and forth across the doorsill where the two worlds touch. The door is round and open. Don't go back to sleep.

"When I am with you, we stay up all night.

When you're not here, I can't go to sleep.

Praise God for those two insomnias!

And the difference between them." Let the beauty of what you love to be what you do. It should be wisely noted that: contemporary life has weaved us into oneness and as evidenced the repercussion of our conducts do immediately effect even the furthest of the globe culturally, politically and financially as the impact of wrong decisions by the mighty is worst on the poverty-stricken societies. And for those most deprived, this should relentlessly remind us of the improper judicious, and often unjustified human criterions, and to warn us all that yes, we do live in a bubble now which can burst at any time if we keep on misbehaving.

EXISTENCE OF GOD

The being of God is a topic of debate that requires philosophical mastery and scholarly information in religious, popular culture, and faith-oriented subjects, where the power of reasoning and inference needs to play a convincing role, since no one has seen or talked to God. A wide range of controversy in metaphysical arguments for the existence or denial of God, leveraged via empirical, logical, or subjective matters, even with scientific issues, have been raised through the course of human history. Epistemology (the nature and scope of knowledge) in philosophy, science, and vast ontological information (study of the nature of existence), is needed to adequately present the "theory of value," to intelligently manifest the perfection of God.

Plato and Aristotle were the pioneers in Western philosophical culture that set forth the discussion for the existence of God, which now will be regarded as the cosmological argument; Ibn Sina, Ibn Rushd (Averroes), Ajuwayani, Alghazali, Thomas Aquinas, Rene Descartes, John Calvin, were among many classical philosophers whom they intelligently argued for a necessary supreme being.

It was Rene Descartes who stated that the being of a benevolent God is logically necessary for the evidence of senses to be meaningful. Ibn Rushed talked about a fine-tuned universe needing an infinitely intelligent tuner; so did Ibn Sina talk about the unmoved mover in the kalam argument. It was John Calvin who argued for a "sensus divinitatis," which renders human beings with the knowledge for the existence of God, and St. Anselm who put forth the first ontological argument.

Philosophers who argued against the being of God include <u>Immanuel Kant</u>, <u>David Hume</u>, <u>Friedrich Nietzsche</u>, and <u>Bertrand Russell</u>. In modern culture, the question of God's existence has been discussed by scientists such as Francis Collins, <u>Stephen Hawking</u>, Richard Dawkins, <u>Lawrence M. Krauss</u>, Sam Harris, <u>Carl Sagan</u>, <u>Neil deGrasse Tyson</u>, <u>John Lennox</u>, and as well as philosophers including <u>Richard Swinburne</u>, Rebecca Goldstein, <u>Alvin Plantinga</u>, Edward Feser, <u>William Lane Craig</u>, <u>A. C. Grayling</u>, David Bently Hart, <u>Daniel Dennett</u>, Neils Bohr, Sigmund Freud, and Peter Higgs.

Scientists comply with the scientific means, within which theories must hold truth via <u>physical experiment</u>, by material evidence. The overall conception of God posits a being which can absolutely not be examined. Hence, the questions concerning the existence of God, for which no evidence can be tested, may by definition lie outside the horizon of contemporary science.

The commencement of many religions affirms that knowledge of the existence of God is the natural light of human reason. They are faith-oriented beliefs that assert that belief in the existence of God is not compliant to proof or rebuttal, but based on <u>faith</u> alone. Classical theism believes in God as the omnipotent, omnipresent, benevolent, transcendent, and metaphysically ultimate being, a timeless, absolutely sovereign being who is bereft (devoid) of all anthropomorphic qualities. This differs from other ideas like open theism, process theism, theistic personalist, and classical theism, which do not accept that God can be wholly defined. They believe it would discredit the <u>transcendent</u> truth of God for simple humans to define him. Robert Barron says by analogy that "it seems impossible for a two-dimensional object to conceive of three-dimensional humans."

<u>Ibn Rushd,</u> a twelfth-century Islamic scholar, philosopher, and physician, explained with rational philosophical argument that there are only two disputations worthy of coherency, both of which are sought in the "Precious Book" (The Qur'an). Rushd cites "providence" and "invention" in using the Qur'an's parables (genres of symbolic literary representation, Allegorical), to claim the existence of God.

Rushd argues that the Earth's weather structured layout is made to support human life; thus, if the planet is so finely tuned to predicate (assert) life, then it suggests a fine-tuner—God. The Sun and the Moon are not just disorderly (random) objects floating in the <u>Milky Way</u>, rather they serve us day and night, and the way nature works and how life is formed, humankind benefits from. Rushd essentially comes to a conclusion that there has to be a higher being who has made everything perfectly to serve the needs of human beings.

Moses ben Maimon, a Jewish scholar, also talked about the heavenly bodies to prove the existence of God. He stated that because every physical object is finite, it can only contain a finite amount of power. If everything in the universe, which includes all the planets and the stars, is finite, then there has to be an infinite power propelling everything in the universe. He believed the only thing that can describe the motion in all things is an infinite being (meaning God), which is neither a body nor a force in the body. Maimonides believed this argument gives us the premises to know that God, but not an idea of what God is. He believed that God cannot be comprehended or be compared.

Abrahamian's religions of Judaism, Christianity, and Islam encourage preamble faith presupposing belief in God and the immortality of the soul, since any other approach including science, philosophy and other analogies do fall short in proving the existence of God.

St. Paul made this debate when he said that pagans should be without excuse because "since the creation of the world God's invisible nature, namely, his eternal power and deity, has been clearly perceived in the things that have been made." In this Paul implied to the proofs for a Creator, later enunciated by St. Thomas, and others, also originally employed by the Greek philosophers.

Other apologetically school of thoughts inaugurated by Cornelius Van Til, known as Presupposition apologetics, or "transcendental" view of God. The principle difference between this doctoring of thought and the more classical evidentialist is that the presupposition list rejects any common denominator between those who believe in God and the nonbeliever, since the nonbeliever denies the assumption of the truth of the theistic view of the world.

Presupposition lists do not accept that the being of God can be substantiated by beseeching to callous, ceaselessly rough facts, which have similar postulated (theoretical, presumed but not proven) sensing for those masses with a primarily different world-vision, as they discredit such a condition is even possible. They say that proof for the existence of God is the very same belief necessary for condition to the intelligibility of all other human experience and action.

They try to prove the existence of God by referencing transcendental importance, the vitality of this belief indicates that all human intelligence, experiences, knowledge, action, (even the situation of unbelief, itself) is the proof for the existence of God. Because God's existence the necessary requirement for their intelligibility.

What Does Modal Logic Mean?

Modal logic is a kind of logical debate that utilizes words like 'possible' and 'necessary' to reach a conclusion.

Plantinga's Modal Ontological Argument

Here's how it breaks down:

1. If God exists, he must exist necessarily
2. Either God exists necessarily or he doesn't
3. If God doesn't have necessary existence, then he necessarily doesn't

Therefore,

4. Either God has necessary existence, or he necessarily doesn't
5. If God necessarily doesn't have necessary existence, then God necessarily doesn't exist

Therefore:

6. Either God has necessary existence, or he necessarily doesn't exist
7. It is not the case that God necessarily doesn't exist

Therefore,

8. God has necessary existence
9. If God has necessary existence, then God exists

Therefore,

10. God exists

Many spiritual people believe that the deduction and philosophical disputation for and against the existence of God does not grasp the point. The word God, which is interpreted in many cultures and history, does not accord with the beings whose existence is justified by such arguments, assuming they are worthy. The real question is not whether, an "uncaused first cause" or, the omnipotent, omnipresent, and the most benevolent God exists.

The real inquiry should be whether Krishna, Zeus, Chinese Shangdi, Sikhism, Christian Yahweh, Jehovah, Allah, or other Gods exist.

And if so, which one, out of thousands of gods sermonized, is the real God? Millions if not billions of the so-called theists do not seem to have an agreement on the only transcendental God that is beyond space and time, and the only cause for all there is, and all there ever will be.

How God is discussed should be of concern, when often no intelligence and cultural dynamics are available to wisely adhere to reasoning power for knowing God, as time parameter should also raise an issue, as most religion's manifestos have originated in the old times, lacking compatibility with evolution trend of thoughts and robust views on philosophical and modern scientific analogies. They demand inference and competency in theoretical proof to correctly argue the premises of God.

Many theists from monotheistic faiths believe their God is the "Henotheism" (most perfect being) from Greek (henos theos, meaning 'one god') and they worship a single God while not denying the existence or possible existence of other deities. Human salvation can only take place in Heaven above, through what some of them prejudicially preach against the others, and vice versa, and no other God is any good.

This hypocrisy of beliefs has led to so many uncivilized behaviors and violence, beyond anyone's imagination, lacking empathy, in which compassion should play a key role in faith-based entities to help others, regardless of who they are and what they believe in.

Most of these arguments do not resolve the issue of which of these Godheads is more probable to exist, since these debates fail to show the difference between immanent gods and a transcendent God.

For the past couple of centuries, many religions, especially the monotheistic faiths, have been subjected to a relentless bombardment of criticism from scientists who have challenged that many historical religious views are wrong; that the universe, and human beings as well, evolved—they were not created; that many religiously based statements of the universe are primitive and mythological; as views on God and man do not comply, and cannot be reconciled with our modem scientific discoveries.

The atheistic conclusion is that the arguments and evidence both show there is insufficient reason to believe that any gods exist. And that believer's subjective religious experiences talk about the human learning, rather than the nature of reality itself; therefore, one has no reason to accept that a god exists.

Some arguments as cosmological, ontological, and theistic' debate stand out among others for proving the existence of God, as they still fall short to adequately prove the existence of God, where faith plays a major role in many religions, since they emphatically express salvation is by having faith in God. The extreme version of this is known as "fideism," which says, if God's existence were rationally evident, then faith in its entirety would become nonessential.

The Cosmological argument

Thomas Aquinas denied the Platonic tie-in of Augustine's theology and constituted his thought on Aristotle. Hence, Aquinas did not bother with "ontological argument," but rebuilt the "cosmological argument." Referencing the question of learning, the difference between these two debates is fundamentally a difference in epistemology.

Augustine believed one can directly go from the soul to God. He did not see the vitality of starting with sensory experiences; but Aquinas deciphered that "The human intellect is at first like a clean slate on which nothing is written" (Summa Theological I, Q:97, 2). It is sensation that writes on the tabula rasa. The mind has no form of its own. All its contents come from sensation; for Aquinas, perception was the key to unraveling the truth about God.

Aquinas initiated with "motion." He argued, it is perceived, as evident to our senses that in our world, some things are in motion. Now, whatever is moved is moved by another, for nothing can be moved except it is in potentiality to that towards which it is moved; whereas a thing moves in as much as it is in act. Motion is the reduction of something from potentiality to actuality.

But nothing can become lessened from potentiality to actuality except by something in a state of actuality. Thus, that which is actually hot, as fire, makes water hot, as water has the potential to be actually hot, and thereby fire moves and changes it, or fire makes wood hot.

Now it is not probable that the same thing could be in potentiality and reality in the same respect, but only in different respects. For what is actually hot cannot synchronously be potentially hot; but it is simultaneously potentially cold. It is therefore impossible that in the same respect and in the same way a thing should be both mover and moved (i.e., that it should move itself.)

Hence, whatever is moved must be moved by another. If that by which it is moved be itself moved, then this also must need to be moved by another, and that by another again. But this cannot go on to infinity, because then there would be no first mover, and consequently no other mover, seeing that eventually movers move only in as much as they are moved by the first mover; as the arrow moves only because it is moved by the hand of the archer, therefore it is necessary to arrive at the first mover, moved by no other, and this everyone realizes to be God.

Thomas Aquinas' intention is to reference a matter of logic, and not a plausible evidence to believe in God. It claims to conclusively prove that God must of necessity exist.

Bear in mind that human intelligence is designed and only potentiated to recognize the traces of God. It is obviously beyond our capability to see God. Is this to say that we will not perhaps one day be able to conquer the universe, as our malleable brain further evolves?

The biological evolution, including human evolution, is basically propelled by environmental changes. Accidental genetic metamorphism (alteration) and innovative outcomes make the successful adaptation possible. Scientists tell us that human evolution started about 7-8 million years ago in the African savannah, where an upright, vertical position became significantly beneficial.

The main reason for improving manual work and tool-making could be to have more food. Our forefathers obtained more meat due to hunting, resulting in more protein and essential fatty acid in the meal. The human nervous system does not proportionally utilize high levels of energy, therefore, a better quality of food was the preliminary reason for the evolution of huge human brain. The size of the human brain was tripled during 3.5 million years; it increased from the average of 450 cm3 of Australopithecinae to the average of 1350 cm3 of Homo sapiens. A genetic alteration in the system controlling gene expression could have occurred approximately 200,000 years ago, which influenced the development of nervous system, the sensorimotor function, and learning capability for motor processes. This is not to believe that the human brain has stopped growing, and that will not further expand.

www.slideshare.net

(Australopithecines are generally all species in the related Australopithecus and Paranthropus genera, and it typically includes Kenyanthropus, Ardipithecus, and Praeanthropus. All these related species are now sometimes collectively classified as a subtribe of the Hominini tribe called Australopithecina.)

I am certain that we sometime in the hereafter will, which should amaze, and alert humanity to forth notice the traces of God as humanity digs more into the so-called nothingness. We should by now know that what we do not see, produces what we see. Our memories, thought process, intelligence, feelings and emotions, our wisdom, and sanity, and hundreds of other things that are not tangible but play an extremely important role in our lives, without which we will not be able to carry on. When a scientist invents and discovers valuable inventions for advancing humanity into the future and for improving human lives, that is admirable. But they cannot not see the mind of their own and the thinking process which materialized the successful result, they can only see the effect of what they have created. We are inhibited to pass the space and time, and to see the almighty God. Simply, because is beyond human brain, and the entire nervous system to decipher that.

"Man is the measure of all things" – Protagoras

Having faith plays a very imperative role in our lives. It engages us consciously, especially in crucial times. It is an intangible agenda that will also subliminally affects us, even if we stubbornly refuse to think about it, which I am afraid is taken for granted.

"We are too weak to discover the truth by reason alone" – St. Augustine

Life for millions often is full of obstacles. Many times we are faced with difficulties in our families, our health, our finances, our work, and a host of other issues. We can either overcome our barriers, or barriers can overtake us. Having faith in God will most definitely help us to fight our way through in difficult times.

Almost everything we do is faith-oriented, when in front line defending our homeland, we expect to come home safe, we have faith in having a pregnant lady to deliver safely, we have faith in seeing a healthy child is borne. We have faith to land safely when taking a plane to our destination. We have faith when we expect to get home safe or to work, when driving, we have faith to make it, when undergoing a surgery, we have faith to make it when stricken with some type of cancer, or any other malignant disease. We have faith to win when entering a race.

For heaven's sake, we have faith in not choking on a bite we take to eat. And thousands, if not millions of other faith-related issues that we deal with in our lives. For the faithful, faith in God is not casual. Faith in God is the heart and the soul of everything they do, and live for, it is the nervous system of their entire being. Let's not make mistake by acting religiously fanatical, and for having faith; they are not the same. Faith in God is to have compassion and believe in peace and humanity.

To expect science to locate God is to behave as imbecilic as one can be, since science operates in laboratories, where the results of real experimentations are manifested and can only deal what is apparent. Science does not delve into the metaphysical realms. As we are not made to fly, and should not expect wings to exude from either our rear end or from our sides to one-day fly. This is anatomically not possible, except in fiction-oriented movies or books. So is seeing God, as it is just beyond human ability. But, not detecting the magnificent traces of God is utterly unwise, and frankly, should designate poor orientation. Ontological argument

An ontological argument is a philosophically based debate for the existence of God dealing with abstract entities, where philosophy, and other contextual words, like dualism, existentialism, dialectical, epistemology, solipsism, sequitur, transcendentalism, and metaphysics, are also discussed. Many arguments fall under the category of the ontological, and they tend to involve arguments about the state of being or existing. More specifically, ontological arguments tend to start with an a priori theory about the organization of the universe. If that organizational structure is true, the argument will provide reasons why God must exist.

Dualism: philosophy, the idea that human mind has a spiritual, non-material dimension that encompasses consciousness, and probably with an eternal attribute, or Good and evil struggling for supremacy. Dualism doctrine in contrary to idealism and materialism, holds that, reality consists of two basic types of substance normally including mind and matter, or two basic sort of entity, mental and physical.

Dialectical thinking indicates the ability to view issues from multiple perspectives and to arrive at the most efficient and reasonable reconciliation of seemingly contradictory information and postures.

Aiming at dialectical reasoning is the process of arriving at truth via a process of comparing and contrasting various solutions. This process, also known as logic, initiated in classical Greece by the philosopher Aristotle and has evolved into the present through the works of other philosophers such as Hegel.

What is Marx's dialectical materialism?

Dialectical materialism is a philosophical view to reality resulting from the ideas of Karl Marx and Friedrich Engels. For Marx and Engels, materialism meant that the material world, perceptible to the senses, has objective reality independent of mind or spirit.

Epistemology is the study of nature and scope of knowledge and justified belief. It analyzes the nature of knowledge and how it connects to analogous (like) ideas such as truth, belief, and what is justified. It also deals with the means of production of knowledge, as well as skepticism about various knowledge claims.

Epistemology is the study of knowledge. Three epistemological factors associated with knowledge procurement (acquisition) are truth, belief, and justification. Truth is an occurrence in which there are no false propositions. Knowledge itself can be defined as "justified true belief." Epistemology basically is a branch of philosophy that investigates the origin, nature, methods, and limits of human knowledge. The terms used to describe epistemological positions differ based on whether it's explaining the origin or the acquisition of knowledge.

Transcendentalism is an idealistic philosophical and social movement that developed in New England around 1836 in response to rationalism. Influenced by Platonism, romanticism, and Kantian philosophy, it arrived at that divinity impregnates (pervades) all nature and humanity, and its members held progressive views on feminism and communal living. Ralph Waldo Emerson and Henry David Thoreau were central figures. A system developed by Immanuel Kant was based on the notion that in order to understand the nature of reality, one needs first examine and analyze the logical process that governs the nature of experience.

Solipsism from <u>Latin</u> souls, meaning 'alone', and ipse, meaning 'self') is the <u>philosophical</u> idea that only one's own <u>mind</u> is certain to exist. As an <u>epistemological</u> position, solipsism holds that <u>knowledge</u> of anything outside one's own mind is unsure; the <u>external world</u> and <u>other minds</u> cannot be known and might not exist outside the mind. As a <u>metaphysical</u> position, solipsism takes an step further to the conclude that the world and other minds do not exist.

A non sequitur is a closure or response which doesn't follow logically from the previous statement. You've probably heard an example of a non sequitur before, therefore bunny rabbits are way cuter than chipmunks.

Non sequiturs are often utilized for comedic effect in movies, novels, and TV shows. When someone says a non sequitur, it usually means the person was off the subject in her own thoughts and not listening to the other person. Image that one girl says, "I'm worried that my mother is mad at me," and her friend responds, "I wonder what you call a male ladybug?" The non sequitur shows the friend clearly wasn't listening.

Idealism.

The idealist philosopher <u>George Berkeley</u> believed that physical objects do not exist apart from the mind that perceives them. An item in fact exists merely as long as it is observed; otherwise, it is not only senseless (meaningless), but simply fictitious. The observer and the observed are one. Berkeley does try to show things can and do exist separate from the human mind and our recognition, but only because there is an all-encompassing mind in which all ideas are perceived— in other words, God, who observes all. Solipsism agrees that nothing exists outside of perception, but would say that Berkeley falls prey to the <u>egocentric predicament</u>— he can solely make his own observations, and therefore cannot be truly certain that this God or other people exist to see "reality." The solipsist would say it is better to ignore the unreliable observations of alleged other people and rely upon the immediate certainty of one's own perceptions.

Rationalism

<u>Rationalism</u> is the philosophical position that <u>truth</u> is best discovered by the use of reasoning and <u>logic</u> rather than by the use of the senses.

What is the philosophy of existentialism?

Existentialism is a philosophy that highlights individual existence, freedom, and choice. Its main thesis suggests that human beings identify with their own meaning in life, and try to make rational decisions even though they live in an irrational universe. The essence of existentialism suggests that existence predates essence, which is a central claim of existentialism. It opposes the traditional philosophical understanding that the essence (the nature) of a thing is more fundamental and ironclad (unchangeable) than its existence.

It says that man is essentially selfish, that man is a rational being. Sartre saying that "the essence precedes essence" means a personality is not constructed over a previously model designed with exact purpose, contrary to metaphysics that says, "the essence precedes existence." Because it is the one who choose one's own destiny. Sartre does not reject constraining positions of human's existence. In response to Spinoza, who ratified (affirmed) that "man is determined by what surrounds him," Sartre says: an oppressive situation is not unbearable in itself, but when considered intolerable by those who feel oppressed the situation becomes unendurable, so, by literally projecting my intentions onto my present position, "it is I who freely transform it into action."

To say that existence precedes essence is to confirm that there is no such thing as predetermined essence to be located in humans, and that an individual's essence is defined by the individual through how that individual defines and lives his or her life. As Sartre puts it in his Existentialism is a Humanism: "Man first of all exists, encounters himself, surges up in the world – and defines himself afterwards."

Ibn Sina was actually the first proponent of the Ontological argument (980-1037), it was Ibn Sina who articulated a proof for the existence of God within a priori premise. existence even though It is common to know Anselm of Canterbury (1033-1109) the first advocator of the Ontological Argument. An ontological debate is a philosophical argument for the existence of God that utilizes ontology. Many arguments are constituted under the category of the ontological, and they mean to manifest arguments about the state of being or existing. Particularly ontological discussion tend to start with an a priori theory about the organization of the universe. If that organizational edifice is true, the argument will substantiate the reasons for God's existence.

The first ontological discussion in the Western Christian tradition was suggested by Anselm of Canterbury in his 1078 work Pros logion. Anselm explained God as "that than which nothing greater can be thought," and argued that this being must exist in the mind, even in the mind of the person who denies the existence of God. He believed that, if the greatest possible being exists in the mind, it must also exist in reality. If it only exists in the mind, then an even greater being must be possible—one which exists both in the mind and in reality. Therefore, this greatest possible being must exist in reality. René Descartes the seventeenth century French Philosopher concocted an equivalent argument of a supremely perfect being. the early eighteenth century, Gottfried Leibniz augmented Descartes' ideas in an attempt to prove that a "supremely perfect" being is a coherent concept. In the early eighteenth century, Gottfried Leibniz augmented Descartes' ideas tried to prove that a "supremely perfect" being is a coherent concept. Other arguments have been categorized as ontological, including those made by Islamic philosophers Mulla Sadra and Allama Tabatabai.

Later, Thomas Aquinas rejected the argument on the basis that humans cannot know God's nature. Also, David Hume offered an empirical objection, criticizing its lack of evidential reasoning and rejecting the idea that anything can exist necessarily. Immanuel Kant's critique was based on what he saw as the false premise that existence is a predicate. He argued that "existing" adds nothing (including perfection) to the essence of a being, and thus a "supremely perfect" being can be conceived not to exist. Finally, philosophers including C. D. Broad dismissed the coherence of a maximally great being, proposing that some attributes of greatness are incompatible with others, rendering "maximally great being" incoherent.

☑ The traditional definition of an ontological argument was given by Immanuel Kant.

He contrasted the ontological argument (literally any argument "concerned with being")[3] with the cosmological and physio-theoretical arguments. According to the Kantian view, ontological arguments are those founded on a priori reasoning.

Anselm of Canterbury was the first to attempt an ontological argument for God's existence.

Main article: Pros logion

Theologian and philosopher Anselm of Canterbury (1033–1109) proposed an ontological discussion in the second and third chapters of his Pros logion. Anselm's debate was not shown in order to prove God's existence; rather, Pros logion was a job of meditation in which he presented the idea of God as self-evident to him.

In Chapter 2 of the Pros logion, Anselm defined God as a "being than which no greater can be conceived." He suggested that even "the fool" can understand this concept, and this understanding itself means that the being must exist in the mind. The concept must exist either only in our mind, or in both our mind and in reality. If such a being exists only in our mind, then a greater being—that which exists in the mind and in reality—can be comprehended (this argument is generally considered as a reductio ad absurdum, because the view of the fool is proven to be inconsistent). Hence, if we can conceive of a being than which nothing greater can be conceived, it must exist in reality. Thus, a being than which nothing greater could be procreated, which Anselm sees as God, must exist in reality.

Anselm's argument summarizes that

It is a conceptual truth (or, so to speak, true by definition) that God is a being than which none greater can be envisaged (that is, the greatest possible existence that can be imagined).

God exists as a notion in the mind.

A being that exists as a concept in the mind and in reality is, other things being equal, greater than a being that exists only as an idea in the mind.

Thus, if God exists only as an idea in the mind, then we can imagine something that is greater than God (that is, a greatest possible being that does exist).

But we cannot imagine something that is greater than God (for it is a contradiction to suppose that we can imagine a being greater than the greatest possible being that can be imagined.)

Therefore, God exists.

In Chapter 3, Anselm presented a further argument in the same vein:

By definition, God is a being than which none greater can be imagined.

A being that necessarily exists in reality is greater than a being that does not necessarily exist.

Thus, by definition, if God exists as an idea in the mind but does not necessarily exist in reality, then we can imagine something that is greater than God.

But we cannot imagine something that is greater than God.

Thus, if God exists in the mind as an idea, then God necessarily exists in reality.

God exists in the mind as an idea.

Therefore, God necessarily exists in reality.

This contains the notion of a being that cannot be conceived not to exist. He argued that if something can be conceived not to exist, then something greater can be conceived. Consequently, a thing than which nothing greater can be conceived cannot be conceived not to exist and so it must exist.

René Descartes

French thinker René Descartes proposed several arguments that could be termed ontological.

René Descartes (1596–1650) proposed a number of ontological arguments, which differed from Anselm's formulation. Generally speaking, they are less formal arguments than natural intuition.

Descartes wrote in the <u>Fifth Meditation</u>:

But, if the mere fact that I can produce from my thought the idea of something entails that everything that I clearly and distinctly perceive to belong to that thing really does belong to it, is not this a possible basis for another argument to prove the existence of God? Certainly, the idea of God, or a supremely perfect being, is one that I find within me just as surely as the idea of any shape or number. And my understanding that it belongs to his nature that he always exists is no less clear and distinct than is the case when I prove of any shape or number that some property belongs to its nature.

Descartes argued that God's existence can be deduced from his nature, just as <u>geometric</u> ideas can be deduced from the nature of shapes—he used the deduction of the sizes of angles in a triangle as an example. He suggested that the concept of God is that of a supremely perfect being, holding all perfections. He seems to have assumed that existence is a predicate of a perfection. Thus, if the notion of God did not include existence, it would not be supremely perfect, as it would be lacking a perfection. Consequently, the notion of a supremely perfect God who does not exist, Descartes argues, is unintelligible. Therefore, according to his nature, God must exist.

Gottfried Leibniz

German philosopher Gottfried Leibniz attempted to prove the coherence of a "supremely perfect being."

<u>Gottfried Wilhelm Leibniz</u> saw a problem with Descartes' ontological argument: that Descartes had not asserted the coherence of a "supremely perfect" being. He proposed that, unless the coherence of a supremely

perfect being could be demonstrated, the ontological argument fails. Leibniz saw perfection as impossible to analyses; therefore, it would be impossible to demonstrate that all perfections are incompatible. He reasoned that all perfections can exist together in a single entity, and that Descartes' argument is still valid.

Mulla Sadra

Transcendent theosophy

Mulla Sadra (c. 1571/2 – 1640) was an Iranian Shia Islamic philosopher who was influenced by earlier Muslim philosophers such as Avicenna and Suhrawardi, as well as the Sufi metaphysician Ibn 'Arabi. Sadra discussed Avicenna's arguments for the existence of God, claiming that they were not a priori. He rejected the argument on the basis that existence precedes essence, or that the existence of human beings is more fundamental than their essence.[26]

Sadra put forward a new argument, known as Seddiqin Argument or Argument of the Righteous. The argument attempts to prove the existence of God through the reality of existence, and to conclude with God's pre-eternal necessity. In this argument, a thing is demonstrated through itself, and a path is identical with the goal. In other arguments, the truth is attained from an external source, such as from the possible to the necessary, from the originated to the eternal origin, or from motion to the unmoved mover. In the argument of the righteous, there is no middle term other than the truth. His version of the ontological argument can be summarized as follows:

There is existence

Existence is a perfection above which no perfection may be conceived

God is perfection and perfection in existence

Existence is a singular and simple reality; there is no metaphysical pluralism

That singular reality is graded in intensity in a scale of perfection (that is, a denial of a pure monism).

That scale must have a limit point, a point of greatest intensity and of greatest existence.

Hence God exists.

Mulla Sadra describes this argument in his main work al-asfar al-arba'a [four journeys] as follows:

Existence

There are two Gods,

There are two Gods in existence. First, the infinitely ethereal (spiritual projection, occult) God that created man, a universally ubiquitous (ever-present) God which is closer to one than one's aorta. The God of the apocalypse (revelation, divine disclosure), love, peace, compassion, kindness, justice, and generosity. And the Other God that is manufactured by man which maneuvers through hypocrisy (the pot calling the kettle black), violence, force, tyranny, genocides, despicably inhumane wars, atrocities, and extreme inequity, all to exert imposition (assignment) for riveting globally classified nations, to exploit and maim solely to ensure maximizing profit. If one cares to meditate on the traces of both Gods, one will be able to clearly discern which one is which, and if so, then enlightenment can prevent moral and spiritual ebb in one's divinity and confessional state of mind. And once this become oriented in one's conscious. It will identify the real culprit, exposing the epidemically disease stricken agent. That is the first step toward collective healing; to further avoid brainwashing, and for eluding against planting fetal mental illness and denial syndrome. Which I am afraid many societies are plotted against, and infected with; where billions live only nominal to God as they behave callous and practice so many misdeeds beyond comprehension, and up to no good criminal activities as if there is no judgment day.

The Cosmological Argument

Everything that exists must have a cause, only correct in our tangible Newtonian's world. Because according to quantum physics things can pop out of nowhere without any cause. Therefore, no flaws by atheists can be materialized in this rather decisive sub-atomic realm. The atheists question that: if God is the cause of everything, then who caused God? Perhaps a make sense question, but certainly not so in the higher realms, since apparently in higher realms no cause is necessary for something to show out of nowhere. Also, you sure cannot pass the bucket and regress to infinity, the bucket must stop at some rather decisive point. Furthermore, Scientists and the mathematicians cannot really calculate infinity as an integer (whole) number or decimal number in their funding's to meaningfully conclude their formulas. Infinity is just a figure of speech, which reason dictates that at least in our material world no open-ended case or idea should make any sense. God created the universe. Nothing can exist outside the universe, but God. Only God can exist outside of time, space, matter and events. Those two things, time and space are really part of the same thing since reason should dictate that: no time can exist without any apace. We can see that we are moving through space, but we cannot see time in the same way, we can only see its effects. And in answering the atheists that why God is an exception to the rules, and why God cannot be seen. we should simply relate that no maker can be seen in one's makings, only the effects and the awesome traces left by the creator should be noticed. Beside thousands, if not millions of other things cannot be seen starting with one's own mind, emotions, feelings and memories. The effects of the material world on our senses cannot be detected which they impact our nervous system and the brain to manage what we must do daily to get by. Have you ever wondered who are you? And if you are inside of you, and where should you be found or seen? look all you want and search for oneself with the most advanced magnifier and try to find you. I am not talking about the apparent physical you with a bunch of muscles, nerves, blood and bones. I am talking about the real you, the one that thinks, feels, falls in love, fears, plays, laughs, cries, is occasionally sad, and perhaps often happy. There are things that are simply above and beyond our human brain and the nervous system to answer. Further, to conceive of God as not existing is not to propagate (procreate, conceive) God.

The Theological argument is that:

The coherency in things is for serving a purpose (for instance, all the complex parts of a watch that allows it to keep time), we need to know that they had a designer who designed them with the function in mind; they are immensely improbable to have arisen by random physical procedures. Saying (A hurricane blowing through a hardware store could not assemble a watch.) Organs of living things, like the eye and the heart, cohere because they have a purpose (for example, the eye has a cornea, lens, retina, iris, eyelids, and so on, which are found in the same organ only because together they make it possible for the animal to see. Further, these things and millions of other products did not have a human designer, hence, they must have had a non-human designer, God. God exists.

The Argument from Irreducible Complexity

Evolution has no ability to predict since each and every piecemeal (gradual, incremental) step must be a progress over the preceding one, letting the organism to subsist and regenerate better than its competitors. In many complicated organs, the removal or metamorphosis (modification) of any part would annihilate the entire functionality of the organ. For instance, the lens and retina of the eye, the molecular components of blood clotting, and the molecular motor powering the cell's flagellum. Call these organs "irreducibly complex." These organs could not have been beneficial to the organisms that possessed them in any simpler forms. The Theory of Natural Selection cannot explain these irreducibly complex systems.

Molecular biology has shown that even the simplest of all living systems on the earth today, bacterial cells, are exceedingly complex objects. Although the tiniest bacterial cells are incredibly small, weighing less than 10-12 gms, each is in effect a veritable micro-miniaturized factory containing thousands of exquisitely designed pieces of intricate molecular machinery, made up altogether of one hundred thousand million atoms, far more complicated than any machine built by man and absolutely without parallel in the nonliving world." — Michael Denton, Evolution: A Theory In Crisis

Michael Behe quote" in Darwin's time all of biology was a black box: not only the cell, or the eye, or digestion, or immunity, but every biological structure and function because, ultimately, no one could explain how biological processes occurred. Michael Behe Time, Black, Eye, Biology, Box, Explain Proteins are the machinery of living tissue that builds the structures and carries out the chemical reactions necessary for life".

The Argument from the Paucity (scarcity, deficiency) of mild Mutations.

Evolution is haphazardly done without conscious decision, or so to speak occurred by random mutations and through natural selection. And since the organism is complicated unlikely systems. Then, by the laws of probability, any change is staggeringly more promising to be for the worse than for the better. The greater numbers of mutation would be detrimental for the organism. Furthermore, the amount of time it would consume for all the benign mutations to assemble an organ to be revealed is ludicrously long time. Therefore, something external, something outside of evolution (the prime Mutator) had to favor the process of mutation, appreciating the number of benign ones, to superintend the evolution to function. The only entity that is both infinitely powerful and purposeful enough to be the essential Mutator is God.

"New mutations don't create new species; they create offspring that are impaired."

— Lynn Margulis

"Life did not take over the world by combat, but by networking."

— Lynn Margulis, Micro cosmos: Four Billion Years of Microbial Evolution

"Natural selection eliminates and maybe maintains, but it doesn't create... Neo-Darwinists say that new species emerge when mutations occur and modify an organism. I was taught over and over again that the accumulation of random mutations led to evolutionary change [which] led to new species. I believed it until I looked for evidence."

— Lynn Margulis

The modern argument from The Original Replicator

It says that evolution is the protrusion (progression) by which an organism evolves from simpler progenitors. Evolution by itself cannot answer how the original archetype — the first living thing — came into existence. The theory of natural selection can accord with this problem solely by manifesting that the first living thing evolved out of non-living matter. That non-living matter (call it the Original Replicator) must be capable of first self-replication, second by producing a practical mechanism out of surrounding matter to protect itself against breaking down, and third, surviving moderate mutations to itself which then will result in fairly different duplicators. The Original Replicator is complicated. The Original Replicator is too byzantine (elaborate, complex) to have hatched from purely physical processes. For instance, DNA, which presently holds the replicated design of organisms, cannot be the Original Replicator, because DNA molecules require a complex system of proteins to remain stable and to replicate, and could not have been born from natural processes before intricate life existed. Natural selection cannot explain the complexity of the Original Replicator. The Original Replicator must have been created rather than have been evolved.

Argument from an unjust point of view.

The argument against God is that the universe seems to be unbelievably brutal and unfair. But how anyone can get this idea of just and unjust? One does not call a line crooked unless one has some concept of a straight line. What is a man comparing this universe with when he/she refers to it as unjust? If the entire show was evil and in vain why did a man who is supposed to be part of the show, find himself in such a fierce reaction against it? Of course one could have given up one's idea of justice by saying it was nothing but a fad, some sort of fancy and wishful thinking. But if so, then the argument against God collapses too–for the argument leans on saying the world was truly unjust. Thus, in the very act of trying to prove that God did not exist and that the entire reality was senseless – one should find that one had to assume one part of reality – namely one's

GOD, MAN, AND THE UNIVERSE

concept of justice – was making a lot of sense. If the whole universe has no meaning, we should never have figured out that it has no meaning: just as, if there was no intelligence in the universe we wouldn't have known about ignorance, or if no goodness in the universe, we wouldn't have known about evil, if no light in the universe and hence no creatures with eyes, we could never have realized it was dark. Dark would be with no meaning.

The fine tuning of the universe.

There are a monumental number of physically potential universes. A universe that would be user friendly to the appearance of life must comply with some very severe situations: Everything from the mass ratios of atomic particles and the number of dimensions of space to the cosmological domain that govern the augmentation of the universe must be just precise for stable galaxies, solar systems, planets, the entire universe and complex life to evolve. The percentage of possible universes that would support life is minuscule. Our universe is one of those diminutively improbable universes. Our universe has been fine-tuned to sustain life. There is a Fine- purposeful Tuner.

Example: neutrons are just a tad heavier than protons. If it were the other way around, atoms couldn't exist, because all the protons in the universe would have decayed into neutrons shortly after the big bang. No protons, then no atomic nucleuses and no atoms. No atoms, no chemistry, no life. Like Baby Bear's porridge in the story of Goldilocks, the universe seems to be just right for life." — Paul Davies

The Argument from the Beauty of Physical Laws

Scientists utilize aesthetic axiom (simplicity, symmetry, elegance) to concoct the laws of nature. They could only use aesthetic principles successfully if the laws of nature were orderly, intrinsically and objectively beautiful. The laws of nature are inherently and equitably beautiful Only a beautiful mind-like being with an appreciation for beauty could have designed the disciplinary physical laws of nature. God is the only being with the power and purpose to design beautiful laws of nature.

The Argument from Cosmic Coincidences

The universe includes so many eerie (unearthly, spooky, uncanny) coincidences, like the diameter of the moon, as observed from the earth, which is the same as the diameter of the sun when is noticed from the earth. That is why we can have exhibition eclipses (when the sun looks like it is completely or partially covered with a dark circle because the moon is between the sun and the earth.) when the corona (a bright circle seen around the sun or the moon) of the sun is shown. Synchronies (coincidences, coexistence) are by definition exceedingly improbable. The overwhelmingly improbable defy all statistical elucidation. These coexistences are such as to ameliorate (enrich, enhance) our petrified appreciation for the beauty of the natural world. Such uncanny coincidences are only possible by an Omnipotent, Omnipresent, Omniscient God. it seems in every situation in which we notice a pattern, someone purposefully set the pattern in our universe to be visualized. Illustrious among the uncanny coincidences that should be injected into this debate are those relating to numbers. Numbers are enigmatic (mystic) to us since they are not physical objects like gravels, chairs, and cars, but simultaneously they seem to be real entities, ones that we can't conjure up with any properties we fancy but that have their own requisite(needful) properties, meaningfulness and relations. Hence, they must, however, exist outside us. We are therefore inclined to attribute magical might to them. And, given the infinity of numbers and the enormous possible ways to make them applicable to our world.

The Argument from Personal Coincidences

Many people experience eerie coincidences in everyday living (for instance, someone you knew long time ago calling you out of the blue just when you're thinking of him or her; or a dream about an episode(event) that proves to have just occurred, or you or a loved one happens to miss a flight which then crashes leaving no one alive. Uncanny Synchronizes (coexistence) cannot be explained by the laws of probability. They are inexplicable but play a significant role in our lives. It sure seems they are as laser likely précised as they are dictated from out of this world. That is why they are known as uncanny behaviors.

The Argument from Answered Prayers

Prayers and curses are energy-oriented thoughts, so is our universe, as people's emotions and feelings are intangible issues as is the prevalent energy in the universe. peoples power of intention has the potential to comply with a prevalently awakened universe which it seems reads people's mind and one's earnest request. which of- course those prayers or curses must justly take place, and not randomly. The reward or the punishment need to be justifying, and not done haphazardly or by coincidence. When a heart-broken mother prays for the life of her only dying child and the child recovers, that is the true power of intention. The well-known phrase that says: what goes around comes around, has infinitely been experienced through the course of human history. It is a definite fact and not just an empty promise. There are many occasions that people have survived death. Patients who flat-line under surgery, or during medical emergencies have indicated an experience of being floated overseeing their bodies and noticed a glimpse of a gloriously shining passage to the other side, all taking place while even being pronounced dead. This out of body experience entails the existence of an immaterial soul.

Argument from Mathematical Reality

Mathematical facts are requisitely true. (There is no probable world in which, can say, 4 plus 4 does not equal 8, or in which the square root of 2 can be expressed as the ratio of two whole numbers. The truths that explain our material world, no matter how elemental (basic, fundamental), are empirical, requiring observational adduce (evidence.) For instance, when waiting for some experimental means to examine string theory, so that we can figure out whether we live in a world of eleven dimensions. Truths that demand empirical evidence are not necessary truths. We request empirical proof because there are probably worlds in which these are not truths, and so we have to test that ours is not such a world. The truths of our physical world are not necessary truths. The facts of our material world cannot explain mathematical truths. Mathematical truths exist on a different realm of existence from physical truths, only something which itself exists on a different plane of existence from the physical can elaborate and describe mathematical truths. Only God can explain mathematical truths. Mathematics is derived through pure reason — what the philosophers call a priori reason — which means that it cannot be debunked by any empirical scrutiny.

The basic question in philosophy of mathematics is: how can mathematics be true but not empirical? Is it because mathematics explains some trans-empirical reality — as mathematical realists accept — or is it because mathematics has no gratification at all and is a purely formal bet agreeing with postulated (posit, stipulate, hypothesis) rules and their consequences? The Argument from Mathematical Reality assumes, in its third premise, the position of mathematical realism, which isn't a sophistry (paradox, fallacy) in itself; many mathematicians believe it, some of them arguing that it follows from Gödel's incompleteness theorems This debate, however, goes further and tries to infer (deduce, conclude) God's being from the trans-empirical existence of mathematical reality.

Trinity Foundation hereby grants permission to all readers to download, print, and distribute on paper or electronically any of its Reviews, provided that each reprint bears our copyright notice, current addresses, and telephone numbers, provided that all such reproductions are distributed to the public without charge. The Reviews may not be sold or issued in book form, CD-ROM form.

It is noteworthy to know that the idea of ethical monotheism, which believes that morality is only possible, coming from God alone, and that its laws are unfaltering, was first instituted in Judaism, but is now a core theology of most modern monotheistic religions, not excluding Zoroastrianism, Christianity, Islam, Sikhism, and the Baha'i faith.

Søren Kierkegaard argued that objective knowledge, such as 1+1=2, is unimportant to existence. If God could rationally be proven, his existence would be unimportant to humans. It is because God cannot rationally be proven that his existence is important to us.

In The Justification of Knowledge, the Calvinist theologian Robert L. Raymond argues that believers should not try to prove the existence of God. He believes all such proofs are basically fallacious and believers should not place their confidence in them, much less resort to them in discussions with nonbelievers; rather, they should accept the content of revelation by faith. Raymond's position is similar to that of his mentor,

Gordon Clark, which says that all worldviews are fundamentally based on certain unprovable first parlor (premises, axioms), and consequently are end-all (ultimately) indemonstrable.

Positive atheism (also called "strong atheism" and "hard atheism") is a form of atheism that avow (affirm) that no pantheon (deities, demigod, goddess) exist. The strong atheist vividly professes the non-existence of gods. Some strong atheists further aver (predicate, say) that the existence of gods is logically impractical, stating that the combination of attributes which God may be declared to have (omnipotence, omniscience, omnipresence, transcendence, Omni-benevolence) are logically contradictory, incomprehensible, or farcical (absurd, ludicrous), and therefore the existence of such a god is a priori false. Metaphysical naturalism is a common worldview affiliated (confederate) with strong atheism.

Negative atheism (also called "weak atheism" and "soft atheism") is any type of atheism other than positive, wherein a person does not believe in the existence of any deities, but does not specifically utter there to be none.

Agnosticism is the behold that the truth value of certain claims—especially rights about the existence of any deity, but also other religious and metaphysical claims—is obscure (not known or unknowable.) Agnosticism as a commodious (broad umbrella) term does not survey one's belief or disbelief in gods; agnostics may still see themselves as theists or atheists.

Strong agnosticism is the belief that it is not possible for human-beings to realize if it is, or not, that any deities exist. Weak agnosticism is the belief that the existence or nonexistence of deities is unknown but not necessarily unknowable.

Agnostic theism is the philosophical view that include both theism and agnosticism. An agnostic theist believes in the existence of a god or God, but accept the basis of this proposition as unknown or inherently unknowable. Agnostic theists may also persist on unawareness regarding the characteristics of the gods they believe in.

Agnostic atheism is a philosophical position that contain both atheism and agnosticism. Agnostic atheists are atheistic since they do not hold a belief in the existence of any deity, and agnostic because they claim that the existence of a deity is either unknowable in principle, or presently not known in truth.

The theologian <u>Robert Flint</u> explains:

If a man has failed to find any good reason for believing that there is a God, it is perfectly natural and rational that he should not believe that there is a God; and if so, he is an atheist, although he assumes no superhuman knowledge, but merely the ordinary human power of judging of evidence. If he goes farther, and, after an investigation into the nature and reach of human knowledge, ending in the conclusion that the existence of God is incapable of proof, cease to believe in it on the ground that he cannot know it to be true, he is an agnostic and also an atheist, an agnostic-atheist—an atheist because an agnostic.

An apatheist is someone who is indifferent, and not interested in accepting, or denying any claims that God or gods exist or do not exist. An apatheist lives as if there are no gods and describes natural <u>phenomena</u> without reference to any deities. The existence of gods is not repudiated, but may be indicated superfluous (nonessential), or worthless; gods neither provide intend to <u>life</u>, nor influence <u>everyday life</u>. Apatheism of <u>apathy</u> and <u>theism</u>) is the attitude of apathy towards the existence or non-existence of god(s). It is more of an attitude rather than a belief, claim, or belief system. An apatheist is someone who does not care, and is not interested in rejecting or believing any claim that gods exist or do not. The existence of God, or god(s) is not refused, but may be indicated not relevant.

Ignosticism and <u>theological no cognitivism</u> are similar although whereas the ignostic utters that "every theological situation presumes too much about the concept of God," the theological no cognitivist claims to have no idea anyhow to label as "a concept of God."

The ignostic (or igtheist) usually concludes that the question of God's existence or nonexistence is not worth arguing about since concepts like "God" are normally not clearly enough explained. Ignosticism or igtheism is the theological discussion that every other theological position (including <u>agnosticism</u> and atheism) presupposes too much about the idea of God and many other theological concepts. It can be described as having two related views about the existence of God. The view that a coherent definition of God must be stated before the question of the existence of God can be meaningfully talked about. Furthermore, if that demarcation is <u>unfalsifiable</u>, the ignostic takes the <u>theological no cognitivist</u> position that the question of the existence of God is basically absurd. In this case, the concept of God is not considered meaningless; the term "God" is considered in vain. The second behold is synonymous with theological no cognitivism, and skips the step of first asking "What is meant by 'God'?" before declaring the original question "Does God exist?" meaningless.

Some prominent philosophers have regarded ignosticism as a variation of agnosticism or atheism, while others have considered it to be unlike. An ignostic says that he is not even able to utter whether he is a theist or an atheist until adequate explanation of theism is rendered.

In the Aristotelian philosophy, God is seen as part of the explanatory structure necessary to support scientific finale, and any powers God own are—strictly speaking—of the natural order that emanate from God's place as creator of nature.

In Karl Popper's philosophy of science, belief in a supernatural God is outside the natural parameter of scientific research since all scientific hypotheses must be falsifiable in the natural world. The view suggested by Stephen Jay Gould also believes that the existence (or otherwise) of God is not relevant to and is beyond the territory of science.

Logical positivists such as Rudolf Carnap and A. J. Ayer believe any sought talk of gods as literal humbug. For the logical positivists and followers of similar schools of thought, proposition about religious or other transcendent experiences cannot have a truth value, and are deemed to be without making sense, because such statements do not have any vivid verification standard. As the Christian biologist Scott C. Todd says "Even if all the data pointed to an intelligent designer, such a hypothesis is excluded from science because it is not naturalistic." This argument limits the territory of science to the empirically observable and limits the domain of God to the unprovable.

John Polkinghorne beholds that the closest analogy to the existence of God in physics is the ideas of quantum mechanics which are seemingly paradoxical (offending against logic) but make sense of a great deal of different data.

Alvin Plantinga compares the question of the existence of God to the question of the existence of other minds, believing both are notoriously impossible to "prove" against a resolute doubter.

Other philosophers, like Wittgenstein, suggest what is known as anti-realist and oppose philosophical discussion related to God's existence. For instance, <u>Charles Taylor</u> argues that the real is whatever will not go away, and not quiescent (inactive, dormant) from talks of existence. If we cannot reduce talk about God to anything else, or replace it, or prove it bogus, then may be God is as real as anything else.

<u>George Berkeley</u> contended that a "naked thought" cannot exist, and that a perception is a thought; therefore only minds can be ascertain to exist, since all else is just an idea transmitted by a perception. From this Berkeley argued that the universe is based upon observation and is non-objective, it is not based on facts, rather than feelings or opinions. However, he noted that the universe includes "ideas" no discernible to mankind, and that there must, therefore, exist an omniscient super observer, which perceives such things. Berkeley considered this proof of the existence of the Christian God.

<u>C.S. Lewis</u>, in <u>Mere Christianity</u> and elsewhere, nurtured the <u>argument from desire</u>. He suggested that all natural desires have a natural object. One thirsts, and there exists water to quench this thirst; One hungers, and there exists food to satisfy this hunger. He then argued that the human desire for perfect justice, perfect peace, perfect happiness, and other unseen strongly implies the existence of such things, though they seem unobtainable on earth. He further furnished that the unquenchable desires of this life strongly imply that we are purposed for a different life, essentially governed by a God who can purvey the desired intangibles.

Philosophical arguments for the existence of God.

Discussing view from beauty.

One form of the <u>argument from beauty</u> is that the grace of the laws of physics, which have been experimentally contrived, or the <u>elegant laws of mathematics</u>, which are abstract but which have empirically proven to be extremely beneficial, is proof of a <u>creator deity</u> who has set up these things to be beautiful and not ugly.

The <u>argument from consciousness</u> claims that human consciousness cannot be described by the physical mechanisms of the human body and brain, therefore, affirming that there must be non-physical aspects to human consciousness. This is held as not so direct evidence of God, prone to the notions that souls and the afterlife in Judaism, Christianity and Islam would be coherent with such a claim. Critics point out that non-physical aspects of consciousness could exist in a universe without any gods; for example, believe in reincarnation are consonant (agreeable, congenial) with atheism, monotheism, and polytheism.

The idea of the soul was created before contemporary understanding of neural networks and the anatomy of the brain. Decades of experimentation lead cognitive science to consider thought and emotion as physical processes although the experience of consciousness still is not understood. The difficult problem of consciousness stays as to whether different people subjectively experience the environment around them in the same way — for instance, that the color red looks the same inside the minds of different people, though this is a philosophical puzzle with both physical and non-physical descriptions. Aquinas profound ways, arguing for God's existence. First cause, the unmoved mover, argument from contingency, argument from degree, or teleological argument.

In his Summa Theologica, Thomas Aquinas generated his five arguments for God's existence. These disputes are foundered in an Aristotelian ontology and utilizes the infinite regression argument. Aquinas did not mean to fully prove the existence of God as he is orthodoxly conceived (a belief or a way of thinking that is accepted as true, or correct), but proposed his Five Ways as an initial stage, which he concocted upon later in his work. Aquinas' Five Ways argued from the unmoved mover, first cause, necessary being, argument from degree, and the teleological argument.

The unmoved mover argument acknowledges that derived from observation, and experience of motion in the universe (motion being the transition from potentiality to actuality) we can see that there must have been an initial mover. Aquinas debates that, whatever is in motion must be put in motion by another thing, so there must be an unmoved mover.

Aquinas' argument from first cause began with the axiom (assumption) that it is not possible for a being to cause itself (because it would have to exist before it caused itself) and that it is impracticable for there to be an infinite chain of causes, which would result in infinite regress. Therefore, there must be a first cause, itself uncaused.

The argument from <u>necessary being</u> affirms that all subsistence (beings) are <u>contingent</u>, representing that it is possible for them not to exist. Aquinas argued that if everything can possibly not exist, there must have been a time when nothing subsisted; as things are now, there must exist a being with need full existence, regarded as God.

Aquinas argued from degree, indicating the event of estate (degrees of goodness.) He believed that things which are known as good, must be called good in relation to a standard of good—a maximum. There must be a maximum goodness that all other goods can relatively be measured with, an absolute good, which causes all goodness.

The teleological argument affirms the view that things without intelligence are carefully organized, controlled towards a purpose. Aquinas argued that unintelligent objects cannot be ordered unless they are done so by an intelligent being, which conveys that there must be an intelligent being to move objects to their ends: God. The idea of the soul was created before contemporary understanding of <u>neural networks</u> and the physiology of the brain. Decades of experimentation lead <u>cognitive science</u> to consider thought and emotion as physical processes although the experience of consciousness still is not understood. The <u>difficult problem of consciousness</u> remains as to whether different people subjectively experience the environment around them in the same way—for instance, that the color red looks the same inside the minds of different people, though this is a philosophical puzzle with both physical and non-physical descriptions.

Aquinas had profound ways of arguing for God's existence. First cause, the <u>unmoved mover, argument from contingency, argument from degree</u>, or <u>teleological argument</u>.

Subjective argument

The sincere seeker's argument, espoused by Muslim Sufis of the Tasawwuf tradition, posits that every individual who follows a formulaic path towards guidance arrives at the same destination of conviction in the existence of God, and specifically in the monotheistic tenets and laws of Islam. This could only be true if the formula and supplication were being answered by the same divine entity being addressed, as claimed in Islamic revelations. This was formally organized by Imam Abu Hamid Al-Ghazali in such notable works as Deliverance from Error and The Alchemy of Happiness, in Arabic Kimiya-yi sa'adat. The path includes following the golden rule of no harm to others and treating others with compassion, silence or minimal speech, seclusion, daily fasting or minimalist diet of water and basic nourishment, honest wages, and daily supplication towards "the Creator of the Universe" for guidance.

Stephen Hawking and co-author Leonard Mlodinow state in their book The Grand Design that it is reasonable to ask who or what created the universe, but if the answer is God, then the question has merely been deflected to that of who created God. Both authors claim that it is possible to answer these questions purely within the realm of science, and without invoking any divine beings. Christian mathematicians and scientists, most notably Leonhard Euler, Bernard d'Espagnat and Lennox, disagree with that kind of skeptical argument.

A counter-argument against God as the Creator tasks the assumption of the cosmological argument ("chicken or the egg"), that things cannot exist without creators, and applies it to God, setting up an infinite regress. The Grand Design / A Brief History of Time.

In his book The Grand Design, Hawkins's conclusion is precisely contrary to what he stated. Professor Hawkins says the universe is not designed, but appeared out of nothing, and into existence; because of some chancy physical laws that just happen to generate universes at will. Then, in his book A Brief History of Time, he claims that "There is a sound scientific explanation for the making of our world – no Gods required." What Mr. Hawking is actually saying is that science in particular physics, and because of some "laws of physics" we now know everything that is requisite to describe the existence of God, and the existence. Professor Hawking is so extremely focused on the laws of physics, he has become one-track-minded, making him irrelevant to the very laws he is proclaiming. He forgets that no law, or laws can ever create anything, they are discoveries from the womb of mother nature. He, as an award-winning physicist, should be applauded for inventing some of them. It is a universe so finely tuned beyond anyone's imagination which requires a must infinitely intelligent programmer.

Hawking states that the reason the universe requires no creator is because of a "new theory" known as the M-theory, (where "M" stands for "membrane," or "murky"1 it has evolved from "strings" to "membranes," although all forms of the theory leads to extra dimensions (11, in fact). However, M-theory is no single theory, but, rather, a number of theories.

The nature of the universe requires that membranes from M-theory must be on the order of Planck length (10-35 m). Such a dimension is much less than microscopic or even well under subatomic particle proportion. In order to validate such objects, one would need an accelerator of 6,000,000,000,000,000 miles in circumference. It should indicate, therefore, that confirmation of M-theory, based upon observable data, would be impossible. Do such a set of theories that forecast everything but are not verifiable through observational data really fall within the realm of science?

Stephen Hawking says, "Because there is a law such as gravity, the universe can and will create itself from nothing. Spontaneous creation is the reason there is something rather than nothing, why the universe exists, why we exist." However, neither gravity nor any other law of physics delivered a mechanism by which universe can be spontaneously created. professor Hawking, and others alike do not know why laws of physics exist? Although in the quantum world, it is relevant for things such as particles to pop into existence from nothing, it has never been exhibited that non-quantum-sized objects can show such feats. Even if it were possible, why would it be even possible that such laws of physics should exist in the midst of the universes that are supposedly created from nothing? If nothing, means no things, not a thing, then, it utterly couldn't have included any laws of physics, or gravity. Why wouldn't an actual nothing agrees with no laws of physics and no possibility of anything popping into existence? Bear in mind that the skeptics always question "who created God?" Why is it so difficult to know that nothing created God, since they are overwhelmed with believing that the entire universe was created by the potent force of nothing. And as the atheists also accept that a nebulous set of theories, which they cannot be corroborated via observation data, can create an infinite number of universes, having been created from the laws of physics. During the entire course of human history so many idolatrous so-called theories is being manifested to explain God and existence, to no avail.

Just "as Darwin and Wallace explained how the apparently miraculous design of living forms could appear without intervention by a supreme being, the multiverse concept can explain the fine tuning of physical law without the need for a benevolent creator who made the Universe for our benefit. Because there is a law like gravity, the Universe can and will create itself from nothing. Spontaneous creation is the reason there is something rather than nothing, why the Universe exists, why we exist."

They then explain the basic theory behind the "multiverse," which presupposes that multiple universes exist. "According to M-theory, ours is not the only universe. Instead M-theory predicts that a great many universes were created out of nothing. Their creation does not require the intervention of some supernatural being or god. Rather these multiple universes arise naturally from physical law."

The conclusion of what Hawking and Mlodinow are claiming is:

Claim 1: Spontaneous Creation is the reason that there is something rather than nothing, including the Universe; ("Spontaneous creation is the reason there is something rather than nothing, why the Universe exists"). This applies to all universes, meaning it applies to the entire multiverse.

Claim 2: Spontaneous Creation requires the law of gravity; ("Because there is a law of gravity, the Universe can and will create itself from nothing"; "Rather these multiple universes arise naturally from physical law").

Claim 3: The multitude of universes are responsible for producing fine-tuned physical laws ("the multiverse concept can explain the fine tuning of physical law").

The bottom line of what they are finalizing is that you can't have a universe without it being created, you can't have spontaneous creation without physical laws, like the laws of gravity, and you can't have physical laws without a universe.

As Hawking and Mlodinow admit, with no Creation, there is nothing. To have anything -a universe, a multiverse, the cosmos, the law of gravity, "finely-tuned" physical laws, anything, anything at all -you must first have Creation. And they've pretty much proven that "spontaneous" creation is impossible, since it needs physical laws like the law of gravity. So without Creation, the universe/multiverse couldn't create itself.

Hawking and Mlodinow may be outstanding physicists, but they sure have shown themselves to be as poor philosophers and logicians as one can be.

THE GOD WE DO NOT KNOW

According to Mr. Leonard Mlodinow science explores the world as it is offered to the five senses and the brain, while spirituality considers the universe to be purposeful and imbued with meaning. In Mr. Deepak Chopra's view, the great challenge for spirituality is to offer something that science cannot provide, which is the realm of consciousness. The worldviews try to explore cosmos, the physical universe, life, the human brain, and to cultivate the mystery of God and consciousness. The perspectives are to know where the universe came from, where did we come from, what is our purpose here, to delve into human nature and to know where we are going.

To grasp the mysteries of our universe, and perhaps someday learn where the universe is heading. Many scientists, innumerable philosophers, and scholarly minded individuals argue about evolution, genetics, the origin of life, Metaphysics, and so on. What we should the least agree on is that: in the visible world existence breeds existence, that something indubitably (irrefutably, unquestionably) comes from something; the womb of nature is practically impregnated with the reality of cause and effect.

Contrary to the invisible world, the scientists and many prominent physicists tell us that: in the sub-atomic realm something can come out of nothing, that things appear out of nowhere without any apparent reason, and the same thing can appear in several places at the same time. We identify with that as magic which no finer word than "miracle" can describe it better.

It seems such phenomena are exclusively dealt with by the unseen God, where the invisible concurs (be of one mind, be of the same mind) with undetectable. It is not a fiction but a fact that dynamics are resolutely (purposefully, decisively) different in the unseen world, as the environment cannot be controlled and harnessed as they are in our tangible world. In the meanwhile, let's suppose as some people believe, that we have evolved from nothing to a self-aware being, if so, what better word than a miracle can define it.

Further, we should agree on the only God that loves beauty. Just look around you and meditate on the radiance (blush, bloom) of the four seasons. The breathtaking views of natural scenery, and uplifting images of nature with truly unbelievable and dazzling ocean sites holding millions of superlative creatures of the sea. Encompassing scarce and diversified forestry, majestic mountains with amazing valleys. How about millions of pristine landscapes and woods filled with infinitely colorful birds and the bees, conveying so many exotic plants and animals, with incredibly tall and diversified trees, unparalleled blue lagoons, exquisite rivers, and splendid streams.

The astounding view of descending dawn, gorgeous sunrise, and the incredible view of the sunset. The wonderful Twilight which is time span between dawn and sunrise, or between sunset and dusk, that is when the light is still seen in the sky due to sunlight scattering off the atmosphere. The unsurpassed view of the moon, the pleasant blue sky and strikingly delightful stars, and the incomparably alluring rainbow, and so on. We should agree on the infinitely intelligent God, a generous God with magnanimity (bounty), an unbiased endowment that is beyond anyone's imagination.

We should agree on, an infinitely resourceful God, so compassionate and kind; an absolute provider that has created a world of plenty, conveyed with infinite diversity in food, and with fresh air and crystal clear water. We should also realize that: wherever there is an injustice, a ruse, a transgression or a curse like behavior, we must look for a cruel culprit, an ugly spirited character within the human race, or an ignorant one.

We should know the root causes of man's ill fate is because of his/her unawareness, and lack of information, and not to blame God. And because we are made in the image of God, we as well need to pursue beauty, seek wisdom and intelligence, have compassion, be generous, resourceful, kind and considerate. And definitely for one not to do evil, but to act in good will.

Eckhart Tolle said quote" you do not become good by trying to be good, but by finding the goodness that is already within you and allowing that goodness to emerge. But it can only emerge if something fundamental changes in your state of consciousness." Eckhart Tolle further said quote "do not get trapped into ego. Change your state of consciousness, be still and know that I am God."

We shouldn't forget that in the material world our mind can deceive us into believing something that might utterly be false, where I am afraid anomalies can become the norms. This often occurs due to relentless conditioning and deceitful conducts, as a toxic environment is construed to make sure citizens are as conclusively biased to take side with the elites and those in power.

To ascertain that consumers can comply with oligopoly politics, for the people to accord with the unjust market mechanism, and with what the corporate culture has to offer. Forcing the inhabitants to live in a world which is misleading and filled with bogus information, deliberately orchestrated to cover up terrible inequality that has caused so much suffering and havoc for billions of human-beings beyond comprehension.

Comparably, Metaphysics, God and spirituality are non-profit issues and are not supposed to be capital driven. They are over and above human senses, they lie in an invisible realm of infinite possibilities which they need to be felt and innately sought. Spirituality looks toward a transcendent phase that lies in the domain of consciousness; it seeks awareness, purpose and looks for the meaning of life. it was Carl Jung who said quote "who looks outside, dreams; who looks within, awakens."

It shouldn't be so riddling (enigmatic) for anyone to see the prevalent traces of God, unless denial is due to perhaps having so much orgulous (pride), with carrying a chip on one's shoulder not to admit that: we live in a universe that everything we witness, all which we observe, and the invisible world is all sign of the incredible God. And yes, it is so true that mind and human brain addresses neuroscience, and escalates the entire matter of mind and body; but the issues of God and spirituality refers not solely to a pantheon (God, Goddesses, deity), also to the broader term that conceptualizes a divine presence in our universe, and the surpassed. Which implies to the unseen realm that lies beyond our five sense and is the key to infinite possibilities, hoping that one day we can unfold the limitless potential in human consciousness, perhaps enabling mankind to further concur with the unseen.

It is further fair to concord with the fact that I exist. I exist because I can think, and also agree that I am incomplete. How do I know that I am incomplete? I know because I have desires, that I do not possess the absolute knowledge, I do not possess the absolute intelligence, I do not have the absolute wisdom. I do not have the absolute wealth, the absolute power, the absolute beauty, the absolute generosity, or the utter compassion, and do not have the absolute prestige, the absolute goodness, that I am fragmented, and so on, hence, I am not perfect?

And unless there is an absolute goodness, an absolutely perfect being that I could envision in my mind, and be comparably aware of and locate with, I would have not known that I am not complete.

As human beings we are bound to our intelligence, and cannot go over what is in our mind, to exceed beyond what exists in our memory; unless there is an idea of the ultimate and the most perfect being in our thought, we couldn't have known about perfectionism.

That is exactly why we are aware of our imperfection since we are able to know about what is to be-all. we could viscerally (by instinct rather than tutelage) compare; otherwise, it would have been impossible to realize that we are not complete since the idea of something perfect wouldn't have registered in our mind. We are not extraterrestrial, some sort of Martian to perhaps know otherwise. The very reason we know that we are not whole is that the concept of a perfect being exists in our mind, which comparably delineates and makes us aware of the deficiencies that we behold.

There must exist an absolute being, that is why we have in our mind the image of a perfect character that we can identify with since we are able to compare and realize that we are not as perfect. And because the only way to know of one's shortcoming is to comparably know of something which is complete, to perceive that the apogee (apex), the absolute pinnacle of perfection, the absolute crown holder exists.

It should remind and make one aware of such utter apex impression. Otherwise, one would be truly exhausted by its awareness, of its existence. Which then, the impression of an absolutely perfect being would have been beyond anyone's imagination; since one couldn't have any idea or any trace of it in one's mind. It simply couldn't have registered in anyone's mind. As Eckhart Tolle said quote "no human being can behave beyond the level of their consciousness." And I believe when you only see within the eyes, then you are easy to fool.

Therefore, if one has an idea of something, that something, that entity must exist, otherwise it is not possible to be mindful of something that does not exists; even a utopian issue, a visionary subject must have the potential, the possibility to exist, for one to be able to imagine it. Having the idea of God in one's mind is not optional, it is a realistic matter. The idea of a perfect being, an absolutely infallible God is riveted in our sub-conscious mind, and because all other things are solely relative in comparison. It was Einstein that said, "there is a hidden reality underlining our universe and quite different from the world we perceive with our senses."

Leonard Mlodinow "Science has revealed a universe that is vast, ancient, violent, strange, and beautiful, a universe of almost infinite variety and possibility one in which time can end in a black hole, and conscious beings can evolve from a soup of minerals."

Where the stars are so fast that no time can possibly get a chance when facing the black holes since gravity devours everything. It seems in such universe mankind are not so significant, since our lives on the planet earth are the byproduct of physical laws. Laws which they no longer seem to matter in the world of black holes and beyond. This is not to say that man's curiosity to discern the avalanche of questions is ever halted where the profound and innumerable unthinking atoms can become intelligently potentiated, galvanized, awakened and mobilized to discover our origin, and the nature of our universe, and the entire cosmos.

To authenticate our knowledge of "singularity" since there is no physic of any kind to explain singularity. To learn what are we here for, and where are we heading. To understand consciousness, to discover the nature of the atom and our DNA, and know about our physical traits, and in heaven sake how did the planet earth get here. To know if animals are machines, since they unexceptionally are driven by instinct, as if they have been so accurately programmed with no flaws. The question which remains is the reality of action and reaction, the result of natural laws relentlessly maneuvering via cause and effect, or is it something else?

Either our reality is encompassed by the visible universe, or it is not. was the cosmos created from the meaningless void, from an empty space, or was not. is a programmer, or a network of analysts is in charge of this superb, and extremely complex simulated computer known as life, or not? And millions of other viable questions which should halt any genius, or smart Alek scientist not to jump into conclusion about infinitely complex and intriguing existence.

We often pause in silence to learn how our brain a computer made of fatty tissues chemically, and hormonally decides how we feel, genetically determines how we grow, then live and expire, and all taking place with an invisible programmer, an unseen analyst working to create thousands, if not millions of software at the cost of lump sum of meat and fatty cluster exhausted of intelligence, and without central processing unit (CPU). What is so strange is that the neuroscience does widely believe that: the mind does not exist but is the by-product of our brain. What is even more strange is that: human mind hatched science, which ironically denies consciousness, its sole creator. Where scientists who deny consciousness cannot explain why the very basic unit of nature called atom becomes extremely small where matter breaks down and then disappears.

They deny that we are part of the fabric of creation which should be free, and not to become enslaved by an industrial lifestyle where technology can overpower us, as Einstein warned us, quote" "I fear the day that technology will surpass our human interaction. The world will have a generation of idiots." If we reject our self and the power of reasoning and our rationale. We then behave like primates, and eventually become lowered to machines, where we become vulnerable to senseless programming, vailed by greed and material wealth seeking excessive pleasure of the flesh, rather than peace in our mind, which can result in our further complicit behavior, not responding to priorities of living, but acting callous towards essentially decisive matters, where even no human life matters any more.

And sadly enough religion has become part of the problem, many religions try to protect God by killing other believers in the name of the same God that we are meant to honor. Most religions I am afraid they also follow the insane rat race activities to maximize profit, to fill their own pocket at the expense of devotees and millions of believers that worship God, and try to seek sanctuary in the house of God. The organized religion is not the same as spirituality, the organized religion may have discredited itself, but spirituality suffered no such defeat. Religions should tune it down to what make sense, rather than insisting on issues that breeds hatred and superstition.

That is why Darwin's explanation of man's decent from the primates overcomes Genesis, and why millions look into the big bang as the source of cultivating cosmos, rather than to creation myth populated by one, multiple or many Gods.

In which the story of the six blind men and the elephant should prove handy, as it befits the position of many religions.

Blind Men and the Elephant – A Picture of Relativism and Tolerance

The Blind Men and the Elephant is a famous Indian fable that tells the story of six blind sojourners that come across different parts of an elephant in their life journeys. In turn, each blind man creates his own version of reality from that limited experience and perspective. In philosophy departments throughout the world, the Blind Men and the Elephant has become the poster child for moral relativism and religious tolerance.

The Story of the Six Blind Men

One day, six wise blind men were walking in the zoo and accidentally came across an elephant that somehow got out of the cage. The first blind man walked right into the side of the elephant. He touched to either side, but all he could feel was the big body of the elephant.

"Boy," said the first blind man. "I think I must have walked into a wall. "The second blind man was becoming more and more curious about what was taking place. He accidentally walked over to the front of the elephant and touched and latched on to the animal's trunk.

He hastily let go and shouted, "This isn't a wall. This is a snake! We should step back just in case it's toxic and mortally poisonous." The third man hurried to figure out what was happening and to let his friends know what they had run into.

He walked over to the rear end of the elephant and touched the animal's tail. "This is no wall, and this is no snake. You are both mistaking once again. I know for certain that this is a rope."

The fourth man also became curious and knelt down and felt around the elephant's legs, as the tame elephant stood still, he said "My good friends,". "This is no wall and this is no snake. This is no rope either. What we have here, gentlemen is four tree trunks. And I am sure.

The fifth blind man walked up to the front of the elephant and touched the elephant's two long tusks. "this thing is sure made up of two swords," said the fifth man. "What I am grasping is long and curved with a sharp tip at the end". I am not certain what this is.

The sixth blind man scratched his head and mediated on the problem. He seemed to be the wisest of all of them and asked for the zoo-keeper to solve the conundrum they were facing. The zoo-keeper being worried about the loose elephant reached them, and tightly grabbed the elephant's collar. And when he was asked about the problem. He said "you are all right, the elephant seems like something different to each one of you. And only in sharing what each of you gentleman knows can probably understand, and collectively resolve the puzzling issue.

The only hope for tolerating others, to show compassion and object to what is not justified, is for bettering quality of human consciousness, to further advance in our awareness where make sense ability can replace ignorance and superstition.

The question is if the laws of nature govern, and they decide our actions, our future, and are the answer to millions of unanswered questions. Then, are this laws orderly, are they purposeful, calculated and meaningful, managed, equitable, balanced and objectified, or not? If the answer is no, and these laws that reign us are chaotic, and are not regulated and carry no meaning, and are exhausted of having any purpose. Then, how scientists, the physicists, the astrophysicists and millions of other intelligently minded researchers do formulate their data, compute and solidify the end result of their significant study. And bear in mind that the core of the physicist's undertaking projects relies on mathematics which is the kernel of their findings, making them able to substantiate dependable theories. How on earth, can this ever be possible to achieve in a world that is muddled, that is disorderly? How can any neuroscience, neurophysiologist, bio-researcher? or any other medical technician work with medical tools that couldn't gather precise measurement from an undisciplined world for the very imperative task of saving lives? Then, if the reply is yes; would you not ask yourself that: if it is a meaningful universe that is attentively managed and accurately programmed, then, it must have a programmer. And if so, who is the planner, the designer? Who is the coordinator, and the software developer?

VAJABALWOOJOOD

God is vajabalwoojood, which means God existence is a must so that other things can relatively exist, they must depend on God existence. God must exist, because God is the creator of all there is, and all there was, and all there ever will be. God is absolute; every other thing is relative referencing the Omni Potent, Omnipresent, Omni temporal and the Omniscient God. God is the absolute truth, that is true at all times and in all places. God is always true no matter what the circumstances. God is a fact that cannot be altered. like for instance, there are no round rectangular, or the angles of a triangle add up to 180 degrees.

It seems math and geometry are the languages of the divine, they can independently be perceived, as they absolutely are necessary for our lives; but numbers as well must be attached to something, like 100 books, 1000 horses, or 1oooo soldiers. They depend on other things; they must be attached to other items to mean something. God is all truths because the existence of God logically makes sense, and is the whole truth. Everything and all that exists depends on God, in which without no relative, or other absolute things can ever exist. Every absolute being depends on the other absolute being, except God. for instance, as long as there is space, time must absolutely exist, there couldn't be time without space. But even time slows down and almost stops for objects going at the speed of light.

There is a phenomenon of relativity known as time dilation, in which time appears to slow down almost to a stop for bodies that approach the speed of light. — Jerry Adler, Newsweek, "Stephen Hawking, Master of the Universe: Our 1988 Cover Story on the Legendary Physicist," 14 Mar. 2018

Is time an absolute? Relating to Newton, absolute time exists autonomous of any beholder and advances at a coherent pace throughout the universe. Thus, every object has an absolute state of motion relative to absolute space, hence, an object must be either in a state of absolute rest or moving at some absolute speed.

There are innumerous absolutes, an infinite number of absolute reasons and issues, but they all one way or another depend on other things, except God. Gravity is an absolute but depends on the Earth mass which is also an absolute, since is the Earth's mass that causes it to have gravity, and so in order to not maintain gravity the Earth must not have mass. But the earth has mass, just like any other solid object does. If the Earth didn't have mass, it wouldn't be there anymore! What we know as an absolute on planet earth, might be relative on other planets, or universes except God that cannot be relative, and is the absolute maker of the entire cosmos. All destructible things are relative, including the entire planet earth' since a couple of colossally atomic bombs can utterly annihilate the entire planet earth, except for God that is the absolute being. All other things either absolute or relative depends on God, the creator of heavens and the earth. The vajabalwoojood argument does not have to be persuasive for piercing the logic of others, it is just a fact since the infinite traces of God are so awesomely impressive that should leave no doubt what so ever for any intelligent mind to decipher.

Notably different experimental truths, all the findings of science, are empirical: they depend on evidence and might be wrong or partial. Also, we can be incorrect about what we think we see or experience. since we rely on science and our senses in practical life. That does not change the fact that absolute truth is only to be found inside a well-defined logical system. That kind of truth may, or may not, correspond to the real world, and if it does in the real world, it must depend on other things, except for God that is absolutely independent.

EXISTENCE PEAKED IN MANKIND

All living creatures are extremely complicated, even the most diminutive(microscopic) single-celled bacteria. However, none exceed the overall complexity of the human being. Each human-being is constructed of trillions of molecules and cells, solely the human brain is filled with billions of cells constituting trillions of trillions of connections. The design of the human brain is rightly remarkable and beyond our comprehension. Every cubic inch of the human brain includes at least a couple of million nerve cells conjoined by ten thousand miles of fibers. It is well known that man's 3-pound brain is the most complicated and orderly arrangement of matter in the entire universe! way more complicated than any sophisticated computer, the human brain is competent for storing and creatively maneuvering infinite amounts of information. Its abilities and potential stagger (offset, displace) the imagination. The more we utilize it, the surpass it becomes. The brain competency of even the smallest insect is astounding. The infinitesimal speck of a brain located in a little ant, butterfly or bee enable them not only to detect, smell, taste and navigate, but even to fly with great accuracy. Butterflies routinely travel tremendous distances. Bees and ants engage in complex social organizations, construction projects, and communications. Comparably these minuscule brains put our computers and aviation to shame.

The prodigy (miracle, marvel) of the bodies of both animals and man are evidently ceaseless. Dr. A.E. Wilder-Smith makes this thought-provoking and humbling statement: When one considers that the entire chemical information to construct a man, elephant, frog or an orchid was compressed into two minuscule reproductive cells (sperm and egg nuclei), one can only be astounded. In addition to this, all the information is available on the genes to repair the body (not only to construct it) when it is injured. If one were to request an engineer to accomplish this feat of information miniaturization, one would be considered fit for the psychiatric clinic.

It is not ambivalent that a machine methodically built by a craftsman cogitate the existence of its maker. It would not be wise to think that time and chance could make a jumbo jet, an automobile a computer, a refrigerator or a typewriter. Where the separate parts could have manufactured by themselves into these elaborate mechanisms based on the physical properties of matter. Yet, life is much more intricate than the most advanced man-made machine. Our planet is filled with infinite forms of life, each conveying massive levels of complexity. Materialists see life in all its wondrous forms concluding merely of atoms and molecules. They acknowledge these atoms and molecules make themselves into millions of complex animals and plants. These kinds of callous behold were materialized of an earlier, unripe period in science when the extreme complexity of living systems was not fathomed. Even if nature could build the necessary proteins and enzymes, it is extremely far away from generating life. Presently so many scientists, the prominent philosopher, and scholarly minded individuals believe that life could have never existed without a highly intelligent planner, a potently wise designer. There is a humongous difference between making a building block and generating a complete operating and serviced 200-story skyscraper made from those building blocks. No building can be erected exhausted of any builder, no program can exist without a programmer, without a studiously smart planner.

When ontology, which is a branch of metaphysics, tests existence and being to prove what it means for something to be a physical object, should one define them by their properties? Is it the size, the color, the shape, or are these properties linked to preceding substance that we need to be aware of? This is referred as the problem of substance, the universal difficulty is posed as how can we know if the problem of color, size or shape are separate from the particular object, and how can a substance or matter change in some ways but still stay the same. Metaphysic examines the essence of mind as contrary to physical object, and if the mind is physical, it is also concern if God exists, and disputes about the nature, space and time. Relating to immaterial issues like beauty, morality, justice, and so on,

313

Plato believed the form was an undeniable fact of nature where principle issues like justice, goodness, beauty are realities perhaps abstract(synopsis) in their own rights.

He pulls distinction between the visible world and the intelligent one, and reckoned it is the absolute fundamental rule and the axiom law that represent a higher form of knowledge which governs and designs the intelligible criterions that are prefect and unchanging. Because our knowledge of the visible world is imperfect and changing, where Plato believed there are those who are stuck in the world of sights and sounds since they relate to human-beings sensory experience; as Plato, a philosopher in classical Greece saw the material world as not real, but rather a shadow of actual world of forms in which nothing alters, and nothing proceeds, and nothing is imperfect, Contrary to the physical world of substance and matter that are constantly altering.

Plato also believed cases of justice in the seen world may be relative, as what seems to one person as just, may seem very unjust to the next individual, but he believed the real world is impregnated with the form of justice itself as absolute and not changeable, in which higher form of intelligent identifies with, so does with beauty, goodness, form of wisdom and host of other vital issues. The world of higher form was the centerpiece to Plato's belief, according to which the object of human experience are just shadows of a higher world of forms that are situated above our sensory world.

Plato's teacher, Socrates, first referred to the idea of the invisible world behind the observable world and the instigator to the world of appearances, that is eternal, immaterial and are inconvertible forms. Hence, the theory of forms is the most vital philosophical and thought provoking idea central to Plato's theme and subject matter referencing the world of unseen, since he believed even though we find so many cases of flaws in justice, goodness and beauty in this world, we still by instinct do sense of true justice, true beauty, true goodness, and what true virtuous conduct is. Plato, like his teacher Socrates, believed soul is what makes us alive and animates us, and it is the spirit or the soul which made life possible. Plato was inspired by the perfect lucidity and durability of mathematics, which was closest to perfect clarity and discipline; he doubted the world of our experience since nothing is perfect or permanent. In his theory he explains that beyond the unfulfilling world of human experience exists a world which holds the form of justice, goodness, beauty and other forms that embodies the perfect expression of these ideas.

In this sense, physics looks into the principles and the reality of nature at its root, which references the idea that there must be invisible principals active in nature relating to which all natural processes can be recognized. And gathered something comes to existence and becomes what it is by obtaining its distinctive form linked to and fed by the essence of nature. For instant a seed which becomes a mature plant, or a baby grown into adulthood, the birds and the bees, the flowers and the trees, and so on. Plato argues that subject matter like justice and beauty exist because they engage in the universal form of beauty and justice as its actual fabric already imprinted in the universe.

In the other hand, Aristotle argues that the universal concept of justice and beauty stems from examples of beauty and justice in this world, since Aristotle places importance on observing the details of this world. Aristotle believes that everything is subject to change and motion, but nothing alters or moves without cause; his theology comprehension is set on his perception that there must be something beyond and above the chain of command for the cause and effect principle to exist, which he sees as the invisible forces and the energy behind the motion and change as a deep mystery.

Aristotle, Plato's student, emphasized on cause and reflected on "change," which ultimately led him to posit the existence of a divine unmoved mover. Aristotle believed what moves the world is consistency in change, he manifested change restlessly takes place in our physical world which is due to motion, and time spent, which in turn requires space. And as much as Plato believed in the invisible intelligent world and its abstract form, Aristotle leaned on the visible world and believed true forms are manifested in substance and the material world we experience.

He believed neither matter nor form can exist without each other; they cannot exist independently. He stated it would not be possible for a form to exist without some matter to depend on. He acknowledged that substance can exist without quality, color, number, or any other category, but it is definitely difficult to imagine any category without substance. He renders an example that illustrates this distinction between form and matter, and to grasp a basic sense of the universe and how laid out it is, via the "bronze statue." The bronze is the matter, while the shape of the statue is the form, which he states even a lump of bronze would have its shape and form.

Aristotle stated that we pay attention to the time that has passed when we notice that something has changed. Put differently, time is a measure of change as space is measure of distance. He denies the possibility of empty time as much as he denies the possibility of empty space, where no time can pass without anything taking place.

Aristotle was the son of a doctor and was interested in biology. He had a keen understanding of anatomy, and in his writing was trying to make sense of the world through biology as a paradigm shift in understanding the world. Aristotle was adamant in finding the purpose to each thing, which he thought was the best way to decipher why things are the way they are, and what goal they are to serve, and pushed on teleology which indicates there must be a reason for everything; where teleological phenomenon (exhibiting design relating to having purpose) is the essence of his doctoring.

I believe every gradual change leads to a new form to serve an exclusive goal, which inevitably sets new agendas and circumstances for the next stage of change to occur, to create new positions and to successively manifest and reach certain objectives, and so on. I believe this is contrary to the idea of accepting infinity, since no change from position or form A to B can ever take place in infinite time, demanding infinite space, where no purpose is ever served or any goal could possibly be reached. Furthermore, the idea of showing out of nowhere and from an infinite time and space sounds ridiculous, because neither time nor space can mean anything without having the inclination to execute a deed.

In today's world, because of advancements of science and technology, the matter in its entirety is in question, since such issues as "antiquark," which means the antiparticle of the quark that deals with the subatomic particle identical in mass but opposite to it in electric and magnetic properties (as sign of charge), that when brought together with its counterpart produces mutual annihilation: otherwise, a subatomic particle not found in ordinary matter, which is big challenge and a game changer for the science to deal with in the world of unseen through the naked eye.

MINDS OF REASON: IT IS NOT WHAT IT IS

In the name of the Omnipotent, Omnipresent, Omni-temporal, Omnibenevolent, and the Omniscient God. The most merciful, the most gracious, and the most compassionate. The proprietor of patience, time, space, and beyond. The Fiduciary, Custodian, the Adjudicator (the Arbitrator, the Judge) to all there is and the nonexistence. In the name of the almighty God.

This collection of essays are strikingly informative since phenomenal strides are taken in search of truth, abating speculation. The well-thought interdisciplinary essays are rare, since they can quench the thirst for studious-minded people in search of knowledge and can bring that inquisitive mind closer to the reality of universal existence. The book is entitled *Minds of Reason* and sub-titled *It is not what it is*, which divulges the most arcane (enigmatic) issues of our time, clarifying imperative subject matter like why there is a God and why not many gods, why we are here, what happens after we die, what existed before the big bang, is our living purposefully driven, if a mind or matter is responsible for creation, and so on.

The book *Minds of Reason* delves into exploring for truth; it unveils the awesome traces of God while leaving no stone unturned, convincing the reader that there's more to life than meets the eye. Quintessential discourse on emerging fields for groundbreaking ideological, spiritual, philosophy, scientific, cultural, psychologic, social, political, economic domains, and the rationale behind these intriguingly intricate subjects, are clearly discussed.

The refined methodology is executed to carefully manifest the essence of what matters, to play a catalyst in intuitively abstract findings, to

317

muster a dynamic form or variation of clear cognizance for illustrating key arguments, to better fathom the essentials of existence. The aim is to insightfully navigate the uncharted territories to further deter obtuse debates; where dogmatic theoretical views can transcend to higher perception planes to further avoid vain acrimony (altercation) for a paradigm shift in meaningful communication, quantifying manna (gratuitous benefit) outcome from both sides of the aisle.

Turn your passion into glory.

1

WHERE DO THE FALLACIES LIE?

Not believing in the Magnificent Designer, the awesome Creator of all there is and all there ever will be, with unimaginable potency as the true reason for existence, bearing infinite wisdom, the superbly intelligent cause behind the majestic universe, the Maker of the exalting cosmos and beyond; and when not realizing the phenomenal traces of the Almighty, and unable to attune to non-anthropomorphic (humanoid, anthropoid) God. And further, unreservedly (reticent, openly) denying the truth, and when demurral (skepticism, reluctant) to essential attributes of the Omnipotent, Omnipresence and Omniscient Ahura Mazda (God, Lord, Spirit.)

One needs to rigorously challenge one's own mind, since one is not fathoming the conscious-oriented universe, literally awakened, as one is not perceiving the miraculous impetus force of God as the sole reason for existence. Where the ambivalence, the mistrust should absolutely not imply to the flawless Creator, or for one to act delusional towards the breathtakingly sacred creation, but to delve into one's own blunt mind.

Or perhaps because someone's diluted (weak) belief is due to extreme hurt facing humanity, blaming God, one ought to further reassess one's paradoxical (unsound) findings since, in good faith, the Merciful Provider has utterly endowed humanity with all of the gratifying resources to live in luxury, in which I am afraid the goods are ungratefully ruined and on the verge of annihilation by mankind without any remorse.

The reality implies the infinite traces of God, where complexity in nature and the immaculate universe are undeniably directed at a splendid designer; and since we are the product of habits, we have the potential to become accustomed to varieties of the atmosphere, we become acquainted with our surroundings, we take even the most wondrous things for granted, acknowledging them as self-propelling, or perhaps gifted by nature, believing that the universe provides, and yes, that is a fact; in the meanwhile, not making much sense when not perceiving the power of intention behind such an astonishing state of being.

It is sad when not realizing that we are the nature, we are an inseparable part of the whole being and the amazing universe; we are part of the cosmic energy, the particles, the electromagnetic forces, the interstellar dust, the nebulas, and beyond which much of the space between the stars is filled with atomic and molecular gas (primarily hydrogen and helium) and tiny pieces of solid particles or dust (composed mainly of carbon, silicon, and oxygen). In some places this interstellar material is very dense, forming nebulas, as we undeniably are made of the same agents which nature, the Milky Way, and the cosmos are comprised of.

We couldn't survive a couple of minutes if we do not breathe, not being able to inhale oxygen and exhale carbon monoxide; we cannot survive a few days with no water, and perhaps a week or two with no food, and if not activated to reproduce, as these events and much more are nature-driven, our survival branches out from the environment that we live in, as it should enlighten us to honor the cause, the almighty God, preserve life, respect nature, validate cooperation, work in unison with nature, believe in collectivism, value mankind, while shedding light on the fact that all men are created equal.

We should be aware of such purveying (provision) and remarkable existence that offers convincingly countless evidences of a mighty cause. And unless we can overcome the notion of acting indifferently towards the miraculously oriented events literally happening around us, then we have acted as blindly as a bat, not showing prudence towards the actual cause of existence and depleted of any reasoning power. Hence, one's wisdom should mature to heighten mental dynamics, avoiding mind traps to further meditate on one's own thoughts for cultivating the facts.

But there is hope, since the human mind is potentiated to unquestionably one day break through the web of uncertainty to truly realize God. Taking enlightened steps toward the right direction, the physicists already have unveiled the absentia world, better known as the subatomic realms empowered by quantum physics.

Making humanity aware of an entirely different set of rules that must be applied in lieu of Newtonian laws are only doable in the empirically oriented world of cause and effect and within the action and reaction events, as they are obsolete in the higher domains, and as scientists are facing mind-boggling dilemmas in the quantum world, while experiencing exciting dare for a thrilling and promising future.

It seems that the secret of God lies in infinite beauty, since everything created in nature is beautiful, indicating that without a doubt, God is a beauty-oriented Being. And since man is made in the image of God, man is also innately attracted to beauty, like beautiful thoughts, beautiful words, beautiful conduct, beautiful songs, attractive bodies, beautiful faces, attractive features, beautiful scenes, beautiful climate, beautiful colors, good-looking creatures, beautiful nature, and so on. Referencing beauty, Aristotle rejected Plato's theory of forms. Aristotle stated that "properties such as beauty are abstract universal entities that exist independent of the objects themselves. Instead, he argued that forms are intrinsic to the objects and cannot exist apart from them, and so must be studied in relation to them."

The next secrets of God are infinite intelligence, infinite wisdom, with an infinitely brilliant imagination. So is man, because we have an idea about absolute perfection and have a notion about the pinnacle of invincibility; we have an idea about quintessential (flawless) being, as if the ultimate characteristic, the most perfect model is imprinted in our mind.

Then, man as imperfect seeking completion searches for knowledge and information, mindfulness, cultivating wisdom, trying for the ability to learn, also with infinite imagination, looking for innovations, abhorring evil, insisting on fair allocation of resources, where covetousness and irrational pile-up of wealth can be stopped. Wanting to dispel violence, persisting to end corruption and ill-behavior.

The next secret of God is doing the infinite good, infinitely resourceful; where divinity finds its meaning. And so is man, as an imperfect being, wanting to do good, seeking perfection, looking for freedom, democracy, justice, peace, and human rights; in which the human heart and brain are the two organs that are infinitely based, since our heart unboundedly desires to the day we physically expire, and our mind infinitely craves progress, is curious, and inclined to acquire wisdom until the day we die.

Where beauty, intelligence, consciousness, mindfulness, imagination, goodness, and God are concept-oriented phenomena, so is heresy, demons, and ill conduct. But the secret is that destructive behaviors are overcome by virtuosity, compassion, caring, through constructive actions in which the overall good reflects living, since virtue overcomes evil; otherwise, life would have been terminated long before, and wouldn't have lasted billions of years and be still in the making.

The hidden issue is that we do not die; yes, we do expire physically, but because we are the only creature that by nature has the outside body experience, as we cannot be found anywhere in our physical body—we cannot be located in our brain, in our heart, kidneys, lungs, bone marrow, in our nerves and veins, or any other part in our anatomy. Because we are conscious-oriented, we are ideas; we are energy-based entities circulating for infinite time, linked to cosmic energy, with much higher frequency rates than any other creature, or substance. We exist to experience higher realms, and we comparably are much in tune with the universe, persisting in revealing the secret of life.

Some so insensibly claim that existence, that we have originated from matter; if so, then we would have no souls, as we would be exhausted of any spirit, and definitely without prevailing to the higher realms. And that would be the end of it, as we perish into dust, since all matter is destructible, as no matter can ever exist forever. But the fact is that the entire existence, that life is thought-oriented, that everything is either animated or not, are energy-oriented with different frequency rates.

There is no nothingness, no impermanent, no impertinence, as all and everything is connected, as human beings are part of nature, spiritually, and through the human consciousness, linked to the universe. Human awakening gives meaning to existence, since there are only consciously based experiences, and an idea-driven universe designed to transcendentally last, architecturally vibrant with the intention to elevate the human spirit to the higher domain, and for the human soul to face a renaissance, a revival, an ecstasy, a trance, a new beginning, an ascendancy.

Further, it would be utterly wacky to accept that an unintelligent, mindless matter, without any emotion, exhausted of any feeling, without sensibility or any wisdom, basically an unanimated being, to create an intelligent, conscious-oriented, thought-driven entity. It is in vain to credit lifeless substance for making an animated being with emotions and feelings, exuberantly pursuing a living; a rational being with the infinite potentiality for progress, and definitely with purpose, that intends to conquer the universe and beyond.

It is acting credulous (gullible) to fancy such tremendously inspiring, highly thought-provoking, infinitely imaginative, immensely curious human beings to be made from decayable matter, without any willpower. If so, that is absolutely a miracle; otherwise, it would be nothing short of a mockery.

You might ask why would anyone believe that matter, an inanimate substance with no mind, no sense, no intelligence, depleted of any knowledge and information, impermanent by nature. Since all matter is perishable, as they can be manipulated, altered to liquid, transferred to steam, gas, and also hardened, to be the cause of existence, as the matter is unstable, and hence, contingent to various circumstances.

The naivety takes over since many believe that what we witness as matter, the world around us, and in what we experience, is the answer. Mainly because science can deal with what is visible and tangible, and so-called the practically experimental issues.

Forget that science is the byproduct of the unseen conscious, where mind utterly governs, enlightening us to disregard such empty manifestos, and in vain doctrines, other than the belief that God rules. In which it believes the matter is the cause of existence, that matter rules? Ignoring that science solely discovers new inventions, as it exploits novelties via intelligence and curiosity, looking at things that are already hidden in nature, since our world is already potentiated with decisive matters, unbounded with disciplinary ideas, and gloriously promising a future, waiting to become exposed.

Furthermore, it is practical to scientifically turn matter into energy, as the scientists have even experienced it with the atomic bomb, but in no way probable to turn energy into matter; it is just not possible. No one can materialize our thoughts, ideas, or substantiate our feelings, our emotions. Because we are a closer part of God, as the Almighty is energy-oriented and beyond reach for such undertakings, we are part of the cosmic energy, part of a holy concept, made because of a sanctified thought.

Intelligence, wisdom, awareness, curiosity, imagination, ambition, rationality, mindfulness, inspiration, love, sacrifice, empathy, dreams, will, intention, and a host of other feelings and emotions, are some of the essences that make us humans. And for punishments and reward, we either are ascended to the higher realms for rewards or descended to the lower domains for chastisement.

2

THE INFINITE FOOTPRINTS OF GOD

"The subtlety of nature is greater many times over than the subtlety of the senses and understanding." (Sir Francis Bacon)

The world's scientific views curiously explore the cosmos, the universe, they cultivate life, delve into the human brain, as they often are eager to know about the human conscience, the mind, and the mysteries of God.

Consciousness is sought, as the quality or state of becoming insightful with something and further awakened within oneself, looking for the awareness with philosophical, scientific, spiritual, mental, psychological, biological, physical, cultural, social, and political concerns, searching for the reasons behind often meandering concepts relating to humankind, through which is the state of being characterized by sensation, emotion, learning, thought, mind, enlightenment, volition (will, the power to make one's decision and choices), and cognition further develops.

In the cosmos, we are perplexed, wanting to know what is the nature of the universe, where the universe came from, and where it is going. In life, we want to know if there is a soul. We struggle to understand the creationist's view, the evolutionary concept, genetics, the effects of the environment on a human's upbringing, and the origin of life. We are inquisitive to know if there are extraterrestrials; why do we think we aren't alone? (Extraterrestrial means originating, existing, or occurring outside the Earth or its atmosphere.)

Extraterrestrial refers to any object or being beyond (extra) the planet Earth (terrestrial), it is derived from the Latin words *extra* ("outside," "outwards") and *terrestrial* ("earthly," "of or relating to the Earth").

Intelligent life may refer to extraterrestrial intelligence – intelligent extraterrestrial life originating from outside Earth's planetary boundaries, whether theoretical, having existence in the past, present or future, yet not discovered by terrestrial intelligence as of today.

Scientists tell us that the chemistry of life may have begun shortly after the big bang, 13.8 billion years ago, during a habitable epoch when the universe was only 10–17 million years old. The scientists further acknowledge that soon after the big bang, primordial protons and neutrons were formed from the quark-gluon plasma. (Quark-gluon plasma is a state of matter in which the elementary particles make up the hadrons of baryonic matter.)

Baryonic matter is made of protons and neutrons that are freed of their strong attraction for one another under extremely high energy densities. Also by definition, baryonic matter should only include matter composed of baryons. In other words, it should include protons, neutrons and all the objects composed of them (i.e., atomic nuclei), but exclude things such as electrons and neutrinos, which are actually leptons. These particles are the quarks and gluons that compose baryonic matter of the early universe as it cooled below two trillion degrees.

A few minutes later, in a process known as big bang nucleosynthesis, nuclei formed from the primordial protons and neutrons. (The plural for the nucleus is nuclei; the atomic nucleus is the very dense central region of an atom. And on the contrary, now that science has relatively advanced, more fundamental and perplexing issues have surfaced leaving scientists and the physicists in awe, since the more they dig into the unknown, the more they face puzzling agendas.)

For instance, in the subatomic world, everything is being quantized, as in the atomic world, energies are also quantized. This means it can have only certain values. In mathematics, physics, to restrict (a variable quantity) to discrete values rather than to a continuous set of values.

In physics, to change the description of (a physical system) from classical to quantum-mechanical usually results in discrete values for observable quantities, like energy or angular momentum. In physics we apply quantum theory to, especially form into quanta, in particular, restrict the number of possible values of (a quantity) or states of (a system) so that certain variables can assume only certain discrete magnitudes, as light is quantized into packets of energy.

In electronics, approximate (a continuously varying signal) by one whose amplitude is restricted to a prescribed set of values distortion is caused when very low-level audio signals are quantized. The physicists are facing pixels, in which a pixel is simply the smallest element in a visual display, billions of times smaller than an atom, where molecules would be too complex to be compared to the relatively simple pixel (any one of very small dots that together form the picture on a TV screen, computer monitor, etc.).

Atoms have smaller components and have too many properties to be compared to pixels, in particle physics, an elementary particle or fundamental particle is a particle not known to have any substructure, thus it is not known to be made up of smaller particles. Quarks: up, down, charm, strange, top, bottom. Leptons: electron, electron neutrino, muon, muon neutrino, tau, tau neutrino. Composite subatomic particles (such as protons or atomic nuclei) are bound states of two or more elementary particles.

For example, a proton is made of two up quarks and one down quark, while the atomic nucleus of helium-4 is composed of two protons and two neutrons. Then the atom was discovered, and it was thought indivisible until it was split to reveal protons, neutrons, and electrons inside; these also seemed like fundamental particles, before scientists discovered that protons and neutrons are made of three quarks each.

Today, we know that atoms do not represent the smallest unit of matter. Particles called quarks and leptons seem to be the fundamental building blocks—but perhaps there is something even smaller. Physicists are still far from understanding why a proton has about 2,000 times more mass than an electron. They've found that an atom has a nucleus, that a nucleus contains protons and neutrons, and that those particles, in turn, are made of quarks and gluons—particles that bind quarks together. But most physicists believe quarks to be the smallest building blocks of matter.

What's smaller than a photon? Smaller than photons include quarks, gluons, electrons, and neutrinos. Then there are the forces that join those things up: light is one of them. Light is carried by little particles called photons. And there is the Higgs boson particle, which scientists recently found that is also smaller than an atom.

The particle duality means being a particle at the same time as being a wave; that they can exist in different places at the same time has further complicated the situation, which implies that the world we live in is apocalyptic, or full of prophecy. Denoting the truth about the world-view spirituality, believing that the invisible wholeness underlies all of the creation, and ultimately it is this hidden realm that matters the most.

Passive observation and probably ignorance render ways to active participation and brilliant new discoveries, telling us that we are part of God's creation while blessing God's creatures with much more pleasant surprises to come. Giving humanity a hint that perhaps our Maker is a God-like computer infinitely imaginative, so genius, simulating a computer-like effect.

A computer made of meat, neurochemical-driven, deciding how we feel genetically, determining how we grow, live, and then die, having an invisible programmer, an unseen analyst dealing with our software department known as the mind, apparently endorsed with the hardware known as the human brain, and lump sum of meat, fat cluster, with seemingly no intelligence, without a CPU (central processing unit) does not make any sense. Ironically, the neuroscientific approach is that the mind is merely a by-product of the brain.

In the meanwhile, long before knowing the true nature of our universe and the world we live in, we were told by the prophets and sages, like Noah, Abraham, Moses, Jesus, Mohammed, Buddha, Rumi, Lao-Tzu, and so on, that a transcendent domain exists and resides beyond the everyday world of pain and suffering; for instance, nirvana means freedom from all sufferings, as Buddha taught.

The ancient *rishis*, or sages, of India suggested that the knowledge of the cosmos is locked inside the human mind. They taught us no sin can go unpunished, where the penitence (contrition, sense of sorrow for one's transgression) should be felt, and one's righteous behavior and humility (modesty, humility, not arrogance) will be rewarded, and that justice will be sought.

The wise remind us that even though the eye beholds the physical world and observes the external existence, this is solely a veil drawn over a vast mystery and the hidden universe that is beyond our five senses and human nervous system, to realize the infinitely unseen realm of possibilities, with the understanding as bio-centric, or Bio-centrism considers all forms of life as having intrinsic value.

In the meanwhile, the core of our curiosity and questioning should focus on what is the reality. Is the reality the consequence of natural laws rigorously operating through cause and effect, or is it something else? Either reality is bound by the visible universe, or it is not.

Either the cosmos was created from an empty, meaningless void, or it was not. Either a programmer, a magnificent designer, and superb analyst is in charge of this super-complex simulated computer called life or not. We can rationally address the whys of the universe, which are gradually answering hows and whats of the universe as they open more doors to the unknown behind the closed doors, eventually shedding light on the mysteries of the universe.

What is even more imperative besides our due diligence persistence on discovering the unknown is that we should not deny ourselves the power of reasoning and the essence of correct thinking. We are not to act like primates; if we do, it will eventually depreciate us into machine-like robots with senseless programming.

We need to be careful of the environment we are living in, since a material-intense society can make people into consumers with one-track-mindedness, veiled and blinded by the industrial societies, hardened by greed, obsessed with material wealth and the thirst for excessive pleasure of the flesh, where every other vital issue can become secondary and not a priority, even as far as doing very little to preserve an innocent human life, as if we are just numbers.

With that said, we ought to be thankful for science, because it is through science that many possibilities for a better world are taking place. For example, science has created a humongous social network that instantly connects the world we live in.

It is through technology and scientific notions that we have conquered many mortal diseases and have the ability to rewire the globe to reach the most remote places and hear the cries of those in pain poking our consciences to do something decisively humane about the victims of countless tragedies and to affect each other often for the best to create a planetary civilization, where cooperative endeavors are gradually replacing competitive agendas. Ironically, it is via science that we are able to know the awesomeness of the almighty God, since it is via science that the wonders of the universe are being incrementally discovered. Scientific methods are deeply rooted in nature; it is the way to comprehend the physical world, as it cannot be falsified.

We also should know that science cannot explain the meaning of life, or why are we here, and if we have a soul, why we feel love, and why we sacrifice and are sometimes sacrificed, gambit (losing oneself) to save another human being. Science cannot tell us how to locate consciousness, nor how to measure consciousness, because consciousness is a concept that cannot be seen, it cannot be sized.

It is not plausible; no magnifier or telescope of any kind can locate the mind. Consciousness is a dilemma that truly has perplexed science, without which, no scientists can ever experience anything, deliver any dependable scientific notion or any reliable output, where nothing is ever possible, since no meaningful communication is ever probable without consciousness.

Bottom line: it is because of consciousness that we experience, discover philosophy (the whys of the world), science (the hows and the ways of the world), and so on. Consciousness can explain science, while science cannot explain consciousness. We are all about intelligence, imagination, emotions, and feelings. Imagine a beautiful face, or let's say Whitehaven Beach in Australia, the sunset, the sunrise, the face of your elementary school teacher, imagine you are walking in the moon, or imagine anyone or anything that you wish to conceptualize or fancy.

The point is that as true as one's imagination is, no picture, no scene, no occasion can ever be located in anyone's brain imagining them. What takes place are known as electrochemical activities manifesting episodes where the mind resides. In reality, we are having a subjective experience, as science cannot describe how electrochemical pursuits manufacture such pictures beyond anyone's imagination, which can solely denote that we are conscious beings.

All of our experiences happen in our consciousness, without which, no experience is ever possible, hence making life as we know it impossible. Where in our brain are memories stored? Making matters more complex, why can we imagine? Why are we creative? Why do we have free will? Why do we have empathy? Why do we care? Where do the laws of the universe come from? Who created them? Why can we not measure the unit of either mass or energy? Why can we turn matter into energy, but are unable to turn energy into mass? Why are we not able to measure reverence? Why do we not have a scientific explanation for consciousness? Is human conscious linked to cosmic conscious? Where in our brain are the experiences made? As Einstein puts it, "If it is a rational world, then it must have a rational source."

In Rene Descartes' *Cogito Argument*, which ultimately results in the famous saying, "I think, therefore, I am," Descartes argues that anything we learn or infer from the senses can be doubted. This is because all sense perception can be deceived. The "I think, therefore, I am" debate can also be interpreted as you and I are concept-oriented beings because we think, therefore, we are, and the only creatures endowed with the out-of-body experience in which, without thinking, we might as well be a piece of rock, dull and with much lower frequencies, without active senses to interact with the energy-based universe.

Our thoughts are energy-based, as nature is, since we are an inseparable part of nature; that is exactly why when our ideas, our thoughts are not constructively managed, then, in one way or another we become punished, since there is nothing unorderly or destructive in our universe except when man's ill-doings take over, often without any remorse, and that is sad, proving the expression of "what goes around, comes around." Which manifests the laws of karma?

Science believes that all sensations come from our brain; they are the byproducts of our brain, insisting that mind, our memories, thoughts, experiences, are the attribute of the brain. Science further says that by titillating (exciting, arousing, stimulating) certain parts of the brain, particular reactions can occur. Yes; of course it is quite natural for the brain to respond when certain parts are triggered, since our brain manages to connect us to the world, just like a smart Samsung or Apple cell phone does.

It seems that as realistic as scientific notions are, even science occasionally can be blinded. It is science that revealed all matter is energy-driven; solely energy-oriented frequencies are operating in subatomic realms where quantum physic is active, as the physicists, the scientists, can observe wavelike particles maneuvering in strange ways.

Particles simultaneously show up at several places and cannot be evaluated, since they show a vibrating, wave-like manifestation, and as delicate as the brain is, it certainly couldn't be an exception, because for the brain to act as an energy-based organ, it would be impossible to connect to the energy-oriented environment.

The human mind is energy-oriented; otherwise, our brain couldn't have so cogently (soundly, rationally) been in tune with our mind, as our brain and mind are vibrantly interconnected, so magnificently in unison, it wouldn't be an easy job to discern which is subordinate to the other.

The dilemmas are that the relationship between neurochemicals and electrochemical activities are utterly not detectable, since any situation, picture, or scene that one is imagining cannot be found in one's brain. There is so far no explanation of any idea to decipher how electrochemical pursuits generate subjective experiences about one's picturing things in one's head.

Hundreds, if not thousands, of subjective experiences happen every day in our consciousness without ever being located by scientists, because consciousness is doing the observing; we are searching for the consciousness, while the consciousness is doing the looking. The mind of science is meshed in with what science is looking for, only making the self-awareness possible.

Most of all science has challenged religions about things that are superstitious and not true, as science has unlocked the secrets that are often beyond anyone's imagination. Science has exposed how the human brain functions, how the universe initiated, how it expanded and exploded to immeasurable reach, how the universe is growing at a very high rate, and how it is going to end. Thanks to God that we live in a world that is hungry for scientific wonders and spiritual longing.

It is because of science the Omnipresent God becomes known because science reveals that an infinite universe was instantly created by the big bang that at the same time showed up everywhere, since cosmic radiation becomes prevalent where radiations impact existence from all sides. Scientists tell us that the big bang did not happen in a particular time or place, since before the big bang there was neither space nor time; it was after the big bang that existence appeared everywhere, radiation coming from all sides, proving the Omnipresent God.

The awesome mechanism of how the big bang was created should make any inquisitive mind wonder about the magic which started with a dot smaller than the tip of a tiny sewing machine needle and stretching it across billions, if not trillions, of light-years of space and time, which should prove the Omnipotent God.

Many sages and enlightened philosophers have redundantly made clear that a universe operating with absolute accuracy, with laws so precise that even the tiniest flaw, does not happen. Because if miscalculation happens for a fraction of a second, no universe, nor any life-driven planet, would ever be possible; which needs to remind us of the Omniscient God, a magnificent Designer absolutely free of any kind of mistake.

Further, what makes the reality of our lives possible is that everything has its opposite, even to the core of existence where matter and anti-matter operate, leaving the concept of good and evil intact. One might ask, why should we have demonic behaviors at all? The answer again lies in the nature of beings, as it seems that without opposite forces, no life is ever possible, and the universe would have been meaningless, as no living is possible without death; telling us perhaps this is a test before entering the next sacred realms or not, where our good deeds should truly matter.

The reality is that opposite forces are constantly at work to make what we know as nature possible, leaving inquiries as such to God's territory since they are beyond human comprehension.

In the meanwhile, the secret lies in harmony, which, along the line of peace and tranquility comes beauty, love, truth, goodness, virtues, justice, equanimity, compassion, forgiveness, transcendence, cooperation, and many other spiritual concepts, since they give meaning to what God is about, rather than evildoings, which signifies satanic behaviors.

Lower selves should be challenged, in which individual's consciousness needs to be refined so that it may reach the radiance of truth, from which one will be cut off by ordinary activities of the world, substantiating that man is made in the image of God where good deeds, clear conscious, and purified souls reside.

To give meaning to human intelligence for understanding that the infinite God cannot conform to human's finite perspectives, but to celebrate our free will, let us either choose destructive impulses to bring out the worst in us, where lower selves and the human flesh is served, or select constructive behaviors, reaching the divinity of mind and manner, and in seeking God.

What should urgently be noticed is that science devoid of spirituality has brought about irresolvable ills condemning humanity with the rise in global warming, Darwinism's survival of the fittest mentality, which dictates kill or be killed behaviors, ethnic cleansing, despicable war crimes, imperialistic exercises, extreme income inequality, precarious living standard for the poor, defunding public education, cutting off social welfare, predatory lending, attacking solidarity movements seeking justice, encouraging digitally oriented violence, placing humanity at the verge of atomic destruction and vulnerable to extinction, arriving with military industrial complex, wherein the wars of aggression globally take many innocent's lives every day, where many bystanders lose their lives and are ignored as collateral lost.

Such atrocities occur because thousands of culprits are spiritually and emotionally disconnected from the grave tragedies they are causing, which should alert humanity that, if we are to expect a mass extinction in our modern era, it would certainly be because of potentiated modern behaviors linked to primitive conduct and savage actions. Therefore, we are left with no choice but to urgently follow the footsteps of God and take the right course for thinking virtue, with good deeds, and with good words, to persist on high caliber moral and spiritual standards, since hoarding wealth, sex, influence, power, and violence have completely blinded us, as we are not noticing the destruction of planet Earth as literally is happening all over the globe.

3

FREEDOM

No capital-intense society can feel true freedom, since capital-driven environments by nature stratify (classify) societies where the poor have to relentlessly struggle to make ends meet and the rich are worried about their wealth and position that might become endangered by those deprived of even the basic necessities in life. It is a no-brainer that millions without financial security will defend themselves against the ravages of poverty through undesirable tactics, where moral depravity can become the norm. Mahatma Gandhi said poverty is the worst form of violence.

I believe poverty is the root of most evil, because of the horrific socioeconomic ills it creates. A free society should mean a society where not only the elites and the super-rich are protected, but the unpopular, the indigent, and the deprived can also feel safe.

The economic onslaught takes the breath out of predominantly poor neighborhoods, leaving them gasping for basic necessities to survive without any life support. The idea of the you are on your own mentality should only work where there are no few robbers among us which, through abracadabra tactics and in the name of the business and law take more than 90 percent of global resources, leaving the majority of the people with dirt to live on.

With so many being exhausted of financial security, neither freedom nor other sacred-oriented concepts, such as liberty, human rights, and the pursuit of happiness, make any sense, reminding us that nowhere in the world should freedom be bestowed to any dictatorial regimes or relinquished to fake democracies where the governors of force under false pretenses arrest, torture, and even kill the crusaders of truth.

"Freedom cannot be bestowed — it must be achieved."

Elbert Hubbard (American writer, publisher, and artist)

You cannot bring out the worst in people and expect to be renowned for protecting freedom, liberty, and human rights; that is hypocrisy in action. You'd be better to refer to intelligence, responsibility, accountability, dignity, trustworthiness, thoughtfulness, which all individuals should uphold.

Yes, any sensible mind ought to agree; but then, put the life of superb luxury you moguls are having in question, and imagine yourselves, your loved ones without food, shelter, clothing, and exhausted of medical necessities, no available schooling; either laid off, or with no promising jobs, having no reliable transportation, and constantly being tempted by luxury living and material extravaganzas in life, and so on.

I am sure you as well would think twice when wanting to talk positive, and acting optimistic, and I doubt that you'd take advice to behave righteously. I sure am not defending any misbehavior, nor am I encouraging uncivilized conduct. Neither am I in any way belittling motivational songs; what I am saying is that desperate times call for desperate measures. It is basic human nature to survive; even if it is at the expense of others, I am afraid.

Conduct that might seem extreme under normal circumstances might seem appropriate during hard times and adversity, which can exert pressure on so many to do the unthinkable. But one cannot even understand what desperate means unless one has experienced it.

I believe that the worst type of moral turpitude (moral turpitude is conduct that violates common moral standards) is to globally inflict a penalty on billions with the crime of poverty they did not commit. It is perhaps true that even in the most perfect world, humanity will fail to deny inequalities, but I am certain that relatively the less class differentiation, the fewer inequalities, the more avoidance of strife (dissension, conflict, wrangling) and bitterness, since seeking balance is always the key.

As in an economically lopsided environment, freedom can manifest its full meaning neither for the poor, as people in need are yoked with having no means to survive, as it makes them worry not knowing where their next meal should come from or how to pay their past-due bills; and for the rich, who employ mercenaries to protect themselves and their wealth, which might find those very guardians to one day turn on them, constantly leaving them with anxiety of how to stay safe.

In an individualistic society is not favorable to the well-being of the society that every member exploits, all of one's talents for personal gains, which the overall intention should be for the common good. The grinding poverty, beggary, starvation, and economic deprivation will eventually afflict all ranks of society, since the millions' desperate struggle for basic needs renders them insensible to all feelings of decency, without right and wrong sensitivity concern, even to the extent of losing self-respect. Nelson Mandela overcoming poverty is not a gesture of charity, it is an act of justice.

We live in an era in which the survival of the fittest attitudes have unfortunately fueled the fire of wrongful competition, deviltry, diablerie (reckless, mischief, sorcery), iniquity, suicides, homicides, genocide, misdeed, offense, sin, wickedness, greed, jealousy, fraud, lies, dishonesty, sexual misconduct, theft, conspiracy, rape, murder, inferiority complex, superiority complex, and other ill-oriented conduct, frequently leading to a crime-infested atmosphere, especially with hardcore criminals that do not mind playing Russian roulette to protect themselves from the hazards of financial insecurities.

"Freedom is nothing but a chance to be better."

-Albert Camus (French author,
journalist, and philosopher)

Occasionally, the rich get caught in this ugly game of greed as they also break the rules, but end up with a slap on the wrist for punishment, since they do have the means to break loose from the clutches of persecution because in a capitalist system, money is the king, playing the role of in God we trust. Dwight Eisenhower said, "You do not lead by hitting people over the head, that is assault, not leadership." I believe no assault is greater than keeping the actual producer of wealth distinctly poor.

It is not a hidden fact that pecuniary (fiscal, monetary) policies run by the few have accumulated most global resources to benefit themselves, where billions are literally being ignored as if they are cursed to tolerate filthy living. The globally rich elites have manufactured scarcities at the cost of human lives, taking the world financially hostage, which it seems they do not even bother to peacefully resolve the issues of predatory lending, hunger, global warming, the wars of aggression, genocide, toxic foods, harmful environment, crippling sanctions—which, in reality, affects the poor and the helpless—the threat of nuclear mayhem, and hundreds of other malaise that have already endangered the very planetary existence.

Critical thinking, unity and mass cooperation, sympathy, moral and legal imperatives, caring, and seeking justice should prevail to deny those mighty few who push the idea of whatever it takes to make money, since I am afraid they have abused their power, utterly neglecting the underlining principle and the morale of the system to exploit and suppress the actual producer of the amassing corporate wealth.

William Shakespeare said, "If the money goes before, all ways do lie open." On the other hand, with financial depravity, all ways remain shut, as well as leaving doors of freedom in question.

4

IS GOD AN ABSTRACT ENTITY?

A concrete noun refers to a physical object in the real world, such as a cat, a person, a building, or a car; an abstract noun refers to an idea or concept that does not exist as concrete nouns in the real world, and cannot be touched, like freedom, virtues, happiness, numbers, brain malleability (elasticity, ductile, flexibility), subconscious mind, mind, atom, subatomic particles like electrons, quarks (which is the basic block of hadrons, as there are two types of hadrons: baryons three quarks, and mesons one quark, one antiquark, and neutrinos with a very tiny mass smaller than any subatomic particle), the universe, the cosmos, infinity, etc.

The sacred concept of the infinite God means there is utterly no limit to Omnipotence, Omnipresence, and the Omniscient God. Rendering no position, leaving absolutely no room for any being or any existence to take over, since infinity is an open-ended expression without any boundary.

Abstract concepts are ideas that cannot be seen, since they cannot be exhibited via concrete (real) examples, but we cannot live without them. Concrete nouns are people, places, or things that we can experience with our five senses; the abstract nouns are the opposite. We can't experience these nouns with our senses. If a noun is abstract, it describes something you cannot see, hear, touch, taste, or smell.

It can be difficult to know when a noun is abstract because there are so many words that can function in different ways, for example, some words might function as verbs in some cases and abstract nouns in other cases; love and taste are two examples. Abstract nouns can be countable or uncountable (mass), they can also be singular or possessive, love, anger, hate, peace, sympathy, pride.

Simply put, describing the progression of logic in a computer program will be possible only if the reader can correctly visualize (imagine) it in his or her mind; therefore, the logical development in computer programing can only be substantiated if the programmer could thoroughly and mindfully imagine.

Abstract reality is a sense tool that empowers us to clarify the world through expressing quality or characteristics apart from the specific object, such as love, hate, anger, frustration, craving, happiness, thrill, hope, desire, imagination, creativity, courage, justice, obedience, honesty, bravery, excitement, poverty, devotion, and other emotions that are abstract nouns, as with so many other feelings that are abstract entities.

A sense of abstract reality is a tool that empowers us to make sense of the world in terms of ideas; this abstract theoretic world can come to appear more real and reliable than the everyday particular world from which it is abstracted. The adjective abstract for things that are not materially oriented objects, or they are general and not related to specific examples, with a word or a phrase naming an attribute added to or grammatically related to a noun to modify or to explain it.

They literally are inseparable from who we really are; also, with the concept of God as an abstract reality that is imprinted in our mind, seeded in our spirit, potentiating humanity with the power of consciousness, empowering us with intelligence, wisdom, freedom, will and the ability to choose, in which if they are activated in the right ways, they clearly distinguish human beings from the beasts.

They are inevitable sources that often flare up in our mind, soul, and body in a variety of ways, as they are not concrete words that can only be sensed. One's senses cannot see, smell, taste, hear, touch, or perceive an abstract noun, since, in essence, an abstract is a quality; concepts are ideas imprinted in our very existence, in which abstract ideas activate thoughts that are not about worldly things, such as reliability, trust, education, faith, knowledge, happiness, empathy, cowardice, freedom, self-expression, peace of mind, safety, etc.

They are the issues that one cannot touch but one can feel them. The existence of abstract objects initially seems like a deep metaphysical inquiry. The view that abstract objects do exist is called Platonism; the view that they don't is nominalism; those who think they do exist, but only in the mind, are conceptualists. Concrete nouns or ideas can normally be experienced with our five senses; concrete nouns are contrary to abstract nouns, which reference concepts that cannot be felt or experiences via our senses.

A concrete thinker will count 50 projects, while a more abstract thinker will meditate on the numbers, for instance, size, length, width, magnitude, scope, volume, amplitude, diameter, depth, radius, and height, are all measures; they are an abstraction in the sense that they do not exist in and of themselves, but they nevertheless explain the real qualities of physical objects. Time is no different; the more one's understanding of physics, the less sense it makes to think of time extending in any direction.

We should utilize the adjective abstract for something that is not a material object. An adjective is a word that modifies a noun or a pronoun to make it more specific: a healthy baby, a sunny day, a humid evening, a kind lady, or a warm glass of milk. You use adjectives to give your nouns a little attitude or to communicate clearly.

The abstract is from a Latin word meaning pulled away, detached, and the basic idea is of something detached from physical, or concrete, reality; and as far as numbers, it is globally understood that numbers and the other objects of pure mathematics are abstract, since numbers cannot really exist without accompanying a concrete object, like 8 books, 12 men, 6 women, or 100 plants, 7 dolphins, 20 monkeys, etc.

Abstract thinking is the empowerment to think about objects, principles, and ideas that are not physically present. It is linked to symbolic thinking, which uses the substitution of a symbol for an object or idea. A variety of everyday behaviors make abstract thinking, like the abstract concept of time.

It begins with awareness and consciousness, as thoughts of the past and future are conceptual ideas that exist in the mind. They are ideas that filter and contort (deform, distort) our realization of factual time. The reference of a word is the relation between the linguistic expression and the entity in the real world to which it refers. In contrast to reference, the sense is defined as its relations to other expressions in the language system.

Thus, there are words that have a sense, but no referents (the person, thing, or idea that a word, phrase, or object refers to) in the real world. Generally, a concept is a function whose value is always a truth value. Concepts are mental representations, abstract objects, or abilities that construct the fundamental building blocks of thoughts and beliefs. They play an important role in all aspects of cognition. In today's philosophy, there are at least three advancing ways to understand what a concept is:

1. Concepts as mental agendas, where concepts are entities that exist in the mind (mental objects.)
2. Concepts as abilities, where concepts are abilities anomalous (strange, deviant, aberrant) to cognitive agents (mental states.)
3. Concepts as Fregean senses (sense and reference), where concepts are abstract objects as opposed to mental objects and mental states.

Concepts are studied as components of human cognition in the cognitive science disciplines of linguistics (the scientific study of language and its structure, including the study of morphology, syntax, phonetics, and semantics. Specific branches of linguistics include sociolinguistics, dialectology, psycho-linguistics, computational linguistics, historical-comparative linguistics, and applied linguistics), psychology and philosophy, where an ongoing debate asks whether all cognition must occur through concepts.

Linguistics is the study of language and its structure; morphology and syntax are two major sub-disciplines in the field of linguistics. The main difference between morphology and syntax is that morphology studies how words are formed whereas syntax studies how sentences are formed.

Concepts are used as formal tools or models in mathematics, computer science, databases, and artificial intelligence, where they are occasionally called classes, schema, or categories, while in an informal situation, the word *concept* often means any idea. An abstract object is an object that does not exist at any particular time or place but rather exists as a type of thing (i.e., an idea, or abstraction). The term *abstract object* is said to have been instated by Willard Van Orman Quine.

Abstract and concrete are classifications that denote whether the object that a term describes has physical referents, as abstract objects have no physical referents, whereas concrete objects do. They are most commonly used in philosophy and semantics. All human feelings and emotions are non-concrete words; they are abstract nouns that can only be sensed, as abstract words may mean two different things to two people or have a different meaning in different contexts, and abstract words are used to describe notions, concepts, and things that can't readily be observed by your five senses.

Abstract words include terms like good and bad, or bravery and cowardice. Abstract objects have no physical referents, whereas concrete objects do. They are most commonly used in philosophy and semantics, the branch of linguistics and logic concerned with meaning. There are a number of branches and sub-branches of semantics, including formal semantics (which studies the logical aspects of meaning, such as sense, reference, implication, and logical form, lexical semantics, which studies word meanings and word relations, and conceptual semantics, which studies the cognitive structure of meaning, the meaning of a word, phrase, sentence, or text.)

Platonism philosophy states that there are such things as abstract objects, where an abstract object is an object that does not exist in space or time, and which is hence utterly non-physical and non-mental. In brief, Platonism refers to the philosophy that affirms the existence of abstract objects, which are believed to exist in a third realm distinct both from the sensible external world and from the internal world of consciousness, and is the opposite of nominalism.

Nominalism doctrine believes that universals or general ideas are mere names without any corresponding reality, and that only particular objects exist; properties, numbers, and sets are thought of as mere features for considering the things that exist. Importantly in medieval scholastic thought, nominalism is particularly linked to William of Occam. The philosophy or Platonism doctrines believe that physical objects are ephemeral (transient, temporary) representations of unwavering (consistent, unchanging) concepts and that the ideas alone render true knowledge as they are known by the mind.

Platonism about mathematics (or mathematical Platonism) is the metaphysical view that there are abstract mathematical objects whose existence is independent of us and our language, thoughts, and practices, just as electrons and planets exist independently (resilient, self-sustaining) of us, so do numbers and sets. Mathematics expresses values that reflect the cosmos, including order-lines, balance, harmony, logic, and abstract beauty. Deepak Chopra.

We ought to realize that the entire beings and whatever is in existence leads to an intelligent designer, as there wouldn't be painting if no drawer, as there is no shape, sketches, and figure of any kind if exhausted of lines, where the fundamentals lay. The term is often applied to movements during the Middle Ages and Renaissance that were set forth by Neoplatonic doctrines; all Neoplatonists, regardless of religious orientation, believe in the superior quality of intangible (ethereal, bodiless, incorporeal) reality, and they consider Plato as the greatest of ancient philosophers.

It is imperative to note that the very essence of our beings, the atom, which is the building blocks to all there is, are not seen with the naked eye, they are irrelevant within our conscious, since they exist independently, as they are not plausible. An atom cannot be felt in any way or shape, but without it, no existence is ever possible. Then, why should anyone be blurred or blinded in seeing God the Creator of the universe and beyond, when one is not even able to notice the very essence of one's makeup, the atom?

Come to think of it, we are all in an abstract, energy-oriented universe, since the entire cosmos and beyond is governed by God, an abstract concept, referencing ideas which serve as the building blocks of what we know as mental delineation or metal rendition (colloquially understood as ideas in the mind), where thoughts are the fundamental cause for the entire existence. Mental portrayal (representations) are the building blocks of what is called propositional attitudes (colloquially understood as the stances or perspectives we take towards ideas, be it believing, doubting, wondering, accepting, etc.). These propositional attitudes, in turn, are the building blocks of our understanding of thoughts that inhabit (dwell, populate) everyday life, as well as folk psychology.

In the philosophy of mind and cognitive science, folk psychology, or commonsense psychology, is a human capacity to explain and predict the behavior and mental state of other people, through which we have an analysis that connects our common, everyday comprehension of our mind, leading to the scientific and philosophical understanding of concepts.

Referencing the human brain and mind, as they are analogs (parallel) to an operational computer, we are basically made similar to a computer comprising of hardware and software.

We are programmed through our software (mind), which literally controls every decision and all the activities that we do. Obviously, living will not be possible without an intelligently designed software (mind) that is certainly potentiated to one day conquer not only galaxies, but the entire universe. But contrary to a computer, which must have an independent programmer to function, our brain is set to relentlessly program our mind and to activate our physical body to execute all sorts of tasks, instruct and manage our body without an external programmer. Meanwhile, it is imperative to know that our mind and our brain are energy-oriented entities, which is the very reason they can relate to the energy-oriented world.

The puzzling issue is that we cannot locate the programmer inside our brain, nor are we; e able to find the consciousness anywhere within. The savvy minded creator who invented computer hardware must have based it on the human brain manifesting magnificent imagination, conceptualizing computer software to simulate the human mind, from simple programming to the most intricate outlets. Yes, we live in a computer-simulated, abstract world, designed by an Omnipotent, Omnipresent, Omniscient Programmer which governs everything from infinitely micro beings to infinitely macro entities in existence.

5

THE ONTOLOGICAL CONCEPT

I suppose therefore that all things I see are illusions; I believe that nothing has ever existed of everything my lying memory tells me. I think I have no senses. I believe that body, shape, extension, motion, location is functions. What is there then that can be taken as true? Perhaps only this one thing, that nothing at all is certain.

— Rene Descartes

The idea of how to integrate concepts into an extended theory of the mind, what functions are permitted or not by a concept's ontology. There are two main philosophical aspects of the ontological concepts: (1) Concepts are abstract objects, and (2) concepts are mental icons. Generally speaking, ontology is a branch of philosophy that is concerned with metaphysics and the nature of existence. What exists their cause, the essence of things, their being and identity.

There are three assumptions in research: epistemological, ontological, and methodological, for instance, in computer science and information science, an ontology encompasses representation, formal naming, and definition of the categories, properties, and relations between the concepts, data, and entities that substantiate one, many, or all domains.

Complicated questions like those are part of a branch of philosophy known as ontology, in which ontology, at its simplest, is the study of existence, but it is much more than that too. Ontology is a part of metaphysics, a branch of philosophy that looks at the very nature of things, their being, cause, or identity.

Epistemology is the study of knowledge, where the methodology is the systematic, theoretical analysis of the methods applied to a field of study; it comprises the theoretical analysis of the body of methods and principles associated with a branch of knowledge. A methodology does not set out to provide solutions—it is, therefore, not the same as a method.

In the simplest terms, a concept is a name or label that regards or treats an abstraction as if it had a concrete or material existence, such as a person, a place, or a thing. It may indicate a natural object that exists in the real world, like a flower, a tiger, or a plant, etc. It may also name a man-made object like a table, car, or a house, etc.

Abstract ideas, knowledge, and domains, such as freedom, democracy, happiness, virtue, equity, science, sadness, etc., are also symbolized by concepts. It is important to understand that a concept is merely a symbol, an indicator of the abstraction. The word is not to be mistaken for the thing. For example, the words Milky Way, Mars, Pluto, or Moon are concepts that represent celestial objects.

Plato was the definite proponent of the realist thesis of universal concepts. In Plato's view, concepts (and ideas in general) are innately inhabited; that was the elucidation (clarification) of a transcendental world of pure forms that lay behind the actual physical world. In this view, universals were described as transcendent objects, in which this form of realism was insightfully tied to Plato's ontological projects.

The concept of mathematics, like Derivative, integral, and so on, are not referring to spatial or temporal perceptions of the external world of experience. Neither are they related in any way to arcane (mystic) limits in which quantities are on the verge of nascence or evanescence; that is, coming into or going out of existence. The abstract concepts are now considered to be totally autonomous, even though they originated from the process of abstracting or taking away qualities from perceptions until only the common essential attributes remained.

It should by now be explicitly clear that the almighty God is an abstract concept beyond space and time, where God's autonomous existence is over the grasp of any mortal, since the realm that we operate in is limited to the human nervous system by which we become aware of surroundings, and the environment we live in; until perhaps the day that our software, the human spirit, the soul, can actually maneuver in transcended heavenly realms.

To further clarify abstract concepts, for instance, it is an abstract idea to question, where did we come from? Why are we here? Where are we heading after we expire? One can answer that we are here to seek beauty, to seek wisdom, to become enlightened, to do good, to gradually progress, to further evolution and reach the pinnacle of perfection, to become part of God, and then, it seems that nothing seems certain, except for what amuses us in our minds, and if so, the mind should not be controlled.

> For, after all, how do we know that two and two make four? Or that the force of gravity works? Or that the past is unchangeable? If both the past and the external world exist only in the mind, and if the mind itself is controllable – what then?
>
> — George Orwell, 1984

The Catechism (confession, creed, dogma, credo) of the Catholic Church says: By his sin Adam, as the first man, lost the original holiness and justice he had received from God, not only for himself but for all humans. It could not be a savvy notion, since this type of interpretation does not correlate with human nature; it does not comply with who we are, as it makes sense to say one as a human being is potentiated to either do good or evil, to act sinful or virtuous, since these, of course, are relative terms.

Furthermore, we first know that we are here, that we are not perfect, we are by-passers that should reach our full potentials, to fill our brain with as much knowledge as possible, to do brilliant works, to be the best that we can be, to do no evil, to do right. Yes, for the afterbirth to fill our clean slate with golden content, on our mind, which should always remind us with the invaluable maxim, to live and let live, and to certainly pass on the good thing we have learned to others before leaving for the next realms of existence.

It seems that we already have an imprint in our mind about God; the concept of beauty, about smiling faces, not liking anger, disdaining pain and suffering, not fond of ugliness, not fond of harsh and rough noises, not attracted towards scary features and ill situations, enchanted with pretty faces, liking good scent, despising fetid (bad odor), pleased with good words, attracted to good behaviors, liking good thoughts, wanting to be educated, trained, seeking perfection, tilted towards a healthy environment and serene atmosphere, as we instinctually are attracted to breastfeeding as infants, since babies innately perform suckling to survive.

6

ONE GOD OR PERHAPS MANY GODS?

One God or perhaps many Gods? The obvious answer to questions as such is that anyone in one's right mind cannot claim seeing God, either seeing one God or many. The closest thing in seeing God is the reasoning power through which the human mind can discern facts from fiction, by which one can identify what makes sense and what does not, since fortunately, the human brain has already reached an evolutionary stage where our resourceful mind can detect decisive issues and meditate on robust discoveries to progress further.

It is true that diabolical behaviors and devil's advocacies are often exhibited by the very human mind in which the same mind is also potentiated with awakening forces which can quash (abrogate, void, overrule) the dark side of its nature, to nullify the mind's ignorance and to acolyte (usher) human beings to enlightenment and guide to where God resides.

Some argue how anyone should know if there is one God in charge, many gods, or perhaps a network of gods that operate in unison. Well, a thorough, logical talk, speech, or statement is expected to make sense and have no discrepancy in what is meant to address. No matter what literary work or dialogue one follows, and no matter in what language that work is presented, it needs to substantiate a clear and viable point.

The whole contextual concept ought to have no disparity or the slightest contradiction, as it is a logical fallacy for instance to say a rectangular circle, rounded square, or deafening silence. There isn't any congruency in the statement. According to Aristotle, the principle (or law) of non-contradiction is the firmest, believing that the principle of non-contradiction is a principle of scientific inquiry, reasoning, and communication that we cannot do without. No one in one's right mind can claim seeing God, as we are utterly left with no choice, as we should steadfastly rely on reasoning power for making sense.

Further, when we say Vahdat Dar Vojood', meaning unity in existence, it means a mighty God that has no cause will absolutely not deteriorate or lessen in any way, which by all means is perfect, that is not contingent to space, time, or any other inhibiting factor; furthermore, one should not extenuate (mitigate, palliate) any disparaging suggestion or claim that otherwise needs to keep up the true meaning of the word unity and the word existence. What unity in existence should mean is that everything from micro to macro, from the tiniest, from the minuscule to infinitely large, are an inseparable part of God.

Here we are accentuating on the word *unity* and the word *existence*. Unity in diversity is used as a popular motto as an expression of harmony. The phrase becomes a deliberate oxymoron when we say or acknowledge unity in existences. There is solely one existence, since the essence of all that exists is latticed (meshed) in God, which adheres to the entire existence, since without God, no existence of any kind is ever possible. For instance, no matter how diversified things or objects are, they are all made of atoms, regardless of their nature or any attribute that each might carry. Everything is made of the atom; our world is apparently unified within the commonality of carrying atom, atom is the common denominator for the entire physical beings.

It means a position whose effect fully identifies with the multiplicities, the entire material diversities, and the spiritual realms. Unity in existence means all existence is interwoven in God, in their actual cause, as everything and everyone is an inalienable part of God's existence.

Either rhetorical or what is literally seen and exercised in every day's routines and work should remind us of the unity in the oneness of God and the existence.

We observe no conflicting manifestation in our universe, since everything in nature and beyond is as patented (not concealed) with absolute discipline, significantly coordinated, where every being is blessed with a purpose. All creatures are mandated towards one goal, as if the designers, architectures, engineers, the surveyors, foundation workers, the roof men, bricklayers, stone and concrete laborers, carpenters, painters, plumbers, electricians, the landscapers, etc., are collectively laboring to build a fine home for its residents to enjoy the serenity of mind with comfortable living.

Furthermore, the whole is made up of the parts, and if the parts have destiny and purpose, in which everything and all is undeniably meant to serve their objectives, then logic dictates that the whole, which comprises of these parts, also has a destiny and purpose. To say we come from nowhere and we are going nowhere simply does not add up, and is both wrong and utterly contradictory. Even the famous phrase the survival of the fittest presupposes the arrival of the fit. If Darwinists wish to maintain this purely biological theory, that the entire vast order around us is the result of random chance and random changes, then they are also saying that nothing of any empirical evidence can ever be confirmed, and no empirical science can be demonstrated, which basically is as good as saying no experimental scientific findings are ever valid.

We are endowed with intelligence, enriched with consciousness, memory, imagination, willpower, and the freedom to choose, and have the ability to discern right from wrong, as we are utterly distinguished from the lower species, from the beasts, that are either devoid of such dynamics, or relatively speaking, have much lower frequencies in comprehension. Therefore, it would make no sense to punish animals, which for humans, contrary to the beasts, it makes whole lots of sense to be reminded of our existence as a test because demonic and bad behaviors shouldn't go unanswered, where good deeds should definitely be noticed and rewarded.

Death does not experience human beings, rather human beings experience death, where everyone according to their deeds will either ascend to higher realms or descend to lower phases of existence, where nominal symbolic such as hell, heaven, and other domains for retribution or reward should be expected to exist. The point is, because we are all organically connected, one's righteous doings, or committing wrongs, will affect the rest. Therefore, it is imperative to behave as mankind is made in the image of God, and definitely not as seeing God in man's image.

The overwhelming complexity in the universe and the awesome precision in design would challenge any inquisitive mind that no polygamy-oriented thoughts about the existence of God can have the unanimity (consensus, assent, union) to agree with all the intricacies that the universe carries. Such genius and the spectacular design can only be manifested from a sovereign mind, a sole Omnipotent, Omniscient Creator, and not creators, since the reality of all beings and the attributes of God do not in any way conflict.

Furthermore, it is not far from reason to fathom that everything starts from one and then expands to multicity, where complexities and further exponential processes occur. No matter how far any phenomenon travels, and how complicated all processes become, they all begin from one; oneness is a common denominator for all there is, and all there ever will be; oneness is the root cause of the entire existence.

Everything in existence is sound and superbly unified without any interruption, propelling from the dawn of time to present days that can only attribute from an absolutely infallible mind. Otherwise, this intricate evolutionary process would have been extinguished in its inception, and couldn't have had lasted for so long as it has and still roaring forward full of zest and absolutely without any interruption, imbued with an extremely intelligent guide, so resilient beyond mankind's comprehension.

Let's maneuver like the sun does, where everyone and everything enjoys its warmth, its goodness, regardless of their biological or social status. Let's make the moral and the legal imperatives universally prevalent so that one can expand onto where God resides in one's soul. Therefore, let's act like eagles, where the eagle can look directly into the sun as a test for their chick's worthiness; the eagle holds them up facing the sun. Let's be worthy of the sun.

The birds that cannot stare into the sun and turn their eyes away are cast out of the nest. Let's not be cast out of fruitful existence, as we should look straight into the eyes of the living, to cultivate prosperity, happiness, caring, peace, and always hope for a much better life; where nothing, even thinking of death, couldn't constrain us to live life to its fullest. Let's believe in God.

7

IN SEARCH OF DEMOCRACY

When adamant to make a free society, and for democracy to be unleashed, there must exist boundless professional counselors, skillful training instructors, quality social services, adept management, and plenty of devoted social workers to educate those in need of mental and behavioral hygiene; when the intention is to build a civilized and rational-minded society. Be aware that in the absence of an informed nation, no democracy can ever flourish except resulting in irresponsible criterions where violence will surely go rampant.

I say it is difficult to implement true democracy when people are famished, where the disease of hunger is prevalent, when illiteracy must be cured, when homelessness and lack of proper medical care must be terminated, when joblessness is often the case, and when transportation is frequently problematic. If the intention is to sincerely lessen the proliferating crimes, ending in too many ills from the criminals, then the above moral, social, and legal imperatives need to be met. I honestly believe that not only is it immoral, but it should be illegal to waste a mind, to force people into unemployment, and not to cure the sick, not feed the poor, and not financially subsidize the needy.

Let me be clear; there is no ambiguity about having freedom and an education going hand in hand for prevailing a civil society. The cultural short-sightedness of extreme inequality has entrapped billions, and is the leading cause for sabotaging a fair and just society as it should be dealt with head on to expose the faces of the underground masterminds behind the very reason for people's misfortune and hellish situation.

The society should be able to absorb the seed of freedom just like a fertile ground that needs irrigation, proper sun, nutrients, and care to grow into a fruitful tree. Priorities should be rendered to those that earnestly believe in acting as true human beings with good conscience. if not, rest assured that our beasty side is to prevail and behave corrupted and become nothing but destructive elements of society.

God endowed humanity with the miracle of brain and mind, so question more to manifest and make good use of your intelligent, your positive emotion, your goodwill, and constructive actions. Nehru puts it this way: "Democracy is good I say this because other systems are worse. So we are forced to accept democracy. It has good points and also bad, but merely saying that democracy will solve all problems is utterly wrong. Problems are solved by intelligence and hard work."

And Thomas Jefferson said, "When the people fear the government there is tyranny; when the government fears the people there is liberty." I say: "The more educated, civilized and opulent the nation, the more democracy is practical and freedom should make sense."

Here is the bottom line: to avoid chaos and bloodbath, we either have to put up with a dictatorial regime of governing, or we must relentlessly work hard to treat and take over our human beastly side, since it can erupt at any time if not fundamentally mended.

This can be manifested through viable education and effective training; and humanity should professionally aim for a gradual introduction of democracy, human rights, liberty, and freedom through which the pinnacle of goodness can be nourished and reached. A sacred realm of existence in tune with the image of God promised can be attained and secured; it is then when human worth and dignity are truly recognized.

8

IN SEARCH OF TRUTH

Many scientists, philosophers, and faith-oriented individuals are engaged in an uplifting quest for truth. Yet, what is the truth and how do we locate it? With the birth of relativistic mechanics, wave mechanics, which in turn evolved into quantum mechanics, the entire classic physics where Newtonian laws govern went topsy-turvy as scientists discovered new dimensions which have perplexed the best minds of our times, as they are not able to grasp the magical world of subatomic particles, where it seems their vibrating, dance-like maneuvers give meaning to the reality of our lives.

Even though quantum mechanics apparently provides the best explanation presently available on a microscopic level, neither the unseen realms of the subatomic nor future scientific discoveries can bring us to the truth. Bear in mind that quantum mechanics took place out of the need to provide explanations for a horizon (domain) of physical phenomena that could not be done by classical physics: blackbody spectrum, photoelectric effect, spectra of the elements, the specific heat of solids. Through the work of Planck, Einstein, and others, the idea shaped that electromagnetic and other forms of energy could be exchanged only in definite quantities (quanta.)

With the work of de Broglie, the concept arose that matter could show wave-like properties. It was Einstein who proposed that waves (light) could behave like particles (photons). Heisenberg proposed the first victorious quantum theory, but in terms of the mathematics of matrices—matrix mechanics. It was Schrodinger who came up with an equation for the waves predicted by de Broglie, and that initiated the wave mechanics. Schrodinger also showed that his work and that of Heisenberg's were mathematically equivalent. But it was Heisenberg and Born who first understood that quantum mechanics was a theory of probabilities.

Einstein would never agree with that, even though he assisted in discovering it! It was the work of Dirac, von Neumann, Jordan, and others, which eventually exhibited that matrix mechanics and wave mechanics were but two forms of a more fundamental theory—quantum mechanics.

Quantum mechanics is a theory of information. It is a set of laws about the information that can be assessed about the physical world. The first hint for a modern physics lay in understanding the genesis (creation) of the blackbody spectrum: A blackbody is an object that captivates all radiation, with whatever frequency, that falls on it. The blackbody spectrum is the spectrum of radiation released by the object when it is in heat.

Yet, recent experiments and new calculations and theories have manifested the existence of finer divisions into much tinier entities— quarks, bosons, leptons, etc., as they are made of even finer strings, as per the string theory. Physics is ever expanding as the reality it attempts to unveil continues to shift. But that reality continues to stay out of the grasp of the latest scientific theories.

Even Einstein seriously doubted its methodology and probability predictions, stating, "I am sure that God does not play dice." It seems that God votes for gradual progress because as every scientific theory runs its course, a new innovation, a fresh discovery replaces it, as the latest one brings humanity a bit closer and in tune with the mysteries of the universe.

For instance, the equation exhibiting the gravitational attraction $F = Gmm'/r^2$ between two masses, in conjunction with Kepler's laws of planetary motion, when dissected on the scale of the universe, has a huge problem. There is apparently not enough mass in the universe to account for the entirety of the gravitational attractions calculated and observed in the universe.

Hence, scientists postulate that there is an elusive element known as dark matter. This hidden dark matter is required to balance the equations of motion for the planets and stars. Yet scientists are baffled as to where this matter is or what it actually is. They can notice its effects by looking at the bending of light from distant stars. In other words, they fathom that the presence of some matter is there, but what that matter is escapes them.

Einstein has proven in his famous theory of relativity that nothing can travel faster than the speed of light or even close to that. Of course, in the contemporary world, it has become the norm to find science fiction-like exceptions to this rule. Truly, it is quite hard to tell if we are dealing with fiction-like scenarios or facts. Either way, NASA spent billions of dollars, and so much time and effort, researching time warp drives—a concept made famous in the popular science fiction show *Star Trek*. The warp drive was utilized to empower the Star Ship *Enterprise*. Another movie, *Contact*, is where a space machine passes through a wormhole, exhibiting a means of travel.

Yes, it is science fiction, perhaps utopia, or exaggerated imagination, but unless our mind can fathom and grasp such so-called dreams, it would be impossible to manifest it, as it couldn't be far from the reality, turning human's passion for magical discoveries into glory. Perhaps movies as such are science fiction, but the best science fiction is always oriented on the actual science and is merely extended by brilliant dreams.

Wormholes are anticipated and learned by moderate physics as doable constructs. They are not fictional—the physics of wormholes is viable in theory. Miguel Alcubierre Moya is a Mexican theoretical physicist who is famous for his paper "The Warp Drive: Hyper-fast Travel Within General Relativity," which stowed the theory of the time warp as a realistic concept.

A great number of scientists mandated his theories viable, although far-fetched to put into practice in any case. The idea of such theoretical physics was regarded practical enough for NASA to explore time warp as a probability as a means of space travel, since they dedicated themselves to such research. Later on NASA halted the endeavor, and stopped their plan. The contemporary science is not progressive enough to resolve many issues of our time. Yet the physics involved in the idea of time warp space travel seems real and theoretically possible. Not all scientific theories materialized through a systematic study of nature, applicable to precise scientific laws of nature, since many wacky imaginations and weird intuition have also ended in great scientific inventions.

For example, the benzene molecular structure was conceived by Friedrich August Kekulé, a German chemist, from a strange dream of a snake chasing its tail. He did not ignore his thoughts from this dream but applied them to his research and thereby reached a great breakthrough.

Many discoveries occurred by those who were not looking for them. For instance, Viagra was discovered by lucky accident, an unexpected but useful side effects from drugs. Saccharine, the artificial sweetener in Sweet'n Low, was discovered by a Russian chemist who forgot to wash his hands after a day's work. Often world-altering findings are the result of creative minds noticing that material or invention could be changed for a different purpose.

The microwave in 1946 was founded by Percy Spencer, an engineer from Raytheon Corporation, as he was working on a radar-related project. While he was testing a new vacuum tube, he realized that a chocolate bar melted in his pocket a bit faster than expected; his curiosity led him to aim the tube at other things, like eggs, more chocolate bars, popcorn, etc., where he drew the conclusion that heating the object experienced was because of the microwave energy.

X-rays

In 1895, a German physicist named Wilhelm Roentgen was working with a cathode ray tube when he realized that a nearby fluorescent screen would keep glowing in the dark room while the tube was on. He replaced the tube with a photographic plate to capture the images, creating the first X-rays. When he put his hand in front of the tube, he could see his bones in the image that was projected on the screen. The technology was then adopted by medical institutions and research departments—unfortunately, it took a long time before the risks of X-ray radiation were learned.

Penicillin. In 1928, Sir Alexander Fleming, a professor of bacteriology, saw that mold had grown on his Petri dishes of Staphylococcus bacteria colonies. While looking for the colonies he could salvage from those infected with the mold, he noticed something intriguing. Bacteria wasn't growing around the mold. The mold actually happens to be a scarce strain of Penicillin notatum that secreted a substance that inhibited bacterial growth. Penicillin was then employed in the 1940s, helping open up the age of antibiotics.

The pacemaker was accidentally invented in 1956 by Wilson Greatbatch, as he noticed the wrong fitting resistor emitted electric pulses, which made him think of the timing of the heartbeat.

The effort that led to the discovery of insulin was an accident.

Albert Hofmann studied Lysergic acid (LSD), a powerful chemical that was first isolated from a fungus that grows on rye, which he first synthesized in 1938. These chemicals he researched were going to be utilized as pharmaceuticals, and many derivatives of them are still used as of today.

Teflon and superglue were accidentally discovered, and thousands of other inventions happened because of accidental discoveries.

This line of reasoning illustrates that the frontiers of science are still vastly short of solving many of the challenges facing them. They are stifled by their small world of limited perception and are further restricted by that science available as tools for their understanding. In general, scientists restrain themselves to the formal thought process, a process that does not allow them to be openminded when considering metaphysical topics in the realms of spirituality and religiosity. Bear in mind that innumerable ideas, like the Pythagorean theorem, the binary number system, decimal system, zero infinity, mathematics, the so-called language of God, evolution, and thousands of others, have their origin ingrained in ancient knowledge and information.

In other words, this ancient system of knowledge was familiar with and illustrated many methods and constructs of math and science that were not even idealized nor founded in the rest of the globe until several millennia later, in which most very old text has eloquently shed light on that. When Heisenberg and Bohr debated about inexorable (certain) disturbances in any conceivable measurement, it was evident to them that this uncertainty was a property of the system, not of the apparatus (machines, devices). In essence, this very important Principle of Uncertainty suggests that we cannot really measure things on a microscopic level with absolute certainty.

Furthermore, Kurt Gödel's Incompleteness Theorem shows that there is a constraint on all but the most basic mathematical systems. These theorems boundlessly show that Hilbert's program for finding a complete and consistent set of axioms for all of mathematics is impossible. These incompleteness findings of Gödel shook the very underpinning (foundation) of twentieth-century mathematics, just as the theory of relativity and quantum mechanics redirected contemporary physical research.

Gregory Chaitlin of the IBM T. J. Watson Research Center takes Gödel's incompleteness results a bit further, and shows with algorithmic (a process or set of rules to be followed in calculations or other problem-solving operation, especially by a computer) information theory that mathematics has more extensive and serious limitations than hitherto (formerly, previously) suspected.

9

IN SEARCH OF HEAVEN

We live in an era where I am afraid hell and heaven play a significant role in innumerable people's psyches, entangling so many with the yoke of uncertainty, nudging believers to do what's right and making non-believers aware of their insensible actions toward religion and God, promising that non-believers will be denied the heaven above and perhaps punished by ending up in hell.

> "Mankind is not likely to salvage civilization unless he can evolve a system of good and evil which is independent of heaven and hell."
>
> -George Orwell.

Oddly enough, not too many look into the mottos for what is right and wrong, which have fundamentally topsy-turvied the entire socio-cultural, socio-economic, and socio-political agendas for the worse, globally denying billions of social and economic justification, forcing millions into doing wrong just to survive. This, I am afraid, has manufactured cut-throat societies beyond correction, as violence has become the norm, as it seems no safe haven is left for the needy to refuge to.

Leaving so many violators with the impression that they shouldn't be a concern with the after-death punishment, as if the retributions would not be so real, that reprisal (payback) will be as fake as voodoo magic (a black religious cult practiced in the Caribbean and the southern US, combining elements of Roman Catholic ritual with traditional African magical and religious rites, and characterized by sorcery and spirit possession) spilled on those wrongdoers. Instead of morally malfunctioning and/or not abiding by the law, the very victims of this whole civilized shenanigans called capitalism must peacefully fight for their rights via non-violent means.

No one should deny that we live in a monetary-oriented environment, where global tendencies are significantly attracted towards the love of money, and rightly so. No proper living is ever possible without it, as so many simply do not have it, where billions are internationally poverty-stricken and without hope for living a decent life.

Wherein the business name has replaced God's name since unduly corporations have even yoked the state and the governments to do as they say is right and wrong, and what is ethical or not, where moral and legal imperatives have shifted to serve the bosses' interest, and not the republic.

The epistemology (the investigation of what distinguishes justified belief from opinion) and meaningful linguistic literature are apparently not intact, as so many interactivities are dubious and incoherent with what is fair and just practice among many social and financial layers of societies; giving meaning to the expression that everyone has a price.

Everybody has a price means that everybody will eventually sell out and do something unethical if they are paid enough. (It doesn't necessarily mean with money—it could be the promise of a great job, higher position, legal protection, sexual favor, or anything else which the culprits might have craving for.)

This is especially true in poverty-stricken atmospheres. If anyone believes otherwise, let them experience having no job, dealing with an empty stomach, no roof over their head, deprived of any education, without viable transportation, with no proper hygiene and medical availability, and without any kind of savings.

Especially when someone's loved one is in need of immediate lifesaving surgery or medical attention, since in many capitalist systems there are no adequate social, medical, or practical economic programs to protect the needy, the elderly, disabled, and the unemployed, making the expression that there is no free lunch a reality. No matter how desperate one's situation happens to be, the real problem is that the capitalist system so cleverly plays double standard, and it is beyond the layman's grasp to detect the cunningly deliberate designs aiming at making the rich richer and the poor poorer.

Institutional religions undeniably play a huge part in feeding consumers with wrong prophecies as well, not finger-pointing the misleading issues to deter believers from such path that leverages the capitalist system to ruthlessly exploit the workers and the actual producer of wealth. Through hard work and backbreaking productivity, the laborers have already created so much wealth for the capitalist's bosses beyond anyone's imagination.

The institutional religions should remind people that hell is here, since billions are deprived of living in peace, as believers are just happy with the promises of the afterlife; reminding them of the ill consequences of hell, and denial of heaven if they dare to do otherwise and as instructed. Placing masses of people in a hard place and a rock, striking them with the double-edged sword of unjustified living conditions and for awaiting the punishment of hell. Like Dante's *Inferno* manifesting a fictional novel which comically draws on the afterlife, just an imaginary fiction not taken as truth.

Many religions capitalize on manufacturing fear and anxiety in a world that is already compounded with stress and pain caused by financially ruling elites. Religion's redundant conditioning of masses promising them hell and heaven should not go any further than Dante's *Inferno* comedy, and many other fictionally based stories uttered in human history.

Accepting that many variables are responsible for one's character and attributes, in which the environmental effects, wrong or right, upbringings are extremely decisive and have a lot to do with one's personality makeup. Therefore, instead of trying to make people fearful and threaten them with the anxieties of the afterlife comedy-like ordeals, promising to torture the sinners in hell, and the expectancy to reward the righteous in heaven.

It would make much sense to establish a thorough social program which could financially sustain citizens in time of need without having paralyzing worries when out of work, or when hit with the recession, depression, and when one has to struggle with a devastating illness, or is faced with any other tragic outcome. By the way, if a society is equipped with proper social welfare and makes sensible social and economic programs, it would significantly lower crime rates.

Perhaps in Dante's allegory, the story of divine comedy can shed some light on the journey of the soul towards God, with the *Inferno* explaining the concession (admission) and the refusal of sin. The *Inferno* tells about the trek of Dante through hell, guided by the ancient Roman poet Virgil, in which Dante the poet perceives to be on the universal Christian quest for God. Concluding that Dante's character is anchored in the everyman allegorical tradition: Dante's billet (position) is meant to show that of the entire human race.

In Dante Alighieri's hell-fire, the poet and pilgrim Dante embarks on a spiritual odyssey guided by the soul of the Roman poet Virgil. Dante travels down through the nine circles of Hell and witnesses the castigation (chastisement, punishment) eternally endured by the souls of deceased sinners.

First Circle (Limbo) Dante's First Circle of hell is virtuous non-Christians and unbaptized pagans who are chastised with eternity in lesser heaven; where they live in a seven-gated castle denoting the seven virtues. Circle 1: Limbo. Resided in by virtuous non-Christians and unbaptized pagans. Circle 2: Lust. The souls here are chastised by being blown about violently by tremendously strong winds, devoid of peace and rest. Circle 3: Gluttony, Circle 4: Greed, Circle 5: Anger, Circle 6: Heresy (eccentricity, nonconforming, dissent), Circle 7: Violence, Circle 8: Fraud.

Being a Christian, Dante adds Circle 1 (Limbo) to Upper Hell and Circle 6 (Heresy) to Lower Hell, making 9 Circles in sum; incorporating the Vestibule of the Futile, this leads to Hell containing 10 main divisions. Thus, Hell has in total 24 divisions. In Canto III of the hell-fire before arriving at the Acheron River and approaching hell, Virgil guides Dante through Hell's Vestibule, where the futile are committed, where those who have exhibited hesitation, indecision after indecision, are forever hustling and bustling (spinning) about without certain objective, exhausted of any goal with indefinite end; they simply are not able to rest eternally.

The Vestibule is the abode of the weather-cock mind (an erratic person, unstable, fickle-minded or often changeable) the obscure (vague, shadowy, puzzling, abstract, opaque) tolerance which will neither ratify nor damn (condemn) the leery, timid, cautious (cowardice) for which no say so or determination is ever final. The spirits rush pointlessly after the aimlessly spinning banner, spurred by the thought that, in doing anything whatsoever certain, they are losing on something else.

Dante conceptualized the recorded entrance to hell: abandon hope all ye who enter here, inhabited by pursuers of pointless endeavors. After going through the gate of Purgatory, Virgil led the pilgrim Dante through the mountain's seven terraces (grandstands.)

These tally (agree, correspond) to the seven mortal sins or seven roots of sinfulness where abomination and wickedness are done, starting with Pride, Envy, Wrath, Sloth, Avarice (greed), Prodigality (spending too much, extravaganza), Gluttony (too much eating or drinking), and Lust (sexual desire, eroticism, libido.)

Historically speaking, the powerful and the financial bullies have always played active roles in setting up states, the way governments ought to be running and how laws should be dictated, since concentration of wealth, which no doubt leads to concentration of power, influencing politics either with direct hands-on or affecting it via covert activities.

Classified societies often leading to extreme income inequality strikes global victims with financial insecurities, leaving them no choice but to sometimes do the unthinkable for subsistence. The powerful and the influential unfortunately have turned living into survival games, where the so-called fittest with the evilest and inhumane ideas conspire against commoners, devouring all of which belongs to the poor. You might ask if greed has anything to do with it.

The answer is yes, but we are faced with a system which relentlessly fuels the fire of temptation, misleading consumers through potently toxic media by setting financial traps with deceiving tactics, which lures millions into a buying spree, continuously brain-storming consumers to hoard things they do not need, and eventually they cannot buy the things they often desperately need. This whole dilemma compounds when people become laid-off or become unemployed, forcing them into the survival mode to the extent of even selling their souls.

The economic insecurity plays like the eye of the storm, whirling so fast into tornado-like worries, bellowing the victims off their feet with anxiety and fear, leaving them with little hope for survival; it is a no-brainer that eventually, every trick in the book is used to cheat, lie, steal, corrupt, and even murder to secure one's monetary position. Especially when there are no meaningful social networks offered in the very unstable capitalist system to temporarily rescue citizens from sometimes horrific financial situations.

The economic supremacism (an ideology which holds that a particular class of people is superior to others and that it should dominate, control, and subjugate others, or is entitled to do so) is exactly what is going on. Bigoted-like behaviors of the oligopolies should vehemently be fought against to awaken the moguls of our time that lives matter.

Global citizenry is running away from this hell we call living in search of heaven, because of the capitalist's atrocious-oriented culture that is designed to exploit people and colonize citizens for the worst, denying so many from God-endowed freedom, liberty, human rights, and the pursuit of happiness, which the good Constitution has also manifested and ratified.

When people desperately are in need of basic resources to survive, loud talks of freedom and human rights can only play an oxymoron with contrasting meaning, such as cruel compassion or living death. Oxymoron: a figure of speech by which a locution (a phrase, a clause, a sentence) produces an incongruous, seemingly self-contradictory effect, as in cruel kindness or to make haste slowly.

Human beings cannot simultaneously live and die, as they could not be free and at the same time left needy, in a system which by nature cannot sustain prolonged social and economic stability that leaves billions monetarily insecure.

Hence, the struggle for ensuring one's financial position will be the norm, and it becomes everyone's priority, with the exception that the rich elites have certainly the means to take all that they can without any remorse, and those deprived of influence and power, the destitute, the poor, end up incarcerated, if they legally malfunction to survive.

The capitalist system cunningly addresses God with the rewards and the punishments of the afterlife to prevent the victims of financial depravity from uprising and to quell resurrections. Telling billions of global hungry people that they might have a terrible situation in this life, but they will have the best of fun in the next life. This type of mental tactics will surely affect so many psychologically, believing what the hell, why bother, since we will be much better off, for our next life, in the heaven above.

With the super-rich possessing all of the resources and leaving the majority of people with almost nothing, the ruling elites would expect violent resurrection by the poverty-stricken dissidents against them. The idea of heaven and hell can to some extent calm them down, especially when people are conditioned that the rich elites must have been blessed with wealth because they are chosen to govern.

As if Jesus agreed with rich landowner Pharisees, and the affluent Sadducees, Essen, and others which in cahoots with Romans crucified him. Jesus rebuked the scribes and Pharisees so harshly in Matthew 23:13–36? In Matthew 23, Jesus pronounces woes on the scribes and Pharisees, the rich religious elite of the day. The word *woe* is an exclamation of grief, denunciation, or distress.

It is further essential to say that not all Jews were responsible for killing Jesus, where people's attitudes toward Jews, as Jewish blame for Jesus' death has long been a linchpin for anti-Semitism, that is neither humane nor right, because most Jews lacked a motive for Killing Jesus. In fact, relating to most historians, it would be most appropriate to blame the Romans for Jesus' death, since crucifixion was a customary punishment among Romans, not Jews.

At the time of Jesus's death, the Romans were imposing a harsh and brutal occupation on the Land of Israel, and the Jews were often unruly. The Romans would have had reason to want to silence Jesus, who had been called by some of his followers King of the Jews, and was known as a Jewish upstart miracle worker defending the rights of helpless, and the needy against the Roman empire. Bottom line heaven means to be one with God Confucius.

10

IGNORANCE OR INTELLIGENCE?

Which faith should one belong to?

Ignoring human intelligence, blunt in moral behavior and experiencing inferior actions will make force, fear, and uncertainty to take over, the absence of civil acts and lack of virtuosity (expert aesthetic, sensibility) can quickly tilt towards ill doings and corrupt activities.

Savagery and dark age mentality historically has left humanity with no choice, but to refuge to legal and moral imperatives, nudging inhabitants to act lawfully, and for the believers to follow spiritual maxims for acquiring a tranquil living. To endure ethical laws, mainly through religion in which most religions unanimously promise brewing punishments in the afterlife when sins are committed, and heavenly rewards when good deeds are done.

It is a no-brainer to realize that in perpetrating transgression or in avoiding sin, one's actions are relatively proportional with one's intelligence, wisdom, and by one's awakened conscience, which can sure play a decisive role in behaving good and humane.

It is relatively true that witted conducts are not born overnight, but for presentable attitudes, civil behaviors, cultured actions with pleasant human interactions also have to forgo enhanced evolutionary process, in which many religions at barbarian's era and through dark ages played viable roles.

In the meanwhile, undertaking fear tactics, denoting punishment and reward mechanism in the afterlife, which once might have been to a certain degrees effective, are no longer of much concern, since time parameter plays a huge role in implementing ideas that are dynamic in nature; or perhaps dull enough to persist on traditionally old creeds that lag behind, not in accord with new information's age. Most of the so-called traditional maxims are not able to meet today's standard since modernism demands an up-scaled paradigm shift in consciousness and civil behavior.

After all, what difference does it make which faith one belongs to when one encroaches on other people's right, infringes on other's sovereignty? Behaves self-centered and arrogant, lies, steals, is cruel, acts vengeful and unconsidered, does not believe in decency and righteous conducts, murders, rapes, and pedophiles, keeps many skeletons in one's closet, and so on?

The crux of the matter is that others should be immune from one's ills, from one's morbid behaviors, and comfortable to benefit from one's kind assistance. Regardless of what one faith is, one needs to believe in the famous maxim, as Confucius stated: "Do not Do unto others what you don't want others Do unto you."

In the meanwhile, it is informing to know what many religions say about the afterlife, which in reviewing various faith-oriented entities, I have noticed that religions have made God's concept of reward and punishment to what mankind imagine and makes it be, making God in man's image, rather than believing that man was made in God's image. the institutional religions constitute the laws of heavens like human's assessment for rewarding, punishing, right or wrong.

They present God as a worldly king that governs through his representatives, ministers, messengers, lecturers, legislative, judicial and executive branches of government, as occasionally retaliatory, or sometimes forgiving. Bottom line, it is most important that state keep away from intermingling with the religion of any kind, and for religion not to infiltrate the government. the state is a legal, earthy entity, and not a heavenly article (to bring someone to a period of service), since the state is responsible for legislative, judicial and executive branches of government to stop wrongdoings, and illegal behaviors. No state should be accountable to make mandatory moral laws, delineate virtuous conducts, and or impose any religious requirements.

No government should interfere to promote religious orientations, or encourage atheism, or dignify secularity. No pope, so the priest, no clergyman of any kind, no mullahs, no rabbi, no monk, nor any other religious head should have merit or priority over others to engage in law.

What should be respected and honored, is the individual right to worship and connect to God in which way one sees fit. An iron-clad of separation between religion and state should be implemented, that needs to be very clear in meaning.

The government cannot make laws that favor one religion over any other, it must not make laws related to the establishment of a religion or the free expression of religious beliefs. What the state should be responsible for, is to exercise contends of the Constitution, and execute the law of the land.

We ought to know that religion is a subject which lies entirely between man and his/her God, that he owes an account to none either for his faith or his homage to his/her God, considering that the legitimate powers of government reach actions only, and not opinions, thus, a wall of separation between state and religion should be built to give the man all of his natural rights, convinced that one has no natural right contrary and opposed to one's social duties.

Most religions and faith-oriented entities emphasis on the influence of divine rewards, and the punishments which stem from man's imagination. A common finding across many cultures is that such doctoring manifests pro-sociability than less or non-religious people who do not believe in an afterlife, and are not foreboding (the feeling that something is going to happen) after we expire. Implicit (implied) religious concepts, or explicit (clearly) said moral declaration and cues (signals) like God, salvation, purgatory, punishment in hell, and rewards of heaven, among many others, rise pro-sociability in religious individuals, groups, or society.

However, such promulgation (creed) and socio-cultural tendency channelized through faith-oriented concepts are mere hypotheses, since the factors underlining such findings are not clear; but it seems the empirical literature encompassing such divine rewards and the fear of punishments in the afterlife are accentuated by many religious customs and traditions that are playing a significant role in pro-sociability.

The objective should hinge on finding the best alternatives for a better living, prioritizing plans which can accommodate people with basic necessities in this life to avoid dismay (very worried, sinking feelings) and crimes, rather than relinquishing unrealistic promises, and in giving believers hope of unsubstantiated claims of afterlife rewards. To let the inhabitants of planet Earth live in peace and not prejudice against viable social welfare which if practiced can constitute good living as it is meant to be for everyone, and not just glorified living for the few, the oligopoly regime, and their gangs.

Religions need to stop belittling an infinite God since no physical, no revival (resurrection), and no being of any kind should define God, as no one has ever seen or talked to God since the Almighty has always existed, as an infinite essential, an infinite priority beyond the space, time, and motion, where no past, present, or future was ever initiated.

The limitless God is over the grasp of any mortal, is so space-less, boundless, timeless, and Omnipresent, which shouldn't be impersonated with any of mankind's attribute, as we are finite beings maneuvering within a limited domain.

Some vital issues in philosophy occur between religious and non-religious people, disclosing whether atheism can better resonate with the ethical environment and for morality to flourish, or theism is more vibrant in accomplishing such task. Theists often debate that Godless views are exhausted of fundamental objective referencing moral virtues which the end result will be immorality and hedonism believing that pleasure or happiness is the most imperative goal in life.

Many atheists and humanists have debunked the theist's view saying that what is presented by religions as moral foundations are functionaries partially rooted in self-interest, which promises divine rewards, for instant eternal euphoria (rapture, bliss, ecstasy), and forever torments promising inferno, which both heaven and hell are as recompense for heaven and acting good, and hell for ill-behaving. In the meanwhile, extensive research shows that what theologians and religious apologists say seems to be true, since many investigative reports have found that religious people behave morally prosocial than less or non-religious individuals.

The religious proclivity towards prosocial attitudes and behaviors is not the sole reason behind people's acting prosocial. Socio-cultural, socio-economic perspectives are certainly not solely influenced by religion, since millions of religious and secularly minded individuals are also influenced by education, enlightenment, the power of reasoning, compassion, civility of mind and manner, which play a pivotal role in reigning good and virtuous behaviors.

Secularity is defined as a secular religion is a communal belief system that often rejects or neglects the metaphysical aspects of the supernatural, commonly associated with traditional religions, instead of placing typical religious qualities in earthly entities. It is further doubtful if religion, per se, is the only underlying cause of the increased pro-sociality; since other factors as economy, good role model, healthy environment, and constructive upbringing also play a decisive role in one's pro-sociability; rather, religion is known to exert its effects indirectly by its appeal to simpler cognitive and effective mechanisms.

For example, Judaism concept of righteous living, and what we should expect in the afterlife.

The promulgation (doctoring) of reward and punishment is an inseparable part of every classical catalog of the primal principles of Judaism. In the Hebrew Scriptures, the creed of reward and punishment (individual, national and universal) is of this world. It is considered as self-evident that God rewards the good folks by granting them prosperity and punishes the wicked with ruins.

It should be clear this is what the American leaders had in mind when they established their Declaration of Independence, which says, "We hold these truths to be self-evident, that all men are created equal, that they are endowed by their Creator with certain unalienable Rights, that among these are Life, Liberty and the pursuit of Happiness." Finally reaching the view that in the end virtue is its own reward, and vice its own punishment.

Most worldviews must accept their belief in the afterlife on untested faith, but the Christian faith believes in the pursuits that first the resurrection of Christ and the testimony of God's Word, accepting that the Bible renders the true view of what occurs after death. Even though many Christians miscomprehend the afterlife.

Some believe that they become one of the angels, others say they go into a state of soul sleep, while some believe they will be floating on clouds playing harps. Christians can be assured that death is not something to be feared. Instead, at death, we will leave our body and are ascended to the next home in heaven.

Believers will be saved through the resurrection of Jesus our Lord. There are differing perspectives on death since the existence of mankind, humanity has wrestled with the question, what occurs after death? What we believe happens after we expire has great innuendos (implication) for our life here on Earth. Even though millions avoid the issue, we ought to sooner or later address the question.

There are many challenging answers to this inquiry. Non-believers, atheists say that at one's death, one ceases to exist. They do not believe in an afterlife or eternal soul and reject any spirit that continues in eon (eternity, the blue moon). They insist on the inevitable death of mankind and the eventual ending of the universe, where there is no meaning or any purposeful life to hope for.

Referencing the pantheistic view, it indicates that one goes through a continuous cycle of reincarnation until the cycle is broken and the person unifies with the divine. What form, what kind of quality life expectancy should endorse the person depends on how one behaved in the previous life?

Further pantheistic belief is that after unification with the divine, one ceases to exist, as the person becomes part of the divine spirit, the life force as if a drop of water reuniting with the ocean. One that believes in pantheism sees God in the entire world around one. Pantheism belief that the entire universe is in its idea of God.

The doctrine of pantheism believes that God is all around us, throughout the whole universe. Pantheism sees everything as being interconnected, as the believers see lack of separation between God, people, and things, they rather see all there is as being interconnected. Pantheism refers to a belief in all gods from all religions, insists on acceptance and tolerance for those beliefs. In Greek, *pan* means all and *Theos* means God.

Those who keep up with the animistic (the belief that natural objects, natural phenomena, and the universe itself possess souls, the belief that natural objects have souls that may exist apart from their material bodies, The understanding that natural objects such as rivers and rocks possess a soul or spirit), or tribal religions which believe that after death the person's soul stays on the Earth, or travels to approach the departed spirits of the ancestors in the underworld, also known as the realm of the shadows.

For eternity they ramble (meander, wander) in darkness, experiencing neither joy nor suffering and pain. Some of the spirits of the dead may be called upon to aid or torment (harm) those on Earth. Some of the most prominent faith do have a common denominator which they are based on, shedding light on the influences in the agendas they respectively share.

Let's start with Zoroastrianism, which is an ancient Persian faith believed to have initiated as early as 4,000 years ago. Probably the world's first monotheistic religion, it's one of the oldest religions still in existence. Zoroastrianism was the state religion of three Persian dynasties, until the Muslim conquest of Persia in the seventh century AD. Zoroastrian refugees, called Parsis, escaped Muslim persecution in Iran by migrating to India.

Zoroastrianism is still practiced today as a minority religion in parts of Iran and India. The prophet Zoroaster (Zarathustra in ancient Persian) is considered as the founder of Zoroastrianism. It's possibly the world's oldest monotheistic faith. Most of what is known about Zoroaster comes from the Avesta—a collection of Zoroastrian religious scriptures. It's ambiguous precisely when Zoroaster may have lived.

Many scholars and historians believe he was a contemporary of Cyrus the Great, a Persian king of the sixth century BC., though most linguistic and archaeological evidence points to an earlier date—sometime between 1500 and 1200 BC. Zoroaster is believed to have been born in what is now northeastern Iran or southwestern Afghanistan. He might have lived in a tribe that pursued an ancient religion with many Gods (polytheism). This religion was probably similar to early forms of Hinduism.

Based on Zoroastrian practice, Zoroaster had a divine vision of a supreme being while participating in a pagan (heathen, idolatrous) purification rite at age 30. Zoroaster started teaching followers to worship a single God called Ahura Mazda. Zoroastrianism formed one of the ancient world's largest empires—the mighty Persian Empire. It was the state religion of three major Persian dynasties.

Cyrus the Great, founder of the Achaemenid Persian Empire, was a devout Zoroastrian. By all means, Cyrus the Great was a tolerant ruler who let his non-Iranian subjects to practice their own religions.

He ruled by the Zoroastrian law of Asha (truth and righteousness) but didn't force Zoroastrianism on the people of Persia's takeover territories. In Zoroastrianism, Ahura Mazda has an adversary called Angra Mainyu (meaning destructive spirit).

Angra Mainyu is the originator of death and all that is evil in the world. Ahura Mazda, who is perfect, abides in Heaven, whereas Angra Mainyu dwells in the depths of Hell. Also within his religion, Zoroaster taught the existence of angels, demons, and saviors, ideas that can also be found in Christianity, Judaism, and Islam. Zoroastrians use the Avesta as their sacred text. The Avesta contains hymns, rituals, and spells against demons.

Some scholars say that credo (tenets, canon law, dogma) of Zoroastrianism assisted to form the major Abrahamic religions—including Judaism, Christianity, and Islam—via the influence of the Persian Empire. Zoroastrian ideas, including the concept of a single God, heaven, hell, and a day of judgment, may have been originally introduced to the Jewish community of Babylonia, where people from the Kingdom of Judea had been living in captivity for decades; hence, Judaism very much influenced with the notions of Zoroastrianism.

When Cyrus conquered Babylon in 539 BC, he freed the Babylonian Jews. Many went back home to Jerusalem, where their offspring (descendants) helped to make the Hebrew Bible. Judaism and the afterlife. Traditional Judaism staunchly (faithfully) believes that death is not the end of human existence. However, since Judaism is originally focused on life here and now rather than on the afterlife, Judaism does not have many credos (confessions, tenets, canon laws) about the afterlife, and leaves it up to individual opinion.

Comparably for an Orthodox Jew to accept that the souls of the righteous dead ends in heaven, like Christian heaven, or they are reincarnated through many lifetimes, or they wait until the arrival of the Messiah, is when they will be resurrected.

Likewise, Orthodox Jews say that the souls of the wicked are tormented by demons of their own creation, or that wicked souls are destroyed at death, simply ceasing to exist. Either way, there is explicit evidence in the Torah believing in existence after death, in which the righteous will reunite with their loved ones after death, where the evil ones will be prohibited from the reunion.

The punishment is indicated to as literally cutting off, which means cut off from his people This is normally translated as spiritual excision, believing that the soul loses its portion in the world to come. What distinguished the Pharisees (intellectual ancestors of Rabbinical Judaism) from the Sadducees is the eventual belief in the resurrection of the dead, since the Sadducees rejected the idea of the resurrection, which is a fundamental belief of traditional Judaism.

The Sadducees stated the concept of resurrection was not explicitly mentioned in the Torah, as the Pharisees claimed the notion implied in some verses as it was founded in the Torah.

The resurrection of the dead will happen in the messianic age, a time indicated to in Hebrew as the Olam Ha-Ba, the World to Come, but that term is also utilized to show the spiritual afterlife. When the Messiah arrives to originate the perfect world of peace and prosperity, the righteous dead will be sent back for the living and given the position to experience the perfected world, where the demonic dead will not be resurrected.

Reincarnation is also part of Judaism. Some sources state that reincarnation is a routine process, while others say it only occurs in abnormal circumstances, where the soul left unfinished business behind. Belief in reincarnation is also one way to describe the traditional Jewish belief that every Jewish soul in history was present at Sinai and complied to the covenant with God. (Another explanation: that the soul exists before the body, and these unborn souls were present in some form at Sinai.)

Why is Mount Sinai important? The biblical Mount Sinai is one of the most important sacred places in the Jewish, Christian, and Islamic religions. According to the Hebrew Bible, it was the mountain where God gave laws to the Israelites. Christians settled upon this mountain in the third century AD. Belief in reincarnation is normally held by many Chasidic sects, as well as some other mystically inclined Jews. The spiritual afterlife is known in Hebrew as Olam Ha-Ba (oh-LAHM hah-BAH), the World to Come, also referred to as messianic age. The Olam Ha-Ba is another, higher state of being.

However, Jews certainly believe that one's place in the Olam Ha-Ba is decided by a merit system based on one's actions, not by who you are or what religion you profess. Plus, Judaism believes that humanity has the competency of being regarded as righteous in God's eyes, or at least good enough to merit paradise after an appropriate time of purification. In Hebrew faith the place for spiritual reward and righteous people is at (Gahn, the Garden of Eden) which those with spiritual perfection end up, many compare the peace, the bliss of afterlife to the joy of sex or the warmth of a wonderful sunny day.

Eventually, the mortals can no more comprehend the nature of such promised land than the blind can realize color, since those dead will be estranged to such notion as heaven. Only the very righteous go directly to GAN EDEN. The average person descends to a place of punishment and/or purification, generally known as Gehinnom (hell). According to one mystical view, every sin one commits makes an angel of destruction (a demon), and then when we expire, we are punished by the very demons that we made. Some views decipher Gehinnom as one of severe punishment, a bit like the Christian Hell of fire and brimstone.

Other sources solely see it as a time when we can see the activities of our lives objectively, become aware of the harm that we have done and the chances we missed to do good, and render remorse for our actions. The limit of time in Gehinnom does not exceed twelve months, and then one ascends to be situated in Olam Ha-Ba.

Only the absolutely wicked do not rise at the end of this period; their souls are punished for the entire twelve months. Sources vary on what takes place at the end of those twelve months: some say that the demonic soul is completely destroyed and ceases to exist, while others say that the soul carries on to exist in a state of consciousness of contrition (regretful, remorse.) Christian views on after death.

The Bible teaches that when we take our last breath, our spirit (soul) will exit the physical body. Then we quickly receive the judgment, which decides our forever destiny. Those who have believed in Christ's being crucified for our sins will enter into eternal life in the presence of God. 2 Corinthians 5:8 states, "We are confident, I say, and would prefer to be away from the body and at home with the Lord." There will be no hesitancy in a state of unconsciousness many call soul sleep. We will instantaneously be in God's presence.

Then, the soul in heaven is made cleansed and unerring (perfect) in holiness and all of our previous sins are wiped out and eradicated. Hebrews 12:23 mentions the spirits of righteous men made perfect. The spirits of the saints are in heaven and they have been made perfect.

The battle with our sin that Paul explained and all Christians face terminating forever after death, as we enter our revered position. Those who deny this blessing will receive what they have chosen, eternity segregated from God in Hell. Hebrews 9:27 states, "Just as man is destined to die once, and after that to face judgment." There wouldn't be a second chance and there isn't any reincarnation. Our eternal fate is decided by the decision we make for Christ here on Earth.

Many presume that after receiving Jesus Christ, all that behold the believer is a blissful entrance into heaven. Scripture instructs that Jesus will reward us relating to how we have lived our life on Earth since Jesus taught us about the axiom and the essence of life in parables.

Each servant was mandated to supervise the talents the master rendered to him. Upon the return of the master, each servant had to give an account for his stewardship (leadership). The wise servants were prized doubly while the wicked servant was removed. Paul said that Christ is our substratum (foundation).

Our works are the making on this foundation. The materials of gold, silver, and precious stones refer to activities done with pure motives for the glory of God. The works of wood, hay, and straw are works done with the wrong motives to praise oneself. The unbeliever will be judged and sentenced to hell. At the end of the time, one faces the Great White Throne judgment. Here, all the unrighteous dead from the beginning of time are judged because of their denial of the Savior Jesus Christ They are then cast into the lake of fire for eternity.

In many religions and folklores (mythology), Hell is an afterlife place, often a location of pain and punishment. Religions with an additive divine background often delineate(describe) hells as eternal destinations while religions with a cyclic history often represent hell as an intermediary (mediator, a link) period between incarnations.

Typically, these traditions locate hell in another dimension or under the Earth's surface, and occasionally include the gate of entry to Hell from the land of the living. Other afterlife destinations include Heaven, Purgatory, Paradise, and Limbo. Other cultures which do not think of the afterlife as a place of punishment or reward, solely see Hell as an abode of the dead, the grave, a neutral location under the surface of Earth (for instance namely Sheol and Hades).

11

WHAT WILL WE BE LIKE IN HEAVEN?

After the soul is departed from the body, it expeditiously enters into the presence of the Lord. Noticing Paul's words in 2 Corinthians 5:8, he says, "We are confident, I say, and would prefer to be away from the body and at home with the Lord." The soul in heaven is made perfect in holiness and our old sin nature is eradicated. As discussed above, Hebrews 12:23 mentions the spirits of righteous men made perfect. The soul of the saints is in heaven and they have been made perfect.

The battle that Paul and all Christians have with sin terminates forever when we after death enter our exalted state. Christianity professes that we will not stay in heaven as a soul with nobody, but rather at God's designated time, there will be a final resurrection where the soul will unite with the body. Philippians 3:20-21 says, "And we eagerly await a savior from there, the Lord Jesus Christ, who, by the power that enables him to bring everything under his control, will transform our lowly bodies so that they will be like his glorious body." 1 John 3:2 promises, "But we know that when he appears, we shall be like him, for we shall see him as he is."

By these two passages, we realize that extolled (glorified) bodies will be akin to that of Christ. We will not be deified, but we will have the same qualities of His revival body. First, our heavenly bodies will be our eulogized (celebrate) earthly bodies. Christ's body that perished on the cross was the same one that was resurrected.

His glorified body was able to permeate through walls, appear suddenly, and ascend to heaven. 2 Corinthians 5:1 reads, "[W]e have a building from God, an eternal house in heaven, not built by human hands." The hands of God will make the resurrected body. 1 Corinthians 15:39-40, 42b-43 tells us. The further belief is that all flesh is not the same. Men have one sort of flesh, animals have another, birds another and fish another. There are also heavenly bodies and there are earthly bodies, but the grandeur (greatness) of the heavenly bodies is one kind and the splendor (grandeur) of the earthly bodies is another.

The body that is perishable, is raised imperishable; it is sown in disgrace, it is raised in honor; it is sown in weakness, it is raised in strength; it is sown a natural body, it is raised a spiritual body.

In responding to the mockers of the resurrection, Paul describes that our heavenly bodies will possess flesh that is of a different variety than our earthly ones. They will be bodies of flesh, but as different from our earthly bodies as humans are from animals. We further conclude that, like a seed, the body will be planted or buried and then one day be lifted to life. It is buried in death, decay, weakness, and disgrace.

When it is revived, it will be changed in every way. It is raised imperishable, glorious, powerful, and spiritual. We will then have eternal, permanent, and perfected bodies. We then will maintain our identities. In Luke 16:23, Lazarus, the rich man, and Abraham all retained their identity. Imagine, one day we will no longer battle with the weakness of sin, sickness, and aging. A great future is in store for those in Christ.

Some even go further and actually profess that they see themselves playing golf for eternity, while others envision the divine souls floating on clouds strumming harps of gold. Although great thoughts, they deficit the glorious future that actually becomes those that await Christ. We are told relatively little about what activities will occur in heaven. We are only given a brief view of our life to come.

Islamic view of after death.

Death in Islam is the ending of worldly living and the beginning of afterlife. Death is grasped as departing soul from the body, and its transfer from this world to the afterlife. There are several elaborate schools of thoughts approaching life after death. But it is not clear what exactly occurs after one dies, since various conclusions are derived from the Quran and other Islamic narratives manifesting life after death scenarios.

One outstanding idea is that angel of death which in the Arabic language means Malak-al-Mout shows up at the instance of death to take one's soul out. Bear in mind that the guilty soul is torturously extracted from the sinner's soul, in which the beatific (righteous, angelic, saintly) are treated with comfort and ease. Another concept is that after one's death two angels called Nakir and Munkar will interrogate the dead person and test his or her faith.

The righteous believer will live in peace and comfort with extravagant amenities if the angels are satisfied with one's answers, if not of course sever punishment pursues. Islam teaches that at the end of history, God will judge the works of all men. Those whose good deeds outweigh their bad deeds will enter into paradise. The rest will be consigned to hell. The Koran teaches that in paradise men will be drinking wine and entertained by heavenly maidens and that they may take several of these maidens for their wives.

To believe in the afterlife is one of the six apprentices of faith in the Islamic religion. Still, the home of the deceased, and where do we end up after we expire is very much questionable, since there are many suggestions in many faith-oriented schools of thought, including Islam. Islam faith believes we might go to heaven, hell, in an intermediary state, or even not become awakened until a great resurrection.

What is at stake, it seems that death is apparently not where our life ends, rather a new stage of living in another form will be the case. Islam believes that God has made us go through a testing ground, endowing humanity with the will to choose, and the responsibility to act right or wrong, giving everyone the chance to prepare oneself for the next life to approach where eventually God judges us according to our good, or bad deeds, where death is recognized as the gateway to the next life. In Islam, the precise time of an individual death is not known since only God is aware of the exact time of anyone's termination of life.

A Muslim is expected to utter their last word in this world would be the admittance of the faith by saying I testify that there is no God but Allah, and Muhammad is the messenger of Allah. Bear in mind that those near deaths are encouraged to say these words before expiring, which occasionally is whispered into the ear of the dying. Islamic faith believes that death is accepted as wholly natural. It solely signifies a transition stage from the material world to the invisible heavens or hell, to the unseen realm.

Many modern writers and believers do not adhere to the depiction of painstakingly torturous punishment after death, where traditionalists often manifest. In the Semitic view (of or relating to the language family that includes Hebrew, Arabic, and Phoenician), man is a union of body and soul/spirit. Muslims especially those predispose by Neo-Platonism, Mu'tazila, traditional Islamic theology, Shi'a and Sufis, considered Ruh unrelated human's immortal spirit.

Therefore, they discern between Nafs (*Nafs* is an Arabic word occurring in the Quran, literally meaning self, and has been translated as psyche, ego and Ruh (spirit, soul), the latter surviving death. In Semitic view (of or relating to the language family that includes Hebrew, Arabic, and Phoenician), man is a union of body and soul/spirit. The Quran itself indicates to run, later utilized as designating human's immortal self, not to the soul, but only to Nafs. Muslims especially those predispose by Neo-Platonism, Mu'tazila, traditional Islamic theology, Shi'a and Sufis, considered Ruh unrelated human's immortal spirit. Therefore, they discern between Nafs.

After being interrogated, depending on the position of the soul, the deceased will experience different journeys. The sinners or the atheists will meet the harsh angels or even the Zabaniyya to take stand in front of him. Then, they advise the soul to come out and appear to the wrath of God.

Being terrified, the soul grievously tries to conceal itself in the body, refusing to extract voluntarily, thereupon, the angels of death commence beating the soul and drag it from the body in a most excruciating way. The painful process of taking out a sinner's soul has been compared with the dragging of an iron skewer through moist wool, tearing the veins and sinews. The soul of the sinner is then wrapped in a filthy cloth which exudes a bad smell. Taking the soul, the angels head towards heaven. On the way, other angels ask about this wicked soul. They are informed this is the soul of that and that sinner person. The angels then arrive at the upper heaven, which is not opened for the evil soul. Eventually, the soul is then thrown into hell or underworld, where it is punished until the Day of Judgment.

The entire scenario alters when a righteous believer dies; glowing-faced angels descend from heaven with divine perfume and cloak (shroud.) Then the angels of death appear and instruct the soul to come out to face the goodness and mercy of God. The soul is then removed as simply as water pours out from the pitcher.

The soul is then wrapped in the perfumed shroud and is ascended to the seventh heaven where God declares: write down his name in Aala'Illiyin and take him back to Earth. I created him from the Earth, and I will raise him the second time from this very Earth. The soul is then pushed back into the body and is questioned by two angels called Munkar and Nakir.

He passes in answering the questions and is blessed with heavenly rewards. Barzakh also retains some resemblance to the Christian concept of limbo, containing some of the souls, which neither go to heaven or to hell, but remain in the grave. It is reminded that the martyrs—persons who die on the way of God—always bypasses Barzakh and the trial of the death angels and go straight to paradise without being questioned.

The Quran redundantly discusses the subject of death. Death is inevitable, no one can escape it since it will reach everyone. Those who deny resurrection and afterlife, and thus challenge God, the Quran challenges them by saying that why these people then do not put back the soul which has reached the throat (of the dying person) and is about to run-off from the body. It also states that when death nears the sinners and disbelievers, and they sense the approaching chastisement, they plead to return to life so that they can do some good deeds, but this will never happen.

The most frequently quoted verse of the Quran referencing death is: Every soul shall taste death, and only on the Day of Judgment will you be paid your full recompense. Elsewhere, the Quran urges mankind: "And die not except in a state of Islam" because "Truly, the religion in the sight of Allah is Islam" Other verses linked to this issue are: "He (Allah) who created death and life, so that He may test you as to which of you is better in deeds. And He is the All-Mighty, the Most-Forgiving" "Certainly, they see it (resurrection) as distant, but We see it as near".

Sufism is a mystical branch within Islam, also known as Tasawwuf or Faqr according to its followers. Sufism and its philosophical custom may be linked to both Sunni Islam and Shia Islam. It has been proposed that Sufism emerged from the Middle East in the eighth century, but believers are now found in many parts of the world. According to Sufism, part of the Islamic teaching deals with the purification of the inner self and is the way which wipes out all the veils between divine and man.

It was estimated 1000 CE (Common Era) and as for BCE (Before Common Era) and for BC (Before Christ) mean the same thing-previous to year 1 CE (Common Era). This is the same as the year AD 1 (Anno Domini); the latter means in the year of the lord, often translated as in the year of our Lord.

Early Sufi literature, in the form of textbooks, dissertation, discourses, and poetry, became the source of Sufi way of life, thinking patterns, and meditations. Sufi philosophy, similar to all another major philosophical modus operand (practice, habit, tradition) has several sub-branches including metaphysics and cosmology as well as other unique concepts.

History of Sufism.

The apparition (emergence) of Sufism is commonly connected to the historical developments of the Middle East in the seventh and eighth centuries subsequent to the life of Prophet Mohammad, and its expansion which took place throughout the centuries after that. Amid the tenth and twelfth centuries, Sufism became a widely spread discipline. One of the most influential early writers on Sufi philosophy was Al-Ghazali (1058–1111). He debated the concept of the self and the reasons of its misery and the causes of its happiness. By the end of the thirteenth century, Sufism had become a well-defined, well-known science of spiritual awakening throughout the Islamic World, an Islamic Golden Age.

No vital domain in the civilization of Islam remained untouched by Sufism in this period. Several tariqahs (Sufi orders) were found. In the meanwhile, a class of prominent Sufi philosophers, theologians, and jurists such as Hankari, Ibn Arabi, Abu Saeed Mubarak Makhzoomi, led this age who taught and produced the historical embodiment of philosophers and geniuses worldwide like Al-Ghazali, Avicenna, etc. An important mark made in the history of Sufi philosophy has been made by Abdul Qadir

Jilani with his jurisprudence and philosophy of Sufism that made him explain the Sufi orders.

Jilani's adopted order was Qadiriyya and the offshoot he started later became known as Sarwari Qadiri. Several other orders were also exposed in this era. Sufis were influential in spreading Islam especially to the furthest garrisons (outposts) of the Muslim world in Africa, flooded south Asia, India and the Far East. Sufism has a history in India evolving for over 1,000 years. The presence of Sufism has been under Persian influence, Sufi thought, syncretic values, literature, education. syncretic values mean Syncretism is the synthesis of various beliefs, while alloying (blending) practices of various schools of thought.

Syncretism (religious syncretism exhibits blending of two or more religious belief systems into a new system, or the incorporation into a religious tradition of beliefs from unrelated traditions), also happens commonly in idioms (expression, phrase) of arts and culture familiar as eclecticism (the practice of deriving ideas, style, or taste from a broad and diverse range of sources.

SUFI Metaphysics

The major concept in Sufi metaphysics has encompassed the notion of Vahdat or Unity with God. Two main Sufi philosophies prevail on this divisive topic. Vahdat-ul-Vojood (Unity of Being) intrinsically (inherently) says that the only truth within the universe is God and that all things exist solely within God. Vahdat-ul-Shuhud (Apparentism, or Unity of Witness), on the other hand, maintains that any participatory of unity between God and the world is only in the mind of the believer and that God and his creation are completely apart. Vahdat-ul-Vojood is the position where there is no difference between God and human being who is trying to obtain a particular state (i.e., 'No One Except God').

The concept of Sufi Metaphysics was first insightfully debated in writing by Ibn Arabi in one of his most fruitful (prolific) works known as Fusus al hikam. Ibn Arabi shows detail analysis on the subject of Oneness through the metaphor of the mirror. In this metaphor, al-Arabi compares an object being cogitated(reflected) in countless mirrors to the relationship between God and his creatures.

God's essence is witnessed (seen) in the existent human being, as God is the object and humans being the mirrors. Meaning two things, that since humans are mere reflections of God there can be no distinction or separation between the two and without God the creatures would be non-existent.

When an individual realizes that there is no segregation between human and God, they start on the path of ultimate oneness. This metaphysics of Sufi philosophy is also narrated (related) in the hadith: Whoever recognized his self, undoubtedly recognized his Rab (Allah).

Baha'i faith, the soul and the afterlife.

In Baha'i religion the soul is regarded not to be subject to natural law; rather, it is subject to spiritual law as a bond between man and God and it appears at the conception of the embryo. Heaven is within the vicinity of God, a soul being close to God, not a location, but a condition, as it ensures an eternal spiritual evolution.

Anyone who adapts and exercise virtues and guidance of God goes to heaven. Hell is being far from God, not a place, but of weakness to understand and practice virtues and guidance from God. Improvement from the worst situation is potentiated even in the next world, but one must Grass-Rooty overcome repelling (repulsive) Godly virtues. Religious labels we are known for, and theologies we are proud to be part of, are not as imperative as the reality of spiritual virtues like freedom, honor. Compassion, courage, justice, love, understanding, etc., which are the choices we make in our lives.

The Baha'i religion believes heaven is a condition more than a place, it is a realm where those who are close to God are also good to each other. It is true that the individual undergoes dramatic changes from birth and the stages of life in this life, then death and life beyond, Bahaism hold it like that the same soul will go through dramatic changes of circumstances. However, they believe life in this world and beyond are actually interwoven since womb of this life and the afterlife are interwoven. It's not like moving to a distant place; the afterlife is also here, but invisible to those living on Earth. Death is about letting go of the physical frame and its demands and has no real identity by itself.

The information about the afterlife is essentially bounded in this life. It is said that the next life is fundamentally different in many ways from this life. The parallel is made when contrasting life in the womb with this life, and the changes after birth, to the changes after death. Realities of the latter are not accessible even as ideas in the former; they are ineffable (unspeakable, unexplainable). The concept of a body in the next world is still present but it is a heavenly body. There is a realm of lights and reunion with descendants (expired) associates.

The sanctity of human nature is confirmed when free from the constraints, it reflects the light of God and the truths of existence become known and fear of death is conquered, and universal acceptance of the religions as coming from one source.

The life of the person initiates at conception when the soul relates itself with the embryo. When a death occurs, the physical body returns to the world of dust, while the soul carries on to progress in the spiritual realms. To consider that after the death of the body the spirit perishes, 'Abdu'l-Bahá has said is like imagining that a bird in a cage will be destroyed if the cage is broken, though the bird has nothing to fear from the destruction of the cage.

Our body is like the cage, and the spirit is like the bird. Once the cage becomes broken, the bird will continue and exist. Its feelings will be even more powerful, its perceptions greater, and its happiness increase. After its association with the body draws to a close, the soul will continue to progress in an eternal journey towards perfection. Bahaullah wrote, "It will manifest the signs of God and His attributes, and will reveal His loving-kindness and bounty."

An illumined spirit continues to have a predispose(influence) on progress in this world and the advancement of its peoples. It acts as "the leaven that leaveneth the world of being, and furnisheth the power through which the arts and wonders of the world are made manifest."

The world beyond, writes Baha'u'llah, is as different from this world as this world is different from that of the child while still in the womb of its mother. Just as the womb made the atmosphere for a person's beginning physical development, the phenomenal world is the arena within which we develop the spiritual characteristics and potentials. that we need for our forward journey.

Both here and in the next life, we propel with the assistance of God's bounty and grace. Also vital to the progress of our souls in the next realm are the good deeds carried out in our names here on Earth. known in this light, death is not to be feared. Bahaullah refers to it as a messenger of joy." He declared that: "Thou art My dominion and My dominion perisheth not; wherefore fearest thou thy perishing? Thou art My light and My light shall never be extinguished; why dost thou dread extinction? Thou art My glory and My glory fadeth not; thou art My robe and My robe shall never be outworn."

Mourning, the suffering and anguish of the absence of contact with family members, friends and kin for Baha'i's is, aside from cultural issues and norms in society, believed to be as another stage of life; a temporary condition that will be altered someday just as someday the infant in the womb comes into the material world through birth and into the company of family and friends. Not avoiding the sense of loss, Bahaullah accentuates the sense of mystery in death, mentioning that The Mysteries of man's physical death and of his return have not been divulged, and still remain unread.

Were they to be revealed, they would evoke such fear and sorrow that some would perish, while others would be so filled with gladness as to wish for death, and beseech (solicit, petition, conjure, request) with unceasing longing, the one true God—exalted be His Glory—to hasten (to happen more quickly) their end. Life after death in Hinduism.

Hindus religion believes that humans are in a cycle of death and rebirth known as samsara. Hinduism instructs that via enlightened knowledge the cycle can be broken. Atman means eternal self.

The atman indicates to the actual self beyond ego or false self. It is referred to as spirit or soul, and indicates our true self or essence which forms the foundation for our existence. it is (Sanskrit: self, breath) one of the most fundamental concepts in Hinduism, the universal self, identical with the eternal marrow (mainstay) of the personality that after death either transmigrates to a new life or obtain release (moksha) from the bonds of existence.

Atman alludes to the essence of each individual living thing; its soul or foremost (preeminent, principle) living energy. Each living thing—people, animals, plants—have an atman that makes each thing's eternal essence, is reborn in a different body.

Some say rebirth happens directly at death, others accept that an atman may exist in other realms. Hindus believe that an atman may enter Swarg or Narak for a period before rebirth. Hindus believe in karma or intentional action. Many believe righteous or evil actions in life leading to positive or negative merit, decides the atman's rebirth. Some Hindus believe that humans may be reborn in animal shape, and that rebirth from human to beast form solely happens if an atman has consecutively failed to learn lessons in human form.

Living life according to teachings in the scriptures will eventually lead to moksha. Some Hindu scriptures describe moksha as the atman becoming absorbed with Brahman, from where each atman is believed to originate. Other Hindu scriptures describe moksha as living in the realm of a personal God.

To know moksha, which means liberation, one must first comprehend several other significant ideas in Hinduism—especially, samsara. Samsara is a Sanskrit word that alludes to the cycle of birth, death, and rebirth, to the transformation of the soul from one life form to another. Moksha: Hindus believe that the soul passes through a cycle of successive lives (samsara) and its next incarnation is always dependent on how the previous life was lived (karma).

Moksha is the end of the death and rebirth cycle and is categorized as the fourth and final artha (goal.) Moksha: Moksha is an idea in Hinduism. Reference: Moksha in Hindu religion indicate to liberation from the cycle of births and deaths as human life is understood to be one full of pains and sufferings. Nirvana: Nirvana in Buddhism is known to be a state of mind that is achieved when one arrives at enlightenment.

The ultimate goal of Hinduism is Moksha or liberation (total liberty, total freedom). This is the personal and direct detection of one's true self, which liberates one's from the cycles of rebirth, or Samsara. This realization is termed Nirvikalpa Samadhi and is the totally transcendent zenith (apex, climax, pinnacle, top) of yoga. Atman (Sanskrit: self, breath), one of the most principle concepts in Hinduism, the universal self, identical with the eternal core of the personality that after death either passes to a new life or attains frees (moksha) from the bonds of existence, Moksha.

Hindus believe that the soul transmigrates through a cycle of consecutive lives (samsara) and its next incarnation is always relating to how the previous life was lived (karma). It is a paradox in the sense that subjugating (defeating, overcoming) desires also includes conquering the desire for moksha itself. The Maitri Upanishad states: Even as water becomes one with water, fire with fire, and air with air, so the atman becomes one with the Infinite Atman (Brahman) and thus attains final freedom. Maitri Upanishad.

What Buddhism believe happens after death.

Buddhism believe that as human beings we have a rare opportunity to try to escape the cycle of samsara. The escape from samsara is known as Nirvana or enlightenment. Once Nirvana is obtained and the enlightened individual physically dies, one will no longer be reborn. However, one's remaining in heaven is not eternal—eventually, they will use up their good karma and will undergo rebirth into another realm, as a human, animal or another being.

Heaven is temporary and part of samsara, Buddhists concentrates on escaping the cycle of rebirth and reaching enlightenment (nirvana). Relating to the Anatta doctrine of Buddhism, at the essence or core of all human beings and living creatures, there is no eternal, essential and absolute soul, self or atman. Buddhism in its main philosophical and ontological texts has denied the existence of the self, soul.

"The kingdom of heaven is like electricity. You don't see it; it is within you." Maharishi Mahesh Yogi.

12

ARTIFICIAL INTELLIGENCE, AND SINGULARITY

The industrial age, the technological progress, and any further development in Artificial intelligence (AI) is undeniably the by-products of human consciousness, which gradually will reach the pinnacle of invincibility by making miracles, not only in the field of artificial intelligence but through which humanity can peak in the unheard of scientific endeavors, where the unthinkable become the norms, assuming that such harbinger of hope does not stray from fundamental human morality and ethics since we are touching on very sensitive agendas, as we should act conscientiously in prioritizing mental wellness, where human behavioral dynamics need to be prioritized, and not to operate as mechanically robotics.

What we might be missing is that human consciousness is an inseparable part of cosmic energy which is the driving force behind all tangible matters and the motivating force in concept-oriented phenomenons, where thoughts and the infinite potentiality for new discoveries originate.

Artificial Intelligence, in fact, is obviously an intelligence transmitted by conscious subject, an intelligence placed in equipment. It has a clear origin, in fact, in the intelligence of human creators of such equipment. Pope Benedict XVI.

The universe decisive interactivities, and the entire nature's mechanism is without a doubt purposefully designed to relentlessly capture new ideas and propel forward for reaching parallel universes, where magical realms will further witness human's ingenious maneuverability and might.

As for the artificial intelligence, the reality is far less dramatic for now, since advancements in AI is certainly linked to progress in human intelligence, which needs to Grass-Rooty be dealt with for further accomplishments in robotics and affiliated fields. In the meanwhile, directing artificial intelligence towards lessening violent criminal activities, where digital gadgets can sure be enhanced further to report crimes instantaneously since time is of the essence to protect victims by informing legal authorities, as soon as possible to prevent tragic situations.

I am afraid Hollywood mentality, and similar media entities where money-oriented culture carelessly encourage violence has taken over the constructive thoughts and humane behaviors, where dystopias (an imagined state or society in which there is great suffering or injustice, typically one that is totalitarian or post-apocalyptic) is wrongly finger-pointed. the actual causes of people's misery are not correctly identified giving millions the wrong impression for their misfortunes. We further explore the possibilities and challenges revealed by this game-changing technology linking to AI.

Artificial intelligence is the concept of expanding intelligent machines—for instance, computer algorithms which function and react like humans. Applications that exhibit speech recognition, natural language processing and interpretation, visual perception, teaching, learning, reasoning, inference, tactical maneuverability, logic-based strategizing, planning, intuition, and decision-making, etc.

It is an undeniable fact that AI is presently very resourceful from saving lives in medical diagnosis, and in dealing with economics, finance, real estates and for processing of loans and mortgage applications, in the legal system, in complex military industrial services, in aerospace, even in our ordinary living like driving fully automated vehicles, and so on. the AI awesome benefits have motivated many multinational corporations, public and private's companies, governmental entities and states to further invest in developing artificial intelligence for better efficiencies and maximizing productivity.

So far, we are witnessing the expansion of much more efficient and smarter machines, that with no doubt are helping us learn new ways to enhance our living which truly gives meaning to the culture of innovation and modernism. Artificial intelligence is also coherent with algorism through which programmers write computer programs, by telling the computer exactly what the programmer wants. The computer then executes the program, following each step mechanically, to complete the end goal. That's where computer algorithms come in.

The algorithm is the basic technique used to get the job done. An algorithm generates the same output information given with the same input information, where several short algorithms can alloy (synthesize, fuse, blend) to exhibit complex tasks like writing a computer program for simple to complex problem solving through which AI systems ameliorate (make better, revamp) their intelligence.

Also, through AI computer hardware processing power and notable speed have increased, where cloud computing empowers so many to share and incorporate data by developing power all over the world; through which billions of dollars are made by multinational companies giving global businesses a tremendous boost in everyday voice recognition communications.

Artificial intelligence is specially very promising in Robotic and automation processes for handling high demands in various industries like aviation, insurance, surveying, statistics, civil and architectural design, accounting, bookkeeping, speech and facial recognition at sensitive places like the airport and many legal, financial, trade and commerce centers, in political arenas, and many other crucial entities that can be targeted by terrorism, where safety and security extremely matters.

Since automated decision makings with precise calculation and accuracy are raising the reliability and scientific bar to the next level for intricate planning, scheduling, optimization, and even more efficiencies. human based decision making and perhaps erroneous judgment will further diminish the risk of inaccuracies.

Currently, robotics is prevalent in wholesale warehouses, retail management, and in many other diversified arenas; where neural-like networks for artificial intelligence in machinery aims at learning capabilities, matching human brain for customers' interactions via speech production and natural language development making it user friendly and as practical as possible for enhancing communications, and thriving more for the pursuit of excellence in technically oriented environment.

Scientific communities expect future evolution in artificial intelligence in which clarity on the probable progression can create miracle like agendas in sensitive fields like space, auto-piloting, auto vehicle driving, medical and other decisive endeavors to even save more lives, and perhaps discover other inhibitory planets. The AI systems are potentiated to expand expertise in a particular domain that extends beyond the capability of humans because of the sheer volume of information they can access to make each decision.

Some of the key issues are how future machines can be designed with having the mind of their own, where they would possess the mental states to sensibly dialogue with humans and other machines, give advice. For example, having a sense of understandings, beliefs, intentions, knowledge, and how their own logic functions. With having the capacity to reason, negotiate, and perhaps help with a global hunger problem, global warming dilemma, finding a better economic system, and how to better cure challenging diseases.

New governing can be employed to avoid nuclear holocaust in which millions can perish, also conveyed with invigorated (energize) new ideas that experts believe such algorithms (a set of steps that are followed to solve a mathematical problem, or to complete a computer process) are present at the development stage, but we can expect to experience them in the near future.

The notion of superhuman is using bio-engineering and artificial intelligence to upgrade human abilities. If they use the power to change themselves, to change their own minds, their own desires, then we have no idea what they will want to do. Yuval Noah Harari.

In the meanwhile, I am not worried about the machinery outsmarting humans, since no matter how artificial intelligence and automation develops, they still would be the byproducts of the ingenious human brain with advancing mind. It might be a race, but a race which humanity never loses, they simply will not exceed the human mind since intelligence, curiosity, motivation, drive, my, mine and I factor rewards, and other decisive variables fuel our spirit.

We should also be reminded that no sophisticated machinery of any kind is linked to universal energy, where the human mind is an integrated part of. Many worries are lurking that at some point may artificial intelligence and dominance in machinery automation supersede human intelligence, where technology might outsmart us. Not realizing that the human brain is an inseparable part of cosmic energy with infinite opportunity in innovation and progress.

Humans are the only beings with the out of body experience, as they are also self-aware creatures, with conscious, will, curiosity, drive, emotions and feelings, creativity, seeking beauty, are in search of excellence, with purpose and setting goals, with spirit, with soul and thousands of other innate means designated as the only source to lead the life's evolutionary concept.

That we will never be able to capture and digitize human consciousness. Despite the fact that many fervently believe that we can one day reach Singularity and Transcendence—this is the idea that the exponential expansion in technology path can lead to a massive expansion in human capability.

We might in the near future, one day be augmented and improved such that could connect our brains to each other and to a future successor of the current internet. collective mind would let us share ideas, solve problems and render others access to our dreams as observers or participants giving true meaning to hive mind which in (science fiction) means a unified consciousness or intelligence formed by a number of alien individuals, the resulting consciousness typically exerting control over its constituent members.

Further, we might also upscale the limits of the human body and connect to other forms of intelligence on the planet—animals, plants, weather systems, and the natural environment. Even to an extent, where telepathy way of communication can become the norm. There are already plenty of envisioning concepts for a smarter world as many scientists and physicists are working hard to develop them in the arena of quantum life and the subatomic particles which it seems the mysteries of our world lay, that I am certain the artificial intelligence will be of huge scientific leverage for more outstanding inventions.

Despite the recent emergence of artificial intelligence AI, several businesses have already developed numerous applications that can replicate human thoughts, performing superior cognitive and creative tasks. Artificial intelligence has quickly grown from being a distant hope to a casual part of the present reality.

Computer programs capable of performing human-like cognitive and computational tasks without human intervention are rapidly growing in capability as well as ubiquity. Every new AI application that emerges expands the limits of what the technology can achieve, leaving us in awe and excitement for what the future holds. Following are a few mind-blowing applications of AI that will definitely make you reconsider the limits of what's possible:

Identifying Criminal Threats, Machine learning-enabled AI applications are being generated and utilized by law legal authorities in some part of the world to foresee and prevent crimes. Japan is considering the use of AI and big data to anticipate criminal activities, which will enable the law enforcement authorities in Japan to prevent crimes by proactively dispatching patrols to high-risk areas. The application also developed in the USA, France, UK, and China.

Providing Personal Assistance, the most commonplace, and hence the most underrated application of AI, are the Personal AI assistants. Personal AI assistants like Siri and Cortana can not only enable you to operate your phones using your voice but can communicate with you like a human and can even engage in banter (joke, jest, pun, quip) in some cases.

The assistant programs use machine learning to relentlessly gather information on users through interaction and provide them with highly effective results and exclusive responses. AI can be programmed to read people's minds. Scientists have researched and made AI programs that can scan one's brain's blood flow to trace mental activities and detect the thoughts associated with brain activity.

The AI system can detect the picture produced in the subject's mind while looking at actual images. In addition to performing cognitive tasks, AI can also be trained to perform creative tasks. Artificial intelligence that can read people's minds but also their hearts! New AI applications powered by machine learning algorithms and trained utilizes historical data on patients with heart problems can often anticipate the risk of heart attacks better than doctors do, that can save so many lives.

The prominent issue is the position of singularity defined as a point at which a function takes an infinite value, especially in space-time when the matter is infinitely dense, as at the center of a black hole. An imaginary point in time when artificial intelligence and other technologies have become so improved that humanity experiences a noticeable and irrevocable situation.

Furthermore, the singularity is described as the hypothetical future creation of super-intelligent machines. Superintelligence is explained as a technologically created cognitive capacity far beyond that possible for humans. The technological singularity, also simply called the singularity is the hypothesis that the discovery of artificial superintelligence (ASI) will unexpectedly actuate (trigger) level technological progress ending in unfathomable alteration to human civilization as technically manifested cognitive potentiality can go far beyond what is currently foreseen by humans.

As far as existence is a concern, it seems that singularity plays a very decisive role in creation. Kurzweil describes his law of accelerating returns, which anticipates an exponential appreciation in technologies like computers, genetics, nanotechnology, robotics, and artificial intelligence. Once the Singularity has been reached, Kurzweil says that machine intelligence will be infinitely more powerful than all human intelligence combined.

Then, Kurzweil foresees intelligence will radiate outward from the planet until it saturates the universe. The Singularity is also the point at which machines intelligence and humans would merge. As far as a singularity and the existence, it seems that singularity has a lot to do with creation since the explosion of the infinitely focused mass in very tiny point can expand astronomically large as physicists tell us have occurred in the big bang, where life has originated from.

The big bang is an event-like singularity; a black hole is like an object. A catastrophic collapse, such as a massive star imploding in a matter of seconds, will produce an event-like naked singularity. When a naked singularity is event-like, it looks like an explosion. If so, the very fundamental life born energy must have been originated, because of the explosive employment in singularity creating the fertile ground for existence to happen, which if not certainly impregnated with required ingredients for life to incept, no Darwinism evolutionary theory, or any other kind of theory could ever have been possible.

According to general relativity, the modern theory of gravity a puzzling issue is known as a singularity, a region with infinite density is situated at the heart of each black hole where space and time as we know it ceases to exist there.

Scientists believe that in the center of a black hole is a gravitational singularity, a one-dimensional point which conveys tremendous mass in a significantly small space with density and gravitational force becoming infinite as space-time curves limitlessly, where the laws of physics as we know them to cease to function. Also known to physicists that (greater mass in a smaller volume = greater gravitational force exerted).

The theory of general relativity anticipates that a sufficiently intense mass can deform space-time to form a black hole. Singularities are predicted to occur in black holes by Einstein theory of general relativity. The boundary of the region from which no escape is possible is by physicists known as the event horizon.

A wormhole is a theoretical passage through space-time that could create shortcuts for long journeys across the universe. Wormholes are predicted by the theory of general relativity, wormholes bring with them the risk of sudden collapse, high radiation and perilous contact with exotic matters. In the vicinity of the singularity, particles and materials are so squeezed. as matter fall apart into a black hole, its density becomes infinitely large as it must fit into a point which relating to equations, is so small that it has no dimensions.

Stellar-mass black holes are basically in the range of 10 to 100 solar masses, while the supermassive black holes at the centers of galaxies are estimated about millions or billions of solar masses. The supermassive black hole at the center of the Milky Way, Sagittarius A*, is 4.3 million solar masses. The event horizon is where the runaway speed passes the speed of light: one has to be going faster than light (which is impossible for any bit of matter) to get away from the black hole's gravity.

A singularity is what all the matter in a black hole gets crushed into. In general relativity, a white hole is a hypothetical arena of space-time that cannot be entered from the outside, which matter and light can escape from it. The white hole is the reverse of a black hole that can only be entered from the outside, and from which matter and light cannot escape.

13

ECONOMIC MISDEEDS

Western societies are heightening consumer-oriented culture, where the exchange of goods and services are done through capital transactions for maintaining a fair balance between supply and demand. It is extremely essential that investors avoid glut since they unnecessarily can flood the market with a certain product. In the meanwhile, scarcity of an item, and not having enough of something to satisfy demand can create a shortage of certain products. The capitalist's system if not monopolized, then must indulge in creativity and innovation, making it possible to survive in a very competitive environment

Some economists believe that the invisible hand of the market or the laissez-faire economy is best since very little interference of the government is required; which can eventually balance supply and demand, where glut or scarcity could barely occur. Many economists forget the element of greed, as so many investors, and so-called businessmen play devil's advocate to disturb the equilibrium of supply and demand, or the absence of a state to allocate proper resources to designated markets were most required, since so many surreptitiously plan to withhold certain products by hoarding them, to be delivered at later times when most requisite (required) for higher profit, and to maximize wealth.

Let's not forget that human beings by nature can become addicted to what feeds them through force of habit. The issue becomes challenging when the force of habit drives so many people to addiction often to the point of no return. As the atmosphere effects are sure decisive in our upbringing and overall behaviors as we are to a large extent the products of our environment. In a culture where so much emphasis is put on money, I am afraid that becomes a serious problem since eventual addiction leads to greed and hoarding wealth which inevitably takes over, driving all sorts off ills and inhumane conducts, certainly resulting in manufacturing evils because of the hell created. It is a no-brainer to conclude that humanity has to put up with countless violence ending in rampant crimes globally leaving billions to suffer the ugly consequences of a system that has gone mad.

In the midst of such anxiety-driven market some economists act like a frightened mouse which closes his eyes, thinking the cat which is about to devour him is not there. They forget that we live in an environment where self-interest, self-preservation, aggressive behaviors, greed, betrayal, misconducts, and wrongful competition has replaced honesty, ethics, righteousness, and good faith, turning business-oriented markets into the cut-throat atmosphere rather than pursuing the fair and justified monetary transactions.

Obviously, the capitalist's market is not mission-driven, as it is not aiming for serving the fundamental needs of the people, but is to maximize profit at the sufferings of others, it is clear that unless citizens are collectively inoculated to Grass-Rooty pull people's power to harness constructive changes, no positive happenings can ever occur to stop the few global financial monsters, making them to unleash their iron-clad hold on global resources where more than eight billion are supposed to live on.

An unregulated market also has something to with the chaotic outcome which will eventually run so many investors out of presumably competitive position destroying their business, their livelihood, and only for a few to reach the pinnacle of financial invincibility by monopolizing the global market. leaving others behind and with no choice but for millions of businesses to quit this shenanigan of the so-called free enterprise notion that can cause irreparable financial damages, and in making a social disaster, since so many become bankrupt as they lose hope of recovery as they perish, because of multinational corporation's take over.

When the market is left unchecked, unregulated, and exhausted from proper state supervision. Concentration of wealth becomes inevitable by the few since they so irrationally handle the market by hoarding, via market manipulation, through outsourcing jobs, where they can seek cheap raw material, dirt cheap labor resources, dodge taxes, and not playing by the rule of the trade demoralizing (disheartening) the rest to vacate, forcing them into bankruptcy, leaving so many to deal with perilously irreparable criterion and with terrifying consequences.

The culprits are influenced enough to cut through the red tapes, and by kicking one's way up through the hustle and bustle of the market to reach the top. the expression of it is not who you are, but who you know can play in one's favor; or simply because of availability of more funds to afford better technology and skilled labors, compounded with having savvy information.

A decisively dynamic means of production can robustly maneuver to distinguish the winner from the losers; and since failure can often occur because of unanimated strategy, dull planning, and not competent enough to intelligently compete in a radicalized market beyond many entrepreneur's capacities, and many business men's potentials. We live in an era where global economy operated by multi-national corporations directly effects local economies all over the globe.

Natives and even the most primitive tribal communities can financially be deranged by a corporate takeover, and since the living dynamics that the natives are accustomed to become quite challenging, as they are not somehow compensated in any way to adjust to the new criteria. One might think that modern life and integrated groups are always better than tribal communities. But put a human face into a socio-cultural, socio-economic situation since the inhabitants are forced to migrate often to nowhere lands, where families become polarized, not because they want to, but because they have to.

Then, perhaps compassion should kick in to call for some type of Grass-Rooty remedy, where constructive social welfare and reliable monetary programs can be implemented to save human lives before forcing locals out of their ancestral homelands, and confiscate their resources through local governments which often play poppets in the hands of the foreign exploiters, as they mostly are in cahoots with multinational corporations.

The problem does not stop there since many of these natives are called xenophobic, which should alarmingly raise the question that wouldn't anyone behave toxic and acting hateful towards those who destroy their lives, as locals passionately disagree with what happens to them as their tribal identity is denied, and their way of making a living is lost forever without any chance for financial compensation, but to expect imprisonment and torture by the bullying state that governs them. The issue sadly remains that when thousands of local business are-driven out of the market, millions tragically lose their jobs, and their means of livelihood, since they are not able to survive the ugly consequence of wrong political, and economic policies, often wreaking havoc on the entire nation.

The point is that even with the absence of the state-regulatory market, any competitive environment can eventually make some businesses to rapidly thrive, where trade and capitalism can expeditiously expand. The greater the demand, the greater the surplus value (surplus value is a central concept in Karl Marx's critique of political economy. According to Marx's theory, surplus value is equal to the new value created by workers in excess of their own labor-cost, which is appropriated by the capitalist as profit when products are sold). Business productivity peaks, creating immense wealth, leaving the market vulnerable to monopoly.

> "In an effort to eliminate the possibility of any rival growing up, some monopolists would sacrifice democracy itself."
>
> — Henry Wallace

Material based societies encourage dreaming big, manufactures perceptual anomalies, dramatic (theatrical) episodes, and maddening temptation, but at whose expenses other than the victims, when millions lose everything by taking the uncalculated risk, as so many do not act diffidence (modest) but emboldened with a trap like a mentality to reach an unrealistic goal. One should acquire leading information through correct competitive market analysis, dynamic strategies, robust planning, devoted experienced crew, knowledgeable personals, reliable partners, professional management, expert book-keeping, and adept accountant.

Dreaming big, glamorizing hype, irrational exuberance and pursuing what is beyond one's means become the very elements of destruction for millions. Capitalist's system is fundamentally designed to have differentiated class. Building up few tycoons, creating an oligopolistic class, where they live opulent living, beyond anyone's imagination, and leaving so many with economic depravity, as billions globally cannot even afford to live beneath the poverty line.

The stratified socio-economic system so unjustly maneuvers that the class system nonetheless bothers to shed light on how global social layers are faring. Let's start with the aristocrats who live by hereditary wealth as they enjoy the high social station. They behave as the common man is indebted to them as ordinary people should pay their dues to the privileged elites, and the gentry class. According to dictionary, aristocracy is defined as a form of government that places power in hands of a small, privileged ruling class, like for example Saudi Arabia, England, Spain, Belgium, Norway, Sweden, Brunei.

Further, the capitalist's society is classified as the upper class, the middle class, the working class, the working poor, the poverty level, and of course billions who live beneath the poverty line. The upper class, which makes up about one percent of the world population, generally consists of those with vast inherited wealth (sometimes called old money). Members of the upper class are such as Rockefeller, DuPont, Walton's, Forbes family, Kennedy, and others. The newcomers with new money are people like Jeff Bezos. Bill Gates, Warren Buffet, Bernard Arnault and family, Mark Zuckerberg, Amancio Ortega, Carlos Slim Helu and family, Charles Koch, also others with new money are people like Oprah Winfrey, Michael Jordan, and other celebrities.

The category known as new money is a relatively new grade on the social ladder and comprises about twelve to fourteen percent of the population. New money includes people whose wealth has been with them only for a generation or two. Also indicated as the nouveaux riches (French for newly rich), they have made their money rather than inheriting it. Unlike the traditional upper class, they do not have a family link with old money. The newly rich do not have every day financially stressful concerns that often plague the rest of society.

> "There is nothing noble in being superior to your fellow men. True nobility lies in being superior to your former self."
>
> — Ernest Hemingway

I am afraid extreme inequality results in bleak outcomes for so many poverty-driven people; that is pitiful, since there are no reliable social programs, and financial safety nets to save those needy, and the destitute that are struggling to survive. We should realize that capitalist's society is confluence with symbolism, since in every field of endeavor only symbolic few can and are apt to reach the pinnacle of success, and leaving others behind, which in some cases most victims have thrived their entire life to objectify dreams, but to no avail.

They are gullible enough to fall into the trap, as they become tempted, and lured into what is beyond their means to accomplish. Typically, the capitalists socio-cultural, and socio-economic agendas destabilize people mentally, pushing them to behave unrealistically. It puts people on the edge of a high-rise and encourages them to jump as if the standpoint is right, and one can land safely without any parachute training, or with no flying equipment's. Unfortunately, so many flies to their death, landing on a concrete and hard floor without any protection. only is a miracle, if one in thousands can occasionally land on a soft material, cushioned and elastic enough to bounce back to safety.

For thousands of years, profits of God, creeds, sages, and the scholarly minded people have relentlessly advised practicing modesty, and against desiring the impractical; they have insisted on equilibrium and in safeguarding balance; they have persisted on compassion and kindness, and they have preached against the obsession with the material world. But then, when looking at the mechanism of monetary, and fiscal policies, and the way the entire capitalist's system operates.

It encourages the exact opposite, and of course for so many to pay the dire price with ill-consequences, often paying with their very own lives, and sometimes so senselessly taking other people's life. Regrettably, so many apparently do not learn any valuable lesson from the misconducts of such wrongful, and morally dysfunctional system. The psychotic behaviors further happen when corporations, the big boys and their goons label those who dare to talk about redistribution of wealth as socialists and radicals.

They are adamant to subsist regardless of harms done to citizens, as they tempt consumers via calculated schemes and relentless advertising tactics which lures people into buying spree as if there is no tomorrow. They utilize extremely effective techniques in commercialism where buyers subconsciously are cornered into acting by instinct, behaving as their will to make sensible decisions become hostage as the consumers become the victims of their own dull decision makings, and in acting like zombies (someone who moves around as if unconscious and being controlled by someone else), ill-responding to crucially decisive matters in their lives.

They become conditioned to behave on impulse since they purchase what they often do not need, making them unable to prioritize, not competent enough to allocate funds adequately. leaving millions with no money available to pay for what they might urgently need because they have already hoarded what they did not need. Regrettably, so many repeatedly pay a dire price, since they must sell what they need for the mistake of buying what they did not need; but avails the businessman a great deal of profit, and of course with luxurious living.

> "If a free society cannot help the many who are poor, it
> cannot save the few who are rich."
>
> — John F. Kennedy.

The problems of the world that we live in, not only include extreme income inequality, and astronomical wealth accumulation. But also immigration, populism, sustainability, peacekeeping, the formation of bubbles in financial markets, or with the global warming, the threats of atomic bombs, wars of aggression, genocide, fascism and dictatorial behaviors, unbearable violence with extreme criminal activities, etc.

Malaise as such need to be watched, it has to be measured, and they should be predicated in terms of ill-consequences. requires an international body, a super-national entity, to watchdog for decisive issues that are out of balance, to prevent lopsided behaviors. we have reached the age of maturity since technology has broken and made the boundaries collapse, making it easy to notice cries of the victims from all over the world, by which many are vigilant, making it a blessing for noticing injustice and in fighting back against it.

14

HUMAN BRAIN AND MIND

Is the brain the cause for our mind, or vice-versa? The fact is that the brain as matter does not exist, what exists as the substantive brain is energy-driven, and for sure not a dull entity with low-frequency rate. It is quite obvious that the human brain by far the most sophisticated product, is dynamic in nature, resourcefully animated, notably energy oriented, and in line with the spirit of the universe, and the immaterial mind.

Traditionally, scientists referred to mind as the consequence of our brain activity, regarding it as a physical substance, saying that the mind is the result of brain firing cells (neurons), but contemporary arguments are that our mind goes far beyond physical activities of the brain. in comparison, most animals are with lower frequency rate brain, and not as robustly as the human brain that is extremely versatile, a consciously based entity, potentiated with a great deal of plasticity.

Yes, the brain is a tangible organ that controls all imperative human functions, but unless it was also energy oriented, it would not be able to accord within the energy-related atmosphere, to vigorously dialogue with our senses, as the brain is an inseparable part of our entire nervous system. In retrospect, our mind percolates (pervade, impregnate) every cell in our body and coordinates with every part to produce action and for what we must do to survive, empowered by the brain which has dominion over our lives.

We know that our senses literally interact with the environment that we live in, as our five senses of seeing, hearing, smelling, tasting, and touching collect information, and data less than a blink of an eye, since they communicate messages back and forth to our brain, and for the brain telling us what to do, making living possible. If so, it seems that without our immaterial senses, our brain will be in vain and of no use. Imagine that we are exhausted of our human senses, utterly without any of our five senses of sight, hearing, smell, taste or touch, then no dynamic brain activity could ever be experienced, except being left with a dull entity, an obsolete organ practically of no use.

It becomes more complicated when we believe that the brain through our senses instructs the ghost within to run the daily chores, commanding us what to do to get by in our lives; but the concern should be which us? To whom are the instructions addressed? When our senses register messages and communicate with the nervous system mainly the brain, telling us to do this or to do that, who are the brain, the mind, and the senses collectively referring to? To whom are they pointing at for executing orders?

The reality is that we are an inseparable part of the universal energy that is fueling the entire existence since all animated beings, the birds and the bees, flowers and the trees, the beasts, the invertebrates, mammals, amphibians, reptiles, fish, and so on, are either instinctually activated by the awesome designer God, or like humans consciously awakened and partially instinctual.

Since being consciously awakened should indicate that human senses, our entire nervous system, our brain is absolutely energy-driven telling us that we are here because of an infinitely insightful creator, because of a boundlessly magnificent mind, in which even the human brain need to subordinate to, for functioning efficiently? Human brain and mind are uniformly active; they are consciously based, as they are linked to the ever-present cosmic energy as both functions with much higher rate frequencies in comparison with other less animated low-frequency beings. The brain assuages (mollify, propitiate, placate, calm) propellant (stimuli) which through our five senses observes the external world and responds accordingly.

The thalamus is the clearinghouse for all sensory information other than the smell. Once sensory information is sorted in the thalamus it is sent to the hippocampus and the amygdala. The smell, however, goes directly to the hippocampus and amygdala. The hippocampus is the place of learning and contrast, the sensory knowledge from the external world perceives how the world should operate as if making quality control for expecting feasible standards.

The hippocampus is the seat of learning and memory and compares the sensory information from the outside world with its perception of how the world should be, like a quality controller checks products to ensure they meet industry standards. The hippocampus indicates any discrepancy or problem to the amygdala which dispatches and accepts information from every part of the brain and body. For instance, bodily hormones are set of very complicated networks which would be fair to link them to literal brain activity, but as dynamic as they are it would be wacky to analyze their superbly intricate activities without a magnificent designer creating them.

With all the brain activities received, we can often be deceived by the fake information through our mind. Five centuries years ago, Michel de Montaigne said: "My life has been filled with terrible misfortune; most of which never happened." Now there's a study that proves it. The study checks into how many of our imagined calamities never substantiate. many subjects were asked to write down their worries over an extended period of time and then clarify which of their imagined trouble did not occur.

Consequently, it turns out that 85 percent of what subjects worried about never initiated and with the 15 percent that did happen, 79 percent of subjects discovered either they could handle the difficulty better than expected, or the difficulty taught them a lesson worth learning. This means that 97 percent of what you worry about is not much more than a fearful mind punishing you with wrong perceptions. The stress it produces makes huge health problems.

The distress hormones dump into one's brain have been linked to shrinking brain mass, lowering your IQ, being prone to heart disease, cancer, and premature aging, predicting marital problems, family dysfunction and clinical depression, and making seniors more likely to develop dementia and Alzheimer's, and other ill health related problems.

Another instance of mind cheating us happens when watching a horror movie as we jump out of our seat thinking that killing, rape or other frightening situations are literally happening, or when some people engage in cybersex, and for the brain to believe the imaginary sex partner is an actual participant, and so on. There is no doubt that our brain, our mind can frequently misinform us, and where are we when imagining things, a feeling that we are not in the real world.

The brain often does not distinguish between reality and fiction, it is accustoming to certain movements, the brain is familiarized with habituated routines making it very difficult to discern another movement than repeatedly perceived. For an instant, it is easy for the brain to detect human-like running by a robot, or any other animal since our brain is aware of the concept of running.

In the meanwhile, it is extremely difficult for the brain to detect plants movement or perceive animal interactions, where it seems cognitive behaviors are surreptitiously designed in which may be and only may be an expert botanist or an experienced ecologist or zoologist can point out certain meaningful maneuvers by the plants and animals since many become acquainted within the uncharted territories where it is beyond human nervous system to extrapolate theoretical precision since creative ability of our mind where great scientific endeavors raises from audacity of imagination, assumption, feelings, emotions, intuition, and dreams which they come out quite handy.

Telling us that the mind of the universe is very much alive with an infinite variety of blueprint for all that exists not excluding human mind, informing us it is wise to pay attention to the cosmic mind where no entity can live without.

Biological intelligence expert Monica Gagliano from the University of Sydney believes it is possible to direct plants in the same way as a dog. Dr. Gagliano quoted her most disturbing find involved a fast-growing and climbing pea plant that developed a Pavlovian response. Ivan Pavlov (1849–1936) was a Russian physiologist who conditioned dogs to salivate every time a bell was rung.

The bell anticipated the arrival of dinner, and yet eventually he rang the bell without bringing dinner and the dogs would continue salivating, Dr. Gagliano said. She stated, "Instead of the bell, we used a little fan, which I knew plants didn't care about. And instead of dinner, I used a little blue light, which I know plants care about very much for growth. The fact many plants grow towards blue light is very well accepted."

The scientific investigators had the fan directed onto the pea plant from a particular direction before they change it with blue light, repeating the fan-light combination from random angles for several days.

Eventually, the fan was blown onto the trained plant from a certain direction.

When the researchers came back the next day to turn on the blue light, they found the plant had bent towards it in anticipation.

"The fan had no meaning whatsoever to start with, but it acquired meaning to the plant through its own experience, the same as the bell did for the dog," Dr. Gagliano said. "The plants don't have brains. They don't have neurons and yet they're still performing the exact same task as the dog. How did they do that? We don't know."

Another experiment with growing pea plants in a maze and running water via one of the pipes shown the plants tilted towards it.

Plants are competent to locate nearby water by sensing its humidity gradient. "But then I recorded the sound of water and substituted the real presence of water inside a pipe with just the sound," Dr. Gagliano said. "Even if the actual water isn't there and it's just the mere sound of it, they will grow towards it." She also tried playing random sounds like white noise but the sound of water managed the greatest effect.

"The experiment showed there is a selectivity in response to sounds around them, and water, of course, is ecologically relevant," Dr. Gagliano said.

She said, "It suggested there was another system of cognition beyond neurons and brains that humans had not yet considered."

Hormones and Neurotransmitters

The endocrine system utilizes hormones and the nervous system uses neurotransmitters to transit between the body and the brain. The endocrine system is the collection of glands that generate hormones that regulate growth, metabolism and development, tissue function, sexual function, reproduction, sleep, and mood, among other things. Hormones are the body's chemical messengers.

They take information and instructions from one set of cells to another. The endocrine system permeates nearly every cell and the function of our body. Hormones are released by endocrine glands into the bloodstream and carry information to and from different parts of the body and communicate with the brain by working on neurons through receptors. Neurotransmitters are chemicals that allow nerve cells to dialogue with each other.

In this case, the nervous system communication between the brain and the body, by hormonal activities and neurotransmitters, report interceptive (relating to stimuli produced within an organism, especially in the gut and other internal organs).

The point is that so many neuroscientists, biologists, psychologists, psychoanalysts, psychiatrists, anthropologists (anthropology is the study of humans, early hominids and primates, such as chimpanzees, anthropologists study human language, culture, societies, biological and material remains, the biology and behavior of primates, and even our own buying habit), and those involved with human anatomy and mind, draw their conclusions based on mechanical activities of hormonal organs as instinctual, as if these apparatus (a complex structure within an organism or system) are self-propelling without a competent fomenter, without an expert programmer.

As sophisticated as this biological maneuverability's are, they seem to see these complex hormonal activities without deliberate and awesome management; where obviously any meddling on the homeostasis or balance of the organism is stressful enough to cause malfunction of the organs engaged in a particular task.

The brain's responsibility is to regulate all stress and return stability to the internal milieu (surrounding), ensue protective actions like increases in blood pressure and serum glucose levels that make us ready for the situation of fight-or-flight; break down health affects the quality of our lives, the same way bad tools and an unreliable situation manifests a hostile work environment. When hormones and neurotransmitters are overworked, they transmit into hypertension, cardiac disease and diabetes, and a host of other ills.

Chronic over-usage results in allostatic the duration by which a state of internal, physiological balance is kept intact by an organism in response to actual or perceived environmental and psychological stressors. Hence, allostasis is the projection that keeps the organism alive and working (i.e., maintaining homeostasis or maintaining stability the cumulative adverse effect on the body).

Homeostasis is the ability or tendency to maintain internal stability in an organism to compensate for environmental changes. An example of homeostasis is the human body keeping an average temperature of 98.6 degrees.

For instance, the nervous system helps keep homeostasis in breathing patterns, because breathing is involuntary, the nervous system ensures that the body is getting much-needed oxygen through breathing the appropriate amount of oxygen. When toxins get into one's blood, they disrupt one's body's homeostasis, this ongoing process continually works to restore and maintain homeostasis. For example, during body temperature regulation, temperature receptors in the skin communicate information to the brain (the control center) which signals the effectors: blood vessels and sweat glands in the skin.

When allostasis happens too frequently (as when the body is subjected to repeated stressors) or is wanting (insufficient, inadequate) over weeks, months, or years, exposure to increased secretion of stress hormones can end in allostatic load and its pathophysiologic (physiopathology is a convergence of pathology with physiology, it can also mean the functional changes associated with or resulting from disease or injury, another definition is the functional changes that accompany a particular disease outcome).

Allostatic load refers to the long-term effects of continued exposure to chronic stress on the body. Colloquially, it is often indicated as wear and tear. Long-term exposure to allostatic load can lead to disease and bodily destruction. Bear in mind that because of today's stressful lifestyle, millions suffer memory loss which, without, life is not worth living.

One should try to dodge distressful living and try to boost one's memory and mind through balanced diet by taking multivitamins, vitamin d, vitamin c, high doses of omega3, fish oil. Whether you suffer from Alzheimer's disease or you simply have memory problems, certain vitamins and fatty acids have been said to slow or prevent memory loss. Know that low blood flow in the hippocampus is the reason for memory loss.

Try to meditate, sleep well, listen to soothing music, eat well, exercise, avoid attention deficit disorder, stay alert, read, and most of all, avoid loneliness. Laugh and enjoy the moment. Avoid lead and mercury and mold exposure, try to learn new things, like a new language, music, solving puzzles, playing chess. Work your memory. Good memory is the most important part of a smarter and faster brain. Make association, make goals, eat food that boosts brain power, think positive, and stay delightful, be happy, play brain games, do mental math.

The long list of potential solutions includes vitamins like vitamin B-12, herbal supplements such as ginkgo biloba, and omega-3 fatty acids. Salmon, gingko, beet, hot peppers, red bell peppers, green vegetables, green tea, blueberry, and should consume lots of leafy green. One needs to drink lots of water, eat as much as organic food as possible, consume fiber, eat spinach, cauliflower, broccoli, cabbage, dark chocolate, nuts, pumpkin seeds, turmeric, ginger, cinnamon, avocado, garlic, onion, mushroom, sweet potato, zucchini.

When people talk about brain foods, fatty fish is often at the top of the list. Coffee, if coffee is the highlight of your morning, you'll be glad to hear that it's good for you, but should be taken within the limit, like one or two cups max a day. Try to lose weight, since being overweight is directly related to memory loss, diabetes, sleep apnea, snoring, stopping breathing, and a host of other troubling diseases.

Memory is all we are; without it, one's living is not worth it. Try to rest, sleep, at least eight hours a day. Avoid caffeine, try to keep your room as dark as possible while sleeping, keep your room rather cool, take magnesium and melatonin for a restful sleep. Know that sleep apnea, snoring, and stopping breathing is directly linked to being overweight.

For the anti-inflammatory diet.

Tomatoes, olive oil, eat green leafy vegetables, such as spinach, kale, and collards. Eat nuts like almonds and walnuts, fatty fish like salmon, mackerel, tuna, and sardines, fruits such as strawberries, blueberries, cherries, and oranges. Curcumin, the active compound in turmeric, is a strong anti-inflammatory agent. It's been found to be more effective than aspirin and ibuprofen at reducing inflammation without the health risks the over-the-counter medicines.

Foods that cause inflammation

The main foods that people following an anti-inflammatory diet should avoid include processed meats, sugary drinks, trans fats, found in fried foods. White bread, white pasta, potato chips, gluten, soybean oil, and vegetable oil, processed snack foods, avoid processed food such as chips and crackers, junk food, avoid MSG and chemically oriented food, food with preservatives and artificial coloring.

Avoiding inflammation.

The fastest way of reducing inflammation in your body: Load up on anti-inflammatory foods, cut back or eliminate inflammatory foods, control blood sugar, make time to exercise. Lose weight, manage stress, do not eat sugar, avoid gum disease.

The actual power of the mind, its influence on our future, our well-being, our health outlook, and self-concept, is an enigma sparking much discussion and arguments for centuries. As food for thought, here's what some of the world's most prominent figures of the past had to offer on this intriguing subject.

The energy of the mind is the essence of life.

– Aristotle

"Physical concepts are free creations of the human mind, and are not, however it may seem, uniquely determined by the external world."

– Albert Einstein.

15

THE WAR ON TERROR, AND THE RHETORIC OF COUNTERTERRORISM

It's not right to respond to terrorism by terrorizing other people. And furthermore, it's not going to help. Then you might say, "Yes, it's terrorizing people, but it's worth doing because it will end terrorism." But how much common sense does it take to know that you cannot end terrorism by indiscriminately dropping bombs?

HOWARD ZINN

The rhetoric of the war on terror is a series of institutional exercise along with a set of political anecdotes (story) which they acquire the methodology of dying discussion analysis. The discourse states that the language of the war on terrorism is not simply a nonaligned or objectified dispersion(reflection) of policy arguments and the actualities of terrorism and counter-terrorism; rather, it is a very precise and deliberately build-up public powwows (seminar)that are particularly orchestrated to make the image of the war appear justified, responsible, and basically good.

The real problem with this whole show is that the talk and practice of the war on terrorism construe radical disputes to the democratic state, not to exclude jeopardizing the legal and moral imperatives of the community, where nation's trust is at stake. The organized terror often is financially fed via umbilical cord attached to many powerful and resourceful entities, in which frequently the head of state from specific developing countries are the actual culprits as they play double standard, exhibiting tolerance as they show apparent concern when terrorism strikes, but in reality they are tied to extremists ideologies and stern radicalism philosophy that are alarmingly dangerous; aiming to destroy animated concepts where progressively faith-oriented credos (ideology, set of beliefs) interpret holy books different than what they approve of, which ironically supposed to worship the same God, and not to follow satanic rituals shedding innocent blood through horrific act of violence and terrorism.

This holocaust view of resolving terrorism must stop which is manufactured through perpetrating wars of aggression, and sanctions, where genocide like extermination is exercised; since millions of innocent people perish, either being slaughtered, via sanctioned therefore hungered to death, a famine like punishment, or banished, being forced to leave their country pushing them into refugee status. They don't leave their countries voluntarily, as they are forced to flee or face ill-consequences, as so many lose their lives while in horrific transitions the midst of this inhumane persecutions. No civil society should ever be dragged down to agree with such barbaric behaviors, since it can entrap a nation of goodwill, making their decency in mind and manner questionable.

But their surreptitious activities do not stop there, since they are also adamant to discredit nations that are the sworn enemy of medieval mentality, and the defenders of freedom, democracy, human rights, liberty and the pursuit of happiness. They camouflage their demonic intention for weakening popular values and civic culture, undermining the legitimacy of democratic institutions and forestalling the enunciation (talk, utterance) of potentially more effective counter-terrorism advances.

It seems that some menacing governments from developing countries are dictating to the west that either turn a blind eye to our inhumane behaviors and atrocious conducts, or else. That is if you want to enjoy billions of dollars' trades in arms deal along with other financially based projects, and for flexible pricing on the oil and gas purchases, also known as the black gold.

Frighteningly enough, we should see the huge ambiguity in the war against terrorism when already the real source of terror is several times identified, but the corporates dynasty convolute people's perception and redirect the culture of thoughts to nowhere land, where facts are somehow misconstrued and eventually denied.

The corporate elites work in cahoots with autocratic regimes to cover up heinous crimes done by the head of states under the banner of national security, which should rather be called for corporate security. This analysis is particularly relevant in the context of the current political climate in the United States, and Europe where the War on terror rhetoric carries on to normalize the logic of Islamophobia aimed at utterly irrelevant places and groups It should remind one of when rubbers plan to rob a bank, and deliberately set fire elsewhere in the vicinity of the susceptible bank in question to distract by standards and the guards, to execute the unethical deed.

> "Wanton (capricious, arbitrary) killing of innocent civilians is terrorism, not a war against terrorism."

> NOAM CHOMSKY

The corporate elites operate beyond the constitution, beyond the government, and act above the will of the people, since they have the entire media to pounce on the incredulous (dubious) images that are meant to be imprinted into people's mind making the victims agrees with their entire ill-natured agendas. It is not so wacky (loony) to believe that like colonialism, fascism, slavery, and piracy, terrorism also has no place or any position in the modern world. But unless those in charge are willing to identify the head of the snake and avoid sleeping with the enemy, as the pythons of terrorism walk the red carpets in the very states that are attacked, but are seen as allies, we are actually just playing with the python's tail.

Look, let's be frank; not a few barefooted Bedouins can create sophisticated plans, facilitate expensive training and equipment's, produce intelligent documents which even the most up to date passenger scanners, and x-ray system with very competent security personals cannot detect the culprits until is too late. They frequently make an extremely effective attack on a foreign soil in which many of those nations are so technologically advanced and brilliantly guarded that even a fly should have a difficult time to infiltrate and pass through, but it happens. Yes, it is true that terrorism has become the systematic weapon of a war that knows no limit or any boundary, and so anonymous which rarely has a face. But there is more to it than meets the eye.

There are powerful people and even governments that play as a wolf in sheep's clothing which they are the financiers and the actual troublemakers defending radical ideologies to protect Islam. Islamophobias shouldn't be of any treatment as so many God-fearing innocent people are either erroneously targeted, or deliberately dealt with as scapegoats, while they throw shindig (big party) to celebrate the big business deals with the perpetrators of the terror, and the actual malefactors against humanity. Either way, it is wrong for great nations to descend to uncivilized mentality, since answering terrorism with terrorism is an impractical idea which should be condemned.

The big threat to America is the way we react to terrorism by throwing away what everybody values about our country—a commitment to human rights. America is a great nation because we are a good nation. When we stop being a good nation, we stop being great. BOBBY KENNEDY, *O Magazine*, February 2007.

The war being fought against terrorism is more than a military discord which needs to be ideologically detoxified from the dark ages mentality, not by coercion and force, or by engaging the military industrial complex, but by practicing what the free world has so much to be proud of against ruthless often religious-based tyranny. It is the decisive ideological struggle of the twenty-first century. On one side are those who believe in the values of freedom and moderation, the right of all people to speak, and worship, freedom of religion, freedom of the press, freedom of assembly and live in liberty with the pursuit of happiness, to even bear arms against despotic and unruly state practices, which dignifies and upholds What does land of the free and home of the brave means.

On the other side, facing those-driven by the images of cruelty and fanaticism, forcing their way in by a self-appointed few which impose their radicalism views on the rest of inhabitants. As veterans, you have seen this kind of enemy before. Comparatively speaking they should remind one of the successors to Fascists, to Nazis, and other totalitarians of the twentieth century. History shows what the result will be, a victory for the cause of freedom, liberty and exercising utter human rights. The object of terrorism is terrorism. The object of oppression is oppression. The object of torture is torture. The object of murder is murder. The object of power is power. Now, do you begin to understand me? GEORGE ORWELL, 1984.

It is not far from reason to see that terrorism is the war of the poor, and war is terrorism of the rich imposed on the poor, since the poverty plays a big role into this whole equation as the nasty aristocrats and the rich elites control the seemingly infinite oil and gas, and other valuable minerals as they play evil in their everyday demonic rituals. Recruiting the financially destitute and naively minded characters, mostly young breeds that easily fall trap into the ludicrous idea of being summoned by God to resurrect against the Kofar (the unbelievers), basically the west, so is the rhetoric of Armageddon which means the final confrontation between good and evil, which by evil it means Satan, but metaphorically implies to other faith, specially Islam.

The impact of fear and anxiety can disorient many people and affect their lives for the worst. Fear is a human emotion that is triggered by a perceived threat. However, when people live in constant fear, whether from physical dangers in their environment or threats they behold, they can become debilitating. Yes, terrorism is no exception and must be dealt with as a prevalent virus. Terrorism is prevalent like a bacterium. There is a global entanglement with terrorism, which follows any system of primacy (supremacy) as though it were its shadow, ready to activate itself like a double agent. Contrary to the violence we watch on movies and allow ourselves to believe it, the objectives of terror are not to perish people but to kill though, to prove a point, to demoralize a nation that it is about to implode (collapse) from within.

Terrorism does not engage in conventional warfare, where two or more military industrial complex becomes involve in a frequently prolonged war. The essence of terrorist's strategy is to camouflage and attack places and people when expected the least, just like a shark or a crocodile, or any other predator with no conscious, as if instinctually programmed to kill. Most crime-oriented activities aim at causing fear to incapacitate the victims. Human beings do vicious, and despicable things to each other. Homicide, betrayal, conspiracy, genocide, torture, mutilation, rape, pedophile at times done while loved ones are forced to watch or public hanging before a crowd, and done intentionally, brutally without conscious and with abusive words and verbal assault to amplify the suffering exerting excruciating pain often to innocent people.

Then, the plagues of poverty, prostitution, homelessness, child abuse, humiliation and hopelessness, racism, sexual exploitation, and other forms of distributed violence; and these are fused by the neglect and carelessness and condescension and insensible rationalizations that add insult to injury, without any remedy for millions entangled in a web of uncertainty and despair.

The troubling issue is that many nations have to deal with their own dictatorial governments that are the actual cause of terrorism, as they are supported by super-powers and are considered as our allies, and if so, then many progressive countries which brag about upholding human rights and democracy, but do not hear the victims outcry and horrific position they are in, are surely behaving double standards. It makes one believe that equity comes with a price, millions are doomed to perish because apparently, they are not able to afford justice, literal hypocrisy in action.

Yes, progressive nations have the very rich lexicon to expose injustice and wrongdoings not to exclude evil, transgression, acting insane, cruelty, savage, sadistic, degrading, inhumane, horrific, ungodly, demonic, atrocious, and the list goes on. But such consensus in words to actually bring any remedy is either futile, skipped or impractical. When millions of victims are experiencing genocide by a racist state, or tortured and incarcerated by their own ominous governments without the world paying any attention.

It brings the worst out of the innocent victims, those who so unjustly lost everything, even their loved ones, that they are left with nothing to live for. Justice is meant to be relevant everywhere and for everyone, it is a sacred word that is rooted in humanity's moral as it is very conscious-driven, it simply must not have toyed with. When fair play is deliberately ignored, and the culprits are not even warned for their wicket crimes because they are in the position of power and influence, not even a slap on the hand. It leaves a ripple effect of deep mental and physical injuries which leaves the victims with no choice but to do the unthinkable terrorist actions, exterminating innocent people which of course is diabolical, but to them, terrorists seem justifiable.

That terrorism is a crime against humanity. One problem is that the attribution is so arbitrary. Hence, the evil needs to be located in those regimes who practice state terrorism, because unless we get rid of the root causes of such ills, it is going to exponentially grow nationally and globally. Terrorism is a crime against humanity, it should warn us not to behave prejudicially in favoring certain so-called ally's terrorists over others denoting us as hypocrites and in denial of the truth, and certainly against our values. It is not so puzzling to know that the root causes of evil are greed and astronomical profits that the arm industries secure from selling a variety of high tech weaponry to globally troubled areas as peace is premeditatively disturbed, where fear is literally manufactured to make sure for the high demand of horrific armaments and inhumane weaponry.

In his final speech from the White House, President Dwight D. Eisenhower warned that an arms race would take resources from other areas; such as building schools and hospitals. On Jan. 17, 1961, President Dwight Eisenhower gave the nation a dire warning about what he described as a threat to democratic government.

He called it the military-industrial complex, a formidable union of defense contractors and the armed forces. As NPR's Tom Bowman tells *Morning Edition* co-host Renee Montagne, Eisenhower used the speech to warn about "the immense military establishment" here is an excerpt. "In the councils of government, we must guard against the acquisition of unwarranted influence, whether sought or unsought, by the military-industrial complex. The potential for the disastrous rise of misplaced power exists, and will persist."

When such terminology as the access of evil or the evil empire denote certain states that probably are at fault and not certain others that are truly at fault, then it solely discredits us as a great nation and puts our leadership in questionable position taking their words as not au+3thenticated but as demagoguery. Phrases as such are contorted to represent and appeal to unwitting and hubris (conceited, arrogance) in order to elaborate the speaker's political potency while lessening public liability (accountability.)

Shrouded in secrecy, executive powers redundantly declare that evil must be fought, which should not give anyone a second thought in wiping evil out, but it must be done without recourse to nefarious activities, if not, what would make a civilized people with progressive government different than the barbarian mentality since they try to bring out the worst in us. We are way past the Machiavellian era, in which he believed that evil exploits goodness governments must be prepared to be not good, so. Machiavelli, states that any means can be used if it is necessary to maintain power.

The word comes from the Italian Renaissance diplomat and writer Niccolò Machiavelli, born in 1469, who wrote *Il Principe* (The Prince.) In today world it is difficult to discern who and what is the actual evil, since many advanced states are also lured into doing the unspeakable crimes beyond anyone's comprehension since they use force exhausted of civil discourse, and without concentrating on the economy of violence.

The heads of many governments maneuver idly by playing to cognitive bigotry (bias) utilizing mass media in which many are in cahoots with the state to easily keep the public at bay which the people are saintly unaware of the often troubling networks of friendship with the fascist regimes and the informal relationships that make the foreign affairs. often the declaration is: You're either with us or against us; you're either evil because you are not as resourceful as we need you to be, or you're good with plenty of valuable resources that you should willingly render if you want to stay in power and as an ally.

One should ask what does the ordinary person that works hard 24/7 trying to make a basic living has to do with taking the side in a military industrial complex confrontation between two oligopolistic governments; which for some odd reason cannot come to term in taking people's resources, since the commoners have to indeed pay a grave price either through war of aggression calling it the good war, or by crippling sanction imposed on them, which only is going to affect the poor and financially deprived, since the rich can afford food and housing at any rate, or take off to dreamland places where they can enjoy their unending wealth.

"The number of people killed by the sanctions in Iraq is greater than the total number of people killed by all weapons of mass destruction in all of history."

NOAM CHOMSKY.

16

SPECULATION ON CONSCIOUSNESS

All matter originates and exists only by virtue of a force
which brings the particle of an atom to vibration and
holds this most minute solar system of the atom together.

Max Planck

The hard problem of explaining the conscious experience is not rooted in
the complexity of whichever kind. The troubling issue is much deeper:
It is permeated in the failure to connect describing the gap between any
level of structure in our neuronal networks and conscious experience. The
conscious experience has its own unique dynamic properties—properties
that do not seem to be 'emerge able' from the complicated buildup of any
kind. This sets it apart from any developing properties. Every incipient
(emergent) property can be elaborated on as an epiphenomenon of the
implicit (implied) procedure in terms of the specific pattern of these
methods (mechanism.)

These arrangements are complex and sometimes stochastic (randomly
determine) or self-regulating so we cannot always foresee or quantify
what is going to take place, but principally we can learn how the property
appears. For every developing property, we have something to say that
convincingly describes in principle how the emergent property arrives
from underlying mechanisms—underlying patterns that are eventually
embedded in the basic laws of physics as we are familiar with today, but for
the conscious experience it looks like being fundamentally unemergeable.

This has made some scientists believe that we must be ignoring a fundamental aspect in our current comprehension of physics—or we have not yet reached the pinnacle laws of physics. Other scientists simply disregard the unemergeability of consciousness by positing that consciousness must be magically emerging somehow from a complex pattern of neuronal networks. Physicists often denote dynamic patterns as fields, and similar ideas are acquired in brain science.

They talk about gravitational fields, temperature fields, electromagnetic fields, quantum fields, information fields, communication fields, and much more. For instance, a temperature field shows that temperature depends on both location and time. In equivalent cases, brain fields might represent patterns of action potentials in individual neurons, synaptic activity, oxygen levels, and so forth in brain tissue with masses of various sizes.

When one exhibits some mental tasks. Certain parts of the brain may be noticed to light up some measure of brain activity, typically electroencephalography (EEG) or functional magnetic resonance imaging (fMRI), will respond as the particular mental task is exercised, while this approach designates important information, but it does not mean a high level of mental activities should relate to more lights burning brighter.

The dynamic aspects of consciousness apparently demand certain kinds of brain activities that insist on for at least a half second or so, furthermore, consciousness is closely linked to special kinds of brain rhythms, registered as electric field (EEG) oscillations. Apparently, brains must be appropriately tuned to be conscious. Finally, there is the matter of the multiscale nature of brain fields, thus, brain fields include dynamic sub patterns within sub patterns within patterns calculated at different organizational levels. In truth, consciousness apparently requires special maneuverability types within high levels of perplexity in brain fields.

It is the shortcoming of such events for a conscious experience that makes the hard problem hard, conscious experience appears to be fundamentally unemergeable. This has convinced some scientists to believe that our physics does not seem to be complete yet, perhaps there are missing links that the physicists are not aware of.

The answer is yes; what is missing is that some physicists do not want to accept that universal consciousness is the cause to what exists, including a human brain that is certainly energy based and able to maneuver with infinite diversity, since there is no limit to the human mind, neither is our heart. Our heart does limitlessly desire and will be in wanting mode to the day we die, so is our mind which possesses the infinite ability to progress in which, if let live.

The collective mind of humanity will one day see God. Implying that conscious awareness must somehow magically emerge from the complex patterns of neurons networks and activities might be true; but it cannot tangibly be located in our brain since it correlates (agree, tally, harmonize, dovetail) with the cosmic energy permeated in the entire existence. It is what the sages have for so long indicated that what is not seen manages what is seen.

In conclusion, the important thing is for humanity to be reminded that we possess two sacred and extremely valuable entity, which they both are coherent with the infinite nature of our creator, and nature itself. One is our heart and the other is our mind, since our heart will not stop craving, and will desire to the day we are alive. Our human mind is potentiated with infinite intelligence that will not stop, and further continues to one day conquer the universe and beyond.

Our heart is correlated with what we know as feelings and emotions, our mind is the spirit which needs to be kept cleansed, and not pollutes with toxic thoughts and desires. Good conscious (thinking), good words, and good deeds become prevalent regardless of race, color. authenticity, ideology, creed, gender or any other factor encompassing humanity.

> The key to growth is the introduction of higher dimensions
> of consciousness into our awareness.
>
> Lao Tzu

17

MAKE SENSE DIALOGUE

The flawed, misleading, and false debates are these days prevalent. A logical argument is intellectual self-defense against imposing assault on reason and avoiding irrational behaviors on logic and what makes sense. Logic, as well as a methodology for quality control, keeps the validity of one's views in check. From the tiniest essentiality to the peak of religious abstraction, from the most primitive man's invention to the modern macro discoveries, everything we are, everything we possess comes from one attribute of man-the function of his deduction and reasoning mind.

> "Man is the only animal capable of reasoning, through many others possess the faculty of memory and instruction in common with him."
>
> Aristotle.

Formal logic is the gateway to a fascinating and elegant branch of dialogue and adequate communication and the very key to philosophy, mathematics, and science since issues as rationality and inference are agendas attached at the hips which without, probing into any viable matter can prove us futile. As no true evaluation and correct assessments can be rendered, as the essence of philosophy is the power of reasoning which demands enlightenment to often contemplate intricate subject and insightful matters beyond the ordinary.

Philosophy gives us the opportunity to ponder and dig into the deepest questions about the world, about our universe, and God. Is there a God?

Does life have an ultimate purpose? Do I have a purpose? What am I? Why am I here? What do I want? How can I serve? What should I be grateful for? How can we be sure that we're not dreaming or in the Matrix? What does it mean to be human—contrary to being an animal or a robot? Does free will exist?

What sort of life is the happiest? What is knowledge? Can we depend on our senses to know what's real? What makes an action right or wrong? Who are we? Where did we come from? Where are we heading? What happens after we expire? How should we live and treat others? Derived from the Greek words, philosophy or love of wisdom is the subject that can come closest to these imperative and intriguing issues.

Making sense dialogues should relate to rationality as wisdom can be applied to complex oriented subjects as their discernibility's can often be difficult, like for instance knowing if our brain or mind, call it spirit or soul if you wish, is playing the decisive role in our lives.

It nudges one toward critical thinking, cultivating logic and ethics, aesthetics, searching for the whys of the world, and much more. The other relatively make sense concern would be: if our brain is the cause for our human mind, or vice-versa? The brain as matter does not exist, what exists as the substantive brain is also energy based, and for sure not a dull entity with low-frequency rate.

It is quite obvious that the human brain by far the most sophisticated product, dynamically animated, which is extremely competent to communicate with energy based thoughts and our senses, traditionally scientists denoted that mind is the consequence of our brain activity, regarding it as a physical substance, saying that the mind is the result of brain firing cells(neurons). But contemporary arguments are that the brain goes far beyond physical activities of the brain.

In comparison, most animals have a lower-frequency-rate, energy-based brain, and not as dynamically oriented human brain extremely versatile, and conscious based entity, the same as our mind. Yes, the brain is a tangible organ that controls all imperative human function, but unless it was also energy oriented, it would not be able to accord and dialogue within the energy-related atmosphere, and with our senses which the brain is an inseparable part of our entire nervous system.

In retrospect, our mind percolates (pervade, impregnate) every cell of our body and coordinates with every part to produce action and in what we must do to survive, which has dominion the brain. Human brain and mind are interchangeably active as they are both consciously based linked to prevalently cosmic energy as they both function with much higher rate frequencies in comparison with other less animated low-frequency objects.

The brain assuages (relieve, alleviate, palliate, abate, soothe) propellant (projectile, stimuli) which through our five senses observes to the external world and responds accordingly. The thalamus is the clearinghouse for all sensory information other than the smell. Once sensory information is sorted in the thalamus it is sent to the hippocampus and the amygdala. The smell, however, goes directly to the hippocampus and amygdala. The hippocampus is the place of learning and contrasts the sensory knowledge from the external world perceiving how the world should operate as if making quality control for expecting feasible standards.

The hippocampus is the seat of learning and memory and compares the sensory information from the outside world with its perception of how the world should be. Like a great manager, the hippocampus indicates any discrepancy or problem to the amygdala which dispatches and accepts information from every part of the brain and body.

For instance, bodily hormones are set of very complicated networks which would be fair to link them to literal brain activity, but as dynamic as they are it would be wacky to analyze their superbly intricate position without a magnificent designer creatively programming them to activate in thousands of different occasions, if not in millions of scenarios.

"The question of science, the authority of a thousand is not worth the humble reasoning of a single individual."

Galileo Galilei

18

ARE WE MADE OF STARDUST?

Nothing is as it appears; what seems to be solid, physical reality is, in fact, a complex system of vibrating energies. What our eyes actually see are dancing patterns that we recognize as objects or living creatures. We are connected with what we see by pulsating waves of light-energy. Karen Wise.

Scientists believe a star exploded, then a big bang someplace in our galaxy happened, which did spread the mass of dust and gas. This supernova (a star that suddenly increases greatly in brightness because of a catastrophic explosion that ejects most of its mass.) which they believe occurred about five billion years ago.

The remnants from the explosion then collided into the near vicinity cloud of gas, together they build up the elements necessary for our solar system. This highly energy-oriented explosion made the dust mixture extremely hot and things began to muster. In the meanwhile, bits of dust started to cluster, constructing bigger and bigger lumps, and the synthesis (alloy, blend) began to pull together under its own gravity.

Later on, the central lump became so hot and tight that it started to produce its own energy, igniting nuclear fires. This is how the sun was born. What remained of dusty mixture whirlpooled around the star, creating a disc. As the sun gradually grew bigger, and the dusty disc cooled off. Then, over millions of years the constellation was made into grains, then lumps, boulders and eventually planetesimal, (is an object formed from dust, rock and other minerals.) chunks of rock big enough to have their own gravitational field. Some of these planetesimals became the emergent forms of the planets in our solar system today.

Gradually, but surely, these rocky planets initiated to organize sitting at a well-off distance from the sun and making their own orbit. Earth detected its path as the third planet from the sun. In the early day's rocky pileups were still common, leaving craters on the surface of all of the planets.

They believe that about 4.5 billion years ago a large planetesimal, about the size of Mars, gave Earth a glancing blow, taking a chunk of Earth's crust out into space. Some of the planetesimals merged with Earth, while the ejected lump began its own orbit encircling the Earth and became the moon. Proof for this theory arrives from samples of moon dust, exhibiting that the moon is made of fairly similar rocks to those detected in the upper layers of the Earth's mantle and crust. The moon formation impact pushed the Earth sideways, altering its angle of tilt to the sun from 0 degrees to 23.5 degrees.

Therefore, the Earth began to have seasons: winter for the hemisphere lifted away from the sun, and summer for the hemisphere inclined towards the sun. Originally the planet didn't have a crust, mantle, and core, and instead, all the ingredients were evenly combined. There were no oceans nor continents and no atmosphere. A meteorite crashed, radioactive dilapidation (decay) and planetary contraction forced the Earth to become hotter and hotter. After a few hundred million years the temperature of Earth arrived at 2,000C—the melting point of iron—and Earth's core was shaped.

Geologists believe there may have been lava (hot liquid rock) ocean at the surface which gradually cooled and the planet made into a mainstay (core), mantle (something that covers) and the hard outer surface, the (crust.) This layering of the planet helped to change the structure of the Earth surface and the Earth began to shape a bit similar to what it is now. Geologists assess that the Earth oceans and atmosphere are because of multiple volcanic explosions that occurred approximately four billion years ago which may have generated mostly from the debris of comets, sometimes debris of asteroids.

The part of a meteoroid or asteroid which survived the passage through our atmosphere and collided with the Earth then released water and gas at the surface. Comets are smaller celestial bodies mainly made of ice and dust. However, scientists say the Earth's situation in the solar system was fortuitous (happened accidentally) Mercury and Venus are too close to the sun, so too hot for oceans to form since they just evaporate, while Mars is too far away because if any liquid it just freezes. Only on Earth, they were just positioned right.

Geologists believe the first single-celled organisms evolved about 4 billion years ago. Gradually the composition of Earth's atmosphere altered chewing their way via carbon dioxide and water and releasing oxygen. By approximately 2.5 billion years ago, significant amounts of oxygen had accumulated the Earth's atmosphere. The site was set for intricate life to emit.

> "The atoms of our bodies are traceable to stars that manufactured them in their cores and exploded these enriched ingredients across our galaxy, billions of years ago. For this reason, we are biologically connected to every other living thing in the world. We are chemically connected to all molecules on Earth. And we are atomically connected to all atoms in the universe. We are not figuratively, but literally stardust."

> Neil DE Grasse Tyson

One scientific analogy is that originally, hydrogen and a little helium existed, and not much of anything else. Our bodies do not convey Helium. Hydrogen is, but that's not the immensity of our weight. Stars are similar to nuclear reactors. They take fuel and change it to something else. Hydrogen is molded into helium, and helium is made into carbon, nitrogen, and oxygen, iron and sulfur—everything that we're building off. As the stars are about to die, they inflate and expand as they fall together, the stars throw off their outside layers.

If a star is a tubby (heavy) enough, it will explode in a supernova (the explosion of the star that causes the star to become extremely bright). Scientists believe that most of the material that we are made of arrives from dying stars, or some stars that expired in explosions. Those stellar explosions carry on. We have stuff in us as old as the universe itself, even some stuff as old as maybe only a hundred years ago. all of that amalgamates (mixes, combine) in our bodies.

> "There's a flame of magic inside every stone & every flower, every bird that sings & every frog that croaks. There's magic in the trees & the hills & the river & the

rocks, in the sea & the stars & the wind, deep, wild magic that's as old as the world itself. It's in you too, my darling girl, and in me, and in every living creature, be it ever so small. Even the dirt I'm sweeping up now is stardust. In fact, all of us are made from the stuff of stars."

— Kate Forsyth, The Puzzle Ring

Many theories of the genesis of life have been suggested but since it's hard to prove or disprove them, no fully depended theory exists. Today, there are several competing theories for how life arose on Earth. Some doubt whether life started on Earth at all, acknowledging instead that life came from a distant world or because of a fallen comet or asteroid. Others believe that life probably has arisen here more than once.

Most scientists accept that life went through a period when RNA was the head-honcho molecule, leading life through its earliest stages. Relating to this RNA World hypothesis, RNA was the nitty-gritty molecule for primitive life and only relaxed when DNA and proteins—which exhibits their jobs much more efficiently than RNA—fostered.

RNA is very similar to DNA, and carries out numerous vital functions in every cell, also acting as a transitional-molecule between DNA and protein synthesis, and functioning as an on-and-off switch for certain genes. But the RNA hypothesis doesn't say how RNA itself first showed up. Like DNA, RNA is a complicated molecule made of repeating units of thousands of smaller molecules known as nucleotides that connect together in very exclusive, patterned ways. While there are those scientists who think RNA could have arisen spontaneously on early Earth, others believe the odds of such a thing taking place are astronomical.

What are the geneses of life on Earth? How did things arrive from non-living to living, from something that could not regenerate to something that could? How can a sum of inanimate atoms become animate? How did organic molecules obtain a high enough level of complicacy to be considered as living? The proper reply is that we do not really understand how life created on planet Earth.

The study of the inception of life on Earth or, more directly, how life on Earth started from inanimate matter, is scientifically familiar as abiogenesis (as opposed to biogenesis, which is the process of lifeforms generating other lifeforms, and as contrary to evolution, which is the study of how living things have altered over time since life first began). The contemporary explanation of abiogenesis is the original evolution of life or living organisms from inorganic or inanimate substances.

It regards the buildup of the simplest forms of life from primordial chemicals. It then becomes the search for some kind of molecule (along the lines of RNA or DNA) which is simple enough that it can be made by physical processes on the young Earth, yet complex enough that it can take charge of constructing more of itself, which most people would detect as constituting life.

Biologist scientists believe that the first living things on Earth, single-celled micro-organisms or microbes without a cell nucleus or cell membrane familiar as prokaryotes, seem to have initially shown on Earth almost four billion years ago, just a few hundred million years after the formation of the Earth itself. By far the longest portion of the history of life on Earth, hence, has contained the biochemical evolution of these single-celled micro-organisms, bacteria, and archaea: we can locate individual fossilized microbes in rocks 3.4 billion years old, yet geologists can only conclusively detect multi-celled fossils in certain rocks younger than 1 billion years.

It is assumed that over a few hundred million years of evolution, pre-biotic molecules gradually evolved into self-replicating molecules by natural selection. While some impression of the subject is well known, others remain puzzling and are the source of much debate among scientists. However, much progress has been made, there is still no single sure theory.

Life for all of its complexity is braided out of about 30 or so different molecules, made from some of the most available elements in the universe: oxygen, hydrogen, carbon, nitrogen, sulfur, and phosphorus. However, no one has yet succeeded in synthesizing a protocell (protocell is a self-organized, endogenously ordered, a spherical collection of lipids suggested as a stepping-stone toward the origin of life) utilizing basic components which would have the required properties of life. The beginnings of life are, strictly speaking, a matter of biology, not physics, which modern science suggests we are. After all, are we made of stardust?

QUOTES BY RUMI JALAL AD'DIN

I died as a mineral and became a plant,
I died as plant and rose to animal,
I died as animal and I was human,
Why should I fear? When was I less by dying?
Yet once more I shall die human,
To soar with angels blessed above.
when I sacrifice my angel soul
I shall become what no mind ever conceived.
As a human, I will die once more,
Reborn, I will with the angel's soar.
when I let my angel body go,
I shall be more than the mortal mind can know.

— Rumi Jalal ad 'Din

He says, There's nothing left of me.
I'm like a ruby held up to the sunrise.
Is it still a stone, or a world?
made of redness? It has no resistance
to sunlight.
This is how Hallaj said, I am God,
and told the truth!
The ruby and the sunrise are one.
Be courageous and discipline yourself.
Completely become hearing and ear, and wear this sun-
ruby as an earring.

If science should be a reliable gauge to depend on, then most scientists acknowledge that approximately sixty tons of cosmic dust fall to Earth every day. Researchers hypothesize that anywhere between 0.4 and 110 tons of the star stuff come into our atmosphere every day. If so, and for billions of years, then why should it be of any doubt that we are an inseparable part of these extremely rich and very valuable mineral soil and the brilliant atmosphere that energizes it with oxygen since without surely not an animated being can ever survive.

The stardust, the cosmos, is within us. We are made of star-stuff. You couldn't be here if stars hadn't exploded, because the elements—the carbon, nitrogen, oxygen, iron, all the things that matter for evolution—weren't created at the beginning of time.

The assay (estimate) is that about 36 and 166 meteorites larger than 10 grams drop to Earth per million square kilometers each year. Over the entire surface area of the Earth, that translates to 18,000 to 84,000 meteorites bigger than 10 grams per year. But most meteorites are too small to fall all the way to the surface.

"You are the universe expressing itself as a human for a little while."

Karen Wise

Many scientists believe, yes, we are made of atoms which perhaps were made up in millions of stars, saying that one's right leg atom might be from an entirely different star than the atoms in one's left leg. In truth our body—and everything in the world around us—is possibly made of atoms from innumerable (incalculable) different stars, originally estranged from each other by millions or even billions of light-years.

Those atoms rambled through space for millions or even billions of years, before eventually summing up in our primeval (prehistorical, primordial) solar system and coalesced (converged) because of gravity, to form the Earth and everything on it; including, ultimately, you and I. Not only are we made of stardust, but the atoms in our bodies are amazingly antiquated (surely billions of years old—at least as old as the solar system itself), and they have traveled an extremely long way, over a very long time, in order to build themselves into us. You are truly a child of God within the cosmic realm.

It doesn't deactivate there, because when living organisms expire, their atoms are reused by the processes of ruination (decay) and pass back into the air, water, soil, and rocks. over millions of years, many of these atoms will gradually become absorbed as food, water or air by ensuing generations of living organisms, and incorporated into their bodies in turn, and fluctuate in the food chain for centuries or millennia, until they are eventually digested into our body as the food, the air we breathe or the water we drink for survival.

So it is entirely probable that we carry atoms in our bodies that once were in the bodies of the first living organisms on planet Earth, and then in the bodies of prehistoric mammals, and in the bodies of apes, and then in the bodies of Neanderthals or homo sapiens and so on, up and up, until they reached you .to here. So as well as being a child of the cosmos, our body is also an atomic microcosm of all the life that has ever lived on planet Earth.

And, assuming the exponentially number of atoms in our bodies, and how they get widespread and mixed up over many centuries and millennia, our physical bodies will certainly have atoms from a considerable proportion of all the human beings who ever lived—as well as a few famous characters or not popular ones; maybe there's a carbon atom in your left pinky that once belonged to Cyrus the great, Plato the Greece philosopher, your eye may once belong to Jesus Christ, or your ear belonged to profit Moses, maybe Buddha, or perhaps one's rear end had belonged to nasty Hitler, may be Mussolini, or a hydrogen or Sulphur atom in your right hand that once belonged to Rumi the Persian philosopher and poet, may the great Shakespeare, or Lenin.

In truth, pick any random person from history, and you've possibly contained a bit of them in you! We know that water and electricity together make a dangerous pair. Mixing water and electricity, either from a lightning bolt or electrical socket in the house, is an extremely dangerous thing to do. Bear in mind that pure water is actually an excellent insulator and does not conduct electricity.

Water that would be considered pure would be distilled water (water condensed from steam) and deionized water (used in laboratories.) Water is an excellent solvent. No matter if the water comes out of your kitchen faucet, comes out of the ground or falls from the sky, the water will contain significant amounts of dissolved substances, minerals, and chemicals.

These things are the solutes dissolved in water. Free ions in water conduct electricity and Water is no longer an insulator once it begins dissolving substances. Even a small amount of ions in a water solution makes it able to conduct electricity. Once water contains these ions it will conduct electricity, such as from a lightning bolt or a wire from the wall socket, as the electricity from the source will seek out oppositely charged ions in the water.

The point is that 97 percent of the human body consists of stardust, claim scientists who have measured the distribution of essential elements of life in over 150,000 stars in the Milky Way galaxy. Body fluid contains electrolytes, chemicals which, when they dissolve in water, produce charged ions.

These ions enable the flow of electrical signals through the body. Electrolytes play a vital role in our body electrolytes that generate ions and enables the body to function. The principal electrolytes convey sodium, chloride, potassium, calcium, and magnesium. These five nutritional elements are minerals, and when minerals dissolve in water they separate into a positive and negative ion. Just like vitamins, minerals help our body grow, develop, and stay healthy.

The body utilizes minerals to perform many different functions—from making strong bones to send (information, sound, etc.) in the form of electrical signals to nerve impulses. Some minerals are even used to make hormones or create a normal heartbeat. The human body conducts electricity, because of minerals and conveying chemicals in our bodies. If any part of the body receives an electric shock, the electricity will go through the tissues with little obstruction. Then, the internal tissues start burning. Electrical current can damage the heart, which could cause the heart to either stop or beat erratically.

The electron current is what causes harm to tissue or nervous system damage, causing death or serious injury. Effects from electrocution can include burns or interference to our body's electric signals. A small current can actually kill you by entering the body, going through the heart, and exiting through the other side. The conductibility of the human body is due to the fact that chemicals and stardust minerals are the building blocks in making what we are, the very elements identified in stars.

Nature is endlessly resourceful, with the advent of new technology, and with the bigger and more powerful scientific equipment we are rapidly improving Earth's view of the universe. It will be at least 50 times more powerful than any telescope on Earth.

NASA is building the biggest telescope the world has ever witnessed and it will render scientists the opportunity to observe cosmic events that occurred about13.5 billion years ago—just 220 million years following the big bang. It is known as the James Webb Space Telescope (JWST), it will be 100 times more powerful than the Hubble Space Telescope, and is estimated to be fully operational within the next three years. It seems that no matter how advanced we become in new technologies, there are continuously recent things in nature that will never quit exhibiting amazing entities and fresh wonders.

Humanity will not see an end to the adventure of our universe since there will not exist blank pages not showing exciting ideas and miracle like resources, they will gradually be invented and explored. The human mind and heart resemble nature and are extremely important and the undeniable extension of this progressively oriented agendas.

Both our heart and mind simulate nature, and the cosmic events, since there is no ending in what our heart carves and desires, and our mind seeks. because the architect of the human brain and heart is born from the same energy-oriented principle that is the literal cause of the entire universe. It is the same precise mathematics that is rooted in plants, the birds, the bees, the flowers, the trees, the stars the galaxies, and the Higgs particles. That is why the view of human aesthetic is as demanding as the aesthetic nature itself. We are not outside observers; we are an inseparable part of this whole magical world anchored inside this magnificent universe.

In the beginning, they thought cells are the tiniest unit, then learned cells are structures that are made up billions of molecules, and figured out that each molecule is composed of atoms (in turn, atoms are made up subatomic particles called protons, electrons, and neutrons, and those are comprised of even smaller particles called quarks). Quarks, like electrons, are fundamentally particles which for now they can't be broken into tinier parts. Scientists believe that the first fount (source) was the big bang that made the universe 14 billion years ago.

When the big bang happened, the elementary particles originally were too hot to make any stable atoms. But after a few thousand years later, when things cooled down a lot, hydrogen and helium got made. Protons, neutrons, and electrons can then form to build atoms. Atoms are then used to create the molecules in our atmosphere. There are about 120 elements that can be sought in the molecules we recognize so far. Smaller molecules can manage together and construct macromolecules.

Then the question which crosses an inquisitive mind is that what comes after quarks and leptons. Quarks are the smallest units or building blocks of the Standard Model of particle physics and therefore cannot be split up into further constituents. On the other hand, if one chooses to believe in string theory, basically everything is made up of tiny vibrating strings, including quarks. Strings or points?

In experiments, tiny particles like quarks and electrons seem to behave like single points of matter with no spatial (having extension in space relating to the position, area, and the size of objects distribution). Quarks represent the smallest known subatomic particles. These building blocks of matter are considered the new elementary particles, replacing protons, neutrons, and electrons as the fundamental particles of the universe. Up and down quarks are the most common and least massive.

Singularity.

If you go back in time as far as you can, you'll find a universe that was hotter, denser, and more energetic. If you were to extrapolate back to an arbitrarily hot, dense state, the laws of physics that describe space, time, matter and energy break down; you'll arrive at a singularity.

Yet a singularity is also exactly what you find if you were to fly inside a black hole, to the final destination where all in-falling matter and energy winds up. These are the only instances in the entire universe's history— past, present, and future—where a singularity occurs. Perhaps the two of them are connected? It's not as crazy an idea as you might think.

General relativity and quantum mechanics, together, do an excellent job of describing the physics of the universe outside of a black hole, like of a gas cloud being torn apart outside the event horizon. But to understand the physics at or near a singularity, a successor theory, like quantum gravity, is needed. Normally, the universe is governed by two sets of rules: quantum mechanics, for particles and their electromagnetic and nuclear interactions, and general relativity, for masses, gravity and the curvature of space-time.

Quantum mechanics tells us that all particles exhibit wave-like properties and have some level of intrinsic uncertainty between position/momentum and energy/time. In particular, every massive particle has a wavelength associated with it: A Compton wavelength, which explains how it scatters in collisions. If you were to take a photon's wavelength and convert it into a mass, via Einstein's $E = mc^2$ you'd get a massive particle's Compton wavelength.

A singularity is where conventional physics breaks down, whether you're talking about the very beginning of the universe and the birth of space and time or the very central point of a black hole. However, we can calculate what happens to space-time inside the event horizon all the way up to (but not including) the central singularity.

Surprisingly, with just a coordinate transformation, the space inside a black hole can be mapped, one-to-one, onto the space outside a black hole. What happens when the universe stops expanding? In a loosed universe, gravity eventually stops the expansion of the universe, after which it starts to contract until all matter in the universe collapses to a point, a final singularity termed the Big Crunch, the opposite of the big bang.

19

THE ANTHROPIC PRINCIPLE

The anthropic principle is a philosophical consideration that by looking at the universe, it must be in harmony with the conscious and sapient life (referring to homo-sapiens, wise) that observes it.

The fundamental laws of nature carry utterly imperative constants, like the gravitational constant, the electric charge, the mass of the electron, the speed of light, plank's constant from quantum mechanics.

For example, gravitational constant: decides the power of gravity, if the strength is lower than stars, the pressure would not suffice to quell(overcome) Coulomb barrier which will result in the stars not shinning, since no thermonuclear composite (alloy, synthesis, mixture) is possible. If higher, stars burn too fast, consume fuel before life has a chance to develop.

Arno Penzias (Nobel prize in physics): Astronomy leads us to a unique event, a universe which was created out of nothing, one with the very delicate balance needed to provide exactly the conditions required to permit life, and one which has an underlying (one might say supernatural) plan.

The Coulomb barrier is the energy barrier due to electrostatic interaction that two nuclei need to overcome so they can get close enough to undergo a nuclear reaction. Electrostatic: relates to stationary electric charges or fields as opposed to electric currents. powerful force coupling constant: keeps particles attached in the nucleus of the atom. If weaker than multi-proton, then, particles couldn't have fastened together, hydrogen would be the sole element in the universe. If stronger, all elements lighter than iron would be scarce. Also, radioactive decay would be less, which heat melts the core of planet Earth.

The electromagnetic coupling constant: Decides the power of the electromagnetic force that joint electrons to the nucleus. If less, no electrons can be held in orbit. If stronger, electrons will not bond with other atoms, if so, then resulting in no molecules. All the above constants are critical for the arrangement of the basic building blocks of life. And, the range of possible values for these constants is with extremely narrow margin only approximately 1 to 5% for the amalgamation (fusion, synthesis) of constants.

Outside this range, and life (specifically intelligent life) could not be possible. what science is not able to answer is that why is there any structure at all to our universe? Why this universal or planetary structure guide to the ability for life to exist? Why does life create intelligence to relatively fathom life's intricacies?

Scientists, the physicists, tell us a universe with a lower gravitational constant would have a weaker force of gravity, where stars and planets cannot form. Or a universe with a highly powerful force would inhibit thermonuclear synthesis, which would lessen the luminosity of stars, then, a darker universe, leaving life without sunlight. Why don't those universes exist? Why does our universe, with its exclusive value exist rather than not, and why not another?

Did you know that not only space but the time itself is distorted by heavy objects since matter, energy, motion, space, and time are intertwined as Einstein's theory of general relativity predicted that the space-time around Earth would be not only warped but also twisted by the planet's rotation? In it, he determined that massive objects cause a distortion in space-time, which is felt as gravity. Since matter carries energy (via Einstein's famous relation that energy is mass times the speed of light squared), such objects will have a gravitational field and so they will distort space-time. So one way in which a charge or a magnet will distort space-time is by virtue of its matter.

The general belief by physics is that the universe is expanding, which is due to the geometry of the universe, at least on an extremely large scale, elliptic. In a closed universe, gravity eventually stops the expansion of the universe, after which it starts to contract until all matter in the universe collapses to a point, a final singularity termed the Big Crunch, the opposite of the big bang. Edwin Hubble space telescope indicated the definitive evidence that the universe was expanding. The idea was that the universe received all the energy required for its expansion in the first few moments after the big bang.

Scientists believe that the curve changes noticeably about 7.5 billion years ago when objects in the universe began flying apart as a faster rate. Astronomers theorize that the faster expansion rate is due to a mysterious, dark force that is pulling galaxies apart. One explanation for dark energy is that it is a property of space. In the 1920s, astronomer Edwin Hubble learned that the universe was not static, rather, it was expanding; a find that exhibited the universe was apparently born in a big bang. After that, it was thought the gravity of the matter in the universe was sure to slow the expansion of the universe.

But what should be clear is that the universal expansion, the gravitational forces, the wonders of millions and millions of black holes, the magic of electromagnetic forces, the atomic forces, the effects of entropy, the subatomic world of particles, the quantum world, the string theory, and the probabilities of some parallel universes, the magical maneuverability's of trillions galaxies, billions of universes, and millions of other perhaps magnificently unknown phenomenon's are breathtakingly operating without the slightest flaw, making the fine-tuning of the universe possible as quoted by the prominent George Ellis (British astrophysicist): "Amazing fine tuning occurs in the laws that make this [complexity] possible. Realization of the complexity of what is accomplished makes it very difficult not to use the word 'miraculous' without taking a stand as to the ontological status of the word.

Further, why should the constants even be present to help with the stability of the universe and lead to the evolution of human consciousness, as they are known as the anthropic principle or the fine-tuning of the universe? This should activate neurons, and raise eyebrows to ask if the anthropic principle has the properties which substantiate intelligent life, then, there must exist a graceful designer beyond human imagination that planned to sustain our universe for reaching specific purpose with having a definite goal, or goals in mind.

GOD, MAN, AND THE UNIVERSE

Declaring the position of the fine-tuned universe states that a slight alteration in several of the dimensionless physical constants would force radical changes in the universe. Stephen Hawking said, "The laws of science, as we know them at present, contain many fundamental numbers, like the size of the electric charge of the electron and the ratio of the masses of the proton and the electron. The remarkable fact is that the value of these numbers seems to have been very finely adjusted to make possible the development of life."

For instance, if the strong nuclear forces were 2 percent more powerful than it is, indicating its strength was 2 percent larger, leaving the other constants unaltered, diprotons would be secure; stated by physicist Paul Davies, hydrogen would fuse into them instead of deuterium and helium. This would extremely alter the physics of stars, and doubtlessly preclude the existence of life similar to what we know on Earth.

The fine-tuned universe is the proposition that the conditions that permit life in the universe can occur only when certain universal dimensionless physical constants lie within a very narrow range of values, so that if any of several fundamental constants were only slightly different, the universe would be unlikely to be conducive to the establishment and development of matter, astronomical structures, elemental diversity, or life as it is comprehended.

Either the entire cosmos, not excluding our universe is a stroke of luck, a lucky accident, a random object that appeared out of nowhere, and we all are the felicitous (fortunate) products. But as experienced for billions of years we should admit that life is robust, and the universe is fined tuned, well-orchestrated and managed, otherwise it certainly would have not lasted as long as it has where scientists do predicate for billions even trillions of years to go; which should imply there can be other forms of life beside the carbon-oriented life that we know.

An ensemble of other different universes is necessary for the existence of our universe (multiple universes.) There are two sorts of anthropic principle issues weak and strong. The weak anthropic principle simply believes that the current universe is of the matrix (form) that allows intelligent spectators. In other words, there is the right amount of complexity and time for intelligent observers to vent (emit, evolve).

Then, is the strong anthropic principle which states that the universe must have these requirements in order to sustain intelligence life (us). Our existence is then the end result of a plan. The strong form seems extreme and the weak form appear not gratifying. The key point here is that a naturalistic view for science requires that the universe is causally closed. That science is whole (full-blown, complete) and the forces of physics are the sole forces in the universe and everything can be described by those forces.

The anthropic principle is observed as a challenge to the naturalistic view and demands an outside an omnipotent force or guiding deity. The philosophical quandary (dilemma) is that the constants of the universe on both microscopic (atomic constants), and macroscopic (electromagnetic forces) and cosmological levels in their entirety appear to be extremely finely adjusted-tuned, in order for life and intelligence to emit.

We should seriously question linking the natural-selection doctrine, and the survival of the fittest theory behind the reason for creating even the simplest living organism which has not only proven futile but the evidence of an omnipotent designer is found in nature and the higher realms that Darwin couldn't have dreamed of.

Darwin argued that the emergence of design could be simplified as the product of a purely unguided mechanism, referencing natural selection and random variation. Modern Neo-Darwinists have likewise indicated that the undirected process of natural selection and random mutation generated the complex designed-like build up in living systems. They state that natural selection can emulate (simulate) the powers of a designing intelligence without itself being directed by an intelligent agent.

As Darwin himself insisted, "There seems to be no more design in the variability of organic beings and in the action of natural selection, than in the course in which the wind blows." Or as the renowned evolutionary biologist Francisco Ayala has debated, Darwin is chronicled for "design without a designer" and showed "that the directive organization of living beings can be explained as the result of a natural process, natural selection, without any need to resort to a Creator or other external agent."

But did Darwin describe all evidence of patent (apparent, obvious) design in biology? Darwin tried to explain the origin of new living forms initiating from simpler pre-existing forms of life, but his theory of evolution by natural selection did not even attempt to fathom the origin of life, the simplest living cell in existence.

Yet, there is now absorbing proof of the intelligent design in the inner recesses of the simplest living one-celled organisms. Furthermore, there is a key component of living cells that convey the intelligent design of life detectable which Darwin was not aware of, and that modern evolutionary theorists have not explained away.

20

HUMAN BEINGS RESEMBLE TREES

Trees and plants create the food they need for living and to grow through photosynthesis, a process that happens in their leaves. To produce food (in the form of glucose and other sugars), a tree, or a plant needs energy from sunlight, carbon dioxide from the air, and water. They make their own food from these imperative elements, like sunlight, water, carbon dioxide and nutrients from the soil.

During the process of photosynthesis, plants use carbon dioxide to make food and release oxygen, as a result. Roots carry water and nutrients to the plant. Trees and Plants absorb nutrients and water through their roots, but photosynthesis—the process by which plants create their fuel—occurs in the leaves.

Therefore, plants need to get fluids and nutrients from the ground up through their stems to their parts that are above ground level. One of the mysteries of nature is how despite the force of gravity water and nutrient go up to reach the branches and feed the leaves, and the entire plant, or the whole tree.

As those trees and plants must have the essential elements to bear fruits, flowers, shade, beauty and release oxygen, the human beings also need clean air, clean water, sunlight, nutrients, rest and productivity which are definitely essential for their existence. these very required elements are absorbed through our digestive system as the sun is via skin to rejuvenate every cell in the human body.

The similarity is that as trees and plants produce astonishing colors, wonderful fruit with great taste, as often exotic flowers do with divine smell; good human beings are meant to bear amazingly fruits like thoughts, and beautiful flower-like minds, with compassionate and kind hearts to make a difference for a better world, creating good thought, with good words, and good deeds; since it is through our mind, heart, and soul that we can cultivate the awesome drive and the impetus to do good, to make it a purposeful living.

A tree requires the four vital elements for survival—soil, water, air, and fire (sun). Human beings also need the same imperative elements.

The soil provides nourishment for the tree, also allows the roots through which the food is absorbed to grow and expand. A person with a great deal of wisdom, but not doing many good deeds is like a tree with numerous branches but with few roots. A brief storm can uproot and destroys it. In comparison, a person whose good deeds exceed his wisdom is like a tree with few branches but whose roots are numerous. It is deeply and firmly planted, and even if many strong windy storms below against it, will not fall apart.

When one belongs, irrespective of his wealth and position, then, there is a strong connection with one's community and people around him which signifies strong roots. But when one does not belong and is behaving like a remote island, even though one might appear wealthy and successful, it denotes much like fancy branches of a tree, but with few roots.

It can easily fall when faced with hardship and lose the challenges that life can unexpectedly throw that are often impossible to overcome. Human beings are group animals they need to collectively thrive to conquer over nature's challenges. Zest, vitality, encouragement, hope, the power of intention, perseverance, blossoming, success, serving others in the name of God and humanity, constructive attitudes, challenging nature, and collectively reaching prosperity, is without a doubt most beneficial to everyone, rather than acting isolated and single-handedly.

WATER

Rainwater is sucked into the ground and through a complex system of roots—it is then carried throughout the trunk, branches, and leaves. Without water, the tree will wither and die. Comparatively, when deprived of water, a person will end up dehydrated and eventually disoriented, even to the point where the victims can lose one's memory.

AIR

Trees and plants need air to survive since the air carries oxygen that trees and plants must have for respiration, also carbon dioxide for photosynthesis. Comparatively, humans also must have oxygen to live, even a couple of minutes with no air to breath, we will expire.

Sunlight

A tree also needs sunlight to survive. The absorption of energy from the light activates the process of photosynthesis, a chemical reaction that is necessary for the growth and health of the tree. Humans also need fire and warmth to survive, the warmth of mankind and community, through which family, friends, and associates can be very helpful and supportive in the times of need. Caring people can boost one's energy and channel that into positive actions. Today's lifestyle has cast us all into the bleak vicinities of fear and anonymity.

The urban culture has pushed so many into cyberspace mentalities. It seems there is no scape, but to behave robotically like, exhausted of nourishing the human soul through caring and warmth, which has I afraid created millions with a psychological problem which has manifested a breeding ground for violence and criminal behaviors, which should demand rationally decisive change if humanity is to pull through.

21

WHAT GOES AROUND, COMES AROUND

Experiencing life is basically channeled through our senses, materially based evidence is executed via our nervous system and through what we see, hear, taste, smell, and touch. When we notice so much injustice, suffering, cruelty, misery, ordeal, and pain on one side in an extremely troubling world, and the absence of God on the other side, it gives the impression that God does not hear our cry for help, then, what most feel is despair, which discords and disorients them from the reality of a living that meant to be good; making it apropos (suitable) and conducive for so many not to realize the infinite traces of God and the consequences of the divine justice.

We ought to know that nothing occurs by chance since everything happens within the universal law of cause and effect, we reap what we saw. It is clearly understood that for every action, there is an equal and opposite reaction. The invisible hand of this divine mechanism is relentlessly at work to make sure that not a single manifestation takes place without being noticed. Yes, so many of man's deed might appear to have no immediate result but concealed. Until eventually all catch up and forms a complex but justified web of cause and effect. As humanity advances in technology, what we presently might consider as miracles, will one day be taken for granted as common.

The endowed human drive will relentlessly push forward for new inventions and magic like concepts to materialize what once was thought as miracle become a contemporary fact. The response often is difficult for millions to link the magnificent design, discipline, and intricacy of this enchanting universe to our Creator.

Traces of God should be quite obvious in God's superb planning, and the ultra-competency of a designer that incredibly manages the cosmos and beyond, which without chaos and definitely perdition (damnation, doom) days should be expected. But the question which most atheists ask is that if God created the cosmos, and if God overseas the divine justice, then, who created God?

Many dilettantes (dabbler, layman, not expert) states that the cosmos is so complicated, it must have been created by a creator, but if that's correct, then, it must alert us that God is even more Byzantine (complicated) than the cosmos. So if the cosmos needed a maker, surely this higher God also needed a creator! Therefore, if it is improbable that the cosmos exists without a beginning, it is even more unlikely that God exists without a beginning. So, why believe in this notably dubious God? Cynic (doubter) and believers both agree that out of nothing, nothing comes. But clearly, if nothing had ever existed, there would be nothing now and nothing endlessly.

Those concerns hence accept that since something exists, something had to exist from all of eternity. In retrospect, the atheists say the cosmos existed from all of eternity, believers say God existed from all of eternity. The famous debate which many creationists have redundantly set forth is that every event has a cause. A universe is obviously an event. Hence, the universe has a cause, and that cause is God. In response, the non-believers have argued that if so, then God must have a cause. But then there is a missing link and a huge discrepancy in the position which the atheists take.

The atheist forgets that the cause and effect events are only authenticated in the observable world, where materially based living can empirically be manifested, and do not make sense in the unseen world since they do not apply to the invisible spiritual realms. They cannot fathom that the physical laws belong to the material world, and are not applicable in the spiritual and the hidden domain.

Edgar Andrews, of the University of London England, an international expert on the science of large molecules, writes this in defense of God's existence: "Because cause and effect are only proven for the physical world, we can no longer insist that cause and effect are relevant when it comes to the origin of a spiritual entity like God. Therefore, God doesn't have to have a cause—he can be the ultimate uncaused cause, a being whom no one has made."

Creationists believe that God is the infinite and perfect spirit in whom all things have their source, support, and end. As mysterious as God is, but certainly not contradictory, when we are faced with the choice of the cosmos existing from all eternity, or the Divine Spirit existing from all eternity, the believers answer is God. The startling discipline, and the mindboggling complexity in the universe and what it holds, is just beyond chance and random maneuverability which should put any inquisitively intelligent mind at awe. Things have to operate the way they originally have, otherwise, we would not be here to question them.

For instance, if the power of the electromagnetic force were just a bit different, atoms would not be secured. Scientists believe that Just a 4 percent alteration would stop all nuclear amalgam (mixture, fusion) in stars. the arrangement which builds the carbon atoms that our bodies are significantly made of. Likewise, there is a sensitive balance between gravity that pulls matter towards itself, and the dark energy, which acts in reverse making the universe grow ever faster, that is required to make the existence of stars possible, while not collapsing the universe on itself.

There is a reason that the neutrons are just a tad heavier than protons, if it were the reverse, atoms would not exist, because all the protons in the universe would have dilapidated (ruination, decay) into neutrons after the big bang. No protons, which then, no atomic nuclei and no atoms. Without atoms, no chemistry, no life.

Adding to the controversy is an unanswered question lurking at the very heart of science -the origin of the laws of physics. do they come from? The wonders of mathematics that correlated with the laws of physics as they comfortably corroborate with the laws of nature. Why do they have the form they do?

We ought to bear in mind that crucial universal functionings are concept oriented which without no decisive living is ever possible, so is the concept of good and evil, as they will be met with divine justice, as they are due in a timely manner.

22

IN GOD, WE SHOULD BELIEVE

Innumerous tragedy and harms behold humanity because of not knowing and lack of information. It is a no-brainer that once one realizes the infinite intricacy of the world we live in and the awesome universe which our galaxy the Milky Way is part of, forth with thousands of other mind-boggling phenomena already discovered, and millions more waiting, if not billions to be contrived. Then, it should nudge intelligent minds to wonder about the magnanimity (magnificent, generosity) of a great designer's footprint in all there is, and all there ever will be.

We should know that our solar system consists of our star, the Sun, and its orbiting planets (including Earth), along with numerous moons, asteroids, comet material, rocks, and dust. Our Sun is just one star among the hundreds of billions of stars in our Milky Way Galaxy. The universe is all of the galaxies—billions of them.

Hence leaving humanity with no choice but to meditate on the enormity of cosmic with limitless universes and infinite galaxies that operate with extreme discipline and accuracy, which ought to leave no doubt that we must be living a purposeful life, since we are an inseparable part of this extremely colossal existence; which should relentlessly spur humanity to delve into the unknown, and to further become competent in discovering the magic that awaits us, to pinnacle the wisdom in searching for God, to tirelessly progress, and for living a life with virtuous intent.

We can communicate through our senses, via our mind, in which our thoughts interact, making it able for limitless messages to get across, they become substantiated because the atmosphere we live in is fundamentally conductive. The environment is an active conductor, where there are no barriers to halt the fluidity of what we think, conducive to our feelings, emotions, and imaginations. The same life force that allows seeds to grow, trees to bear fruits, potentiates embryos to mature, and basically allows any animated activity to take place; it is the entity that deals with the entire universal maneuverability.

The cosmic forces not to exclude electromagnetic forces, gravity force, the strong and weak atomic forces that are engaged in making it a fertile ground for prolific mind and ideas to function and revolutionize the world we know. The same life force that makes it possible to invent x-rays machines, MRI, SCANS of many sorts, EKG/ECG machines, which renders an extremely measured atmosphere so disciplinary that makes it possible to materialize all kinds of scientific inventions, and so reliable making our life easier, not to exclude the internet, satellites, GPS, and other media feats.

A life that we can resonate with and function through our everyday living, since the atmosphere that we operate in, is not insulated, but a great conductor for mandating infinite possibilities in the near and far future, where kneeling next to the gates where God resides becomes an option.

The reason for our brain which apparently is energy based that can produce thoughts, and for our mind to communicate and interact is because of the conductibility of the surroundings which makes it possible. It is because our brain also is a fabulous conductor compatible with the environment in which we operate. Our thoughts, feelings, desires, and emotion can interact just because the fertile ground already providing the means absolutely necessary to produce such tasks, and relate to employing science, manifest philosophy, constitute arts, music, creativity, imagination, and host of modern socio-cultural, socioeconomic activities conveying wonderful ideas, and innovations.

Our mind and hearts ought to act as awakened agents to simultaneously accord with the extremely alert environment that we live in since we are an is an inseparable part of nature, nature so robustly impregnated with magic and never-ending surprises which has amazed the most talented and magnificent minds of our times.

Gradual brain neuroplasticity is directly proportional to the brain producing more brain cells, and in creating billions of neurons firing at trillions of synopsis (junctures) to produce millions of thoughts every day to make magic, that is because of the fluidity of mind and its congruency with the universally exuding energy that is prevalent in our world, in our universe, and billions of other universes having their own solar systems.

Our solar system consists of an average star we call the Sun, the planets Mercury, Venus, Earth, Mars, Jupiter, Saturn, Uranus, Neptune, and Pluto. It includes the satellites of the planets; numerous comets, asteroids, and meteoroids; and the interplanetary medium.

It seems promising that one-day people are able to communicate thoughts by means other than known senses known as telepathy. Telepathy falls into two parts: Telepathic communication, that is the ability to delegate information from one mind to another, and telepathic perception, which is the power to receive messages, information from another mind that sounds colossally exciting, since reading minds can encourage good thoughts, good words and good deeds, perhaps a wonderfully effective way to lessen wrongdoings and violence behaviors.

It is a blessing knowing that the human mind and soul, our heart and imagination is so coherent with the energy-driven universe that is infinite in nature, so is our mind and our heart. There is no limit to our heart desiring and our mind imagining to the day we take our last breath, which should excitingly get ready for our next step up adventure in the next runner up living. Otherwise, transparency of human communication and any other activity for that matter would have been insulated and absolutely futile.

What we see and feel as solid matter is made of nuclei and electrons, and when we get down to investigate the really small things like atoms and nuclei and the distinction between matter and empty space, we confront a much different meaning. We face solid matter as what we cannot penetrate and walk through it, because what we know as mysterious forces connect the nuclei and the atoms so tight to each other, making it into the solid position that is impermeable.

Liquids, the life force, or if you like the mysterious fields and forces hold the atoms less tightly over each other, and more loosely than the position of atoms in solids, making it possible to wall through water, and of course not as fast as one can walk through air than the water. Walking through the gas is easy, since the atoms in the gas are not tied together, but rather whizzing freely.

Let's look at a few things out of thousands of wonders taking place in our own body. If we pay attention to so many things happening in our own body, it should put anyone at awe since amazing mechanisms occur in human anatomy which we take for granted. For example, if the tongue gets caught between two layers of sharp teeth every time we eat, or when talk, it would be extremely painful. But the tongue by instinct maneuvers so magically, moving side to side, bouncing food up and down without getting caught and becoming injured by our sharp teeth.

The miracle of saliva, and other wonderful digestive hormones; and no matter how much food and drink a healthy digestive system can take in, until one is full, one does not feel any discomfort as food gradually travels through the digestive system. What we experience is feeling full, and quenching our thirst, enjoying the ride. Many frequently question how can human spirit experience the joy of lovemaking, playfulness, experience fear, or any other human feat, as there is no live physical body after we expire?

What I can say is, one should think about one's dream in which our mind, the spirit, or the soul, call it what you wish, often does the unthinkable as we are very well alive in our dreams, without our body lifting a finger when deep in its sleep.

Obviously, billions of phenomena, if not trillions of cases are so precisely calculated that is utterly infallible, making life possible; which should put any intelligent mind at awe and reverence for the infinite mind of a creator with such incredible fist beyond imagination. A magnificent designer beyond space and time, that is over the human mind to assess its infinite abilities and greatness.

In the end, we should pound on science, philosophy, and seek poetry and art as they all play great roles in our lives, as for science it is enormously important since scientists relentlessly delve into nature to discover the infinite resourcefulness of the world we live in. They insist on looking into the root-causes of all things as their findings will never face any unwritten page, as the infinite universe would constantly expose new ideas to inquisitive minds, surprising them with fresh concepts to the end of times.

DR. FERIDOUN SHAWN SHAHMORADIAN

A society without philosophical endeavors is empty of wisdom, where a society without poets has no soul, and a nation without artists has no beauty, and gatherings without music can seldom be happy, as music can excite the body, and thrill the soul, as these entities and the like bring us closer to God.

23

TESTOSTERONE AND AGGRESSIVE BEHAVIORS

Lack of information, and for some not even willing to talk on the subject of sex, and evaluate why for example some men are more aggressive, and to some extent violent than other sexually timid ones. So many are irrelevant to correctly evaluate this rather decisive subject as millions carelessly are inclined to harsh and often inhumane punishment as they are for sexual predators to forgo life imprisonment and even death in many developing nations, and third world countries, reminding one of the dark age mentality where cruel and savage retaliations often the case.

To act incredulous (cynical, dubious) referencing men's motive for sex as many females say or believe that men's brain is between their legs can biologically be better described as men's brain being located directly in the testes the male's testosterone factory. What undeniably is medically known aside from any baffling (confusing, mix up) psychological factors which initially been decided on that men's sexual craving is solely related to the amount of testosterone in a male's system.

If male's testosterone, also called T-level, is high, then more tendencies should be expected towards the opposite sex. That is how sex drive, also known as libido, is described by how much (T) one produces. Apparently this is correct for both male and females, knowing that on average basis males produce about ten to twelve times as much of this sex hormone as do females which should explain why men commonly have more irrepressible sex drive urges than women.

Stressful positions, such as trauma and the like, inflict significant inhibition on testosterone secretion. High testosterone levels or an increase in basal (relating to bottom layers) concentrations are associated with aggressive manifestations, whereas high cortisol concentrations are linked to submissive behaviors. Aggression has been differently described and it is shown with a broad spectrum from the tendency to verbal abuse and physical violence.

It is a primitive and common social behavior that the media report with covert gratification as if it is something to hurray about using it as a leverage for describing exciting news, in which the people of civilized nations accept its manifestation with horror and a subconscious disturbance, because such declaration yanks (uproot) the comfortable belief of the difference of human conduct from that of animals.

Violent and aggressive behavior is a natural and physiological element that rules beastly living, driven as it is by the instincts of survival and the preservation of species through reproduction. Attenuated (diluted, weak) remains of these instincts stay in humans, albeit (although) repressed by homey and social inhibitions, but it still patents (manifest) in transformed and various forms in accordance with the idiosyncrasy (mannerism, eccentricity), temperament (individuality, makeup, disposition) and the psychological state of each person.

Atavistic ancestor residues of belligerent behavior victorious (prevailing) in animal life, ruled by testosterone, stay diluted in man and choked via domestic and social reticence (inhibition.) Thus, it still manifests itself in different intensities, shape, and forms including thoughts, verbal aggressiveness, anger, frustration, offensiveness, competition, dominance behavior, physical aggression and violence conduct.

Testosterone plays a decisive role in the arousal of aggressive behavior in the brain centers involved in offensive conducts and on the growth of the muscular system that help with their findings. There is proof that testosterone levels are higher in people with aggressive behavior, those who have committed violent crimes.

Also, there is evidence that testosterone levels increase during the highly intensified sports games and other radical situations, where the victor's testosterone rises. Just like the fight or flight situation the sympathetic nervous system sends out impulses to glands and smooth muscles and instruct the adrenal medulla to relinquish epinephrine (adrenaline) and norepinephrine (noradrenaline) into the bloodstream.

These stress hormones make several changes in the body, including an increase in heart rate and blood pressure. In response to extreme stress, the body's sympathetic nervous system is invigorated (activated, quickened) because of the sudden rush of hormones. The hormone is known as the catecholamine, which includes adrenaline and noradrenaline.

The autonomic nervous system has two elements, the sympathetic nervous system, and the parasympathetic nervous system. The sympathetic nervous system works like a gas pedal in a car. It triggers the fight-or-flight response, providing the body with a burst of energy so that one can count to received dangers.

Many studies have shown that offensive behavior appreciates in the brain via interaction between subcortical structures in the amygdala and the hypothalamus in which emotions are generated and the prefrontal cognitive centers where emotions are perceived and controlled. Subcortical structures. The subcortical structures of the nervous system have a complex motor and non-motor functions.

The subcortical structures include the limbic system, the diencephalon, and the ventricles. The activities of testosterone on the brain initiates in the embryonic stage. It seems that in the beginning development of the DNA level, the number of CAG repeats in the androgen receptor gene seems to play a role in the expression of aggressive behavior. A (DNA) segment known as a CAG trinucleotide repeat.

This part is a buildup of a series of three DNA building blocks (cytosine, adenine, and guanine) that appear multiple times in a row. Neuroimaging testing's in adult males have shown that testosterone motivates the amygdala ameliorating (improving, enhancing) its emotional activity and its resistance to prefrontal curbing (restraining) control. This maneuverability is countered by the action of cortisol which simplifies prefrontal area cognitive control on impulsive inclinations (tendency) awakened in the subcortical structures.

The degree of impulsivity is regulated by serotonin inhibiting receptors, and with the meddling of this neurotransmitter, the major agents of the neuroendocrine influence on the brain process of aggression form a triad. Testosterone activates the subcortical areas of the brain to cause aggression, while cortisol and serotonin act antagonistically with testosterone to lower its consequences.

Inducing testosterone is biologically demanded as it is urged to literally guaranty the survival of the species. So it must be seen positively, and it should not be lightly. Still, given the constraints of civilization, and the nature of the human psyche, it also guarantees colossal frustration and sorrow—and possibly as much for men as for women. When a male's T-levels rise beyond a certain degree he can barely help but have sex on his mind virtually (practically, almost) all the time.

That's why it's not at all uncommon to hear a male's behavior described as testosterone-driven. Undeniably for males in their later teens and early twenties (when their T-levels rush), their thoughts and feelings are permeated hugely by what really is going on between their legs. They experience an almost continual thrilling in their genitals—sensations that howl (scream) for attention but that society does not permit being fully signified.

Knowing that, regardless of such austerity (inhibition, self-control), the very sight of a female can't be helped, but fan this not-to-be-denied and burst of libidinous flame. Generally speaking, many adolescent girls and women correctly criticize that they feel de-valued and less worthy when men look at or treat them, as sex objects. But obviously, this criterion shouldn't be loggerhead (state of strong disagreement) situation, since it is debatable that so many adolescent boys and men, tempted, and seduced from within by elevated T-levels, can't much help but be lured into very difficult position.

Like animals in heat, males under the influence since the beastly part of human being acting by instinct, will kick in harder when no sex education is ever presented to them as millions if not billions are exhausted from having the opportunity to become enlightened. so many are hardly alerted not to perceive females other than one-dimensionally—as objects for sexual pleasure.

These hormonal activities should remind one of not having a choice to either being born in ghetto, any other Godforsaken place and so many condescending hoods, or to be born in an upgraded, affluent family that are highly luxurious with money, influence, and prestige in which the difference would be like growing up in hell or heaven. Without having the slightest choice or say so, referencing where and whom one should be born to, or to what nationality, religion, race, clan and so on. They are mandatory, and thanks to God there is no prejudice to whom these hormonal activities should belong to since everyone is unanimously born with them without any exception.

Expect those with having good opportunities and decisive means which are able to better control aggressive behaviors, since they can identify with good education, and equate to constructively respond for great upbringings, and can accord with reliable role models, which most indigenous and poor are exhausted from having such prominent variables for making a better difference in their lives.

The harsh reality is that so many poor people will face stringent punishments, without having the knowledge or opportunities to be aware of the reason behind their anger and frustration which has a compounding effect when they are born into poverty and within desolate condition not being aware of the trouble inside which certainly would be mitigated and healed with education and through professional therapeutic procedures that they are denied of since they cannot afford such bonuses available to the rich.

What I mean is that we are part animal and part human, as there is not much we can do to stop instinctual mechanism which they make us partly beast, since our physical body must breath, must be nourished, must sleep and have rest, need to keep up with good hygiene, must have intercourse to produce life, must work to survive, and so on, which they are also blessings since they keep us afloat to survive for reaching our objectives which by having conscious, being mindful, and through our will, also for being free to choose we can reach our goal in life, as we are potentiated to reach stars.

Hence, we need good education and professional training to constructively manage human instinctual apparatus that are probable for civil and cultured nations in which they realize the human malaise (anxiety, heebie-jeebies), feeling of distress brought by uncertainties early in life, as they ought to prioritize devoting time, allocate more funds, with plenty of accessible expertise and sincere intention to capitalize on improving people's mind and behaviors.

To mold and better condition people from the early ages, so that the overall society can live in tranquility and peace, where aggression and violence can alleviate. It a fact that environment plays a huge catalyst in shaping people's mind and conducts, either a product of a constructive atmosphere which should relatively result in fruitful personality or born to the destructive and toxic environment which can introduce menacing characters to the society.

Bottom line, a curse should be upon those deprived victims if they are overflowed with testosterone since hormones as such cause aggression, belligerency and apparently forces one to act violence; also, because proper education, training, financial empowerment, social recognition, and prestige are available to the elites as they can buy the most prominent attorneys, if they ever face any legal trouble, as obviously the poor are exhausted from having them.

No wonder so many poor and financially deprived are incarcerated, as they globally have saturated prisons with some facing inhumane retaliations from the so-called law authorities. Just like when a heroin addict chases a substance-induced high, sex addicts are bingeing on chemicals which is their own hormones. as heroin addicts need professional medical therapeutic, sex addicts must also be treated medically and professionally attended to, and not by forceful means.

Many advance God-fearing nations slogan that in God we trust where liberty, human rights, democracy and pursuit of happiness should mean something, as millions know that some behavioral malfunction in human beings is due to hormonal abnormality such as testosterone-driven personalities that are much more inclined to act belligerent and have anger issues.

Making them much more vulnerable to do wrong, since this should be detected early in people's lives to avoid disaster, and stop tragic events. millions end up in overcrowded jails and prisons, causing the taxpayers billions, and society is ridden with violence and crimes which many innocent victims pay with their lives for heinous crimes committed by offenders that could have been avoided.

I gather you have heard of the yin and yang, which believes that the principle of Yin and Yang in all things exist as inseparable and contradictory opposites, for example, female-male, hot-cold, dark-light and old-young. The principle, dating from the third century BCE or even earlier, is a fundamental concept in Chinese philosophy and culture in general. (in Chinese philosophy and religion) two principles, one negative, dark, and feminine (yin), and one positive, bright, and masculine (yang), whose interaction influences the destinies of creatures and things.

Testosterone brain hormones natured for aggressive behaviors originates in brain centers that instigate metabolic stimulation of the neuroendocrine system, this guides the feeling of aggressiveness via the mobilization of the body's muscles. The neurons of the prefrontal area, the hypothalamus, and amygdala that are regarded with aggression show significant quantities of androgen and estradiol receptors, along with the enzymes imperative for the steroidogenesis of these hormones.

The local production of testosterone in neuroendocrine neurons introduces a new factor into the interpretation of the interaction of this hormone with offensive, bright manifestations as yang, and cortisol's hormones can play the role of ying. Thus, it makes sense that the hormonal axes that regulate testosterone levels and cortisol levels are antagonistic. According to research, chronically elevated cortisol levels can produce impotence and loss of libido by inhibiting testosterone production in men.

The effect of testosterone maneuverability on the brain initiates in embryonic life. Testosterone receptors are shown in the fetus earlier than the biosynthesis (the production of complex molecules within living organisms or cells of testosterone) which happens in the seventh to eighth week of pregnancy. In the fifth month, the testosterone values in male fetuses reach a max with levels approaching those of adult men. This secretory surge lasting for a few weeks inundates the brain with testosterone, prompting anatomical and organizational alteration that mark the sex disparity (separation, polarity) of the male brain in adulthood.

The first study in prisoners was initiated in 1972, soon after the accessibility to testosterone estimation, by Kreutz and Rosel, who captured that prisoners who had committed violent crimes when adolescence had higher testosterone levels (13). In a single sample size of free testosterone in the saliva of 89 prison inmates, it was revealed that at the extremes of the testosterone distribution, the relationship between testosterone to aggressive behaviors was more striking (14).

Ten out of eleven prisoners with the highest testosterone concentrations had committed violent crimes, whereas nine out of eleven who had committed non-violent crimes had the lowest testosterone activity levels.

The question of fairness does not apply in the above situation, when the administration of hyper physiological doses of testosterone does increase aggression and violent behavior, compounded with lack of opportunity to escalate wisdom and intelligence that is also depleted in some people, because of deficiencies in funds, which sure in capitalist system money is so decisive for good and manageable upbringings that would make one much prone to luck for making it.

It is a fact that environment plays a huge catalyst in shaping people's mind and character, as we are either a product of a constructive atmosphere which should relatively result in fruitful personality, or born into a destructive and toxic environment which can introduce menacing personality to the society. Often in the dark ages, castration is also known as gonadectomy was performed on slaves, prisoners of war, violent criminals and so on. is a surgical procedure (excision of both testes), also chemical castration that utility pharmaceutical drugs to incapacitate the testes, and by other cruel means of removing one's testicle to ensure sterilization (preventing the victim from reproducing).

It is meant to significantly lower the production of specific hormones like testosterone, treating humans just like animals that were neutered that is the surgical castration for animals to prevent reproducing. Castration was also applicable for females in which they removed the ovaries, also known as oophorectomy. If so, the estrogen levels lower precipitously (hastily, hurriedly), and long term effect of drastic lowering of sex hormone should be expected.

The term castration may occasionally be used to indicate emasculation where both the testicles and the penis together are taken out, since in certain cultures, and in some translations, no distinction is made between the two. It was sometimes utilized to prevent overpopulation.

Castration was often performed for religious or social reasons in some cultures in Europe, South Asia, Middle East, Africa, and East Asia, and many other places. After battles in some cases, winners castrated their captives or the corpses of the defeated to represent their victory and seize their power.

Castrated men known as eunuchs were frequently accepted to special social classes and were used especially to staff bureaucracies and palace households, in designated harems. Religions, such as Judaism, were strongly opposed to the practice. The Leviticus Holiness code, for instance particularly denies eunuchs or any males with defective genitals from the priesthood, just as castrated animals are removed from being gambit (sacrificed.)

In antiquity era castration frequently involved the utter removal of all the male genitalia. This made the victims much more inclined to death because of profuse bleeding or infection and, in some states, like for example the Byzantine Empire, it was seen similar to the death sentence. Removal of only the testicles had a much lower risk. Either surgical removal of both testicles or chemical castration may occur in the case of prostate cancer.

Testosterone-depletion treatment (either surgical removal of both testicles or chemical castration) is done to slow down cancer which greatly reduces sex drive or interest in those with sexual drives, obsessions, or behaviors, or any combination of those that may be considered as deviant. Castration has also been performed in the United States for sex offenders. Involuntary castration appears in the history of warfare, often used by one side to torture or demoralize their rival enemies. It was exercised to exterminate opposing male lineages and thus let the victor to sexually own the defeated group's females.

Historically, because of ignorance, lack of education and because of not having skillful training to implement corrective means, and for non-availability to learn and accentuate on good habits; that, compounded with instinctual necessities for humanity to survive which often has gone way overboard also because of self-interest and greed, which these shortcomings have affected so many for the worst, causing heartbreaking pain and suffering beyond belief.

It is an undeniable fact that testosterone and other forceful hormones as such can either be a blessing if one is enlightened to leash them and a demon like if unleashed and not intelligently enabling one to reign them.

When in the qualm (stabbing pain, pang) of starvation, our senses are without a doubt emphatic on food. Wretchedly (unpleasant state of emotion) exhausted of an essential requirement, the dire (critical) quest for sustenance overpower and determine any other concern, which at the moment must feel absolutely immaterial, inorganic, and impertinent. The state of hunger has no conscience.

Ethical regards become secondary bearing no impact in situations where the excruciating ache of starvation must overcome any other thought.

It's easy enough to criticize a testosterone-driven man for his one-track mindedness. As Darwin say? After all, is it not part of "evolutionary wisdom" to make sure that the virile sperm carrier is distracted with spreading that sperm? A male's conscious reasons may not be to procreate his seed. Experiencing an almost overwhelming sexual tension—which is inseparable from carnal (bodily) desire—he may simply feel coerced to alleviate (soothe) it.

Besides, his beastly physical (and unconscious mind) has evolved exactly to make him concentrate on attaining this natural act. Therefore, how much can one be blamed for approaching his genital prime many years prior to his capturing maturity in wisdom, emotional intelligence, and ethical progression to adequately deal with his sexual needs, wants, and feelings of the objects he desires for?

After all, it sure is a blessing that biological imperative is extremely resilient since it surely gifts us the most potent imaginable defense mechanism contrary to extinction. Yet, I am afraid it seems what needs to be celebrated, is predominantly looked upon as a curse in many naïve and backward cultures, often leaving behind many socio-cultural ills, and psychological ailments, mental gridlocks where millions of men and women literally are infected which some are negatively impacted for life.

It is a no-brainer to know that the primitive message which a male perceives by his amoral (not moral) sex hormone is to pursue females not for their selves but for their bodies. The same so-called testosterone culprit which without no life is possible, go figure. yes, societal hindrance can wrongfully inhibit what nature has endowed humanity to pursue life, but it sure wouldn't be without its dire and irreparable damages often reflecting the entire society for the worse. It is not a lie that everyone rich or poor, young or old, pretty or not, wise or dull, intelligent or not and so on can indiscriminately become gloomy and sad, occasionally get depressed with much anxiety.

They say is all about behaving positively and not acting pessimistic. Yes, true to some extent, but we should not forget that we cannot help it when certain stressful and sad hormones force their way in because of the ugly circumstances which one is faced with, or when one is so mal-nutrition beyond grasp and born into broken family and a violent atmosphere which the ends justifies the means just to survive.

The hormonal brain is activated by the occasions and the atmosphere which we are engaged in and is part of. But it seems we just do not care to deal with the reality of what is happening. Planting oak seeds in a pot will certainly affect the ability of the oak tree to grow and reach its full potential since the tree is inhibited with the circumstances that are not suitable for its true nature to expand which demands different criterions.

Our brain dialogues with itself by delegating chemicals from one neuron, or nerve, to the other, which this natural rapid-fire messaging enacts a big role in how one feels and function every day. There are two categories of neurotransmitter that are known as excitatory, meaning they arouse brain activity, and inhibitory, meaning they have a more relaxing effect.

For an instant, serotonin plays a huge role in sleep and in depression, but this inhibitory agent also plays a major role in many of your body's imperative functions, not to exclude appetite, mood arousal. Etc. Many antidepressants aim at serotonin receptors to better one's mood and mitigate depressive symptoms. Bear in mind that serotonin is also accumulated in our intestine which helps with the digestive work mechanism too.

Dopamine controls many activities, including emotion, conduct, and cognition. This chemical also interacts with the front part of our brain, that is linked with pleasure and reward, it helps motivate you to work toward reaching one's goal and a reward. because dopamine is linked to the movement as well, low levels of dopamine have also been connected to Parkinson's disease.

Glutamate, this is the most common excitatory neurotransmitter, located throughout one's brain and spinal cord. Glutamate has many vital functions, for example, brain development, cognition, learning, and memory.

Norepinephrine

Its original role is part of your body's stress response, it assists with the hormone adrenaline to make the fight-or-flight feeling. Norepinephrine which is as well utilized as a drug to elevate or maintain blood pressure in some illnesses. Norepinephrine and other related hormones, like adrenalin, melatonin, adrenaline, and other neurotransmitters affect our moods, even can change the health of our brain.

Cortisol is exuded when one is stressed. It's often helpful, but for too long, and too much of it can cause memory loss as we get older. Hormonal imbalances in neurotransmitters can potentiate many ill-conditions, including schizophrenia, depression, bipolar disorder, autism, Parkinson's disease, and host of other incurable diseases. Keeping a balance in the hormonal brain, and chemicals are the essence of a savvy mood which tightly depends on having balanced nutrition, good rest, exercise, avoiding stressful lifestyle, meditation, listening to relaxing music, enjoying family, friends and all of which can uplift one's spirit.

The point is that human behaviors are not all discretionary (optional) for example, we simply cannot help it when frightened and scared, or when become excited and the adrenaline hormone is secreted by the adrenal glands, especially in conditions of stress, increasing rates of blood circulation, breathing, and carbohydrate metabolism and preparing muscles for exertion. In fact, hundreds of brain and bodily hormones are mandatory since they are activated when they see it fit.

We need to realize that there is a beast within all of us that needs to be balanced and tamed, but when a rogue system realizes that and feeds the animal within us, tempting us in a clandestine manner, rather than educate and train people to wisely harness the animal inside by capitalizing on the enormously potentiated human intelligence.

Then, living can eventually be more peaceful and tranquility of mind and manner can become the norms. You might inquire that is it our genes, or is the environment and upbringings responsible for our ill-behaving or good conduct?

The answer is that we all are affected by our genes and of course the relative products the environment that we live in, which must be paid attention to.

In the meanwhile, also keep in mind that most poverty-stricken neighborhoods, atmospheres, and cultures are the embodiment of cruel and unjustified criterions where millions live way under the poverty line devoid of good nutrients, proper rest with good hygiene, with lack of proper education or proper medical coverage, as they live an extremely stressful life, and most with no hope for either recovery, or upper mobility exponentially impacts so many when not wise enough to think twice in the verge of doing wrong, and not potentiated to correctly discern they are the victims of the circumstances which they must overcome that is extremely difficult.

All of the resources are congealed and taken by the rich elites that literally play the devil's advocates and are not willing to constructively invest and are refusing to believe in human spirit and productivity, where nations would not go to devastating wars, leaving behind horrific consequence just because the rich elites must add a dollar more to their already humongous concentration of wealth. Come to think of it, all ills return to malnutrition, stressful living, with lack compassion, lack of love, being born in a broken family exhausted from any financial remedy and living in toxic environments, which no doubt can affect our genes for the worse, wherein the long run abnormal living can make genes to go berserk and haywire, leaving one vulnerable to irreparable damages.

Why shouldn't we believe that genes can be ill effected because of toxic food, wrong upbringings and poisonous atmosphere potentiating one to wrongfully coexist with the beast inside, and often paying the price with their lives. After all, balance is the virtue, where wisdom and the impetus to gain conclusive information and knowledge can sure help with breaking the vicious cycle of greed, lust, and temptations to avoid ill desires, where good judgments can detour one from doing wrong.

24

GOD AND SCIENCE

Science does not need God to explain the universe, as Einstein said, "Only two things are infinite, the universe and human stupidity, and I'm not sure about the former," which signifies those with callous minds that expect God to explain the universe, which has unnecessarily become a human dilemma.

What should be of concern is that when science is unquestionably the product of human consciousness which without no experience of any kind either scientific or not would ever is ever possible, as it cannot be identified and be located anywhere in the human brain should not be considered a fact and a priority not only over science, but the entire existence, and is the cause behind all there is, and all there ever will be. should hold true to the day science can examine and test it in scientific laboratories as it should remind any savvy and intelligent mind that would be to the day which hell freezes since it is utterly beyond the scope of scientific endeavors to deal with locating God or even consciousness.

It is hilarious that the subject of science which is the byproduct of human consciousness and intelligence, somehow for certain people is naively refused to see, not grasping the fact that what we do not see, manages and controls what we see. Stephen Hawking said in his book *The Grand Design* that God did not create the universe. He then, says that our universe followed inevitably from the laws of nature, and people like Hawking capitalize on such shallow rhetoric. The point is if so? Where did these irrefutably disciplined laws of nature come from?

Then he said that the search for this particular Holy Grail is over, now that scientists have come up with a type of theory, known as M-theory, that may describe the behavior of all the fundamental particles and force, and even account for the very birth of the universe. If this theory is backed up by experiment, it might perhaps replace all religious accounts of creation.

Mr. Hawking got excited about something that cannot be authenticated, which is not true since it cannot be tested. Here is what the scientists are saying on M theory: M-theory is a new idea in small-particle physics that is part of superstring theory that was initially proposed by Edward Witten.

The idea, or theory, often causes arguments among scientists, because there is no way to test it to see if it is true, which I am afraid is already taken place in Mr. Hawking's capricious mind. It seems Mr. Hawking is saying that accepting God-made the universe can be replaced with a belief in M-theory, a good candidate for a Grass-Rooty theory of nature at its finest level, as its potentiality which can be promising, as we should believe in human intelligence that might one day be as competent to conquer galaxies and perhaps the universe, since it is the human intelligence which gradually exploits the mysteries of nature arrow headed by further human awakenings.

But the shortcoming with the theory is that it looks as though it will be exorbitantly (excessively) difficult to test unless scientists can build a particle accelerator the size of a galaxy. Even if that hypothetically becomes probable, and the M-theory succeeds in all related tests, the cause behind mathematical order at the heart of the orderly universe order would remain an irresolvable mystery What prominent physicist are saying is that one notable feature of string theories is that these theories, not hypotheses coming about not from just any layman, but from precious scientific evaluators, which they say it requires extra dimensions of space-time for their mathematical consistency. In bosonic string theory, space-time is 26-dimensional, while in superstring theory it is 10-dimensional, and in M-theory it is 11-dimensional.

The point is that for string theory, M theory, superlative theory and theories alike the scientists are searching for higher dimensions, since obviously we do not live in a 10, 11, or 26 dimensions since they all need extra dimensions of space and time; but oddly enough when believers say the almighty God is beyond the existing space and time, the atheists are reluctant to accept it. perhaps we should attach the word science to God as the scientific God for them to comply.

As Hawking justly stresses, it is clear that Einstein did not think of God as a white-bearded benefactor capable of interfering with the functioning of the universe. Rather, Einstein followed closely the views of the philosopher Spinoza, for whom the concept of God is an expression of the underlying unity of the universe, something so wondrous that it can command a spiritual awe. Something as potent as mathematics which patterns in the basic fabric of reality—the mathematical laws that rule the workings of nature at its finest level.

There is plenty of evidence that these laws hold good all the way back to the origin of time, that is how scientists have put together an exorbitant detailed and well-tested theory of the big bang.

> "The remarkable fact is that the values of these numbers
> seem to have been very finely adjusted."

> Stephen Hawking

What we should pay attention to is that human mind and heart are potentiated with infinite urges in which both seek wants to the day we expire. furthermore, if brought up in a constructively dignified the environment which humanity inclusively deserves, then, rest assure that human heart is filled with good intentions and infinite compassion, and our mind with infinite intelligence craving wisdom and persisting on progress, manifesting the God within.

If endowed with such blessings then when one hears of, or sees a misdeed, a crime or a tragedy about to happen, one most probably will go to an extent sacrificing one's life to stop it, yes, because the infinite compassion and the infinite intelligence are an inseparable part of what God is all about substantiating the fact that we are made in God's image.

Now science which by the way is a product of human conscious ironically cannot be dragged into any laboratory and is absolutely not found anywhere in our brain. science advances over the wreckage of its theories by relentlessly placing theoretical ideas to empirical testing; which does not matter how impressive a theoretical concept might be, it must be discarded if not coherent, or at odds with experiment. This indicates that like any other human endeavor or activity, science also has flaws which often do not always comply or go smoothly as scientists expect.

We should appreciate science, because science assist humanity to understand the world, and underpin technology which is the vehicle that without we would have still been in the dark ages territory, which should also inform us not to expect science to divulge whys of the world, since this inquiry encompasses millions of mysterious unanswered questions beyond scientific capabilities to shed lights on. Bear in mind that Newtonian theory is the nervous system of the material world, which without its magnificent scientific reality has already proven deficient in non-material realms that has become identified literally because of advancement in human intelligence which constantly deals with the idea of Pragmatism.

Pragmatism is a philosophical movement that includes those who claim that an ideology or assertion is true if it works satisfactorily, that the meaning of an assertion (proposition) is to be found in the practical consequences of accepting or rejecting it. Does pragmatism also deal with an educational philosophy that says that education should be about life and growth?

Two important elements of pragmatism include practical learning, which focuses on the real-world applications of lessons, and experiential learning, which complies with learning through experience, contrary to idealistic is pragmatic, a word that explains the philosophy of doing what works best. From Greek pragma deed, the word has historically described philosophers and politicians who were concerned more with real-world application of ideas than with abstract notions, knowing that it is through the idea of real-world applications which scientists gradually divulge the abstract notions which initially seem beyond our reach.

Einstein's views were predominantly shared by his friend Paul Dirac, the great English theoretician since Newton. For Dirac, the biggest mystery of the universe was that its most fundamental laws can be stated in terms of beautiful mathematical equations. At the end of his life, in the 1970s and early 1980s, Dirac often uttered that mathematical beauty "is almost a religion to me."

Earlier in his life, Dirac was an outspoken atheist, attracting his colleague Wolfgang Pauli to say that There is no God and Dirac is his prophet. Decades later, in 1963, Dirac was eager to use theological imagery: God is a mathematician of a very high order. He was talking metaphorically, but we know what he meant. perhaps reminded him of the infinite disciplinary precision in mathematics that is the kernel of any scientific endeavor, which without no scientific manifestation should be possible.

An entity imbued with logic and reason that cannot be seen or touched, but so prevalently real in our lives helping scientific empirical come alive.

Then when theists ask the non-believers what has caused life to come about? What is the cause of existence? They respond to nature is the cause. By the way, do they mean matter? As any savvy mind would perhaps hastily say that matter has no intelligence, and is not imbued with any common sense, and since I am afraid we cannot think beyond what our mental capacity is, and over the grasp of our nervous system, then we need to accept an infinitely intelligent designer behind this miraculously oriented universe, as we should refuse a senseless matter exhausted of any intelligence to have caused a magnificently intelligently life bearing criterions.

Furthermore, when believers inquire that if the nature you atheists talk about, or matter in which you believe in has any motion? They say everything has motion, nature has motion. When we ask does this motion which evidently is incorporated in the tiniest to the most grandeur demands time and space? The non-believers say yes, again the right answer. But when we ask any motion must have an origin and a final destiny to serve a purpose.

They so illogically refute the fact of having a beginning, an end as they do not budge to a purposeful life. The further inquiry that no perishable matter can be the cause of an infinitely durable life beyond anyone's imagination, as no matter is stable enough since matter can appear in the form of Solids. In a solid, particles are packed tightly together so they are unable to move about very much.

Liquids.
Gases.
Plasma.
Bose-Einstein condensates.

Melting and freezing
Sublimation.
Vaporization.

Then, we have those who pull their hair and insist on the laws of physics, and the world of science like Newton's laws and other affiliated scientific methods, as they say, it runs the real world as no God is necessary.

That might be true, but it absolutely should not mean that the almighty creator is not the real cause to all that exists. as is the nature of science to discover new things, as it historically has, then science found out that in general, the behavior of the subatomic particles cannot be explained by Newton's laws.

Here are how the Newtonian's laws of motion can be explained. There exist particles with a peculiar position and velocity interacting with each other via means of force. There are several kinds of forces in Nature, in which they can act between two particles, and their strength and direction are based on the position and the velocities of those particles.

Newton's first law states that every object will remain at rest or in uniform motion in a straight line unless compelled to change its state by the action of an external force. Newton's second law of motion describes the relationship between an object's mass and the amount of force needed to accelerate it. Newton's second law is often stated as F=ma, which means the force (F) acting on an object is equal to the mass (m) of an object times its acceleration (a) Newton's second law of motion pertains to the behavior of objects for which all existing forces are not balanced.

The second law states that the acceleration of an object is dependent upon two variables -the net force acting upon the object and the mass of the object. The third law states that for every action (force) in nature there is an equal and opposite reaction.

As many sages and philosophers of past and present indicated, there is more to life than we grasp out of our limited human sense, as we should not be hasty and finalize that science and the laws of physics are what the universal magic is all about, which then the quantum world appeared.

Saying that the laws which rule the action of the subatomic particles are entirely different since it is not possible to commit a particular position and velocity to a specific particle. Each particle can be in a superposition of various states, which means it is found simultaneously in a whole region of space conveying a whole range of velocities.

When one measures the position or the velocity of the particle, one obtains certain values from that range, randomly so, possibly with various probabilities for each value. Yet, this is not because the particle truly had secured that position, not knowing the particle in actuality had a whole range of positions just before the moment of measurement. many physicists admit it is very strange and in the meanwhile beautiful. Einstein was the first physicist to say that Planck's discovery of the quantum (h) would require a rewriting of the laws of physics.

The ability of the particle to be in several different states simultaneously results in a well-known wave-particle duality: the subatomic particles (electrons, neutrons and other) can behave like waves and show interference. Suppose we have a particle source aimed towards a wall with two slits where the particles can pass and a detecting screen beyond this wall. First, we allow the particles to pass only through one of the slits, and then only through the second one.

In a third experiment, the particles can pass through both the slits. When looking at the results, the results of the last experiment seem to be completely unrelated to the results of the first two. This happens because when particles are allowed to pass through both slits it's not that some of them pass through the first slit and some of them through the second one, but in some sense, each particle passes through both of them. On the detecting screen, we see a picture identical to the one which is obtained from the interference of waves.

The faculty (ability, competency) of the particle to be in many different states at the same time indicates a wave-particle duality: the subatomic particles (electrons, neutrons and other) can act like waves and exhibit interference.

The theory which is able to describe the subatomic particles is quantum mechanics. In quantum mechanics, a system (sometimes a single particle) can be explained by a wave function (or by a vector in a multi-dimensional space). The information conveyed in the wave function is just the weight of each possible state in the current state of the system.

Therefore, we should notice that there is much more to the reality of life than what we as human beings decipher through our five basic senses of sight, hearing, smell, taste, and touch which in association with our brain can understand and perceive the world around us. Knowing that it is the invisible realm that manages the visible materially based world.

Furthermore, many believe that we are the products of our environment, that is fundamentally a materially based atmosphere which we have to deal with where no spiritual laws are applicable, and since it has nothing to do with innate variables that might lightly or heavily affect the outcomes of our lives. Mostly encouraged by Marx and Angles proponents which dictate Dialectical materialism, a philosophical approach to reality derived from the teachings of Karl Marx and Friedrich Engels.

For Marx and Engels, materialism meant that the material world, perceptible to the senses, has an objective reality independent of mind or spirit. Dialectical materialism looks at the process of change and how the physical world and individuals move from one state to another, basically through historical class struggle.

Marx proposed that this evolution occurs through conflict and opposition in contrary to Hegel's materialist history in which Hegel claimed that history occurs through a dialectic, or clash, of opposing forces. Hegel was a philosophical idealist who believed that we live in a world of appearances, and true reality is ideal. However, so many inquisitively minded individual, philosopher, scientists, and scholarly mind people objected and elaborated on the fact that genes and other prominently innate factors also were decisive of who we are.

Either way, this was dubiously dealt with until the birth of quantum mechanics, or better known as quantum physics which completely altered the concept of materially oriented nature since physicists unanimously agreed that no substance or entity of any kind is-driven or is exhausted of energy, since solid, liquid and gas are all energy-driven and of course made of atoms through which subatomic particles play I huge role.

The external world is energy-driven human mind is capable to correlate and accordingly respond to the outside world, because our mind, conscious and human spirit are energy-driven as well making the environmental conductibility and human intelligence to actively interact to accomplish our daily tasks and substantiate what needs to be done for further progress.

The Einstein theory of relativity of $E=MC^2$ basically states that mass is another form which energy can be altered too. For instance, if you collide particles with a very high kinetic energy in a particle accelerator, one can make that kinetic energy to convert into a mass, and thus create particles with much higher mass than the particles one collided. $E=mc^2$ explains nuclear fusion, how matter can be annihilated and converted to energy and energy can flip-flop back to mass.

It describes the atomic energy generated by nuclear power plants and the atomic energy relinquished by atomic bombs. Neither would be possible without Einstein's equation. Energy equals mass times the speed of light squared. On the most fundamental level, the equation states that energy and mass (matter) are interchangeable; they are various forms of the same thing.

Under the right conditions, energy can become mass, and vice versa, as if an androgynous with (having both male and female characteristics or qualities.) then when the theists related to the non-believers that things can appear and disappear out of nowhere, they said that is superstitious magic, that cannot be, as many blatantly rejected the idea.

At the quantum level, matter and antimatter particles are constantly popping into existence and popping back out, with an electron-positron pair here and a top quark-antiquark pair there. This is what the physicists are saying quote, between the plates, only waves (particles) with wavelengths smaller than the separation between the plates can exist.

They further say that quote, the quantum effects are probabilistic, not deterministic. Therefore, a quantum fluctuation has no cause. Quantum fluctuations are a point change in the energy of a volume of space due to the Heisenberg Uncertainty Principle. Zero point zero is extremely precise, and in quantum mechanics, unstable. According to quantum mechanics, a vacuum isn't empty at all. It's actually filled with quantum energy and particles that blink in and out of existence for a fleeting moment—strange signals that are known as quantum fluctuations.

There are no particles there, and nothing to interfere with pure physics. In fact, old explanation of gravitation is not capable to resolve quantum vacuum problem. Relating to Heisenberg uncertainty principle a vacuum isn't empty and filled with particles-antiparticles that appear and disappear randomly fashion.

Mr. Hawking believes that gravity is the cause for existence, gravity with having no intelligence, weaker than other forces, depends on mass, which without its existence is very much questionable is the cause to exist. let's elaborate a bit on the forces of our universe.

Gravity is relatively simple to understand: any two things that have mass (atoms, rocks, people, planets, stars) are pulled towards each other. The bigger the mass, the stronger the pull.

Electromagnetism? It's electricity and magnetism squashed. The electromagnetic force describes how things that are electrically charged (positively or negatively) they interact with each other, a magnetic charge can create an electric charge, and vice versa. Those interactions are responsible for electric power production that is vital.

Electromagnetism and the way it pushes and pulls objects are responsible for the energy in things such as batteries and magnets, but it also includes light, which is about waves of electromagnetic radiation.

For the weak and the strong nuclear forces since they're both stronger than gravity they only act in diminutive (tiny) spaces between atoms when even smaller spaces where quantum physics makes everything really strange.

The strong nuclear force is indeed the strongest of the four known forces and fundamentally the glue that binds everything together. It is responsible for keeping protons and neutrons (which along with electrons make up atoms) stable and then lets those to cinch (bind) into atomic nuclei. In the meanwhile, the weak force o is liable for radioactive decay, the opposite of the strong force, it controls how things on a nuclear level fall apart, also it's accountable for fusion, and keeps our sun bright, nice and warm.

Surprisingly enough now the physicists talk about the fifth force, which they say we need to realize what makes other forces of the universe do their tasks. They believe since one body with mass does not just magically start moving towards another massive thing, scientist anticipates that this moving mechanism possibly happens by force carrier particles.

Force carriers are the particles that carry information between things and alert them on how to maneuver and forces them to behave by the rules, which should remind one belief in a committed and purposeful life. The force carriers for gravity are hypothetical things called gravitons, for electromagnetism they're the photons. For the weak nuclear force, the carriers are called W and Z particles, and for the strong nuclear force, gluons. These force carries are all known as examples of bosons.

But he adds, "There are many experimental groups working in small labs around the world that can follow up the initial claims, now that they know where to look." We should bear in mind that without mass no gravity is possible. The Moon's surface gravity is weaker because it is far less massive than Earth. A body's surface gravity is proportional to its mass but inversely proportional to the square of its radius. The Moon's surface gravity is about one-sixth as powerful, or about 1.6 meters per second.

Gravity in our universe. Gravity is what keeps the planets in orbit around the sun and what holds the moon in orbit around Earth. The gravitational pull of the moon fancies the seas towards it, producing the ocean tides. Gravity not only pulls on mass but also on the light. Gravity from Earth keeps the Moon and human-made satellites in orbit.

It is true that gravity lessens with distance, so it is possible to be far away from a planet or star and feel less gravity, or perhaps in some state no gravity. Earth's gravity arrives from all its mass. All its mass generates a combined gravitational pull on all the mass in your body, which you weight. if you were on a planet with less mass than Earth, you would weigh less than you do here. Therefore, there is no question that gravity depends on mass, which without it wouldn't exist.

Mr. Hawking believes that a force without intelligence, weaker than other forces in our universe, which must depend on mass to exist, as it alters with distance and weight, an unseen force should replace the omnipotent omnipresent creator, which its magnificent traces should be seen and felt. As the traces of Gravity can only be felt, as it cannot be seen, and in some states, it does not even exist.

Then, oddly enough gravity is the God known to Mr. Hawking and alike and the cause for our existence. Gravity is most accurately described by the general theory of relativity (proposed by Albert Einstein in 1915) which describes gravity not as a force, but as a consequence of the curvature of space-time caused by the uneven distribution of mass.

Albert Einstein's general theory of relativity is one of the towering accomplishments of twentieth-century physics. Published in 1916, it says that what we know as the force of gravity in true sense arises from the curvature of space and time. Einstein suggested that objects like the sun and the Earth alter this geometry.

In the presence of matter and energy, it can evolve, stretch and warp, forming ridges, mountains, and valleys that make bodies moving through it to zigzag and curve. So although Earth appears to be pulled towards the sun by gravity, there is no such force. It is simply the geometry of space-time around the sun telling Earth how to move. The general theory of relativity has far-reaching outcomes. It not only describes the motion of the planets; it can also elaborate on the history and development of the universe, the physics of black holes and the bending of light from distant stars and galaxies. Bear in mind that as you move faster in space, time goes slower.

However, it is the undertaking of science which teaches us about the magnanimity (generosity) of nature since science delves into the unknown and discovers the wonders of our universe to progress and for a better living. In the meanwhile, we should give credit where credit is due, as we should not believe that science can replace our creator, as science has not to exhibit why the universe came into existence nor what preceded its inception in the big bang.

Furthermore, biological evolution has not shown humanity how the first living organisms arrived from inanimate, unintelligent matter, and how progressive eukaryotic cells-highly structured building blocks of advanced life forms did emerge from simpler organisms. Why consciousness escalates in living things? Where do thoughts come from?

Where does self-awareness come from? What is consciousness? And since no one can be located anywhere in one's body, why do we have out-of-body experience? Why are we potentiated to understand the magic of science, physics, mathematics, biology, botany, engineering, medicine, architecture, literature, philosophy, astronomy, art, music and so on? Why are we here, where did we come from, where are we going, what is our purpose in life? Science cannot explain these and with thousands of other abyss mysteries that science is not able to figure out by any scientific methodology.

The more intriguing question should be why the fine-tuning of the universe, why is our universe is so tailored for the emergence of life? We should delve into the infinite mysteries of the universe, like a daunting task as it is, but through human drive and perseverance, we can gradually reach the hidden wisdom and the blueprint of what life is all about.

The cosmological constant (Λ, Lambda) constant is a term in Einstein's theory of gravity that influences the expansion rate of empty space. It can be positive or negative (unless it is within an extremely narrow range around zero, the universe will either collapse or expand too rapidly for galaxies and stars to form).

25

THE BIG BANG

People cited a violation of the First Amendment when a
New Jersey schoolteacher asserted that evolution and the
big bang are not scientific and that Noah's ark carried
dinosaurs. This case is not about the need to separate
church and state; it's about the need to separate ignorant,
scientifically illiterate people from the ranks of teachers.

— Neil deGrasse Tyson.

Is a cosmological model, a theory utilized to explain the beginning and how
the universe has evolved? It states that the universe was in an extremely hot
and dense position prior to expansion 13,.7 billion years ago. This theory
is based on fundamental observations:

In 1920, Hubble detected that the distance among galaxies was
increasing all over in the universe. should decipher that galaxies had to be
closer to each other in the past.

In 1964, Wilson and Penzias found out that fossil-like cosmic
background radiation emitted throughout the beginning of the universe
when it was hot and dense, since the cosmic background radiation is
observable everywhere in the universe.

The composition of the universe, for example, the number of atoms
of various elements is consistent with the big bang Theory. The big bang
theory is so far the only theory that can describe why we observe an
abundance of primeval (pre-historical, primordial) elements in the universe.

I believe the mechanism of a huge volcano eruption should resemble, and perhaps give us an idea about the big bang, but with a colossally bigger magnitude in eruption. Geologists tell us that Volcanoes are made by eruptions of lava and ash when magma rises through cracks or weak spots in the Earth's crust. A buildup of pressure in the Earth is relinquished, by things such as a plate movement which forces molten rock to explode into the air causing a volcanic eruption. The scientist also tells us that Volcanic gases are harmful to health, vegetation, and infrastructure, but the most abundant volcanic gas is water vapor, which is harmless.

Either way, scientists also believe that significant amounts of carbon dioxide, sulfur dioxide, hydrogen sulfide, and hydrogen halides can also exude from volcanoes. Pyroclasts (a dense, destructive mass of very hot ash, lava fragments, and gases ejected explosively from a volcano and typically flowing downslope at great speed) also known as (tephra) are materials forcefully thrown to the atmosphere via explosive eruptions. When loose materials (like volcanic bombs, volcanic blocks, and gases, which are expelled during violent eruptions) are mixed with ashes, the so-called pyroclastic deposits are formed.

Therefore, after becoming aware of volcanic mechanism, logic should dictate two probable scenarios. First, either the big bang occurred out of nowhere, exhausted of any prior preparation, appeared out of nothing and without any evolutionary process, if so, it must have been a miracle, which certainly calls for the hands of God. Or, it must have happened because of the gradual accumulation of lava, the concentration of extremely hot ashes, volcanic gases, molten rocks, magma and because of other volcanic depositories, etc.

This should confirm matter, since matter should confirm motion, where motion demands space, time, direction and purpose, causing a build-up of intolerable pressure which eventually substantiated enormously huge explosion, namely the big bang beyond anyone's imagination, and if so, then, because logic dictates, it should remind any savvy-minded person to notice the prior existence of matter, certainly before the big bang explosion.

The further noticeable issue is that any explosion should bring destruction, chaos and disorder as big bang explosion must have brought, which on the contrary the big bang evidently must have resulted in an orderly, extremely intricate life, infinitely disciplined nature and magnificently organized, if so, again we need to see the undeniable hands of God in making of a masterpiece design, creating an awesome universe, which I am afraid is taken for granted by unmediated minds unreasonably denying the indisputable facts about a superbly dazzling (brilliant) creator.

"It is either coincidence piled on top of coincidence, or it is deliberate design."

Robert J. Sawyer, *Calculating God.*

26

THE MEANING OF LIFE

Humanity is potentiated with the gift of intelligence as everyone is blessed with the miracle of awareness which needs to be invigorated to give meaning to one's life, which no doubt is correlated with having the opportunity to grow in a decent environment free form societal ills and suppressing factors that can impact people for the worse.

It is true that some are more ambitious than others, but many are also equipped with positive variables that millions if not billions are deprived of in which they play a huge catalyst in their being successful.

Meaningful lives are for extraordinary people: teachers, scientists, philosophers, professors, saints, artists, scholars, doctors, surgeons, nurses, writers, poets, engineers, politicians, ministers, bankers, researches, musicians, activists, explorers, national leaders, and so on, and since life can become meaning with purposeful livings, then, there are those behaving idol without having a mission or a purpose in life, and not able to make sense of what they are here to accomplish.

"I don't believe people are looking for the meaning of life
as much as they are looking for the experience of being
alive."

Joseph Campbell

People that are professionally engaged are more focused as they are more in tune with their lives. Meaningful living also is relatively linked with happiness that often materializes when one is on top of what one does for a living and has not lagged behind. As accountability is frequently an issue for so many as they care about their profession and the excellent work they are committed to doing.

When people's duty at work, with daily chores, weekly plans, monthly outlooks, even yearly agendas are intact as they feel orderly and not behind their responsibilities, it makes them less stressful and more relaxed without much anxiety or pressure for performing their daily tasks right, as many meticulously pursue what must be done daily, weekly, monthly, even annually, making them happy and with much less distressed. No doubt that stressful lifestyle and happiness are correlated, which will tremendously help, if one can disentangle oneself from doing what one does not love to do.

Either way, people should not be devoid of caring, attention, tenderness, connection, wanting to belong, sympathy, compassion, opportunity, education, intelligence, relationship, commitments, responsibility, accountability, honesty, reliability, love, devotion, dreaming, imagination, creativity, and millions of other things that we should have to collectively help give meaning to our lives, which without we would be much prone for not making it than when we do. Humanity should be bonded to a social contract not only among those living but also for the sake of future generations.

It is an undeniable fact that Godly societies are more in accord with morality, as millions believe in virtue, belief in destiny with purpose, as they believe in a creator, which no doubt is fueled with doing good. That I am certain is accordingly sealed with believing in some sort of divine reward or ugly punishment in people's mind, and rightly so, since no fool would believe in the same consequences for doing right and for acting wrong.

Either way, people should not be devoid of caring, attention, tenderness, connection, wanting to belong, sympathy, compassion, opportunity, education, intelligence, relationship, commitments, responsibility, accountability, honesty, reliability, love, devotion, dreaming, imagination and creativity, and millions other things that we should have to collectively help give meaning to our lives which without we would be much more prone to not making it than when we do.

Let's not forget that many people are frustrated with the word God, as I do not blame them. Innumerous charlatans and so-called preachers, priests, Mullahs, Rabbi, monks and so on with deep pockets have belittled the word God showing huge discrepancies between their words and their action for the worst beyond belief; which has apparently become an issue with the non-believers, atheists, agnostics, etc.

I rather say, Creator, to perhaps mitigate their reluctance approach to even discuss the sacred word of our God. The point is that discussing and talking or preaching about the creator demands sacrifice. What I mean is you are damned if you understand and are conscientious, and you are damned if you don't, an individual without conscious that is used to constantly feed the beast inside which is irrelevant to what is moral.

When you are enlightened, obviously you will not stand by and let what is not just to take place, as in one way or another you will get involved, even if it is to call for the law to intervene. That is of course if circumstances permit, if not so, then most probably you even might sacrifice your own life to avoid a tragedy of certain kind. I am sure you have heard about the phrase that says no good deed goes unpunished.

Well, when one is enlightened with having a sharp conscious, a compassionate heart, one will perhaps go to the extreme to save an innocent life, which should expect not only praise but sometimes punishment, if one is dealing with an emotionally unintelligent person or perhaps an immorally oriented individual. But overall human beings are of good nature, imagine if you are certain that an innocent female either of proper age or not is going to be raped, or you are sure that in a rubbery about to happen someone is to get killed, or probably of proper age to go to war for your country's sake, and might happen that a child is about to be drawn where you are present, or may be struck by a moving car or a truck, and when a terrorist attack of some sort is going to endanger many lives.

Experience has shown that many individuals volunteer to help by instinct and without any hesitation, sacrificing their own lives to save others, this is a fact. So when we hear the creator made human beings in his image, "Don't you know yet? It is your light that lights the world." Rumi

It should dictate that so many willingly pay a huge price and sacrifice time, money and even their own lives to avoid a tragedy, or to stop an innocent by-standard from not getting killed or even hurt. Because of the enlightenment, the wisdom and the compassion within you, you will not remorse your heavenly actions, no matter what punishment beholds you, which certifies the phrase that says what goes around comes around. This is when the law of karma makes sense.

This is why you should resist anyone trying to devoid awakening the heavenly giant within your heart to do good, and challenge those who perhaps plan to stop the infinitely potentiated cells and neurons in your brain from progressing and from living your full potential where the sky is the limit. One will awaken when one finally stopped agreeing to things that insult one soul. This ought to happen despite any system with corrupt motives or shortcomings imposed on you because of wrongful cultural upbringings and toxic environment.

You must try to belittle the beast within you and activate the spirit, the divine soul, the revered conscious that is waiting to become materialized. "The awakening of consciousness is the next evolutionary step for mankind." Eckhart Tolle

> "Your vision will become clear only when you can look into your own heart. Who looks outside, dreams; who looks inside, awakens."

> Carl Jung

As Plato said, "good is its own virtue", and as the nature of good is "higher consciousness" so is the nature of evil which is "lower consciousness" embrace the fact that: You are your mind, your thoughts, you're conscious. If you see yourself as able as having strength and achievement you possess a conscious with reactive respond.

If you are frightened, where you are in survival mode, and your life is at stake, you possess a conscious of fight or flight. If you are progressing, growing and are in an evolution mode, your conscious is of intuitive response. If you are relaxed, calm and focused, yours is serenity of mind and awareness. If you are the dreamer, making your dreams a reality, you have a mind for creativity.

If you possess a visionary mind, you are potentiated with making miracles to happen. if you possess a mind of deity, yours is conscious of sacredness. The mystery which we need to solve is who is overseeing the above and millions more if not billions of organic responses which literally dictate who you are. You might say I am the one who makes my choices as I decide what to do, correct, but where are you truly located either in your brain or within your body. Let's both of us work on that since so far, the predominant finding is to do good and avoid evil.

When endowed with a good conscience, then all good deeds seem mandatory, as you see no choice but to help those caught in a helpless position, and since your high conscious will constantly remind you of yours being a reluctance to assist when you should have, but did not. As your awakened conscious will cause you tremendous pain, that is if you could have helped it, but did not. Hence, no matter if your kind intention and good work are appreciated or not, your reward is with an Omnipresent Creator.

27

IS IT GOD OR HUMAN GREED?

Then, a great deal of concern arises stating that even with a finely tuned cosmos and/or since the intricate life should remind us of a first cause/ designer, there's too much suffering in the world to believe in God. That certainly is true as there exists so much pain in our world beyond anyone's imagination as it should not be denied. But the blame is wrongfully directed and not justifying so.

If honesty, truth, intelligence, decency, and courage should mean something, then, we should aim our anger towards the actual culprits and target the real source of the problems. Humanity should hold those accountable that relentlessly push for the well-being of the very few against the will of many.

Governments are in cahoots with the rich elites and the multifaceted corporations in an oligopolistic atmosphere to globally suppress the basic needs of billions of deprived people as they are struggling to barely live way under the poverty line, without any mercy from those controlling the world by policing and the military industrial complex; as God has nothing to do with it, because the atrocities are caused by our own kind as the fault should be directed at them.

It looks like global citizens are colonized by the moguls of our time where masses of commoners are exploited by surreptitious means forcing billions to leave below the poverty level, as the multi-national corporations have taken people's right and their freedom away by taking their resources and livelihood. The monumentally rich elite have the means to loudly trumpet freedom and human-rights, forgetting that no freedom and no right of any kind can exist without having the means to survive, as they are not in the same boat as globally billions of poverty-driven people are. Money is the worst discovery of human life. But it is the most trusted material to test human nature. Buddha

The point is that need and having freedom are attached at the hip, the more need one has the less free one can be, another word if you are needy, relatively speaking, you cannot be free. We by nature need to breathe, to consume food, must drink water, must rest, need to work, need be sexual, must reproduce to avoid extinction.

These factors are extremely essential for humanity to survive. But this naturally driven requirements should not be mistaken by artificially manufacture needs created by monumental corporations that keep millions out of work when they feel like it, or when they see it fit to maximize their profit. Hence taking millions of worker's freedoms away since workers can no longer afford basic living with being unemployed.

It is a no-brainer that economic bondage and forcing millions to unemployment can sure inhibit people's freedom no matter how much of empty rhetoric is hollered into people's ear with no substance. No one can actually feel free when one cannot feed one's family, not able to keep a roof over their head, not affording education, and not able to afford proper medical for themselves and their loved ones.

They have enslaved masses of global inhabitants through huge class differentiation, where extreme economic inequality has exhausted so many from any hope of recovery and for a better living. This is not rocket science to understand since it is deliberately formulated by big corporations, designed to keep the status quo, that is I believe a recipe for disaster, where the poor get poorer and the rich get richer. This occurs through the barrel of guns, as they immediately extinguish any fiery voice demanding justice, which instead they need to stop fueling the fire of poverty, as there is a limit to everything, including suppressing humanity. Hence, in our contemporary living, we are left with a clear-cut choice, a definite choice which must not be played with. Either to save capitalism and ditch the planet, or get to rid of capitalism and save the planet. Then Jesus said be aware! Guard against every kind of greed. Life is not measured by how much you own.

28

MORAL ABSOLUTISM

Further question branches out by the atheists that a moral life doesn't need God. Not so, true morality requires a transcendent standard God. Before elaborating on this rather imperative concern. We ought to know that Science affirms that the finely tuned cosmos was created out of nothing.

Life's order, design, purpose, the infinite complexity, they all demand an Intelligent Designer, as our response to pain and suffering is relative to our knowledge of right and wrong/good and evil in a fallen world. God has gifted humanity with conscious and a potentiated entity called the brain, that if just given a chance to grow. It will stop all the anguish and the sufferings of the world and will proceed to conquer the entire universe which with no doubt must believe it to succeed and overcome all the burdens in our lives.

As for morality, no human being can claim knowing it all, besides no human-being is free from making mistakes, as no one is absolutely perfect, referencing our behaviors human beings are relative to acting either good or bad, everyone as the saying goes everyone has skeletons in their closet. No man should be trusted with absolute moral laws. As we are all relative beings, as with no prejudice everyone makes mistake.

The sole absolute conscious is God which oversees the mind of the awakened universes with no flows.

Absolute morality is when universal standards of right or wrong apply to all people at all times irrespective of their culture or beliefs. Relative morality is based on the theory that truth and rightness are different for different people or cultures. Hence no man can morally be in a position to globally, universally be followed because of diversity in so many socio-cultural beliefs and what should define what is moral. Bottom line, what is crucial to the human soul, is to educate the heart as well as literacy for the mind. "Educating the mind without educating the heart is no education at all." Aristotle.

Absolute means any theory in which its rules are absolute: they cannot be altered as they are universal. Relative means any theory in which something is judged in relation to something else and thus is open to change. Absolute laws or rules of morality will never change. Moral Relativism (or Ethical Relativism) is the position that moral or ethical criterions do not reflect objective and/or universal moral truths, but in lieu (alternatively, instead) make claims relative to social, cultural, historical or individual circumstances.

Moral absolutism asserts that there are certain universal moral principles by which all peoples' actions may be judged. It is a form of deontology, in which deontology derives from the Greek words for duty (Deon) and science or study of logos. In contemporary moral philosophy, deontology is one of those kinds of normative theories concerning which choices are morally necessary, forbidden, or allowed.

The challenge with moral absolutism, however, is that there will always be strong disagreements about which moral principles are correct and which are incorrect. Moral Absolutism is the ethical belief that there are absolute standards against which moral questions can be judged and that certain actions are right or wrong, regardless of the context of the act. One should further bear in mind that we are partially instinct-driven animals with physical needs as we must satisfy our instinctual urges to survive. This often can compromise our judgments for the sake of bodily pleasures. or our spiritual and moral guide.

> I count him braver who overcomes his desires than him who conquers his enemies, for the hardest victory is over self."

> — Aristotle.

29

MULTIVERSE UNIVERSES

Multiverse universes are apparently raised in our contemporary life by non-believers to state their case. Science has realistically brought us a colossal amount of realization. It is understood that the sum total of human knowledge doubles approximately every couple of years or less. of physics and cosmology, we astoundingly know what happened to our universe as early as a tiny fraction of a second after the big bang. In chemistry, we understand the most complex reactions among atoms and molecules, and in biology, we know how the living cell works and have mapped out our total genome. But can this enormous knowledge base reject the existence of some kind of pre-existent outside force that may have launched our universe to be the way it is?

The scientific atheists have tried to describe this problematic mystery by offering the existence of a multiverse—an infinite set of universes, each with its own parameters. In some universes, the conditions are wrong for life; thus, by the sheer size of this alleged multiverse, there must exist a universe where everything is right. But if it takes a massive power of nature to make one universe, then how much more strength would that force have to be orderly for creating infinite universes? Therefore, the sole hypothetical multiverse does not resolve the problem of God. The incredible fine-tuning of the universe indicates the most powerful debate for the being of an imminent creative entity we may well call God. the fact is that we must have a powerful creator to essentially force all the parameters we require for our existence.

"I believe we live in a multiverse of universes."

Prominent physicist Michio Kaku.

What is fine-tuning? What is a multiverse? The multiverse is a hypothetical group of multiple universes including the universe in which we live. Together, these universes include everything that exists: the entirety of space, time, matter, energy, the physical laws and the constants that describe them.

In summary, the fine-tuning argument points out some of the physical properties of our universe that are meant to prominent the right circumstances for making atoms, stars, planets, galaxies, the universe, and life. If the outcomes were even a bit different, life could not form or survive in the universe. Any savvy mind would see God crafting and sustaining a universe to accomplish his purpose of making it just right for humanity to exist.

The multiverse shows a model where our universe is one of many universes, and each of the universes has a variety of physical properties. But this should not be so wacky to reject the omnipotent, omnipresent and the omniscient God, it should indeed manifest the infinite power of God beyond anyone's imagination, since the infinite God is the cause for the unbounded cosmos as mankind should expect more philosophical and scientific surprises as humanity grows to achieve more knowledge and information to discover more dimensions, and to further divulge the mysteries of the cosmos.

It is surprising that some high caliber philosophers and well known scientists would doubt God, knowing that human intelligence and awareness give rise to scientific discoveries that are often bound to be wrong, as this cannot be historically denied, since new things have consistently come along to replace the old, as many scientific ideas either had to be corrected, or previous founding's had to be improved to make sense.

The point is we are not flawless, as we do not possess the absolute wisdom and the utter intelligence, so is many of our findings. No scientific theory can be the answer for millions of complex questions to quench humanity's thirst for the answer to many curious oriented inquiries.

Renowned physicist Stephen Hawking said, "A combination of quantum theory and the theory of relativity would better explain our existence than divine intervention."

It shouldn't be surprising if the next scientific Joe to show up next and say what I claim is the solution to all the puzzling question in which humanity is grappling with, that my so and so theory is the answer to all there is and no divine intervention would be necessary, because through modern history is not the first time such title is raised and wouldn't be the last. whenever the hypothesis on the multiverse universe become a reality for conveying life, then, the fine-tuning of those universes without any doubt must have occurred by a higher power to make them fruitful.

It is a fact that rigorous mathematical structures are behind the quantum theory, string theory, gravitational forces by the physicists and cosmologists tied up with the probabilities of multiverse universe. But no matter how advanced we become in our scientific discoveries we should never disregard the infinitely intelligent mind of our creator orchestrating the entire show.

> "String theory envisions a multiverse in which our universe
> is one slice of bread in a big cosmic loaf. The other slices
> would be displaced from ours in some extra dimension
> of space."
>
> Brain Greene

If scientists are correct, then all the stars and galaxies we can observe in the clear night are just a tiny fraction of an unimaginably huge assemblage that scientists call the multiverse. The whole universe may be just one element—one atom in an infinite quintet (combo) of heavens, a cosmic wonder. So far physicists have put forth three exclusive debate for the existence of the multiverse.

First is the big bang, the catastrophic event that made the universe into existence about 13.8 billion years ago. Some physicists believe the big bang happened by a random fluctuation which they call quantum foam The big bang is thought to have been triggered by a random fluctuation in what physicists call the quantum foam, a vortex (whirlpool) of virtual particles that pop into and out of existence. as many scientists claim that there could have been many such events leading to multiple universes. The second argument for the existence of a multiverse arises from string theory, in which string theory says that matter is eventually made not of particles but of unthinkably small, vibrating strings or loops of energy. Physicists believed that string theory might afford a theory of everything that is, a system of equations that could describe why our universe has the precise properties that it does. For instance, why is the mass of a proton 1836.15 times greater than that of the electron? No one has a convincing expiation.

String theory's equations seem to have an amazing number of probable solutions (that's a one followed by 500 zeros). Strangely enough, some string theorists debate that each of these solutions can explain a different universe, each with its own physical properties. String theory is a theoretical framework that tries the idea that the point-like particles of particle physics can also be modeled as one-dimensional objects called strings. String theory attempts to unite the four forces in the universe—the electromagnetic force, the strong nuclear force, the weak nuclear force, and gravity into one unified theory.

Physicists believe string theory is a potentiated theory for everything, perhaps able to unite all matter and forces in a single theoretical framework, which could explain the fundamental level of the universe in terms of vibrating strings rather than particles. In the meanwhile, superstring theory formally known less as string theory is occasionally called the theory of everything because it is a uniting physics theory that reconciles the differences between quantum theory and the theory of relativity to explain the nature of all known forces and matter which if so, it would be huge breakthrough for science and the scientist's mind behind it.

One imperative component of string theories is that these theories demand extra dimensions of space-time for their mathematical consistency. In bosonic string theory, space-time is 26-dimensional, while in superstring theory it is 10-dimensional, and in M-theory it is 11-dimensional. Spatial dimensions. Classical physics theories describe three physical dimensions: from a particular point in space, the basic directions in which we can move are up/down, left/right, and forward/backward. Time is often thought of as the fourth dimension. Time plays a key role as a dimension in mathematical formulations of physical laws and theories such as general relativity and string theory. The qualitative maneuverability of time as the fourth dimension is arguable.

The third argument for the multiverse arrives from quantum theory. even though it's has been around for more than a century now and has shown to be very successful in explaining the nature of matter on the smallest scale, quantum theory guides us to a number of existential probabilities that defy common sense, known as many worlds translation of quantum theory began in the 1950s, the universe necessarily splits in two each time there's a quantum event. Niels Bohr suggested the Copenhagen interpretation of the quantum theory, which indicated that a particle is whatever it is measured either to be for instance a wave or a particle, in which cannot be assumed to have specific properties or even to exist until it is restrained and measured. Quantum mechanics is the body of scientific laws that shows the preposterous (bizarre) function of photons, electrons and the other particles that make-up to the entire universe.

Wave-Particle Duality of Light.

Quantum theory indicates that both light and matter consist of tiny particles which have wavelike properties linked with them. Light is made up of particles known as photons, and the matter is composed of particles named electrons, protons, neutrons. In our contemporary lifestyle the most exact clocks in the world, are atomic clocks, able to utilize the foremost behavior of quantum theory to measure time. They monitor the specific radiation frequency required to make electrons jump between various energy levels. Modern quantum mechanics came about in 1925 by German physicists Werner Heisenberg, Max Born, and Pascual Jordan generated matrix mechanics, and Erwin Schrodinger the Austrian physicist which invented the wave mechanics and the non-relativistic Schrodinger equation.

Some elementary notion of quantum mechanics is the Bohr theory which constitutes the idea of energy levels but does not succeed to divulge the details of atomic structure. It is the theory utilized for extremely small particles, such as electrons in atoms. Quantum theory is the theoretical fundamental of modern physics which explains the nature and behavior of matter and energy on the atomic and subatomic level. The nature and behavior of matter and energy at that level is occasionally indicated to as quantum physics and quantum mechanics.

30

ONENESS VS. NOTHINGNESS

As demanding as technology is, I am afraid it can be troubling too. It seems that industrialization and technology advance people's IQ while people's empathy for their fellow human beings and the environment keeps declining. We live in a progressive era which ironically violence and criminal conduct has rampaged as people's faith has deteriorated, even replacing God with science.

So many are losing sight, ignoring that scientists conduct scientific research to advance knowledge in an area of interest. In reality, they discover the truth by plying (draw on, exploit) facts; they act as gynecologists relentlessly pursuing new scientific ideas from the womb of mother nature. It seems they are probing for the Oneness, and look for the root causes of the infinite possibilities. Hoping that perhaps one day they could detect the point of singularity where Oneness resides.

Scientists are adamant to discover the mysteries of our universe, to find the real source of existence where they research for the absolute power of intention behind this extremely mind-boggling cosmos. Misinterpreting modernisms by millions and miss understanding science and technologies by lots of people, they have caused a lack of collective awareness, as often neighbors are completely cut off from each other as they do not exist. Millions are so individualized, they have become robot-like, mimicking mechanical routines like they have no soul. They relentlessly engage in electronic plays, incessantly pursuing cyber-oriented activities, often with sexual bearings, and so many are obsessed with diversified gadgets like there is no tomorrow.

People's priorities have changed, these days one is more concern with let's say a dead Raccoon in their backyard than a child dying because of hunger in Asia or in Africa. As if we live in the Paleolithic (periods of the stone age) era. We should know that spiritual and moral values gravitate humanity towards the culture of tolerance and understanding.

Compassion plays a decisive role in refuting cruelty, and being considered keenly draws on wisdom, while kindness, pursuing art, creativity, and beauty are to appreciate soul searching. the spirit does not work with the hand, there is no art. Leonardo da Vinci. Nations can resort to progressive cultures to collectively harness science, exchange art, and manifest civilized conducts to mandate freedom, glorify democracy and reach the pinnacle of human rights so that everyone can taste the sweetness of life as it is meant to be.

The principle of causality and the axiom of non-contradiction is to avoid ambiguities and dissension (discord, disharmony) in all propositions, which without nothing in the material world should actually work. since both doctrines not only apply to the tangible world but are certainly decisive in conceptually oriented phenomena for validating logic in philosophy, science, socio-cultural, socio-economic, socio-political and certainly for reaching God, spirituality and the existence.

Coherency in moral behaviors should be sought, to avoid hypocrisy in one's conduct, and not stray from the path of righteousness and what is just. Good and evil are not just nominal, as good is its own virtue, so as evil is repugnant, which if moral turpitude (degradation) shall somehow overcome, then human demise will be on the ballot.

The point is that all pluralities initiated from oneness, the entire cosmos started from singularity where everything in existence shall purposefully return to God the creator of heavens and Earth. Consider one's own place in the universal unity in which we all belong, and the Oneness of which we are all a part of, from which we all depart and to which we all return.

Many scientists, prominent philosophers believe that accidental behaviors will never verify unity, they so confirm that no accidental motion can purposefully reach unity, but in contrary, they generate chaos and disharmony.

"Technology is destructive only in the hands of people who do not realize that they are one and the same process as the universe."

Alan W. Watts

Further, let's put the search for traces of God to test. let's imagine that nothing exists. I often did so, but with no avail. I just am not able to delineate (portray, depict) nothingness. I mean to imagine no light, no darkness, an imagination barren of stars, planets and galaxies, no universe of any kind to dwell on.

I mean, can anyone imagine no space, no time, no matter, an idea devoid of any sentient life, to utterly imagine nothingness. I mean an absolute vacuity (void), just nothing. It neither is conceptually nor physically possible. begs the end-all question from curious minds? Why is there something rather than nothing? To envisage nothing is nonsensical (not sensible, absurd.) It is not practical to fancy nothing—not only no space, time, matter, energy, light, darkness or any aware beings, but no consciousness at all to perceive void, to behold nothingness. In this sense, the question is literally not probable.

Nothing, nil, naught, is something. A fallacy, a deductive paradox, inferential sophistry, a wrongful reasoning or non sequitur (Latin for it does not follow) is a flaw in the structure of a logical argument which renders the argument invalid. It obviates (preclude) balderdash (nonsense, bunk.)

The absence of all there is. Perhaps so many people think that how insignificant nothing is but far from it; the idea of nothing is primal to our universe. It is awkward to imagine absolute nothingness. If we are able to remove all there is from inside of a small container box: all the air, molecules, atoms, particles, until not a thing is left in it. At this stage, we should see and feel that there is nothing in this empty box since we have removed everything from the inside since the box literally looks empty. But what we know as emptiness is not corollary (by-product) to what we see, since such void arranges most of the universe; which are the atoms forming everything and not excluding us.

Hence, it is deductive sophistry (fallacy) to talk about nothing like it was a something that ceases to exist, is not. Here we are faced against the puzzling issue of describing what we mean by nothing and the exclusion that language intrudes on the problem. The very act of trying to dialogue about nothing makes it a something. Alternatively, (otherwise) what are we saying? should, in reality, be abjured (formally rejected) since contextually does not make any sense.

31

NOTHING WOULD HOLD GOD'S NONEXISTENCE

In the classification of nothing let's categorize some of the issues that perhaps can encompass something that would be contradicted by nothing: since in the material world nothing does attribute to anything physical, mental, moral, spiritual, platonic love and God, etc. If by nothing is meant no physical objects or matter of any kind, for example, there can still be energy from which matter may arise by natural forces guided by the laws of nature. Physicists, for example, talk about empty space as seething with virtual particles, from which particle-antiparticle pairs come into existence as a consequence of the uncertainty principle of quantum physics. From this nothingness, universes may pop into existence.

Nothing excludes creation ex nihilo. If by nothing is meant that there is no physical, mental, platonic or nonphysical entity of any kind, then there can be no God or gods, which means that there cannot be anything outside of nothing from which to create something.

This negates the Christian theologian argument that God created the universe ex nihilo, or "out of nothing," based on the English translation of Genesis 1:1 that "in the beginning, God created the heavens and the earth." This is misleading. Recent scholarship has suggested that the Hebrew word for "creation" in Genesis 1:1 is bara ()—a verb that more accurately translated means to "separate" or "divide." Genesis 1:1 should read, "In the beginning, God separated the heavens and the earth." Separated from what is not indicated.

Nothing is unstable; something is stable. Asking why there is something rather than nothing presumes nothing is the natural state of things out of which something needs an explanation. Maybe something is the natural state of things, and nothing would be the mystery to be solved.

In his sweeping narrative, *The Greatest Story Ever Told—So Far*, a sequel to his 2012 book *A Universe from Nothing*, Krauss notes that Einstein was one of the first physicists to demonstrate that the classical notion of causation begins to break down at the quantum realm. Although many physicists objected to the idea of something coming from nothing, he observes that this is precisely what happens with the light you are using to read this page.

Electrons in hot atoms emit photons—photons that didn't exist before they were emitted—which are emitted spontaneously and without a specific cause. Why is it that we have grown at least somewhat comfortable with the idea that photons can be created from nothing without a cause, but not whole universes?

One answer has to do with our discomfort with the Copernican principle, which holds that we are not special. We prefer religious and anthropic explanations that the universe was created and fine-tuned for us because they put humans right back in the center of the cosmos anthropocentrically—it is all about us. But 500 years of scientific discoveries have revealed that it isn't about us. From this fact, we may gain purchase on a perspective that engages both the religious and scientific impulse toward a sense of awe one gains from contemplating nothing.

32

MIND CONTROL

Human beings are potentiated to learn, to reason and solve problems. We're self-aware, and we're conscious of our surroundings, the presence, thoughts, and feelings of others. We make tools and practice the art of deception, we're creative. We think abstractly. We have language and use it to concoct complex ideas. All of these are relative signs of intelligence—we are highly intelligent beings. I say relative, since not everyone is endowed with great IQ, or born with golden opportunity to raise at the top. Even when one is highly intelligent one must be educated, trained and have the financial means to succeed in life.

Historically speaking, those at the top, the ruling class, the elites, do not easily let go of their power without a bloody encounter. They will resort to anything and everything to subdue and quell (end) any uprising, peaceful or none, either through force or by mind manipulation. The rich elites, the ruling class, the state, and the media work in cahoots to control the commoners, and fundamentally they have the resources and all the technological means to mentally exploit and control people's mind.

The authorities utilize propaganda and censorship to keep the population at bay (preventing them from reaching, attacking, or affecting) the status quo, to make certain that people are thinking in a proper way. The idea of overcoming and making the citizens subservient to the system is not new, but the modern approach in the technology of mind control is extremely sophisticated. The commoners cannot even fathom the tactics and the strategy that the system uses against them since the system buys the most intelligent and extraordinary minds to work for them often against the will of the people.

For instance, one of the techniques used to substantiate mind control was developed by Dr. John C Lilly, when he was working for the US National Institute of health. Dr. Lilly found out that certain wavelength format could control the water molecules inside the subject's brain which could intrinsically (essentially) alter the undertakers think and feel. Evidently, the technology utilizes frequency waves of 40hz, not needing the use of electrodes. According to Melissa and Aaron Duke of Truth stream Media, the Lilly wave is solely the tip of icebergs.

The couple believed that a man known as Hendricus G. Loos patented a grotesque (bizarre, unheard of, extraordinary) invention called Nervous System Manipulation via electromagnetic fields from monitors. Mr. Loos claimed that his invention when utilized can change human's emotional state by altering the electromagnetic fields around them through devices like a television screen and computer monitors.

Loos wrote, "It is, therefore, possible to manipulate the nervous system of a subject by pulling images exhibited on a close by computer monitor or TV set." Probably the most sinister part of this invention is that it can be exploited without the subject of the mind control ever being aware of what has occurred.

Furthermore, Aaron and Melissa Dykes also have indicated brain mapping technology, according to Truth Stream Media brain mapping technology is enabled to decode human brain which means it can render the ability to the user to read thoughts of other people. It is literally a big problem since there are no laws against covertly monitoring people's trend of thoughts and the invasion of the inhabitant's privacy, as it is presently legal, although not ethical at all.

33

WHAT SCIENCE SAYS ABOUT THE MATTER AND AFTER WE DIE

If the matter can neither be generated nor obliterated, then how was the universe was hatched? Scientists agree that the entire amount of energy and matter in the universe stays constant, solely altering from one form to another. Further, $E = mc^2$, an equation derived by the twentieth-century physicist Albert Einstein, in which E represents units of energy, m represents units of mass, and c^2 is the speed of light squared, or multiplied by itself. Energy equals mass times the speed of light squared. On the most basic level, the equation says that energy and mass (matter) are interchangeable; they are different forms of the same thing. Under the right conditions, energy can become mass and vice versa.

Then it shouldn't make any difference to either say that matter can neither be generated nor destroyed, which you can say the same thing for energy too. $E=mc^2$: Einstein's equation that gave birth to the atom bomb. It says that the energy (E) in a system (an atom, a person, the solar system) is equal to its total mass (m) multiplied by the square of the speed of light (c, equal to 186,000 miles per second). Therefore, if matter and energy are interchangeable, then it should really not matter. The first law of thermodynamics doesn't actually specify that matter can neither be created nor destroyed, and instead it says energy can neither be created or destroyed.

It should say either matter, or energy cannot be created or destroyed, since once again matter and energy are equivalent or better yet, are identical. It states that the total amount of energy in a closed system cannot be created nor destroyed (it can be changed from one form to another). It was after nuclear physics told us that mass and energy are essentially equivalent -this is what Einstein meant when he wrote $E = mc^2$ that we realized the 1st law of thermodynamics also applied to the mass. Mass became another form of energy that had to be included in a thorough thermodynamic treatment of a system. Hence, the total amount of energy in the universe has to remain the same, from the beginning of the universe until the present.

The overall understanding is that total energy in the universe is constant, and scientists believe that the universe is expanding. There are infinite stars, planets, galaxies and with prevalent globular clusters, matter and energy seem to commute, rushing off everywhere in many directions. The scientists say that the expansion of the universe does not have to consume more energy as the universe expands, since the distance between stars or galaxies increases. Therefore, the gravitational energy between them decreases to compensate.

Further, thermodynamics does not know what value the total energy should carry, since the physicists believe that the amount can be colossal (huge), but constant that is known as an open universe, where the amount of matter/energy exceeds a definite so-called cut-off density level. in our universe. It is now believed zero which is called a flat universe, as many physicists agreed that the matter-density in the universe is equal to the cut-off density. It could also be negative, even an encircled, a closed universe where the amount of matter is less than the cut-off density.

Finally, they say it could be anything, but whatever the value is at the present, it was at the very beginning too. According to the science of physics, the entire matter and energy in the universe now existed in some form or shape at the big bang. Once again, the notoriety of the point to make shown through the image courtesy of NASA, stating that The expansion of the universe doesn't have to take more energy -as the universe expands, the distances between stars or galaxies increases, and thus the gravitational energy between them decreases to compensate. Quantum mechanics indicates that an extremely tiny scale and for an extremely short period of time, energy can be spontaneously being made and destroyed. Similar to boiling water, where bubbles spontaneously show up and burst, energy—in the form of particles—can very quickly appear from the void of space-time, exist for an immensely short amount of time, and disappear again.

Normal time and length scales average out to what thermodynamics indicated. It should hold true (that no energy is created or destroyed within the closed system of the universe). But eventually, what they mean is that if there was such a tiny fluctuation at the beginning of time, it could have made the total energy of the universe at creation a bit more than zero, and hence, the universe will always carry that total amount of energy, since such a fluctuation could have been what made the universe to begin in the first place.

The scientific field of cosmology, also the growing field of string theory, is trying to answer this ultimate question, how did the universe start? But so far, no one knows what occurred at the moment the universe initiated. The First Law of Thermodynamics (Conservation) states that energy is always conserved, it cannot be created or destroyed. In essence, energy can be converted from one form into another. The Second Law of Thermodynamics is about the quality of energy. It states that as energy is transferred or transformed, more and more of it is wasted.

The bottom line with infinite interactivities in stars, planets, galaxies, and in the entire universe, one should expect some type of lop-sidedness and imbalances causing energy shortage in some part of the universe, or energy abundant in other parts, even causing energy exhaustion in the heavens above. Instead, energy transferability is awesomely at work converting the precise amount of energy required to where is designated to go and vice versa without any malfunction, which should definitely alert us with the immense discipline and magnificent power of an infinitely competent designer overseeing everything in existence.

If we are also energy-driven, and an inseparable part of nature, then what happens to us when we die? We know we are here temporary which sooner or later we expire. Scientists say that after we pass on, the atoms in our body will forever remain here. but most of the atoms in your body are forever. Alternatively, we are either buried, embalmed (to treat a dead body with specials to prevent it from decay) or not, or buried. If so, then one's soft tissues are eventually consumed by bacteria and tiny organisms. Also if one is burned, one's soft tissues are consumed by oxygen and made into carbon dioxide, water, and sulfur oxides and nitrogen. The long-term effect is that we become food for other organisms.

The dead person's bones also will decay, but more slowly than the soft tissue, which then phosphorus and calcium in dead body's bones will end up into the soil and taken by the plants. Then, some plants will be eaten by animals, where eventually the animals die, some consumed by humans and cycle through biosphere redundantly, over and over again. So one wouldn't know how much of and which predecessor's body one has taken in. There are some radioactive elements, not many which few of them decay and turn into other elements before they can arrive into the biosphere.

Radioactive potassium will become calcium, small amounts of thorium and uranium will eventually turn into a lead, with most of this decay, the new elements made the stay here on planet Earth. In the process helium is also formed as Earth gravitational force cannot hold helium, hence a bit of it will take off into space. Some of it will get away from the solar system and shift to the stars, and some will be caught by Sun and other planets like Jupiter which is the fifth planet from the Sun and the largest in the solar system. It is a giant planet with a mass one-thousandth that of the Sun, but two-and-a-half times that of all the other planets in the solar system and Mars.

The point is that no matter what happens to you after you die, or how you expire, your atoms do not care since they just stay the way they are, and start a new life elsewhere doing the same job they did for you.

Most of your atoms commute and do their thing. Our body continuously dies and rebuild itself as it constitutes our genetic pattern as the atoms and molecules in changes. Most of the atoms that build your body today are not the same atoms that made your body a few months or years ago.

34

ENLIGHTENMENT; AN EXTREMELY POTENT AGENT

For this enlightenment, however, nothing is required but freedom, and indeed the most harmless among all the things to which this term can properly be applied. It is the freedom to make public use of one's reason at every point. But I hear on all sides, 'Do not argue!' The Officer says: 'Do not argue but drill!' The tax collector: 'Do not argue but pay!' The cleric: 'Do not argue but believe!' Only one prince in the world says, 'Argue as much as you will, and about what you will, but obey!' Everywhere there is a restriction on freedom."

— Immanuel Kant

An answer to the question: What is enlightenment?

There are two fundamental issues, one is that life is hard, so they say, which it is not supposed to be, life is meant to be good, and the second is that there are opportunities, but not available to everyone. These two troubling states are manufactured, they sure stem from people not getting their fair share out of life, and often for millions that are exhausted of any given chance. One might ask if so, why intelligent communities and savvy minded people do not do anything about it.

Historically speaking inhumane behaviors happened through the dark ages, force and savagery by the powerful and the mighty were the norms, and not so surprisingly common, that has caused beyond repair damages to mankind. Violence and exerting brute force was the key for the strong to rule and create masses of slaves and millions of subservient individuals to do as the violators and the tyrants desired. The point is that stupidity and ignorance played a big role in dwelling on (populate) atrocious behavior.

Perhaps not much of criticism should behold the culprits since civility of mind and manner were just simply absent. Societies were thoughtfully barren, and not mentally fertile enough to fight back, where most victims were not mindfully potentiated to realize their rights as a human being which they should not have been exploited, and lowered to the animal level. God or gods also did not mean much, again because of lack of human intelligence worshiping idols and man-made agents of some sort. As Immanuel Kant said: "How then is perfection to be sought? Wherein lies our hope? In education, and in nothing else."

Then, of course, there are those who believe that God will punish the evil doers, even so, they do not realize that the good God has endowed humanity with all the tools and the resources to live happy and free. The mind of man is not to be taken lightly, as God has made it possible for the mankind to conquer the universe in which far exceeds for solving the problems made by our own kind, and not wait for the creator of heaven and earth to save us from the torts (misdeed, felony) of bad characters.

"Space and time are the frameworks within which the mind is constrained to construct its experience of reality."

Immanuel Kant.

People should realistically confront abuse of power and injustice by the few and not wait for so long that one day Messiah, or any other faith-related Icon to appear from beyond the space and time to free us from the clutches of so much economic inequality and extreme financial transgressions by the moguls of time, which have resulted in people's suffering and despair, it just does not make any sense.

"All our knowledge begins with the senses, proceeds then to the understanding and ends with reason. There is nothing higher than reason."

Emmanuel Kant.

The violator's irrelevancy to God and acting far away from good conscious has made life miserable for billions, and unreasonably very hard for the global commoners, as they literally feel the horrific financial impact imposed on them, leaving so many destitute as the victim's cry for help do not reach those in position of power and fame.

The Persian poet Saadi Shirazi said that:
Human beings are members of the whole.
In the creation of one essence and soul.
If one member is affected with pain.
Other members uneasy will remain.
If you have no sympathy for human pain.
The name of human you cannot retain.

35

LIFE AFTER DEATH

Theories of where humans go when they expire have been the question since humans have lived. Many religiously oriented thoughts believe that there is a God and that heaven is where the righteous souls end up, and Inferno (hell) is where the evil souls go. Some are Polytheism (from Greek polytheisms) is the worship of or belief in multiple deities, which are usually assembled into a pantheon of gods and goddesses, along with their own religions and rituals.

As those gods have no control of where humans go. Some believe that souls are reincarnated. Some believe that nothing happens when people die. Others believe that after a person dies, they are gone forever. Some believe all go to the same place when they pass on. As far as the human soul, the overall understanding is that human soul or spirit is energy-oriented and runs through our vein and permeates brain waves, the nervous and so on, is any different than the energy that science says is never created nor destroyed?

Either way, it seems that the energy is being recycled in a matrix world which all things are conserved, which can shed lights on the idea of reincarnation that believes after death, reincarnation occurs depending upon the accumulated karma, rebirth occurs into a higher or lower bodily form, either in heaven or hell or earthly realm. No bodily form is permanent: everyone dies and reincarnates further. It is believed that some people remember past lives.

The data from their lives are still preserved within the soul.

36

INFINITY VS. FINITE WORLD

Infinity can only correlate with the infinite God.

Physicists have to deal with math to make sure their experimental assessments, either at the cosmological level, like the big bang model, or any other scientific hypothesis that they are working on makes sense before establishing a theory that assuredly can be relied on. Hence, if we should accept the big bang as our best accomplished cosmological model, then the big bang should be considered as the beginning of the universe, which initiated about 14 billion years ago. But then, realistically acknowledging this time period is not feasible, it can only be a prediction which seems not applicable to our actual universe because of scientist's findings based on relate to numbers.

But numbers do not exist, they are simply adjectives, which definition of an adjective is that it is a word that describes or clarifies a noun. Adjectives describe nouns by giving some information about an object's size, shape, age, color, origin or material. It's a big table (size). It's a (round) table, they are not nouns. If one says, round you should ask round what?. The natural numbers also do have a start, but not an end, they do not possess any finality.

For instance, if one says 100, then, you ought to inquire 100 what? Let's assume for an instant, we ask an accountant to show us 5 he/she perhaps hold up 5 fingers. But we did not inquire about showing us fingers. When he/she decides to withdraw the fingers, then the adjective five also vanishes.

Then, another accountant or mathematician writes a 5 when is asked to exhibit 5 but 5 is not a number, it is the symbol that represents a number. The Romans used the symbol V for five, and the roman symbol for 1 through 10 are as follows I, II, III, IV, V, VI, VII, VIII, IX, X.

We shouldn't be deceived by numbers since they only exist as concepts or thoughts in our minds, they truly do not have an independent reality of their own, Numbers must be attached some type of names for them to make sense. One cannot find a number not being attached to something to make sense. But they are concepts which we cannot do without.

Have you ever seen a number line? That is how a math teacher, a mathematician or any math student will describe a number line: In math, a number line can be defined as a straight line with numbers placed at equal intervals or segments along its length. A number line can be extended infinitely in any direction and is usually represented horizontally.

A number line can also be used to represent both positive and negative integers as well, but number lines do not exist in the real world. If one tries to draw a number line one can only draw a line that can go so far, can go a definite length, it will never be infinite. Some mathematicians, physicists or others in affiliated fields relate to space and indicate the line can go on forever, but in actuality, no line will go very far in the real world.

Infinity (symbol: ∞) is a concept describing something without any bound, or something larger than any natural number. In mathematics, infinity is often treated as a number (i.e., it counts or measures things: an infinite number of terms) but it is not the same sort of number as either a natural or a real number.

When used in the context infinitely small, it can also describe an object that is smaller than any number. It is important to know that infinity is not a number; rather, it exists only as an abstract concept. Infinity Symbol Meaning Revealed. Many utilize infinity for symbolizing its modern interpretation of eternity and everlasting love, or the infinite God.

However, occasionally infinity draws from its traditional understanding as the symbol of perfection, duality, and empowerment.

Further, Infinity is an invaluable abstract concept in mathematics, physics, and philosophy. Isaac Newton used the abstraction of infinitely small times and distances to formulate the calculus upon which all modern physics and much of mathematics relies. The question centers on whether

Infinity (∞) is a quantity or an amount. One can enjoy the symbolic infinity as a sign of limitless love, empowerment, and other positive affirmations.

No doubt that mathematics is the heart of many scientific discoveries, especially physics. What one should notice is that as meaningful as numbers are, they are a concept that we cannot do without, as they seem to be the language of God. Italian astronomer and physicist Galileo Galilei said:

Mathematics is the language with which God has written the universe. It is imperative to know that mathematicians do not operate in the real world.

They operate in the realm of concept which they have no physical reality, since numbers do not exist, they are not subject to the boundaries of physics. Numbers are not influenced by factors such as pressure, gravity, statics, hot, cold, humidity, light, dark, snow, rain, wind, heat, and so on.

That is why if an experiment is mathematically compatible and correct, can most probably be relied on to constitute a theory. It also should be noticed that no equation can fully regard every probable physical effect that is involved, the reality is simply too complicated than it looks.

There are many imaginary ideas in mathematician's view of infinity which can only be true in their minds. For instant when a math-oriented individual, a mathematician, an accountant or anyone in related field states that there is an infinite number of numbers or points between any two given points.

This can solely be true in their minds, where a point has no width. In reality, we cannot find a number thin enough, with absolutely no width to fit the infinite points between two designated marks, even as smallest as an atom, since atom also has width. There is just no way that one can fit an infinite number of the point between to marks or two points. yes, multi-millions of the atom, perhaps billions can be placed in a line that is one or two millimeters long, but nothing can ever come close to fitting infinite numbers or points between two indicated marks or points.

It is just not practical in the real world even electrons that smaller than atoms that are as close to having no width as we cannot know how small they are. So we could get possibly an infinite number of electrons into our millimeter line. But be also aware that electrons carry an invisible something called charge. Therefore, put two electrons close together and they will repel each other. I am afraid most people's judgment is in their eyes, they believe what they see, as it is often difficult for so many individuals to grasp abstract concepts.

The imperative point is that most concepts like, God, time, gravity, energy, universe, numbers, consciousness, sub-conscious mind, thoughts, ideas, memories, emotions, feelings, infinity and millions of other things are concepts that are just not tangible, in which without we cannot carry on, where they should be realized, if we are to present a make sense view of our world. As for making sense, do mathematicians not know we live in the rounded world, and no imaginary number line can go to infinity since our planet has no edge and what one imagines is to make sense, because what in our world goes around, comes around, obviously, they imagine otherwise.

Hence, In the real world, there is no infinity. Infinity can never start and never stop. As such, nothing in our real world is infinite. Anything that starts is limited by its beginning and thus cannot be infinite, not excluding how life started. Only something that never initiates can never terminate, as we cannot locate such a thing in the real world of three-dimensional physics. Everything in our world has a beginning, that is why we cannot practically relate to infinity; which with a beginning logic dictates to expect an end, at least in the materially based world.

Let's be clear that infinity can only be a property of higher realms, the spiritual domain with beyond grasp dimensions, an unimaginable concept that can solely be attributed to the almighty God.

37

WHO IS RUNNING THE SHOW IN OUR BODY AND MIND?

What we so far know is that through our senses we learn about the outside world, and become aware of our surroundings. Dynamic interactivities with our environment happen through our nervous system, via our five senses of seeing, hearing, smelling, tasting and touch impacted by the outside world. The information accordingly is taken by our nervous system to the brain, which our brains interpret, assesses and apparently re-arranges them sending them back again via the nervous system and our senses to our limbs, the same senses that delivered messages to our brain in the first place, now telling our limbs what to do.

Further, the outside world couldn't have been the same as what our brain interpreted afterward. The external world should be different and not the same to our brain before the human brain produces a subsequent translation and in making sense of them. what is imprinted in our senses as certain figures, shape, colors, sound, noise, smell, taste and touch are much different to millions of other creatures besides us. So, it seems that what we see, hear, taste, smell, and touch, what we experience in the so-called the real world is not the same as what we comprehend them to be, the external world is not as we know it to be.

Then, for the outside world what we know as matter is nothing but condescend energy, the same energy as our immaterial senses and the nervous system, otherwise, they wouldn't have been conductible, and transparent to our senses. Now, what our senses, our nervous systems including our brain are made of? The dynamics in more details are: The nervous system draws in information through our senses, processes the information and triggers reactions, such as making one's muscles move or causing one to feel pain.

The central nervous system (CNS) includes the nerves in the brain and spinal cord. Central nervous system: a part of the nervous system includes the brain and spinal cord. The parasympathetic nervous system, part of the human nervous system that unconsciously controls our organs and glands when the body is at rest. The brain is the body's main control center. The main function of the Central nervous system is the integration and processing of sensory information; it synthesizes sensory input to compute an appropriate motor response or output. The central nervous system is made up of the brain and spinal cord.

The peripheral nervous system is made up of the nerve fibers that branch off from the spinal cord and extend to all parts of the body, including the neck and arms, torso, legs, skeletal muscles and internal organs. Cerebrum: is the largest part of the brain and is composed of the right and left hemispheres. It manages higher functions like interpreting touch, vision, and hearing, as well as speech, reasoning, emotions, learning, and fine control of movement.

Cerebellum: is located under the cerebrum. The cerebrum, the large, outer part of the brain, controls reading, thinking, learning, speech, emotions and planned muscle movements like walking. It also controls vision, hearing and other senses. The cerebrum is divided into two cerebral hemispheres (halves), the left halves, and the right halves.

How does the nervous system usually communicate with the rest of the body? Peripheral nerves carry information to the central nervous system, which then processes the info and dispatches a message back telling the body how to react. While the function of the dendrites (which dendrites are components of neurons, the nerve cells in the brain, neurons are large, tree-like structures made up of a body, the soma, also known as the cell body with numerous branches called dendrites extending outward) of neurons is to pick up signals and send them to the cell body.

Emotions, like fear and love, are carried out by the limbic system, which is located in the temporal lobe. While the limbic system is made up of multiple parts of the brain, the center of emotional processing is the amygdala, which receives input from other brain functions, like memory and attention.

The nervous system has three main functions: To collect sensory input from the body and the external environment. To process and interpret the sensory input. It controls all parts of the body. It receives and interprets messages from all parts of the body and sends out instructions. The three main components of the central nervous system are the brain, spinal cord, and neurons.

The brain forwards messages by the spinal cord to peripheral nerves throughout the body that serve to control the muscles and internal organs. The somatic nervous system is made up of neurons linking the central nervous system with the parts of the body that communicate with the external world.

The central nervous system deals with the rest of the body by sending messages from the brain through the nerves that branch off of you. Muscles move on commands from the brain. Single nerve cells in the spinal cord, called motor neurons, are the only way the brain links to muscles. When a motor neuron inside the spinal cord fires, an impulse goes out from it to the muscles on a long, very thin extension of that single cell known an axon.

These messages go through specialized cells called neurons. Unlike most other cells, neurons have the competency to interact with other cells and transmit information across relatively long distances. Notice that such intricate transactions for making one aware of its surroundings through one's senses and the central nervous system happens very quickly. On average non-voluntary reflexes (which is actually information going to the central nervous system, being processed, and then going out to the motor neurons) take about 0.3 seconds. However, the average human can blink in about 0.1 seconds, which is probably a better measure.

But for instance, imagine one's sense of touch is lost known as hypoesthesia (also spelled as hypoesthesia) is a common side effect of various medical conditions which manifests as a reduced sense of touch or sensation or a partial loss of sensitivity to sensory stimuli. In an everyday speech, this is commonly indicated as numbness. Is part of the somatosensory system, the sensory system concerned with the conscious perception of touch, pressure, pain, temperature, position, movement, and vibration, which arise from the muscles, joints, skin, and fascial.

if one is to touch an extremely hot stove, one's safety is radically compromised, since the sense of touch is dead to immediately alert one of the killer heat. is applicable to other senses of vision, hearing, smell, and taste resulting in different kind of ills if not properly functioning. without our senses, basically the entire central nervous system can go obsolete because obviously they are awakening factors in linking us to the outside world and the central nervous system, they are as imperative as the spinal cord and our brain.

The point is that our senses and the central nervous system, our brain, work as mediators, or if you like, like a cell phone connecting us to the world outside. The more opening cells in one's brain the better connectivity to our external environment, just like an up to date apple cell phone, or any smartphone made of dynamic components, and with many ABS, and not a regular cell phone without having complex amenities, and exhausted of complicated functions.

Bottom line, consciousness, the mind, is managing our senses, and is running the central processing units (CPU) in our brain, denoting that it is our mind that is linked to the universal energy inclusively functioning as one, and as an inseparable part of what is permeating in all beings, and the entire creation. should make one wonder, who is running the show, if no one can be found inside of any one of us, except for a bunch of bones, muscles and nerves and other necessary affiliated parts.

What about having the outside of the body's experience. Why this conscious which is as real as one's breathing, and much closer than our aorta to us, cannot be located anywhere in our brain or any place in our entire body. Hence, before one should question God's existence, one should try to get to know oneself.

As Rumi said There is a candle in your heart, ready to be kindled. There is a void in your soul, ready to be filled. You feel it, don't you? Before doing so, one should shed bad habits and stay alive to do no evil and to uphold what is righteous. And as Rumi said: "Be like a tree and let the dead leaves drop." And in the road of cultivating your soul no one can help you; it is you that should feel the emergence of God within you.

Dig into your soul which is as deep as an ocean, which Rumi again said "I have been a seeker and I still am, but I stopped asking the books and the stars. I started listening to the teaching of my Soul." And be aware that: the most difficult things to do is to know yourself, before knowing God, so let silence to accompany you in that.

38

WHAT EXACTLY IS INSTINCT BEHAVIOR IF NOT SOFTWARE PROGRAMMING?

Growing up human is uniquely a matter of social relations rather than biology. What we learn from connections within the family take the place of instincts that program the behavior of animals; which raises the question of how good are these connections? Elizabeth Janeway

It is questionable how animals acquire the instincts that enable them with awesome innate behavior. It seems some behaviors are taught to animals by their parents and some traits are instinctual which animals are born with.

For instance, instinctive behavior in human-like Rooting reflex in babies is a primitive reflex that is seen in normal newborn babies, who automatically turn the face toward the stimulus and make sucking (rooting) motions with the mouth when the cheek or lip is touched. The rooting reflex helps to ensure successful breastfeeding. Originally when animals ascended out of the primordial sludge (muck, mud), and as our ancestors began to walk upright, the evolutionary process helped us to survive and reproduce.

If instinct is purpose-oriented and innate formats of action which are not the outcome of either learning or any experience. Then what other alternatives are left except believing in a magnificent designer which has programmed all there is in existence.

For instance, relating to instinct theory of motivation all organism is born with innate biological propensity (inclination, disposition) that assists them to survive. This theory suggests that instincts drive all behaviors,

Instincts are goal-directed and innate which are not the result of education or any experience.

If so, then what prominent psychologists like Sigmund Freud, Abraham Maslow, and other like William James are saying? Who orchestrated theories that supposedly are to resonate with the idea of behaving instinctual ambiguity since they say, quote instinct is a term used to describe a set of behaviors that are both unlearned, not experienced, set in motion as the result of some environmental trigger. Are they not saying that instinctual behaviors are caused by environmental trigger?

Therefore, when animals not excluding humans, mate, enjoy groupings, as social pleasure for humans, and as herding for the beasts, breeding, getting hungry, consume to survive, etc. Are they triggered by their atmosphere to function as such? Or are they natural agendas that we are born with?

Instinctual behaviors are often discussed in relation to motivation since they can also occur in response to an organism's need to satisfy some innate internal drive tied to survival. The question is that if instinctual behaviors are innately-driven, then what does environmental triggering has to do with it? since no experience, learning or triggering of any kind is basically required.

Referencing motivation again, if the initial conducts are innately maneuvered, then no outside force or cause is needed to motivate the animals to perform what they can so adeptly do because of their natural biological capabilities. This is not to say there are no learned behaviors, where environmental factors are sure decisive, but psychologist should make sure to prominent and discern (distinguish) instinctive actions from learned behaviors. What am saying if animals where exhausted of innate behaviors, and were not instinctually programmed, then, no outside forces of any kind could truly precipitate (prompt, provoke) them to do what they so naturally do.

> "Trust the instinct to the end, even though you can give no reason."
>
> — Ralph Waldo Emerson

As for mankind, this is what Charles Darwin believed:

"The following proposition seems to me in a high degree probable—namely, that any animal whatever, endowed with well-marked social instincts, the parental and filial (particular blood relationship, avuncular, fraternal, maternal, paternal) affections being here included, would inevitably acquire a moral sense or conscience, as soon as its intellectual powers had become as well, or nearly as well developed, as in man. For, firstly, the social instincts lead an animal to take pleasure in the society of its fellows, to feel a certain amount of sympathy with them, and to perform various services for them."

— Charles Darwin, *The Descent of Man*

As for the human mind and man's psychological behaviors, there are some truth to Freud's role of mind that Freud redundantly disclosed, since he believed that the mind is responsible for both conscious and unconscious decisions related to drives and mental forces. The id, ego, and superego are three impressions of the mind in which Freud mentioned to make up a person's personality. Sigmund Freud emphasized the imperative of the unconscious mind, as the primary assumption of the Freudian theory, is that the unconscious mind rules behavior to a greater degree than people realize.

The focus of psychoanalysis is to make the unconscious conscious. The id is an important part of our personality because as newborns, it let us get our basic needs met. Freud believed that the id is based on our pleasure principle. In other words, the id inquires whatever feels good at the time, with no consideration for the reality of the situation.

Freud believed that events in our childhood have a great influence on our adult lives, forming our personality. Freud believed dreams represented a disguised realization of a repressed wish. He believed that investigating dreams indicated the simplest road to comprehending the unconscious activities of the mind.

According to the concept that Freud suggested, the dream is regarded as the guardian of sleep. According to Sigmund Freud, human personality is complicated and has more than a single component. In his famous psychoanalytic theory of personality, personality is composed of three elements. These three elements of personality—shown as the id, the ego, and the superego—work in concert to make complex human behaviors.

Further, the Freudian theory also segmented human personality into three major components: the id, ego, and superego. The id is the most primary part of the personality that is the source of all our most basic urges. Then, the superego comprises of two systems: The conscience and the ideal self. The conscience can punish the ego by causing feelings of guilt. For example, if the ego gives in to the id's demands, the superego may make the person feel bad through guilt.

Relating to Freud's psychoanalytic theory of personality, the id is the personality component made up of unconscious psychic energy that works to satisfy basic urges, needs, and desires. The id operates based on the pleasure principle, which demands immediate gratification of needs. In order to understand the role of the ego in one's life, one must first detect its purpose. The ego is the human consciousness part of you. It was designed to ensure one's security.

According to Freud, the unconscious continues to influence our behavior and experiences, even though we are unaware of these underlying influences. The unconscious can include repressed feelings, hidden memories, habits, thoughts, desires, and reactions. According to Freud, psychological development occurs during five psychosexual phases through a person's life: oral, anal, phallic, latency, and genital.

Latency Period: The period of lessened sexuality that Freud argued occurred between approximately age seven and adolescence. Freud believed that children went through a latency period during which we can notice a halt and retrogression in sexual development Latency is the fourth stage in Freud's Psychosexual theory of development, and it happens from about age 5 or 6 to puberty.

During the latency stage, a child's sexual impulses are suppressed. Freud believed that the nature of the conflicts among the id, ego, and superego change over time as a person grows from child to adult. Specifically, he stated that these conflicts develop via a series of five preliminary stages, each with a different focus: oral, anal, phallic, latency, and genital. Freud's structural model posits that personality consists of three interworking parts: the id, the ego, and the superego. The five stages of Freud's psychosexual theory of development include the oral, anal, phallic, latency, and genital stages.

During these stages, a person's id, ego, and superego develop, and each stage is dependent upon the fixation of the libido. Freud developed the psychoanalytic theory of personality development, which argued that personality is formed through conflicts among three fundamental structures of the human mind: the id, ego, and superego. According to Freud's psychoanalytic theory of personality, the superego is the component of personality composed of the internalized ideals that we have acquired from our parents and society. The superego works to suppress the urges of the id and tries to make the ego behave morally, rather than realistically.

In Freudian psychoanalysis, the pleasure principle is the instinctive seeking pleasure and avoiding pain in order to satisfy biological and psychological needs. Specifically, the pleasure principle is the driving force guiding the id. Sigmund Freud (May 6, 1856, to Sept. 23, 1939) founded psychoanalysis, a treatment technique that involves the patient talking to a psychoanalyst.

Even though Freud's ideas were disputes, he was one of the most influential scientists in the fields of psychology and psychiatry. Consistent with the psychoanalytic perspective, Sigmund Freud's theory of dreams suggested that dreams represented unconscious desires, thoughts, and motivations. According to Freud's psychoanalytic view of personality, people are-driven by aggressive and sexual instincts that are repressed from conscious awareness. Sigmund Freud's work and theories helped shape our views of childhood, personality, memory, sexuality, and therapy.

Meanwhile, the most reliable answer is that we do not yet understand the functions of dreaming, this shortcoming should not be surprising because despite many theories we still do not fully understand the purpose of sleep, nor can we gather the functions of REM (rapid eye movement) sleep, which is when most dreaming occurs. According to Freud's psychoanalytic theory of personality, the superego is the component of personality composed of the internalized ideals that we have acquired from our parents and society.

The superego works to suppress the urges of the id and tries to make the ego behave morally, rather than reality in which I am sure the environmental impact has a lot to do with triggering such human behavior like our dreams, and the functioning of id, ego and the super-ego. As far as for human instinctual behavior, we sure are programmed to eat when hungry, sleep and rest when tired, breath to stay alive, live in groups, defend ourselves, have the urge for having intercourse, and dream.

As for newborns, fetuses spend most of their time sleeping. At 32 weeks, your baby sleeps 90 to 95 percent of the day. During REM sleep, his eyes move back and forth just like an adult's eyes. Some scientists even believe that fetuses dream while they're sleeping. Further, a reflex action, also familiar as a reflex, is an involuntary and instantaneous movement in response to a stimulus. When a person accidentally touches a hot object, they automatically jerk their hand away without thinking.

A reflex does not require any thought input. Decided that it was not wisdom that enabled poets to write their poetry, but a kind of instinct or inspiration, such as you find in seers and prophets who deliver all their sublime messages without knowing in the least what they mean. Socrates

Instincts are innate complex patterns of behavior that exist in most members of the species, reflexes, which are simple responses of an organism to a specific stimulus, often triggered such as the contraction of the pupil in response to bright light or the spasmodic movement of the lower leg. Extensor spasticity is an involuntary straightening of the legs, which may also occur in the arms.

Instinct, or innate behavior, is an action that is impulsive or immediate based on a particular trigger or circumstance. Many scientists believe that most human behaviors are a result of some level of both instincts and learned behavior. other Reflexes normally solely observed in human infants are:

Asymmetrical tonic neck reflex (ATNR)

Palm omental reflex. The palm-omental reflex is a primitive reflex consisting of a twitch of the chin muscle elicited by stroking a specific part of the palm. It is present in infancy and disappears as the brain matures during childhood but may reappear due to processes that disrupt the normal cortical inhibitory pathways.

Moro reflex, also known as the startle reflex. The **Moro reflex** is an infantile **reflex** normally present in all infants/newborns up to 3 or 4 months of age as **a response** to **a** sudden loss of support, when the infant feels as if it is falling. It involves three distinct components: spreading out the arms (abduction), pulling the arms in (adduction), also meaning the movement of a limb or other part toward the midline of the body or toward another part.

Newborn **reflexes**. Newborn babies can become startled by a harsh noise, a jerky movement, or feels like they're falling, they might respond in a specific way. They might unexpectedly extend their arms and legs, arch their back, and then curl everything in again. This is an involuntary **startle** response called the **Moro reflex**.

Palmar grasp reflex. Palmar grasp reflex (sometimes simply grasp reflex) is a primitive reflex found in infants of humans and most primates. When an object is placed in an infant's hand and the palm of the child is stroked, the fingers will close reflexively, as the object is grasped via palmar grasp.

Rooting reflex. **Rooting reflex**: A **reflex** that is seen in normal newborn babies, who automatically turn the face toward the stimulus and make sucking (**rooting**) motions with the mouth when the cheek or lip is touched. The **rooting reflex** helps to ensure successful breastfeeding

Sucking reflex. The **sucking reflex** is probably one of the most important **reflexes** your newborn has. It is paired with the rooting **reflex**, in which a newborn searches for a food source. When he finds it, the **sucking reflex** allows him to **suck** and swallow the milk.

Symmetrical tonic neck reflex (STNR) is a primitive reflex found in newborn humans.

Tonic labyrinthine reflex (TLR) The tonic labyrinthine reflex (TLR) is a primitive reflex found in newborn humans.

Call these involuntary behaviors what you want, either instinctual or reflexes, the point is that they are not done by choice. Therefore, when psychologist Abraham Maslow argued that quote humans no longer have instincts because we have the ability to override them in certain situations.

He might have felt that what is called instinct is often imprecisely defined, and really amounts to strong drives. Otherwise, it is hard to gather what Mr. Maslow is actually talking about? As if, we can override breathing, as if, we do not have the natural instinct to protect ourselves, even when not triggered by the environment, or as if humanity can override propagation (procreation), or as if we can forego sleeping and rest, and so on.

All animals, including humans, are potentiated with innate instincts, as innate programming is the primary cause for their automatic actions; where the particular situation or certain environment can perhaps play as a catalyst for activating them, as their atmosphere cannot be the actual cause, or the primary reason for their instinctual mechanism, this naturally innate instinct are already endowed to them long before birth.

> "A young child can sense danger even if you repeatedly say, "I love you". There are those who can console a baby with their first touch and there are those who can make a baby scream, no matter what they try. Our basic animal instincts are suppressed by the subliminal messages fed to us by society. This leads to some surprising truths, such as this one: If the first kiss doesn't convince you, then nothing ever will"

> — Reham Khan

The mechanism of sexual intercourse, the interaction between the male and female reproductive systems results in fertilization of the woman's ovum by the man's sperm. These are specialized reproductive cells called gametes, created in a process called meiosis which can occur without any learning, they are often triggered by the opposite sex that is instinctual. When organisms that reproduce through asexual (without having sex) reproduction tend to grow in number exponentially. Thus, because they depend on mutation for variations in their DNA, all members of the species have similar vulnerabilities.

The beasts, for instance, the ambient behavior of ducklings, turtles, frogs, toads, seals and hundreds if not thousands of other animals, they are programmed since they are innately designed before even being born, like being able to live in water and dry land, where the Innate behavior comes from an animal's heredity.

An animal's instincts are examples of its innate behavior. For example, migrating birds use innate behavior to know when to incept their migration and the route they should take. Learned behavior arrives from watching other animals and from life experiences. Some birds even predict where they should be heading, flying for thousands of miles to reach climates contingent to their survival.

Birds can foresee the climate. Most birds have what's called the Vitali Organ, an exclusive middle-ear receptor that can sense an extremely small shift in atmospheric pressure. when you observe that birds are flying high up in the sky, the weather is most likely clear. An if birds fly low in the sky, you can be sure of that, a weather system is approaching. since bad weather is linked to low pressure.

Birds on a telephone wire predict the coming of rain. When the birds flew off, the storm was still hundreds of miles away, so there would have been few anticipated changes in atmospheric pressure, temperature and wind speed. Scientists think that this sixth sense that birds possess has to do with their power to hear sounds that humans cannot.

Furthermore, Rats, weasels, snakes, and centipedes reportedly left their abode and ran for safety several days before a destructive earthquake could occur. Also fish, birds, reptiles, and insects performing strange behavior weeks, days to seconds before an earthquake.

Certain behaviors, called instincts, are automatic, and they occur without the animal even noticing them. Instincts are inherited from parent organisms. Each year birds such as Canadian geese fly south for the winter. These animals know to migrate and hibernate because their instincts tell them.

Birds Learn to fly with not much help from their ancestors. It is true that birds learn to fly through practice, gradually refining their innate competency into a finely tuned skill. Thus, according to a psychologist, these skills may be easy to refine because of a genetically specified quiescent (dormant, shelved, temporary inactive, latent) memory for flying.

In addition to utilizing the Earth's magnetic field to orient themselves, some birds take advantage of the Sun and the stars to find their way. Whooping cranes, for instance, learn migration routes from older birds. When birds are migrating, they always know exactly where they are going, unlike us, when we're driving, we need a Sat-Nav, GPS, their sense of direction is dependent on a combination of three 'maps' of their own. Birds have a substance called magnetite, which is located just above their beaks.

Also, camouflaging is a physical adaptation in which the animal's body is colored or shaped in such a way that enables the animal to blend in with its surroundings. Like camouflage, mimicry discourages predators and improves the animal's rate of survival. Instinct is a behavior pattern that an animal naturally follows. Prey animals often use camouflage to hide from predators.

Camouflage is a way of hiding that allows an animal to blend in with its environment or otherwise go unnoticed by predators. Predators also sometimes use camouflage so as not to be detected by their prey. Have you not seen a bobcat, a cheetah, lion or a tiger in action, they act so cunningly when in hunting mode, as if they have earned a post-doctorate degree specialized in camouflaging trying to corner, and kill their prey from Stanford, or Berkley University?

There are four basic ways animals camouflage themselves. Most butterflies and moth protect themselves from predators by using camouflage. Some butterflies and moths blend into their environment so well that is it almost impossible to spot them when they are resting on a branch. Some butterflies are poisonous.

There are four basic types of camouflage:

Concealing Coloration. Concealing coloration is when an animal hides against a background of the same color.

Disruptive (uncontrollable) Coloration.

Disguise.

Mimicry.

Innate behaviors do not have to be learned or practiced. They are also called instinctive behaviors. Instinct is the ability of an animal to perform a behavior the first time it is exposed to the proper stimulus. For instance, a dog will drool any time it is exposed to food. Based on what one means by instinct, there is the breathing instinct, belief instinct, instinctive fear of snakes, among many others. Survival is our prime instinct which we will resume accordingly.

Like all animals, humans have instincts, genetically hard-wired behaviors that enhance our ability to cope with vital environmental contingencies. Our innate fear of snakes is an example. Other instincts, including denial, revenge, tribal loyalty, greed and our urge to procreate, now threaten our very existence. Hibernation is an innate behavior that is not learned after birth.

Animals that hibernate are born with an internal sense, or instinct, that tells them when they need to hibernate. During hibernation, an animal's body temperature drops, they take fewer breaths for a minute, and they do not need to eat. Some of the animals that hibernate include Hedgehogs, bats, snails, box turtle, garter snakes, bears, and so on.

The survival of 'the fittest of animal behavior and the awesome mechanism of how they are instinctually tuned to hunt. Like eagles, whales, cheetahs, lions, tigers, lizards, etc. and the speed in which they maneuver. Birds have something of an advantage when it comes to speed, for obvious reasons.

The peregrine falcon is particularly swift, capable of reaching speeds of up to 200 mph while at a dive, making it a fearsome hunter. The rest of the time it does not fly this fast, but that hardly matters to its prey. It is the fastest animal on the planet when in a dive. The eagle's eyes are very sharp and can see fish when the bird flies over the water. The eagle can look directly into the sun. As a test of the worthiness of its young, the eagle holds them up facing the sun.

In humans, the contemporary human brain (frontal cortex) is accountable for resolving problem, thoughts, memory, language, impulse control, judgment, and reasoning power. The primal brain (hindbrain and medulla) is responsible for survival instinctual mode, drive, and other instincts. When the primal brain is engaged (sympathetic response), one's modern brain is not active much. Learned behaviors, although they may have innate feature or foundations (motive, underpinning, cornerstone), they permit an individual organism to adapt to changes in the environment.

Learned behaviors are modified by previous experiences; examples of simple learned behaviors include habituation and imprinting (in psychology, imprinting is defined as a remarkable phenomenon that occurs in animals, and in humans, in the first hours of life. In humans, this is often called bonding, and it usually refers to the relationship between the newborn and its parents). Innate behavior comes from an animal's heredity. An animal's instincts are examples of its innate behavior.

For instance, migrating birds deploy innate actions to determine when to initiate their migration and the route that they should follow. Learned behavior comes from watching other animals and from life experiences. Behavior is decided by a combination of inherited traits, experience, and the environment. Some behavior, called innate, comes from your genes, but other behavior is learned, either from interacting with the world or by being taught. Examples of behaviors that do not require conscious will include many reflexes.

Examples of instinctive behaviors in humans include many of the primitive reflexes, such as rooting and suckling, behaviors which are present in mammals. further, there is not much that we know on how and why we laugh, except it bonds us via humor and interplay. It is a hidden language that we all speak, as it is not a learned collective or group reaction but instinctive conduct programmed through our genes.

Infant swimming or diving reflex. Most human babies exhibit an innate swimming or diving reflex from birth until the age of roughly six months, but babies this young cannot swim, due to their barrier of body features and strength. Survival instinct is present in all creatures with not excluding humans. Beasts such as dear, Gazelle, small mammals, and lizards often rely on their speed and quickness to escape predators, and many birds rely on the flight as their primary defensive strategy.

Some organisms, like a tortoise, armadillos, porcupines, and thorny plants, utilize armor, quills (any of the main wing or tail feathers of a bird.) and thorns to defend themselves against predators. In communal defense, prey groups actively defend themselves by grouping together, and sometimes by attacking or mobbing a predator, rather than allowing themselves to be passive victims of predation. Mobbing (to crowd around excitingly, to the multitude, to mass, to hoard) is the harassing of a predator by many prey animals. Other defensive mechanisms for some animals include:

live in groups (herds or shoals)

built for speed.

defenses such as poison or stings.

camouflage to avoid being seen by predators.

eyes to the side of the head to get a wide field of view (monocular vision).

39

HOW DO ANIMALS AVOID PREDATION?

Most animals face predation pressure and must avoid or defend themselves against predators for survival to successfully reproduce. Beside physical traits such as armor and camouflage, animals use behavior to avoid and survive predation; Prey detection is the process by which predators are able to detect and locate their prey via sensory signals.

Predators are an imperative part of a healthy ecosystem. Predators cull (select, choose) vulnerable prey, such as the old, injured, sick, or very young, leaving more food for the survival and prosperity of healthy prey animals, also, by controlling the size of prey populations, predators assist with lessening the spread of disease. Animals are far more intelligent than we ever recognized; the one thing that we've been educated within our research from the past is that so many species have much more going on inside their brains than we previously thought.

We know now that animals can solve puzzles, learn words, and interact with each other in complex ways. Crows can solve puzzles as well as five-year-olds. These remarkable birds are capable of constructing tools, using them and saving them for future use. Their cognitive abilities include problem-solving, reasoning and even self-awareness. Despite their relatively small brain, they have a good memory. They can remember other members of their own species and even recognize humans when they pose a threat.

A series of recent experiments exhibited crow's magnificent ability in troubleshooting and problem-solving with highly skill maneuverability. In one study conducted at the University of Auckland, researchers realized that when tubes of water that contained a floating treat were made ready, crows figured out that dropping other objects into the tubes would cause the water level to rise, making the treatment accessible. They also figured out that they could get the treats much fastest if they selected tubes with higher water levels to start, and if they dropped objects that sank, rather than ones that floated.

Other research, meanwhile, has shown that crows can intentionally bend a piece of wire in order to fish a treat out of a narrow tube. On the whole, researchers put their problem-solving skills roughly comparable with those of 5 to 7-year-old children. Researchers further experienced that cockatoos, like crows, can solve not so easy puzzles in order to get treats. In a research done in 2013 study, they required the birds to open a box (which contained cashew) by removing a pin, unscrewing a screw, pulling out a bolt, circling a wheel, and finally sliding out a latch.

Obviously, this takes a long time for an animal that doesn't have opposable thumbs. It took one cockatoo a full two hours, eventually solving the puzzle exposing that the birds are competent in striving towards goals that are much more distant than the researchers had previously believed. Other birds in the experiment, meanwhile, learned from the first bird and completed the whole puzzle much more quickly. when the puzzle was altered so that the five steps had to be completed in a different order, the birds seemed to detect this and responded accordingly instead of trying to replicate the previous solution.

Chimpanzees.

These are mankind's closest relatives. Chimpanzees are sociable animals and form elaborate communities. They are skilled at using different types of tools to carry out complex tasks, such as thin sticks to extract termites and rocks to open fruits. Combined with a powerful memory, these abilities make the chimpanzee the most intelligent (non-human) animal on Earth.

Dolphins are outstandingly smart in all sorts of ways. when captured, they can be quickly trained to complete tasks in exchange for treats and are known to mimic human actions just for the fun of it. In the wild, they've been seen to cover their snouts with sponges for protecting themselves against spiny fish while hunting and terminating spiny fish so they can use their spines to extract eels from crack (fissure, cleft, cranny, slot, fracture, crevices).

A dolphin's whistle seems to be similar to its name. It is interesting to know that each dolphin seems to own a characteristic whistle that represents itself, a dolphin's whistle sounds much like its name. Experiments show that dolphins swim towards the speaker emitting whistle of a family member much more often than an unfamiliar dolphin's, and when a mother dolphin is apart from her calf, she'll vent the calves' whistle until they're reunited.

Researchers also found that dolphins act differently upon hearing the whistle of a dolphin they'd last seen 20 years earlier, in comparison to a stranger's—they're much more tuned to approach the speaker and whistle at it redundantly, trying to make it respond back to whistle.

Dolphins are extremely sociable creatures with a highly developed ability to adapt to their habitat. They help one another when injured or ill and, thanks to their individually distinct calls, they're able to pass on their knowledge to others. In fact, the list of high-level cognitive abilities—including identification, differentiation, and behavioral control.

Elephants can cooperate and show empathy. Field researchers have realized that elephants cooperate in complex ways. Elephants have the largest brain of all land animals. Elephants notoriety is for their sociability and can express emotions, including happiness and compassion, as well as pain and grief. They show acts of altruism and self-awareness. With a greater memory than even us humans, an elephant truly never forgets!

Many families of related elephants travel together in clans, interact via low-frequency rumbles (finding out, come upon.) At times, they'll form circles around calves to protect them from predators, or carry out coordinated kidnappings of calves from competing clans (extended family, tribe) in the performance of dominance. Levels of coordination have been shown in controlled experiments, where pairs of elephants quickly learned to instantaneously pull on a rope to get a treat, and not to pull alone, as they would have risked ruining the chance of getting it.

Other studies, the researchers found out that elephants seem to show genuine empathy.

Contrary to many beasts that exhibit little interest in dead members of their species, typically, they either briefly sniff them before walking away or eating them. Elephants, however, show a special interest in elephant remains, lingering near them and in some cases becoming agitated as one can notice an ill-effect on their peace of mind. Field researchers have also noticed that elephants consoling, comforting each other—something seldom seen in other species. Typically, when an elephant becomes perturbed, it'll make squeaking noises and perk its ears up. often, other elephants from the same clan will come and stroke its head with their trunks, or put their trunk in its mouth.

It is a difficult task to study octopuses since they're aquatic, also a bit hard to keep them alive in captivity, and also because octopuses relatively live deep in the ocean. The imperative point to realize is that octopuses maneuver in an environment very different than ours, so basically their intelligence is directed at solving divergent (disparate, not the same) oriented goals. By far the world's smartest invertebrates, octopuses can manage intricate tasks, like opening a jar to get to its contents. They possess a good short- and long-term memory but also an outstanding ability to learn new skills from the moment they're born.

For instance, the mimic octopus (Thaumoctopus mimicus) can impersonate other species in order to save itself from predators.

Many scientists believe that they're smart in ways that are qualitatively different from us and the other species. They have the largest brains of any invertebrate, they also have more neurons than humans, sixty percent of these cells are in their arms, not their brains. Thus, their arms look like being individually intelligent: when the arms are cut off, they can crawl away, grab food items, and raise them up to where the octopus' mouth would be as if they were still linked.

Meanwhile, octopuses seem to have a keen sense of aesthetics, even though they're likely colorblind. Field researchers have observed octopuses gather Intelligence which is one of the prominent features of being human and it comes in various forms.

For example, there's verbal-linguistic intelligence (communicative ability), interactive ability. spatial intelligence (the competency to observe the world with the mind's eye), logical-mathematical intelligence (the power to solve mathematical problems) and potentiated with emotional intelligence (the ability to identify and manage your own emotions and the emotions of others), investigative ability. There are also other types of intelligence which, in the process of comprehending the workings of the human mind, we have tried to disentangle and define.

However, when we talk of animal intelligence, we talk in quite different terms. The study of animal intelligence has a long history. We can describe animal intelligence as the combination of skills and abilities that permit animals to live and adapt to their particular environments. Animals possess the ability to adapt to their surroundings by learning to change their habits and behaviors. Many species are also capable of forming social groups. All of these characteristics are based on the animal's capacity to process information and, by assessing this capacity.

Parrots

These birds have an incredible ability to know different human faces and have a high aptitude for communication, as can be seen by their aptitude (prowess, knack) for impersonating human voices. Parrots also possess an incredible memory, which assists them to solve complicated problems.

Rats

Rats dream in a similar way to that of humans. Thanks to their ability to process different sensorial cues, they can analyze situations and make their way out of mazes (confusing, labyrinth, puzzling) system. Interestingly, they have been found to display high levels of empathy, making sacrifices for other members of their species. Rats can even make calculations in order to obtain food from a trap without being caught.

Many animals depend on such a clock to maintain their circadian rhythm (If you've ever noticed that you tend to feel energized and drowsy around the same times every day, you have your circadian rhythm to thank). What is it, exactly? Your circadian rhythm is basically a 24-hour internal clock that is running in the background of your brain and cycles between sleepiness and alertness at regular intervals. It's also known as your sleep/wake cycle.

Animals that use sun compass orientation are fish, birds, sea turtles, butterflies, bees, sand hoppers, reptiles, and ants. While they usually use it together with other navigational methods, animals also use the Earth's magnetic field as their compass. While they use the sun and the stars to navigate, birds also use the Earth's magnetic field.

Loggerhead turtles can even sense the direction and strength of Earth's magnetic field soon after hatching, and later use this skill to navigate along their regular migration route. Other animals use land features such as mountain ranges and rivers, and dolphins use the shape of the ocean floor. The sun compass plays a role in homing pigeons which have the ability to return home after a great distance and may be used by birds that migrate during the day. Many songbird species, however, migrate at night. For many years' scientist suspected that birds take advantage of the stars for navigation.

Magneto-reception: The homing pigeon can return to its home because of its ability to sense the Earth's magnetic field and other cues to orient itself. Magneto-reception plays a part in guiding Loggerhead hatchlings to the sea. Some animals sleep for a long time in the winter, but they do not go into true hibernation. Their heart and breathing slow down, but often their body temperature does not drop as Bio-magnetism. Bio-magnetism is the phenomenon of magnetic fields generated by living organisms; it is a subset of bio-electromagnetism.

In comparison organisms' use of magnetism in navigation is magneto-reception, a sense which allows an organism to detect a magnetic field to perceive direction, altitude or location. This sensory modality is used by a range of animals for orientation and navigation, and as a method for animals to develop regional maps. the study of the magnetic fields' effects on organisms is magneto-biology.

Stimulus *modality* in humans also called *sensory modality*, is one aspect of a stimulus or what is perceived after a stimulus. For example, the temperature *modality* is registered after heat or cold stimulate a receptor. Some *sensory modalities* include light, sound, temperature, taste, pressure, and smell.

A **sensory modality is related to** sensing, like vision or hearing. **Modality** in someone's voice indicates a sense of the person's mood. In logic, **modality** has to **do** with whether a proposition is needed, possible, or impossible. In general, a **modality is a** particular way in which something exists.

Scientists who study whales believe the animals utilize a combination of senses to find their path, in a way that helps them observe the ocean floor, spot landmarks along the way and navigate in the proper direction. Enthusiasts have known for decades that whales use noises to communicate. When in search of food they circle around making a huge pond where they collectively make a horrifyingly loud noise which scares thousands of little fish as they pop up to the surface dead, and then are consumed by wales.

The point is that one shouldn't ignore the evolutionary impact of these marvelously disciplinary actions which ought to put any curiously inquisitive mind at awe. But why? Why should evolution, or any other force for that matter play such an active role in these incredibly complex procedures? One can use any lexicon which one desires, such as instinct, instinctual, or any other word to describe this magnificently awakened animal's maneuverability. But without considering a disciplinary awakened force, a magnificent designer implementing such intricate tactics and strategy in the animal kingdom, programming them for their survival must not make any sense.

Biology is the study of complex things that appear to have designed for a purpose. Richard Dawkins

Nothingness

We ponder on this controversial issue about if things are created from something, or perhaps are made out of nothing. But then, the proper question should be addressed as: Is nothingness impregnated with an infinite number of things or not? if not, then, quintillions of scientific discoveries which scientists and scholars have divulged and employed should mean fiction and no more. It should be harboring that our inventions have stemmed from nothingness and transmitted into actuality from the unknown; in which we either have already concocted or hope to excogitate in the future. if yes, then we should tirelessly dig into nothingness to further get closer to the truth.

We are conducive to perceive and define nothingness according to available human resources and competency. The term nothingness can be alarmingly deceptive since what we know as nothing, is actually everything; but since nothingness is incomprehensible to us at certain times, not realizing when and where, or by whom, nothing is going to give birth to our next scientific breakthroughs. Then we are deluded into believing nothingness as literally meaning being immaterial and barren to us which is based on our limited senses.

The consensus should be in accepting nothingness as the holy grail of creativity and where the real potential lay for things we persist on to decode and eventually conquer. if not, then, we have acted shortsighted in all of which we have discovered and hope to invent. We are faced with no choice but to delve into the reality of nothing and realize there is no such thing as void. Hence, it would make sense to switch and replace the word nothingness for the word unknown.

To say life came out of nothing is honestly an insult to reason since literally should mean God is in charge of the womb of what we know and grant as emptiness which in contrary is filled with propitious prospects. That gave birth to all there is and all of which there will ever be. Through the eyes of quantum physic which represent the world of unseen, renowned physicists like Niels-Bohr, and many of his colleagues accept and say quote: atomic uncertainty is truly intrinsic to nature: the rules of clock might apply to familiar objects such as snooker balls, but when it comes to atoms and quarks, and other subatomic particles, the rules are those of roulette. Many scientists believe these subatomic particles are being thrown around by an unseen ocean of microscopic forces.

It is therefore apparent that we must refuge to bounds of our senses to acquaint and to comply with the world outside of us, since as humans we cannot reconnaissance with what is beyond our ability and knowledge to decipher. should not mean that there is no magic in the air, or perhaps we need to quit searching for miracles, since the history of evolution should validate the human mind that progresses into dynamic stages of enlightenment where boundaries are magically torn and miracle like discoveries become the norm.

It seems beautiful minds are impacted with premonition and are mandated with a mission to seek and to perform gynecology into the womb of mother nature to give birth to yet another treasure, leaping into unveiling the mysteries of nature's obscurities to emancipate man from the clutches of ignorance.

Our curiosity into the realms of speculation and probabilities is fostered and potentially backed up by hidden agenda conveyed into the unknown ready to be exploited and burst into reality. of course it is inclined to action by passion, human drive, time consumed, and keen enough to feel and detect the maturity and the magnificent moment of delivery. That is encouraged with hope, perseverance, and bearing hardship through many trials and errors; and then occasionally bull-eyed into steppingstones for other miracles like disclosures. sometimes a huge leap into successful challenges where our struggle in bettering human life pays off generously.

MENTAL METAMORPHISM

In the name of the omnipotent, omnipresent, omnipotent, omni temporal, omnibenevolent, and the omniscient God. The most merciful, the most gracious, and the most compassionate. The proprietor of patience, time, space, and beyond. The Fiduciary, Custodian, the Adjudicator to all there is and the nonexistence. In the name of the almighty God.

Mental metamorphism conveys philosophy, science, ideology, spirituality, biology, history, culturalism, economics, and social and psychological endeavors through which the inquisitive minds can discern facts from fiction. Historically, keywords like what, where, when, why, and how are often the quintessence (extract) of arriving at the principal reason for many imperative subject matters of human concern. One can grasp the core cause and effect of events or phenomena where mental metamorphism can occur via sincere adjudication (umpiring, judging) to embody the true meaning of living for serving one's objective, since inspiring topics as such require humble attributes and devotion.

Diggar diseeye fekery (Mental Metamorphism) is my school of thought where I have collectively substantiated the vast vicinities of decisive matters so that the essence of vital subjects is sought, gradually disclosing the traces of God to viewers' attention through make-sense dialogue and explicit communication since man, the universe, the cosmos, are the byproducts of the almighty, awesome design. God willing, it might help me to learn more and perhaps I also could contribute to this sacred task of mutual knowledge and understanding. This sure reminds me of Rumi's quote: "Stop acting so small, you are the universe in ecstatic [euphoric, elated, thrilled, joyful] motion." Despite the advice of many sages, enlightening prophets, insightful advisers and philosophers, where does humanity really stand?

To answer that, imagine the globe without any law enforcement, exhausted of mandatory policing; then, honestly think to decipher if those so-called civil societies can still prevail to conserve the status quo where a relatively peaceful environment can be attained. Hence, to arrive at the sacred stages of moral conduct where decency of mind and manner can prevail, humongous steps should be taken to preserve mental metamorphism (a change in physical form or substance).

Immanuel Kant, the founder of critical philosophy, puts it this way in the categorical imperatives, a moral law that is unconditional or absolute for all agents, the validity or claim of which does not depend on any ulterior (hidden) motive or end. "Act as if the maxim [saying, motto] of your action were to become through your will a universal law of nature."

It is only through acting in the image of God that no tramping, no dictatorial regimes or fascist entity should exist to straighten anyone by force and through aggression when one has managed to consciously behave awakened where no policing is necessary. We are most definitely potentiated with such power; the power of waking morally and spiritually up. With that said, the key is to cognize the reality of the exceptionally mosaic (complex) universe that we live in. To apprehend (perceive) the authenticity of the world we live in, we ought to grasp the reason for cause and effect, which most definitely ensues for a reason, a reason baffling enough that it has caused some people to behave as if they are hallucinating, since it seems they are so disengaged with the miracle-like universe that should awaken any studious (attentive) mind.

It is a no-brainer that the law of attraction between cause and effect happens because of infinitely empowered original sources in which such uncompromisingly dynamism that is extremely disciplined renders stability to all scientific findings, since no reliable experience could have ever occurred without God's magnificent planning where no chaotic environment can ever lead to such an awesome, orderly cosmos.

The natural events that force the law of cause and effect are precisely controlled by an Absolute Power. They are not driven innately from any matter, and couldn't have been experimental if not designed to behave the way they do. This should remind us of the complexity of the universe, indicating, for example, the quantum world is not engaged with the theory of cause and effect as they function in the visible world. Quantum mechanics holds nonlocal causality. Quantum mechanics challenges our commonsense picture of causality by implying that some things happen at random, with no apparent cause, or that an action in one place can seem to have an effect elsewhere, even if the two locations cannot interact. This has become a serious dilemma for the scientific community, showing God works in strange ways, so much so that it seems Professor Max Planck, Werner Heisenberg, and other very prominent physicists are saying what the idealist philosopher George Berkeley prophetically argued centuries ago, saying that the physical objects do not exist independently of the mind that perceives them. An item truly exists only as long as it is observed; otherwise, it is not only meaningless, but simply nonexistent. The observer and the observed are one. "Do you really believe the moon exists only when you look at it?" Albert Einstein famously asked. (Einstein, born in Germany, played an important role in developing quantum theory.)

Perhaps he was referencing how **wave-particle duality can help,** since a subatomic particle can exhibit properties of a wave and a particle. But at any one time it will only show attributes of being either a wave or a particle. **Wavicle** is a term invented in 1928 by the British physicist Arthur Stanley Eddington to convey the duality of light and radiation as being both waves and particles, although they never appear to be both at the same time. It has to do with particles in the quantum world having the weird capacity to exist in all possible states (or positions) at once, called **superposition** (in quantum physics), the ability of some minute subatomic-scale particle to be in more than one place at the same time. Therefore, referencing matter as the cause for all that exists can only prove one's utter shortsightedness in this rather extremely complex universe, which hold criterion beyond anyone's imagination.

In Mulla Sadra's view, one cannot have access to the reality of being, since only linguistic analysis is available. Comparatively, that is what Werner Heisenberg noted: "What we observe is not nature itself but nature exposed to our method of questioning. Our scientific work in physic consists of asking a question about nature in the language that we possess and trying to get an answer from an experiment by the means that are at our disposal." This is perplexing enough to remind one of what Socrates said centuries ago, reaffirmed as well by Plato.

"The only thing I know is that I know nothing." Socrates

"That man is wisest who, like Socrates, realizes that his wisdom is worthless." Plato.

But why such an analogy? Perhaps Anaxagoras has better understood the sap, or the nature, of such a claim by saying, "In everything, there is a share of everything." If so, I say it will be of no possibility to exponentially fathom the infinitely driven share of everything in everything else, since consequentially every entity conveys the share of every other entity, escalating to countless events where perhaps only collective understanding can divulge bit by bit and make sense of the world, which no man should single-mindedly claim knowing it all.

Frankly, despite the hassle and bustle of very busy life, billions are consciously and sublimely captivated with questions like, is mind or matter the source of life? Where did we come from? Why are we here? Where are we going? What is the purpose of life, if any? What is my goal in life? Do we face punishment or reward after we die? And if yes, how is it done? What are the dynamics of such reprisal (retribution, wrath, revenge) or clemency (leniency, grace)? Is there a God? If yes, one God, or many gods? Is God the rationale (motive) behind the suffering of the world? If God is so omnipotent, so omnipresent, so omniscient, then why did God not make it a just world?

If God created everything, then who created God? Is mankind the cause of repression and pain? Why are some evildoers? Why are others saint-like?

Most intrusive thoughts happen that are not invited by you. They may be sexual, aggressive, religious, or anything that might disturb you; but where do they come from? Most of the thoughts that pass through your mind are not invited by you, they just happen. But why? Is the big bang the inception, the origin of existence? Was there any being (actuality) before the big bang? Or was there trace of any substance before the big bang? Are space and time a reality? Is the universe a reality? Are there other living creatures in trillions of galaxies, billions of universes, and countless planets? Any extraterrestrial anywhere in the cosmos? Does anything exist beyond space and time? Is nothingness impregnated with everything and the source of all there will be? Are our senses telling us the truth? Is the outside world a reality? Can one innately feel or be aware of anything if one is removed from all of one's senses?

Hence, because of the intricacy of the subject matter, one has to vigorously cultivate the philosophy of metaphysics, explore science, seek knowledge, learn about the origin of existence, investigate dialectics, dialectical materialism, and so on. Strenuously dig into the physical world where the mind and the matter are of concern, delve into the world of the atom, the subatomic particles, subatomic realm, the quantum world, and so on. But before we probe into so many rather enigmatic-oriented concepts, it is essential to know if "matter" is the cause of it all, and perhaps is the reason for life. Or is "mind" responsible and the creator of what is in existence?

I believe if humanity was not pressured with so many hurdles to make ends meet, millions would be perceptive to fathom what is at stake, where an incredible number could conveniently arrive at truly believing in God, making so much hypocrisy past tense. Why do I say so much hypocrisy? Well, for one to be convinced, one should seek the daily crime statistics and the global violence rates to realize that humanity, I am afraid, is in a real mess, which should awaken us to spiritually, with religion—preferably not the institutional religions, but those that truly mend broken hearts and are sincerely there to help millions of desperate victims of financial ills and other malignantly horrifying troubles.

Bear in mind that in theology, or the theist's view, divine light (also called divine radiance or divine refulgence) is an aspect of the divine presence, specifically an unknown and mysterious ability of God, angels, or human beings to express themselves communicatively through spiritual means, rather than through physical capacities. Comparatively for materialists, or the atheist's opinion,

"The basic Marxist idea is that everything can be explained by one thing: matter. That spontaneous generation of matter is the key and the answer to the human brain that is assessed by the most prominent neuroscientists, psychologists, philosophers, and other magnificent scientific-minded of our time as the most complicated entity in the face of planet Earth. Here is what they say referencing matter. Matter is the total explanation for space, nature, man, psychic consciousness, human intelligence, and every other aspect of existence.

Marxism then assigns the task of knowing all truth to science. But this analogy, I am afraid, is perforated beyond repair since it holds no common sense, where disparaging approaches from Darwinism to Marxism have left the philosophical, ideological, and scientific reasoning mortified. People worldwide should not trust such hallucinating views because nonbelievers have so cunningly divulged manicured ideas often relating to rather very sensitive issues that the common man cannot easily discern.

It seems that the atheists either deliberately or unknowingly do not pay attention to the miraculously oriented quantum world that is mind-bogglingly strange, since they so naively simplify the infinite intricacy of our universe to senseless matter as the cause for existence. We know by now that no matter how hard physicists investigate, they still puzzle over the universe's deepest secret, the quantum realm. For example, in the quantum world, scientists can predict where the particles might be, but they never know where they are since they could be found anywhere, and definitely locating one of these particles is next to zero. The atheists so simplemindedly attribute the jaw-dropping mysteries and the infinitely goal-oriented phenomena (event) of the omnipotent God to simple matter, giving any novice the impression that they might have lost their mind.

Bear in mind that the quantum world is the world that's smaller than an atom. Things at this scale don't behave the same way as objects on the scale that we can see. Bohr argued that a quantum theory can never explain classical physics. Some physicists argue that we just haven't worked hard enough, and that we do fundamentally live in a quantum world, and that we can reproduce classical physics from purely quantum rules. The subatomic bits of matter don't function with the same rules as objects that we can see, feel, or hold. They behave ghostly and very strange. Sometimes, they are like lumps of matter. They also exhibit spreading out like waves, as ripples behave on a pond. Although they might be found anywhere, the certainty of finding one of these particles in any particular place is zero. Scientists can predict where they might be, yet they never know where they are.

"The bottom line is, the quantum world just doesn't work in the way the world around us works," says physicist David Lindley. "We don't really have the notion to deal with it." He further says, "Here's a taste of that weirdness: If you hit a baseball over a pond, it sails through the air to land on the other shore. If you drop a baseball in a pond, waves ripple away in growing circles. Those waves eventually reach the other side. In both cases, something travels from one place to another. But the baseball and the waves move differently. A baseball doesn't ripple or form peaks and valleys as it travels from one place to the next. Waves do."

But in experiments, particles in the subatomic world sometimes travel like waves. And they sometimes travel like particles. Why the tiniest laws of nature work that way isn't clear to anyone.

Photons are the particles that build up light and radiation. They're tiny packets of energy. Centuries ago, scientists accepted light traveled as a stream of particles, like a flow of tiny, bright balls. Then, 200 years ago, experiments showed that light could travel as waves. A hundred years after that, newer experiments found that light could sometimes act like waves, and sometimes act like particles, called photons. Those findings caused a lot of confusion, frustration, and arguments. Wave or particle? Neither or both? Some scientists even offered a compromise, using the word "wavicle." How scientists answer the question will depend on how they try to measure photons. It's possible to set up experiments where photons behave like particles, and others where they act like waves. But it's impossible to simultaneously measure them as waves and particles; it does not work that way. At the quantum scale, things can show up as particles or waves—and exist in more than one place at the same time.

This problem is not limited to photons. It expands to electrons and protons and other particles as small or smaller than atoms. Every rudimentary particle has holdings of both a wave and a particle. That concept is known as *wave-particle duality*. It's one of the biggest conundrum (puzzles) in the study of the smallest parts of the universe, known as *quantum* physics. Quantum physics will play a critical role in future technologies—in computers, for instance. Ordinary computers run calculations using trillions of switches constituted into microchips. Those switches are either "on" or "off." A quantum computer, nevertheless, utilizes atoms or subatomic particles for its computation. Because such a particle can be more than one thing at the same time until it's sized—it may be "on" or "off" or somewhere in between, elucidating that quantum computers are competent to simultaneously run many calculations. They have the capability to maneuver thousands of times faster than today's fastest contemporary machines.

Experiments based on quantum knowledge have produced astonishing results. For example, in 2001, physicists at Harvard University in Cambridge, Massachusetts, manifested how to stop light in its tracks. And since the mid-1990s, physicists have based peculiar new states of matter that were anticipated by quantum theory. One of those, called a Bose-Einstein condensate, forms only near absolute zero. (That's equivalent to −273.15° Celsius, or −459.67° Fahrenheit.) In this state, atoms lose their individuality. Expeditiously, the group conducts as one huge mega-atom.

Quantum physics isn't just an electrifying (thrilling) and weird disclosure. It's a body of scientific enlightenment that alters in unforeseen ways how we see the universe and how we interrelate with it. *Quantum* theory describes the behavior of things, particles, or energy on the smallest scale. In addition to wavicles, it predicts that a particle may be found in many places at the same time. Or it may tunnel through walls. (Imagine if you could do that!)

If you measure a photon's location, you might find it in one place and you might find it somewhere else. You can never know for certain where it is. Although quantum theory is quirky, it should be extremely valued, since scientists have demonstrated how pairs of particles can be connected even if they're on different sides of the courtyard or opposite sides of the universe. Particles linked in this way are said to be *entangled*. Scientists presently have been able to entangle photons that were 1,200 kilometers (750 miles) apart. Now they want to extend the proven entanglement limit much farther.

Quantum experiments signify the accuracy of quantum predictions. It also has been compellingly decisive to technology for more than a century. Engineers used their findings about photon behavior to build lasers. Their understanding about the quantum behavior of electrons has helped with the invention of transistors, making modern devices such as laptops and smartphones possible. "If you can think about quantum theory without getting dizzy, you don't get it," says Danish physicist Niels Bohr. Bohr was another pioneer in the field. He had a famous debate with Einstein about how to understand quantum theory. Bohr was one of the first people to explain the strange things that pop out of quantum theory. "I think I can safely say that nobody understands quantum [theory]," noted American physicist Richard Feynman once said. And yet his work in the 1960s helped show that quantum behaviors aren't science fiction. They really happen. Experiments can demonstrate this.

In 1935, Austrian physicist Erwin Schrödinger described such a thought experiment about a cat. First, he imagined a closed box having a cat inside. He presumed the box also conveyed a device that could release a poison gas. If released, that gas would kill the cat. And the possibility the device released the gas was 50 percent. (That's the same as the chance that a flipped coin would turn up heads.) The only way to know if the poison was released and the cat was dead or alive was to open the box and look inside. To check the status of the cat, you open the box. The cat is either alive or dead.

But if cats behaved like quantum particles, the story would be stranger. A photon, for instance, can be a particle and a wave. Likewise, Schrödinger's cat can be alive and dead *at the same time* in this thought experiment. Physicists call this "superposition." Here, the cat won't be one or the other, dead or alive, until someone opens the box and takes a look. The fate of the cat, then, will depend on the act of doing the experiment. Schrödinger utilized that thought experiment to delineate (illustrate) a huge problem. Why should the way the quantum world behaves depend on whether someone is watching?

Nobel prize physicist Anthony Leggett simply says: "Things that right now seem fantasy will be possible." Some physicists have offered even rampant solutions to the "cat" problem. For instance, our world could be one of many. It's possible that infinitely many worlds exist. If true, then in the thought experiment, Schrödinger's cat would be alive in half the worlds and dead in the rest.

Quantum theory describes particles like that cat. They may be one thing or another at once. And it gets more bizarre than that: Quantum theory also predicts that particles may be found in more than one place at a time. If the many-world idea is true, then a particle might be in one place in this world, and somewhere else in other worlds. You possibly choose which shoes to wear in the afternoon and what to consume for your evening. But based on the many worlds idea, there is another world where you made different choices. This wacky concept is familiar as "many-world" rendition (interpretation) of *quantum mechanics.*

It is thrilling to meditate on it, but physicists have not discovered a way to test whether it can become authenticated or not yet. Quantum theory includes other fantastic ideas, like that entanglement. Particles may be entangled or connected, even if they're separated by the width of the universe.

For example, in the lab, a physicist can entangle two photons, then send one of the pair to a lab in a different town. If the physicist measures something about the photon in the lab, like how fast it moves, then the physicist instantly knows the same position about the other photon. The two particles act as though they send signals instantaneously. And this will be true even if those particles are apart by hundreds of kilometers.

Quantum entanglement is really strange. Particles maintain an enigmatic link that persists even if they are separated by light-years. As in other parts of quantum theory, that idea makes a big problem. If entangled things send signals to each other at the same time, then the message might seem to travel faster than the speed of light—which, of course, is the speed limit of the universe! So *that cannot happen.*

In June, scientists in China stated a new record for entanglement. They utilized a satellite to entangle six million pairs of photons. The satellite beamed the photons to the ground, forwarding one of each pair to one of two labs. The labs sat 1,200 kilometers (750 miles) apart. And each pair of particles stayed entangled, they demonstrated. When they measured one of a pair, the other one was affected immediately. They released those findings in *Science.* Scientists and engineers are presently trying ways to use entanglement to connect particles over ever-longer distances. But the rules of physics still stop them from sending signals faster than the speed of light.

And as for our physical world, the most critical concept-oriented entities in the visible world are not tangible, meaning they are extremely decisive in sustaining a living, influencing the entire existence. They maneuver within the vicinity of life and death criteria; by nature, they cannot be tested or experienced in any laboratories of our time.

Thought experiments are the mathematical analyses of ideas, situations, or events. They are not based on real-world tests in a lab or the environment. They instead use numbers and relationships between mathematical operations to test whether something can or will happen. This is also known as **theoretical** research.

I am afraid their extremely pivotal position so absentmindedly is taken for granted. For example, God, time, space, the universe, mind, memory, intelligence, wisdom, consciousness, sub-conscious mind, the soul, our emotions, feelings, our senses, our imagination, hopes, desire, inspiration, passion, intuition, the way our senses take order from our nervous system and the brain, are so camouflaged that no one can sense the slightest activity since their innate behaviors, their dynamic interactivities, can absolutely not be seen, heard, or even felt. We know faith, self-awareness, earth going around its axis, earth moving around the sun, numbers, geometry, gravity, electromagnetic, strong and weak atomic forces, infinity, the invisible realm, quantum world, the sub-atomic particles, the energy-oriented movement within matter, extension, motion, how our bones stretch from the day we are born making us taller, why we are by nature prone to be linguistically oriented from a very young age, why we sacrifice, why a guilty conscience may bother us sometimes so much so that many commit suicide, why we fall in love, why sympathy, why empathy, why caring, why so much curiosity, why pride, why self-preservation, why so much pain and grief over the loss of loved ones sometimes ending in suicide, why do we seek justice, peace, tranquility, why so adamant to breed, why seek freedom, liberty, and the pursuit of happiness, and millions of other things that decisively impact human beings. We live in an imaginary, concept-related world where millions of very essential entities cannot be tested in scientific laboratories, miraculously giving us the impression that it is a real world.

The Principle of Non-contradiction

Many philosophical debates often intend to discover the root causes of knowledge and enlightenment, since inquisitive minds want to know the origin of intelligence, sagacity, and awareness, and where it comes from. What is the principal reason for man's thoughtfulness, rationality, comprehension, and the factors that distinguish us from the animal assisting humanity in all of their endeavors and daily tasks?

But before any rather intricate argument, you should be potentiated with the knowledge and understanding to correctly defend the philosophical, scientific, biological, environmental, or any other mental aspect and challenge of the debate that you might be faced with. One ought to thoroughly know about the subject in question and insightfully possess the competency, the knowledge, to correctly evaluate and analyze it; *otherwise personal biases, ideological impositions, and sometimes bullying one's idea* forward, acting dogmatic, can disturb the tranquility and calmness of the cogitation, which can adversely impact the accuracy of a just conclusion, ending in a bitter experience for participants.

There are things and occurrences in life that are grasped by our senses, like cold, heat, sound, light, sweet, sour, bitter, soft, rough; they are external, and do not need much intelligential support. They are apparent; they can be held by our senses. But when you say it is cold because of the winter, the sun is the cause for heat, the sun is shinier than the stars, the Earth is not flat, the atom bomb can explode and kill us all, or metal can expand if heated, motion is the cause for heat, matter can turn into energy, then the presence of intelligence and mindfulness is called for, since one manifests rationality, astuteness (keen, awareness), and strives to arrive at what makes sense where logic lies.

For instance, we cannot materialize the motion of the Earth but we can calculate its speed. At the equator, the **Earth** is **spinning** at 1,000 miles per hour about its axis and moving at 67,000 miles per hour around the Sun. With all this motion, you would expect to **feel** something, right? Well, **we don't feel** anything because all of the motions are almost completely constant. Since **speed** is equal to the distance traveled over the time taken, **Earth's speed** is calculated by dividing 584 million miles (940 million km) by 365.25 days and dividing that result by 24 hours to get miles per hour or km per hour. Further, there are **more** stars **than grains of sand**. **There** are 10 times **more** stars in the night sky **than grains of sand** in the world's deserts and beaches, scientists say.

Astronomers have worked out that **there** are 70 thousand million million million—or seven followed by 22 zeros—stars visible from the Earth through telescopes. No such limitless expansion can be materialized, like if you unraveled all of the DNA in your body it would span 34 billion miles, reaching to Pluto (2.66 billion miles away and back six times). Your body contains cosmic relics (remains, artifacts) from the creation of the universe. Almost all of your hydrogen atoms were formed in the big bang about 13.7 billion years ago. Many of the atoms you are made of, from calcium in your bones to the iron in your blood, were brewed up in the heart of an exploding star billions of years ago. Almost all of the ordinary matter (99.9999999%) is space. If you took out all the space in your atoms, the entire human race, all seven billion of us, would fit in the volume of a sugar cube.

The above are abstract concepts; they cannot be materialized. Hence, one needs to clearly distinguish between what is attributed to our mind power and what is grasped via our senses.

We need to differentiate between these two entities since one is understood via our senses and one is the attributes of our mind and the power of inference. They are the essence of what stems from within the self. We have to bear in mind that all scientific, philosophical, or experimental views cannot truly be substantiated if exhausted of mindfulness and without rationale where the presence of intelligence and consciousness is absent. God, God-awareness, self-awareness, hunger, thirst, love, pain, intuition, faith, space, motion, time, the universe, cosmos, extension, infinity, and so on, cannot be grasped by our senses. They are abstract entities that need to be sensed, felt; they carry their dependency, their reliability, their proof. They simply cannot be unfolded (typified).

Emmanuel Kant believed that trigonometry, space, and time existed before the human mind experiencing them. Kant argues that when one so renders a triangle to perform the auxiliary (additional, aide) constructive steps necessary for geometric proof, one does so a priori (based on hypothesis or theory rather than experience) whether the triangle is produced on paper or only in the imagination. He argued that the color or size of objects can change, but space and time in which they might go through any alteration cannot be changed. "A priori and intuitive truth" are those that are in the mind independently of all experience, not being derived from experience nor limited by it. For instance, the whole is greater than the part, or things which are equal to the same thing are equal.

One should bear in mind that no empirical theory or scientific experience can identify the origin of causal mechanism, clarifying why there is an attraction between the cause and the effect. No human senses

DR. FERIDOUN SHAWN SHAHMORADIAN

or feelings can either manifest the actual reason behind such magnetism or prove the interactions between the two. Therefore, signifying that not only does the enigmatic metaphysical concept require mindfulness, enlightenment, and the power of inference, but also definitely the materially oriented world essentially demands insightfulness, wisdom, and the power of intelligence, since consciousness is a priority to all scientific experiments and philosophical endeavors.

All intuitive truth is transcendental. But *transcendental* is a wider term than *intuitive*, including all within the limits of thought that is not derived from experience, as the concept of space and time. Being is transcendental. As being cannot be included under any genus (type, group, genre) but transcends them all, so the properties or affections of being have also been called transcendent. Kant believed that God, space, time, and motion, are constant.

Kant argued that adequate judgment is derived from the power of rationality, understanding, and comprehension; after what is sensed and felt within the vicinity of time and subject to space, then through mindfulness, they become information and knowledge in which the intelligence analyzes them for an appropriately decent verdict (acumen, judgment, discernment). It is important to mention that we do not carry any thought when born. We are a clean slate but certainly potentiated, capacitated with the essence of knowledge from within, inherited with not so apparent intelligent entities or wisdom as newly born, but equipped with the heightened power of inner feelings, discernment, and self-awareness.

The human's inner thoughts are seeded and so gradually are cultivated within the self as we mature. They are enhanced and are incorporated inside the subconscious mind, where they eventually thrive and appear in a conscious mind as "self or Nafs" evolutions. **Kant** believed when it comes to the **self**, we all have an inner and an outer **self** that together form our consciousness. The inner **self** is comprised of our psychological state and our rational intellect. The outer **self** includes our senses and the physical world.

John Locke, in his work the *Essay on Human Understanding*, **Locke** set out to offer an analysis of the human **mind** and its acquisition of knowledge.

He suggested an empiricist **theory,** according to which we obtain ideas via our experience of the world through our senses. In another words, he is saying we are the products of our environment. He believed what cannot be obtained by our senses is also out of our mind, another world; our knowledge of the world around us happens via our senses. John Locke was among the most famous philosophers and political theorists of the seventeenth century. Locke aspired to suggest an analysis of the human mind and its procuring (acquiring) of knowledge. He offered an empiricist theory relating to how we gain ideas through our experience of the world. The mind is then able to test, compare, and combine these concepts in countless various ways.

Knowledge consists of a special kind of relationship between different ideas. Locke insisted on the philosophical examination of the human mind as preparatory to the philosophical study of the world. The *Essay* conveys a series of more concentrated arguments on important, and widely divergent, philosophical themes. In politics, Locke is famous as a proponent of limited government. He utilizes a theory of natural rights to put forth that governments have obligations to their citizens, have only limited powers over their citizens, and can eventually be overthrown by citizens under certain circumstances. He also provided powerful arguments in favor of religious toleration.

John Locke's philosophical view on validating our experiences and the decisive roles human senses play as the only way to acquire knowledge is questionable. He does not clarify why there is an attraction between the cause and the effect that results in human experiences. And yes, we sense the mechanism of any cause and effect, but Locke and his peers cannot disclose the actual attraction between the cause and the effect. For example, we grasp through our sense that the metal expands when heated, but why such a dynamic must take place, what is the actual attraction between the two entities of the metal and fire, we do not know. We know that water will boil when arrived at **100 °C or 212 °F; but why? What is the attraction between the water and the heat that results in boiling at certain degrees? Why does such maneuverability, such precision, occur? No human senses of any kind answer that. Hence, Locke's analogy of experiencing the cause and effect mechanism through** our senses is true. But they never disclose why these interests and magnetism among objects take place.

For someone, like Mulla Sadra, the existence was of importance where the essential motion is the essence of running through all that exists. Mulla Sadra's philosophy is the theory of substantial motion, which is based on the premise that everything in the order of nature, including celestial spheres, undergoes substantial alteration and transformation as a result of the self-flow and penetration of being, which renders every concrete individual entity its share of being. In contrast to Aristotle and Avicenna, who believed change only in four categories: quantity, quality, position, and place, Sadra defines change as an all-pervasive reality permeating through the entire cosmos, including the category of substance Mulla Sadra debated the view that reality is existence. He believed that essence was by itself a general concept, and therefore does not, in reality, exist.

Existence is the only reality. Existence and reality are therefore identical. Existence is the all-comprehensive reality and there is nothing outside of it. Negative essences require some sort of reality and therefore exist. Existence, hence, cannot be denied. Therefore, existence cannot be negated. As existence cannot be negated, it is self-evident that its existence is God. God should not be searched for in the realm of existence but is the basis of all existence. The reality in Arabic is "Al-Haq," and is stated in the Qur'an as one of the names of God.

To paraphrase Mullah Sadra's *Logical Proof for God*:

1. There is a being.
2. This being is perfection beyond all perfection.
3. God is perfect and Perfection in existence.
4. Existence is a singular and simple reality.
5. That singular reality is graded in intensity on a scale of perfection.
6. That scale must have a limit point, a point of greatest intensity and greatest existence.
7. Therefore, God exists.

Sadra argued that all contingent beings need a cause that establishes their balance between existence and non-existence in favor of the former;

nothing can come into being without a cause. Since the world is therefore contingent upon this first act, not only must God exist, but God must also be responsible for this first act of creation. Sadra also believed that a causal regress was impossible because the causal chain could only work in the matter that had a beginning, middle, and end: 1. a pure cause at the beginning; 2. a pure effect at the end; 3. a nexus of cause and effect.

Causal nexus in Latin means "to bind." it means to link a cause and effect. A **causal nexus** exists if the result is a natural and reasonable outcome or consequence of the activity. For Mullah Sadra, the causal "end" is as unpolluted (pure) as its correlative "beginning," which instructively places God at both the beginning and the end of the creative act.

God's capacity to measure the intensity of existential reality by measuring causal dynamics and their relationship to their origin, is contrary to knowing their effects. For Mullah Sadra, a true statement is a statement that is true to the solid facts in existence. He believed a metaphysical and not a formal idea of truth, arguing that the world is made of mind-independent objects that are always true and the truth is not what is rationally acceptable within a certain theory of description. In Mullah Sadra's view, one cannot have access to the reality of being, since only linguistic analysis is available. Comparatively, that is what Werner Heisenberg said: "What we observe is not nature itself but nature exposed to our method of questioning. Our scientific work in physic consists of asking a question about nature in the language that we possess and trying to get an answer from an experiment by the means that are at our disposal."

The law for mind-oriented and conscious-related entities is quite different from those subjects that can be sensed or felt via seeing, hearing, tasting, smelling, and touching. Because internal concepts are felt from within, they are specific; they are beyond what can be experienced from outside. Their innate and visceral (nonrationality) reality carry different meanings from those external mechanisms where the interpretation of cause and effect are manifested.

Innate **ability** is a trait or characteristic that is present in an organism at birth. It is always present in the organism and is not a learned behavior. For instance, humans have the **innate ability** for language; it occurs in all humans naturally. Other examples are like having the feelings of where do we come from, where are we going, why are we here, what happens after we die, does life has a purpose, is there a God, and hundreds if not thousands of other related inquiries, self-awareness, the concept of God, and so on.

Comparatively, **perceptual** learning is the process by which the **ability** of sensory systems to respond to stimuli is improved through experience. Examples of **perceptual** learning include developing an **ability** to distinguish between different odors or musical pitches and an **ability** to distinguish between different shades of colors, to discern beauty and the beast. **Perception** refers to how we interpret stimuli such as people, things, or events. **Our perception** is vital to recognize because it is the driving force behind **our** reaction to the outside world.

All visible acts—for instance, consuming food via our hand—is an apparent motion where the entire mechanism is fueled by an unseen motion without which no visible or practical activity can ever occur, further signifying that the operation of our five senses must also be fueled by this obscure motion-oriented, energy-based truth.

A proposition is true if it corresponds to things in reality; and manifesto (proposition) can be true if it conforms with the actual thing itself. What Mulla Sadra is saying is, there are two kinds of truth: one that is our impression of what we think is true, and the other the actual truth about existence.

We should also realize the power of meditation, which can shut us off from the outside world, help us focus on the inner self, and access agendas that are induced from within. Meditation can help people arrive at a certain level of spiritual maturity; they can activate the same prophetic dream experience as when they are awake, which one can observe and hear things veiled to others since ecstasy is to be known from within. It can clear our mind so that "Mutakhayyila" or the sense of imagination, can better connect to divine power, where the divine imaginings and creation takes place when in the state of ecstasy.

We are part of God. We imagine, and the potency of our imagination gives birth to creativity, signifying the sense of prophetic dreams. Our sense of imagination can potentially be activated like the sap of a tree through which the inspiration approaches via the unseen realm and pours into the outer senses, making one see and feel magnificent events while the person is still sound asleep. A **recluse (loner, hermit, monk)** values an environment where no one is talking so they can be more focused on their inner state. It is easier to reach the inner state via meditation.

The purpose of **meditation** is to lower your brain waves so that you can veer (redirect) your attention from the external to the internal, access your **subconscious** mind, which can only happen when your brain is in the theta range. **Theta (θ)** is the angle of rotation, a measurement of the amount (the angle) that a figure is rotated about a fixed point—often the center of a circle. **Meditation** is the answer to many of our deep-rooted problems. It **does help** us connect with our **subconscious** mind. To change anything, you need to have a proper understanding of the subject and you need to change the process that you are applying to. The purpose of your **subconscious** is life-ward. People who **meditate** appear to be **more aware** of their unconscious mind.

Scientists have found evidence that people who practice mindful **meditation** are **more aware** of their unconscious brain activity, leading to a feeling of **conscious** control over their bodies. Closely allied with the **conscious mind** is the **preconscious**, which includes the things that we are not thinking of at the moment but which we can easily draw into **conscious** awareness. Things the **conscious mind** wants to keep hidden from awareness are repressed into the **unconscious mind**.

Meditation can help connect to our inner state of mind, the inner self; it can help us much better to connect to God. Because the truth is of two kinds; one is externally grasped through our senses and the other is from within. It is intuitionally manifested, so much so that if one is separated from one's five senses, the person can still feel self-awareness, feel one's mind, feel God.

And finally, the matter is not but our imagination of the outside world. And the motion within the matter is the mobility mechanism that conforms and correlates with the interpretation of the dynamic forces within nature and the entire universe. The matter has condensed and stored energy, which functions not by its innate activities, or via independently maneuvered accord, but is driven by the outer forces. The triad of **thesis, antithesis**, and **synthesis is the dialectical doctoring of "material dialectics" of Marx and Ingles,** which denotes that dialectical materialism is an approach to reality, meaning that the material world perceptible to senses has an objective reality independent of mind or spirit.

It is true that the particle of matter continuously moves because of kinetic energy, and that is why they are in motion, which might operate under progression because of the so-called contradiction where dialectical materialism is concerned. But contradiction within any matter cannot occur simultaneously, making thesis, antitheses, and at the same time, building synthesis. That might be true in converse related behaviors where dialogues could persuasively culminate to a better stage of any argument arriving at its objective, but not true for every aspect of nature and the entire universe, as I am afraid Marxism claims.

The same procedural mechanism cannot at the same time happen and not happen, but such dynamics from potentiality to actuality can exist within an entity or matter. To take place from amplification to manifestation, but certainly not an innate force which can at the same time play the cause and the effect, to simultaneously act subjectively and objectively, making it impossible for such dynamics to substantiate, since all movements in the matter and the entire universe is leveraged by a magnificent outside force to occur gradually from possibility to certainty, conducting them with phenomenal precision. There surely exists inside change within matter taking place from strength to actuation, to evolution from having the likelihood, the probability to transfer into reality. To substantiation from competency to the substance.

Like a chicken egg that is potentiated to become a chicken, or from human embryo to a fetus, or any seed that grows into a plant or turns into a tree, and millions of other instances happening in our world. Hence, it is not true when Marx and Engle say "contradiction means motion." or when Henry Loffler says that no movement can occur in something with no contradiction.

The atheist's ideology does emphatically allege (claim) a spontaneously based force exhausted of any intelligence, no conscious, no will, no emotion, and without any feeling, dulled nature with having no purpose is responsible to play God in an infinitely complicated and astronomically resourceful universe. Not believing in an imminently (brewing, looming) awakened external force couldn't be sensibly oriented. The basic **Marxist** idea is that everything can be explained by one thing—**matter. Matter is** the total explanation for space, nature, man, psychic consciousness, human

intelligence, and every other aspect of existence. **Marxism** then assigns the task of knowing all truth to science.

What dialectic ideology professes is that we are the product of a senseless matter, where the motion or the mobility within matter occurs innately without any outside interference, since no external force can be responsible for such events. In other words, the matter can simultaneously play the subject and the object, behave as the cause and the effect of its bilateral (collective) action, its motion, and the changes in progress. As odd as it sounds, this is an ideology that also believes in evolution, meaning gradual movement from simple or not so perfect to more sophisticated and complete.

But no imperfect, immature mechanism at its very preliminary stages can cause its objectified perfection exhausted from the external force. The matter does not have what it takes to evolve, reaching its objective via motion. Entire activities within any matter must be fed beyond what it possesses because it certainly has no mind, lacks intelligence, knowledge, information, wisdom, will power, choice, creativity, imagination, inspiration, memory, or other dynamics to substantiate such potentiated intricacy for arriving at its goal to serve its purpose. Marx and Ingles's dialectic ideology is saying that matter created itself; it conveys the innately oriented essence, the sap that manipulates motion to get any job done.

It is potentiated to gradually arrive at the peak of its evolutionary process where the action in any matter is completed. Material dialectics drive the biological evolution, the socioeconomic upheaval, the class war of labor against capitalism that one day, as they claim, peaks to revolution with the same stick as if we are hallucinating. For Marx, the ideological, philosophical, scientific, cultural, educational, economic, social, biological, physical, spiritual, and other imperative findings are all matter-infused, matter-related concepts. For example, the social, economic, and historical changes pursue the same biological dynamics of how a caterpillar evolves and finally, via leap revolutions and turns into a butterfly since the contradicting forces fuel everything and is the essence of all changes without any guide, exhaustive of any external interference as if we live in a vacuum where a senseless, unstable matter is the creator, the designer, the planner, the programmer, and the conductor. It can play God in all there is and all there ever will be. May God help us all.

Furthermore, Marx, Angles, and their affiliates have mistaken the dynamics of the thesis, antithesis, and synthesis in daily dialogues, contentions, and social interactions for biological criteria, baselessly extending them as a contradiction within all matter and the entire existence. According to the German philosopher Walter Kaufmann, Fichte introduced into German philosophy the three steps of *the thesis*, antithesis, and *synthesis*, using these three terms.

Dialectic comprises three stages of development: first, a thesis or statement of an idea, which gives rise to a second step, a reaction or antithesis that contradicts or negates the thesis, and third, the synthesis, a statement through which the differences between the two points are resolved. Synthesis, in philosophy, is the combination of parts, or elements, in order to form a more complete view or system.

The term *synthesis* also refers, in the dialectical philosophy of the nineteenth-century German philosopher G. W. F. Hegel, to the higher stage of truth that combines the truth of a thesis and an antithesis. Hegelianism is the philosophy of G. W. F. Hegel, which can be concluded by the dictum that "the rational alone is real," which means that all reality is capable of being expressed in rational categories. His goal was to reduce reality to a more synthetic unity within the system of absolute idealism.

You Are God

> *"Awakening is not changing who you are, but discarding who you are not."*

> *Deepak Chopra*

It is fascinating to grasp the meaning of the mere act of observation affects, the experimental findings of manifesting the very difference between the existence and the nonexistence. Exhibiting the incredible traces of life so infinitely vast that even mammoths with inversely related brain size and intelligence would kneel to the awesome power of God, since it cognitively shouldn't take much to realize the real cause behind the marvel of the cosmos and beyond.

As for mankind, Socrates's view on the faculties of man is apparent in his saying: "Oman, know thyself," which drew attention to the role of humanity since he believed that in human beings there are hidden treasures of life that should be discovered, as the modern era has prominent man in the technology of the "observer effect," "biocentrism," and the like, accrediting man as the actual reason and the principle focal point behind the existence after God, further reinforcing the expression that says, "Man is made in the image of God."

When a quantum "observer" is watching, and when not observing quantum positioning alters, stating that particles can also behave as waves. In other words, when under observation, electrons are being "forced" to behave like particles and not like waves. Thus the mere act of observation affects the experimental findings.

1. A human being is a part of the whole called by us universe, a part limited in time and space. Albert Einstein.
2. He experiences himself, his thoughts and feelings as something separated from the rest, a kind of optical delusion of his consciousness. Albert Einstein.

The above assessment of the man and the universe should be enough for distancing the heavenly manifested mentality from the inferno-like ideologies of Nihilism, Atheism, and the like, believing there is no God, no heaven or hell, no reincarnation, no judgments, no hope, so screw it. Thus, there can be no right or wrong. If so, can you even imagine the ill consequences of such a curse, like doctoring dragging mankind into demonic vicinities and the territory where Satan maneuvers? The realization one has in this life will no doubt influence one's attitude.

Awaken the God within you; what does it mean? Where inside shall we look to find God, or at least a portion of God-like character? Knowing that the good God has also given us a choice to choose what is heavenly and what is demonic, this is not fiction, since every day we see both angel-like behaviors and satanic similar actions performed by man which is made in God's image. This is a question that not only holds intellectual traits where rationality should play a crucial part to either philosophically relate to it or try scientifically to reject it, which is not possible since entities such as consciousness, mind, spirit or soul, heart, emotions, and faith, couldn't be confined in any laboratories.

Starting with consciousness or mind; is anyone able to see, touch, pinpoint, or limit mind? The answer is no. Consciousness gives us a clue to God's attributes. Can anyone see, touch, limit, or locate emotions, something as grand as love? No, since we can only know the traces of emotion, we can only feel love, delightfulness, sorrow, pain, suffering, etc. What about our senses and how they maneuver to make our lives easy so we can deal with the outside world? We sure cannot locate their mechanism as dynamically as they operate; they invisibly function and are applicable through our nervous system and brain. Same with God. We can't see or touch God, we are solely able to see the effects of the Almighty as the universe, cosmos, and beyond manifests as they play an extremely significant role in existence.

Can we stop thinking until the day we die? Certainly not, as infinite as our thoughts are we cannot halt thinking. Same with God, since he is infinite, and in no way limited. The same goes for our feelings and emotions; they are an infinitely oriented phenomenon. So is God of infinite essence. Can we terminate our hearts from desiring and stop wanting things? Not possible; we will desire love and want things to the day we expire. They are also of invisible and infinite nature. So is God of infinite essence and unseen.

Further, we wouldn't be able to turn energy into matter. No one can take your mind, your energy-oriented thoughts, your feelings, and turn them into visible matter, to substantiate, to materialize them. Same with God, since no man can claim to see or touch the energy-oriented God sacredly prevalent where no goodness or sin can go undetected. God witnesses everything since what goes around, definitely comes around.

Keep in mind that scientists are able to make matter into energy, as they do with atomic bombs, but not vice versa. These are the sacred places where we should explore and look for the God within, and not in our instinctually animal-oriented behaviors like eating, drinking, resting, sleeping, making love, and so on that are only the fuels for running the main show, to live a life with purpose and not aimlessly wander in the living of luxury and carelessness as if depleted of intelligence and wisdom, exhausted of any responsibility and without making enlightening choices to constructively help self and others in need, which is the actual reason for living, to cooperate, to make others and self-happy, to believe in a life with spiritual and moral destiny by helping humanity to constructively challenge nature, to make people's lives better regardless of their faith, race, or nationality, to believe in the God within. The catastrophe occurs when demons get a chance and fools raise the so-called scientific theories that flagrantly but perhaps so naively excite the self-interest part of man; it's when obnoxious greed, avarice, and self-centeredness is encouraged to accumulate wealth at any cost as social Darwinism exercised it for more than a century, leaving behind devastating cultural and social mishaps and disastrous consequence for millions, if not billions, to bear.

> "It seems sensible to discard all hope of observing hitherto unobservable quantities, such as the position and period of the electron. Instead, it seems more reasonable to try to establish a theoretical quantum mechanics, analogous to classical mechanics, but in which only relations between observable quantities occur. Since the measuring device has been constructed by the observer. we have to remember that what we observe is not nature itself but nature exposed to our method of questioning. Our scientific work in physics consists of asking questions about nature in the language that we possess and trying to get an answer from an experiment by the means that are at our disposal."

> Werner Heisenberg.

What Darwinism conceptualized has done more damage than any good. Right or wrong, the Darwinism evolution might have contributed to the science of biology, but it has destructed the civility of mind and manner, giving the impression that we are brutal, savage animals that operate by instinct, and through nature controlling rather than loving creatures with conscious that is happiest when it belongs, is cooperative, and is socially accepted. Social Darwinism's vicious trend of thought relies on animal instincts and beastly attitude, for some so unconsciously condemn human beings as non-loving that should believe in the "survival of fittest" mentality, which left so many driven to act psychotic, conditioning them to behave as ruthless as animals proliferating the unthinkable deeds of genocide.

What happened when Charles Darwin presented his idea of natural selection in his momentous book *On the Origin of Species,* employing natural selection, was the excuse that we have barbaric, savage, brutish, bestial, primitive, and essential animal instincts within us, availing his findings with biological basis through the misleading concept of natural selection as survival of the fittest creatures. Social Darwinism a set of squandering ideologies arrived in the late 1800s in which his theory of evolution via natural selection was welcomed by influential people and many Godless elements in the authoritative position used to justify certain political, social, and economic views.

Social Darwinist's core view is that certain people become powerful in society because they are innately superior. Social Darwinism has been utilized to justify imperialism, eugenics (ancestry-genetics), racism, acting prejudice, and with extreme social inequality even genocide. The United Nations Genocide Convention defines genocide as "acts committed with intent to destroy, in whole or in part, a national, ethnical, racial or religious group," leading to the most brutal and savage conduct that mankind perpetrated at different times which proliferated (mushroomed) over the past century and a half.

Some say we are pre-programmed to try to dominate others and be a winner in the battle of life; and our preoccupation with sexual conquest is due to our primal instinct to sow our seeds; and men behave abominably because their bodies are flooded with must-reproduce-their-genes-promoting testosterone; and we are conquerors induced with wanting lands and big places to live since by nature are we innately territorial; and fighting and war is just our deeply rooted combative animal nature expressing itself; and religions are merely our survival-driven group mentality expressing itself; and the most common saying of all, it's just human nature to be selfish.

Some recognize that we progress because of our testosterone-driven nature. Testosterone plays a role in certain behaviors, including aggression and dominance. Just as sexual activity can affect testosterone levels, taking part in competitive activities can cause a man's testosterone levels to rise or fall. Low testosterone may result in a loss of confidence and a lack of motivation. In other words, we are robots mechanically fueled by testosterone programmed to reach the so-called pinnacle of invincibility no matter how vulture-like (rapacious-hunting) the behavior; at what price and at whose expenses emboldening the ruthless expression which believes the end justifies the mean? It is so unfortunately sad that the God within us is betrayed so much that no good social theories are heightened with causing cataclysmic (calamity, disaster) affect often beyond repair.

The idea of natural selection, later interpreted by others like the British philosopher and scientist Herbert Spencer to survival of the fittest, held that the life of humans in society was a struggle for existence ruled by survival of the fittest. The ideas about survival of the fittest hugely influenced commerce and human societies as a whole and led to many social ills, such as atheism, sexism, inequality, racism, and imperialism, which I am afraid was justified because of lack of minds of reason and depletion of emotional intelligence. Social Darwinism is further linked with nationalism and imperialism.

Many Social Darwinists embraced laissez-faire capitalism and racism. They argued that the government should not interfere in the survival of the fittest by helping the poor, and encouraged the idea that some races are biologically superior to others, such as a "Hitler mentality." Social Darwinism was the application of Charles Darwin's scientific theories of evolution and natural selection to contemporary social development, believing in nature only the fittest survived, as well as in the marketplace.

The list of genocides by death toll includes death toll estimates of all deaths that are either directly or indirectly caused by genocide. It does not include not strictly genocidal mass killing (variously called mass murder, crime against humanity, politicized, classicized, war crimes), Japanese war crimes (3 to 14 million deaths), the Red Terror (100,000 to 1.3 million deaths), the atrocities caused in Congo (1 to 15 million deaths), the Great Purge (0.6 to 1.75 million deaths) or the Great Leap Forward (15 to 55 million deaths). The Great Leap Forward campaign began during the period of the Second Five Year Plan, which was scheduled to run from 1958 to 1963, though the campaign itself was discontinued by 1961. Mao unveiled the Great Leap Forward at a meeting in January 1958 in Nanjing.

The above statistics do not include the rise in global crime against humanity where wars of aggression and other inhumanely oriented and heinous behaviors have led to displacement of hundreds of millions of innocent people from their homeland, as so many are murdered and as so shamelessly are counted as collateral damage without any impunity for the real culprits. The consequences of staying in a state of ignorance can lead to serious social and economic downfalls like relationship crises, legal issues, and more. Ignorance can hurt individuals and societies; ignorant people believe in rumors and behave herd-like, often causing irreparable damage because of a lack of awareness where minds of reason are lost. For instance, having a negative attitude about another race.

> *"Darwinism by itself did not produce the Holocaust, but without Darwinism... neither Hitler nor his Nazi followers would have had the necessary scientific underpinnings to convince themselves and their collaborators that one of the worlds greatest atrocities was really morally praiseworthy."*
>
> *— Richard Weikart, From Darwin to Hitler: Evolutionary Ethics, Eugenics, and Racism in Germany*

1. Holocaust
   German occupied Europe 1941–1945 about 6,000,000 Jews were murdered.
2. Genocide of Ukrainians through starvation by the Soviet regime. At least 10% of Ukraine's population perished. Holodomor 1932–1933 Ukrainians Soviet Holodomor (Ukrainian genocide which is part of greater Soviet (Famine of 1932–1933) in which 7,500,000 Ukrainians were murdered.
3. Nazi genocide of German-occupied Europe
   In 1939–1945, 3,000,000 or about 17% of Poland's population, was killed WWII.
4. Democratic Kampuchea
   Cambodian genocide,10–33% of the total population of Cambodia

killed about 3,000,000 people were killed by 100% of Cambodian Viets.

50% of Cambodian Chinese and Cham
40% of Cambodian Lao and Thai
25% of Urban Khmer
16% of Rural Khmer

5. Kazakh genocide during the Soviet Union 1931–1933, about 1,750,000 perished. Some historians assume that 42% of the entire Kazakh population died in the famine. The two Soviet censuses show that the number of the Kazakhs in Kazakhstan dropped from 3,637,612 in 1926 to 2,181,520 in 1937.

6. Armenian genocide (Medz Yeghern, "Great Crime")
by the Ottoman Empire (territories of present-day Turkey, Syria, and Iraq).
1915–1922 At least 50% of Armenian in Turkey were slaughtered by the Turks.

7. The Rwandan genocide in 1994, a loss of 77.0% of the Tutsi population of Rwanda killed in the genocide.
20% of Rwanda's total population killed.

8. Indonesia genocide in Indonesia 1965–1974 about 4,000,000 were massacred.

9. Greek genocide including the Pontic genocide
by the Ottoman Empire
(territories of present-day Turkey), 1914–1922, more than a million were killed.

10. Genocide by the Ustase, including the Serbian genocide.
The Independent State of Croatia (territories of present-day Croatia, Bosnia, Herzegovina, and Serbian Syria 1941–1945; 320,000 and 600,000, 13% to 21% of the Serbian population within the NDH was killed.

11. Genocide in Bangladesh, East Pakistan, 1971; more than 3,000,000 Bengali Hindus were slaughtered, over 20% of Bengali Hindus were killed.

12. Pacification of Algeria, French Algeria 1830–1871.
10% to 33% of Algeria's population died during the period.

13. Genocide of indigenous peoples in Brazil, 87 out of 230 Brazilian tribes went extinct from 1985–1900 when 235,000 and 800,000 were wiped out by genocide.
14. Assyrian genocide by the Ottoman Empire (Seyfo, "Sword") 815–1923 about 1,000,000 people were killed.
15. Romani genocide German-occupied Europe 1935–1945. 25% of Romani people in Europe were killed.
16. Polish genocide by the Soviet Union in 1937–1938; 22% of Poles perished.
17. Soviet deportation of Chechens and other Vainakh populations. The Soviet Union, North Caucasus, 1944–1948; 24% to almost 50% of the total Chechen population perished.
18. Darfur genocide, 2003, Darfur, Sudan, 98,000 and 500,000 were killed.
19. Kurdish genocide, Iraq 1977–1991. 8% of the Kurdish population of Iraq was killed.
20. East Timor genocide 1975–1999. 13% to 44% of the East Timor population killed.
21. Genocide of 5% Burundian population occurred in 1972, and as much as 10%–15% of the Hutu population was killed.
22. Libyan genocide in Italian Libya, plague, 1923–1932 in which 125,000 Libyans were murdered.
23. Bambuti Genocide North Kivu Democratic Republic of Congo, 2002–2003; more than 100,000 people killed, 40% of Congo's Pygmy population perished.
24. Massacres of Poles in Volhynia and Eastern Galicia, Eastern part of pre-war Poland 1943–1945; more than 300,000 perished.
25. Genocide of Isaaqs, Somalia, 1988–1991; more than 200,000 people were killed.
26. Bosnians and Croats by Chetniks, the independent state of Croatia (territories of present-day Croatia, Bosnia, Herzegovina, and Sandzak), 1941–1945; more than 100,000 people were slaughtered.
27. Deportation of the Crimean Tatars, Crimean Peninsula, 1944–1948; the deportation of Crimean's Tatar reduced the population by about 40% to 46%, enforced by the Soviet Union.

28. Genocide in German southwest Africa, 1904–1908; left more than 200,000 people from the Herero and Nama population murdered.

29. Jewish Genocide during the Russian White Terror in what is now Ukraine, 1918–1923; more than 500,000 were slaughtered.

30. Guatemalan genocide, 1962–1996; more than 200,000 were killed, leaving more than 40% of Mayan people in the Guatemala and Rabinal region killed.

31. Genocide of Burundi, Burundian Tutsis, 1993; about 75,000 to 80,000 were killed.

32. Punjab, India, 1937–1938; about 50,000 were killed.

33. Latvian operation, Soviet Union Latvian genocide, 1937–1938; about 17,000 were killed.

34. California genocide, California, 1846–1873; approximately 150,000 Amerindians killed. Their population declined by 80% during this period.

35. Queensland, Australia, Aboriginal genocide, 1840–1897; more than 80,000 aboriginals were killed, over 50% of the aboriginal population.

36. Rohingya Myanmar genocide, 2017; about 70,000 Muslims were murdered.

37. Former Russian Empire De-cossackization, 1917–1933; about 1,000,000 perished.

38. Chittagong Hill Tract genocide, Bangladesh, 1977–1997; about 20,000 killed.

39. Selknam genocide, Chile, Tierra del Fuego, Late nineteenth century to early twentieth century; more than 2,500 perished.

40. Genocide of Yazidis in northern Iraq and Syria in 2014 to present; more than 6,000 slaughtered.

Bear in mind most of these savage killings of innocent people were race, religion, and nationality related.

THE DEVIL INSIDE

The angel is free because of his knowledge, the beast
because of ignorance. Between the two remains the son
of man to struggle.

Rumi

Our subconscious mind is 30,000 times more powerful
than our conscious mind.

Brian Tracy

When babies are born, the subconscious mind takes over where no mind
sensibility and mature functioning is a factor until about 7–8 years old,
doing things as they see fit without much of rationale, lacking the power
of reasoning without much intelligence competency. During this time,
no will or choice-oriented issues are involved and if possible, it will most
probably be immature and mainly about monkey see monkey do business.
Children's critical mind solely develops from about the age of eight, hence,
whatever they hear, see, feel, goes straight into the subconscious mind
without examining, and is believed as fact, as the subconscious mind never
sleeps; the amount of data that goes directly into their subconscious mind
is phenomenal. Learning how to correctly prod (stimulate, encourage) the
communication between the conscious and the subconscious minds is a
potent instrument leading to success, riches, and happiness.

When intelligence can overcome the brainwashing of our subconscious
mind via resoluteness and mindfulness of conscious awareness, better and

much healthier living is inevitable. The subconscious mind is a databank for everything, in which the conscious mind is deprived of it. The first five years of a child's life are fundamentally important, since children learn more quickly during their early years than at any other time in life. They need love and nurturing to develop a sense of trust and security that turns into confidence as they grow. One's subconscious mind will not forget anything, since all incidents stick into the memory bank, it stays aware and alert at all times. The subconscious mind is a store for everything; it has powers that the conscious mind lacks and stores what the conscious mind might do on a daily routine.

The subconscious mind is not separated, not an autonomous or visible entity of the body; no outside force can inflict harm or physically damage it. Our thoughts directly affect the internal system of the mind. The damaged mind loses its control over the body and action. The deeper brain structures are indicated as sub cortex, or under the cortex. The function of your subconscious mind is to gather, store, and retrieve data. Its job is to ensure that you respond precisely to the way you are programmed. One's subconscious mind makes everything one says and does fit a motif (shape, pattern) congruent with your self-concept.

The subconscious mind is the master program; it is a part of your mind that works without your awareness and over which you do not have agile (nimble, ready) control.

The term *self-concept* is a general term used to refer to how someone thinks about, evaluates, or perceives themselves. Baumeister (1999) manifested the following self-concept definition: "The individual's belief about himself or herself, including the person's attributes and who and what the self is." Our self-concept is important because it influences how we think, feel, and act in everyday organizational life. Our self-concept behaves like a filter that lets some information in and keeps other information out.

According to Carl Rogers, self-concept has three components: self-image, self-esteem, and the ideal self. This is based on a combination of self-esteem (how a person feels about themselves), self-image (how a person sees themselves), and how they are viewed by others. A person's self-concept is affected by age, appearance, gender, culture, emotional development, education, relationships with others, and sexual orientation.

Factors that can influence an individual's self-concept are education, media, appearance, culture, abuse, relationships, gender, income, and age. Education can impact a person's self-esteem. If they cannot get into the workforce, the person will get a negative self-image and low self-esteem. The self-concept is a knowledge representation that contains information about us, including our beliefs, way of life, our personality traits, physical characteristics, abilities, values, goals, and roles, as well as knowing that we exist as individuals.

The part of your mind that makes your dreams is an instance of your subconscious; it is the link between your subconscious mind and your dreams. When you fall asleep, it is your conscious mind that is sleeping. However, your subconscious mind will never fall asleep. And that simply leaves your unconscious mind only accountable for your dreams. Bear in mind that 95 percent of brain activity is over and beyond our conscious awareness. Many cognitive neuroscientists have tested studies showing that only 5 percent of our cognitive abilities for (decisions, emotions, actions, behavior) are conscious, whereas (although) the remaining 95 percent is only produced in a non-conscious manner.

It is your conscious recall that is suspect. The function of your subconscious mind is to store and retrieve data. Its job is to make sure that you respond exactly the way you are programmed. Your subconscious mind makes everything you say and do fit a pattern consistent with your self-concept, your master program.

And when the conscious mind is potentiated to act resolute and starts to activate, it is the time we need to be educated, to intelligently progress, to learn and be trained for life, to appreciate in wisdom for overcoming the ravages of the subconscious mind which is enforced 24/7 wanting to accommodate the urges of the flesh where the mind of reason cannot stop us from doing sometimes the unthinkably wrong stuff in a crime-infested environment, where for so many the gratification of the flesh and hedonism (pleasure-seeking) is of priority. And if the atmosphere for equipping and empowering the mind with right thought processes is not available, there is no doubt that most will become the victims of forceful urges pushed by the subconscious mind, causing irreparable damage. It is so sad that many countries suppress biologically related impulses, like sexually oriented urges related to subconscious ills via fear and hate-mongering and not through professional help and educational therapy.

The subconscious works on manipulating the animal instincts, spurring them to activate with no wit or reasoning power. Hence malignant environments with no good upbringing where suitable opportunities are lost can only feed the subconscious with dirt-like mentality, exacerbating the situation against having quality life experiences, which can lead to one's ugly position without a promising future. You should ask why millions are incarcerated because of crime-related reasons where cultural decency and social civility deteriorate every day, and where economic prosperity is nowhere to be found for the countless number of masses.

This, I am afraid, happens despite advancement in modernism and revolutionary progress in technology and industrialization. Darwinism theory and the affiliated trend of thought gives the green light to the many exploiters for believing in the nonsense of the survival of fittest mentality to hoard galactically units of wealth and force the majority to live in poverty for the sake of maintaining an absurd classified society to acquire power and influence for satisfying their greedy and psychotic urges. The subconscious mind is the product of the environment, which relentlessly gathers information via our five senses, and since the environment is materially oriented and is all about money, wealth, prestige, and power, it creates a culture of hypocrisy where billions behave theater-like, acting where no "categorical imperative," no morals exist. As Kant said, an imperative is "categorical" when it is true at all times, and in all situations. Bear in mind that there are decisive matters that are driven by the inner self and they cannot be received by our senses. For example, the concept of God-awareness, self-awareness, self-consciousness, motion, space, the universe, the concept of infinity, the mind itself, the human soul, the human spirit, and so on.

Grasping concepts as such are an irrelevance to our senses. They need to be felt. They need to be meditated on to deepen one's knowledge about them. It should trouble us when barely any time, energy, effort, or money is spent on the issue of "categorical imperative" to educate people about moral and vitreous behaviors, since maximizing profit is instrumented via capitalist systems where often activities are all about emphasizing money. The subconscious in many cases does not believe in God and righteousness since 24/7 it is being fed through a malignant atmosphere where toxic behaviors and violence are encouraged by many entertaining media corporations and ill-intended programs where countless people cannot afford the education, the right training, the skill, the wit, and the knowledge to distinguish between fact and fiction. They are easily conditioned and deceived; that is the aim of many propaganda machines and monetary-based systems.

The subconscious, 95 percent of brain activity is beyond our conscious awareness. Numerous cognitive neuroscientists have conducted studies that have revealed that only 5 percent of our cognitive activities (decisions, emotions, actions, behavior) are conscious, whereas the remaining 95 percent is generated in a non-conscious manner. That means that the subconscious or unintentional aspect of your mind represents around 90 percent of your total brain function.

Your subconscious is a vast collection of unintentional, habitual thoughts, behaviors, and actions. Therefore, the phrase that best describes the subconscious mind is *NO CHOICE*. Think about it; no state or government is stupid enough to not know about this shortcoming and how vulnerable one is because of one's subconscious mind, since without a doubt many politicians and the so-called correctional institutions, corporations, and states creepily take advantage of the people's mental mechanism, making it suitable for the rulers to easily brainwash, condition, to harness, and lead the masses to where they want.

The inner driven abstract concepts are mostly conscious-related; they consume much more time and effort to flourish, to substantiate, and not profit-oriented entities, which is contrary to the nature of the monetary system since the resources are expended on bringing about quick results by feeding the subconscious mind through our five senses, capitalizing on sex, money, power, and violence. In any case, the end should not justify the means. The intentions shouldn't justify the means. Intentions must not ever justify conduct. If intentions were to justify actions, the entire world would be thrown into a chaotic state. Occasionally, situations might exist where we act less than honest, but the idea of these actions should prevail to perhaps save lives and to do good for the benefit of others in urgent need.

The problem mainly occurs because not enough resources are allocated to educate and constructively empower the conscious mind, since those in power control the resources for their luxury-seeking extreme comfort and pleasure rather than caring about global billions that are devoid of any opportunity to fight against illiteracy and the ever-present rise in violence and crimes. The super-rich are well-equipped with indomitable (invulnerable, bulletproof) strategy and tactics because they can afford to bribe the media and buy the best advisers in diversified fields to maintain the status quo by conditioning people, telling them it is the military-industrial complex that we need to keep us safe, which feeds the weapon industry's vampire-like nature, like Lockheed Martin, Boeing, Raytheon, Northrop Grumman, and others, since they must suck the blood of innocent people in wars of aggression to keep afloat.

Feeding these fat cats with billions and billions of dollars like money grows on trees has created trillions of dollars of deficit, financially driving many states into cul-de-sac situations where economically there is no way out, rather than doing what is urgently required in many so-called modern societies. Instead they should improve in real subjects like employment, education, health-related issues, housing, transformation, infrastructure, to challenge crime-ridden environments, to fight against global warming, and so on, rather than killing innocent children, elderly, and women in many wars of aggression, counting them as collateral damage, and to top it all off addressing it with "in the name of God." Yes, right, as if God is the devil's advocate wanting to perish planet Earth through the wrongdoings of morally bankrupt psychotic governments since they, on false premises, savagely attack any country that is blessed with valuable resources like it ought to be free for taking by force. Instead they should try to make it a winning situation for all engaged parties in a civilized manner and the name of God, humanity, and good business so that the entire international community can benefit from fair and balanced trade.

People need to be inspired to be more, to become more humane, rather than to have more beyond anyone's imagination only to further create extreme inequality where many deprived individuals commit suicide, setting themselves on fire or cutting their wrist, their throat, via shooting, or by hanging, to let the rest know the evils live among us since in thousands of ways the super-rich have manufactured an oligopolistic global state, making living for the rest as miserable as it can be, fettering billions, slapping them with unemployment, or paying the minimum wage to barely keep them alive, to further exploit them to the day that most victims prematurely die. The super-rich manipulate the economy as they create a recession, depression, manufacture an inflationary situation, stagnation, leaving billions desperate to fight for survival against a heinously operated financial system that is rotten to the core.

They execute war crimes in many parts of the world, making it look like they are endowed with moral, legal, and absolute authority to abuse their power, not considering God in their ruthless actions, like the Almighty is absentminded and cannot notice their cruel and atrociously oriented behaviors, forgetting that no bad deed goes unpunished.

Is it fair to say that Communism, where many believe the allocation of resources is just, will be the answer? I say no because no one is and nothing is more communist than God, the absolute communist without the tiniest un-justification or prejudice in giving the sun, the moon, the stars, the rain, the beauty of nature with all of its amenities, and millions of other safe havens provided for everyone to enjoy. And any school of thought or theory that so dogmatically denies the utter source of life, our God that is the absolute reason for the entire existence and beyond, should, in my opinion, not be relied on. Take God out of the scene and there would exist nothing to collate men to set side by side, to show likenesses, to aim at relative values or excellences by bringing out the God-image qualities from within the man.

The solution's bottom line is to free natural resources and invest more in education, literacy, skill, and training for bettering people's lives. Challenge the robot-like subconscious mind with constructive awareness and dynamics, giving a chance to mindfulness to powerfully face the ills of the subconscious, to save one from the bondages of an invisible entity that maneuvers surreptitiously, enslaving the victims; where consciously driven testosterone, the malaise of unfettered freedom, without a competent and resolute mindfulness can affect people for the worse.

I. Thoughts of Sages and Insightful Philosophers

Socrates's beliefs were nonconformist. He often referred to God rather than the gods and reported being guided by an inner divine voice. For

Plato, man is not an animal, though he is born in the same manner. Plato believed that man had a soul that is a part of the Divine Soul. This helped him to know the eternal laws and the secrets of the universe. He said that man's body, or matter, tries to subjugate his divine soul and attracts him towards itself. The man should seek to control it and rise above matter or body to reason.

Aristotle bequeathed (commit, grant) rationality, intelligence, perception, language, and science to mankind. Man is blessed with a divine spark and this very spark is the spirit, the soul, of gaiety (happiness) in man. Even though an animal, he executes great tasks because of the divine spark. He ascends to the length and breadth of the universe where the mechanics that man has invented to discover the visible and the invisible are also a benevolence (gratuity) of the divine spark. Aristotle views on God and existence. Aristotle made God passively responsible for the change in the world in the sense that all things seek divine perfection. God imbues all things with order and purpose, both of which can be discovered and point to his (or its) divine existence.

God, according to Aristotle, is divine intellect or nous, the unmoved Mover that stands as the final cause responsible for the intelligible motion of the cosmos. Aristotle's philosophy emphasis is on biology, instead of mathematics, like Plato. He believed the world was made up of individuals (substances) happening in fixed natural kinds (species). Each discrete entity has built-in patterns of development, which help it develop toward becoming a fully grown individual of its kind.

Aristotle believed in an unmoved Mover and explained the unmoved Mover as being perfectly beautiful, indivisible, and beholding only the perfect contemplation: self-thoughtfulness. He equates this concept also with the active intellect. "The All" is the impervious (seal) version of God. It has also been called "The One," "The Great One," "The Creator," "The Supreme Mind," "The Supreme Good," "The Father," and "The Universal Mother." The All is understood by many to be a panentheistic conception of God, embracing everything that is or can be experienced.

Aristotle defined and ranked the various branches of knowledge. He classified them into physics, metaphysics, rhetoric, psychology, poetics, reason, and logic, and hence laid the foundation of most of the contemporary science.

Darwin's view on religion and God.

Though Darwin thought of religion as a tribal survival strategy, Darwin still believed that God was the ultimate lawgiver, and later recollected that at the time, he was convinced of the existence of God as a First Cause and deserved to be called a theist.

Stoic's view on mankind.

According to the Stoic school of thought, man is a microcosm of the whole of the universe. Thus, in man, as in the universe, reason empowers, and he should subordinate himself to the laws of the universe. The study of the universe reveals that it is ruled by reason whom the Stoics call Divine Reason. Hence, man ought to follow inference and not become a slave to his belly and body. Stoics believe that everything has a specific place in the divine order. Therefore, man is urged to explore his place and fit himself into it. Thus, man should live according to the laws of nature.

Therefore, he will be happy if he comprehends the laws of nature and obeys them at will. That was addressed and contributed in the sacrifices of scholarly minded scientists and philosophers like Galileo, Kepler, Copernicus, Pythagoras, Newton, Einstein, Rumi, Ibn Sina, Berkley, Kant, Bacon, Spinoza, Confucius, Rene Descartes, and millions more, if not billions. After Spinoza comes the philosophy of George Berkeley, John Locke, and David Hume. According to them, everything is contained within the human mind; nothing is outside it. This whole universe, for whose mastery scientists are striving, has been reduced to man's imagination only.

Bacon, a modern philosopher, accentuated the reason for a meticulous and correct study of the universe with an open mind. He acknowledged that man is obligated to believe in religion and God and through his wit should quell (triumph) the powers of nature in intelligent ways. He said the "best of men are like the best of precious stones." Bacon believed that philosophy and the natural world must be studied inductively, but argued that we can only study arguments for the existence of God. Information on his attributes (such as nature, action, and purposes) can solely arrive from special prophecy (revelation, divination). Bacon took up Aristotelian concepts, debating for an empirical, inductive (causative) approach, familiar as the scientific method, which is the foundation of modern scientific inquiry. He was called the father of empiricism. Sir Francis Bacon is credited with establishing and popularizing the "scientific method" of inquiry into natural phenomena.

Bacon argued that the purpose of the scientific method was to not rely on past knowledge of ancient authorities but to depend on observation imperative to the evolution of science in the modern world. Hobbes believed that human beings naturally desire the power to live well and that they will never be satisfied with the power they have without acquiring more power.

Thomas Hobbes believed that people acted in their self-interest. Thomas Hobbes believed that government, an absolute monarchy, is needed to mandate order and demand obedience. Locke's political theory was founded on social contract theory. Unlike Thomas Hobbes, Locke believed that human nature is characterized by reason and tolerance. Like Hobbes, Locke believed that human nature potentiated people to be selfish. This is clear with the introduction of currency.

The sovereign would make and enforce the laws to secure a peaceful society, making life, liberty, and prosperity possible. Hobbes called this agreement the "social contract." Hobbes believed that a government headed by a king was the best form the sovereign could take. Hobbes defines a *contract* as "the mutual transferring of right." In the state of nature, everyone has the right to everything—there are no limits to the right of natural liberty. The social contract is the agreement by which individuals mutually transfer their natural rights. Throughout his entire life, Hobbes debated that the only true and correct form of government was the absolute monarchy. He believed this most coercive in his landmark work, Leviathan.

This belief stemmed from the central tenet of Hobbes's natural philosophy that human beings are, at their core, selfish creatures. Because of Hobbes's pessimistic view of human nature, he believed the only form of government strong enough to hold humanity's cruel impulses in check was an absolute monarchy, where a king wielded supreme and unchecked power over his subjects. Both Hobbes and Locke said that people in the state of nature need to get together and make a society. The ruler has to be absolute if society is to survive. The major difference, then, is that Locke visualized a very restricted government while Hobbes believes in the need for an utter monarchy. Thomas Hobbes, however, did away with this dualism and went over completely to the scientific position.

Everything in the universe, including man, is, for Hobbes, material, and is in constant motion. Thus, man's task is to understand the laws of motion and thereby to understand the universe. Having gained this understanding, man could adjust the laws by his will. Hobbes believed that in man's natural state, moral ideas do not exist. Thus, in speaking of human nature, he defines good simply as that which people desire and evil as that which they avoid, at least in the state of nature. For Locke, in the state of nature, all men are free "to order their actions, and dispose of their possessions and persons, as they think fit, within the bounds of the law of nature. The state of Nature has a law of Nature to govern it," and that law is the reason.

Rene Descartes wrote his famous book *Meditations on First Philosophy* and first published in 1641. The book consists six meditations in which he argues that mind and body are separate and in his familiar cogito "I think, I exist" he indicated the "Cognito" as being the essence of existence of a human being, the human nature for Descartes is made of mind and body and how they are distinct from each other. In the last of the six meditations, "Relating to the Existence of Material Things and the Real desperation between Mind and Body," Descartes says that the body and the soul are not similar, and called his findings "mind-body dualism."

Therefore, a human being exists and is capable of thinking. Descartes confirms that a human being is "a substantial union," a unified entity of a body and mind where each one of them is distinct, and this realization leads to human nature and the body and mind being apart. The mind-body dualism describes that the body and mind can grasp things apart from each other since God made everything separate and independent from each other. He indicated the mind as "I"; hence, he reached an argument that he is a thinking thing, "A thing that doubts, understands, affirms, denies, is willing, is unwilling and also imagines and has sensory perceptions" (Descartes).

Therefore, the mind is indivisible, clear, and unalike, contrasting from the body while the body is an extended, divisible, and non-thinking entity. The nature of a body can realize and perceive the shape of other bodies. The quintessence (gist, main) or the nature of the mind can discern between the power of imagination and comprehension, where imagination is the picturing of things and understanding is the awareness of things without cognizing (grasping, fathoming). He also discussed that something exists because there is something that already exists and creates it; this directs to his belief about the existence of God as being perfect who creates a human being. We, as human beings, are not infinite or perfect beings and we are susceptible to committing errors and mistakes because we don't have the infinite power to recognize the truth.

Friedrich Nietzsche (1844–1900) advocated that the principle thing in man is the passion for power and this passion, the basic element in the universe, dominates everything. The passion for power is so potent that it spares none; whosoever came in its way faces destruction. The wheel of the universe continues revolving regardless of who faces destruction and in what condition. Man is at the mercy of storms, earthquakes, floods, and many other calamities. Thus, life is a misery. Nietzsche regards man to be the barbarous animal who does anything to master power. Reason and morality are helpless against this passion for power, they are but weapons in his hands, tricks of his game. Nietzsche attested, behind all "morality" is a secret desire for power, possession, or superiority. Therefore, man's struggle shouldn't be to be good. It should be to be powerful. Such societies would come to an end as cannot produce "the superman."

Referencing Friedrich Nietzsche and his book *Twilight of the Idols*, meaning the waning, the declining, the half-lighteners of icons, God, Nietzsche contested and was against the philosophy of Descartes's "the mind-body dualism" and that the body and mind are separate. He also discarded the Christian doctrines that deny the ideology of a human being. He believed that the mind and body are one entity and are one aspect of the nature of human beings. He stated that a human being can define himself by accessing "the will to life," which leads to the "will to power." He explained the will to power as being the impetus (motive, force) for winning and leadership by the human beings in the face of the miseries of human nature.

Nietzsche's doctrines concerning the will to power and the will to live are contrary to the doctrines of Christianity; therefore, Nietzsche opposed Christianity as being anti-life weak. Christianity teachings promote self-sacrifice, devotion, and quietude, which denies the values of human beings and their momentum, their crusade "will to power."

Nietzsche believed that human beings are having innate human natures and desires. The desires exist within our form and define the state of the human being; a reasonable, strong human being can control himself and avoid drawbacks in life and a weak human being is the one who doesn't have self-control and denies these desires or passions. Therefore, Nietzsche finalized that a human has to lodge (put up) with his human nature and passions, which in the end leads to the finest moralities.

JOHN PAUL Sartre, born in Paris on June 21, 1905; Sartre's early work relates to existentialism and humanism. He was incarcerated for nine months as a German prisoner of war in 1940. Jean-Paul Sartre started to expand on the meaning of freedom and free will. He focused on his principal philosophical work—*Being and Nothingness: a phenomenological essay on ontology*. The pain of freedom: "Man is condemned to be free; because once thrown into the world, one is accountable for everything one does." Jean-Paul Sartre argued that human beings live in constant anguish, not because life is miserable, but because we are "condemned to be free." While the position of our birth and upbringing are beyond our reach, Sartre manifests that once we become self-aware (and we all do eventually), we have to make choices that define our very essence. Sartre's theory of existentialism says that "existence precedes essence," that is only by existing and acting a certain way do we give meaning to our lives.

According to him, there is no fixed plan, design, or pattern for how a human being should be and no God to render us a purpose. Thus, the onus (burden, load) for defining ourselves, and by extension humanity, falls heavily on our shoulders. I believe Sartre is right, since the choices that we are free to make are not all educated ones, and many are exhausted of intelligence and with no rationale, which often is the reason shit hits the fan. And here is when we go down and sometimes destroyed to the point of no return. Billions are born into poverty with no literacy, without any training, frequently depleted of any role model and without any purpose, barely hanging on to survive. And when decisions are wrongfully made, then guess who benefits other than the state in cahoots with those at the top, the aristocrats, the oligopoly system, the super-rich, their affiliates and mercenaries that are adamant to keep the status quo.

This lack of pre-defined purpose, along with an absurd existence, delivers us infinite choices and is what Sartre characterizes as the "anguish of freedom." With nothing to confine us, we have the arbitrator, the adjudicator (judge) to take actions to become who we want to be directing us to the life we want to live. Sartre believed each choice we make defines us while at the same time showing us what we think a human being should be.

And this unimaginable burden of responsibility that the free man has to tolerate is what commits him to constant suffering. Living in bad faith, as Sartre says, "Everything has been figured out, except how to live." He denounced the concept of living without pursuing freedom. And I say freedom must be accompanied with educated, enlightened choices and the courage to change for the better, taking calculated risk imbued with knowledge and wisdom.

Let's be cleared that freedom so sacred, it is next to God, and when not abused, it brings out the best in man; it substantiates the essence of humanity. It is not ill-treated when imbued with enlightenment and sagacity, it is then when freedom makes miracles, manifesting heaven promised right here on Earth. The phenomenon (sensation, event) of people accepting that things have to be a certain way, and subsequently refusing to employ other adequate options, is what he called "living in bad faith."

According to Sartre, people who convince themselves that they have to do specific work or live in one particular city are living in bad faith. In *Being and Nothingness*, Sartre's renowned discourse for philosophy on ontology (metaphysical) about the nature of existence, he explains the concept of bad faith via exemplifying a waiter who is so immersed in his job that he regards himself to be first a waiter rather than a free human being. In the example of the waiter, Sartre says the waiter is so persuaded that his present job is all that he is competent to do, that it's all he's meant to do, he never considers other alternatives and the option of doing anything else in life.

Sartre argues that we alone are responsible for everything that we are, and by not prospecting the countless possibilities life presents to us we are responsible for restricting the freedom we deserve. "We are left alone without an excuse," he said. With fury against the machine, an avid believer in the Marxist school of thought, Jean-Paul Sartre acclaimed money as the one factor that limits a person's freedom. The need for money, he acknowledged, is the excuse people give themselves when they shut down the idea of discovering unconventional life choices.

Society's acquiescence (agree to) of money enraged Sartre, and capitalism was the political system he found liable for the situation. He likens capitalism to a machine that traps people in a vicious cycle of working in jobs they don't fancy so they can buy things they don't need. This necessity of material things, he debated, did not exist in reality but rather was a man-made construct that led people to refuse their freedom and consider living recklessly without constructively oriented purposes. Sartre was a vocal opponent of capitalism and participated in several Parisian protests in 1968 against the system.

As a Marxist, he hugely admired Fidel Castro and Che Guevara, both of whom were vehemently against capitalism and were establishing a communist state in their respective countries. "We do not know what we want and yet we are responsible for what we are—that is the fact." Ultimately, Sartre was a humanist who advocated that people break free of becoming free from self-shackling and acquire their massive potential. He wanted us to know our freedom, to not be constrained by the popular definition of reality, and live life as we wished to live it; that is what he thought makes us happy.

Spinoza, like Descartes, also argues the universe to be a machine. For Spinoza, God is a part of this machine and so is the man. The machine is viable much more than its parts. This machine is due to the forceful and compulsory operation, bereft of thought. As man is intertwined in its rotation, he cannot free himself of the laws of nature. Relating to Spinoza, the will of God and the laws of nature are the same. He believes the mind of God is the collective of all thought spread all over in time and space.

He sees reason and will to be the same thing. Free will has no existence; the mind is deprived of an absolute will. When the mind wills something, it is determined by some reason, which is the result of other causes.

Spinoza regards human actions to be limited by laws that are absolutely like mathematical laws. According to Spinoza, our self is a delusion. We are part of the stream of laws and sequence of causes. We are an undeniable part of God. We are transient forms of a Being that is the greatest of us all. We are mortal and finite, while he is immortal and infinite. Our bodies are modes of making, our race is an incident of the mode of life. One may call this the philosophy of positivism or compulsion. In a way, it is the philosophy of pantheism (that all the forces in the universe are God, worship that admits or tolerates all gods) because man is held to be a part of God. Spinoza was considered a true Naturalist.

Spinoza's philosophy conveys almost every arena of the philosophical subject, not to exclude metaphysics, epistemology, political philosophy, ethics, philosophy of mind, and science. It gained Spinoza a lasting reputation as one of the most imperative and resourceful thinkers of the seventeenth century. Samuel Shirley, who translated Spinoza's entire works into English, concluded the significance of Spinoza's philosophy as follows: "To my mind, although Spinoza lived and thought long before Darwin, Freud, Einstein, and the startling implications of quantum theory, he had a vision of truth beyond what is normally granted to human beings." Which, by the way, Spinoza was Einstein's favorite philosopher of all times, since it is said that Einstein identified most with Spinoza's views on God and existence.

In Spinoza's ethics, titled *Treating of God and What Pertains to Him,* he indicated, "Whether there is a God, this, we say, can be proved." His proof for God follows an alike structure as Descartes's ontological debate. Descartes tries to prove God's existence by saying that there "must be someone thing that is supremely good, through which all good things have their goodness." Spinoza's argument varies in that he does not conceivably arrive at the greatest being to the existence of God, but rather uses a deductive argument from the idea of God. Spinoza debated that man's ideas do not come from himself, but some sort of external cause. Hence, the things whose attributes a man comprehends must have come from some external, prior source. So, if man has the concept of God, then God must exist before this thought because man cannot create an idea of his imagination.

Spinoza argued that God is "the sum of the natural and physical laws of the universe and surely not a discrete (single) entity or creator." Spinoza strove to prove that God is just the substance of the universe by first stating that substances do not share attributes or essences and then demonstrating that God is a "substance" with an infinite number of attributes, thus the attributes possessed by any other substances must also be possessed by God. Thus, God is just the sum of all the substances of the universe. God is the only substance in the universe, and everything is a part of God. "Whatever is, is in God, and nothing can be or be conceived without God." Bear in mind that this stone-age mentality as seeing God as matter like was driving before the modern physics discovering "quantum mechanics," which states that without a doubt all matter is energy-oriented, signifying there is no matter, only condensed energy, concluding that nothing can exist outside of the mind. If so, then the mind of God is the actual cause to all that exists.

But for Spinoza, nature is everything. Not a nature that is incompetent, but on the contrary, an infinitely resourceful entity; in other words, nature is God. Perhaps Spinoza had difficulty to just digest the word of God since he replaces God's attributes with prevalent, omnipotent nature.

Locke states that besides the human mind and body, there is God, who made the universe. For him, man's reason is the yardstick (criterion) of everything in the universe. Locke holds to the view that if we would exist, so God also exists. But George Berkeley eliminated the material world. For him, there is no universe outside the mind. Existence is that which is perceptible and nothing means anything; nothing exists if there is no mind to recognize it. Hence, all there is, is within the mind of man and nothing is outside it.

David Hume's logical conclusion is that God made man, and man alone is the center and the total of the universe. All that we know is our imagination. There is no material or spiritual substance outside that would generate our ideas. All that can be said about this universe is that the universe is our ideas in succession. A genius in his analytical assessment, he is seeing the universe just as an abstract concept in our mind. From where these ideas come to our mind, Hume has no answer. According to him, these ideas arise from unknown causes. He further argues that we are incompetent to prove their ideas by any rational method known to us.

French philosopher Jean Jacques Rousseau (1712–1778) believed that man is good by nature. Jean-Jacques Rousseau was a French philosopher and writer of the *Age of Enlightenment*. His political philosophy, particularly his formulation of social contract theory (or Contractarianism), strongly influenced the French Revolution and the development of Liberal, Conservative, and Socialist theory. He argued that people in the state of nature were not at fault and innocent at their best. He indicated that people were corrupted by the not so natural civilization. The state of nature, for Rousseau, is a morally neutral and peaceful condition in which (mainly) solitary individuals act according to their basic needs, like hunger and self-preservation.

General will, in political theory, is a collectively held will that directs the common good or common interest. In *The Social Contract* (1762), Rousseau argues that freedom and authority are not contradictory, since legitimate laws are founded on the general will of the citizens. Rousseau states for the subject on inequality in *The Social Contract*, the state of nature is the hypothetical, prehistoric place and time where human beings live uncorrupted by society. Jean Jacques Rousseau holds that man is not a machine or its part. The man is an ideal of feeling and sentiments. Science and civilization have bound him in chains and are destroying all that is human. Rousseau proposed to cast off this shell of civilization to free man for the full development of all his capabilities.

Jean Jacques Rousseau had a major impact on modern governments through the advancement of the philosophy of social contract. Rousseau was able to transform mostly fascist government institutions into democratic institutions founded on individual freedoms. He believed human nature is the total of our species' identity, the mental, physical, and spiritual characteristics that make humans uniquely, well, human.

He was an advocate for direct democracy. This is the only form of government that Rousseau believed would give expression to humanity's innate freedom and autonomy that was graceful before the advent of civilization. Rousseau famously stated, "Man is born free and everywhere he is in chains." Rousseau's theory of education emphasized the importance of expression to produce a well-balanced, freethinking child. He believed that if children are allowed to develop naturally, without constraints imposed on them by the society, they will develop towards their fullest potential, both educationally and morally.

Jean-Jacques Rousseau strongly believed in the innate goodness of man and basic human rights sought based on universal natural law; plus, he debated that both rulers and the citizens have natural human rights, as well as obligations to each other, which should be manifested in a social contract. The contract essentially binds people into a community that exists for mutual preservation. Rousseau strongly believed that only by arriving at the social contract can we become fully human. Rousseau confirms that modern states repress the physical freedom that is our birthright, and take no action to secure the civil freedom for the sake of which we enter into civil society.

Kant's discussion from morality is the reason for the existence of God.

Immanuel Kant (1724–1808) was a prominent German philosopher who argued that the goal of humanity is to achieve perfect happiness and virtue (the summum bonum) and believed that an afterlife must exist for this to be possible and that God must exist to provide it. He denied materialism, fatalism, and mechanism. He argued that there is a higher kind of truth than science and other knowledge and that truth is the moral nature of man. All virtues are within man and it is his inner voice without the need for any outside proof. Man's moral being and his inner voice, the good inside, motivate him to do right. This proved that God exists and he is the Creator of man and the universe.

Kant believed that if God did not exist, man's necessity would demand his existence. Kant insisted on the world of reason and action, which he believed is beyond the world of experience and science. He says our reason directs us to God and our moral being compels us to believe in God. It is our mind that arranges experiences and sensations into orderly thought to reach conclusions. Kant believed we are potentiated for doing good; we have a sense of immortality since we feel the next life awaits us after this life and if the perception of the next life was missing, man would choose the path of immediate gain rather than acting good and righteous.

Arthur Schopenhauer (1778–1860) was a German philosopher that advanced skepticism in philosophy. He considered man to be a supernatural animal but chained to his passions, in which reason subordinates his desires. Occasionally it seems as if the reason is not enslaved by desires, but is the guide. On the contrary, this guide intends to go to where that is already addressed for visiting. For Schopenhauer, the "will" is the powerful blind man who carries on his shoulders the lame man who can see. For him, the will is the only enduring and immutable element in the human mind. According to him, man cannot free himself from desires since desire after desire is consecutively initiated, often leading to passion-oriented behaviors. He is recalled for his pessimistic views on human nature. Freedom is possible only if desires are subordinate to knowledge and reason, but such a possibility does not exist.

Life is evil and full of continuous struggle and every human being is entangled in a continuous compulsive chain. In his most famous work, *The World as Will and Idea*, he states the concept that the will is a universal and omnipresent force that is independent of the individual. In other words, he is saying that the will or the desire for things in life control us rather than vice versa; that we are animals that must live by instincts, as if conscious, and will live in two different worlds because a person victim to his will could not be accredited with wit, and couldn't be relied on since apparently mindfulness cannot play a decisive role in making choices.

Auguste Comte, a French philosopher (1798–1857), founded sociology, or the scientific ways for studying society. He was a positivist, which is the concept that solely scientific facts are the real truth. Positivism is a Western ideology that believes in any system that confines itself to the data of experience and excludes a priori (deductive, reason) or metaphysical speculations. This French philosopher was known as the founder of sociology and positivism. Comte gave the science of sociology its name and systematically accomplished the new subject. He was a philosopher who is also known to be the father of sociology, the study of the development and function of human society, and of positivism, a means of using scientific evidence to perceive the causes for human behavior.

The law of three stages is an idea generated by Auguste Comte in his work the course in positive philosophy. Comet states that society as a whole, and each particular science, develops through three mentally conceived stages: (1) the theological stage, (2) the metaphysical stage, and (3) the positive stage. Auguste Comte first used the term "sociology" in 1838 to refer to the scientific study of society. He believed that all societies develop and progress through the following stages: religious, metaphysical, and scientific. Positivism is the state of being certain or very confident of something. An example of positivism is a Christian being certain there is a God.

He described sociology as a positive science. Positivism is the search for "invariant laws of the natural and social world." Comte's ideas created a major role in developing structural functionalism, which is the perspective in sociology according to which society consists of different but related parts, each of which serves a particular purpose.

Bertrand Russell (1872–1970) wrote, "I think all the great religions of the world - Buddhism, Hinduism, Christianity, Islam, and Communism - both untrue and harmful. It is evident as a matter of logic that, since they disagree, not more than one of them can be true." Bertrand Russell wrote these words in his famous essay "Why I Am Not a Christian." Russell is generally credited with being one of the founders of analytic philosophy, but he also produced a body of work that covers logic, the philosophy of mathematics, metaphysics, ethics, and epistemology, which is the theory of knowledge; it is the investigation of what distinguishes justified belief from opinion.

He saw the universe as a great mathematical machine ruled by scientific laws that are inexorable (relentless, not stoppable), unfaltering. Man is a very small and not so significant part of it. Man is caught in the on rolling of the great machine, and its wheel grinds everything regardless of what is thrown into it. The machine of the universe does not care who comes in its ebb and flow. In the theory of the machine of the universe, an individual has no place. Russell believed that mankind is like a group of shipwrecked sailors on a raft in a vast sea at night. There is darkness all around; they are at the mercy of the waves. He pessimistically viewed they all one by one fall off the raft into the water and disappear. The process will continue until the last man has fallen. The nature of the sea does not value man.

John Stuart Mill (1806–1873) further developed this thought by showing how a man should discover relationships within the universe. We say that we see many events in which there are similarities. We study the sameness and find consistencies. Since man is a part of the universe, this uniformity and sequence should also show by his actions. He argued that man is an extremely complex being. Every action of man is the result of an expansive number of factors.

These fundamental facts apply both to the universe and man, but recognizing them is easier in the universe but difficult in man. For instance, it is possible for an astronomer, based on observation and experience, to anticipate with utter accuracy the time of the appearance of a comet, but to foresee whether a newborn body will be a lawyer, a physician, an engineer, a nurse, or a thief, is impossible, apparently for the reason that the factors behind the appearance of a comet are easy and somewhat constant and factors behind the man are very complicated.

John Stuart Mill believed in the philosophy of utilitarianism. He would describe utilitarianism as the principle that holds "that actions are right respectively and in proportion, they tend to promote happiness, they are wrong as they tend to produce the reverse of happiness." The ethical theory of John Stuart Mill is to justify the utilitarian principle as the foundation of morals. John Stuart Mill was an English philosopher, economist, and exponent (advocator) of utilitarianism. The main characteristics of utilitarianism are as follows: utilitarianism holds that morality is universal, that the same moral standards apply to all people and all situations.

The standards that define what is right are the same for me and you, regardless of who we are. Utilitarianism believes that pleasures are all qualitatively alike; however, they can be graded based on intensity, length, certainty, temporal closeness, fruitfulness, and purity. Ethically, the main concept of utilitarianism is that an action is right if it results in the happiness of the greatest number of people in a society or a group. However, if you choose to do something morally wrong, even though it may be legal, your happiness will decrease.

Utilitarianism is a theory in philosophy about right and wrong actions. It argues that the morally best action is the one that makes the most overall happiness or "utility" (usefulness). Bentham wrote about this idea with the words: "The greatest good for the greatest number." Utilitarianism states that actions are considered moral when they promote utility and immoral when they promote the reverse. The utility itself is explained by Mill as happiness with the absence of pain.

Many utilitarians believe that pleasure and pain are objective states and can be, more or less, quantified. Jeremy Bentham and John Stuart Mill both were towering British philosophers and political thinkers. Four vital categories of the ethical theory include deontology, utilitarianism, rights, and virtues. The deontological class of ethical theories says that people should adhere to their obligations and duties when they are ethically involved in making decisions. Comparatively, Kantianism and utilitarianism have different ways of deciding whether an act we do is right or wrong. According to Kant, we should look at our maxims, or intentions, of the specific behavior. On the other hand, utilitarianism argues that we should do actions that generate the greatest amount of happiness.

Kantian ethics indicate to a deontological ethical theory ascribed to the German philosopher Immanuel Kant. Central to Kant's makeup for the moral law is the categorical imperative, which acts on all people, regardless of their interests or desires, in moral philosophy, deontological ethics, or deontology (from Greek Deon, "obligation, duty") and is the normative ethical theory that the morality of an action should be based on whether that action itself is right or wrong under a series of rules, rather than based on the consequences of the action.

Utilitarianism defines the morality of actions, as suggested by Jeremy Bentham and John Stuart Mill. The greatest happiness principle states that a moral action is one that maximizes utility, or happiness, for the greatest number of people. For example, most people would agree that lying is wrong. But if telling a lie would help save a person's life, consequentialism says it's the right thing to do.

Two examples of consequentialism are utilitarianism and hedonism. Utilitarianism judge's consequences by a "greatest good for the greatest number" standard. Deontology is a set of moral theories that place themselves opposite to consequentialism.

While consequentialism determines the right actions from good ends, deontology asserts that the end and how it is arrived upon are intrinsically linked. A good end will come about as a result of good or right means. Bentham defined as the "fundamental axiom" of his philosophy the principle that "it is the greatest happiness of the greatest number that is the measure of right and wrong." Not so much leaning on the means and how that pleasure and happiness for the greatest numbers are reached, but the result that is objective and is best valued.

Herbert Spencer (1820–1903) is famous for his doctrine of social Darwinism, which asserted that the principles of evolution, including natural selection, apply to human societies, social classes, and individuals, as well as to biological species developing over geologic time. Herbert Spencer, an English sociologist, took Darwin's theory and applied it to how societies change and evolve. As a sociologist, Spencer did not feel the need to correct or improve society, for he felt that societies were bound to change automatically. He takes the position that man can be identified solely by his experiences.

He is certain that the experiences must have a cause; that there must be a universe beyond our experiences which becomes the cause of our experience. Although he called this the "unknowable," he translates it in terms of what he found in man. And because man has subjective feelings and sentiments, the "unknowable" is of the same nature. Thus, the fundamental principle of the universe is also the fundamental principle of man.

The "unknowable" is a creative force and remains active according to definite laws of development. Man is the result of this creative development and a part of the evolutionary processes found in the universe. The law of evolution is the universal law of things and is also applicable to man. Moreover, everything in the universe, not excluding man, adapts itself to the environment.

Man is the product of the universe and his environment. William James (1842–1910), also belonging to the "positivist" school, believed in the universe of observation and experience. He placed man at the center of the universe. For him, the experience is real. Therefore, based on our experience, we build a theory of the universe. For James, what satisfies man is true, and that which does not satisfy him is false.

Man finds certain consistencies in his experience. These apply to the universe too. We act upon them, and the results we predict follow. Therefore, the reality is this experience, and the universe then is the universe of human experience. Through his philosophy of pragmatism, William James justified religious beliefs by using the results of his hypothetical venturing as evidence to support the hypothesis's truth. Thus, this doctrine lets one assume belief in God and prove its existence by what the belief brings to one's life.

William James's lectures, writings, and theories were organized around the dual principles of functionalism and pragmatism. Functionalism considers thought and behavior in terms of how they help a person adapt to their environment. In other words, how they help a person function in the world and be successful. William James wrote *The Principles of Psychology* (1890), *The Will to Believe*, and *Other Essays in Popular Philosophy* (1897), *The Varieties of Religious Experience* (1902), *Pragmatism: A New Name for Old Ways of Thinking* (1907), and other accomplishments. Among his many works, he was the first to teach a psychology course in the US and is often known as the father of American psychology. James was also noticed for contributing to functionalism, one of the earliest schools of thought in psychology, the theory of emotion.

Pragmatism is a philosophical approach that measures the truth of an idea by experimentation and by examining its practical outcome. According to James, truth should be evaluated based on its impact on human behavior; hence, one's religious faith can be justified if it makes a positive difference in one's life.

DEWEY'S view:

Dewey believed that human beings learn through a hands-on approach. This places Dewey in the educational philosophy of pragmatism. Pragmatists believe that reality must be experienced. From Dewey's educational point of view, this means that students must interact with their environment to adapt and learn. John Dewey admits that the universe is that which man experiences. He, however, does not admit this world of experience to be real. He says it is foolish to go beyond the experiences and to try to learn from where this world initiated and where it will last, as no man can get outside his experience. Relating to Dewey, the reality is changing and extending according to laws that are the laws of human experience. Man is a part of this process of evolution, which we find everywhere. The difference is that man can comprehend the universe. He says that as in man, we find uncertainty and doubt; the same is the case with the universe. Man's experience is, thus, the only measure that helps him understand the world.

Buddhism is a spiritual tradition that concentrates on personal spiritual development and the attainment of a deep insight into the true nature of life. There are globally about 400 million believers. Buddhists try to reach a state of nirvana, following the path of the Buddha, Siddhartha Gautama, who went on a pursuit for enlightenment around the sixth century BC. There is no belief in a personal God. Buddhists believe that nothing is fixed or permanent and the state of change is always possible. The path to enlightenment is via the practice and development of morality, meditation, and wisdom. Buddhists believe that life is both endless and subject to impermanence, pain, suffering, and uncertainty. These states are called the *tilakhana*, or the three signs of existence. Existence is endless because individuals are reincarnated over and over again, experiencing anguish throughout many lives.

It is impermanent because no state, good or bad, lasts forever. Our wrong belief that things can last forever is the principal cause of suffering. Siddhartha Gautama, the Buddha, was born into a royal family in present-day Nepal over 2,500 years ago. He lived a life of privilege and luxury until one day he left the royal enclosure and encountered, for the first time, an old man, a sick man, and a corpse. Disturbed by this, he became a monk before adopting the harsh poverty of Indian asceticism. Neither path satisfied him and he decided to pursue the "Middle Way"—a life without luxury, but also poverty. Buddhists believe that one day, seated beneath the Bodhi tree (the tree of awakening), Siddhartha became deeply absorbed in meditation and reflected on his experience of life until he became enlightened.

By finding the path to enlightenment, Siddhartha was led from the pain of suffering and rebirth towards the path of enlightenment and became known as the Buddha, or "awakened one."

There are over 150,000 Buddhists in Britain. The two main Buddhist sects are Theravada Buddhism and Mahayana Buddhism, but there are many more. Buddhists can worship both at home or a temple.

Some Weird Scientific Stuff

Separation of the observer from the phenomenon to be observed is no longer possible.

Werner Heisenberg rewarded the 1932 Nobel Prize for Physics.

You can't have two electrons occupying the same space doing the same job. This also means that atoms are pretty effective at blocking other atoms from getting all up in their space. This is what makes solid objects solid, and keeps them from passing through each other. Walk-Through-Wall effect might be possible with human-made Object, Physicists Predict. If you've ever tried the experiment, you know you can't walk through a wall. But subatomic particles can pull off similar feats through a weird process called quantum tunneling. Tunneling would be an even bigger achievement. The reason two solid objects can't pass through each other is from the pauli exclusion principle that states that two identical fermions. A fermion is any particle that has an odd half-integer (like 1/2, 3/2, and so forth) spin. Quarks and leptons, as well as most composite particles, like protons and neutrons, are fermions. Atoms are made of fermions, but themselves may be fermions or bosons. Fermion is a name given to a particle with a half-integer spin. Electrons, protons, neutrons are fermions.

But if you take two electrons, their combination is not a fermion, 1/2 + 1/2 = 1 or 0 (depending on the directions of spin) so can't occupy the same state at the same time. It feels solid because of the dancing electrons. If you touch the table, then the electrons from atoms in your fingers become close to the electrons in the table's atoms. As the electrons in one atom get close enough to the nucleus of the other, the patterns of their dances change. Particles Walk Through Walls While Physicists Watch. Electrons bound to an atom can sometimes escape, even if they lack the requisite energy, through a phenomenon known as quantum tunneling. Atoms are indeed mostly space. But atoms can't overlap because only a limited amount of electrons can be in the same orbit. The reason for this is what's called the Pauli Exclusion Principle.

The Pauli exclusion principle also states that, in an atom or molecule, no two electrons can have the same four electronic quantum numbers. As an orbital can contain a maximum of only two electrons, the two electrons must have opposing spin. Electrons have spin. The reason solid objects do not pass through each other. To pass through another atom, the electrons of the first atom would have to exist, however briefly, in the same atomic space as the electrons of the second atom.

Can we phase through objects? Phasing happens when the speedsters vibrate their bodies at the same frequency as that of the object they are phasing through. Running fast does not matter here. And yes, if you can vibrate your body fast enough, and at the same frequency as that of the molecules of an object, you can phase through it. Can a gas pass through a solid? Yes, some gases (the smallest molecules) pass through some solids.

But normal gases don't pass through normal solids under normal conditions in normal amounts! We walk through the air because when we move, the loosely packed molecules give way to the tightly packed molecules (i.e., the body). In the case of water, the molecules are more tightly packed than the air molecules. Solid substances have very tightly packed molecules. And you already know that you cannot walk through a wall. This molecule vibration made the Flash go through objects.

Superman is capable of maintaining higher molecular energies than Flash and hence, to be clear, Superman can do that phasing through the objects thing.

Researchers have made light act like a solid, bringing the lightsaber to life (sort of). Photons, the particles that make up light, don't behave like particles of matter. They can pass right through each other, and they don't bind together to make bigger structures. And as in the rest of physics, its nature has turned out to be mind-bendingly weird: Space is not empty because nothing contains something, seething with energy and particles that flit into and out of existence. Physicists have known that much for decades, ever since the birth of quantum mechanics.

Particles are, by their very nature, attracted to particles with an opposite charge, and they repel other similarly charged particles. This prevents electrons from ever coming in direct contact (in an atomic sense and literal sense). Their wave packets, on the other hand, can overlap (ride, protrude) but never touch. There isn't anything to touch; even electrons are made of massless energy particles. We know that splitting an atom creates a lot of energy.

That is because there is a lot of pure energy bound in matter as mass. This same intense power in a small space is essentially why nothing ever actually touches. The objects feel solid because of the dancing electrons. Do you never actually touch anything? Two particles can never touch because of a force between them. Always an amount of space will remain between two particles as long as they don't merge. We can't touch anything but can feel it. When we press something soft, it will bend or dent, but we cannot go beyond the force between our skin and the object we touch. In other words, we feel like we are touching the chair we sit on, but in actuality, we are not touching the chair at all. Or when grabbing the steering wheel as we drive, we are not touching the steering will because of electron repulsion.

And as for all matter ultimately being made out of photons (electromagnetic radiation), it is not true, since photons have no electrical charge. Hence, one can't make a charged particle out of them, as 99.9999999 percent of all of the matter around us is space. That means if you took the space out of every human on Earth, you could compress the entire human population down to an object smaller than a sugar cube. If that is not a miracle; I do not know what is.

If we are 99.9999999 space but feel as solid as we do, that should give us a clue how strange and enigmatic our world is. Atoms are the building blocks of matter. They, quite literally, make our universe what it is. When we die, our bodies do not turn into anything; rather, they are broken down into their constituent parts and recycled into the ecosystem. And the first law of thermodynamics, also known as the law of conservation of energy, confirms it, stating that energy can neither be created nor destroyed; energy can only be transferred or changed from one form to another. In other words, energy cannot be created or destroyed.

Even though electrons, protons, and neutrons are all types of subatomic particles, they are not all the same size. Because protons and neutrons are so much more massive than electrons, almost all of the mass of an atom comes from the nucleus, which contains all of the neutrons and protons. A photon is produced whenever an electron in a higher-than-normal orbit falls back to its normal orbit. During the fall from high energy to normal energy, the electron emits a photon—a packet of energy—with very specific characteristics. Quarks are subatomic particles and are the most basic building blocks of matter that make up protons and neutrons. They're held together by the strong interaction or strong force; it is what holds matter, which is one of the four fundamental forces in nature. (Electromagnetism, weak interaction, and gravity are the other three.)

The reason we do not fall through the floor is that when we are standing on the floor, the pauli exclusion principle prevents the electrons in our feet or shoes from getting too close to electrons on the floor. This is because they are not allowed to occupy the same electron orbit. This means an electromagnetic repulsion between feet and floor is generated. In an atom, three fundamental forces keep atoms together: The electromagnetic force, strong force, and weak force. The electromagnetic force keeps the electrons attached to the atom. The strong force keeps the protons and neutrons together in the atom.

What causes the force that holds atoms together? The answer is electricity and magnetism. The atom's center, or nucleus, is positively charged and the electrons that whirl around this nucleus are negatively charged, so they attract each other. The reason the force is strong is that the atom is so small. Gravity affects atoms the same way it affects all other matter. Every atom creates its gravitational field, which attracts all other matter in the universe. If you put a lot of atoms together, like in a planet or a star, all of the little gravitational fields add together, creating a much stronger pull.

Your atoms would either have to shrink or you would have to be made out of fewer atoms. Atoms don't shrink. The average distance between the protons and neutrons that make up the nucleus of an atom and their surrounding electrons can't be changed. How small is an electron? Together, all of the electrons of an atom create a negative charge that balances the positive charge of the protons in the atomic nucleus. Electrons are extremely small compared to all of the other parts of the atom. The mass of an electron is almost 1,000 times smaller than the mass of a proton. Most of the energy that can be found in an atom is in the form of nuclear mass. The nucleus of an atom contains protons and neutrons, which are held together by the strong nuclear force.

And why objects do not fall to the center or below the surface of the Earth is because if one runs over a deep enough hole, one will fall to its center. So why does no one fall to the center anyway? Because the earth already blocks the space.

As most of it is either heavier than you are or at least is solid and sticks together, it's on you to stay on the outside of the ball. If the matter below you is light and doesn't "stick together" then, you will fall to the center (i.e., until you land on something that again is solid and/or heavier than you are). In the case of a hole, this lighter material is air; in case of, for example, the ocean, it is water.

In both cases, you "fall" to the ground; that is, toward the center of the Earth. So why does matter block us at all? Why can't we go through walls or fall through the ground to the center of the Earth? The reason is electromagnetic forces between the atoms of the matter. They prevent the atoms from colliding. Electromagnetism is the force that acts between electrically charged particles.

Electromagnetic forces are tremendously stronger than gravity. The "weak" nuclear force is 10 to the 25th power stronger than gravity. That's 100,000,000,000,000,000,000,000,000 times stronger!

Electromagnetism—the force we know best—is 10 to the 36th power stronger than gravity. The bottom line is the electromagnetic force behaves as an insulator, an impasse preventing objects from falling to the center of the Earth.

Quantum Mechanics and the Human Brain

It seems sensible to discard all hope of observing hitherto unobservable quantities, such as the position and period of the electron. Instead, it seems more reasonable to try to establish a theoretical quantum mechanics, analogous to classical mechanics, but in which only relations between observable quantities occur. Since the measuring device has been constructed by the observer, we have to remember that what we observe is not nature itself but nature exposed to our method of questioning. Our scientific work in physics consists of asking questions about nature in the language that we possess and trying to get an answer from an experiment by the means that are at our disposal.

Werner Heisenberg.

Scientists are not so far away from understanding the relationship between quantum mechanics and the human brain, since quantum mechanics explains the extremely small world of things, the world of the atom and its affiliates where subatomic particles function. The presence of the quantum has made a breakthrough, reaching not only into the invisible realms where our minds and thoughts are engaged but a drastic change into the entire Newtonian's laws and our notion of realizing space and time not as boundary-oriented entities but as abstract concepts that can only take place in our mind where no such things as materially existing properties can ever be manifested because of the intangible world where the basic laws of physics are not applicable, but also realizing that scientists are still short of manifesting a link between quantum mechanics and consciousness.

This leaves many scientists to behave dogmatically, with no availability to resolve their predicaments unless they can accept the view that conceptual realities must exist to oversee the materially based world where they are not analogous (corresponding, identifying) to the physical universe. The dichotomy of the material territory, the actual physical world, and the concept-oriented entities have forced many scientists to behave not so realistically, and I am afraid adamant to unreasonably stick to their guns since not many physicists want to believe that some strange force or interactivity can take place with zero travel time from one particle to its apparent twin, giving the impression of eerie (ghostly) action at a distance. Quantum theory was originally challenged by some physicists, such as Einstein, who had a different view than Neil Bohr. They engaged often in heated clashes contesting the very nature of science. The Copenhagen translation of quantum mechanics by Bohr and Werner Heisenberg in the 1920s believes that physical systems have only probabilities, rather than specific properties, until they're measured, which basically refers to the credibility and the decisiveness of "the observer effect."

Becker stated that trying to dissect how this interpretation reflects the world we are engaged in is acting in obscurity, exhibiting that the evolution of science is influenced by historical events not to exclude cultural, biological, sociological, political, and economic factors. The disagreements between Bohr, Einstein, and others, including Erwin Schrödinger and Louis de Broglie, materialized since Bohr suggested that entities (such as electrons) had only probabilities if they weren't observed. Einstein argued that they had independent reality, prompting his famous claim that "God does not play dice." Years later, he added a gloss: "What we call science has the sole purpose of determining what is." Suddenly, scientific realism, the idea that confirmed scientific theories roughly reflect reality, was at risk.

Quantum phenomena were perplexing to many physicists because of wave-particle duality, in which light can act like particles and particles such as electrons interfere like light waves. Relating to Bohr, a system behaves as a wave or a particle depending on the context, but you cannot anticipate which it will do. Heisenberg demonstrated that uncertainty, for example about a particle's situation and momentum, is hard-wired into physics. Bohr argued that we could have only probabilistic knowledge of a system and that particles can become entangled. For instance, two particles might have opposite spins, no matter how far apart they are. If you measure one to be spin up, you instantly know that the other is spin down. (Einstein called this "spooky action at a distance.")

It seems that God plays dice, despite Einstein believing otherwise. They seem to ignore that the independent incidents, free proceedings, can occur non-local at the microscopic level. As in the Einstein theory the episodes, the events in space and time, can be measured in respect to each other, but quantum mechanics focuses on the actuality of the measurement, which makes the nature of computation itself very vulnerable to risk, threatening the very fundamental objectivity of the experience.

Scientists believe their incompetency to figure out the "quantum uncertainty" is because of not having accesses to adequate technology, which has centrifuged them from the decisive issues like "Bio-centrism," the "quantum world," and the "conceptuality of space and time," since quantum uncertainty hits at the very heart of Einstein's concept of space and time, saying that the speed of light is constant, and an episode, an incident in one place, cannot synchronously (at the same time, simultaneously) affect events or occurrences in another place, but it does. This has amazed millions of inquisitive minds, since the above has exhibited to be true for so many years, grasping the fact that in a vacuum, the speed of light is 186,282.4 miles per second.

Albert Einstein explicitly dismissed quantum entanglement—the ability of separated objects to share a condition or state—as "spooky action at a distance." Over the past few decades, however, physicists have demonstrated the reality of spooky action over ever-greater distances—even from Earth to a satellite in space. Like Einstein, the physicists Rosen and Podolsky, Schrödinger was dissatisfied with the concept of entanglement because it seemed to violate the speed limit on the transmission of information implicit in the theory of relativity. They rejected the idea that a particle can know what another one that is separated in space is doing, dismissing such findings as to some unknown and yet unidentified local impurity, some type of pollutant interfering with the results of the experience, where Einstein jokingly arrives at "spooky action at a distance," and further saying, "God does not play dice." Which, by the way, indicates Einstein's belief in God.

John Bell, an Irish physicist, employed an experiment that exhibited that separated particles can influence each other at the same time over a far distance and that Einstein was wrong. Bear in mind that quantum theory discloses that everything in nature conveys a particle reality and a wave nature in which the object's conduct exists solely as probabilities, since no tiny object truly takes on a specific motion or place until its functional wave collapses. As strange as it seems to be, when particles are entangled, the pair share a functional wave, and when one member's wave function collapses, so does the other's, even though they might be apart by the width of the universe, showing that when one particle maneuvers with an up spin, the other simultaneously behaves from being a sole probability wave to an actual particle with opposite spin.

It is freakishly oriented since they demonstrate being connected, as there is no space between them or no time to affect their actions. The bottom line that traditionally was grasped by "locality," meaning measuring, that nothing can affect anything else at "the speed of faster than light" is not true. The innovative notion is that the properties that we observe are maneuvering in the field of our mind, manifesting "the observer effect," which does not correlate with the Einstein theory of space and time events, which is solely practical in the physical world where Newtonian laws of physics are exercised. This has come to the attention of so many physicists, such as John Wheeler, who said, "No phenomenon is a real phenomenon until it is an observed phenomenon."

When Death Approaches as Quiet as a Weaving Spider

If we didn't have a soul, no mind, we couldn't have felt pain and suffering; we couldn't have felt happiness. If we did not have a soul, we couldn't have felt either love or hate. If we didn't have a soul, we couldn't have thrived, have imagination, dreams, no intuition, no compassion, no sympathy; couldn't have cared, no curiosity, no ingenuity, no IQ, no passion, no thrilling, no pride; couldn't have sacrificed. If we didn't have a soul, no crying, no laughing, no mindfulness, no memories, no worries, no hope, no faith, no inspiration, no aspiration, no desires, no relief, no anger, no peace or tranquility could have been felt. If we didn't have a soul, no fear, no anxiety, no stress, or any distress, could have been sensed. If we did not have a soul, we wouldn't have courage, couldn't have the spirit to protect ourselves and our loved ones. If we did not have a soul, we couldn't have cared about not belonging. If we did not have a soul, we could have tolerated loneliness, we couldn't have connected to God and thousands of other sacred feelings and emotions that are an inseparable part of the reality of our spirit, our human soul. No global coherency and collective resonance would be possible between the Earth's magnetic fields and the human heart and brain. If nature's energy-oriented fields were not magnificently designed to fluctuate with coordinated frequencies of the human body and other animated beings, no living would have been possible.

The heart's **magnetic** field **is the** strongest rhythmic field produced by **the human** body, and not only influences **every** cell of **the** body but also extends out on all sides into **the** space around us. **The heart's magnetic** field can be measured several feet away from **the** body by sensitive magnetometers. Blood viscosity can **be** reduced 20–30 percent by subjecting it to a small **magnetic** field, lowering potential damage to blood vessels and the risk of **a heart** attack. The **human body** generates intricate electrical action in several different types of cells, including neurons, endocrine, and muscle cells—all called "excitable cells." As all electricity **does**, this activity as well produces **a magnetic field.**

Science confirms: the **heart** is **stronger than the brain**! No doubt, the **brain** has its electric and magnetic field, but they are relatively weaker than the **heart's,** which are about 100 times **stronger** electrically and 5,000 times **stronger** magnetically. We should know that tiny electrical currents exist in the **human** body due to the chemical reactions that occur as part of normal bodily functions, even in the absence of external electric **fields.** They cause current to flow through the body to the ground. Low-frequency magnetic **fields** induce circulating currents within the **human** body. Wherever there's a nerve cell, there's electricity. Being an electric field, all those convergence (overlaying, circuit) electric wave patterns that make one's brain waves are ruled by the same equations governing the **electromagnetic** spectrum, light, particles, and everything else in the universe, which a slight change in Earth's magnetic fields can throw off the balance and the tranquility in our heart and brain and other vital nervous systems and organs. Many enlightening and eye-opening phenomena, often beyond our understanding, should spur our curiosity to diligently probe the mysteries of life, including the so-called death, which has historically perplexed mankind with its enigmatically oriented nature.

Death, so-called, is a thing which makes men weep, And yet a third of life is pass'd in sleep.

Lord Byron

It shouldn't be surprising to know that because of the law of the conservation of energy, no one is wasted; we become a bit disorderly. Realizing that photons that emitted from anyone were gathered in the particle detectors that photons made within constellations of electromagnetically charged neurons whose energy will carry on for infinity and perhaps alter in many forms of life; that all of one's energy, every quivering (vibration), every bit of heat, hundreds of trillions of particles and eternal waves that one might have been engaged in and with many activities, is not destroyed but maneuvering in higher realms since according to the laws of thermodynamics, energy is never lost, nor created in the universe. We simply change the state. Everyone is so afraid of death, but the real Sufis just laugh; nothing tyrannizes their hearts. "What strikes the oyster shell does not damage the pearl." Rumi

According to the laws of thermodynamics, energy cannot be created nor destroyed. It simply changes states. The total amount of energy in an isolated system does not—cannot—alter. And as Einstein indicated, matter and energy are interchangeable. We live in an enclosed universe, but human bodies and other ecosystems are not closed; they're open systems. We exchange energy with our surroundings. If we memorized that we would soon undeniably die, our situation would be entirely different.

"If a person knows that he will die in a half-hour, he certainly will not bother doing trivial, stupid, or, especially, bad things during this half-hour.

Perhaps you have half a century before you die—what makes this any different from a half-hour?" (Leo Tolstoy).

We know we are not just physical; we are not just senseless matter. We are mind and body. We have consciousness, and consciousness cannot be confined. Our mind is simply energy-oriented, an inseparable part of the universal energy. Scientists tell us that neuro-electrical resources within us operate with 100 watts of energy, equivalent to bright, 100-watts bulb, and no doubt our body exudes heat; no wonder in extreme cold those who cuddle can keep much warmer. We should be reminded that when the body expires, this energy does not just vanish, because the way energy operates in our universe, no energy gets wasted, it just transforms. But destined to what form, only God knows; this is something that no one can correctly envision.

What is known is that the energy continues changing but does not diminish, it never terminates, since we are just energy-oriented entities. We are conscious beings fueled by intelligence endowed with miracles of love, empathy, beauty, dreams, imagination, inspiration, hope, and thriving, and many other heavenly attributes made in the image of God. Our death is our wedding with eternity, Rumi. Death permanently ceases all biological functions for the living of physical organisms. There is no doubt that life and death are intertwined, since every breath one takes is a step away from living and towards death. Francis Bacon puts it this way: "Men fear death, as children fear to go in the dark; and as that natural fear in children is increased with tales, so is the other."

Energy is gained via chemical processes, and we can lose energy by off-loading waste or releasing heat. In death, the collection of atoms of which we are comprised is obtained for a different reason. Our energy is redistributed after we expire. The human body, which conveys matter and energy, is both electrical impulses, signals, and chemical reactions. Comparably, plants are influenced by photosynthesis, a process that allows them to produce energy from sunlight. The process of energy generation is much more complex in human beings. Transforming energy takes place not only in death, but also when alive. We receive it via consuming food, which avails us chemical energy. That chemical energy is then transformed into kinetic energy that is burned to empower our muscles. Death is only a change that gives the soul a partial liberation, releasing us from the heaviest of our chains. Death is the greatest of earth's illusions; there is no death, but only changes in life-conditions. Annie Besant. It is one of nature's enigmatic works that we live as we at the same time die.

Ephemerality (transience), or temporariness, confirms that all governed existence, with no exception, is temporary, evanescent (fading, perishing), and varying. All worldly things, either material or mental, are compounded objects in fierce (cruel, constant) changes and subject to determination and ruin.

Some believe that we, to a certain degree, keep some perpetual, everlasting because if we didn't, we would not be here. Being volatile (mutable, changeable, capricious) is something that is inclined to alter often without obvious or compelling (convincing, cogent) reason. Evanescent is bound to disappear like vapor. Transient is something lasting a very short time. Death happens to everything; everyone expires. And it is impossible to know when one will die unless one chooses to commit suicide or has premediated to kill someone, an act of homicide. One of the reasons people do not think or fathom death is because it is not an easy subject to deal with; death cannot easily be defined.

Therefore, acting fearful of the unknown makes no sense. We need to be educated on death since everyone has those times when they fear death. But it's not the fear of death, it is more about the absence of life. But how can you have a life without death? How can something so wonderful have an end? But what is "end"? Because all and everything is interactively connected, then, how can you have death without life? And how can one die without becoming alive again? Perhaps appearing in other forms? Yes, they tell us that the body annihilates, but if the mind, the soul, our conscious, a drop of the cosmic energy, an inseparable part of the ocean of life leaves our body, where does it go? Goodbyes are only for those who love with their eyes. Because for those who love with heart and soul there is no such thing as separation. Rumi

It seems that the mystery of consciousness is correlated with resolving the puzzling issue of death and the human soul, which probably can shed light on the whereabouts of our consciousness, perhaps even realizing what happens to the "soul" after we die and during near-death experiences, or when a person expires. Many scientists are striving to know if the properties of the quantum world and consciousness are somehow linked.

But what exactly is consciousness? Where does it come from and can it be scientifically proven? When the heart stops beating, the blood flow stops and the microtubules lose their quantum state. Microtubules are hollow, fibrous shafts whose main function is to help support and give shape to the cell. They also serve a transportation function, as they are the routes upon which organelles (any of several organized or specialized structures within a living cell) move through the cell. The medical scholars believe once the heart stops beating and the blood stops flowing, the microtubules lose their quantum state. According to Socrates, true philosophers spend their entire lives preparing for death and dying, so it would be uniquely odd if they were to be sad when the moment of death finally arrived. Death, Socrates explains, is the separation of the soul from the body.

It is evaluated that the quantum information in the microtubules isn't destroyed, it permeates the universe at large, and if the patient comes back to life and is revived, then, they believe that the quantum information is retrieved to the microtubules. On the occasion that the patient is not bounced back to life, "it's predicted that the quantum information can exist outside the body, probably indefinitely, as a soul," knowing that so far, nobody has convincingly pierced through this rather viable but controversial issue. Believing that as our consciousness dies at the same time as our bodies, scientists have noticed repeated evidence that once one dies, one's brain cells take days, even longer, until atrophied too far to ever be viable again. This does not mean you're not dead; you are dead. One's brain cells, however, may not be. "What's fascinating is that there is a time, only after you and I die, that the cells inside our bodies start to gradually go toward their process of death," Dr. Sam Parnia, director of critical care and resuscitation research at New York University Langone Medical Center told *Newsweek*. "I'm not saying the brain still works, or any part of you still works once you've died. But the cells don't instantly switch from alive to dead. The cells are much more resilient to the heart-stopping—to the person dying—than we used to understand."

Die happily and look forward to taking up a new and better form. Like the sun, only when you set in the west can you rise in the east, Rumi. And as Avicenna (Ibn Sina) puts it: "And whenever sleep seized me I would see that every dream; and many questions become clear to me in my sleep." On a larger scale, it seems some of our impossible to answer questions are probably answered after we die, such as what happens to our soul, the spirit, our minds.

The human brain grasps information, but receiving information and accumulating knowledge happens as wave transfer photons in the form of energy and not matter. Some believe the energy-oriented soul can enter into another body after one expires and if we can build something to obtain data and substantiate meanings from them, like messages are made via media communication devices, perhaps then we can make sense of them. But not remembering our past living is probably because of awesome design, bearing in mind that frequency waves can transfer energy.

There are several kinds of energy transformation. Since there is energy vibration in all forms of beings, for instance in electromagnetic waves, energy is transferred by vibrations of electric and magnetic fields. In sound waves, energy is transferred via the vibration of air particles or particles of a solid through which the sound travels.

In water waves, energy is transferred through the vibration of the water particles. Light, heat, radio, and similar types of energy are carried by a variety of waves in the ELECTROMAGNETIC SPECTRUM. Radiofrequency energy is another name for radio waves. It is one form of electromagnetic energy that consists of waves of electric and magnetic energy moving together (radiating) through space. The area where these waves are found is called an electromagnetic field.

Some energy waves need a medium, like water or air, through which to travel. The medium moves back and forth as waves carry energy through it, but in actuality, it doesn't travel along with the wave. Waves transfer energy particles. All matter conveys heat energy. Heat energy is the result of the movement of tiny particles called atoms, molecules, or ions in solids, liquids, and gases. Heat energy can be transferred from one object to another. The other types of radiation that make up the electromagnetic spectrum are microwaves, infrared light, ultraviolet light, X-rays, and gamma rays. The sole difference between them is their wavelength, which is directly related to the amount of energy the waves carry. The shorter the wavelength of the radiation, the higher the energy. The rainbow of colors that we notice in visible light shows only a very small portion of the electromagnetic spectrum.

The transferor motion due to the difference in temperature between the two objects is called heat. Energy is not made of anything; energy is a concept to explain a characteristic of matter and non-matter fields. When the matter has velocity, for example, it is known to have kinetic energy. There are also different forms of potential energy. High Energy Particles from Space. The gamma rays are specific particles thought of as photons because that is how they are noticed. A particle is a small portion of matter.

The word conveys a huge range of particle sizes: from subatomic particles, such as electrons, to particles large enough to be seen, such as particles of dust drifting (moving) in the sunlight. Thus, energy isn't a particle or a wave, but it is something consumed by a particle or a wave by which the particle or the wave can do work. Everything, not ostensibly, in the universe, has energy in one or the other form. Scientists noticed that everything in the universe is made out of energy. Quantum physicists revealed that physical atoms are made up of vortices of energy that are constantly spinning and vibrating, which definitely without life is not possible. "Cowards die many times before their deaths; The valiant never taste of death but once. Of all the wonders that I yet have heard, it seems to me strangest that men should fear; Seeing that death, a necessary end will come when it will come." (Shakespeare, Julius Caesar Act II, Scene II).

We Don't Die.

> Don't grieve. Anything you lose comes around in another
> form.
>
> *Rumi.*

Planck believed in life after death. He believed in the existence of "another world, exalted above ours, where we can and will take refuge at any time." (Planck, as cited in Heilbron 1986, 197).

The scientific notion is that matter doesn't disappear, but is simply transformed. If so, then why should anyone be afraid of dying? Is there life after death? It depends on what one acknowledges by life. Logic dictates that the next life will not be similar to this life, so what will it be? It makes sense to say life after life, since the energy does not terminate. The first law of thermodynamics expresses that energy can't be created or destroyed. It can only change forms. Although bodies self-destruct, this energy doesn't go away at death.

It should be something awesome, something extraordinary. Maybe when we die we wake up in an alternate parallel universe. Referencing parallel universes, they are hypothetical and independent of external influence. A specific group of parallel universes is called a "multiverse," also known as an alternative reality. The multiverse is the hypothetical set of probable universes, including the universe in which we live.

Together, these universes constitute all that exists: the entirety of space, time, matter, energy, and the physical laws and constants that explain them. The different universes within the multiverse are known as "parallel universes," "other universes," or "alternative universes." It is imperative not to be subdued by ignorance, which can only be challenged through daring to question and by the way of dialogues via thesis, antithesis, synthesis:

(1) a beginning proposition called a thesis, (2) a negation of that thesis called the antithesis, and (3) a synthesis whereby the two conflicting ideas are reconciled to form a new proposition.

It is human nature not wanting to live forever. We like diversity. Humans like change. We like variety; we adore new things. Redundancy for us humans eventually brings boredom. Immobility does not make us happy. Having the idea to live forever is not savvy. Scientists believe that a proton will last 10 to 32 power years. An electron will last 6.6 x 10 to 28 power years. The universe will continue for 13.8 x 10 to 9 power years. Human life does not die since the energy, our minds, the soul, is carried by photons to dreamlands. Human life was here before we were born and human life will be active in some other kind of being after we expire, which means that you could have another life. People do not realize the past and future in a big scope; all they care to see is their lifespan. We ought to know that other lifespans came before us where we respectively showed up in this era, and that future lifespan will either live or expire depending on if humanity can behave sanely and not annihilate it all. Letting go is a must, potentiating us for a new beginning, new dawn, and for surprisingly experiencing many things, perhaps magnificent living with exciting adventures.

Human bodies (and other ecosystems) are not closed, they're open systems. We exchange energy with our surroundings. We can repeatedly gain energy through chemical processes, and we can lose it by discharging waste or emitting heat, in which the entire scenario is well managed and balanced; otherwise, it would lead to a chaotic atmosphere. I am certain the discipline is well-intended and part of the immaculate design.

The energy-oriented universe.

Science is the most reliable way to understand the real world, and what science indicates is true awareness, since within the sphere of conscious able nature, and meticulously disciplined universe our findings, and experiences become possible. It is no longer an enigma that formless, shapeless energy-oriented, and the unobserved thought molds, and controls what is formed.

The conscious is the universe, it is the reality in which we experience the physical world, and it is within the light of human awareness that we make the actual physical world possible. We see a subjective self, and the outside objective world, in which we acquaint to the substantive matter through our senses.

wherein reality this duality does not exist; the body and mind conceptualizes through consciousness experiencing itself, body and mind are the experiences in the consciousness, in which consciousness is the universe, manifesting infinite possibilities, infinite imagination, infinite creativity, infinite intuition, infinite synchronization, infinite liberation, infinite insight, infinite love, infinite freedom, infinite aspiration, infinite beauty, for the mind of man to perform magic, that is an undeniable part of the wholeness of this miraculous event we call life.

With riveted might, and destined to harness the Neuroplasticity of man's brain where equanimity (balance) of mind is molded and made to collectively conquer what seems impossible is to optimize, and lay the fertile ground for the next stage of our evolutionary life process possible.

Man cannot hold on to what is an impertinence. Once we realize the transcendence part of humanity is not constrained within life and death, we can let go of the fear of holding to what does not pertain, then we have discarded the fear of death.

The truth will set us free, it will trigger self-awareness, and potentiate one to discover a self that is interwoven with the might of the universe. And yes, we sometimes go through so much pain and suffering that can break us, but difficult times mold us into a sturdy and tough individual that often morphs, and transcend us to discover higher self, to mature us despite the dark seasons for fulfilling enormous task.

It seems that the almighty God mold, and make us through the darkness, as The caterpillar crawls, and twists and turns, not realizing is destined to become a beautiful species with wing, to elegantly fly, as butterflies play a critical role in our environment, it's a purpose other than being part of an evolutionary Ecosystem, is just to allow the more conscious mind to enjoy its grace and colorful wings.

TRIBALISM VERSUS SUPER GROUP

No problem can be solved from the same level of
consciousness that created it.

-Albert Einstein

It is a good task to promote freedom as a global brand, but then, only to
brandish it will not help, and could also backfire; it should be substantiated
with good intention, and money well spent. It ought to become a way of
life, where it is desperately needed. It should be implemented through
constructively peaceful means, and not exported via wars. If done through
violence, it will make a bitter experience for everyone, rather than becoming
a potent force for a good cause and a savior. In the meanwhile, it sure would
be helpful if the fascist villains that are our so-called allies could stop
forcing their religious-based dictatorial laws on helpless people where fear
rules and not human rights.

Furthermore, the governments and the affiliated agencies in charge of
sociocultural and socioeconomics are the real problems, where no good can
come out of them to constructively correct their nations. A new trend of
thought, a cultural revolution, is needed for cultivating new social, political,
and economics. To re-do, to educate the masses, to uproot and rejuvenate
the fundamentals. To boost the averagely backward intelligence for cutting
the inhibiting chains of ignorance, to break the yoke of enslavement often
linked to no good customs and traditions.

"A civilization which leaves so large a number of its participants unsatisfied and drives them into revolt neither has nor deserves the prospect of a lasting existence"

-Sigmund Freud

Westerners' view of the developing nations is so shallow that every time they try to help, they unquestionably fail. Not realizing that devolving the nation's sociocultural, sociopolitical, and socioeconomic agendas are fundamentally different than ours since they wrongly perceive the dynamics and the interactivities of the decisive forces in action there, making huge mistakes, therefore causing more trouble for the people that they mean to help. Because the truth about many third world countries, if you like, is no so illuminating that I am afraid many politicians think that for instance they can export freedom, liberty, democracy, accountability, responsibility, upper mobility, the pursuit of happiness, and so on, to no avail. Let's elaborate on some of Carl Marx's doctrines about socioeconomic and sociocultural findings, which can shed light on the development of different societies.

The principles of superstructure design. "A Superstructure is the building's shell which includes all the walls, roofs, windows and doors. It situates on the top of the substructure (Foundations). From the base arrives a superstructure in which laws, morality, metaphysics, politics, religion, and literature legitimize the power of the social classes that are formed in the base. As the Mode of production refers to the varied ways that human beings collectively produce the means of subsistence to survive and improve social beings. Marx believed that human history could be characterized by the "dominant modes of production." This indicates a particular economic system. Marx himself gives a definition: "The totality of these relations of production constitutes the economic structure of society, the real foundation, on which arises a legal and political superstructure and to which correspond definite forms of social consciousness." The superstructure of a building is the part that is entirely above its foundation or basement. Marx puts it this way, the "base" is the foundation of our society. It is the thing that is truly vital. In comparison, the superstructure comprises of things that are made upon that base.

In Marxist theory, human society consists of two parts: the base (or substructure) and superstructure; the base comprises the forces and relations of production—employer-employee work conditions, the technical division of labor, and property relations—into which people enter to produce the necessities and amenities of. To elaborate a bit further, historical materialism is a theory of history laid out by Karl Marx and Friedrich Engels that says that a society's economic organization, Grass Rooty, determines its social institutions. The mode of production for a society changed when the productive forces came into conflict with social relations. The four factors of production are land, labor, capital, and entrepreneurship. They are the inputs needed for supply. They produce all the goods and services in an economy.

Marx argued that because of this uneven arrangement, capitalists exploit workers. Another imperative theory generated by Marx is known as "historical materialism." This theory says that society, at any given point in time, is inevitably ordered by the type of technology used in the process of production. Marx saw the progression in the means of production, technological development, advancement in the tools of the trade as a very decisive force in constituting a social and economic relationship, as they gravely influence the making of a stratified society where different sociocultural and socioeconomic classes are based upon.

With that said, thanks to freedom, human rights, liberty, and democracy, many politicians do not realize that in a short period, for example, America and many of the European nations, have managed to expeditiously become industrialized where technological development has revolutionized their awareness in becoming a "super group" maneuvering advanced ideologies where decisive socioeconomics, sociocultural, and socioeconomic renaissance propelled them into the peak of the twenty-first century, overcoming many tribal mentalities that essentially are accompanied by feudalism culture and the agricultural societies, which I am afraid many of such countries behave backwards since the industrialized forces where advanced technology play an imperious role for making such nations to leap forward into modernism are not present.

One might disagree, saying that many of the third world countries do practice capitalism where the market of supply and demand is actively in force and alive. But one should realize that "dependent market capitalism" is quite different than naturally structured capitalism where in Europe, the West, and in North America, the market dynamics, the technical information, the human resources, the productive dynamics, the skills, are not imported but a byproduct of actual industrialized nations making the culture of the super group possible, where many people's attitude and conduct has moved on beyond tribalism mentality and far away from our primate predecessor's behavior, making super group and the collective identity possible where by law no prejudice, no racism, no religious discrimination, no gender bashing, not allowing bullying or tolerating any finger-pointing is allowed. Encouraging even the smallest group, the minorities, to flourish, to let the sub-groups advance not because of their race, religion, or any identity group, but based on their good deeds, civilized conduct, talent, enthusiasm, skill, and good human relationship creates a melting pot of immigrants that are willing to play by the rules of civil society, at least that is what constitutionally we are aiming at.

Let the criteria for constitutional freedom and democracy prevail. In the meanwhile, we have to persist on the constitutional objectives, since it seems that some of us have forgotten about the vehicles and constructive variables like freedom, democracy, human rights, accountability, responsibility, and the pursuit of happiness for everyone; that no man is above the law, and that we are all created equal, which has so far rendered us the pinnacle of invincibility in being the superpower, endowing us with the "super group" idea and away from tribal mentality.

We should not fall into the trap causing so many ills and misconduct as at one time in history the British Empire did, placing people and minorities against each other, victimizing millions and in different parts of the world through the ugly notion of "conquer and divide policy," which by the way they have still not quit in doing wrong since many of their evil plans are hurting countless innocent people all over the world, leaving the victims of their atrocities economically broke and socially stranded, taking people's happiness away and leaving so many without laughing faces but gloomy, experiencing pain and suffering. We are in the twenty-first century but the British monarchy operates as if we are still living in the fifth or tenth century, operating in medieval and the dark ages where the kings and the queens exploit citizens and claim to be the sovereign proprietors of the entire land.

The British and Denmark, along with the rest of them, are so naïve that they are still pushing the backward idea of a king and the queen as if people should live like bee colonies where the queen bee is the heart and soul of the honey bee colony. She is the reason for nearly everything the rest of the colony does, while millions are annually spent on the queen and the royal family for no good reason, where so many nowadays, even in places like England, cannot make ends meet.

We must get away from the position of "market-dominant minority" where the majority are financially suppressed and left without social protection.

Many politicians do not realize that in many developing nations, certain minority groups have for ages ruled over the majority for one reason or another, suppressing them to the bone with discriminatory actions by policing and through inhumane actions, and as for the victims, they wait to break loose and take revenge at any cost, aiming to destroy their long-time enemy, often causing civil war as soon as the opportunity presents itself either via majority voting to elect their representatives or through coup data or social uprising, like, for instance, putting Shia faith against dominant Sunni minorities. Saddam Hussein was part of creating a bloodbath in Iraq and in many African and South American countries, wanting to export freedom and democracy, not fathoming pulling people away from their tribal mentality and beliefs is not as easy as they think because the very fundamentals required for modernization have not yet been established in developing countries, where there are a variety of hyper-conscious group identities at force not letting democracy produce what it is meant to produce. I am afraid it seems that the beacon of democracy in America is gradually moving toward a minority-controlled corporate oligopoly, which has already caused so much suffering beyond comprehension.

Senator Bernie Sanders this year (2019), at the Democratic presidential debate, said that the three wealthiest Americans have more money than the bottom half of all Americans—an assertion he's made before, including at the Democratic debate in June. Sanders is referring to billionaires Bill Gates, Jeff Bezos, and Warren Buffett. And according to the fact-checking news organization Politi-Fact, Sanders is right that they're richer than half of all Americans.

Not only that, people have to watch for the warning signs, even in the progressively advanced nations where the super group mentality and the melting pot identity could become gravely at risk because the overarching super group protection must not be compromised for the sake of any tribal group identity, since no specific minority should be able to impose their group identity, causing shortsightedness and divisions among the nation. Constitutional principles should relentlessly be enforced to act as an iron-clad umbrella to protect the nation and integrate people into super group mentality where everyone is bound to behave as a member of the human family and with open-mindedness, where no one is left behind or polarized, treated or finger-pointed as no-good foreigners, where xenophobia, which is the fear or hatred of foreigners or strangers, is embodied with discriminatory attitudes and behavior and often culminates in violence, abuses of all types, and exhibitions of hatred that can gradually bring chaos, even at a national level.

In conclusion, people ought to be able to speak their mind, with freedom of expression, freedom of assembly, have the freedom of religion, freedom of the press, and gender equality. They need to exercise democracy, liberty, and human rights. They must be encouraged with accountability, responsibility, and be conditioned for upper mobility with the pursuit of happiness, and so on, where the undeveloped nation can be assisted with technological innovations, expert instructions, and advice so that they as well can become a part of industrialized nations oriented with advanced technology, where the infrastructure and the requirement for global melting pot societies can become an alternative.

> "It is not the strongest of the species that survives, nor the most intelligent that survives. It is the one that is most adaptable to change."

> Charles Darwin.

This is only possible if tyrants and despotic rulers in many autocratic regimes are not adamantly supported by the superpowers of our time, which is also the reason for the people to become victimized through force and suppression, as most are deliberately kept illiterate and uninformed to avoid establishing progressive laws for the despotic regimes to fear that perhaps one day the people can become enlightened and aware of the truth and perhaps arrive at their own super group mentality.

If they do, I am sure everyone will be better off, since many of these nations are enriched with raw materials, with plenty of natural and human resources that can be put to good use for both advanced and underdeveloped nations rather than being squandered by the fascist regimes that I am afraid are absolutely in charge of people's wealth, as they do not hesitate to plunder what belongs to the actual citizens as people's backward belief systems can be overcome through progressive thoughts and behavior to negate cultural impediments where everyone can be guided to access and exploit decisive pieces of information and knowledge, which eventually can deliver them with a super group attitude and belief system for experiencing the sweet taste of equality and liberty. I think even nation-states should be and will be obsolete.

> "I think nationalism will be seen in the future as a form of tribalism and I think what we call Democracy will be Netocracy where people globally can work on issues."
>
> Deepak Chopra

THE VITAL COSMIC FORCE

The transparency of traces of God should be known even to the most naïve-minded individuals because it is perplexing to know that there are those people who do not realize the driving force behind everything that we do is the animated Force, the sacred energy-oriented Entity, an infinitely brilliant Conscious that sustains and embodies the entire existence since cosmic energy provides vitality in all animated bodies. Many of the ancient cultures of the globe have some concept of life energy as they arrive at various names to perceive it as they accordingly relate to the idea of energy. There are indeed many of the same meanings to the life energy concept. We know it from the Latin *spiritus*, the Greek *pneuma*, the Indian *prana*, the Chinese *qi* (or chee), the aborigines of Australia, for example, call it "Jojo."

Even early scientists searched for something they called "élan vital," an unseen force giving rise to life, where Japanese call it *Ki*, meaning life force, *gi* in Korean, *mana* in Hawaiian. In Persian it is known as *Joon*, named vital energy in Western culture or the lively force, the innate energy that gives life to the entire living, the Spirit, the Essence of the universe, and so on. The life force or prana energy is all around us; cosmic energy that every mystery tradition worked for to master it, to amplify the human experience. We feel lifted by some ever-present Power that gives us grace. It is at death in fact that our life force stops and our soul is freed from the bondage of the human body where our spirit blends with the energy-oriented universe, impregnating the womb of Mother Nature with excitingly diversified ideas and new horizons in life-bearing force.

Cosmic energy is the prevalent life force. It is present in the cosmos, the universe, between the galaxies, molecules, and in the space. It is essential to manifest the order of our life and expand our consciousness. Life one force or "Parana" supplies energy directly to the brain. This cosmic energy comes

632

from outside the body, enters the brain, and keeps the cells charged with life. Life force is the intelligent power that infuses food matter, oxygen, and sunshine into living matter.

It is unbecoming when so many do not fathom the driving force behind every nutritious food that we consume to keep us going, not realizing the driving force behind billions if not trillions of species and plants which for one reason or another must exist to make the balance in nature possible, not asking what is the driving force behind the biological, biomechanical, biochemical, bio-centrism, and trillions and trillions of interactivities taking place causing a decisive chain reaction to make living possible, not curious about countless environmental requirements that bring about just the right atmosphere for living, and for the entire Earth's inhabitants to enjoy life, taking for granted all the celestial bodies not to exclude the heavenly stars, the Sun, the Moon, the wondrous forces of the universe with infinite planets, countless galaxies, billions of universes, and the amazing world of black holes, and the entire cosmos as if they have no order as an amazingly mindful Conductor, an awesome Creator, can ever be absent.

Any orderly organization must have an intelligent Planner, a must-have Programmer, a phenomenally orderly mind because such an infinitely gargantuan universe cannot operate without a superbly rational designer? Scientists say that matter, the way we know it, the way we think of it, doesn't exist. Fundamentally, all that exists in our world is made of energy. The entire materials that make up our world, every component, every part, every element on the periodic table, are all comprised of atoms. The particles that makeup atoms—protons, neutrons, and electrons—are nothing but a condensed manifestation of energy that interacts with each other and brings about an element's characteristics, making life possible.

When one touches any solidified item, any object—an iron plate, a wooden chair, someone's face, a tree, an avocado, or some seeds—one is just touching energy that has been compressed into a specific shape or form. A brick, a rock, an iron door, or a wooden wagon may seem hard to the touch, but in reality that's just an illusion generated by the energetic forces of the object thrusting against particles that make up the feeling on your hand. Contemporary physicists and modern scientists believe that all particles are precisely vibrating energy. In reality, all that one sees is made up of space. The atoms that create matter are all made up of energy. That means you too are made up of energy, just like the Sun, the Moon, the stars, planet Earth, the forces of the universe, and so on.

Energy is extremely vital because it's what makes everything that exists. Energy is the invisible power machine, the imperative force necessary for growth, progress, development, and change. Based on a natural and holistic health point of view, having an "energy apparatus system" that is working properly is the key to health—not only physical health, but mental, emotional, and spiritual health, which are linked to each other through the functions of the nervous and endocrine systems.

Energy makes up your body and mind, and it is the mode of communication between the two. In the East, people have long believed that life energy flows through all things in the universe. They have addressed this energy over thousands of years and have influenced a set of rules and beliefs by which this life energy force maneuvers. In many ways, the essence of what Berkley argued centuries ago correlates with perceiving the universal animated force influencing all biologically driven species, known as "biocentrism," where human consciousness plays a very decisive role in identifying the external existence.

What we perceive as real is not, but an illusion, since our senses also immaterially based as they communicate with the shadowy world, an apparition (phantom) entity where its real existence is questionable. If the physical world as we know it exists, then it must exist in space and time; it must be conveyed within the space and time. But this does not make any sense because space and time are not materially oriented to hold anything, to grasp what we know as the universe since space and time are just abstract concepts, they are the byproducts of our mind. So is the universe; they are immaterial instruments and variables.

They are not accessible to the five human senses of sight, hearing, smell, taste, and touch. The parameter of space and time are not plausible; they are not materially oriented. They cannot hold a so-called materially based world. What we see as real is all just a mirage; they are nothing short of theoretical ideas, nonrealistic phenomena (events). In the realms of quantum mechanics and in dealing with the behavior of subatomic particles, all particles and objects are dependent on the presence of an observer, known as the observer effect. Denoting that without consciousness, matter resides in an unproven, indefinite state of probability. Any universe or anything that could have existed before consciousness only existed in a probability state. The external and our internal perceptions, our senses, are inseparably interlaced.

Berkeley was right. A practical idealist, he believed that objects are only collections of ideas; that things are mind-related. He argued that there are no material substances. There are only finite concepts and an infinite mental substance, namely, God. George Berkeley theorized that matter does not exist, it comes from the belief that "sensible things are those only which are immediately perceived by senses." Berkeley held that there are no real matters of any kind; that what is designated as objects or the physical world are in reality collections of ideas that originate in the mind of God. From his ontological views, Berkley argued God is himself a Spirit, but an infinite one. Berkeley's famous principle is esse is percipi; to be is to be perceived.

Berkeley was a true idealist. He believed that ordinary objects are mind-dependent, as it should remind us of the observer effect in modern physics, as it also credits Berkley's view where the subatomic world of quantum mechanics can relate to Berkley's idealism doctrine. He would answer that it can be said to exist if we can perceive it, but that it cannot be said to exist if we cannot perceive it. The theory that all knowledge comes from sense-experience, instigated by the rise of experimental science, happened in the seventeenth and eighteenth centuries, expounded by John Locke, George Berkeley, and David Hume.

Empiricism is the theory that the origin of all knowledge is sense experience. It emphasizes the role of experience and evidence, especially sensory perception, in the buildup of ideas, and believes that the only knowledge humans can possess is some posterior (i.e., based on experience) knowledge that is known to be true based on reason alone, popularized by Emmanuel Kant.

Moderate empiricists believe that significant knowledge comes from our experience, but also know that there are truths that are not based on direct experience. For example, a math problem, such as 12 + 12 = 24, or 20 – 10 = 10, is a fact that does not have to be investigated or experienced to be true. Rationalism is a belief or theory that opinions and actions should be based on reason and knowledge rather than on religious belief or emotional response. The theory is that reason rather than experience is the foundation of certainty in knowledge. The practice of dealing with a reason as the ultimate authority in religion. Rationalism finds that facts are held by the intellect. For example, the statement: "Rape is wrong" is an example of ethical truth, which makes it a rational belief. Rationalist thinkers believe that knowledge, or our understanding of truth, is acquired without sense perception.

Rationalism is the view that regards human reason as the primary means of discovering knowledge and determining what is true or false. Rather than emotions, experience, or religious doctrine, a rationalist would rely on reason and logic to make sense of the world. Rationalism was a major theme of the Enlightenment Summary. Modern, or continental, rationalism refers to the works of the seventeenth-century philosophers René Descartes, Baruch Spinoza, and Gottfried Leibniz. Scientific rationalism encouraged people to think for themselves instead of relying on Church authority. Some political thinkers applied scientific rationalism to the government. René Descartes is generally considered the father of modern philosophy. He was the first major figure in the philosophical movement known as rationalism, a method of understanding the world based on the use of reason as the means to attain knowledge.

Rationalists claim that there are decisive ways in which our concepts and knowledge are learned independently of sense experience. Empiricists argue that sense experience is the ultimate source of all our concepts and knowledge. Rationalists develop their views in two ways. French philosopher René Descartes, who said, "I think therefore I am," is regarded as the father of rationalism. He believed that eternal truths can only be revealed and examined via reason. The two principle answers are reason and experience. Relating to the choices you make, you'll either be categorized as a rationalist, which corresponds to reason, or an empiricist, which corresponds to experience.

Rationalism prioritizes reason and factual analysis and argues that truth can best be known by logical power and not through faith, dogma, or religious teaching. Empiricism is contrary to rationalism, the view that mental ideas and knowledge exist in the mind before experience; that there are abstract or innate ideas. Subjective idealism, or empirical idealism, is the monistic metaphysical doctrine that only minds and mental contents exist. It entails and is generally identified or associated with immaterialism, the doctrine that material things do not exist. The mind is not an idea but holds a mental substance that is different from ideas. It supports ideas but is entirely distinct from them. By ideas, Berkeley refers to the immediate perception of sensible things (in contrast to inference). Ideas are sensible things, objects of thought, and objects of perception.

Berkley contests Locke that says all knowledge comes from experience. There are no innate ideas. The structure of the universe is describable only through our human mind and consciousness. The universe is fine-tuned for life, since life creates the universe; it is not that the universe brings about life. The universe is and simply exists in both space and time, "spatiotemporal," having both spatial extension and temporal duration and both mind-related concepts which, without comprehension in our mind, they both will be unclear and solely fit in a probability state, since neither time nor space have a real

QUANTUM MECHANICS AND CONSCIOUSNESS

> I regard consciousness as fundamental. I regard matter
> as derivative from consciousness. We cannot get behind
> consciousness. Everything that we talk about, everything
> that we regard as existing, postulates consciousness.

Max Planck (as cited in de Purucker, 1940, Ch. 13)

The question of what kinds of physical systems are conscious "is one of the deepest, most fascinating problems in all of science," wrote the computer scientist Scott Aaronson of the University of Texas at Austin. "I don't know of any philosophical reason why [it] should be inherently unsolvable"—but "humans seem nowhere close to solving it."

Conscious awareness is one of the most staggering—and most complex—aspects of the human brain. We are special since we are self-questioning (introspection, self-contemplating, soul-searching) creatures. Because we are a consciousness-oriented species, we can experience and react to our surroundings in a self-directed way. We have come so far in understanding the human brain but there still are much more puzzling issues that scientists cannot figure out about the human brain. For instance, how the brain produces consciousness, how it generates remarkable experience or qualia. Neuroscientists do not know how incoming sensations happen and are translated into subjective impressions like color, taste, happiness, or pain. Or how is it that we can invoke a mental image in our minds at will. As Minsky notes, "Consciousness is a word that you use to not discuss the 40 or 50 different processes that are going on at various times..."

We further do not know how much our personality is decided by our brain and whether our mind manifestation and potential is the byproduct of innate activities or externally permeated agendas, a conundrum still not resolved to whether nature or nurture is the cause for our character build-up since it is believed that we are all born with genetic predispositions that influence our psychology and who we are, which contests the blank slate position, saying that the mind has no innate traits of its own and believes that most of our personal preferences are socially caused since our brain is continuously engaged in progress, relentlessly being fed via the environment and the atmosphere we are engaged in. The other imperative issues are what happens to our consciousness when our mind wanders, when our brain is at rest and sleeps? And why is it that we must sleep to stay alive, and why do we dream? Conscious alertness is disengaged because our brain shuts off, leaving us unaware of our environment and utterly vulnerable when we are deprived of sleep.

We would eventually expire if not allowed to sleep, which makes sense that our brain needs to recharge and for our body to become refreshed so that conscious vitality and our body's energy can be restored. It further puzzles us all, how does our brain store and access memories and how information is registered in the human brain not to exclude short-term memories and long-term memories? There's also declarative memories (names and facts) and non-declarative (like so-called muscle memory).

And inside our long-term memories, we possess flashbulb memories since we're able to remember the exact details of what we were doing during so many events. Neuroscientists think that memory storage depends on the link between synapses and the strength of their relation; memories aren't so much encoded as discrete bits of information, but rather as relations between two or more things, for instance, touching a hot item or surface causes pain or thinking about squeezing a lime produces saliva, getting aroused thinking about one's lover. Scientists think memories of an event may be stored in a matrix of interconnected neurons in our brains called "memory trace."

And how do perceptions work? Do we have free will or are we all predestined and deterministically at work?

Can human consciousness be replicated? Neuroscientists think not, because its characteristics are nonlinear, unpredictable where interactions occur among billions of cells. How we do a fascinating job moving and controlling our bodies through space and time stays a mystery. There's something very intricately happening between our motor cortex and the cerebral cortex that allows for such smooth, efficient actions to take place.

Where do our thoughts come from? What are they made of? What is the mind? What is consciousness?

Where does consciousness come from? To the above and countless other insightfully complicated questions, the atheist answers that nature is simply the cause of it all. If so, the question is, does nature convey reliable information? The atheist's answer is yes, since they have no choice but to agree. Otherwise, no scientific inquiry of any kind can be cultivated from a chaotically stated nature exhausted of valuable information and data. Hence, if an entity conveys information as decisive as nature does, then it must have intelligence because information and intelligence are attached at the hip, and therefore, if the footprints of information and unimaginable intelligence are traced, there must exist a Magnificent Designer, an extremely competent Programmer, indicating that God must exist.

The relevancy of consciousness and quantum mechanics are not so far apart, as both maneuver in an invisible hemisphere as they fundamentally are the very reason for existence, where quantum mechanics deals with the subatomic world of infinitely dancing particles, not only making modern technology like laser and advanced computers, quantum chemistry, quantum optics, quantum computing, superconducting magnets, light-emitting diodes, and the laser, the transistor, and semiconductors, such as the microprocessor, medical and research imaging, such as magnetic resonance imaging, and electron microscopy possible, but acting as the substratum to the physical world itself. And consciousness for having the ability to experience and reason with it all. It seems that quantum mechanics challenges the critical and utter idea of not only space and time, but the very notion of the Newtonian law that deals with what we take as the reality of the physical world.

"I cannot define the real problem, therefore I suspect there's no real problem, but I'm not sure there's no real problem." Richard Feynman.

American physicist Richard Feynman said this about the infamous (well-known) puzzles and anomaly (ambiguity, paradoxes) of quantum mechanics, the theory physicists use to describe the tiniest objects in the universe. But the issue of equally, if not a more shackling (fettered) problem of consciousness is also very enigmatic. Quantum mechanics is the finest theory we have for fathoming the world at the nuts-and-bolts level of atoms and the tiniest world of subatomic particles. Probably the most prominent of its mysteries is the fact that the outcome of a quantum experiment can alter depending on whether or not we choose to measure some property of the particles engaged.

When the observer effect was initially realized by the earlier scientists of quantum theory, they were deeply concerned. It seemed to sabotage (threaten) the fundamental assumption behind all science: that there is an objective world out there, heedless of us. If the way the world behaves depends on how or if we look at it, what can "reality" really mean? Some of those researchers felt compelled to conclude that objectivity was an illusion and that consciousness has to be permitted to have an active role in quantum theory. To others, it was very perplexing. Albert Einstein once complained the Moon does not exist only when we look at it!

Contemporary physicists indicate that whether or not consciousness influences quantum mechanics, it might arise because of it.

They think that quantum theory is probably required to fully grasp how the human brain works, and quantum objects can be in two places at the same time, so a quantum brain can hold onto two mutually exclusive concepts at once. Newly driven experiences have perplexed the scientific communities as many mathematical notions such as infinity and the square root of minus one have since infinity is not a real number, mostly is used as a figure of speech, a metaphor, and as an imaginary number and the ($\sqrt{-1}$) (the square root of minus one) which they utilize as an imaginary concept, leaving many scientists to behave dogmatically with no availability to resolve their predicaments unless accepting the conceptual realities that exist to oversee the materially based world as they are not analogous (corresponding, identifying) to the physical universe. The dichotomy of the material territory, the actual physical world, and the concept-oriented entities have forced many scientists to behave not so realistically, and I am afraid adamant to unreasonably stick to their guns.

They seem to ignore that the independent incidents, free proceedings, can occur non-local at microscopic level, as in the Einstein theory the episodes, the events in space and time, can be measured in respect to each other, but in which quantum mechanics focus on the actuality of the measurement that makes the nature of computation itself very vulnerable to risk, threatening the very fundamental objectivity of the experience.

The point is that there is more to the universe than meets the eye, that the entire existence is mind-made, where the entire cosmos and beyond are consciously driven. Since matter, the human body, and the universe grew from this fact, and not this fact from matter, the universe and human body, and that all and every theory of existence should subordinate to infinite mindfulness of God since behind all theories, not to exclude the theory of materialism (matter-centrism), the observer effect, the bio-centrism, naturalism, the big bang theory, Darwinism, existentialism, or human centrism (a philosophical theory or approach that emphasizes the existence of the person as a free and responsible agent determining their development through acts of the will), and so on, lays the driving force of cosmic energy prevalently executed and impetus to all there is and all there ever will be. A brain scan can show that one's decisions are made seven seconds before one decides to dismiss the claim of the free choice and rational thoughts where determinism kicks in.

Scientists at the Max Planck Institute for Human Cognitive and Brain Sciences exposed that our choices are made seconds before they become known to us. By looking at the micro patterns of activity in the front polar cortex, the scientists could anticipate the participant's decision-making seven seconds before the participants make them. "Your decisions are strongly prepared by brain activity. By the time consciousness kicks in, most of the work has already been done," said study co-author John Dylan Haynes, a Max Planck Institute neuroscientist. "I don't even know where to begin here! I know from the hypnosis research that the unconscious pretty much controls everything and that consciousness is extremely limited." He goes on to say, "I am not the only one." Further, Marcus Du Sautoy (Professor of Mathematics at the University of Oxford) went through the study himself. The 7-second delay was in full effect.

Marcus claims he is disturbed here and brings up the subject of free will. Does this mean we do NOT have free will? This should spur us to pay more attention to the unseen spooky agendas of the quantum world, the conscious mind, the subconscious mind, where they are the driving forces behind our thoughts. The solution to the above dilemma is to Grass-Rooty create a healthy environment with golden opportunities, since the non-prejudiced subconscious mind collects everything from a very young age, putting the conscious mind in a very vulnerable position. If the mind is not educated, intelligent, and not wise enough to discern wrong from right, then often every choice made is bound to mistakenly orient toward free choosing, which not only affects the conscious mind but the subconscious as well because the subconscious mind records everything; it does not discriminate, leaving one with miscalculated and misdirected will to substantiate "determinism," often manifesting ugly outcomes.

A collective intelligence should relentlessly activate to preserve the human spirit for building a globally constructive environment for not only the deprived people but the entire humanity to indiscriminately grow where man's glory can reach the glittering stars and the freedom to truly follow the pursuit of happiness. "A drop from the ocean cannot survive, if not preserved as part of ocean." There is a natural order to this intricately designed world which, if defied, will eventually bring nothing less than destruction. Any centrifugal force or deliberate attempt away from what is intelligently devised will be bound to failure. We are to coagulate our position to what is destined and purposefully directed to reach its objective.

HAVE FAITH

Over the entrance to the gates of the temple of science are
written the words: ye must have faith.

Max Planck

And the best proof for God is to have mercy, to believe in empathy as Jesus
showed the way to glorification, where grace finds its meaning, compassion
arrives at its source, wisdom is pinnacled, magic is performed, miracles
happen, the souls are freed, peace becomes reality, tranquility is sought,
and mankind reaches hope. It is then when man is exalted, can exhibit he
is no stranger to Godly attributes where angels reside.

In our human journey, we should not bypass the fact that the human
heart and mind are interactively connected where a cruel and perturbed
(agitated) heart manifests a disturbed, unrestful, and often angry character
with no peace and serenity in spirit, neither composure in mind nor the
body. A quiet heart will bring about calm, rational, caring, and peaceful
attributes; it can explore the God within. It gives birth to longevity, good
health, and contentment. "My heart is glad, and my flesh also will rest in
hope" (Psalm 16:9).

What signifies a cruel heart is a fit of jealousy, venomous intention,
resentment, vengeance, and a host of inhuman conduct. Awaken the God
of love, God of mercy, God of empathy, the God of caring and kindness
within you because for one, you will live a much healthier, happier, and
longer life, make a better world, be a mentor (confident, guide), a role
model for the rest to follow, knowing that amelioration (betterment,
goodness) is contagious, and so is evil.

Kant's theory is an example of a deontological moral theory—according to these theories, the rightness or wrongness of actions does not depend on their consequences but on whether they fulfill your duty. Kant believed that there was a supreme principle of morality, and he referred to it as The Categorical Imperative.

In moral philosophy, deontological ethics or deontology is the "normative ethical theory," which states that the morality of an action should be based on whether that action itself, under a series of rules and principles, is right or wrong rather than because of the consequences of the action. In other words, it shouldn't be the outcome of an action that is morally decisive, but the nature of the action itself.

Deontology states that an act that is not good morally can lead to something good, such as shooting the intruder (killing is wrong) to protect your family (protecting them is right). For instance, in a self-defense situation, even though it is rational to protect oneself or loved ones from a vicious attack by harming or killing the offender, still it is not morally the best thing to do.

A system of ethics that judges actions based on whether they adhere to a rule or a set of rules, deontological ethics are different from teleological ethics, which states that the rightness of an action is based on the goal that the action is meant to achieve. Deontological theories believe that certain acts are always wrong, even if the act directs to an admirable outcome. Kant is responsible for the most prominent and well-known form of deontological ethics. Kant's moral theory is based on his view of human beings as having a unique capacity for rationality. The core theory of deontology states we are morally obligated to act by a certain set of principles and rules regardless of the outcome. Comparatively, in religious deontology, the principles derive from divine commandment so that religious laws say we are morally responsible and obligated not to steal, lie, or cheat.

You might say temptation is very yearning (craving) and sometimes enforcing and that revenge is sweet. But I say to you the power of love, peace, and tranquility is so significant and a lot stronger. "For peace to reign on Earth, humans must evolve into new beings who have learned to see the whole first" (Immanuel Kant). But the fathoming whole is to conceptualize infinity that's beyond anyone's grasp, since even collective intelligence and reasoning power are not potentiated to fully realize the vastness of God.

And because the principles for a methodological inquiry, whether intellectual, scientific, philosophical, moral, aesthetic, or religious, are a constraint to the human brain, the nervous system, and the senses that are limited within the space and time, "Space and time are the frameworks within which the mind is constrained to construct its experience of reality" (Emmanuel Kant). Thus rules of logical inference or the embodied wisdom are only applicable to see the amazing traces of God, where having faith comes in handy knowing that belief is a product of the mind, but faith is not. Faith is a product of the spirit, therefore, strengthen your faith to empower your spirit.

Let's adhere to caring and peace. Let's make it a better world knowing that temptation is a desire to engage in short-term urges for enjoyment that threaten the long objectives and goals, where often self-control is lost incurring addiction to sex, fornication, and because the appetite for excessive lewdness (sexuality, drive) can take over, leading to dependency, obscene behaviors, and lustfulness in offensive ways. Human beings are bound to make mistakes, since no man is perfect. We all make mistakes. As Jesus said: "It is better to take refuge in the Lord than to trust in man" (Psalm 118:8). The above testimony by the Lord Jesus Christ, that all men either sometimes or frequently do wrong, is a very potent example. Another is where Jesus said: Let him who is without sin cast the first stone.

According to the Gospel of John, the Pharisees, in an attempt to discredit Jesus, brought a woman charged with adultery before him. Then they said to Jesus that adultery was punishable by stoning under Mosaic law and wanted him to judge the woman so that they might then accuse him of disobeying the law. Jesus thought for a moment and then answered, "He that is without sin among you, let him cast the first stone at her." The people crowded around him were so touched by their consciences that they departed. When Jesus found himself alone with the woman, he asked her who were her accusers. She replied, "No man, Lord." Jesus then said, "Neither do I condemn thee: go and sin no more."

Is it about the frequency of doing wrong, and how appalling, how relatively corrupted, the culprits are or the degree of acting improper which can indicate how serious is the wrongdoing, how horrified or the wretchedness of the crime? No moral absolutism can be held by any mortal, denoting that only rules of God should be followed since solely God is absolute and utterly free from making mistakes. Therefore, for some to claim that we live in a twenty-first century with an awakened conscious, where the civility of mind and manner prevails that can replace the commandments of God, is simply not true; no man can ever be the total moral compass or potentiated to carry the ultimate reference point for the rest to follow.

Plus, I will say, do not be hasty, since humans are Spirit in the flesh, and because both mind and body can be weak, demanding and bounded for satisfying the urges raising from our animal instinct and essentials without which we perish, is not a feeling, but an innate, "hardwired" tendency toward a particular behavior or need. No man's moral principle has the competency to ever replace God's absolute moral dogma (law).

In time, the betterment of human behavior advances, or you might say progressively evolves, but eventually it's not good enough to make any human 100 percent immune from doing wrong and universally virtuous. Perhaps in other realms where the very nature of our being, our soul, can transcend to the heavens, as we are vulnerable to so many often irresistible temptations not to exclude gluttony (over-indulgence), greed (avarice), sloth (laziness), wrath (anger), envy (jealousy), pride (vanity) and as all of the deceits of the material world with deadly sins attacking us, leaving millions with no way out of their misery.

Jesus was tempted three times. The temptations were hedonism (hunger/satisfaction), egoism (spectacular throw/might), and materialism (kingdoms/wealth). John the evangelist, in his epistle, calls these temptations "in-world" as "lust of eyes" (materialism), "lust of body" (hedonism) and "pride of life" (egoism).

And as for wrath, Jesus says this about turning the other cheek. In the Gospel of Matthew chapter 5, an alternative for "an eye for an eye" is given by Jesus: "You have heard that it was said, 'An eye for an eye and a tooth for a tooth.' But I say to you, do not resist the evil one. But if anyone slaps you on the right cheek, turn to him the other also." Referencing virtues and dignified behaviors one should practice, chastity (purity) is the key, starting with temperance (self-restraint), charity (giving), diligence (zeal, integrity, labor), forgiveness (composure), kindness (admiration), and humility (humbleness).

In a materially oriented society where consumers are incessantly bombarded with luxury items and ranking where the rich and famous are relentlessly being propaganda as the cream of the crop since not their dignified personality, their character worth, honesty, understanding, loyalty, wisdom, intelligence, trustworthiness, courage, integrity, dependability, compassion, with many other virtuous allots (traits) matters so much, no, but their material wealth, prestige and power is what I am afraid dictates the norms that make them who they are.

The New Testament quotes Jesus as saying, "It is easier for a camel to go through the eye of a needle than for a rich man to enter the kingdom of God." So powerful a metaphor cannot come from mankind. Realize that practicing virtues is not an easy task, which helps when one has in mind a salvation reference point. Salvation, in religion, states the deliverance of humankind from such fundamentally negative or disabling conditions as suffering, evil, finitude (limitedness), and death. In some religious beliefs, it also entails the restoration or raising of the natural world to a higher realm or state. "The angel of the Lord encamps all around those who fear Him and delivers them" (Psalm 34:7).

Can you not think of a time when you were spared from potential harm or position, from being destitute but turned into your favor much better than expected? If so, the evidence of the almighty God should be cultivated, since there are no accidents. We are all fate-related and destined accordingly since our good deeds and righteous conduct, or demonic behaviors, ill-manners, and inhumane actions, deterministically reserve us a seat either next to the glory of God or neighboring Satan. It is not a lie to believe in what goes around, comes around. Hence, remember what Jesus of Nazareth said: "Do to others whatever you like them to do to you" (Matthew 7:12).

Believe in a judgment day tailored for each person immediately after one is gone, so justified, so meticulously precise, utterly leaving no doubt even for the most skeptical of men to see the truth behind God's decree (command, edict) as one will feel remorse one's punishment for one's sins, and pride in one's reward, since the grace of God receives the righteous and corrects the sinful. It is a purposefully driven universe; what once the wisest of men took as superstitions are giving birth to scientific reality. There is a prayer in a Persian saying that:

"I belong to the other world, burn me, God, burn me, turn me into Homaay." Turn me into a fortunate angel, ascend me, take me into the higher realms. The dialogue means so much for the worshiper, as the request often carries so much passion asking the Creator of heavens, the omnipotent, the omnipresent, and the omniscient God for mercy, requesting for the prayers to come true, to free one from the suffering of this world.

THE WONDERS OF OUR UNIVERSE

Not only is the universe stranger than we think, but it
is also stranger than we can think." "What we observe
is not nature itself, but nature exposed to our method of
questioning." "There are things that are so serious that
you can only joke about them.

Werner Heisenberg.

One of the foremost wonders of the universe is without a doubt how
the human brain functions. The human brain is the largest brain of all
vertebrates relative to body size. The cerebrum makes up 85 percent of the
brain's weight. It contains about 86 billion nerve cells (neurons)—the "gray
matter." It contains billions of nerve fibers (axons and dendrites)—the
"white matter." White matter is found in the deeper tissues of the brain
(subcortical). It contains nerve fibers (axons), which are extensions of nerve
cells (neurons). Many of these nerve fibers are surrounded by a type of
sheath or covering called myelin. Human cognitive ability has helped us
to even land on the moon.

The brain has three main parts: the cerebrum, cerebellum, and brain
stem. Cerebrum is the largest part of the brain and is made of right and
left hemispheres. It maneuvers higher functions, like interpreting touch,
vision, and hearing, as well as speech, reasoning, emotions, learning, and
fine control of movement.

The cerebrum is the thinking part of the brain and it controls your
voluntary muscles—the ones that move when you intend to move them.
Your brain produces enough electricity to power a lightbulb. Your brain is
made of approximately 100 billion microscopic cells called neurons. Your

neurons create and send more messages than all the phones in the entire world. Eighty percent of the brain's volume is made up of glial cells. In terms of volume, brain tissues help in maintaining the metabolic activity of the human body. Most of the energy to the brain is provided from glucose.

Chimpanzees are our closest living relative in the animal kingdom. An international team of researchers has sequenced the genome of the bonobo for the first time, confirming that it shares the same percentage of its DNA with us as chimps do. Since it controls vital functions such as breathing, swallowing, digestion, eye movement, and heartbeat, there can be no life without it. Bonobos and humans are the only primates to typically engage in face-to-face genital sex. Bonobos do not form permanent monogamous sexual relationships with individual partners.

Humans have five vital organs that are essential for survival. These are the brain, heart, kidneys, liver, and lungs. The human brain is the body's control center, receiving and sending signals to other organs through the nervous system and secreted hormones. Your brain's autonomic nervous system signals your heart to pump its oxygen-rich blood, and your heart responds by delivering blood to your entire body, including to your brain. Fortunately, the steps you can take to protect your heart are also ways to protect your brain. The hippocampus is a structure in the brain that has been associated with various memory functions. It is part of the limbic system and lies next to the medial temporal lobe.

The human brain weighs about 3.3 pounds. The average male has a brain volume of 1,274 cubic centimeters. The average female brain has a volume of 1,131 cm3. The brain makes up about 2 percent of a human's body weight. Traditionally, scientists have tried to define the mind as the product of brain activity: The brain is the physical substance, and the mind is the conscious product of those firing neurons, relating to the classic belief. Many evidence exhibits that the mind goes far beyond the physical workings of your brain. The human brain is primarily composed of neurons, glial cells that are known as the "supporting cells" of the nervous system.

The four main functions of glial cells are to encircle neurons and hold them in place, to supply nutrients and oxygen to neurons, to insulate one neuron from another, and to destroy and remove the carcasses (corpses) of dead neurons neural stem cells and blood vessels. About 60 percent of our adult body is water. The brain and heart are made of 73 percent water and the lungs are about 83 percent water. The brain works like a big computer. It processes information that it receives from the senses and body and sends messages back to the body.

Brain tissue is made up of about 100 billion nerve cells (neurons) and one trillion supporting cells that stabilize the tissue. It is one of the most complicated structures in the universe and contains an average of 100 billion neurons, each one linked to 10,000 other neurons, resulting in 10,000 synapses per cell. Every synapse passes an electric signal around the brain telling your body when to do things. Each synapse is a data point, every signal is a 1 or 0; in total, about one quadrillions of ones and zeros. Our brain works as fast as a computer that processes 100 trillion bits per second. It can contain up to one thousand terabytes of data, a hundred times the size of the US Library of Congress. Most of that power is hiding below the surface.

April 13, 2008 - Brain Scanners Can See Your Decisions Before You Make Them. Experiment by the late Benjamin Libet, who motor activity fired a fraction of a second before test subjects chose to push a button a theory that subconscious activity preceded and determined conscious choice.

Unconscious cognition is the processing of perception, memory, learning, thought, and language, without being aware of it. The role of the unconscious mind on decision-making is a topic greatly argued globally by neuroscientists, anthropologists, linguists, and psychologists. Truly, a lot of human behavior branches out from our subconscious mind. Scientists say the subconscious helps to initiate goal-orientated behavior, creativity, insight, memory consolidation, and decision-making. Relating to cognitive neuroscientists, human beings are conscious of only about 5 percent of our cognitive activity, so most of our decisions, actions, emotions, and behavior depends on the 95 percent of brain activity that goes above our conscious alertness. Your subconscious mind is an unquestioning servant that works day and night to make your behavior fit a pattern consistent with your emotionalized thoughts, hopes, and desires. Your subconscious mind is what is called homeostatic (equilibrium, balance, equanimity). Several studies conclude that up to 90 percent of the decisions we make are based on emotion. We use logic to justify our actions to ourselves and others. Summary of the most important ways to control your subconscious mind. The subconscious mind is a data bank for everything that is not in your conscious mind.

The subconscious stores your beliefs, your previous experience, your memories, your skills. Everything that you have seen, done, or thought is also there. Experts estimate that the mind thinks between 60,000–80,000 thoughts a day. That's an average of 2,500–3,300 thoughts per hour. That's incredible. Other experts estimate a smaller number of 50,000 thoughts per day, which means about 2,100 thoughts per hour. Numerous cognitive neuroscientists have conducted studies that have revealed that only 5 percent of our cognitive activities (decisions, emotions, actions, behavior) are conscious, whereas the remaining 95 percent are generated in a non-conscious manner.

Emotions are more potent than reasoning power. When someone is in a state of rage, with extreme emotional disturbance, he or she loses all of their wit and reasoning power; it frequently occurs when one is deeply in love with someone or in a position of dislike and hate. Love makes us blind because we cannot clearly distinguish between right and wrong; we cannot discern the most obvious fault of the beloved one when in love.

About 95 percent of brain activities are utterly subconscious. Statistically, every second our subconscious mind grasps about two million bits of data. Cognitively random thoughts can come to anyone's mind from nowhere, which neurologists call intrusive thoughts, in which some are weird, goofy, strange, creepy, and dark. Our subconscious mind is not an analytic mind, whereas our conscious mind is a calculative one that can make sense of things. The subconscious mind does not like to be questioned, but our conscious mind can be rational and objective so that it can prevent much trouble, since our subconscious mind acts like a robot, which is contrary to our conscious mind that can deal sensibly with the reality of what is happening around us.

Our subconscious pretty much controls all that occurs in our body. The subconscious mind cannot tell the difference between what is fact and what is fiction. Our conscious mind takes all of the information the subconscious mind takes in and makes sense of it; it absorbs all the information the subconscious mind takes in and rationalizes it; it distinguishes between what is real and what is not; it reacts to what is true and otherwise.

That is the reason why we sometimes become frightened and panicked, because of being fearful because our subconscious mind thought it was a real danger, not being able to recognize the difference. That is why often our conscious mind kicks in, trying to make sense of the nonsense. Our brain is not designed to work 24/7; on the contrary, our subconscious mind does, even when we are not awake.

In our childhood stages, in premature development, we cannot tell what is real and what is not since we operate subconsciously until about 7–9 years old because as children, we have not developed a conscious mind yet. What is called cognitive chunking is when we group a similar type of information in our memory and then when we are dreaming, our subconscious mind tells us what to think before we think it.

The field of neuroscience is remarkably one of the most prominent fields in discovering new brain activities where dynamic behaviors can be accomplished, referencing force of habit and brain plasticity via persistence and repetitious behavior, which new neurons and synopsis (synapses are the connecting points between one's 100 billion brain cells) can be created for dynamic approaches in everyday living, realizing that creating new behaviors can be done by rewiring the brain. People can be professionally empowered to reach positive changes, arrive at new objectives, approach constructive behaviors, not to exclude health, sport, nutritional, business-oriented ventures, become a success through motivational scenarios and a host of other things by grasping the neuroscience of behavioral changes.

Neural pathways, comprised of neurons connected by dendrites (dendrites are the segments of the neuron that receive stimulation for the cell to become active. They conduct electrical messages to the neuron cell body for the cell to function), are created in the brain based on our habits and behaviors. The number of dendrites increases with the frequency of behavior, since through the neural pathways, our brain cells communicate with each other by a process called "neuronal firing."

Many psychologists believe that when brain cells often interact, the link between them strengthens and the messages that repeatedly travel the same pathway in our brain start to transmit faster and faster. With enough repetition, these behaviors become automatic. For example, almost effortless driving, learning a new language, reading, swimming, and riding a bike are some of the rather intricate behaviors that we do automatically because neural pathways have shaped.

Neuroscientists tell us that it takes approximately 3–6 months for a new behavior to become a habit; this estimate differs in each person. Linking a new behavior to as many areas of the brain as possible supports to create fresh neural pathways. By tapping into all five senses, we can make what the experts in the field of neuropsychologists call "stickiness" that helps shape neural pathways.

The more science advances, the more scientists are baffled with the way our universe operates, which often admits it is the craziest place you might ever witness. It's full of exploding stars and immortal jellyfish and it's been hanging around for approximately 14 billion years.

Let's put some of the wonders of our universe into perspective. The most noticeable wonder of them all should be the human mind, because the mind of man resembles the mind of God, since our Creator made man in his image. As neither the mind of God nor the human mind can be seen, they are both invisible and energy-oriented; only the effects and traces can be identified. No existence is ever possible without the mind of the Creator. The mind of man is made of ascending qualities; its attributes are potentiated to function as a drop in an infinite ocean of the mind of the Creator.

Our mind is energy-oriented, and cannot be transferred into matter or into any other entity. The mind of God is also beyond reach; it is an abstract concept that we cannot do without, signifying the crucial requirement for God. But unlike energy, matter can be transferred into energy.

We have been endowed with love, the most powerful emotion in human beings; something as miraculous as the human mind, sensational heart, the soul and with a sacred emotion like love through which we can escalate to the heavens. God has even honored man with choice and the will to utilize that right or to abuse it; given a choice to control the will of passion which, if not intelligently managed, can either make us or break us. Your mind, your heart, the feelings and emotions, soul and the spirit, are God-like differentiated properties that are infinitely oriented energy. They will not exterminate when the physical body expires but return to the original Source where we came from to be accordingly judged and perhaps reincarnated to where we are destined.

Which should remind us what Rousseau says about human nature. The belief that man, by nature, is good, was espoused by the French philosopher Jean Jacques Rousseau (1712–1778). He believed that people in the state of nature were innocent and at their best and that they were corrupted by the unnaturalness of civilization. Rousseau believed modern man's enslavement to his own needs was responsible for all sorts of societal ills, from exploitation and domination of others to poor self-esteem and depression. Rousseau believed that a good government must have the freedom of all its citizens as its most fundamental objective. And I say that man, unlike other animals, is potentiated with virtuousness; he should be encouraged to do good, to reach his full potential, to bring about the God within him.

Many of the atoms you're made of, from the calcium in your bones to the iron in your blood, were brewed up in the heart of an exploding star billions of years ago. One's body conveys cosmic relics (the cosmic microwave background, or CMB), in big bang cosmology, it is electromagnetic radiation as a remnant from an early stage of the universe, also known as "relic radiation." The CMB is faint cosmic background radiation filling all space. The cosmic microwave background is landmark evidence of the big bang origin of the universe from the creation of the universe. Almost all of your hydrogen atoms were formed in the big bang, about 13.7 billion years ago, before the digital television. If you tuned your TV between different channels, trying to reach various stations, a small percentage of the static visible to you would be the afterglow of the big bang.

Other wonders include light from some stars takes so long to travel to our eyes that when you look at the star-speckled night sky you're staring, peering deep into the past. NASA's Hubble Telescope can look as far back as 13 billion years ago. Forty-seven years ago, man put its first steps on the moon and the boot prints will probably still be there a million years from now since the moon has no atmosphere, so there's no wind or water to wipe out and sweep through and erase any evidence or marks.

Outer space is silent. Eerily silent (strange and mysterious). That's because sound waves need some sort of medium to travel through. And space is a vacuum, a dark, silent vacuum. Did you know that one year on

Venus is equal to the orbital period of 225 Earth days? Venus is the second-closest planet from the Sun. It is named after the Roman goddess of love and beauty. As the second-brightest natural object in the night sky after the Moon, Venus can cast shadows and, rarely, is visible to the naked eye in broad daylight.

The tallest mountain on Venus is Maxwell Montes, standing over 20,000 ft./8.8 km high. What makes a day on Venus longer than a year? Venus is the sole planet in our solar system that rotates backward.

The Sun makes up 99.86 percent of the mass of the solar system. It's so big that you could squeeze 1.3 million Earths inside of it.

There might be as many as three sextillion stars in the universe. That's 3 followed by 23 zeros, or 300,000,000,000,000,000,000,000. That's more than all of the grains of sand on Earth. When a massive star explodes, its scrunched-up (squeeze, bent) core forms something called a neutron star. Neutron stars are so dense that just about a teaspoon of their material would weigh more than Mt. Everest. The explosion can spin the neutron star to unbelievable speeds, up to 600 rotations per second. Ordinary, observable matter (like stars and planets) make up a measly (inadequate) 5 percent of the universe. The other 95 percent of the universe is made up of invisible dark energy (68 percent) and dark matter (27 percent). That means there's 95 percent of the universe that we don't know about yet.

The universe is estimated to be around 13.7 billion years old, 93 billion light-years wide, and contains over 100 billion galaxies, each galaxy with hundreds of billions of stars. Estimated numbers start to overwhelm anyone's mind when one thinks about it. Stars are made of balls of gas adhered together by gravity and made of helium and hydrogen. The hottest stars are blue-white whilst the coolest stars are red, relating to their temperature. Stars are the reason for most of the naturally occurring elements; without stars, we would not be here. The calcium in our bones and the iron in our blood came from inside stars that terminated long before the solar system was ever constituted.

The most imperative star is the Sun, which is the temperature of 5,500 degrees Celsius, and is the closest star to the Earth. But why should the Sun exude the precise amount of heat and light for life to so carry on orderly? This wouldn't be a mystery if one is rationally minded and sees a highly intelligent Designer behind this fascinating task. The Earth is the third planet out from the Sun and is our home planet. It is the only planet in our solar system that we know of that can sustain life, and the only planet that we know of that has liquid water on its surface.

The distance the Earth keeps from the Sun is beautifully balanced, just perfect for our survival. A little further away or closer to the Sun and life would not be possible. We should have in our mind and realize the goodness that God has blessed us with and pursue a living with a purpose, following with how and why we are here!

As far as the wonders of the black holes, black holes behave like utter quicksand. They are created when a giant star collapses, imploding into a tiny area with enormously intense gravity where it even sucks in the surrounding light. We've had an idea, a sense of how black holes work, but we've by this time never actually seen a black hole—there are no apparent to telescopes that pick up electromagnetic radiation, light, or X-rays. We can only guess what they probably look like on the inside.

We already know that no light can escape from black holes. We also realize that they are the terminal, the verge (border on) of huge stars. Black holes utilize the power of gravity for not letting anything escape as they pull things towards them. Black holes are made of three layers, starting with the outer layer, which is called the outer event horizon. Within the outer event horizon, it is not too strong; things can still escape from a black hole's gravity. The middle layer is known as the inner event horizon, the gravity in this layer is much stronger and will strongly hold objects it captures. Then falling toward the center of the black hole, which is called the singularity, a point in space beyond the knowledge of present-day science, since no one knows what takes place there as gravity is the strongest, no scientists can grasp what is exactly happening at the center of the black holes known as the point of singularity.

Dark matter is a form of matter thought to account for about 85 percent of the matter in the universe and about a quarter of its total energy density. Most dark matter is thought to be non-baryonic, possibly being composed of some as-not-yet found subatomic particles. The known material of the universe, familiar as baryonic matter, is composed of protons, neutrons, and electrons. Dark matter may be made of baryonic or non-baryonic matter. To hold the elements of the universe together, dark matter must make up approximately 80 percent of the universe.

Astronomers know that dark matter is vital and it plays a role, but what is that role? In our universe, dark matter outweighs normal matter, the everyday stuff we see all around us, by a factor of 6 to 1. The gravitational effect of all that matter holds together galaxies and galaxy clusters. That includes its gravitational pull. Dark matter is made of particles that do not absorb, reflect, or emit light, so they cannot be detected by observing electromagnetic radiation. Dark matter is material that cannot be visible directly. We realize that dark matter exists because of the effect it has on objects that we can observe directly. Then we have the giant void which, unlike a black hole, is not a hole in space, it is empty of both matter and dark matter.

Contrary to a black hole, light can pass through the void, though scientists believe it conveys dark energy. It's not the only void in space, either, although it is the largest, with an estimated diameter of 1.3 billion light-years. Dark matter is still a mystery, but we're depending on it to assist in describing some of the unknown and puzzling positions of our universe. Cosmologists believe as much as 27 percent of the universe is dark matter.

As for the dark energy, in addition to the 27 percent of the universe that's believed to be dark matter, a lot more is in the form of dark energy, which makes up about 68 percent of everything surrounding us (the "normal" matter we all know and love is only 5 percent of the universe). And like dark matter, scientists don't know much about dark energy, but the present hypothesis is that it's what's behind the increasing expansion of the universe (whereas dark matter slows it). Much of our understanding of dark matter and energy comes from the Cosmic Microwave Background, a snapshot of thermal radiation "soon" (380,000 years) after the big bang when hydrogen atoms were first formed.

In the meanwhile, there is something really attractive 220 million light-years away, and it's dragging our whole galaxy toward it. Ever since the big bang, the entire universe has been expanding, so it makes sense that our galaxy would be moving. But not in the direction it is going. Some point to dark matter as the cause of this. And others claim that our galaxy, the Milky Way, is blocking our view of whatever it is that's pulling us towards it at 1.4 million mph.

A brief look into the multiverse, also familiar as a mani-verse, mega-verse, metaverse, omniverse, or meta-universe, is an assumption group of multiple universes. Together, these universes form everything that exists: the entirety of space, time, matter, energy, and the physical laws and constants that explain them. The multiverse: If we define "universe" as everything and "all there is" or "all that exists," then as defined there can be only one universe, otherwise many. If there is a limited possibility of something occurring, for example a planet, or a galaxy forming, then in an infinite universe there will be an infinite number of that thing. Therefore, there would be an infinite number of galaxies and planets in an infinite universe. What the multiverse universe model says is that there are many other universes plus our own, and each universe possesses various properties and with different values, believing that only some of this universe is appropriate for living since they have the basic constants of physics, for instance, having gravity set just right to form stars. But many universes would not, as we are living in one of those (because we couldn't survive in the others).

The different multiverse models come from theoretical physics and cosmology and the leading ones have a rich mathematical basis. One version of the multiverse arises from string theory. String theory is the best theory so far developed to unify the four fundamental forces of physics, by considering each particle as a tiny, vibrating string operating in 11-dimensional space. String theory was not explored to describe the fine-tuning or multiple universes; the multiverse prediction arose out of the math of the theory. String theory hasn't been confirmed experimentally yet; testing it will be very demanding, since it requires large, high-energy experiments like the large hadron collider and more. It is an extremely challenging task. Physicist Gerald Cleaver writes: "if multiverse theories are shown to be correct, it would be "the next step in understanding the beauty, splendor, complexity, and vastness of God's creation."

A parallel universe, also known as a parallel dimension, alternate universe, or alternate reality, is a hypothetical self-contained plane of existence, coexisting with one's own. The aggregate of all potential parallel universes that make the reality is often called a "multiverse." Together, these universes comprise everything that exists: the entirety of space, time, matter, energy, and the physical laws and constants that describe them. And as for the quantum world, the word *quantum* is obtained from the Latin, meaning "how great" or "how much."

The discovery that particles are distinct packets of energy with wave-like properties led to the branch of physics dealing with atomic and subatomic systems, which is today called quantum mechanics. The universe is all of space and time and their contents, including planets, stars, galaxies, and all other forms of matter and energy. The geometry of the universe is, at least on a very large scale, elliptic. The presumption is that in a closed universe, gravity eventually halts the progression of the universe, after which it begins to contract until all matter in the universe collapses to a point, a final singularity termed the "big crunch," the opposite of the big bang.

No doubt that the position of constants in the universe and the conditions of the early universe are elegantly fine-tuned for life, with several theories in physics anticipating that our universe may be one of many, an idea familiar as the multiverse universes. Some believe that fine-tuning is proof of God's existence, while some others argue that the multiverse replaces God. In reality, linking the matter for the existence of God should reference the ability to reason and address it with the power of inference and with since no scientific approach, can manifest the proof of God because the existence of God is not a scientific question, but to discover the magnificent traces of an infinitely wise Designer via the competency of intelligence and realizing the awesome orderly conducts, precision with exquisite life-bearing criteria where an inch of disorderly behavior can mean annihilation of the entire universe, where chaos (mayhem) can result from the exhaustion of infinitely wise and immaculately oriented supervisor since logic resonates and dictates the creation is so harmonized and with delicate congruency that fit for life.

Plus, multiverse should further remind us that the multiverse itself would still be God's creation, where God's authority is infinitely expanding. We need to know that for a habitable planet such as Earth to even exist, so many Grass Rooty constants should exactly and correctly maneuver to create the right values for fine-tuning a dial most appropriate for living. If the universe was made of any physical constant with even slightly different value, the universe simply could not support life: it would expand too quickly, or never form carbon atoms, or never make complex molecules like DNA. The multiverse is the idea that our universe is one of the possibly infinitely many universes.

Out of the many possible universes that may exist, each with different strengths of forces and properties of particles, our universe is one of very few that is empowered with hosting life as we know it. What the science is further saying should remind anyone of the very fine-tuning of our universe since the physicists believe that when the big bang happened billions of years ago, the matter in the universe was consistently disseminated (distributed). There was the exhaustion of stars, planets, or galaxies, just particles floating about in the dark void of space. As the universe was built up outwardly from the big bang, gravity pulled ever so gently on the matter, gathering it into clusters that at the end became stars and galaxies. But gravity had to have just the right force—if it was a bit stronger, it would have pulled all the atoms together into one big ball. The big bang—and our prospects—would have ended quickly in a big crunch. And if gravity was a bit weaker, the expanding universe would have distributed the atoms so widely that they would never have been gathered into stars and galaxies.

The strength of gravity has to be exactly, precisely right for stars to form. But what do we mean by "precisely"? Well, it indicates that if we change the gravity by even a tiny fraction of a percent—enough so that you would be, say, one billionth of a gram heavier or lighter—the universe becomes so different that there are no stars, galaxies, or planets. And with no planets, there would be no life. Change the value a bit, slightly, and the universe moves along a very different path. And remarkably, every one of these different paths leads to a universe without life in it. Our universe is user-friendly, but only because the past 13.8 billion years have unfolded in a specific way that has guided to a habitable planet with liquid water and rich chemistry. These millions of other extremely disciplinary events are exposed by the very science that utterly cannot function without orderly conduct or within a disorderly nature, which should make scientists the adamant believers of a rational world with a miraculously rational Operator.

Note that carbon is the very decisive element upon which all familiar living is oriented. Carbon atoms shape in the cores of stars by fusion reactions. In these reactions, three helium atoms bang (crash) and amalgamate (fuse) together to make a carbon atom. However, for that combined reaction to work, the energy levels must be compatible and match up in exactly the right way, or the three helium atoms would bounce off of each other before they could fuse. To create this atypical (uncommon) match-up of energies, two physical forces (the strong and electromagnetic forces) must cooperate in just the right way. The slightest change to either the strong or electromagnetic forces would change the energy levels, resulting in a great reduction for the production of carbon. The values are so harmonized and coordinated that carbon is generated efficiently, leading to abundant amounts of an element we require for life.

Each atom has a nucleus of protons and neutrons and a cloud of electrons whirling (causing it to move in a twisting or spiraling manner) encircling it. When an atom coheres (ties-up, binds) with another atom to make a molecule, the charged protons and electrons interact to keep them together. The mass of a proton is nearly 2,000 times the mass of the electron (1,836.15267389 times, to be exact). But if this ratio changed by only a slight amount, the steadiness and the balance of many common chemicals would be compromised which, eventually, would inhibit the formation of many molecules, including DNA, the building blocks of life. As theologian and scientist Alister McGrath pointed out, the entire biological evolutionary process depends upon the unusual chemistry of carbon, which allows it to bond to itself, as well as other elements, creating highly complex molecules that are stable over prevailing terrestrial temperatures and are capable of conveying genetic information (especially DNA).

As agnostic Steven Weinberg, a Nobel Laureate in Physics wrote, how surprising it is that the laws of nature and the initial conditions of the universe should allow for the existence of beings who could observe it. Life as we know it would be impossible if any one of several physical quantities had slightly different values.

And as for anthropic doctrine, it is defined as of or relating to human beings or the period of their existence on Earth as the weak anthropic principle saying that the current universe is of the form that permits intelligent observers. The strong anthropic principle states the universe has these conditions because it *must* have them to have intelligence life (human beings).

The key role of the anthropic principle in cosmology is in helping to explain why our universe has the properties it does. It used to be that cosmologists believed they would discover some sort of fundamental property that set the unique values we observe in our universe. The anthropic principle, in cosmology, any regards for the structure of the universe, the values of the constants of nature, or the laws of nature that have a bearing upon the existence of life. The weak anthropic principle is the fact that the universe must be found to have those properties required for the existence of observers. Rather, it is a methodological principle.

It is admirable, and science should be proud of behaving realistically towards the cause and effect principle for arriving at make-sense conclusions in its discoveries, as their findings are often true in the tangibly oriented world as by now any sluggishly minded person should realize the actual cause to all and every entity, every being in the realms of the subatomic particles, as the unseen world of the quantum mechanics, is the actual reason for what we in our daily living experience. I am afraid many nonchalantly shrug their shoulder and refuse to notice what is so crucially demanding, even in their own body to exist, where countless atoms invisibly swirl around in empty spaces, in the fields comprising human body, which is 99.9999999 percent empty, which ought to puzzle anyone since only miracle-oriented phenomena should come to mind for an answer.

The human body comprises matter and energy. That energy is both electrical (impulses and signals) and chemical (reactions). The same can be said about plants, which are powered by photosynthesis, a process that allows them to generate energy from sunlight. Physics says it does not matter what anyone touches, in reality, no one can touch anything, any object, whether be it one's pants, shirt, shoes, comb, table, chair, one's loved one or a stranger. It sure would give you the impression that you are touching what you are coming into contact with, but physicists tell us that we are not. Physics reasoning is that everything you can see, touch, and feel is composed of atoms, the minuscule small parts of matter.

Evidently, quantum physics, delivers us a lot of mind-boggling stuff about our world to meditate on, particularly the identical activities happening at an atomic scale. We ought to be reminded that the subatomic realm is relevant to our existence, as we should also realize that the four forces make up the physical world as they play a very significant role in comprehending our universe. It is a no-brainer to know that one can't understand how large things work without knowing the details of the small stuff, too. Among many phenomena we specifically have to deal with: quantum entanglement with particles that pop in and out of existence; the particle-wave duality, particles that shape-shift at random; strange states of matter; and even strange matter itself. Quantum mechanics also deciphers that we are made up of particles, which means that microscopically, all sorts of crazy things are happening within us that aren't detectable to the human eye—things that seem to make no sense. Physics states one can never truly touch anything. Grasping the structure of an atom probably is going to give us a clue why we cannot come in contact with anything.

Within these premises, it is also vital to realize how electrons function. Almost the entire mass of an atom is focused on an amazingly small space known as the nucleus. Around the nucleus is a whole lot of space, except for the place within an atom where electrons (and protons) can be located orbiting the central nucleus.

The number of electrons within each atom depends on the element an atom is expected to carry. For instance, photons that are subatomic particles also show the particle-wave duality, which means that the electron has the attributes of both a particle and a wave, which also have a negative charge. Particles are naturally attracted to particles with an opposite charge, and they repel other similarly charged particles. This stops electrons from ever coming in direct contact, where their wave packets can overlap, but never touch.

Human beings are of no exception, since every time we come into contact with, let's say, the seat in our car, the electrons within our body repel the electrons that make up the seat in the car or in any seat that we might be touching or sitting in, as with any object at all since we hover about anything we touch by unexpectedly small distance. But on the contrary, we have the idea that we do touch things, but why?

The scientists tell us that even though electrons in any object repel each other, our brain translates the world around us since the mechanism of the nerve cells that operate within our body forward signals to the brain that then relates to us that we are touching an object. The sensation of touch is because of electron's interaction by their repelling apparatus from the electromagnetic field getting into space-time, which is the medium that electron waves propel forward. Bear in mind that our bodies are also made of particles that at the micro-level behave quantum mechanically because these particles that are the building block of everything made, including the human body, are extremely and unfathomably small.

The particles that our bodies are made of, for instance, convey about 0.2 milligrams of gold, most of it in our blood. One would need 40,000 people to sum up enough gold to make one 8g sovereign. About 99 percent of your body is made up of atoms of hydrogen, carbon, nitrogen, and oxygen. We also have much smaller amounts of the other elements that are necessary for life. And yes, the sensation of touch is almost delusional, manufactured by the brain's wave interpreting interactions between our electrons and the sacred electromagnetic fields. It is a scientific fact that things are often not as they seem, or as they are perceived to be, leaving us with the impression that the external reality is no more than an illusion.

The fine-tuning of our universe should remind us of the many wonders taking place to make life best suited for living. Taking the fine-tuning argument for just a lucky accident should without a doubt give legit reason for those who make such shallow and irresponsible comments to see a reliable psychologist, since some agnostics and certain atheists are still not awakened to so many facts produced by the very science that they rely on, which on the contrary has helped a lot to bring us much closer to God, telling us what you see is not what you get since there are an infinite number of machines that are invisibly manifested to the so-called material world. Astronomer Fred Hoyle wrote, "A common-sense interpretation of the facts suggests that a super-intellect has monkeyed with physics, as well as with chemistry and biology." Physicist Freeman Dyson wrote, "The more I examine the universe, and the details of its architecture, the more evidence I find that the Universe in some sense must have known we were coming."

AMAZING DNA

All living organisms store genetic information using the same molecules—DNA and RNA. Written in the genetic code of these molecules is compelling evidence of the shared ancestry of all living things. In all organisms alive today, the hard work is done by proteins. However, the information needed to make proteins is stored in DNA molecules. You can't make new proteins without DNA, and you can't make new DNA without proteins. Benjamin Libet.

Our cells require elaborating tasks and many kinds of activity to maintain health, which relies on finely tuned circuits involving multiple genes and molecules. Hence, to understand the genetic and molecular basis of circuits inside cells is very essential; it is vital to realize the impact of genetic variations on these circuits. To deny that it takes far more intelligence than we can ever comprehend for the dynamics of natural selection to happen is just wacky. This occurs by random mutation filtering out what works and deletes what does not, a complex biologically oriented process that cannot occur disorderly, with no purpose, no direction, and exhaustive of any supervisory environment.

A mutation is an alteration in DNA. Mutations are hereditary events of life. An organism's DNA fundamentally affects how they behave, how they look, the physiology that denotes the entire feature of a species, as the mutation is critical to evolution as they are the raw material of genetic variation.

Mutation, natural selection, genetic drift, and gene flow are the principal driving forces behind evolution in any population progression. Evolution is a process that results in alteration for the genetic material of a population over time. Evolution reflects the adaptations of organisms to their changing environments and can result in changed genes, novel traits (novel traits are characteristics in an organism that have been created or introduced through a specific genetic change using modern biotechnology or techniques specified in the definition of living modified organisms (LMOs), or by mating with initial LMOs and that make the LMO different from the unmodified organism and new species). "Living modified organisms" means any living organism that possesses a novel combination of genetic material obtained through the use of modern biotechnology; living modified organisms (LMOs) are also commonly referred to as genetically modified organisms (GMOs).

In biology, evolution is the change in the features of a species over several generations and depends on the process of natural selection. The theory of evolution is fundamentally grasped on the idea that all species are related and gradually change over time. If the mutation is fruitful, the mutated organism survives to reproduce, and the mutation gets passed on to its offspring. In this way, natural selection directs the evolutionary process to solely engage the good mutations into the species and get rid of bad mutations.

Evolution is not a random process. The genetic variation on which natural selection behaves may happen randomly, but natural selection itself is not random. The survival and reproductive success of an individual are linked to the ways its inherited characteristics work in the context of its local atmosphere. Mutation maneuvers a vital role in evolution. The final source of all genetic variation is mutation. Since mutation in the evolutionary process, it creates a new DNA sequence for a specific gene, creating a new allele. A gene is a portion of DNA that determines a certain trait or quality. An allele is a specific form of a gene.

The extensive biodiversity on planet Earth evolves as it accepts natural selection and three other forces of evolution as its requirement; they are a mutation, random genetic drift, and gene flow. Gene flow occurs when genes are transferred from one population to another. The genetic variation that occurs in a population because of mutation is random, but natural selection cannot be random since it acts on that variation in a very non-random way, because any selection that leads to life-bearing agents must endure good choosing, leading to intelligence. It expands what we think evolution is capable of. It shows that natural selection is sufficient to generate significant traits of intelligent problem-solving. For instance, a key characteristic of intelligence is the competency to foresee actions and the mechanism that will lead to future benefits.

The idea that the mechanism of natural selection through mutation has randomly and without any guidance or meaningful direction caused the existence and the appearance of every design does not make any sense. It brings to mind that before any biological attempt or life-bearing perspective was to initiate, there must have existed the preludes, the chemical and environmental necessities, the primary soup potent enough to feed such a hugely significant task. And as for the big bang, the theist views are that life has a beginning and is purposely driven, which eventually comes to an end knowing there was a start to the universe in which both time and space began from nothingness, bearing in mind that nothingness is impregnated with an infinite existence.

The atheist persists on the big bang as the beginning of the world; if so, any evolutionary process taking off from the big bang signifies gradual motion in time, which should remind us that motion, even randomly driven natural selection via mutation, should be destined, no matter how long that departure might take. Bear in mind that science is dealing with assessing billions of years of space-oriented events, naturalism, biological, and so on that any inquisitive mind should be skeptical, since so many hypotheses and the so-called scientific theories have historically been discarded concerning the origin of existence where the power of collective reasoning should play a decisive role in either accepting them or not, including the big bang, creationism, and Darwinism, etc.

Intelligent design is an evidence-related scientific theory about the origins of species—one that exclusively challenges materialistic views of evolution. According to Darwinian biologists like Oxford's Richard Dawkins, living systems "give the appearance of having been designed for a purpose." But for modern Darwinists, that appearance of design is misleading. They believe that the undirected processes of natural selection acting on random mutations can generate the very complex structures detected in living organisms. Bear in mind that the theory of intelligent design believes that there are revealing characteristics of living systems and the universe that is described by a magnificent Programmer. Design theory accepts the idea of evolution explained as alteration over time, and even common ancestry; what it disagrees with is Darwin's theory that the cause of biological changes is wholly blind and undirected.

It is a fact that contemporary biologists have found significant discoveries of complex nanotechnology inside the living cells so awesome that they should awaken any studiously curious mind of the wonders of God. For instance, sliding clamps (a DNA clamp, also known as a sliding clamp or β-clamp, is a protein fold that serves as a process-promoting factor in DNA replication. As a critical component of the DNA polymerase III holoenzyme, the clamp protein binds DNA polymerase and prevents this enzyme from detachment from the template DNA strand). Complex circuitry, energy-producing turbines, and extremely micro machines where bacterial cells are catapulting (forcing, propelling) by tiny rotary engines called flagellar motors that rotate at speeds up to 100,000 rpm with many distinct mechanical parts made of proteins including rotors, stators, O-rings, bushings, drive shafts, and U-joints.

The bacterial flagellar motor (BFM) is a rotary electric Nano machine that drives swimming in a wide diversity of bacterial species. There have been many milestones, both theoretical and experimental, that have extended our realizing of this tiny motor since the first swimming flagellated bacteria was known. Biochemist Michael Behe points out that the flagellar motor depends on the coordinated function of 30 protein parts. Remove one of these necessary proteins and the rotary motor simply doesn't work. In Dr. Behe's terminology, "irreducibly complex."

Further referencing the flagellar motor does not work unless all of its 30 parts are available; hence, natural selection can "select" or preserve the motor when it has been formed as a functioning whole, but it can't generate the motor gradually and in a step-by-step fashion. Natural selection allegedly (supposedly) makes complex systems from simpler structures by keeping a series of intermediate structures, each of which must exhibit some function.

It is different in the case of the flagellar motor. Most of the imperative intermediate stages—like the 29- or 28-part version of the flagellar motor—perform no function for natural selection to preserve. The origin of the flagellar motor and many complex cellular machines remains unfamiliar, indescribable by the mechanism "natural selection" that

Darwin particularly suggested replacing the "intelligent design" thesis (a proposal, hypothesis).

In the year 1953, James Watson and Francis Crick explicated the structure of the DNA molecule; they made a surprising discovery. They experienced that DNA's structure permits it to store information in the form of a four-character digital code. Strings of exact-sequenced chemicals known as nucleotide bases store and transfer the assembly guide, the directive, the information for building the crucial protein molecules and machines the cell requires to survive. Mr. Crick later developed this idea with his famous "sequence hypothesis," in his finding the chemical constituents in DNA act like letters in a written language or symbols in a computer code. Bill Gates has since indicated that "DNA is like a computer program, but far, far more advanced than any software we've ever created." There is simply too much information in the cell to be described through chance. No laws of chemistry or any biological findings have to date been able to expose why and how the information in DNA is installed, since DNA functions like a software program.

Russian scientist Alexander Oparin envisioned a complex series of chemical reactions that gradually increased the complexity of the chemistry involved, causing life as we know it. That was the standard theory, but it started to clarify in 1953 with the discovery of the structure of DNA and its information-bearing properties, and about proteins and the complex information within the cell, the way the proteins were processing the information on the DNA. The common problem is that they can't explain the origin of the information in DNA and RNA as Darwin neither understood the origin of life nor attempted to pursue such a vital task.

It is fairly safe to say that biocentrism and the way biology operates is quite important, since many scientists have detected the essential operation known as digital information or digital coding within each cell that is the decisive factor that must be paid attention to. Apparently, digital information or digital coding was discovered by James Watson and Francis Crick that within the DNA molecule there are chemical activities that encode information in alphabetic order, where digital characters are encoded and written for forming specific language. As the pioneering information theorist Henry Quastler observed, "Information habitually arises from conscious activity." So the discovery of information in the

DNA molecule provides strong grounds for inferring that intelligence played a role in the origin of DNA, even if we weren't there to observe the system coming into existence.

It is a no-brainer that no senseless matter is imbued with any intelligence to carry such infinitely exquisite programming that manifests the DNA digitally coded information that must lead to an utterly magnificent mind. What is known to biologists and affiliated scientists is that we have digitally oriented nanotechnology taking place inside our cells, so meticulously programmed that without a doubt indicates a predominantly supreme God, an infinitely ascending mind, since trying to randomly create new proteins or genes from the subunits of molecules is just not possible where the arrangements are so managed and disciplined to perform a particular function. It just refers to strings of characters that need to be arranged in a very precise way to perform a function. If they are arranged in a precise way such that they perform a function, they are not just complex but specified in their complexity.

The arrangement is specified to perform a function utterly, leaving no chance for any chance position to deliver such an awesome endeavor. Many philosophical inquires and scientific research is done that attributes such intelligence, drive, pride, imagination, inspiring, curiosity and passion play to very decisive roles to fathom the secret behind the infinitely enormous agenda we call life. Scientific fields of study like archeology, biology, geology, anthropology, paleontology, botany, neurology, history, cosmology, physics, and other related fields are relentlessly engaged to make sense of it all with no consciousness, absolutely no experience or any outcome is ever possible, which should nip it in the bottom that intelligence, the consciously oriented human mind is the key element behind making it possible. Not only is it rational to believe that nature is extremely intelligent but it is practical to know without a savvy-minded nature all scientific inquiries would prove futile. Nature is intelligent, which leaves no room for anyone to be concerned with senseless, dull-minded matter as the initiator of life leaving no doubt that we are an intelligent and rational-minded species because we are created by an utterly rational-minded Spirit.

If we choose to believe that we are the result of a senselessly unintelligent matter, then we have no choice but to believe in miracles. Think about it and tell me now what other option is left unless accepting the invisibly interactive mechanism that must be fueled and well-directed to bring living out of spiritless dead matter to make the evolutionary process possible for billions of years that must have extinguished long before if not being very well realized and fabulously directed, indicating God had put design and order in fathomable pattern. Kepler said that scientists have the high calling of "thinking God's thoughts after him." If the modern scientists, the philosophers, and the contemporary researchers wouldn't have believed in and didn't already have the assumption that nature is designed as a fundamental part of their knowledge, then most probably no attempt for any research could have happened because no reliable finding, theory, or dependable answer could ever be possible.

THE EXISTENCE OF GOD

The Cosmological Argument

The cosmological argument that stresses everything that exists must have a cause should be revised and instead say that everything within the physical boundaries must have a cause, since the material world is based on the cause and effect reality, but this theory does not apply to the unseen realms

The universe must have a cause. Referencing that, the universe has a cause, the almighty God.

Nothing can be the cause of itself. Yes, true, only in the material world, but not in the invisible world of the subatomic because particles proliferate and show up out of nowhere without any cause.

The universe cannot be the cause of itself. Quite true, but where is the universe? If the universe is only an abstract concept, then are we in the universe or is the universe within us? Modern science believes one cannot exist without the other, but either way, yes, only God can create countless numbers of the planets, trillions of galaxies and billions and billions of universes.

Something outside of the universe must have caused the universe. Yes, the almighty God existing outside of time and space, and beyond cosmos, since God is the cause of the entire existence, God caused the universe. God exists.

We just cannot assess such reasoning about what exists beyond space and time since our nervous system and our senses simply cannot grasp what is immaterial, which only through footprints and traces of God we can conceptualize and try to search for meaning. Let's not forget that scientists, specifically the physicists, are perplexed, not knowing the proper answers to many phenomena such as, was anything in existence before the big bang? How did the big bang occur? What is the nature of dark matter? What is the nature of cosmically prevalent dark energy? How did life happen? Why is there something rather than nothing? What is consciousness? Where did consciousness come from? Why is the universe so finely tuned? Why do we precisely have four forces in our universe, or are there more forces that we have not yet discovered? Is there life after death? Why are the constants behaving the way they do? Who are we? Where do we come from? Where are we heading? Why are we here? Why can no one be found in one's body or mind? Why do we have the outside of body experience?

Does life have a purpose? Why do numbers, mathematics, and geometry, as abstract as they are, make a lot of sense, so much so there are no flaws in their compatibility with the scientific laws and nature? Why we can perish without love? Why do we commit suicide? Why do we commit homicide? Why do we commit genocide? Why rape? Is it God inside, or is it the devil? If God, why for some is God inside? And why do some people act as if the devil is in charge? Is justice going to be served after we expire? If no punishment or rewards, why not? If our feelings, emotions, imaginations, and dreams are the byproducts of neurochemicals and neurotransmitters, how and why? Are we connected through matter or are we consciously linked? Why we can imagine what we desire, but no one can find any image anywhere inside?

And millions of mind-boggling questions which frankly neither philosophy nor science knows the answer to as of the present time.

Bear in mind that DNA carries the most detailed information on everything and everyone, without which, no adequate living is possible. All living organisms store genetic information using the same molecules, DNA and RNA. Written in the genetic code of these molecules is compelling evidence of the shared ancestry of all living things. In all organisms alive today, the hard work is done by proteins. However, the information required to make proteins is stored in DNA molecules. One can't make new proteins without DNA, and you can't make new DNA without proteins. Genetic technologies are also being used to help reach targeted medicines for certain diseases. Plus, for being beneficial in health care, genetics has a host of other very helpful offerings. For example, the police can use genetic fingerprinting to deal with criminals.

The effect of discovering DNA on scientific and medical progress has been enormous, detecting those genes that trigger major diseases, or for the creation and manufacturing of drugs to treat many life-threatening diseases. DNA contains the precise instructions needed for an organism to develop, survive, and reproduce. To carry out these functions, DNA sequences must be transferred into messages that can be utilized to generate proteins, which are the complex molecules that do most of the work in our bodies. DNA replication is the process by which DNA makes a copy of itself during cell division. How are these extremely delicate applications occurring in our bodies without us feeling or noticing them and why? Who or what exactly is the nature of these very significant and lucrative mechanisms taking place inside of us so meticulously, so surreptitiously, without which we cannot survive?

Why should neurochemical activities play God and resonate to our happiness, being thrilled, exuberance, calm, peaceful, feeling love, feeling good and pleasured, acting positive, compassionate, courageous, sacrificing, inspiring, hopeful, and a host of other goods, and occasionally play demonic, making so many of us frightened, depressed, anxiety-driven, hateful, vengeful, and hundreds of other ill-willed scenarios behaving deterministically toxic where no goodwill is an option, sometimes ending for the worse, and thousands if not millions of decisive tasks as if the Ghost inside called the subconscious mind is deliberately set to challenge our conscious mind, which is supposed to intelligently save us from the damages of the subconscious mind because the subconscious mind is addressed as not able to tell the difference. Let me know if you find the answers to the above and countless other enigmatically vital issues facing us in our life. A further question on the cosmological argument, some like to play devil's advocate and as they bluntly put it say: if God caused everything, then, who caused God?

There are fallacies in the cosmological argument when invoking God to resolve some problems. For example, if everything must have a cause, why doesn't God have a cause? The proponent of the cosmological argument would say that God is an exception, and although God exists, God does not have a cause, which expresses not so savvy debate since there is a contradiction in the power of reasoning behind such an analogy because it does not explain why God must be uniquely exceptional. And if nothing is self-caused, why should God be clear from such premise and reasoning and act as self-caused? Reference the question that asks if God caused everything and everyone, then who caused God?

This concern will automatically bring us to the regression analysis since such decisive premises cannot be left open-ended. Infinity is just a concept of endlessness, and can only be used symbolically to represent numbers going on forever. Negative infinity is the opposite of (positive) infinity, or just negative numbers going on forever, as statisticians and mathematicians believe that "any mathematical operation on infinity would output infinity, including infinite values in one's regression analysis data this would not lead to any meaningful results. Most software would prohibit you from using infinite values. Moreover, no real-life data contains infinite values." Therefore, the buck must stop somewhere, and that is with God.

Plus, this concern is only applicable where the Newtonian laws of physics relating to the material world apply, and not practical to the invisible realms where the particles in the quantum territory are dancing to a much different song, since cause and effect dependency are not as reliable, as they do not mean much.

The ontological argument carries on to say that nothing greater than God can be conceived. It is greater to exist than not to exist. If we conceive of God as not existing, then we can conceive of something greater than God. To conceive of God as not existing is not to conceive of God. It is inconceivable that God does not exist. Hence, God exists. This argument, first articulated by Saint Anselm (1033–1109), the archbishop of Canterbury, proceeding purely on the conceptual level.

Immanuel Kant said that everyone agrees that the sole existence of a concept does not mean that there are examples of that concept. Many people know what a unicorn is and simultaneously say unicorns don't exist. The ontological argument claims that the concept of God is the one exception to this rule. The very concept of God, when defined correctly, entails that there is something that satisfies that concept. Further, it is not conforming to give the example of a unicorn, since a unicorn is often considered the most wondrous of all mythical creatures, a fiction, the unicorn is also a symbol of magic, miracles, and enchantment. The magical and enchanting unicorn appears to only a rare few and can bestow magic, miracles, and wisdom to those who are pure of heart and virtuous in their deeds in which people like the late legendary Joseph Campbell dealt with. He was an American professor, writer, and orator, best known for his work in the fields of comparative mythology.

But concepts like the almighty God are abstract concepts like the universe. Are we saying that the universe does not exist even though no one knows exactly what the universe is? And where precisely is the universe? Or where is the soul, the spirit, even our mind, the consciousness? The unicorn we can live without, since we are giving it property in our mind. It does not have to exist. Immanuel Kant points out the fallacy in the ontological argument by choosing to give property to the concept for the existence of God, like "being fat" or "having ten fingers." And further says, "We could, with the wave of our verbal magic wand, define a unicorn as 'a horse that (a) has a single horn on its head, and (b) exists.' So if you think about a unicorn, you're thinking about something that must, by definition, exist; therefore, unicorns exist. This is absurd: we could use this line of reasoning to prove that any figment of our imagination exists."

Yes, the very nature of the unicorn example is wrong since God, universe, mindfulness, and consciousness is, as Immanuel Kant said, figments of our imagination, space and time, quantum and subatomic realms, and so many other abstract concepts cannot be proven, but we cannot live without them. Most are closer to us than our aorta. The aorta is the main artery that carries blood away from your heart to the rest of your body. As for the design argument, behind the reason for any design is a purpose or a function in which the parts must cohere to objectify the task. For instance, all the intricate parts of a watch are to keep time, which should prove that the designer had a reason in mind for making it, or in designing an automobile, knowing that all the global hurricanes blowing through any junkyard could not build a car. Bear in mind that these and other examples couldn't in any way be as sophisticated as the universe, since only the infinitely intelligent God could have made an extremely complicated world. Organs such as the eye and the heart, the kidney cohere only because they have a function. The purpose is to properly see (for instance, the eye has a cornea, lens, retina, iris, eyelids, and so on, which are found in the same organ only because together they make sense and as potentiated for seeing).

They demand an infinitely intelligent Designer; without which it would have been impossible to complete such a grave task. Simply put, these organs were not designed by man, since God could only be a true designer of such very complex organs. God is the non-human designer. God exists.

Referencing the above, the non-believers say that Darwin showed how the process of replication could bring about the illusion of design without the foresight of an actual designer, since replicators make copies of themselves, which make copies of themselves, and so on, producing an exponential number of descendants. Since no copying process is perfect, errors will eventually crop up, and any new experience happening because of an error made causes a replicator to reproduce more efficiently than its competitors and will result in the replicators predominating position for population growth.

After many generations, the dominant replicators will appear to have been designed for effective replication, whereas all they have done is collect the copying errors which in the past did lead to effective replication. Therefore, they so callously say no designer is needed, which should further tell us no evolutionary process at all can take place in a vacuum. For any evolutionary process or any natural selection to occur it must have, not should, the necessary atmospheric requirements to compete, develop, and survive, as many scientists adamantly believe that in any finite environment, the replicators must compete for the energy and materials necessary for replication. The survival of living things is affected by changes in the air with the precise temperature, food, water, shelter, and space available to them and how they will access the must-have resources, living things adapt to changing environmental conditions or they may become extinct. An organism must be able to adapt to changes in the environment or move to another location, otherwise, it will die.

This scientific finding without a doubt is telling us that any biological species must have environmental support in the original stages before they can genetically compete or not, live or die. Note that much research puts emphasis on the exact and proper situation required for natural selection to biologically occur.

Natural selection is the process by which organisms that are better suited to their environment than others produce more offspring. As a result of natural selection, the proportion of organisms in a species with characteristics that are adaptive to a given environment increases with each generation. In any finite environment, the replicators must compete for the energy and materials necessary for replication.

One can come up with any fancy theory relating to evolution, since the power of reasoning should distinguish fact from fiction.

It is imperative to grasp that no biological or genetic transformation can ever materialize unless extremely decisive ingredients, the very organic resources, and the environmental criteria are originally in place to set the stages for any evolutionary Darwinism to happen and because no suitable and befitting atmosphere with such complicity and magnitude can just occur haphazardly and by chance to lay the foundation for evolutionary dynamics to substantiate, there must be an extremely intelligent Creator behind the make-ready circumstance which leads to life. The significant point is that either one is a creationist or evolutionary minded individual. One should realize the essence of life, the very significant requirement behind all the biological mechanisms which imbue (permeate, diffuse) life into leaving creatures and the entire universe and beyond.

No species of any kind can make it in an unsuitable environment; for every species to survive, it must face a correct and orderly atmosphere that is bound to countless variables to potentiate life. What some so shallow-mindedly take as randomly accidental is exactly deterministic, since there is no accident in what God patterns. There is neither accident in nature, nor should there be in our lives. It is only because of our shortsightedness seeing it that way. There is no accident in life. What we consider as the accident is people's lack of attention and ignorance about their surroundings. It is about not focusing, not paying attention, not being able to concentrate, since one's mind can often wander elsewhere and not exactly where it is supposed to be, making one vulnerable to an accident that sometimes proves to be fatal.

The argument from irreducible complexity intelligent design advocate William A. Demoski gives this definition: A system performing a given basic function is irreducibly complex if it includes a set of well-matched, mutually interacting, non-arbitrarily individuated parts such that each part in the set is indispensable to maintaining the system's basic, and therefore original, function. The set of these indispensable parts is known as the irreducible core of the system. The argument from irreducible complexity is a descendant of the teleological argument for God (argument from design or complexity). This says that since certain things in nature appear extremely complex, they must have been designed.

William Paley famously argued in his 1802 watchmaker analogy that complexity in nature implies a God for the same reason that the existence of a watch implies the existence of a watchmaker. Evolution has no forethought (foresight, anticipation), and every gradual step must be an upgrade over the preceding one, letting the organism survive and reproduce better than its competitors. In many complex organs, the removal or change of any part would annihilate and ruin the entire function. For instance, the lens and retina of the eye, the molecular components of blood clotting, and the molecular motor powering the cell's flagellum (a flagellum is a whip-like structure that permits a cell to move. They are found in three domains of the living world: bacteria, archaea, and eukaryote, also familiar as prosits, plants, animals, and fungi. While all three types of flagella are used for locomotion, they are structurally very different), make these organs "irreducibly complex." Molecular biology is a field of science that explores and studies the structures and functions of cells on a molecular level.

A molecular biologist is preoccupied with exploring, understanding, or teaching the concepts behind the cellular structure and function on a molecular level. These organs could not have been beneficial to the organisms that have them in any simpler forms. The theory of natural selection cannot describe these irreducibly complex systems.

The Darwinians have nothing better to say as for being critical of irreducibility complex as flaws, stating that FLAW 1: For many organs, the irreducibility of a part is false. An eye without a lens can still see, just not as well as an eye with a lens. Exactly; but how well the eye without a lens can see is very questionable. And natural selection is not the way out of the conclusions of the classical teleological argument since the natural selection in its argument completely ignores the very preliminary life-ridden environment and the Grass Rooty resources requirement necessary for any biological transformation to occur, and is wrong to claim that natural selection is the only way out of the conclusions of the classical teleological argument. No reliable scientific theories can ever be formulated if the idea behind any of them does not apply to nature's orderly conduct, where not so many random acts and accidental behaviors happen not as exceptions to the rule, but for accidents to occur in making the essence of Darwinism and the spinal cord of Darwinism theory. There are many ifs and buts engaged in the so-called natural selection, since one should ask who is the ghost inside doing the proper selection? What is the actual cause or reason behind such disciplinary evolutionary behaviors?

"The Fallacy of Arguing from Ignorance: There may be biological systems for which we don't yet know how they may have been useful in simpler versions. But there are many things we don't yet understand in molecular biology, and given the huge success that biologists have achieved in explaining so many examples of incremental evolution in other biological systems, it is more reasonable to infer that these gaps will eventually be filled by the day-to-day progress of biology than to invoke a supernatural designer just to explain these temporary puzzles."

Yes, only true for saying that the incremental progression in biological developments happen where gaps will be eventually filled. But false in saying no outside force is responsible to originally implement such dynamics because if the evolutionary process or any gradual changes taking as long as it has for billions of years beyond anyone's imagination was not superbly guided and directed for so long, it would have been extinguished in its primary stages without a trace, ending life as we know it. And certainly, there are things that we cannot explain yet, but the miraculously intelligent-minded men and women will, by the grace of God, one day reach the pinnacle of invincibility where all enigmatic issues will be resolved, bringing humanity next to the angels where God resides.

WHERE THE UNSEEN RULES

If ordinary people really knew that consciousness and not matter is the link that connects us with each other and the world, then their views about war and peace, environmental pollution, social justice, religious values, and all other human endeavors would change radically.

Amit Go swami

The magic of the quantum world, consciousness where human mind resides, knowing of the space, time, the universe, and the entire cosmos, are not things that we can experience; they are not tangible. We just by intuition and instinctively are aware of them, since no physicists or scientists can deal with them in any laboratory. They are not an object of any sort; they are not real, merely conceptual, as they are of specific subjective parameters which without life, would not make any sense. They cannot be constrained within walls and are not separate entities. They are of abstract concepts; their very material existence is in question because they can only exist in human perception.

Referencing Einstein's relativity, Einstein exhibited that no space is constant, neither absolute, as no space and time are materially oriented and insignificant. Hence, if one can travel by very high speed, perhaps by the speed of light, then the intervening space and time will contract and shorten to zero. This is just one example telling us that space, time, the universe, and the wonder of how far and vast the heavens and celestials are in the universe is questioned and not separated from our mental maneuverability and the observer effect.

683

Kant's views largely contend that space and time are nothing but forms of intuition, a view connected to the claim in the transcendental aesthetic that we have pure intuitions of space and of time. Kant tells us that space and time are the pure (a priori) forms of sensible intuition. Intuition is contrasted with conceptualization (or categorization) performed by the understanding and involves how we passively receive data through sensibility. "The belief in an external world independent of the perceiving subject is the basis of all-natural science" (Einstein). His "biggest blunder": Convinced that the universe is static and eternal. But Einstein's view of the external world is not in accord with experimental findings of quantum theory where modern interpretation of scientific data lay because quantum theory casts doubt on classical physics, which sees the external world as a separate entity where individual items truly exist independent of our mind to make their experiments possible contrary to the quantum theory, which doubts the distance between items can truly exist.

Lorentz transformation (1904) was based on the fact that electromagnetic forces between charges are subject to slight alterations due to their motion, resulting in a minute contraction in the size of moving bodies. Lorentz is also best known for his work on the FitzGerald-Lorentz contraction. In 1904, he introduced his transformations, which described the increase of mass, the reduction of length, and the time dilation of a body that is moving at speeds closest to the velocity of light. And as real as space, distance, time, and the universe, the cosmos is in our mind human perception receives them instinctively where they cannot exist without the observer effect.

As for consciousness, the reality of consciousness is decisive even after we die. There is no doubt that we should, in our daily life, rely on the power of reasoning, especially for correct analytical views on conceptual energy-driven issues that are not so plausible, where their traces should make a difference in acknowledging their existence. This does not mean that the whole universe is not energy-based, since all of so-called matter is just condensed energy, giving us the impression of their not so real solidified state. It comes to mind that if we are as science says also energy-related, then after our body dies and our corpse disintegrates to dust, what happens to our mind, thoughts, and consciousness, since they are also energy-driven entities? Science tells us that the average human, at rest, produces around 100 watts of power. This equates to around 2000 kcal of food energy, which is why your recommended daily intake of calories is around 2,000 kcal.

Science also believes that 80 percent of an average human's body power is given off as heat. We radiate ~350,000 J of energy per hour. Since watt is just joules per second, this is roughly equal to the energy given off by a 100-watt light bulb! Most body heat is generated in the deep organs, especially the liver, brain, and heart, and in contraction of skeletal muscles. Most of the molecules in the human body interact weakly with electromagnetic fields in the radio frequency or extremely low-frequency bands. One such interaction is the absorption of energy from the fields, which can cause tissue to heat up; more intense fields will produce greater heating.

It is not an exaggeration to say that consciousness is the core component of our being, even after we die, since our corpse disintegrates to dust but the energy-driven mind or consciousness does not, since a neuro-electric-oriented fountain utilizing about 100 watts of energy having the same power as a light bulb, also carrying the same heat as a light bulb, cannot just die. One skeptical person might play a devil's advocate and say after we expire the energy as well will perish, but not true, since energy neither can be created nor destroyed and because consciousness only identifies with energy. Therefore, it should relate to immortality. Further, it seems that consciousness in some ways aligns with quantum mechanics, which is the bedrock component of the invisible energy-driven world.

The enigmatic state and paradoxes (ambiguity, anomaly) of quantum mechanics have perplexed the most notable physicists and scientific minds of our times when trying to explain the tiniest beings in our universe that are no less complex than the problem of exploring into the consciousness. Quantum mechanics, also known as quantum physics, quantum theory, the wave mechanical model, or matrix mechanics, including quantum field theory, is a fundamental theory in physics that intends to describe nature at the smallest scales of energy levels of atoms and subatomic particles.

In particle physics, a massless particle is an elementary particle whose invariant mass (rest mass, intrinsic mass, proper mass, or in the case of bound systems, simply, mass), is the portion of the total mass of an object or system of objects that is independent of the overall motion of the system. The two known massless particles are both gauge bosons: the photon (carrier of electromagnetism) and the gluon (carrier of the strong force). Neutrinos were originally thought to be massless.

Fisher says that the quantum-mechanical behavior of these nuclear spins could plausibly resist DE coherence on human timescales. Fisher argues phosphorus spins could resist DE coherence for a day or so, even in living cells. DE coherence is the study of interactions between a quantum system (generally a very small number of microscopic particles like electrons, photons, atoms, molecules, etc., often just a single particle) and the larger macroscopic environment, which is normally treated "classically," that is, by ignoring quantum effects. That means they could influence how the brain works.

As for consciousness, consciousness relies on quantum mechanics because quantum mechanics is the foundation of all mechanics—it describes the behavior of all particles that make up our bodies. So far, no reliable findings have structurally been constituted to unanimously convince the scientific community to substantiate a definite location for consciousness. Logic dictates that the behavior and the properties of the energy-oriented quantum world, which deals with the tiniest scale of energy levels of atom and subatomic particles, should not be unfamiliar with the operations of our mind and consciousness since the brain is also made of atoms and is undeniably energy-based. Our mind invisibly and not tangibly interacts with nature and the world around us. Furthermore, it should not be a surprise for anyone to know that the quantum spheres are the substructure and the underlining for all beings, since what exists is made of the atom where atom and the subatomic particles are the territorial and the vicinities of the quantum world.

Somehow linking consciousness and quantum mechanics has led to quantum mysticism, which is a set of metaphysical beliefs and related practices that seek to associate consciousness, intelligent energy, spirituality, or mystical worldviews to the concept of quantum mechanics and its elucidation (demystification). In physics and chemistry, a quantum is a distinct packet of energy or matter. The term *quantum* indicates the minimum value of a physical property involved in an interaction. For instance, a photon is a single quantum of light. Light and other electromagnetic energy are absorbed or emitted in quanta, or packets.

It is the body of scientific laws that describe the unearthly behavior of photons, electrons, and the other particles that make up the universe where nothing is static. Everything and all is about motion regardless of the rate of their speed. Any motion, either at the micro or macro level, is magnificently programmed to serve an objection, for reaching a purpose, to serve a thought that at its core is disciplined with commitment and reliability since an unwavering force has from infinitely oriented nothingness propelled and is intelligently conducted to guide life forward, leaving no living entity without a mission. This has endowed them with the power of intention that is innately ingrained in every being to specifically maneuver without a flaw or a lapse in action, as they were designed. It is noteworthy that at the scale of atoms and electrons, many of the inquiries of classical mechanics, which describe how things move at everyday sizes and speeds, stop to be of benefit.

It sure seems we have already entered into the higher realms, into the mystifying world of quantum mechanics where the heavens are more in tune with the miraculously functioning environment, where energy-oriented frequencies sure sing a much different song since countless particles manifest an enigmatic dance, encouraging the most prominent physicists and scientific-minded people of our time to relentlessly pursue this puzzling but extremely exciting endeavor until may one day humanity can fully respond to the way the almighty God has guided us for finding the shortest way to reach and kneel at God's feet and say mission accomplished and that we are ready for the next phase of human glory since our mind and our heart is made of the infinite properties which they will never stop but propel forward to give real meaning to the expression "man is created in God's image." To fulfill what is persistently flaring inside of us for becoming better and to improve more and more until no evil spirit can ever reach us, but for man to tango with the angels until millions and millions of galaxies and billions of planets and celestial bodies outside of the Earth's atmosphere can be reached, since man has already visited planets Mercury, Venus, Mars, Jupiter, and Saturn, which have all had human probes crashed (or landed) on them. Luna and Titan are moons that have had probes land on.

Quantum mechanics deals with the behavior of matter and light on the subatomic scale, trying to explain the properties of molecules and atoms and their affiliates—electrons, protons, neutrons, and other more profound particles such as quarks and gluons. Quantum theory is the theoretical basis of modern physics that explains the nature and behavior of matter and energy on the atomic and subatomic levels. Quantum superposition happens since at the quantum level, particles act like waves. In the meanwhile, multiple waves can overlap each other to make a single new wave; quantum particles can exist simultaneously in multiple overlapping positions. Quantum activities have shed light on the fact that there is more to life than meets the eye, even to a point of making many scientists hope to explore more, to perhaps one day locate consciousness, since a great deal of them are becoming aware of the idea that many of the quantum behaviors indeed reference the way our mind functions.

And with the birth of quantum mechanics, the classical physicist's views toward the laws of physics was revolutionized. Einstein was the first physicist to eloquently say that Planck's discovery of the quantum would require a rewriting of the laws of physics. In 1905, he exposed that light sometimes acts as a particle, which he called light quantum.

Imperative applications of the quantum theory include quantum chemistry, quantum optics, quantum computing, superconducting magnets, light-emitting diodes, and the laser, the transistor, and semiconductors such as the microprocessor, medical and research imaging such as magnetic resonance imaging and electron microscopy.

Some scientists believe that quantum events might have influenced the whereabouts of the consciousness, believing that we have already grasped where consciousness comes from as they behave illusion, as there is not an inkling of evidence where the consciousness comes from or where it resides. The perpetual (eternal, perennial) mystery of consciousness has even guided certain researchers to implore quantum physics to describe consciousness, but others believe it is not wise to explain one mystifying issue with another. It seems that the human mind has the properties of a quantum world where many of its characteristics simulate quantum theory, like being at more than one place at the same time; like thought showing and disappearing more than the speed of light, not tangible, not observed with a naked eye, and so on.

And as far as the brain using quantum mechanics? Fisher says the brain is composed of atoms, and atoms follow the laws of quantum physics.

Whether or not consciousness can affect quantum mechanics, he said, perhaps quantum mechanics is involved in consciousness.

Consciousness relies on quantum mechanics because quantum mechanics is the foundation of all mechanics. It describes the behavior of all particles that make up our bodies. Perhaps the apparatus of quantum entanglement furnishes the sub-structural dynamics, which produces collective human thought process and mindset, which should indicate to millions of our common thought processes and goals, since also intuition, telepathy, reading minds, and a host of other intelligently related ideas are occasionally manifested since quantum entanglement is a physical phenomenon that occurs when pairs or groups of particles are generated, interact, or share spatial proximity in ways such that the quantum position of each particle cannot be defined independently of the state of the others, even when the particles are apart by a large distance. In quantum physics, entangled particles stay connected so that actions exhibited on one affect the other, even when separated by great distances. The phenomenon so vexed (provoke, riled) Albert Einstein he called it "spooky action at a distance."

Experiment in space confirms that reality is what you make it. An odd space experiment has confirmed that, as quantum mechanics says, the reality is what you choose it to be. As for our brain, Fisher says the brain is composed of atoms, and atoms follow the laws of quantum physics. Some theories state that the brain behaves like a quantum computer. The idea that consciousness arises from quantum mechanical phenomena in the brain is intriguing, yet lacks evidence, scientists say. Higher consciousness is the consciousness of a higher Self, transcendental reality, or God. It is "the part of the human being that is capable of transcending animal instincts." The concept was significantly developed in German Idealism and is a central notion in contemporary famous spirituality. "Yes, Your Thoughts Can Change Reality. Before your thoughts can change the world, they must change you.

When the dialogue shifts to the power of positive thinking, dreaming it, imagining it, setting intentions, focusing and acting with one-track-mindedness, *Think and Grow Rich*, *The Law of Attraction*, fake it until you make it, mindfulness and more, are the positions maneuvered in the territory of quantum dynamics. But one important point often gets lost. Whether or not consciousness can affect quantum mechanics, physicists believe perhaps quantum mechanics is involved in consciousness, indicating that one's brain is a quantum computer. Scientists believe that the brain functions as a biochemical and bioelectric system. Individual brain cells, so-called neurons, fire in intricately coordinated patterns, and their chemical and electrical discharges build up a network that processes information.

Physicists have long known that a quantum of light, or photon, will behave like a particle or a wave depending on how they measure it. Quantum reality: The many meanings of life. Quantum particles such as atoms and molecules have an eerie (uncanny, ghostly) supernatural ability to appear in two places at once, spin clockwise and anticlockwise instantaneously, and influence each other when they are half a universe apart. In physical terms, the reality is the totality of the universe, known and unknown. The quantum mind or quantum consciousness is a group of hypotheses that proposes that classical mechanics cannot explain consciousness.

It is not yet possible to perform experiments designed to prove the validity of the ideas involved in quantum consciousness. Other mystifying and shadowy concepts besides quantum consciousness that have also engaged some of the most scientific and scholarly minds of our times are issues like the string theory, parallel universes, traveling through space and time, etc.

The phrase *alternate reality* is frequently stated as a synonym for a parallel universe. It may also refer to alternate universe (fanfiction), fiction by fan authors that purposely change facts of the canonical universe (the term "canon" refers to all activities of fiction within a franchise's fictional universe, which are considered to have happened within the fictional universe they belong to the universe they are writing about). This reminds us of virtual reality. Virtual reality is an artificial environment that is created with software and presented to the user so that the user "suspends disbelief," or has a willingness to suspend one's critical faculties and believe something surreal (unearthly, freakish), negating realism and inference for the sake of enjoyment. On a computer, virtual reality is primarily experienced through two of the five senses: sight and sound. VR is the use of computer technology to produce a simulated environment. By simulating as many senses as possible, such as vision, hearing, touch, even smell, the computer is transformed into a sentry (guard, doorman) to this artificial world, creating a simulated reality.

Whether fiction or not, an item truly exists only as long as it is observed; otherwise, it is not only in vain but simply nonexistent. The observer and the observed are one as the first clue was manifested in the vicinity of the quantum mechanics that appeared in the German *Quanten Mechanik*, by the group of physicists including Max Born, Werner Heisenberg, and Wolfgang Pauli, at the University of Göttingen in the early 1920s, and was initially utilized in Born's 1924 paper "Zur Quantenmechanik." The observer effect brought about the culture of quantum mysticism, indicating a set of metaphysical beliefs and associated practices that seek to relate consciousness, intelligence, spirituality, or mystical worldviews to the ideas of quantum mechanics and its interpretations.

And as for string theories, the principle of quantum superposition states that if a physical system may be in one of many configurations— arrangements of particles or fields—then the most general state is a combination of all of these possibilities, where the amount in each layout (format, design) is indicated by an intricate number. String theory is meant to model the four known fundamentally interactive forces of our universe— gravitation, electromagnetism, strong nuclear force, weak nuclear force— together in one unified theory. Einstein had tried a unified field theory, a single model to describe the principle interactions or mechanics of the universe.

In the 1980s, supersymmetry was found in the context of string theory, and a new sort of string theory known as superstring theory became the center of attention. Superstring theory is also named the theory of everything, because it is a unifying physics theory that conforms (adapts) the contrast between quantum theory and the theory of relativity to explain the nature of all known forces and matter.

The main concept of string theory is quite simple. If one puts to test any piece of matter ever more finely, initially one will see molecules, atoms, subatomic particles. Then examine the smaller particles, you'll get something else, a tiny vibrating filament of energy, an extremely tiny vibrating string. As the string theory seeks extra dimensions for all practical purposes, we should know that we live in a world with three spatial dimensions, normally called Cartesian coordinates or spherical coordinates.

It is a misapprehension that the world is four-dimensional and that time is the fourth dimension. The eleventh dimension is a characteristic of space-time that has been suggested as a possible answer to questions that come up in superstring theory. The theory of superstrings involves the existence of nine dimensions of space and one dimension of time (a total of ten dimensions). One noticeable feature of string theories is that these theories demand extra dimensions of space-time for their mathematical steadiness. In bosonic string theory, space-time is 26-dimensional, while in superstring theory it is 10-dimensional, and in M-theory it is 11-dimensional.

In physics, string theory is a theoretical structure (fabric) in which the point-like particles of particle physics are replaced by one-dimensional objects called strings. It describes how these strings spread through space and interact with each other. These dimensions are mathematical, not dimensions in space, and each one is a number that saves information.

Does string theory demand the concept of 11 dimensions? Bosonic string theory requires 26 dimensions, but can only model bosons and not fermions, making it a bit frivolous, as it cannot describe important natural phenomena. Bosonic string theory is the actual version of string theory, produced in the late 1960s. It is called boson because it solely keeps bosons in the spectrum.

The main concept in string theory deals with tiny elementary particles. When you hear *particle*, you think of a dot, like a point in space or the period at the end of the sentence. But in string theory, instead of a dot, a particle is seen instead as a tiny vibrating string that's closed up to form a loop. The strings of string theory are unimaginably small. If an atom were magnified to the size of the solar system, a string would be the size of a tree. The fundamental premise of string theory is that the basic objects in nature are not point-like, but rather string-like. It is exactly this fact that makes string theory such a cogent (captivating) prospect for a unified theory.

What must be realized is that without consciousness, no experience of any parallel universe or with any scientific approach reaching them is ever possible, since consciousness is the status or the recognition or of being aware of an external object or something within oneself. Many believe that there is a broadly common upholding intuition about what consciousness is. Despite what some philosophers claim consciousness is, there are many mysteries about the reality of consciousness. It seems that quantum mechanics and consciousness manage to have some like qualities when it comes to their position and criterions and the vicinity within which they function. A quantum system is a portion of the whole universe (environment or physical world) that is taken under consideration to make analysis or to study for quantum mechanics about the wave-particle duality in that system.

The quantum realm is a dimension in the multiverse only accessible through magical energy, mystical transportation using a Sling Ring, or by tremendous subatomic shrinking caused by the Pym Particles. In the quantum realm, space and time are believed to be irrelevant.

The Pym Particles work by shunting (turning, or choosing different path) matter into the cosmos dimension when shrinking a subject or accruing extra matter from that dimension when enlarging. In their original formula, these Pym Particles existed in a liquid elixir form that would shrink objects or living beings to which it was applied. Henry Pym not only discovered the existence of the Pym Field, through its corresponding Pym Particle, but also how to vary the coupling between atoms and this surrounding field, thereby making them larger or smaller on demand. The two-sided nature of the electron is grasped as the wave-particle duality: The property of particles behaving as waves and the property of waves behaving as particles as well as waves, where this duality is not effective at the macro level, not decisive in the large matter.

It is interesting to know that no space, no time, no consciousness, no innate activities of the physical world, nor any biocentrism behavior, no human soul or spirit, no universe, not the quantum world, no parallel universe and all the forces of the universe are ever tangible. They are abstract ideas, but so real. They are the reason, the cause to all that exists. They are extremely complex as they perplex us as if they do not exist but it's not possible to live without them because they sacredly carry some of God's attribute.

The bottom line with the emergence of the universe in your mind, or for example what consciousness is, and because you already have an inkling about God, then no denial or deprogramming of any kind can clear imperative concepts as such from your mind or delete the above ideas from your memory unless stricken with Alzheimer's disease, because if such notions can arrive within your conscious, since you can mentally grasp them, then they must exist; otherwise, no human can idealize or imagine what one's mind is exhausted of and is out of the boundaries for collective thoughts and beyond our perception when we have no clue, since our human mind is completely unaware of them. We will be utterly bewildered (baffled, mystified) and irrelevant to an idea if beyond our grasp and out of our thought process where we would not have a clue of its existence, since it is otherwise for the existence of God that is frequently in our subconscious and occasionally in our conscious mind. And as for the physical body our heart and gut instinct, or intuition, is the immediate knowing of something.

Your intuition arises as a feeling within your body that only you experience. Descartes clearly and distinctly realized the mind exclusively by itself, apart from the body, and the body all by itself, separately from the mind. Relating to Descartes, his ability to clearly and distinctly grasp them separately from one another implies that each can exist alone without the other.

Socrates and Plato believed that the mind and body are made of different substances. Plato argued that the mind and body are fundamentally different because the mind is rational, which means that examining the mind can lead to truth. Typically, humans are characterized as having both a mind (nonphysical) and body/brain (physical). This is known as dualism. Dualism is the view that the mind and body both exist as separate entities.

Descartes's Cartesian dualism argues that there is a two-way interaction between mental and physical substances. In the Fifth Meditation and elsewhere, Descartes says that God's existence follows from the fact that existence is contained in the "true and immutable essence, nature, or form" of a supremely perfect Being, just as it follows from the essence of a triangle that its angles equal two right angles. These facts and millions of others, like adding numbers, subtracting them, multiplying, division, calculus, algebra, differentiation, integration, logarithms (a quantity representing the power to which a fixed number, the base, must be raised to produce a given number), binary numbers, thousands of geometrical facts and so on are ingrained in the very essence of existence. As abstract as they are, they are the true reality of what gives meaning to order.

The world of science has already realized that quantum consciousness is not a mystical woo (support) but an entity linked to the fundamental forces of our universe. And if quantum computers are anticipated to be capable of accomplishing extraordinary tasks more so than other computers, then it should remind us of the most advanced inventions solely as derivative of human brains that can achieve things beyond any artificial intelligence. The perplexing issue is the observer effect, which seems to undermine (sabotage, erode, weaken) the basic assumption behind all scientific endeavors since the outcome of a quantum experience can be altered relating to whether or not we choose to evaluate some property of the particle engaged, which questions the position of science that there is an objective world out there irrespective of us, and if irrelevant to the observer effect, then how would that world be presented?

And if the world behaves depending on how or if we look at it, then what can reality mean? The critical issue is the primacy of consciousness that all facts, all knowledge, the essence of what we grasp, all the principles of existence, must initiate with personal sensation of mind and self, as many prominent philosophers like Kant, Berkley, Ibn Sina, Rumi, Descartes, Leibniz Bergson, and Schopenhauer believed in, not to exclude Zen-oriented beliefs, several branches of Buddhism, and some sects of Hinduism. It's only when Kant and Descartes come on the scene that we begin to get more of a focus on introspection and understanding ourselves by looking from within.

The absorbing incursion (meddling) of the mind into quantum mechanics arrives at a double-slit experiment, even to the extent of forcing some scientists to judge that objectivity was not real but an illusion. Surely, Albert Einstein once complained, the Moon does not exist only when we look at it! or when staring at the rainbows delightfully pleasant but does the rainbow or the beauty of a clear night filled with amazingly stars exist without you observing them. Either way, the question of consciousness has sure left the consequences of whether or not consciousness influences quantum mechanics.

Many researchers believe that quantum theory might be required to fully understand how the brain works, and just as quantum objects can simultaneously be in two places, so a quantum brain can hold onto two mutually exclusive ideas at the same time. In neuroscience, quantum brain dynamics is a hypothesis to describe the function of the brain within the framework of quantum field theory. I am afraid that despite the very powerful evidence referencing the decisiveness, the make-sense derivatives and the validity of the unseen world which comprises the invisible structures to all that exists, we still have many dogmatically and so-called physicists that persist with the Newtonian approach to the physical world, trying to emphasize what any novice should accept: that Newtonian's law of physics are most definitely the foundation of what is truly happening in our life.

Callously refusing to recognize that it is ironically the science that is the pioneer in discovering amazing realms where the world of subatomic particles has taken a new turn in revolutionizing millions of scientific minds since it has opened new ideas for advancing even more dynamic endeavors in the field of physics for further revealing the majestic reality of our universe. For instance, let's elaborate on the double-slit quandary (dilemma), a brief testimony to the prominence of the observer effect.

Imagine shining a beam of light at a screen that contains two closely spaced parallel slits. Some of the light passes through the slits, whereupon it strikes another screen. Light can be thought of as a kind of wave, and when waves emerge from two slits like this, they can interfere with each other. If their peaks confirm (equate, coincide), they reinforce each other, whereas if a peak and a trough (groove, trench) coincide, they cancel out. This wave interference is called diffraction, and it produces a series of alternating bright and dark stripes on the back screen, where the light waves are either reinforced or canceled out.

The idea seems to be that each particle passes at the same time through both slits. The double-slit experiment can also be shown with quantum particles like electrons, tiny charged particles that are parts of atoms; these particles can behave like waves. That means they can sustain diffraction (the slight bending of light as it passes around the edge of an object.) The amount of bending depends on the relative size of the wavelength of light to the size of the opening. If the opening is much larger than the light's wavelength, the bending will be almost unnoticeable. When a stream of them passes through the two slits, producing an interference (the process in which two or more light, sound, or electromagnetic waves of the same frequency combine to reinforce or cancel each other, the amplitude of the resulting wave being equal to the sum of the amplitudes of the combining waves pattern).

Now imagine that the quantum particles are sent through the slits one by one, and their arrival at the screen is seen one by one. In the meanwhile, there is nothing for each particle to interfere with along its course—but regardless, the pattern of the particle effects that buildup over time, exhibiting interference bands. The thought seems to be that each particle passes simultaneously through both slits and interferes with itself. This fusion (union, alloy) of "both paths at once" is known as a superposition state. The principle of superposition states that when two or more waves of the same type cross at some point, the resultant displacement at that point is equal to the sum of the displacements due to each wave.

If we put a device to detect inside or place it behind one slit, we can find out whether any given particle passes through it or not, and if so, the interference disappears. Simply by observing a particle's path—even if that observation should not disturb the particle's motion—we alter the outcome.

Physicist Pascual Jordan, who worked with quantum guru Niels Bohr in Copenhagen in the 1920s, put it like this: "Observations not only disturb what has to be measured, they produce it...We compel [a quantum particle] to assume a definite position." In other words, Jordan said, "We produce the results of measurements." If that is so, objective reality looks like going out of the window. If nature seems to be changing its behavior depending on whether we "look" or not, then what we understand as reality should tightly be linked to human observation, since the utter act of noticing, rather than any physical disturbance caused by measuring, can cause the collapse.

It is as if nature "knows" not just if we are looking, but if we have decided to look, and as Bohr confidently anticipated, it does not matter whether we delay the measurement or not, as long as we measure the photon's path before its arrival at a detector is finally registered, we lose all obtrusion (interventions). Researchers have further stated that when we have discovered the track of a quantum particle, its cloud of probable progression "collapses" into a single, well-defined state. Furthermore, the delayed-choice experiment indicates that the pure act of noticing, rather than any physical disturbance made by measuring, can cause the collapse. But does this mean that true collapse has solely occurred when the result of a measurement infringes (affect) on our consciousness? It is hard to avoid the innuendo (hint, insinuation) that consciousness and quantum mechanics are somehow linked. Hungarian physicist Eugene Wigner noted: "It follows that the quantum description of objects is influenced by impressions entering my consciousness," he wrote. "Solipsism may be logically consistent with present quantum mechanics."

Solipsism from Latin soul's, meaning "alone," meaning "self," is the philosophical concept that solely one's mind is certain to exist. As a metaphysical position, solipsism goes further to the conclusion that the world and other minds do not exist. Solipsism is the theory that only the self is real and that the self cannot be aware of anything else except itself. Solipsism believes the idea that nothing matters except yourself.

Wheeler even addressed the thought that the presence of living beings, which are capable of "noticing," has transformed what was previously a multitude of possible quantum pasts into one concrete history. In this sense, Wheeler said, we become participants in the evolution of the universe since its very beginning. In his words, we live in a "participatory universe." Either way, it is difficult to ignore the suggestion that consciousness and quantum mechanics are somehow linked.

Other physicists have suggested that the connection might be valid the other way around, whether or not consciousness can influence quantum mechanics, saying that perhaps quantum mechanics is involved in consciousness. We cannot figure out how thoughts work, for instance. We know what the color blue is like but in no way can resonate with the sensation we get from noticing so and so color, or the beauty of a rose, the shining moon and the glittering stars. One particularly complex question is how conscious minds can experience unique sensations, such as the color green, the smell of chicken barbeque, or the sound of a passing train.

We all know what yellow is like, but we have no way to communicate the sensation and there is nothing in physics that can indicate what it should be like. Sensations as such are called "qualia." We perceive them as unified properties of the outside world, the material world, but in fact, they are products of our consciousness—and that is hard to describe. "If you want to find the secrets of the universe, think in terms of energy, frequency, and vibration" (Tesla).

It is the awakened, oriented universe seeded with infinitely enlightening information that is purposefully cultivated by scientific discoveries, making man's mind a truly a magnificent agent by which the essential life-bearing communications are transparent, since our brain and the nervous system so magically reflect the intentions of the observing self and the existence that we are undeniably part of as they place us in the mainstream of challenging nature for more intelligent discoveries and a meaningful living, leaving no doubt that humanity is meant to play a very decisive role in this dream-like scenario known as life that is imbued with hopes, vision, and imaginations, miraculously designed by absolute, consciously natured phenomena beyond anyone's expectation, denoting that it is the biological states and not any matter-based or substance-related reason that dynamically sets forth the cause behind what we call living.

The mind of man simulates an inkling of the infinitely manifested image of God because man's curiosity and due diligence for finding the unknown is never-ending until humanity's sacred intention is incrementally met, where human objectives are progressively followed by relentlessly asking why, how, who, where, and when, for ultimately reaching the universal goal until man can kneel at God's presence. "You are not IN the universe, you ARE the universe, an intrinsic part of it. Ultimately you are not a person, but a focal point where the universe is becoming conscious of itself. What an amazing miracle" (Eckhart Tollie).

In the meanwhile, we need to see things as realistic as they are, not only in the obvious world but definitely by digging into the unseen realms where the essence of existence is prevalently lurking. It is so crucial for the scientific community to put more weight on the consciously driven agendas than behaving absent-minded toward the real essence of existence.

"Do not be dominated by your ego, we are infinite and spiritual beings undergoing a collective human experience" (Eckhart Tollie).

"Ignorance is the curse of God; knowledge is the wing wherewith we fly to heaven" (William Shakespeare).

Occasionally, the human mind or the observer self is distanced as far as the universe and the infinite cosmos from reality, often not grasping that our human existence is laid at the heart of the very existence whose foundation is inseparable from the laws of the entire universe. What has so far been accomplished has thrown off the scientific society either by deliberate attempt on the part of scientists, or somehow by ignorance, since the further science peers into matter, energy, time, space, planets, galaxies, and the universe, the further it fails to recognize the actual awakened life-bearing Entity behind it all. Name it what you wish: consciousness, awakened energy, an enlightened Promulgator, the Cause of all causes, or the omnipotent, omnipresent, omniscient God.

There is so far much emphasis on science taking the essence and the reality of consciousness for granted, which precedes not only science but the entire existence since without mindfulness, no experience can ever substantiate, leaving any scientific testing futile, resulting in no discovery. Not realizing without a sheer disciplinary environment and a precisely calculated atmosphere that is amazingly and correctly resourced, neither can any scientific testing be formulated nor scientific theories manifested. It simply applies that no practical scientific founding can be materialized in a chaotically oriented world.

Many do not grasp that what we do not see manages what we see, for instance, our minds, our memories, our feelings and emotions, the way our surroundings impact our nervous system and senses and communicate and take orders from our brain. None of these dynamic activities are seen. The sensory system is a part of the nervous system responsible for processing sensory information. A sensory system consists of sensory receptors, neural pathways, and parts of the brain involved in sensory perception; taking in the world around you through your senses, making sense of it, and responding appropriately to it. Sensation refers to the process of sensing our environment through touch, taste, sight, sound, and smell.

This information is sent to our brains in raw form, where perception comes into play. Perception is the way we interpret these sensations and therefore make sense of everything around us. The sensory system is part of the peripheral nervous system. The sensory system is composed of organs and tissues that provide the sensations from sight, hearing, smell, taste, and touch (along with the nerves and brain tissue that process the sensations). The external world must come to terms and be correlative with consciousness to mean something, since the external world and consciousness are as demanding and inseparable parts of each other as the oxygen in the air, since one cannot exist without the other.

Besides the five senses, people also have a proprioceptive system that tells you how much effort is being used to move your body and regulates both emotional responses and sensory input. Everyone should learn how to use the vestibular and proprioceptive systems, just like the other five senses. Proprioception is the way we can notice when flexing our neck, or lifting our leg, lifting our shoulder and tell when our eyes are shut; these are examples of proprioception. Other examples may include your ability to sense the surface you are standing upon, even when you are not looking at the surface. And vestibular sense is gross motor skills: crawling, walking, running, jumping, throwing a ball, etc.

We take these and so many valuable dynamics for granted, as if science is God, the magnificent designer, not wanting to accept that science should be thankful for these available resources already rooted like things endowed to human beings, potentiating them for even more marvelous tasks. Furthermore, we should know that our world is energy-oriented, all matter is energy, frequency-based, depending on the rate of their frequency things are made into either solid, liquid, or gas-related.

One should not deny that human beings are the only creature with out of body experience, since no one can ever be found inside one's anatomy because we are also energy-oriented beings; that is where the souls and human spirit comes to play. We need to realize that all animated beings are innately invigorated. Biocentrism and the way we look at existence, known as the observer effect, decisively matters to the extent that if observed, no existence or external reality should mean anything. As for space, time, and even the entire universe, they are abstract concepts that obviously couldn't have existed if there is no one to perceive them as such.

The question is: can what we know as the material world exist if no one is alive to observe it? A reasonable question; but unless an available conscious force existed to reflect it, then it really wouldn't matter, would it? By observer effect I mean because of our sight, hearing, touching, smelling, and tasting, which make the external world possible since each sense from seeing to the other senses in communication with our brain generate sensations whose existence lies within our mind, indicating a material world out there.

It is true that because of the presence of our senses, along with the activity of our brain and mind, make the wonders of the electromagnetic activities in our world possible. Otherwise the electromagnetics, gravity, and other vital forces of our universe are just invisible entities. Plus, there is no doubt that all and everything in existence is made of atoms except for energy. For example, when we do not observe the sun, the sun disappears; if we do not look at the stars and the moon or anything else for that matter, they won't exist, telling us that if no consciousness existed, in what sense can any object that is subjective to our seeing, even our feelings; would they persist, and to what form for reliability?

In several experiences made by scientists, they exhibited that our brain neural impulses and electrochemical links speed at about 268 mph. Signals travel along an alpha motor neuron in the spinal cord, the fastest such transmission in the human body, telling us that the human brain, as well as the mind, can perform by themselves without any interference by our thoughts. There is no actual discord between the internal and the outside world. We can sum it up by saying that all cognition, comprehensions, are the combination of the experimental self and the energy field permeating the universe. It is true that there are 100,000 miles of myelin-covered nerve fibers in the brain of an average 20-year-old.

For instance, if one touches a door, then the electrons from the atoms in one's fingers become close to the electrons in the door's atoms. So pushing just two atoms close to each other takes energy, as all their electrons need to go into unoccupied high-energy states. When two atoms come together and have empty spaces in their electron shells, they will share electrons to fill in the spaces in both of their shells. Yes, the electrons dance back and forth between atoms and they do so pretty fast. Atoms are the building blocks of matter. Everything is made of atoms (except energy). Atoms, quite literally, make our universe what it is.

When we die, our bodies do not turn into nothing; rather, they are broken down into their component parts and recycled into the ecosystem. Electrons are made of massless energy particles. We know that splitting an atom creates a lot of energy. That is because there is a lot of pure energy bound in matter as mass. This same intense power in a small space is essentially why nothing ever actually touches.

Scientists tell us that in fact, 99.9999999 percent of all of the matter around us is space. This means if you took the space out of every human on Earth, you could compress the entire human population down to an object smaller than a sugar cube. Atoms are bound into molecules, and molecules are bound into everyday objects by the electromagnetic force. The bottom line is, nothing solid ever bumps or meets any other solid, since everything is made of space conveying energy field since literally atoms comprising things are just as empty as they can be.

If two atoms are held a meter apart, they are touching each other through all four fundamental forces. Weirdly enough, space is not empty because nothing contains something; boiling with energy and particles that zoom (dash, speed) into and out of existence. Physicists have known that much for decades, ever since the birth of quantum mechanics. Physicists also tell us that objects feel solid because of the dancing electrons. If you touch any hard object, for example, a table, then the electrons from the atoms in your fingers become close to the electrons in the table's atoms.

Come to think of it, an empiricist like George Berkley is much closer to the reality than other so-called positivist's point of view (a philosophical system that holds that every rationally justifiable assertion can be scientifically verified or is capable of logical or mathematical proof and that therefore rejects metaphysics and theism), since Berkley believed what is perceived through the mind is what should count. Since scientists considered Berkeley's argument as an idealist, not so credible, they carried on to build physical models based on the assumption of an outlandishly separate universe into which we have each individually come about. This so-called realistic model entails (presuming) the existence of one essential reality that prevails either with us or without us. But if without us, then how would anyone know that the universe still prevails with no one available for grasping it? Which begs the question that if no collective thoughts are present to conceptualize such grave task as the magnificent universe, then trying to substantiate such reasoning remains futile.

The physical model relied on Newtonian's law, which justly expresses that in the materially visible world, "what you see is what you get." An actual breakthrough occurred because quantum physics experiments have routinely exhibited the external reality, depending on whether anyone is observing. This is explicitly illustrated by the famous two-slit experiment.

When someone looks at a subatomic particle or a bit of light pass through the slits, the particle behaves like a bullet passing through one hole or the other, and if no one observes the particle, it shows the behavior of a wave that can inhabit all possibilities—including somehow passing through both holes at the same time. This should hint to any reluctant mind that we do matter and that the nature of existence is an umbilical cord to the human consciousness. We are truly a decisive force to reckon with since the universe couldn't have existed without us observing it. This controversial issue for millennia has entangled even the most prominent minds where materialists and the idealists have ideologically challenged each other's point of view to figure out the essence of existence, and if man had anything to do with it.

An empiricist is one who believes that our knowledge is limited by the data provided to us via our perceptions of the external world. The principal founders of empiricism were John Locke, David Hume, and George Berkeley. For Berkeley, all that existed was what we perceived. Berkley even argued against Descartes's rationalism and materialism. He also criticized Locke on many points. He noted that most philosophers make an assumption that has no proof: the existence of matter.

Trying to asses and figure out the nature of the real world, the Irish empiricist George Berkeley contributed a particularly visionary, prophetic observation: The only thing we can perceive are our perceptions, he said. In other words, consciousness is the matrix upon which the cosmos is apprehended. Color, sound, taste, smell, touching, temperature, and the like, exist only as perceptions in our head, not as absolute essences, as he categorically denied the external world and was utterly not sure of an outside universe.

Through quantum mechanics, physicists have been able to shed light on a more reliable model for explaining the world of the atom, which also has revolutionized the position of conscious perception, an undeniable integral to the dynamic interactivities of our universe. Quantum physics indicate that an unobserved small object (quarks, electron, or a photon—a particle of light) exists only in a shadowy, unforeseen state, without clear and well-defined location or motion until the instant it is seen, following Werner Heisenberg's famous uncertainty principle.

Physicists describe the phantom, not-yet-manifest position as a wave function, a mathematical state utilized to locate the possibility that a particle will show up in any given place. When a property of an electron suddenly shifts from possibility to reality, physicists acknowledge that its wave function has collapsed.

In religion, transcendence refers to the aspect of God's nature and potency, which is entirely independent of the material universe, beyond all physical laws. This relates to the immanency, where God is fully present in the physical world and therefore accessible to the whole existence in infinite ways, also indicating that the human mind is an inseparable part of the universal dynamics with the set of cognitive faculties including consciousness, imagination, perception, thinking, feelings, emotions, will, judgment, language, and memory that are immaterial. They reside in the brain (sometimes including the central nervous system), indicating that mental human attributes happen instantaneously, which should remind us about the position of the quantum world where things also occur on the spot faster than the speed of light.

"You are the universe; you aren't in the universe"

Eckhart Tollie

Quality consciousness is designated as the highest degree of development of its consciousness. That means that someone conscious of himself can have different degrees, or levels, of consciousness. And it also means that it is possible to develop the quality level of your consciousness. Level of consciousness is a measurement of a person's heightening and responsiveness to stimuli from the environment. A mildly depressed level of consciousness or alertness may be classed as lethargy; someone in this position can be aroused with some difficulty. Higher consciousness is the consciousness of a higher self, transcendental reality, or God. It is "the part of the human being that is potentiated in transcending animal instincts."

Consequently, evidence reveals that humans are not the only species possessing the neurological substrates. Neurological substrate may mean the natural environment in which an organism lives or the surface or medium on which an organism grows or is attached. That generates consciousness. Biologists, zoologists, and others in the related field believe that non-human animals, including all mammals and birds, and many other creatures, including octopuses, also possess these neurological substrates.

Human consciousness has been defined as awareness, sentience, a person's ability to experience and feel. But despite the important role it plays in our lives and making us who we are, we know very little about how consciousness works. Consciousness refers to individual awareness of your unique thoughts, memories, feelings, sensations, imagination, dreams, and environment. Topics such as hypnosis, hallucinations, meditation, and the effects of psychoactive drugs are just a few of the major topics linked to consciousness that psychologists study.

Traditionally, scientists have tried to define the mind as the product of brain activity: The brain is the physical substance, and the mind is the conscious product of those firing neurons, according to the classic argument. But growing evidence shows that the mind goes far beyond the physical workings of your brain. Scientists differ on the difference between consciousness and self-awareness, but here is one common explanation: Consciousness is awareness of one's body and one's environment; self-awareness is recognition of that consciousness—not only understanding that one exists, but further understanding that one is aware.

Researchers for so long have thought that consciousness resides somewhere in the cortex—the outer layer of the brain—but no one has been able to pinpoint where. A Harvard team identified not only the specific brain stem region linked to arousal but also two cortex regions that all appear to work together to form consciousness. It is surprisingly sad when some of the scientific communities still insist on finding consciousness in the brain, not realizing that our mind, our brain, both energy-oriented entities, are part of the bigger picture where the universal energy maneuvers through every bit and piece of the entire existence. And yes, it is our brain which communicates with our senses and fluently dialogues with the so-called outside world that we are an inseparable part of placing us in the mainstream of challenging nature for more intelligent discoveries and a better life for generations to come.

"Whatever you think the world is withholding from you,
you are withholding from the world"

Eckhart Tollie

What should amaze humanity is that all baryonic matter, everything that we see, all energy-oriented entities and everything that has formed, only comprises 4 percent of the universe. By definition, the baryonic matter should only include matter composed of baryons. In other words, it should include protons, neutrons, and all the objects composed of them (i.e., atomic nuclei), but exclude things such as electrons and neutrinos, which are lepton. All the stars, planets, and galaxies that can be seen today make up just 4 percent of the universe. The other 96 percent is made of stuff astronomers can't see, detect, or even comprehend. These mysterious substances are called dark energy and dark matter. The universe is known to consist of three types of substance: normal matter, dark matter, and dark energy. Normal matter consists of the atoms that make up stars, planets, human beings, and every other visible object in the universe. It happens that roughly 68% of the universe is dark energy.

Dark matter forms about 27 percent. The rest—everything on Earth, everything ever seen with all of our instruments, all normal matter—adds up to less than 5 percent of the universe. Space that we can see is very empty. If you ignore the galaxies and stars, then the rest of the space is just a vacuum, so there are no particles at all. The particles that are there are mainly hydrogen and helium, which form a plasma called the Intergalactic Medium. Millions if not billions of astonishing things occur in the 5 percent of the universe that scientists and physicists claim we know of, for instance in biocentrism, cell reproduction is the process by which cells divide to form new cells. Each time a cell divides, it makes a copy of all of its chromosomes, which are tightly coiled strands of DNA, the genetic material that holds the instructions for all life, and sends an identical copy to the new cell that is created.

THE OBSERVER EFFECT / ABSTRACT CONCEPTS

> So Einstein was wrong when he said, *"God does not play dice." Consideration of black holes suggests, not only that God does play dice, but that he sometimes confuses us by throwing them where they can't be seen.*
>
> Stephen Hawking

It is not fiction, or perhaps hallucination, to realize that abstract concepts are as realistic as life itself, without which no existence would be practical. Concepts like The four fundamental forces of nature are gravitational force, weak nuclear force, electromagnetic force, and strong Nuclear force. The weak and strong forces are effective only over a very short range and dominate only at the level of subatomic particles. Gravity and electromagnetic force have infinite range. They are esoterically active forces, as they behave beyond human senses as the absentia world operates mystically, bewildering since the unseen forces function so intelligently and majestically disciplined that no flaws could ever be possible because with even the slightest mistake, the entire existence could fundamentally collapse, which should remind us of the miraculously disciplinary layout of the universe, making the innate behaviors of entire biocentrism possible.

There surely exists a deep correlation within the universally oriented forces, where the interrelated activities of the biosphere and biocentrism make living collectively possible. I should start with consciousness, because the awakened oriented forces of the universe and the animated organisms of nature are innately programmed to behave the way they do, where billions of majestically abstract phenomena are steadfastly at work to make life as naturally pleasant as their inner behavior is absorbingly puzzling since they cannot be seen, smelled, or touched.

It is essential to hold that without consciousness, without any thought process, no perception would ever be possible since as George Berkley puts it, "To be is to be perceived." What I am saying is that without an intelligently conscious able Creator as an abstract concept that can oversee the validity of any being, no existence can or will be possible, which should shed light on the practicality of the observer effect, which carries some of the traits of God in the expression that says, "God made man in his image."

Scientists are already aware of the fact that no subatomic particles truly exist in any certain place, but they only exist as possibilities that are not manifested. The term *observer effect* indicates that the act of observing will affect the phenomenon being watched which in physics, a more routine observer effect can be the result of instruments that by necessity change the position of what they measure in some way. In physics, the observer effect is the theory that the sole observation of a phenomenon unavoidably alters that phenomenon. A specifically uncommon version of the observer effect happens in quantum mechanics, exhibited by the double-slit experiment. When a quantum "observer" is watching, quantum mechanics states that particles can also behave as waves.

When under observation, electrons are being "forced" to behave like particles and not like waves. Hence, the mere act of observation affects the experimental findings. The term observer effect refers to the possibility that an act of observation may influence the properties of what is observed. Observer effects are a threat to validity in much of educational research. Some believe consciousness relies on quantum mechanics because quantum mechanics is the foundation of all mechanics; it describes the behavior of all particles that make up our bodies. The term *observer effect* means that the act of observing will penetrate the phenomenon being observed. For instance, to "see" an electron, a photon must first interact with it, and this interaction mechanism will change the path of that electron, but the entire mechanism is not detectable with the naked eye, which should alert us to value the decisively unseen apparatus in all of which is happening in our so-called physical world.

In the absence of an observer, each one's wave function collapses and it resumes an actual state, a physical actuality. Essentially, you would indeed need a mindful organism to grasp and give meaning to life, without which no independent existence can be possible because it should make a great deal of sense that where there is no mind to experience the external world, and when there is no mindful feedback of any kind to recognize the external universe, why should the universe matter? And without perceiving the external universe, how should we know that it exists? Of course, man has not reached a point to experience the entire universe since apparently we are dealing with trillions of galaxies, leaving us with the choice for only conceptualizing such a magnificently absorbing task. We should be aware that we are not in the universe, but the universe is within us, since for anything to exist it must be perceived.

It was Wayne Dyer who said, "If you change the way you look at things, the things you look at change." But not only that, by now it is clear that nothing even exists if there is no one present. And when some say that man is the center of the universe, that is a shortcoming because we *are* the universe, and if perhaps not because of our collective consciousness, which is giving reality to life rather than the other way around, then it is either that or some intelligent being in the higher realms, some sort of extraterrestrials ought to be actively present, probably in a parallel universe or even someplace in trillions of planets, galaxies, and billions of universes that are empowered to perceive and observe the existence besides human beings for existence to be manifested, which brings us to square one that without an intelligent entity or any awakened responsible organism to perceive the external universe, the rationality behind the fact that life can exist, it will collapse.

Abstract concepts are ideas without concrete form that cannot be adequately explained scientifically. For instance, one is the feeling of happiness, which comes with thoughts of wellbeing, content, satisfaction, safety, connection, time, belonging, love. Another abstract concept is beauty. God and other abstract concepts like knowledge, compassion, courage, anger, honesty, trust, bravery, hate, pride, misery, numbers, etc. also impact our lives in subtle ways, as if we are detached from them but in contrary, we utterly cannot do without them. They are ingrained within our human spirit, our minds, within our soul, since there is nothing substantive about them, as if they are playing ghost with us that we cannot do without.

As for abstract numbers, a concrete number is a number linked to the things that can be counted, in comparison with an abstract number or numerous, numerous which is a number as a single entity. For example, "10 oranges" and "half of a pizza" are concrete numbers, while "10" and "one-half" are abstract numbers. The connotation here is about a physical object. Something that is concrete is physical. Abstract, on the other hand, means to take something away. So something abstract is drawn away from the real, from the concrete, from the physical. Abstract terms indicate ideas or concepts; they have no physical reference. For instance, abstract terms include consciousness, mindfulness, love, compassion, failure, success, democracy, freedom, good, moral, evil, etc.

Mathematics and numbers also play a role in abstract concepts, without which no testing or technological endeavors, and so many scientific undertakings, would be without transparency where no meaningful transaction could happen. Let's take length or any other measure-oriented entity—length is an abstraction in the sense that it does not exist in and of itself, but it explains the real qualities of physical objects. Time is no different. The more you know of the science of physics, the less sense it makes to think of time relating to any direction.

The abstract concept of time begins with sensing and mindfulness, so as with any other abstract behavior. Thoughts of the past and future are conceptual ideas that exist in our minds. They are ideas that filter and fudge (twist, falsify) our understanding of the reality of what is happening. The concept of time is self-evident. An hour consists of a certain number of minutes, a day of hours and a year of days. The passing of time then (in effect, indeed) is closely linked to the concept of space. According to the general theory of relativity, space, or the universe, arrived in the big bang about 13.7 billion years ago.

Time is a theoretical build-up created by humans for keeping track of their activities, their works, where objectives can promptly be served. Humans explored the idea of time to measure the interval between events based on the standard unit of measure, for instance seconds, minutes, hours. The prospect that abstract objects do exist is known as "Platonism." The perspective that they don't is "nominalism." The conceptualists reply: the fact that the concepts exist even just as explanation exhibits that they do exist in our mind. Abstract objects seem to behave as mental fictions, but they so realistically define our purposeful living that often without, no existence would be possible; therefore, as such, they truly exist.

Abstract concepts refer to the ideas which are not concerned with materialism. For example, God, compassion, love, cosmos, universe, literacy, knowledge, wisdom, fear, anxiety, happiness, courage, cowardice, liberty, freedom, assertiveness (individualism, creativity), tranquility, and peace of mind, etc. They are the things that you cannot either see or touch but you can feel and see the effects. Time is a basic quantity of different measurements utilized to order occurrence to compare the duration of events or the intervals between them, and to quantify rates of change of quantities in the material world or the conscious experience.

Time in physics is definitive working expounded as what a clock shows. Physicists define time as the progression of events from the past to the present into the future. Fundamentally, if a system is resolute (steadfast, unwavering), it is timeless. Time can be regarded to be the fourth dimension of reality, used to describe events in three-dimensional space. According to theoretical physicist Carlo Rovelli, time is an illusion: our naive perception of its flow doesn't correspond to physical reality. He suggests that reality is just a complex network of events onto which we project sequences of past, present, and future. Einstein's theory of relativity states that time and space are not as constant as everyday life would suggest. He suggested that the only true constant, the speed of light, meant that time can run faster or slower depending on how high you are, and how fast you are traveling.

Time has no dimension, not an absolute physical quantity. Time cannot play the role of the independent variable (time, t, is frequently the x-axis on graphs that exhibit the evolution of a physical system). In reality, we cannot measure t. What we are doing is measuring an object's frequency, speed, etc. What experimentally exist are the motion of an object and the sound of a clock, and we relate the object's motion to the tick of a clock to measure the object's chronicity (frequency), speed, etc. By itself, t has only a mathematical value, and never original physical existence. Time is referenced with space rather than with the idea of absolute time. Hence, it is more becoming to imagine four dimensions of space than three dimensions of space and one dimension of time. The roots of this idea come from Einstein himself. "Einstein said, 'Time has no independent existence apart from the order of events by which we measure it,'" Sorli says. "Time is exactly the order of events: this is my conclusion."

An example of the abstract concept of time is to imagine a photon that is moving between two points in space. The distance between two points is made of Planck distances, Grass-Rooty based on Planck time, each of which is the smallest distance that the photon can move. When the photon moves a Planck distance, it is moving only in space and not in absolute time, the researchers explain. The photon can be grasped as moving from point 1 to point 2, and its status at point 1 is "before," its status at point 2 in the sense that the number 1 comes before number 2 in the numerical order. Numerical order is not equal to temporal order; the number 1 does not exist before the number 2 in time, only numerically. Physicists believe that we can explain the physical world more precisely without using time as the fourth dimension of space-time.

Another famous delineation for indicating the abstract-concrete distinction holds that an object is abstract if it does not have any causal strength. Causal powers have the competency to causally affect things.

Thus, the empty set is abstract, since it is unable to act on other objects but only so in the visible world because it seems that in the abstract subatomic world, the quantum environment, the reality, is gravely different, since what we do not see is the cause for all and the underlining reality for every occurrence that we see. It shouldn't be of any surprise to decipher that each natural operational mechanism in our universe is fueled by a dynamically invisible force that innately affects them to decisively maneuver the way they do, which it seems without observing them, no existence of any kind could be possible. Come to think of it, most conceptual entities are ingrained into our spirit, into our soul, since our mind is constantly in one way or another engaged with them and as the concept of God is a divine manifestation of that.

A bit of history about abstract language.

Abstract language refers to qualities and ideas. Concrete language appeals to the senses. For a time, as an abstract, the difference between past, present, and future is merely a naively persistent illusion. Hipparchus and other Greek astronomers employed astronomical techniques that were already instituted by the Babylonians who resided in Mesopotamia. The Babylonians made astronomical calculations in the sexagesimal (base 60)

713

system they inherited from the Sumerians, who developed it around 2000 BC. The B-theory of time is the name given to one of two positions regarding the philosophy of time. B-theorists discuss that the flow of time is an illusion, that the past, present, and future are equally real, and that time is a temporal meaning (tense-less).

This would mean that practicing temporal is not an objective portent (trait, feature) of reality, just an abstract concept. But whatever the intention, we have to deal with it to make sense of our disciplinary living, no matter how illusive we behave, and because of the spatial and temporal dimensions of human interactivities in complex ecosystems, this does not mean the conceptual universe is or can be contained within any time parameter or space, which should so weirdly remind us of the non-existence of time and the non-existence space, grasping the non-existent universe since they solely are nothing less than abstract entities in our mind but so practical that we cannot live without them. It sure ought to remind us of the Almighty's magnificent approach to existence; extremely strange but without question, awesomely designed.

NOT SO MUCH OF A FICTION

*Consideration of particle emission from black holes would
seem to suggest that God not only plays dice but also sometimes
throws them where they cannot be seen.*

Stephen Hawking

The human mind and heart are the two organs that are infinitely oriented
phenomena, since neither heart stops desiring nor mind halts thinking, as
both often pursue wellbeing and progress to the day we expire, like they
are part of God and are linked to the Almighty's infinite quality, giving
reality to the expression that says man is created in the image of God.
Human beings will innovate to the end of time where man's curiosity and
the pursuit of excellence will carry humanity to one day kneel and bow
to God, knowing the mission is accomplished, giving meaning for living
with purpose. Humanity will one day fulfill his dreams where human
curiosity and imagination fuel and propel progress with revolutionary
ideas like teleportation and other groundbreaking ventures in space-time
endeavors with imperative inventions where challenging nature will fulfill
man's mission in this exciting phase of existence known as life.

We should mentally register what we want, believe it, persist to make
it an embodiment of who we are so much so like an inseparable soul,
since we should become obsessive and infatuated with the thought and so
mindful of it, perceiving it as it already happened, then see where this is
not the other way around, it is not to see what you crave, what you desire
first, then believe it, but the expression of "seeing is believing" aside on the
back burner because that is for trivially material stuff, for mechanically
natured situations, for physically manifested everyday work and so on.

But for reaching your big dreams one must imagine it, become obsessed with it, our brain neurons, the junctures, the synopses, capillaries, and the decision-oriented parts our brain is made of delicately potentiated tissues that can be empowered to make the impossibilities a reality and possible. The human brain is the most complex organ with the most intricate structure; the gray matter is made up of approximately 100 billion neurons that collect and transmit signals while the white matter is made of dendrites and axons that the neurons use to transmit signals.

The brain is composed of about 75 percent water and is the fattiest organ in the body, consisting of a minimum of 60 percent fat. The brain has three main parts: the cerebrum, cerebellum, and brain stem. Cerebrum is the largest part of the brain and is composed of the right and left hemispheres. It performs higher functions like interpreting touch, vision, and hearing, also for speech, reasoning power, emotions, learning, and fine control of movement. Slicing down the center of the brain exhibits its main parts: the cerebrum, the cerebellum, and the brain stem. The large, wrinkly cerebrum is the most competent part of the human brain, responsible for all your conscious actions, speech, emotions, and feelings.

You see, our brain cannot distinguish between fact and fiction; it believes what it is fed. Have you not experienced a horror movie when a murder is about to happen? Many jump out of their seat and want to alert the victim, and hundreds of other scenarios which we decide not to yearn it, not to let those untrue events trick us, avoid becoming delusional by fictions even when we know what ill is about to happen is not real, but so many still react to, let's say, an acrobat carrying a pole (it's called a balancing pole, more specifically) horizontally in their hands walking on a tightrope. The tightrope walker that is about to fall from a high-rise where people jump out of their seat hoping for the acrobat's safety.

The point is that when one sincerely prays or justifiably curses a culprit and becomes obsessed with the notion of wishing for the faulty person to be punished, it will eventually happen. The expression that says imagine it, believe it, and become obsessed with it, as the thought becomes the embodiment and the focus of your attention, then, definitely see your desire and what you have wholeheartedly wished for turn into reality. Believe that your conscious, your mind, and heart, are part of the energy-sacred cosmos, part of God. They must be kept sacred and not abused with demonic and ill thoughts carrying toxic emotion and ill will.

Space-time is a mathematical model that joins space and time into a single idea called a continuum. Also, the strength of any gravitational field slows the passage of time for an object, as it is noticed by an observer outside the field. With the emergence of space-time, exciting undertakings such as quantum teleportation are manifested, by which quantum information, for example (the exact position of an atom or photon), can be transmitted (in principle) from one location to another, with the assistance of classical communication and previously shared quantum entanglement between the sending location the departure and receiving destination. Perhaps teleportation is presently an unreasonable concept to expect, as it is with traveling through the wormhole. But even the most revolutionary ideas at first seem unlikely, which eventually become realities. Wormholes are solutions to the Einstein field equations for gravity that act as tunnels, linking points in space-time in such a way that the trip between points via wormhole could consume way less time than the trip through normal space.

Referencing gravity is crucial, since gravity plays a decisive role in the entire existence. Gravity is the powerful force that pastes our universe together. Gravity helped form our solar system, the planets, and the stars. It keeps the planets in orbit around the Sun, and hold moons in orbit around the planets. The gravitational pull of the Sun and Moon generate the tides on planet Earth. The gravitational force is also accountable to the shape of the stars and planets, as well as many other objects in space. The beginning motion of all the material in the universe was later affected by gravitation, resulting in the rotational motion of the galaxies and the orbits of the planets in our solar system. We should further know that there is a difference between intrinsic and extrinsic curvature in gravitational theory.

An object is indeed intrinsically curved if it can't be "flattened out" without garbling (twisting out, distorting) its surface. The surface of the Earth, for instance, is intrinsically curved, which is why you can't make a flat map of the entire Earth's surface. General relativity solely relates to the intrinsic curvature of space-time, not the extrinsic curvature. Our space-time could be hard-cored in some higher-parameter space, just as the cylinder is enrooted in three-height space. But those higher facets (magnitude) are obscure, and not possible to be attained. Bear in mind that

DR. FERIDOUN SHAWN SHAHMORADIAN

the workings of gravity in our four space-time dimensions aren't affected by extrinsic curvature, only intrinsic curvature. No matter what new invention and progressive-oriented space-time venture beholds us, scientists will always need to incorporate gravity in their perspective (outlook) agendas for any scientifically meaningful space-time undertaking.

And as for teleportation, in which we can step into a giant scanner of some kind and instantaneously arrive at our destination with mind, body, and soul safe and sound, perhaps an outlandish thought but since it is being fueled with human imagination and drive, it couldn't be too farfetched from reality. What we mentally should perceive is the likelihood of physical decomposition, deconstruction at point A and reconstitution at point B, or the translation of one's person into data to be transmitted, then changed back into matter, like being transmitted through a huge fax machine, or perhaps in some sort of super-advanced MRI machine. The inkling of hope is gained when a pair of photons manage to simultaneously share the same position, even when they are apart by a very long distance.

Alter the state of one particle and strangely enough, the other changes too. In 1993, an international group of six scientists exhibited that complete teleportation is probable in principle, or at least not against the laws of physics. Recently Chinese scientists were able to "teleport" photons to a satellite 300 miles away, using a phenomenon called quantum entanglement. Making this significant and chilling behavior possible shortly where a pair of photons can at the same time share a similar state, even when apart by great distances. Change the state of one particle, and the other changes too.

Scientists have started to work on the phenomenon to pass information between the two entangled particles. Entanglement is a state of correlation between two or more quantum objects. They need not even be the same object. Hence, the momenta (mass times velocity) of the photon and atom are entangled. Entanglement is a natural happening in quantum mechanics. Quantum entanglement benefits terminate and is done with after links are broken. The concept of quantum entanglement is where objects can magically become linked and instantaneously affect one another notwithstanding (nevertheless, regardless) how far apart and distanced they are from each other.

Scientists have noticed that a third particle can be used to entangle one of the original particles and control the state of the distant particle. This will tremendously affect the internet system since quantum internet will be born much faster, with huge power and not possible to hack, and even making it practical for science to beam us to where we need to go, establishing a new world order. A breakthrough will perhaps occur when able to teleport photons, atoms, then molecules—shortly which is not an easy task for scientific discovery, as the prominent physicist Michio Kaku has stated. The amount of bits to record and transmit is unthinkable. Even an E. coli bacterium contains 9×10 to the power 10 atoms; you are made of an estimated 32 trillion, or about 31.2tn (trillion) more cells than there are stars in the known universe.

According to University of Leicester research into the computing power demanded to teleport a human being, your cells, broken down into data, equates to around 2.6×1042 bits, which is 2.6 followed by 42 zeroes; utopia, yes, but again we should remember that the means, the technology and the science of such a fascinatingly grave task, will not behave stagnant, as progressive parameters will gradually or occasionally in leaps be available then to expeditiously support the intention behind many groundbreaking ideas.

You would need enormous bandwidth and approximately 10tn gigawatt-hours of power. Teleporting one human being would, therefore, require dominating the entire UK power supply for more than a million years and take some 4.8 million years to transfer, or about 350,000 times longer than the universe has existed. And after such a long wait, you might not even survive the transfer. Not a practical task with having the present technological ability, since even the most advanced 3D printers, materials, and scanners are not able to realistically reproduce an excrete, much less a human with their neurons, memories, thoughts, or personality. Let's say that becomes possible; but are you not transferring solely a copy? What happens to you at point A when you at point B show up? Will original you be zapped? Yet Kaku is a positivist physicist, since he believes these difficulties are resolvable and that human faxing, yes, that's what Kaku predicts, may be possible within 100 or 200 years. Mr. Kaku fancies a teleporter that works as an ultra-high-res MRI scanner, with preciseness at the single-atom-per-pixel level.

To transmit this data, Kaku suggests utilizing x-rays, which have super-short wavelengths and high frequencies that carry 1m times more data than normal optical fiber. One's data would be ciphered (written in code, encrypted) and beamed into space, bounced around a satellite network, and then beamed to a quantum computer on the other side of the world to unpack. The elephant in the room remains when Kaku does not disclose what happens to the original you but goes so far as to anticipate the transport of a simple molecule in the next 10 years, soon to be pursued by DNA. Professor Michio Kaku says that human teleportation may be possible within 100 years.

In the meanwhile, no matter how much difficulty a dream-big task would be, it couldn't have been accomplished if we didn't have an inkling of an idea in our mind about the specific mission in which we plan to devote valuable resources in accomplishing it. It just couldn't have existed if outside of our mind. If we can imagine, grasp big events and fictionalize such scenarios for creating science fiction movies and other media entertainment, then they couldn't have been much further from the truth. In other words, if we have an inkling of thought that they can one day exist, then they couldn't be beyond the scope of the human mind and man's dreams, which makes it possible for humanity to conquer them, to one day make it happen. Otherwise, they couldn't ever be deciphered in any shape or form, if not shadowed within the scope of the human mind.

Science fiction is defined as a genre of fiction in which the stories frequently talk about science and technology of the future. It is imperative to note that science fiction has a relationship with the principles of science— these stories involve partially true/partially fictitious laws or theories of science. The world of science fiction and fantasy is rich and varied. Isaac Asimov, once asked to talk about the difference between science fiction and fantasy, answered that science fiction, given its grounding in science, is possible; fantasy, which has no grounding in reality, is not.

Other alternatives are the "folded paper analogy and plasma beams" hypothesis, which indicates bringing two distance points together by "folding" space-time to create an "Einstein Rosen Bridge" analogy. The impracticality of it is that this whole concept stays solely theoretical, since being associated with black holes makes it awkwardly disadvantageous of stretching out one's body into a line the width of a single atom before one can get anywhere.

That leaves other options, like a plasma beam that could theoretically blast you from Washington to China in about a minute. Or perhaps more "conventional" vehicular travel, empowered by something akin to NASA's highly promising EM drive, which might be able to transport humans using a so-called "warp-bubble" to locations near and far at faster than the speed of light. The warp bubble is a detached region of space-time which is theoretically capable of moving faster than the speed of light. Warp drive doesn't exist yet, but, it's theoretically possible. It allows science fiction ships to get across space by moving faster than the speed of light. According to Einstein's theories on relativity, it takes an infinite amount of energy to accelerate an object with mass up to the speed of light.

Robert Winglee and his colleagues, encouraged by the Sun's effect on Earth, are developing an interesting approach to space momentum. The craft visualizes travel through space on sails made of magnetic fields. The sails soar upward under pressure from the solar "wind"—electrically charged particles from the sun—or from intense man-made plasma beams, which special satellites would aim at the sails. These approaches could shorten the travel time to Mars from about six months each way to 40 days, indicate the body of scientists, led by Dr. Winglee, director of the University of Washington's Research Institute for Space Exploration. No-Man space exploration to the edge of the solar system itself could be compromised from roughly 40 years to a decade or so.

Winglee believes it is possible to design a Mars mission that would last 90 days instead of the 950 days that the National Aeronautics and Space Administration uses as its reference or baseline for planning. A shorter mission increases its chances of success. "A lot of the technologies we need already exist," he says. "We're just trying to pull them together into something special." In fact, "the enabling technologies may not be available today and the science may not be completely understood," says director Robert Cassanova. But the ideas are conceptually sound, he continues, and holds the promise of revolutionizing space travel over the next 10 to 40 years.

For Winglee and his colleagues and others working on space, the driving ideas ranging from space engines, the contest is to overcome the limits imposed by current chemical rockets. What is the cause for the sudden warp-drive fancy known as the Electromagnetic Drive, or EM Drive? It's an innovative thruster that was made to steer rockets without the use of a propellant. The hype over the EM Drive is all about record-timing interstellar (occurring between stars) travel elevators and tethers (secured, ropes) to antimatter; *antimatter* is a term in particle physics. Antimatter is a material composed of antiparticles. These have the same mass as particles of ordinary matter but have opposite charge and properties, such as lepton and baryon number. Encounters between a particle and an antiparticle lead to both of them being destroyed.

According to scientists, if this antimatter is made of antiprotons, antineutrons, positrons, or some combination of those, it could be utilized to release a lot of energy. It would annihilate a gram of matter and release 180 trillion Joules (50 million kWh) of energy. So a gram of antimatter could be used as a weapon of mass destruction. Antimatter was generated along with matter after the big bang, but antimatter is scarce in today's universe, and scientists aren't certain why.

To better understand antimatter, one should know more about matter. Matter is comprised of atoms, which are the basic units of chemical elements like hydrogen, helium, or oxygen.

Thanks to a NASA physicist, the notion of warp speed might just travel out of sci-fi and into the real world. The aim is to develop the wrapped drive that allows spacecraft to travel. And as for traveling back in time, the problem with traveling backward in time is that we don't see anybody coming back from the future. If that would be practical, then no that our offspring, our children perhaps thousands of years from now, would make a time machine and come back to spend time with us. Optimistically enough, it seems this predicament would be resolved with the making of wormhole time machines, which are meant to commute in time. Physicists tells us that if, for instance, the first wormhole time machine was built in the year 4000, there could not be any time tourists in earlier years, it would be on from the year that the anticipatory machine is built.

We have entered into a new era which ironically the scientific findings are fathoming what for thousands of years the sages and the scholarly minded philosophers have been professing, that mankind is the very reason for the existence of the universe; that you are not in the universe but the universe is within you. It is because of the almighty God that you exist and it is because of you that the universe exists, since the quantum world of the infinitely dancing particle where the substratum, the subatomic realm of the unseen world and the observer effect arrives at making it all possible as it renders meaning to countless probabilities as they are validated with how you look at the universe, knowing that the sole act of observing will influence the phenomenon being observed. Thus, it is fascinating to grasp the mere act of observation affects the experimental findings, manifesting the very difference between the existence and the nonexistence. The traces of the almighty Creator are so infinitely vast that even mammoths, with inversely related brain size and intelligence, would kneel to the awesome footprints of God since it cognitively shouldn't take much to realize the real reason behind what is at stake.

"There's no way to remove the observer - us - from our perceptions of the world"

Stephen Hawking

THE PRICE OF FREEDOM

When money and evil combine the most infamous human conducts are experienced since nowhere in the culprit's trait should one look for decency unless searching for vile; it is where the hellions reside and the demons ruthlessly operate leaving so many plagues behind, and you might as why mayhem, because the moguls of our times chose not to grasp that living is a right and not a privilege that must not be cornered by the few against the world's populace as the modern Barons so sadly are taking the basic rights of living away from the rest of the humanity.

They leave billons financially coerced often for the poor thinking it is the wrath of God that perhaps has unjustifiably ill-fated them, not knowing it is the corrupted propaganda machines in cahoots with religious institutions that so cunningly have conditioned the indigents to believe in such bizarre plot as the modern tycoons make a biased decree against the impoverished as if the command is from the heavens above which can only mean that the merciless charlatans are the real cause to people's misery. Thus with the grace of God and with the help of globally awakened masses, this malignancy of thought for keeping extreme income inequality intact will Grass-Rooty alter giving birth to more equitable societies where God is realized and the global resources are fairly allocated leading to the pursuit of happiness for all and a better life for everyone not just hype with memory left behind.

Some people are so poor, all they have is money.

Bob Marley

The price of freedom also is in an obsequious (soft, docile) way tied to capital as it should not be so costly as to rob people from their peace of mind since millions live below the poverty line, frequently worrying about their next meal, a place to live, and deteriorating health condition. So many lives are at the mercy of prayers for their children not to get shot at school and their loved one becoming the victim of rampage shooting where innocent bystanders get killed, even at the so-called safest places like a church, synagogue, mosque, and other sacred and worship-oriented entities for no reason at all. And so not sadly knowing where the next carnage is going to happen.

The price of freedom should not manufacture a crime-infested society where no one is safe, and is exponentially unsafe for those who are exposed to everyday sweeping violence in harsh neighborhoods since lack of funds and opportunities have deprived them of being guarded against savagely oriented plots marginalizing the indigents (broken, barren), implying that the poor should not belong. Taking these beastly behaviors as they are normal, as they are part of life, there is not much we can do. This is the price we pay for being free. What an odd analogy! So distasteful and bitterly sad it does not make any sense. One should dig into corporate culture to realize there is no limit to ill-doings for the love of money, since they even bribe the government to hush and work in cahoots to control the republic, the people. The price of freedom is not to run an economy that every time it fails, horrifyingly destroys families and so many lives beyond imagination since millions lose their jobs unexpectedly, leaving them financially stranded, tearing families apart, impoverishing them from their livelihood frequently to the point of no return.

The price of freedom shouldn't have to perpetually (continuously) worry about paying so much taxes so the state can doggedly invest in the military-industrial complex for wars of aggression, and to build up even more incarcerations, the **prison industrial complex** (PIC) to manage the overlapping interests of government and **industry** that use surveillance, policing, and imprisonment as solutions to economic, crime-ridden society, social and political problems giving anyone the impression that we are heading for a Gestapo-like policing as so many surveillances and technological gadgets are activated, spending billions of dollars to watch the citizens and even frisk anyone they wish without due process of the law creating fear, anxiety, and torment, menacing the so-called suspects often proving them being wrong. Annually thousands of unconstitutional and illegitimate activities are far from civil society, and very unbecoming from Godly nations that are meant to lead the way and guide the rest for reaching liberty, freedom, human rights, and the pursuit of happiness. The price of freedom is not to let children, even at very young ages, die in their parent's arms trying to emigrate, and for many human beings to be drowned at sea for seeking freedom and happiness.

The price of freedom shouldn't be global prejudice against billions because of their poor financial status, race, nationality, faith, and favor others because of their wealth, power, and influence. The price of freedom must be not to displace and force so many from their homeland, making them refugees, leaving them with no choice but to wither away in transition, to bear inhumane treatment in refugee camps and from the so-called host nations (a **nation** that receives the forces and/or supplies of allied **nations**, coalition partners, and/or NATO organizations to be located on, to operate in, or to transit through its territory). The price of freedom is not to collude (alliance) with fascist regimes to pillage the weak country's entire resources, abuse and by the millions evict them from their own home as if God is not watching.

The price of freedom is not to support monstrous states with savagely fierce human rights records since they annually put hundreds to death and imprison and torture thousands furtively (hiding, covertly) as the powerful governments globally turn a blind eye from so much atrocities done against humanity, not freeing the innocents from being maliciously persecuted by these barbaric governments that maneuver in a tortuous (twisting, indirect) manner, leaving the populace with no choice but to live in utter misery since there is no alternative but for those awakened to raise their voice to aid the helpless. After all, God only works through the enlightened, the savvy-minded and the compassionates, those Jesus-like, those who are not hypocrites in either words or actions and truly mean to discard malaise of living to establish a just and fair global society, one nation under God, where humanity can truly seek our Creator, relevantly taste life and passionately pursuing happiness.

The price of freedom is not letting presidential candidates buy their way to the presidency via illegal campaign funds and camouflaged contributions, unjustifiably leaving the deserving and legit nominees (contender, hopeful) behind, and with thousands, if not millions of painfully agonizing (excruciating) conducts facing humanity. The price of freedom is not for so many soldiers to return home with PTSD (post-traumatic stress disorder) and intense depression in which they must undergo psychiatric and psychological treatment, often with no cure since many either have radical behavioral change for the worse or commit suicide. Bear in mind that over the last 15 years, more US troops have died from suicide than have been killed in Afghanistan. The gruesome effect of wars that have arouse the God within them since the punishment of awakened conscious can be very devastating on the combatants because of the troubling images of badly injured or killed comrades, remembering the killing or maiming of innocent people taken as collateral damage, the nightmares and the ugly nature of the war itself, which can unyieldingly reflect in their minds, pushing them to the limit.

I am afraid the estimated number of combat service members, veterans, who suffer from signature wounds such as invisible injuries of combat trauma, traumatic brain injury (or both) is 1 in 3. These signature wounds include painful symptoms such as flashbacks, avoidance, isolation, and hyper-arousal reactions including anger outbursts.

Lone Survivors Foundation's focus is to educate service members, veterans, and their family members on the warning signs, symptoms, and characteristics of these injuries to better prepare the soldiers when returning home; good, but not good enough. The price of freedom is not to execute innocent prisoners, then call it a mistake since they shouldn't have been arraigned (prosecuted, indicted) in the first place, since the state refuses to allocate funds and proper resources for thoroughly investigating a suspect before putting them to death, indicating that they prefer money over lives.

No doubt the redundancies of such awful mistakes and the calamities (disaster) of such irresponsibility will lessen if allegations and frequently baseless accusations are taken more seriously to prevent the tragedy of murdering innocent people. The price of freedom is not to let go of the wealthy and the very well-off criminals with a slap on the wrist because of being highly influential, and since most can afford a competently sharp attorney to free them from the legal bondage, the clutches of the law and jail comparably with the poor with the same crime or less serious ones have to rot in prison or worse. Yes, people are holding the short end of the stick and are paying the real price for what freedom is costing them, but do not get what they are sacrificing for.

The price of freedom is not for many to senselessly die not being able to afford their utility bills in below-zero climates or expire because of extreme heat. The price of freedom is not for millions of good souls to globally become horrifyingly homeless, especially the children, exposing them to corruption and making them vulnerable in a jungle-like world to so many misdeeds. The price of freedom is not for any human being to perish because of not being able to pay for medical care for saving one's life. It is inhumane to forsake the children of God, which certainly deserve better living, which ironically you as well are the sibling and brethren. You ought to realize that you are who you are because of the grace of God and because of the trust put in you.

Billions after God believe in you to globally make it a more equitable world not by stirring trouble via the divide and conquer strategy as the British Empire once did, but through your love for mankind, your compassion as Jesus did, which have drawn so many towards what you are claiming to stand for: freedom, liberty, human rights, and the pursuit of happiness, where the upper mobility is encouraged; undeniably the hallmarks of a free and proud society.

Bear in mind that the world is attracted to the West's renaissance-oriented ideas and the sociocultural, socioeconomic innovations since they are originally designed to bring prosperity and happiness to everyone regardless of who they are and from what orientation or background. You have the power, the means, to make the wildest dreams for every human being possible. You should not lose this heavenly mission, should not turn your back from God and God's children. Do not deny your siblings the right to live happily. Help them, help themselves. You have what it takes to make it a peaceful world.

GOD PARTICLE?

> All matter originates and exists only by virtue of a force
> which brings the particle of an atom to vibration and
> holds this most minute solar system of the atom together.

> Max Planck

In 2012, scientists confirmed the detection of the long-sought Higgs boson, also familiar by its nickname the "God particle." This particle helps render mass to all elementary particles that have mass, like electrons and protons. The Higgs particle is one of the 17 particles in the Standard Model, the model of physics which explains all known basic particles. The Higgs particle is a boson. Bosons are thought to be particles that are causing all physical forces. The theory of Higgs boson, known by the media as the God particle, was discovered by physicist Peter Higgs and his colleagues in 1964, which states it is an elementary particle in the standard model of particle physics theory generated by quantum excitation of the Higgs field with more reliably precise measurement. The media calls the Higgs boson "the God particle" because, according to the theory laid out by Scottish physicist Peter Higgs and his colleagues in 1964, it's the physical proof of an invisible, universe-wide field that gave mass to all matter immediately after the big bang, forcing particles to coalesce into stars, planets, and so on.

The Higgs boson particle is so important to the Standard Model because it signals the existence of the Higgs field, an invisible energy field present throughout the universe that imbues other particles with mass. The Higgs is the particle that gives other particles their mass, making it both fundamentally important and magical. We think of mass as an

729

intrinsic property of all things, and yet physicists believe that without the Higgs boson, mass Grass-Rooty doesn't exist. Higgs boson gives particles mass, letting them fasten together and make things, like stars and planets, galaxies, etc. Infinite Higgs boson particles constitute an invisible force throughout the entire universe know as a Higgs field. Scientists are almost certain it's the elusive Higgs boson, a particle that gives all other particles their mass through the Higgs field.

If it is the Higgs, it will not have an anti-particle, says Taylor. "At the elemental particle level bosons do not have anti-particles." The Higgs boson is the subatomic particle associated with the Higgs field, an energy field that transmits mass to the things that travel through it. Technically, the Higgs boson doesn't give other particles mass; the particle is a quantized position of a field (the Higgs field) that produces mass through its interaction with other particles. Quantization is the idea that a physical quantity can have only certain discrete values, for instance, matter is quantized since it is made of individual particles that cannot be subdivided. It is not possible to have half an electron. Also, the energy levels of electrons in atoms are quantized. The Higgs boson helps explain how particles obtain mass, so it looks like the Higgs boson might help to find the key to comprehend dark matter, which is the dominant form of matter—that, along with dark energy—makes up 95 percent of all there is in the universe.

Dark energy is thought to make up 73 percent of the total mass and energy in the universe. Dark matter accounts for 23 percent, which leaves only 4 percent of the universe composed of the regular matter that can be seen, such as stars, planets, galaxies, and people. Dark matter is a form of matter thought to account for approximately 85 percent of the matter in the universe and about a quarter of its total energy density. The majority of dark matter is thought to be non-baryonic, possibly being composed of some as-yet-undiscovered subatomic particles. Baryonic matter means that it should only include matter made of baryons; it should include protons, neutrons, and all the objects composed of them for example (atomic nuclei), but deprived of things like electrons and neutrinos, which are leptons.

Light is composed of photons, so we could ask if the photon has mass. The answer is then definitely no: the photon is a massless particle. According to the theory, it has energy and momentum but no mass, and this is confirmed by experiments to within strict limits. After all, it has energy, and energy is equivalent to mass. Photons are traditionally said to be massless. This is a figure of speech that physicists use to describe something about how a photon's particle-like properties are described by the language of special relativity.

The speed of light in a vacuum is 186,282 miles per second (299,792 kilometers per second), and in theory, nothing can travel faster than light. In miles per hour, light speed is, well, a lot: about 670,616,629 mph. If you could travel at the speed of light, you could go around the Earth 7.5 times in one second.

Matter is the "stuff" of the universe—the atoms, molecules, and ions that make up all physical substances. Matter is anything that has mass and takes up space. Energy is the capacity to cause change. Energy cannot be created or destroyed; it can only be conserved and converted from one form to another. Einstein called these energy packets photons, and these are now recognized as a fundamental particle. Visible light is carried by photons, and so are all the other kinds of electromagnetic radiation like X-rays, microwaves, and radio waves. In other words, light is a particle. Photon, energy. The amount of energy is directly proportional to the photon's electromagnetic frequency and thus, equivalently, is inversely proportional to the wavelength. The higher the photon's frequency, the higher its energy. Equivalently, the longer the photon's wavelength, the lower its energy.

What is inside a quark?

A quark is a tiny particle that makes up protons and neutrons. After the invention of the particle accelerator, it was discovered that electrons are fundamental particles, but neutrons and protons are not. Neutrons and protons are made up of quarks, which are held together by gluons. There are six types of quarks. There are no free quarks. Other particles— electrons, neutrinos, photons, and more—can exist on their own. But quarks never will. The Higgs boson (or Higgs particle) is a particle in the Standard Model of physics. The Higgs particle is a boson. Bosons are thought to be particles that are responsible for all physical forces. Other known bosons are the photon, the W and Z bosons, and the gluon.

> "It seems probable to me that God, in the beginning, formed matter in solid, massy, hard, impenetrable, moveable particles"

Isaac Newton

Black holes form almost entirely out of normal matter no matter where they form. The ones that form where the density of matter is low—like out where we are—will have a substantial portion of that growth come from dark matter, but that growth is (on average) negligible compared to the initial black hole's mass. As it turns out, the mysterious substance is almost everywhere, drooping throughout intergalactic space to form an all-encompassing web of matter. Dark matter is invisible: It doesn't interact with light, so astronomers cannot see it. In physical cosmology and astronomy, dark energy is an unknown form of energy which is hypothesized to permeate all of space, tending to accelerate the expansion of the universe. Dark energy is the name given to the force that is believed to be making the universe larger. Distant galaxies appear to be moving away from us at high speed: the idea is that the universe is getting bigger, and has been since the big bang. Conventional black holes are formed by gravitational collapse of heavy objects such as stars, but they can also, in theory, be formed by other processes.

A photon is massless, has no electric charge, and is a stable particle. A photon has two possible polarization states. In the momentum representation of the photon, which is preferred in quantum field theory, a photon is described by its wave vector, which determines its wavelength λ and its direction of propagation. In particle physics, proton decay is a hypothetical form of particle decay in which the proton decays into lighter subatomic particles, such as a neutral pion and a positron. Despite the significant experimental effort, proton decay has never been observed. In physics, exotic matter is a matter that somehow deviates from normal matter and has "exotic" properties. A broader definition of exotic matter is any kind of non-baryonic matter—that is not made of baryons, the subatomic particles (such as protons and neutrons) of which ordinary matter is composed.

How fast is the universe expanding? In 2001, Dr. Wendy Freedman determined space to expand at 72 kilometers per second per mega parsec—roughly 3.3 million light-years—meaning that for every 3.3 million light-years further away from the Earth you are, the matter where you are is moving away from the earth 72 kilometers a second faster. The speed of light in a vacuum, commonly denoted c, is a universal physical constant important in many areas of physics. Its exact value is 299,792,458 meters per second (approximately 300,000 km/s (186,000 mi/s).

Consciousness relies on quantum mechanics because quantum mechanics is the foundation of all mechanics. It describes the behavior of all particles that make up our bodies. The quantum mind or quantum consciousness is a group of hypotheses which propose that classical mechanics cannot explain consciousness. And since energy and matter are the same relating to Einstein's theory and the formula of ($E=mc^2$), matter can also appear and disappear.

At the quantum level, matter and antimatter particles are constantly popping into existence and popping back out, with an electron-positron pair here and a top quark-antiquark pair there. A controversial theory suggests the brain acts like a quantum computer. The idea that consciousness arises from quantum mechanical phenomena in the brain is intriguing, yet lacks scientific evidence. Many scientists believe that an item truly exists only as long as it is observed; otherwise, it is not only meaningless, but simply nonexistent.

The observer and the observed are one. What is clear is that without consciousness, no perception or any experience is ever possible, therefore halting progress. Even the idea of the observer effect wouldn't be possible since with conscious depletion, no observer effects and the material world are of any good if they cannot be empirically doable. The reality is that every creature, to a certain extent, perceives the environment around them and experiences their specific world. The bottom line is we need to realize the task of the cosmic and universal energy force thought that not only creates biocentrism but is imbued in the entire existence as, for example, the contemporary scientists denote that it is the Higgs boson that is causing the energy force in the physical world.

Furthermore, quantum mind and the quantum world are not apart, as the human brain is so intelligently designed and has gradually evolved to peak performance and is expecting to improve to reach the pinnacle of invincibility beyond our imagination. It is no doubt that the entire existence is a benefactor of the omnipotent, omniscient God. The fact that the human brain is endowed with many abs is undeniable, which is bound to step by step grasp the essence of life. Like the Apple cell phone or the Microsoft cell phone, our brain is much more complex, as it can better comply with universal consciousness that is an inseparable part of where the bigger picture should be realized.

Virtual particles do not necessarily carry the same mass as the corresponding real particle, although they always conserve energy and momentum. The longer the virtual particle exists, the closer its characteristics come to those of ordinary particles. Quantum level may refer to energy level. A particle that is bound can only take on certain discrete values of energy, called energy levels. The quantum realm, also called the quantum scale, is a physics term referring to scales where quantum mechanical effects become important.

Consciousness is the state or quality of awareness or of being aware of an external object or something within oneself. Despite the difficulty in definition, many philosophers believe that there is a broadly shared underlying intuition about what consciousness is.

Quantum biology refers to applications of quantum mechanics and theoretical chemistry to biological objects and problems. Many biological processes involve the conversion of energy into forms that are usable for chemical transformations and are quantum mechanical. The word *conscience* derives etymologically from the Latin *conscientia*, meaning "privity of knowledge" or "with knowledge." The English word implies internal awareness of a moral standard in the mind concerning the quality of one's motives, as well as a consciousness of our actions.

With higher intelligence and the advent of technology, the overall progression in miraculous discoveries, humanity can gradually reveal the role of the quantum world where it seems that the human mind is an inseparable part of the magical quantum realm, the invisible world linked to the prevalent universal consciousness, since it is the thought transactions, with the exchange of information, which identify with the character of the quantum phenomenon, as the mind can dialogue and communicate through the awakened energy-oriented concepts we know as thinking.

The essence of what is not tangible, namely consciousness in the material world, has perplexed even the most inquisitive scientific mind as so many of them resist the fact that the universal consciousness has the characteristics of God, which cannot be located and utterly not seen but is prevalent and the fuel for propelling what we know, like existence in its entirety, and unless that is reckoned with, then no matter how we preserve and challenge to overcome the hurdles of how existence initiated, why we are here, where do we come from, and if living has a purpose, where are we heading, if there is living after we expire, or if there are rewards and punishments in the next realm, and so on, will be hopelessly in vain.

Scientists have so far been able to enter the vicinity of the subatomic particles where information and magical behavior of the invisible world maneuvers through wave-like apparatus, puzzling the most promising minds of our time. Quantum mechanics is defined as the body of scientific laws that describe the wacky behavior of photons, electrons, and the other particles that make up the universe. At the scale of atoms and electrons, many of the equations of classical mechanics, which describe how things move at everyday sizes and speeds, cease to be useful.

In the quantum life, entangled quantum particles can "communicate" through time. When two quantum particles interact, and if one can place them at opposite ends of the universe, and then measure one, whatever the measurement, the other particle also takes on a corresponding quality at the same time, no matter the distance. Quantum entanglement occurs relating to physical phenomenon when pairs or groups of particles are produced, interact, or share spatial proximity in ways such that the quantum state of each particle cannot be described independently of the position of the others, even when the particles are apart by a long distance. Scientists say that entangled quantum particles can "communicate" via time.

Why is quantum entanglement important? Entanglement can be utilized as a tool in quantum computing, for instance, in "super-dense" coding—which can transport two bits of classical information via a single entangled qubit. The best thing about qubits is that they can exist in a superposition of multiple states. Quantum entanglement can be key to that. Can quantum entanglement happen between people? A qubit is short for a quantum bit, which is the fundamental unit of quantum information. A qubit also has two states, but this time they are two quantum states. The difference between a bit and a qubit is that the qubit can exist in a quantum superposition. Concept: the principle of quantum superposition says that if a physical system may be in one of many configurations—arrangements of particles or fields—then the most general position is a combination of all of these possibilities, where the amount in each configuration is indicated by a complex number.

Referencing consciousness, imagination, dreams, and the infinitely potentiated human mind and heart, we can identify with the properties of the quantum interactivity where magic can happen: what scientists call entanglement. People get entangled with each other when they fall in love, and it can start when they're nowhere near each other, perhaps catching each other's eyes for the first time across a crowded room.

How does quantum communication work? Using the principle of entanglement, researchers have used entangled photons to transfer information between two nodes, in which the sender holds half of the entangled photons and the receiver holds the other half. How do particles get entangled? Entanglement occurs when a pair of particles, such as photons, interact physically. A laser beam fired through a certain type of crystal can cause individual photons to be split into pairs of entangled photons. Can more than two particles be entangled? Entanglement is a counterintuitive quantum physics phenomenon, in which a particle influences all the others with which it's entangled—even if the particles are far apart. If one particle is in one state, for example, the others might be in the same state. Usually, it's easier to entangle only two photons at once.

Can we create entangled particles? In other words, the two atoms are now entangled. Any time you can bring two systems together in such a way that the final state of one particle depends on the input state of the other, you can make an entangled state by making that input state a quantum superposition. Physicists believe that quantum entanglement transfers information at around 3 trillion meters per second—or four orders of magnitude faster than light. This is a lower speed limit, meaning as we collect more precise data, you can expect that number to get larger.

Quantum entanglement benefits exist after links are broken. "Spooky action at a distance" is how Albert Einstein famously derided the concept of quantum entanglement—where objects can become linked and instantaneously influence one another regardless of distance. Quantum entanglement benefits pass after links are no longer intact and are broken.

Is man the decisive force in the world around us, or is it as Marx and Angles believed we are the products of our environment and that it is the matter and the environment that plays a decisive role in our lives and in who we are? Historical materialists Marx, Engels, and Lenin are, without a doubt, the proponent of the economic decisiveness for what is happening in our world. But other variables, other elements, also haunt human minds that play a part, but not a fateful one, arguing that history is the result of material conditions rather than ideas.

Idealists' mentalist monism holds that only mind or spirit exists. Mentalism (psychology) refers to those branches of study that contemplate perception and in grasping the thought processes related to mindfulness, consciousness, cognitive behaviorism, imaginations, and dreams, where idea-oriented perspectives should be noticed. Mentalism is a psychological theory that believes human beings have a conscious mind that can affect conduct. Dualism is an idea that there is a body and there is a separate soul. Materialism is the notion that consciousness is created by the body in one's brain. In materialism, the idea is that we are just a body since in reality, no spirit or soul ever exists because our body can do a lot of very complicated things. We should know there are many bodily sensations that scientific theories cannot explain.

In the *Fifth Meditation* and elsewhere, Descartes says that God's existence follows from the fact that existence is contained in the "true and immutable essence, nature, or form" of a supremely perfect being, just as it follows from the essence of a triangle that its angles equal two right angles. As a result, he clearly and distinctly understands the mind all by itself, separately from the body, and the body all by itself, separately from the mind. According to Descartes, his ability to clearly and distinctly understand them separately from one another implies that each can exist alone without the other. The mind is the set of cognitive faculties including consciousness, imagination, perception, thinking, judgment, language, and memory, which is situated in the brain and the central nervous system.

Descartes's Second Proof of the existence of God: Axiom: The same power and action is needed to preserve something as would be needed to create something anew. Axiom: There must be at least as much reality in the cause as in the effect. Neutral monism believes that one sort of thing fundamentally exists, to which both the mental and the physical can be reduced. Material monism (also called physicalism and materialism) states that the material world is primary, and consciousness arises through the interaction with the material world. Materialism is a form of philosophical monism that holds that matter is the fundamental substance in nature, and that all things, including mental states and consciousness, are results of material interactions. Materialism is closely related to physicalism—the view that all that exists is ultimately physical since the only supreme entity is matter, which is the fundamental reason for all beings, and we are all the byproduct of matter. It is a theory or doctrine that denies the existence of a distinction or duality in some spheres, such as that between matter and mind, or God and the world. The doctrine says only one supreme being exists, and that is matter.

Materialism is a philosophical doctrine that postulates (puts forward, posits) a limited assertion (upholding, defense) of consciousness to that which is observable and subject to the scientific method. As philosopher George Santayana puts it, "If philosophy is based on science, science, in turn, is based on the premise of materialism—namely, that all exists is a matter in the motion of which materially we, the thinkers and logicians are a part." Excuse me, but any motion must have an inception, a starting point, and an ending, a destiny, a purpose to serve, as it is true with all animated beings regardless of their micro or macro behaviors since a senselessly dull, decayable, will-less, and utterly unintelligent matter cannot be the driving force behind such an amazingly sensible, phenomenally willful, awesomely intentional, wonderfully disciplined, and infinitely intelligent task we call life.

Material is a synonym for a matter that sees (no exception for the material brain) in which materialist psychologists believe that consciousness (the mind) is the byproduct and the function of the material brain. Materialists are entitled to their opinion, but any idea should at least make a bit of sense since it is odd not seeing the oxymoron behavior in the material brain and the immaterial mind. How can an immaterial mind come from a material brain, since no matter is conveyed with intelligence or any sense at all that we should know of? They believe in two opposite ideas making sense, like "living death," because if we choose to accept that living can come from death, then we must believe in miracles and certainly the act of God. Materialists are not in accord with any tautology where the meaning is to make sense, as they should be in accord without any flaws. They deliberately choose not to see that there is no material brain according to the very science they are proud of, which clearly says we are all about energy since matter is nothing but condensed energy, especially when it comes to the thinking brain.

Scientific naturalism states that all objects and events are part of nature, for instance, they all belong to the world of space and time.

Not to exclude the mental realm of human beings, which is also subject to scientific inquiry. Historical materialism, also known as the materialist conception of history, is a methodology utilized by many communist and Marxist historiographers that concentrate on sociology and human societies and their progression via history, believing that history is the outcome of material conditions rather than ideas; go figure. The question that should be asked is are "material conditions" static or dynamically oriented entities since one cannot be influenced from a dull, spiritless, mindless, and clueless environment where no fluidity of thought can ever be grasped or communicated because no conditioning impact can ever become manifest. Further, again by taking science as witnessed, it is precisely the observer effect and one's mindfulness that can give meaning to the external world and not the other way around. Simply put, "We do not simply live in this universe. The universe lives within us" (Neil de Grasse Tyson). We are the byproduct of an infinitely magnificent idea and not the other way around.

In philosophy, naturalism is the "idea or belief that only natural (as opposed to supernatural or spiritual) laws and forces operate in the world." Such an absolute belief in naturalism is commonly referred to as metaphysical naturalism. Charles Darwin was a naturalist. Marx, naturalism, and affiliates believe that religion is the grievance of the deprived, sigh of the oppressed creature, the heart of a cruel world, and the soul of spiritless conditions. It is the opium of the people. Marx claims that the abolition of religion as an illusion, the illusory joy of the masses is the demand for their real happiness. What Marx propagates branches out of the roots of materialistic doctoring, since the atheists address that human beings are the products of their environment since soulless, spiritless, and mindless matter is the sole cause to the entire existence, forgetting that man is much more complex than what Marxism believes. The atheist should realize that since human beings are group animals, they must belong; we must connect emotionally; we must communicate and exchange feelings; we cannot remain as remote islands; we are thoughts, imaginations, hopes, and dreams. Take that away from us and we will appear with a host of psychological disorders: loneliness, anxiety, and manic (insane, frenzied) depression. Individualize us and witness crimes going rampant, not to exclude so many suicides and often very senseless homicides.

People are about the power of intention, about will power and in making choices. People are not some type of robots programmed by history or their atmosphere. And yes, the human being is influenced by their environment, but they can always challenge and change their position and often revolt against any odds facing them. Human beings make history; it is not the history that makes them. That is why humanity will by nature seek an answer to the very existence they have, starting with where do we come from? Who are we? Why are we here? Where are we heading? Is doing right rewarded after we expire or not? Are wrongdoings at the end punishable or not? if not how can an orderly, well-disciplined and extremely intelligent universe lack from acting justify? Is there a soul? And millions of other innately oriented questions. Therefore, if not religions, either way, human beings will find anything to replace religion with something to comfort them and deliver their spiritual longings for answers and connections.

The spiritual wellbeing has two components: religious wellbeing, which refers to the connection with God or a Supreme, a Higher Being, and existential wellbeing, which pertains to the meaning and purpose in life. Raise children without love, compassion, deprive them of a happy living and a warm environment, abuse and deprive them of the necessities required for a decent living where they cannot belong, then expect from them the exhaustion of the happy hormones that are biologically driven. The four primary chemicals in the brain that affect happiness are dopamine, oxytocin, serotonin, and endorphins, so one should expect sadness, cruelty, and lack of loyalty.

Other biological hormones that affect our mood are adrenaline, cortisol, melatonin, and other hormones can affect your mood or even influence the health of your brain. Cortisol is a hormone released when you're stressed. A shift in these hormones can cause both physical and emotional symptoms. Changes in estrogen and progesterone levels also influence serotonin levels. This is a neurotransmitter that helps regulate your mood, sleep cycle, and appetite. Low levels of progesterone also affect our mood and cause us to feel irritable, anger, and rage. There are many literary readings and perhaps awakening analogies that Marx and Angles have made for only making some sense into the socioeconomic aspect of our lives. But they sure have both gone lopsided and in vain trying to ideologically explain religion and address God, the universe, and man.

Here is a quote that points to the economics and today's ethics gone wrong since economic tyranny has forced millions to behave unethically, where crimes have gone rampant and violence has globally ridden (harassed, oppressed) every nation.

"Do I obey economic laws if I extract money by offering my body for sale? Then the political economist replies to me: You do not transgress my laws, but see what Cousin Ethics and Cousin Religion have to say about it. My political economic ethics and religion have nothing to reproach you with, but—But whom am I now to believe, political economy or ethics? The ethics of political economy are acquisition, work, thrift, sobriety—but political economy promises to satisfy my needs. It stems from the very nature of estrangement that each sphere applies to me a different and opposite yardstick—ethics one and political economy another; for each is a specific estrangement of man and focuses attention on a particular field of estranged essential activity, and each stands in an estranged relation to the other."

Some research indicates a link between your beliefs and your sense of wellbeing. Positive beliefs, comfort, and strength gained from religion, meditation, and prayer can contribute to wellbeing. It may even promote healing. Improving your spiritual health may not cure an illness, but it may help you feel better. What is spiritual health? Spirit is what cannot be defined as part of the body or as part of the mind. Body, mind, and

DR. FERIDOUN SHAWN SHAHMORADIAN

spirit all affect one and other. Spiritual health is obtained when you feel at peace with the Creator and with life. It is when one is competent to find hope and comfort in even the hardest of times, where one struggles to overcome and out of being submerged with crippling difficulties only to seek God for help.

Marxism and affiliates reject human spirit, mind, and soul, since they one-track-mindedly see only matter as their groundbreaking and fundamental reason for making history as they try to ideologically grasp a base for addressing class struggle against capitalism, therefore making a hodgepodge (assemblage, collection) of wrongful doctrines with the mistaken identity of who and what is the nature of human beings that is much more sophisticated than invented by atheists. The bottom line is the decisive force of biocentrism that is innately maneuvered for managing life as we are experiencing.

Marx was right when he addressed that no one should be superior to anyone. The quotation "all men are created equal" is part of the US Declaration of Independence, which Thomas Jefferson penned in 1776 during the beginning of the American Revolution. The phrase was present in Jefferson's original draft of the declaration. Let's treat humanity as it is meant to be, with reverence, dignity, equity, justice, and pride, where confidence and self-respect should be expressed among those socially marginalized, based on their shared identity, culture, experience, or any other divisive factor, since there's no doubt that we are made in the image of God and we must rebel against any other prejudice and less-ranking notions or belittling ideas.

Do not search for God,

persist on awakening to grow if so, rest assured God will be as crystal clear water to you as without a speck of doubt your thirst for finding God will be quenched as indisputable claim demand extraordinary clue which one should possess to rebut the challenge of any denial of God; it is in truly knowing God that one avoids toxic thoughts, misconduct and ill- oriented behavior that is the only way to human survival.

THE QUEST FOR GOD

Like Plato, Boethius divides substance into the corporeal and the incorporeal in a manner that does not match the Cartesian division between physical and mental substance. Boethius divides the incorporeal substance into the rational and non-rational. He regards the animating spirit or soul of beasts to be non-rational incorporeal substances. God is accounted to differ from other rational substances because He is by nature immutable (permanent-constant) and impassible (trackless, unpassable), while angels and souls are only immutable and impassible by divine grace. To be a person, according to Boethius, is to be a particular substance that has a mind or intellect, or is rational, and he believes God to be a person insofar as He is an incorporeal particular substance with a mind.

Now from all the definitions, we have given it is obvious that Person cannot be confirmed of bodies which have no life (for no one ever said that a stone had a person), nor yet of living things which lack sense (for neither is there any person of a tree), nor finally of that which is bereft of mind and reason (for there is no person of a horse, ox or any other of the animals which dumb and unreasoning life a life of sense alone), but we say there is a person of a man, of God, of an angel.

Like Descartes, however, Boethius regards God to be an incorporeal mind (that which possesses intellect or reason). As Boethius makes it clear, being a person implies having a mind. However, when Boethius considers God to have a mind, he does not believe that God has what would be called psychological states with having desires, needs, instincts, requirements, communicating, ideas, emotion, and feelings, or any kind of mental image. Thus, even though Boethius alleges that God is a person and has a mind or intellect, it would be an utter mistake to denote God's attributes to man's position.

Boethius takes God to be a substance; for that all persons are substances, and God is a person. This is also a claim on which there is no unanimity (unity- consent). Avicenna, for instance, debated that God is not a substance; even though he conceded that there is a sense in which one could say that God is a substance. If by "substance" one meant whatever is not an accident, then one could consider God a substance. This would be misleading, however, from Avicenna's, view because it would suggest that substance could be considered a genre (type) which God would also be included along with other substances.

While Boethius categorizes God with other rational substances (with the difference being that His immutability and impassibility (calm- unmoved) are by nature rather than by grace), Avicenna considers the distinction between substance and accident to be a difference in protest and since God lacks any crotchet (oddity- weirdness) other than His existence, it is inappropriate to consider God as a substance. Contrast among characteristics into substance and another kind only appropriate for contingent entities. Avicenna provides a reason for emphasizing divine transcendence: God transcends the categories related to contingents.

And I say God is not temporal, God is not spatial, God is all-cause, God is the existence, God does not emanate wisdom, God is the wisdom, God does not emanate intelligence, God is intelligence, God does not emit rationality, God is rationality, God is not of Justice, God is justice, God does not percolate (permeate-impregnate) divinity, God is divinity (deity- holiness), God does not exude compassion, God is compassion, God is empathy, God is mercy. God does not ooze goodness, God is what good means, God does not convey consciousness, God is consciousness, God is not of mimetic, delineative (represent-portrait) knowledge, God is knowledge, God is not of the truth, God is the truth, God is not of any essence, God is the essence, God is the quintessence (spirit-ethos-soul.)

God is not of creation, God is the creator, God is not of inspiration, God is an inspiration, God is not of spirit, God is the spirit, otherwise God couldn't be "Omnipotent and Omnipresent." He couldn't be ubiquitous (everywhere), God is not within infinity, God is infinity, God gives meaning to the word everlasting. No attributes behold God because God is the primary source for all there is and all of which there will ever be. For Avicenna, however, the work of the active intellect is not only to contain forms that would be reflected in human intellects; the active intellect is taken to emit the matter of the sublunary (earthy, transient, temporary) world, to emanate natural forms on the appropriate sublunary matter, and the emanation of human knowledge.

While Avicenna's theory of prophecy is centered on the notion of union with the active intellect, the idea can be glimpsed in Fārābī, as well, who argues that since the active intellect emanates from the existence of the First Cause, that is, God, it follows that God is the source of revelation for man through the active intellect. In the subsequent traditions of Islamic philosophical thought, there is an increasing emphasis on the transcendent nature of God, so that if Avicenna considered God to be the wājib al-wujūd (that which about existence is necessary), by the time of Mulla Sadra God is realized with pure existence.

In this doctrinal, it is denied that God has a mind, intellect, personhood, or substantiality. Hence, God is the creator of all intellects and is beyond intellect. God does not think, but knows and wills without thinking. Likewise, one could define "soul" in such a way that to say "soul (Nafs.) To have a soul is to be governed by some principle under which one can be said to have various aptitudes or faculties (knack- adroitness- quality) such as intellection, perception, volition (discretion- option) nutrition, reproduction, and growth. Concerning spirit, too, the interpretation is that God created spirit, not that He is spirit.

Ghazālī disagreed with Avicenna believing that Avicenna limited God's knowledge to universals. With Mulla Sadra, God does not have representational knowledge at all. Instead of a hylomorphic (the doctrine that physical objects result from the combination of matter and form) model of intellectual knowledge, Mulla Sadra bases his analysis of divine knowledge on the idea of the immediate presence of the existence emanating cause to its effect.

God's knowledge is described as knowledge by presence. So, God's knowledge is not using immaterial forms or representations of the known, but, rather, His knowledge of them is the same as their existence, since He is existence and the cause of all lesser extent (existents.) Accordingly, God's creation and sustenance of things are the same as His knowledge of them. Divine knowledge is the presence of whatever exists to the source of its existence. Whoever tries to prove one's knowledge of things through one of one's creations like the soul, the intellect or says that His complete knowledge is posterior (comes after) to his Essence, this is due to the imperfection of his vision and weakness of his knowledge.

With Mulla Ṣadrā's analysis of divine knowledge, there is no room left for the attribution of mind in the sense of intellect to God. God does not make use of concepts. He does not have propositional knowledge, only presentational knowledge. This means that God does not have a mind and is not a person, at least according to the notion that persons are concept users or substances with minds.

If having a mind means knowing universals, or knowing things through universal concepts, God does not have a mind because He knows without making use of universal concepts, or anything else. God knows everything that exists, because He is the existence granting a cause of everything, and Sadra argues that immaterial causes may be said to know their effects. In Mulla Sadra's view, existence has a continuum of gradations, from the lowest material to the very essence of God, who is pure existence and is purely immaterial.

GOOD TO KNOW

The heart's magnetic field, which is the strongest rhythmic field generated by the human body, not only enfolds every cell of the body but also widens in all directions into the space around us. The heart's magnetic field can be measured several feet away from the body by sensitive magnetometers. Blood viscosity(stickiness) can be lessened 20-30 percent by subjecting it to a small magnetic field, lowering potential harm to blood vessels and the risk of heart attack, conforming to a new study. If a person's blood develops too thick it can damage blood vessels and raise the risk of a heart attack. Do Humans Have a Magnetic Field? The human body produces complex electrical activity in several different types of cells, not to exclude neurons, endocrine, and muscle cells – all called "excitable cells". As all electricity does, this activity also makes a magnetic field. Science confirms: the heart is stronger than the brain! No doubt, the brain has its electric and magnetic field, but they are relatively fragile compared with the heart's that is about 100 times stronger electrically and 5000 times tenacious (vigorous, stronger) magnetically!

Some Philosophical Views Referencing Man

Some groups of philosophers see man as animal-like. They believe that man will meet the same fate as beasts. Man has no precedence over them, claiming that differences in certain characteristics are not imperative, as similar differences are also noticed among the animals themselves. Next are those philosophers who see man as part of a universal machine, where the machine is vital and not of the part. The wheel of the universal machine is turning and man, like other things in the universe, is functioning, living his position since man is tied to the machine and his end is attached to it. This is Spinoza's assessment of man.

The third group is of those for whom a man is a reason and a fundamental purpose of existence for the universe. He is the pinnacle of creation and the whole universe has been formed to his purpose. This is the school of thought of Socrates, Plato, Aristotle, Kant, Berkley; the sophism school of thought. The contemporary philosopher, because of the influence of science, manifests that man will soon conquer the universe via science and will perhaps manipulate to control it. He does not link it to God and is visualizing to master the universe himself.

The fourth group, Grass Rooty, see matter and nature as the principal reason for existence where no intelligence, information, will, design, or any purposeful conduct had to be imbued in the origin of the species, just randomness, chance, which has for billions of years so oddly guided the universe to where we are. Notice they say "natural selection," but selecting should remind us of choosing. But then how can choosing or selecting occur exhausted of mindfulness, depleted of information where species without any planner, no programmer, could blindly, through natural selection and mutation, last for billions of years without interruption, leading the overall evolutionary impetus to the present time?

The fifth are those who believe no leaf can ever drop from any tree without God's knowledge, where God is present everywhere. God exists in every particle of the universe, cosmos, and beyond, and mankind is God's best creation. God is closer to us than our aorta and has endowed man with some of God's attributes. They do not believe that man exterminates like other animals, and the universe is deprived of its purpose and responsibility. Can it be said that an amazing universe full of wisdom, with infinite, intelligently based information, is rendered without a purpose, maneuvering aimlessly? If so, no good can ever come out of delusional minds where absurdity arrives at its meaning.

THE GOD WITHIN

While the global financial meltdown and its aftershocks have unleashed a flood of indignation, condemnation, and protest upon the ills of corporate monopoly, the crisis has exposed a deeper distrust and implacable (immitigable, not appeasing) resentment of capitalism itself. Historically, capitalism might have been the greatest engine of prosperity and progress ever devised, but it has done so while exploiting the very nucleus of its productivity: the workers, since billions are disgruntled with the implicit nature of the monetary system and its hidden agendas of surplus values that are so unfair to the actual producer of wealth, which denies to fairly govern the responsibilities of businesses and corporations towards the workers, deprived, and the poor.

The global economy and the Internet have heightened our sense of interconnectedness and sharpened our awareness that the real reason for corporation should not be to concentrate solely on enriching the shareholders, the investors, the CEOs, the managers, but to also boost the interests of their low-rank employees, globally billions of workers, communities, and the welfare of the customers; and of course, the fate of planet Earth. It is time to demand a new form of capitalism, something like a progressive social-democratic system or fair co-op system which is a function of an alternative economy and was built out of the necessity to provide an alternative system outside of capitalism and merge many autonomous movements and networks to form a society based on each community's values. That can truly comply with the twenty-first century, one devoted to encourage and promote a greater wellbeing rather than the single-minded pursuit of growth and profits; one that would have the interest of the entire nation at heart and not only the stakeholders; and a system that will hold those financially in charge responsible, the leaders accountable for their actions and the consequences and the way it creates value.

A system which does not sacrifice the wellbeing of the future generations, a profoundly governing one that is fundamentally principled toward the wellbeing of all of its citizens and not only a few; one that is socially accountable and is designed to have meaningful social safety nets where no citizen will be exhausted of the very basic needs. New revolutionary social and economic changes are more urgent than ever— not just as empty rhetoric, but an effort to genuinely reform and abide by the Grass Rooty rules and regulations that can restore the public trust, to repair the moral fabric of the system and to unleash the innovation required to tackle the world's most pressing and important challenges, prioritizing the ever-growing needs of the global citizenry, the one that truly emphasizes the progressive practices and disruptive (dissimilar, divergent) concepts that can tackle the challenges of the new world order where the legal, ethical, and moral imperatives of the system are not undermined, where the corrupt activities of multinational corporations are questioned; a system that hedges against favoritism and nepotism where the few thrive while billons are left gasping for air, worn-out because of striving for survival.

We live in a society that worships the wrong god, that worships violence and militarism, that is in favor of the war of aggression and is complicit to find the truth, since even the most tragic events are dealt with casually and soon forgotten as fads (crazes, weaknesses, whims) as social and economic justice are put on the backburner as if human lives are just numbers. Poverty and inequality do not happen by chance; poverty, inequality, and injustice occur because of the pursuit of greed, since wrong monetary systems are preplanned and actively at work and need to be overhauled by peaceful means via progressively organized sociopolitical and socioeconomic undertakings by a peaceful cultural revolution. Capitalism cannot maneuver in a social vacuum and put so much emphasis on profits and growth; it must come to terms with so many urgently needed social requirements if it is to save the freedom of choice, the liberty, and the human rights of the republic.

It is a fact that no empty rhetoric can practically resolve the actual reason behind so much hurt, often deviltry and decadent conduct caused in today's world, as one should not expect an easy solution to this rather very crucial but difficult task that can manifest hope only if the experts in the fields of law, legislative, judiciary, executive, economics, politics, psychology, psychiatric, linguistic, anthropology, sociology, neurology, neurochemistry, biology, and moral, spiritual, and religious-based entities or any other discipline or branch of science that deals with human behavior in its social and cultural aspects can act and interlink in unison for finding an answer to explain the different areas of human life and their relationships to each other and God.

This is not to say that a fundamentally oriented cultural revolution is not necessary, because it surely is if we should expect a Grass-Root change in all aspects of global monetary systems that are broken from the inside out, leaving so many victimized, certainly because of horrifying implemented policies since for the sake of maximizing wealth, millions of lives are annually trampled on and wasted, linked to one abusively demented policy or another, as people are struggling to survive on a daily basis not knowing where their next meal should come from.

Almost all probable consequences of poverty have an ill impact on children's lives. Not to exclude poor infrastructures, unemployment, lack of basic services, and income reflecting on their lack of education, malnutrition, violence at home and outside, child labor, diseases of all kinds transmitted by the family's poor living standards or through the environment. If a man is made in the image of God, then it is the God inside that is being trashed and humiliated.

The urgent needs are to prognoses why in the twenty-first century, where most contemporary cultures are grasped as civilized, they are the least concerned with propagating the negative agendas and tempting people with inhumane ideas, encouraging consumers with out-of-reach so-called dreams that certainly some violently contribute to Hollywood-style conduct, which as they say the sky is the limit for acting immoral and ill-willed to reach one's objectives since so many ruthlessly premeditate and are wrongfully aimed at others where the behaviors of the most savage beasts look pale in comparison to the ill-conducts of the so-called human beings. No savvy explanation should convince anyone for thousands of misdeeds globally happening every day without the tiniest positive response to assist millions of victims crying out loud for help as no genuine attempts are made even by law authorities, which so many of them either turn a blind eye or are bought and bribed to the teeth to keep their mouth shut no matter how grave the crimes or executed atrocities, and because the poor simply do not have the means to cut through the red tape so they can effectively be heard, which globally leaves billions without any legal or social protection. The truth is that even the evilest man is imbued with a drop of God's image that needs to be constructively fed at birth no matter how disgraced the genes, but it does not because so many destructive variables are actively at work awaiting the innocents before they are even born into a prevalently oriented toxic environment.

Perhaps the experts in human behavior should pay more attention to this fact that the saintly side of the man is extremely sensitive and can easily rebel when maltreated and can execute demonic conduct against others, even at a very young age. They ought to know this is where the foundation lies, since no human child must be dealt with deeds that can potentially resonate hurt and an inferiority complex in them.

It is very challenging to deal with and correct neglected individuals living for so long in filthy environments where the building blocks of their character become cemented for the worse since no love and caring, no hope for a better living becomes them, as most are synonymous with violence, crimes, incarceration, with many mentally disturbed where the state resumes to inhumane punishments, perhaps for making a bit of sense to them but often with no avail as most come from broken and scattered families due to hard times. Human beings can go berserk when they realize they do not belong, as so many are stranded and ignored. It is part of God within them that rebels and often so justified.

It is precisely the man's feeling that becomes hurt and injured, making one prone to rebellion. It is the God within one that is stepped on, that is humiliated and bashed (struck violently), where no remedy can quench one's thirst for not intending to take revenge, as frequently the inferiority complex takes over with inhumane residue left in them often to the day the victims expire, and sure in the long run affecting the overall society that is compelled (cogent, not able to be refuted) to deal with. We are human. We are wired to be social. Conditioning factors that contradict collectivism with close social interactions can only make things worse since the philosophy behind individualism is pragmatically divergent and not socially conducive, in which the culture of remote island attitude conquers millions leaving them with a host of irreparable psychological and behavioral disorders.

According to Freud, many psychological disorders can overcome us if we are not brought up in a healthy and upskilled environment where adequate training and professional behaviors are taught from the very early ages, as Freud believed the superego starts to arrive at about age five. The ego is fully conscious, while the id and superego are unconscious. The ego is solely concerned with pleasure, while the id and superego deal with what is socially acceptable. Your ego is your conscious mind, the part of your identity that you consider your "self." If you say someone has "a big ego," then you are saying he is too full of himself. The superego consists of two systems: The conscience and the ideal self. The conscience can punish the ego through causing feelings of guilt. For instance, if the ego gives in to the id's demands, the superego may make the person feel bad through guilt. Ego indicates the realistic and controlling component of the psyche. In comparison, the superego is the last component, which refers to the critical and moralizing part. The ego tries to maintain a balance among reality, superego, and id. Superego confines both ego and id for consequences of actions. Freud divided the superego into two parts: the ego ideal and the conscience. The ego ideal is the idealistic view of what is right, while the conscience is that sense of guilt, or the view of what is considered wrong.

What I mean is that a loving atmosphere must not be denied to any human child, any human being, even an animal, for that matter, since love is too potent and is imprinted to soothe man's feeling of hurt and to make one's emotions serene for preventing violent conduct. Compassion and kindness must be exercised at a very young age. The real problem is the elephant in the room; billions have to run for their lives to make a living, leaving no time to closely and watchfully attend to their loved ones. Unending poverty is one of the very decisive factors that has depleted so many from having the time or the financial means to properly attend to their families, since often the entire family has to work toward making ends meet. So many persevere to make a basic living and cannot, forcing them to lose priorities for a good living that is frequently lost forever, not to exclude spending time with their children.

Due to not belonging and becoming exhausted of the financial means to upgrade one's status, countless people flock (congregate, flight) with the wrong groups; therefore, no correct upbringing, no right training. Without proper education, and because the absence of role models are leaving them mentally and emotionally stranded, ill-fated, and not inspired to do good, this results in ugly consequences which blazon (announce) war on one's God-image, injuring their soul as their spirit collapses, sometimes doing the unthinkable as often hopelessness and despair haunts them without any constructive social welfare or professional remedies because I am afraid many so-called civil societies have already quit on the wrongdoers, labeling them as felons since millions are financially despaired and talking of them as either unfit or as collateral damage.

I frequently have wondered about this expression that says "the greatest good for the greatest number." A goal put forth for governments: that they should be judged by the results of their policies, and specifically, whether those policies benefit the majority. If so, I am puzzled; what about the ones that are left out, since they are not included in the majority? It's certainly not a progressive slogan.

It should remind us of the Lord Jesus in the passage: Jesus sat down in the temple to teach some of the people after he spent the previous night at the Mount of Olives. A group of scribes and Pharisees faced Jesus, disturbing his teaching session. They dragged in a woman, accusing her of committing adultery, claiming she was caught in the very act. They asked Jesus whether the punishment for someone like her should be stoning, as prescribed by Mosaic Law. Jesus first tried to ignore the interruption and wrote on the ground, ignoring them like he did not hear them. But when the woman's accusers persisted their challenge, he stated that "the one who is without sin is the one who should cast the first stone." The accusers and congregants departed, realizing not one of them was without sin, leaving Jesus alone with the woman. Jesus asked the woman if anyone had condemned her. She answered that no one had condemned her. Jesus said that he, too, does not condemn her, and told her to go and sin no more.

We ought to know that deprived people are the world's greatest entrepreneurs, since they have to relentlessly challenge their fund-depleting situation to satisfy their hunger and put a roof over their head. They must innovate to stay alive; living has practically become a game of Russian roulette since most are not guaranteed with any life-bearing plan, as people are financially exhausted. Money is essential for fueling and undertaking constructive agendas. They remain poor because they do not have the opportunities to turn their creativity into sustainable income, leaving no doubt that it is not the poor people that are the root cause of the problem, but the system that has yoked them. And you should ask why is it that the monetary system places so much emphasis on individualism? Why would it philosophize that it is solely the individual that is responsible for one's wellbeing?

Perhaps it's true to some extent, but surely not to a point that can leave the system to act carefree from its obligations and responsibilities toward its citizens, where millions are unemployed, with millions discouraged because they cannot find jobs, with so many homeless, without having access to education, medical, and transportation, and exhausted of the very basic needs that often economically paralyzes the entire society with prolonged depression. The culture of policing must become activated to prevent the destruction of a nation. Human beings are potentiated to progressively become so witty that no police would be needed to keep the peace, where people's conscience can be awakened to police themselves without any military or police interference. Why is it that even the most civilized nations must be restrained and policed over to maintain tranquility? Professor of social work and social policy Iain Ferguson has argued, "It is the economic and political system under which we live—capitalism—which is responsible for the enormously high levels of mental health problems which we see in the world today."

The alleviation of mental distress is only possible "in a society without exploitation and oppression." Highly materialistic people believe that owning and buying things are necessary means to achieve important life goals, such as happiness, success, and desirability. However, in their quest to own more, they often sideline other important goals, forgetting that we are here for a very short time and our priorities in life should be to help others in need because the very nature of the capitalist system is deliberately designed to manufacture stratified societies, often with inhumane economic inequality. And those who have inherited so much wealth without lifting a finger, won the lottery, or even worked hard for their money, should realize that realistically the odds must have played in their favor for becoming billionaire buffoons. Why buffoons? Because only fools stand by and watch their kind being wasted in front of their eyes and nonchalantly (unconcerned) shrug their shoulders believing that it is their fate, knowing as they do. We truly are living in a casino-like economy, leaving so many losers with only very few winners having it all since playing with people's lives and annihilating the God within them is taken as being lucky for the super-rich and being unlucky for the poor.

I am certain that no nation can survive a day in the absence of a police force because no nation has genuinely reached a state of enlightenment these days to restrain themselves from the clutches of the crime-ridden activities, since resources that are vital to accommodate people's basic needs and to awaken and raise people's consciousness, to enlighten them, are not available or are misallocated. That is why thousands and thousands of incarceration and detention centers are well, alive, and kicking.

"Insanity is the only sane reaction to an insane society"

Thomas Stephen Szasz

A culture of collectivism, cooperation with liberty and freedom, seeking justice, emotional stability, awakening, wisdom, patience and understanding, caring, not self-centeredness, loving, kind and compassionate, peaceful atmosphere, serenity of mind and spirit, happiness, professionalism, humbleness, open-mindedness, acting insightful, having inner strength, good leadership, accountability, responsibility, loyalty, faithfulness, unity, trustworthiness, self-awareness, proper hygiene, behaving ethically, mindfulness, sacrifice, and hundreds of quality-oriented attributes as such will awaken the God within you that would definitely demand and eventually force the state to act responsibly and fairly toward its citizens. Let's raise the God within humanity, without which the stability of the entire nation will be at grave risk. Otherwise, in a capital-intense society where money has replaced God, the God within is going to constantly be stepped on.

BELITTLING THE GOD WITHIN

We are the only creature with outside body experience, meaning no one can be located anywhere in their bodily anatomy, no one can be found in their brain, heart, limbs, spine, bones, nerves, and ligaments, bloodstream or within their gut. No tearing or an autopsy conducted with heavily guided magnifier anywhere in man's physical can ever locate one at all because we are having outside body experience, the mysterious force that makes the conductibility of our inner self and the outside world possible, the interactivities with the atmosphere enabling us to understand our environment is the human spirit, soul, or if you like, our mind that is in accord with our senses and the nervous system, as they also are energy-oriented, which should denote the ever-present awakened human spirit after we physically expire.

The ever-present human spirit can either transcend to the higher realms or descend to lower phases accordingly. Our brain is neither digitally nor analog-based. It is not in any way manufactured to exude thoughts where one can push a variety of designated buttons to become imaginative, creative, relaxed, complicit, or aggressive, often doing heavenly tasks. Any curious-minded person should meditate on a real cause that is beyond space and time, an omnipotent, omnipresent God, which is the actual source of making the miracle-oriented phenomena like the human brain and mind possible.

One should ask if we cannot be found in our body, and what comprises us is nothingness but a load of bones, fatty tissues, organs, nerves, and blood, then who on God's green Earth is this Ghost within that is thoughtful, titanically emotional and with a host of feelings, with colossally driven dreams and imagination? Who and what is this Ghost within that frequently rebels when stepped on and humiliated and reaches the stars when praised and admired? And how can this Ghost within communicate with the awakened forces outside of self if not an inseparable part of the energy-oriented universe?

The human psyche, our mind, is what makes the world practical, making living possible, but is not limited to what is clear and obvious in our material world. It is potentiated to dig into the so-called nothingness where the infinite realm of possibilities are hidden as humanity must cultivate the so-called darkness, the invisible world, to experience the nature of what is unknown, to shed light on the reality of the unseen, to make sense of the world around us, where the spirit of animated beings, the soul, finds its meaning. Precious pearl or another bivalve mollusk highly valued gem can only be found in the deep, dark-blue ocean while another antiquated rarity can be cultivated in remote historical sights attempted by the know-how experts and experienced. The spiritual world where the enlightenment is pursued is no exception. It can only be sought through long and deep meditation, making it probable to enter the immaterial world by feeling the suffering and often the excruciating pain of loneliness in search of soul-seeking, delving into the unknown where the birth for every being is manifested.

The mental exclusivity and the human soul is to carry on after we expire, leaving our human body because we should not expect an energy-oriented entity such as the human soul not to follow the energy-based patterned universe, as no energy is lost but is transferred into infinite numbers of other potentiated energy-based entities, which common sense and as disciplined as our universe is should further follow the rule of action and reaction and the cause and effect principle that we are bound to hint to awaken humanity that this is just a test where the human conscious, intelligence, wisdom, will, and freedom of choice should play an extremely imperative role to either pass the test or not. This certainly is beyond human comprehension to grasp why it is what it is, but it sure seems that all roads lead to Rome, where no good deeds can go unpunished and escape judgment or righteous behaviors go without being rewarded.

And as progressively intelligent as humans are and as complicated the essence of our consciousness is, we can never behave as the absolute moral where flaws are not committed. The simple fact is that despite man being potentiated with intelligence and consciousness, and for some reaching the pinnacle of wisdom, no man can become the absolute moral and spiritual role model because human beings are also driven by instincts, since everyone must drink, eat, have sexual intercourse, work, rest, and sleep to survive, which sure makes us all dependents one way or another. Man's conducts are relative and proportional to one's intelligence and smarts, in how strong his moral and righteous conducts are since wisdom and compassion play a big role in acting wrong or right.

Relatively speaking, the wiser and educated the person, the higher the moral and the spiritual beliefs and the lower the wrongdoings. But even the most righteous man is vulnerable for his/her needs being met since anyone's moral standing can be negotiated when their basic need to stay alive is at stake, since so many can act on impulse when desperate, even the wisest among us. Because of these compulsory human needs and innately instinctual properties, we can never have peace, since our dependency on valuable resources to survive, which often kicks in the greed factor, makes millions blind, not believing in equity and the fair allocation of resources, as we cannot be free from flaws and wrongdoings.

Statistically speaking, poor do more crimes than the rich, which should not surprise anyone since the rich can buy their way out and quench their thirst for being tempted. They can satisfy their urges for living a luxury life while the poor are frequently deprived and gradually reach an inferiority complex state of mind, since most are vulnerable to everyday temptation that worsens when people's needs are not met, and are not able to justify the root causes of a world that is gone wrong as millions of youth feel trapped and frustrated and they resort to ugly means for a way out of their difficult situation.

Freud believed that man is a sexual being; perhaps true to some extent. It is a no-brainer that millions of crimes are sexually related, where many sell their soul to achieve sexual gratification. Sociocultural, sociopolitical, and socioeconomic inequality has brought us to the brink of destruction, not to exclude prevalently horrifying sexually oriented crimes where so many children are neither safe at home nor school, since they must relentlessly be watched and safeguarded because of the very basic human need, since "sexuality" is wrongly addressed for financial reasons, forcing millions to sell their body to survive. And as we speak, in many countries, parents sexually compromise their loved ones, since they are left with no choice but to do the unthinkable, raising the demons inside and belittling the God within them.

Printed in the United States
By Bookmasters